MANAGERIAL ACCOUNTING

AN INTRODUCTION TO CONCEPTS, METHODS, AND USES

SIXTH EDITION

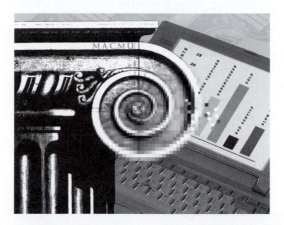

MANAGERIAL ACCOUNTING

AN INTRODUCTION TO CONCEPTS, METHODS, AND USES

SIXTH EDITION

MICHAEL W. MAHER | *University of California—Davis*

CLYDE P. STICKNEY | *Dartmouth College*

ROMAN L. WEIL | *University of Chicago*

THE DRYDEN PRESS
Harcourt Brace College Publishers

Fort Worth   Philadelphia   San Diego   New York   Orlando   Austin   San Antonio
Toronto   Montreal   London   Sydney   Tokyo

Executive Editor: **Mike Reynolds**
Acquisitions Editor: **Sara Tenney**
Developmental Editor: **Craig Avery**
Project Editor: **Jim Patterson**
Art Director: **Brian Salisbury**
Production Manager: **Eddie Dawson**
Art & Literary Rights Editor: **Annette Coolidge**
Product Manager: **Craig Johnson**
Marketing Coordinator: **Michelle Dunagan**

Copyeditor: **Carolyn Crabtree**
Proofreader: **Clifford Crouch**
Indexer: **Cherie Weil**
Compositor: **The Beacon Group**
Text Type: **10/12 Times**

Address for orders:
The Dryden Press
6277 Sea Harbor Drive
Orlando, FL 32887-6777
1-800-782-4479

Address for editorial correspondence:
The Dryden Press
301 Commerce Street, Suite 3700
Fort Worth, TX 76102

ISBN: 0-03-018193-3

Library of Congress Catalog Card Number: 96-85709

Printed in the United States of America

6 7 8 9 0 1 2 3 4 5   0 3 9   9 8 7 6 5 4 3 2 1

The Dryden Press
Harcourt Brace College Publishers

FOR OUR STUDENTS, WITH THANKS

Whatever be the detail with which you cram your students, the chance of their meeting in after-life exactly that detail is almost infinitesimal; and if they do meet it, they will probably have forgotten what you taught them about it. The really useful training yields a comprehension of a few general principles with a thorough grounding in the way they apply to a variety of concrete details. In subsequent practice the students will have forgotten your particular details; but they will remember by an unconscious commen sense how to apply principles to immediate circumstances.

Alfred North Whitehead
The Aims of Education and Other Essays

THE DRYDEN PRESS SERIES IN ACCOUNTING

Introductory
Bischoff *Introduction to College Accounting* Third Edition

Computerized
Wanlass *Computer Resource Guide: Principles of Accounting* Fourth Edition

Financial
Hanson and Hamre *Financial Accounting* Eighth Edition
Porter and Norton *Financial Accounting: The Impact on Decision Makers*
Porter and Norton *Financial Accounting: The Impact on Decision Makers* Alternate Edition
Stickney and Weil *Financial Accounting: An Introduction to Concepts, Methods, and Uses* Eighth Edition

Managerial
Maher, Stickney, and Weil *Managerial Accounting: An Introduction to Concepts, Methods, and Uses* Sixth Edition

Intermediate
Williams, Stanga, and Holder *Intermediate Accounting* Fifth Edition

Advanced
Pahler and Mori *Advanced Accounting* Sixth Edition

Financial Statement Analysis
Stickney *Financial Reporting and Statement Analysis: A Strategic Perspective* Third Edition

Auditing
Guy, Alderman, and Winters *Auditing* Fourth Edition
Rittenberg and Schwieger *Auditing: Concepts for a Changing Environment* Second Edition

Theory
Bloom and Elgers *Foundations of Accounting Theory and Policy: A Reader*
Bloom and Elgers *Issues in Accounting Policy: A Reader*

Reference
Bailey *Miller Comprehensive GAAS Guide* College Edition
Williams *Miller Comprehensive GAAP Guide* College Edition

Governmental and Not-For-Profit
Douglas *Governmental and Nonprofit Accounting: Theory and Practice* Second Edition

PREFACE

The changing role of managerial accounting in organizations includes calls for managerial accountants to expand their horizons to incorporate a broad range of issues that they have traditionally not considered to be in their domain. In targeting this book toward prospective managers in graduate programs, we have addressed this expanding role of managerial accounting in a number of ways.

THREE NEW CHAPTERS ON MANAGERIAL ISSUES

First, we have written three new chapters that discuss emerging issues that were traditionally outside the domain of accounting:

- *Managing Quality and Time* (Chapter 8) discusses the "quality is free" concept as well as issues in measuring quality, potential conflicts when companies install total quality management but reward employees based on traditional accounting measures, and the importance of time in a competitive environment.
- *Nonfinancial Performance Measures* (Chapter 12) discusses the balanced scorecard, ways that companies communicate their values, nonfinancial performance measures, and the importance of worker involvement for the organization to achieve its goals.
- *Incentive Issues* (Chapter 14) discusses the economic value added concept, the nature of incentive compensation plans, and incentives for managerial (or corporate) misconduct.

EXPANDED DISCUSSION OF DIFFERENTIAL COST AND REVENUE ANALYSIS

Second, we have expanded the discussion of differential cost and revenue analysis from one chapter in the previous edition to two chapters (6 and 7) in this edition. We have added discussion of life cycle product costing and pricing, target costing based on target pricing, customer costing and profitability analysis, and the theory of constraints and throughput contribution analysis.

ADDING VALUE TO ORGANIZATIONS: A NEW THEME THROUGHOUT

Third, an important theme in the Sixth Edition is the idea that students should seek ways to add value to the organizations in which they will work. We emphasize this value-added concept in several ways:

- We discuss ways to identify and eliminate nonvalue-added activities in several chapters (for example in Chapter 1, *Managerial Uses of Accounting Information,* and in Chapter 5, *Activity-Based Management*).

- We use the value chain as a unifying concept for discussing topics in several chapters including Chapter 2 (*Cost Concepts for Managerial Decision Making*); Chapter 5 (*Activity-Based Management*), Chapter 6 (*Differential Cost Analysis: Marketing Decisions*), and Chapter 12 (*Nonfinancial Performance Measures*).
- We develop a value-chain-based income statement in Chapter 2, which we believe is unique to this text.
- We develop a value-based income statement that reports unused resources (resources supplied minus resources used) in a cost hierarchy framework in Chapter 5, which we believe is unique to this book.
- We emphasize the importance of using incentive plans to add value to organizations in the new chapter *Incentive Issues* (Chapter 14).
- We emphasize the importance of using quality management methods to add value to organizations in the new Chapter 8.

EMPHASIS ON EMERGING THEMES IN MANAGERIAL ACCOUNTING

Fourth, we have added discussions of emerging themes in managerial accounting throughout the book. Several of these themes are mentioned above, including quality, nonfinancial performance measures, incentives, theory of constraints, life cycle product costing and pricing, target costing, customer costing and profitability analysis, value chain, and identification of nonvalue-added activities. In addition, we have expanded our discussion of activity-based management, just-in-time methods, and ethical issues from the Fifth Edition. We discuss strategic uses of cost analysis in our coverage of cost structure and operating leverage in Chapter 4 (*Cost-Volume-Profit Analysis*), behavioral and implementation issues involved in advanced cost management systems in Chapter 5 (*Activity-Based Management*), behavioral issues in making capital investment decisions in Chapter 9 (*Capital Expenditure Decisions*), and how target costing and *kaizen* costing contrast with traditional standard costing and variance analysis in Chapter 11 (*Evaluating Performance*).

REORGANIZATION TO EMPHASIZE MANAGERIAL CONCEPTS

Fifth, we have reorganized the book to emphasize managerial concepts. We have reduced the material on traditional cost systems that were formerly Chapters 3 through 5 to two chapters and moved them to the end of the book as Chapters 15 and 16. This reorganization enables instructors to teach the entire course covering just managerial topics, starting with Chapter 1 and continuing through Chapter 14. Because Chapters 15 and 16 are self-contained, however, instructors can still teach them before the managerial chapters or insert them anywhere in the course. In addition, we have substantially reduced the material on standard cost systems, keeping the most important topics as an appendix to Chapter 11, *Evaluating Performance.*

MAJOR FEATURES OF THIS BOOK

Enhances Critical Thinking Skills
Users of previous editions and reviewers have always regarded this book to be one that requires critical thinking. A critical thought approach views accounting as a

process of reporting information for people to use, as opposed to a view of accounting as a set of rules or procedures to follow. We have encouraged the development of critical thinking skills since the First Edition of *Managerial Accounting: Concepts, Methods and Uses.*

In short, we are preparing the next generation of managers and managerial accountants to think through specific situations for themselves using the concepts explored in this book.

To enhance instructors' ability to get students into critical thinking mode, we have added a new section of assignment materials called *Critical Analysis and Discussion Questions.* We have found these questions to be particularly useful for in-class assignments to groups of students who discuss the issues and report the results of their discussion. These questions are also good for take-home group or individual writing assignments.

Here are typical examples (from Chapter 8):

CRITICAL ANALYSIS AND DISCUSSION QUESTIONS

9. Discuss how a restaurant might differ under a quality-based view versus the traditional view of managing quality.

15. Southwest Airlines has particularly emphasized the importance of on-time flight arrivals. Why?

16. Allegiance Insurance Company sends a questionnaire to policy holders who have filed a claim. The questionnaire asks these claimants if they are satisfied with the way the claim has been handled. Why does Allegiance Insurance do this?

CONCEPTUAL APPROACH

The Sixth Edition emphasizes concepts over procedures. We believe students in MBA managerial accounting classes should understand the fundamental concepts and see the "big picture," leaving more detailed procedures to cost accounting classes and on-the-job training. Although a minority of students taking managerial accounting classes will become accountants, all will use managerial accounting concepts during their careers. We intend this book to give them a solid grounding in those concepts.

VARIETY OF ASSIGNMENT MATERIALS

Accounting instructors know the value of interesting and accurate assignment materials. We have written many exercises and problems to reflect the new material. We have extensively class-tested the assignment material and worked every question, exercise, problem, and case at least twice in preparing this edition.

The variety and quantity of end-of-chapter assignment materials makes the book suitable for various levels of courses. To help the instructor assign homework and select items for class presentation, we have divided the assignment materials into four categories.

- *Review Questions* are straightforward questions about key concepts in the chapter.
- *Critical Analysis and Discussion Questions* are thought-provoking questions about the challenging issues that managers and accountants face. These questions are particularly good for written essays and class discussions.
- *Exercises* reinforce key concepts in the chapter, often referring the student to a particular illustration. Exercises typically deal with a single topic and are particularly useful for classroom demonstration. To enhance the self-learning dimension of the book, we include fully worked-out solutions at the end of the chapter to the even-numbered exercises. (For convenience, we also place these solutions in the Solutions Manual.)
- *Problems* challenge the student to apply and interpret the material in the chapter, many with thought-provoking discussion or essay questions.
- *Cases* encourage students to apply concepts from multiple chapters and their other courses to deal with complex managerial issues. These are particularly good for advanced students and graduate students with some previous background in managerial accounting.

SELF-STUDY OPPORTUNITIES

Better and more motivated students take every opportunity to test their understanding. Students who find managerial accounting at the MBA level more challenging need additional resources for self-help.

We have designed this book to make it easy for students to learn the basic concepts on their own, thereby making more class time available for discussion. Like most managerial accounting textbooks, this one includes *Self-Study Problems* placed at key points in each chapter. (Their answers appear at the end of the chapter.) Unlike other managerial accounting textbooks, the worked-out solutions to half of the exercises in each chapter give students ample opportunity to test their knowledge of the basic concepts. Ideally, they will come to class with a solid understanding of the basic ideas, and instructors can devote class time to provocative discussion.

MANAGERIAL APPLICATIONS

Students become more highly motivated to learn the material if they see its application to real-world problems, particularly ones they believe they will face. This book contains *Managerial Applications* that are like sidebars in news magazines. These allow the student to explore company practices that illustrate concepts discussed in the text without disrupting the flow of study. *This edition includes more Managerial Applications for service and governmental organizations than before.* Here are selected titles of Managerial Applications:

- Chapter 1: "Will L.A. Cut Costs by Eliminating Nonvalue-Added Activities?"
- Chapter 2: "Dispute Over Indirect Costs Between Stanford University and the U.S. Government"
- Chapter 3: "United Airlines Uses Regression to Estimate Cost Behavior"

- Chapter 5: "Contrasting Activity-Based Costing with the German/Dutch Cost Pool Method"
- Chapter 5: "Using Activity-Based Management to Control Health-Care Costs"
- Chapter 6: "Pricing Practices in Various Countries"
- Chapter 7: "Using Differential Costs to Estimate the Costs of the Baseball Strike"
- Chapter 8: "Measuring the Cost of Quality in a Nonmanufacturing Setting"
- Chapter 9: "Environmental Investments"
- Chapter 10: "Conflicts Between Meeting Performance Standards and Behaving Ethically"
- Chapter 12: "Does Effective Total Quality Management Require Nontraditional Performance Measures?"

ORGANIZATION AND USE OF THIS BOOK

We divided the book into five major parts, as follows:

Part One, Fundamental Concepts, Chapters 1–2 → **Essential background**

Part Two, Managerial Decision Making, Chapters 3–9 ⎫

Part Three, Managerial Planning and Performance ⎪
   Evaluation, Chapters 10–14 ⎬ **Teach in any order**

Part Four, Cost Systems, Chapters 15–16 ⎭

Part Five, Overview of Reporting, Chapter 17 → **Overview—optional**

Part One covers fundamental concepts and provides an overview of managerial accounting. Instructors may cover the other parts in any sequence, or omit them, after Part One, as the diagram below shows:

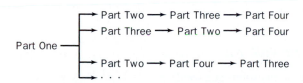

Part Two discusses concepts and methods useful for managerial decision making. Chapter 3 discusses methods of estimating cost behavior. Chapter 4 covers cost-volume-profit analysis. Chapter 5 discusses activity-based management. Chapters 6 and 7 discuss differential cost and revenue analysis. Chapter 8 discusses quality management. Chapter 9 discusses the use of accounting in long-run decision making involving capital budgeting.

Part Three concentrates on managerial planning and performance evaluation. Chapter 10 provides an overview of planning and control, and discusses development of budgets as tools for planning and control. Chapter 11 presents the fundamental cost variance model that applies to any type of manufacturing or nonmanufacturing cost. Chapter 12 discusses the use of nonfinancial performance measures. Chapter 13 focuses on performance evaluation in decentralized operations. Chapter 14 discusses a variety of incentive issues.

Part Four describes cost methods and systems. Chapter 15 focuses on alternative production settings. Chapter 16 discusses cost allocation.

Part Five presents an overview of financial reporting and analysis for readers familiar with financial accounting. This chapter will serve as a review. Readers who have not studied financial accounting can use this chapter as an introduction to the concepts, methods, and uses of analyzing financial information. It is independent of the rest of the book and may be read at any time.

Appendix The Appendix to the book discusses compound interest calculations used in discounted cash flow analysis. It is also independent of the rest of the book.

Glossary The Glossary defines comprehensively the concepts and terms used by managers and management accountants.

RELATED MATERIALS ACCOMPANYING THE TEXT

INSTRUCTOR'S MANUAL AND TEST BANK

The Instructor's Manual, by Steven R. Jackson (University of Southern Maine), includes chapter overviews, learning objectives, lecture notes with teaching suggestions, and suggestions for group discussion, all focusing on the needs of MBA instructors. A master list of Check Figures is available.

The revised Test Bank, also by Steven R. Jackson, includes a mix of questions and Problem Essays tuned to the lasting needs of MBA instructors.

SOLUTIONS MANUAL BY THE AUTHORS

This manual contains responses to questions and solutions to all exercises, problems, and cases.

COMPUTERIZED TEST BANK

The test bank is available in EXAMaster+ computerized formats for PC and Macintosh computers.

REQUESTEST

Call (800) 447-9457 toll-free to order custom test masters by chapter or by criteria, including specific test items if preferred, through the HB RequesTest service. Allow 48 hours for compiling the test in addition to first-class mail delivery (fax delivery available). RequesTest service and software support are available Monday through Friday, 9 AM to 5 PM (Central Time) for questions, guidance, or other help.

STUDY GUIDE

For each chapter and the appendix, the Study Guide written by Anne J. Rich (Quinnipiac College), includes

1. A brief summary of the chapter.
2. An outline of the chapter with emphasis on key points.
3. Several self-test and practice exercises, with answers or suggested solutions. Included are matching exercises and short problems.
4. A study plan designed to help students solve the problems in the text. Included here are references to test exhibits for review and coverage of those text problems solvable using the spreadsheet templates available to adopters.
5. Instructions on how to use the student software (see the following for more details).

MANAGEMENT TEMPLATES

This supplement gives students experience in solving management accounting problems using electronic spreadsheets. It enables students to solve selected problems from this text using the templates provided. It requires Lotus 1-2-3 or Microsoft Excel (PC). End-of-chapter items workable using the templates are identified with a disk icon in the margin.

TRANSPARENCIES

Acetate teaching transparencies are available to enhance classroom instruction. In addition, Transparencies are now available for solutions to Exercises, Problems, and Cases found in the Solutions Manual.

ACKNOWLEDGMENTS

We are grateful for comments, criticisms, and suggestions from the following reviewers of the Fifth Edition: Timothy A. Farmer (University of Missouri, St. Louis), Douglas A. Johnson (Arizona State University), Karl Putnam (University of Texas at El Paso), and Jacci Rogers (Oklahoma City University). We are also grateful for the efforts of those who reviewed chapters of the manuscript for the Sixth Edition: Michael Alles (University of Texas at Austin), Joseph Bylinski (University of North Carolina, Chapel Hill), Dan Edwards (Indiana University, Purdue), George Klersy (Birmingham-Southern College), Lawrence Lewis (Gonzaga University), Ella Mae Matsumura (University of Wisconsin, Madison), Monte Swain (Brigham Young University), Helen Traugh (University of Alabama, Birmingham). We would also like to thank those who contributed syllabi in the course of researching this revision: Edward Blocher (University of North Carolina, Chapel Hill), Dan Elnathan (University of Southern California), James O'Meara (St. John's University, Minnesota), Rebecca Oatsvall (Meredith College), Karl Putnam (University of Texas at El Paso), C. E. Reese (St. Thomas University), Jacci Rogers (Oklahoma City University).

During the course of research, other instructors responded with useful comments: Ramji Balakrishnan (University of Iowa), Ann O' Brien (University of Iowa), Kenneth Pelfrey (Ohio State University), K. V. Ramanathan (University of Washington), and Rajendra Srivastava (University of Kansas).

Thomas Horton and Daughters, Inc., has given us permission to reproduce material from *Accounting: The Language of Business.* The following have consented to let us use problems or cases they prepared: Case Clearing House, David O. Green, David Solomons, George Sorter, Jean Lim, and Robert Colson. Material from the Uniform CPA Examinations and Unofficial Answers, copyright by the American Institute of Certified Public Accountants, Inc., is adapted with permission. The Institute of Management Accountants has given us permission to use questions and unofficial answers from past CMA examinations.

We further thank certain individuals who have made this book possible: Kathryn Rybowiak, Kurt Heisinger, and Reita Wilkinson. Cherie Weil prepared the index. Vanetta Van Cleave contributed to the entire development and production of this book. Thank you, Vanetta.

We thank those at The Dryden Press who have contributed their expertise to this project: Mike Reynolds, Sara Tenney, Craig Avery, Jim Patterson, Eddie Dawson, Brian Salisbury, Craig Johnson, Annette Coolidge, and Michelle Dunagan.

Finally, Sidney Davidson. What can we say? For over twenty years he has taught us and guided us and wrote with us. Thank you.

M. W. M.
C. P. S.
R. L. W.

BRIEF CONTENTS

CONTENTS

PART FOUR
COST SYSTEMS   501

CHAPTER 15
Managerial Accounting Systems in Alternative Production Settings   502

CHAPTER 16
Cost Allocation   546

PART FIVE
OVERVIEW OF REPORTING   565

CHAPTER 17
Introduction to Financial Statement Analysis   566

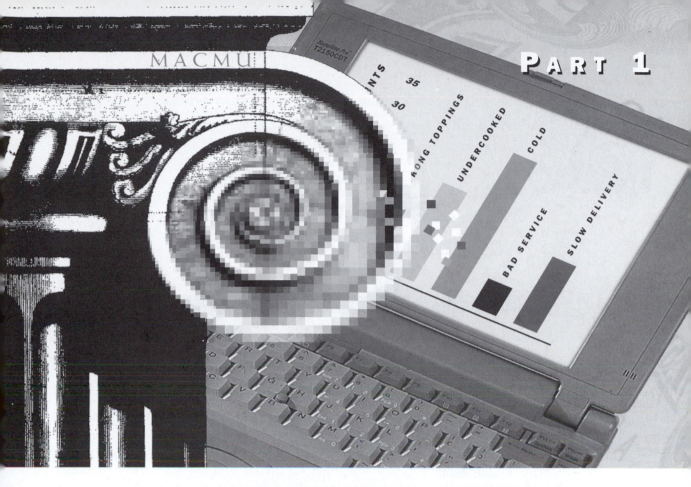

FUNDAMENTAL CONCEPTS

Noted management writer Peter Drucker calls accounting the most intellectually challenging and turbulent area in the field of management. Whether or not your career plans include work in accounting, the ideas in this book will help you meet those challenges.

Part One has two chapters that lay the foundation for the rest of the book. Chapter 1 provides an overview of managerial accounting and shows how decision makers use managerial accounting information. Chapter 2 discusses important managerial accounting concepts that we use throughout the book.

MANAGERIAL USES OF ACCOUNTING INFORMATION

LEARNING OBJECTIVES

1. Distinguish between managerial and financial accounting.
2. Understand the use of accounting information for decision making, planning, control, and performance evaluation.
3. Identify the key financial players in the organization.
4. Understand managerial accountants' professional environment and ethical responsibilities.
5. Explain the benefits of activity-based management and application of the value chain.
6. Describe how managerial accounting supports the new production environment.
7. Understand the importance of effective communication between accountants and users of managerial accounting information.
8. Understand the ethical standards that comprise the Institute of Management Accountants' Code of Ethics (Appendix 1.1).

Managerial accounting affects virtually everyone. Workers in fast-food restaurants may not use accounting themselves, but their managers use it in deciding whether to increase or decrease employees' hours. Recently, Kmart closed numerous stores, Nike sold a new type of shoe, and a local grocery store began staying open all night. These decisions involved the use of accounting information.

About 80 percent of new businesses fail within five years of opening their doors. Often they fail because management does not have adequate accounting information to make good decisions, plan for growth, and forecast cash needs. Organizations with poor accounting systems also have difficulty obtaining financing from banks and shareholders.

MANAGERIAL APPLICATION

Why Managers Need Cost Information

Domino's Pizza nearly went bankrupt until the owner discovered that the company was losing money on 6-inch pizzas; the company dropped the product line and went on to become a multibillion-dollar company. Many hospitals that thrived when insurers fully reimbursed health-care costs are now facing large deficits. Many airlines that were successful when regulated have since gone bankrupt.

What do all these stories have in common? They all represent situations in which a better understanding and management of costs would have helped the organization to succeed. In general, an organization's ability to manage its costs becomes more important as the environment becomes more competitive. Hospitals, airlines, and many other organizations face increasingly stiff competition. As a result, they are seeking better ways to measure productivity and costs.

USER ORIENTATION

We make an assumption about you as a reader of this book. You will use accounting in your career.

- Marketing managers will use accounting information to help price products and assess their profitability. Using product cost information, marketing managers will determine how low they can drop their prices and still be profitable.
- Financial managers will use accounting information to project future earnings in investment decisions.
- Production managers will use accounting information for control and production design decisions.
- General managers will use accounting information to measure employee performance and create incentives.

Consequently, we take a user's perspective of accounting. We want you to understand accounting so you can effectively use the information that accountants provide.

The Managerial Application, "Why Managers Need Cost Information," gives examples of companies that struggled because managers did not use cost information. Perhaps you know of organizations that have struggled because they did not use cost information to manage costs. (One such organization is the U.S. federal government.)

COMPARING FINANCIAL AND MANAGERIAL ACCOUNTING

Accounting is part of an organization's information system. Information systems include both financial and nonfinancial data. Accounting commonly divides into financial accounting and managerial accounting. **Financial accounting** deals with preparing general purpose reports for people outside an organization to use. The users include shareholders (owners) of a corporation, creditors (those who lend money to a business), financial analysts, labor unions, and government regulators.

External users wish primarily to review and evaluate the operations and financial status of the business as a whole.

Managerial accounting provides information for managers inside the organization to use. The information provided to a particular manager will be based on that manager's wishes. Managerial accounting is not bound by rules and regulations, such as Generally Accepted Accounting Principles. The following chart spells out the fundamental differences between managerial and financial accounting:

Financial Accounting	Managerial Accounting
Users	
External users of information—usually shareholders, financial analysts, and creditors.	Internal users of information—usually managers.
Generally Accepted Accounting Principles	
Compliance with generally accepted accounting principles.	Need not comply with generally accepted accounting principles.
Future versus Past	
Uses historical data in evaluating performance of the firm and its managers by outsiders.	Uses estimates of the future for decision making and historical data for internal performance evaluation.
Reporting Requirements	
Regulations often specify how much information to report.	Internal cost/benefit evaluation dictates how much information is needed.
Detail Presented	
Presents summary data.	Presents more detailed information about product costs, revenues, and profits.

Note these important distinctions:

1. Financial accountants are concerned with external reports; managerial accountants are concerned with internal reports.
2. Managerial accounting need not comply with generally accepted accounting principles. This surprises many nonaccountants who assume generally accepted accounting principles apply to managerial accounting. Not so.
3. Unlike financial accounting, which must use historical data, managerial accounting can, and does, use projections about the future. After all, managers make decisions for the future, not the past.
4. How much accounting is required? Managerial accounting must meet a managerial cost-benefit test whereas financial accounting is more subject to what regulations require. For managerial accounting, the benefit from having the information must be greater than the cost of collection.
5. Managerial accounting presents data that managers can use for decision making—that is, details about particular costs, revenues, and products. By contrast, financial accounting provides aggregate data.

USES OF ACCOUNTING INFORMATION

Accounting provides information for (1) managerial decision-making and planning, (2) managerial control and internal performance evaluation, and (3) financial reporting for external performance evaluation by shareholders and creditors.

RELATIONS AMONG THE THREE USES OF ACCOUNTING

Exhibit 1.1 illustrates the relationship among the three principal uses of accounting information discussed in this section. This book deals with the first two principal uses of accounting information. Note the close relation between managerial decision-making and planning and the internal performance evaluation process. In making a decision, management forms expectations about performance if everything goes according to plan. The results of the internal performance evaluation in one period become inputs into the planning and decision-making process of the next period.

EXHIBIT 1.1

Managerial Processes and Accounting Information

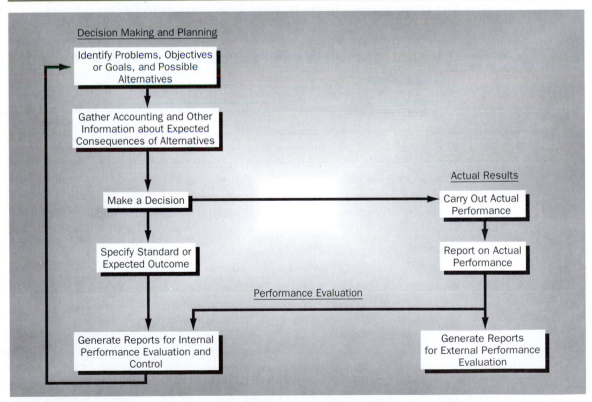

Looking at Exhibit 1.1, where is financial accounting? Where is managerial accounting? (Answer: Financial accounting is generating reports for external performance evaluation. Managerial accounting is part of the entire decision-making and planning process. It is also generating internal reports.)

MANAGERIAL DECISION MAKING AND PLANNING

The decision-making and planning process includes the following steps, as Exhibit 1.1 shows:

1. Identify a problem requiring managerial action; specify the objective or goal to be achieved (for example, maximize return on investment); and list the possible alternative courses of action.
2. Gather accounting and other information about the consquences of each alternative.
3. Make a decision by selecting one of the alternatives.
4. Specify a standard or target specifying what actual performance should be.

Managerial accounting plays a role in all these steps, particularly steps 2 and 4.

Example A health maintenance organization is considering adding dental care to the services it provides. Management wishes to predict the expected costs of operating the proposed dental care service. The managerial accountant must obtain cost data from the records of costs incurred in the past for providing similar types of services. Management and the accountants then use these data to help project the costs they expect to incur from the proposed dental care service.

CONTROL AND INTERNAL PERFORMANCE EVALUATION

The control and internal performance evaluation process includes the following steps:

1. Measure the results of actual performance.
2. Compare actual performance with the standard or budget. This evaluation helps management assess actions already taken and decide which courses of action to take in the future.

Managerial accounting plays an important role in the control process. It helps establish incentives for good performance, and it reports actual results to compare with expectations.

Example Assume the health maintenance organization in the previous example decided to add the dental care service. Management expected the first year's operating costs to be $5 million. This $5 million cost projection could serve as the budget or standard for evaluating the performance of the dental service managers.

If the costs varied significantly from $5 million, management would make an effort to find the cause of the difference, or *variance*, as accountants call it, between anticipated and actual costs. If factors the dental service managers could not control caused the variance, management probably would not hold them responsible for it. For example, a dental technicians' strike might cause a labor shortage, thereby resulting in a loss in patient revenue that dental service managers could not control.

PROBLEM 1.1 FOR SELF-STUDY

Differences between financial and managerial accounting. What are the differences between financial and managerial accounting?

The solution to this self-study problem is at the end of this chapter on page 21.

MISUSE OF ACCOUNTING INFORMATION

Managers and other users of accounting information often mistakenly use data for one purpose that were intended for another. For example, many companies use various inventory cost flow and depreciation methods for tax purposes; however, these data are not necessarily appropriate for managerial uses.

Further, most managerial decisions require more detailed data than external financial reports provide. For instance, General Electric's external financial statements present a single amount for inventory valuation and a single amount for cost of goods sold expense summarized for all product lines. For decision-making purposes, however, management wants detailed data about the cost of each of several hundred products.

Managers sometimes assume that they must use the same accounting data for their decision-making, planning, and other managerial activities as presented in tax returns and financial statements. That is not correct. In fact, many companies are developing managerial accounting systems independent of financial accounting.

Many organizations have tried simply to take their financial accounting systems as given, and modify them a little for managerial uses. The results are often disastrous, because managers do not get the information they need for decision making.

Many proponents of improvements in business have been highly critical of the cost accounting practices in companies. One such critic even produced a film titled *Cost Accounting: Enemy Number One of Productivity.*[1] It turns out that, though some of these criticisms have been exaggerated, many have identified important problems that companies should address. Most problems with accounting systems appear to occur when managers attempt to use accounting information that was developed for external reporting instead of the type of accounting discussed in this book.

Companies must realize that different uses of accounting information require different types of accounting information. "One size fits all" does not apply to accounting.

KEY FINANCIAL PLAYERS IN THE ORGANIZATION

As managers, you need to know the key financial players in organizations. Who in the organization will help you get the information you need to manage the company? Exhibit 1.2 shows a typical organization chart—an abbreviated version of du Pont's organization chart. The shaded boxes represent the financial managers at the corporate level.

---

[1]E. Goldratt, *Cost Accounting: Enemy Number One of Productivity*, Avraham Goldratt Institute, 1983.

EXHIBIT 1.2

E. I. du Pont de Nemours and Company

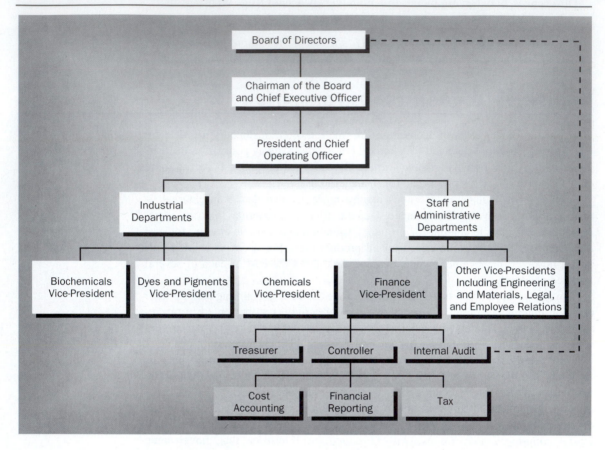

FINANCIAL VICE-PRESIDENT

The top financial person is usually a senior vice-president in the company, the **financial vice-president.** This person is in charge of the entire accounting and finance function and is typically one of the three most influential people in the company. (The other two are the president and the chief executive officer.)

CONTROLLER

The **controller** is in charge of cost and managerial accounting in most organizations. The name *controller* sounds like someone who "controls things." In fact, the controller's office is involved in planning, decision making, designing information systems, designing incentive systems, and helping managers make operating decisions, among other things. If you have a career in marketing, production, or general management, you will have frequent interactions with controllers.

TREASURER

The corporate **treasurer** is in charge of raising cash for operations and managing cash and near-cash assets. The treasurer normally handles relations with banks and other lending or financing sources, including public issues of shares or debt.

COST ACCOUNTANTS

Cost accountants record and analyze costs. They also work on teams with people from marketing who decide whether to keep or drop products because of product profitability. They work with people from operations to find ways to redesign products to save money.

The key to successful cost accounting is for cost accountants to have a thorough knowledge of the business. They also should constantly look for ways to add value to their organization. Merely keeping records is only the beginning of a cost accountant's job. Cost accountants must constantly analyze operations and costs to find ways to improve operations and product quality while reducing costs.

INTERNAL AUDIT

The **internal audit** department provides a variety of auditing and consulting services. Internal auditors are often helpful consultants to managers because they provide an independent perspective on managers' problems. Auditors who focus on operations as well as finance are particularly helpful to managers. Such auditors are called *operational auditors.* In some companies, like General Electric, internal auditing is an important training ground for managers.

Notice in Exhibit 1.2 that the internal audit manager reports to the controller's superior at du Pont. This is true in many companies. The controller is in charge of the accounting systems audited by the internal auditor. If the internal auditor reports to the controller, then he or she would be auditing his or her boss. The dotted line between Internal Audit and the Board of Directors indicates that internal auditors can communicate directly with the audit committee of the board of directors. That allows internal auditors to "blow the whistle" on anybody in the company—even the president—if they believe it's necessary to do so.

PROFESSIONAL ENVIRONMENT

Accountants are not only part of the management team, they are also professionals. Their professional environment influences the types of reports and databases they develop.

GENERALLY ACCEPTED ACCOUNTING PRINCIPLES

Firms use **generally accepted accounting principles (GAAP)** for guidance in preparing their external financial statements. Managerial accounting does not have to follow generally accepted accounting principles or the income tax laws. Nevertheless, even managerial accountants learn about GAAP in their studies, so GAAP influences their perspective. Some managerial accountants have to be trained not to allow GAAP to constrain them.

INSTITUTE OF MANAGEMENT ACCOUNTANTS

The **Institute of Management Accountants (IMA)** has thousands of members who work in management accounting. It publishes a journal called *Management Accounting,* numerous policy statements, and research studies on accounting issues. It also sponsors the Certified Management Accountant (CMA) program, which is the major certification for managerial accountants.

CERTIFIED MANAGEMENT ACCOUNTANT

The **Certified Management Accountant (CMA)** designation recognizes educational achievement and professional competence in management accounting. The examination, educational requirements, and experience requirements are similar to those for a CPA, but they aim at the professional in management and cost accounting. We have included many questions from CMA examinations in this book.

CERTIFIED PUBLIC ACCOUNTANT

The designation **certified public accountant (CPA)** indicates that an individual has qualified to be registered or licensed by passing a written examination and satisfying audit experience requirements. The CPA examination includes questions on managerial accounting.

INTERNAL REVENUE SERVICE

Income tax legislation and administration have influenced the practice of accounting, although income tax requirements in themselves do not establish principles and practices for external or internal reporting. The *Internal Revenue Code* (passed by Congress), the regulations and rulings of the Internal Revenue Service, and the opinions of the U.S. Tax Court form the basis for income tax reporting rules.

COST ACCOUNTING STANDARDS BOARD

If you work in the defense industry, you will hear about the **Cost Accounting Standards Board (CASB).** The U.S. Congress established the Board in 1970 to set accounting standards for contracts between the U.S. government and defense contractors, such as Boeing, Honeywell, and General Dynamics. Accountants apply CASB standards to many transactions between defense contractors and the U.S. government.

CANADIAN CERTIFICATIONS

Two Canadian organizations provide designations similar to the CPA designation in the United States. The Canadian Institute of Chartered Accountants provides the

Chartered Accountant (CA) designation, and the Certified General Accountants' Association of Canada gives the Certified General Accountant (CGA) designation. The Society of Management Accountants in Canada gives a Certified Management Accountant (CMA) designation similar to the CMA in the United States.

ETHICAL ISSUES

Companies hold managers accountable for achieving financial performance targets. Failure to achieve these targets can cause great difficulty for managers. If a division or company is having trouble achieving financial performance targets, managers may be tempted to manipulate the accounting numbers to make themselves look better.

For instance, managers whose compensation is based on their profits may wish to record sales that have not yet occurred in order to boost the bottom line. This early revenue recognition usually occurs just before the end of the reporting period, say, in late December for a company using a December 31 year-end. Management may have rationalized the early revenue recognition because the firm would probably make the sale in January anyway; this practice just moves next year's sale (and profit) into this year. This is unethical. Also, the information may be used to generate external reports, thus exposing the company to charges of fraudulent reporting.

We include discussions of ethical issues throughout this book. We hope these discussions will help alert you to potential problems that you and your colleagues will face in your careers. Many accountants and businesspeople have found themselves in serious trouble because they did many small things, none of which appeared seriously wrong, only to find that these small things added up to a major problem. If you know the warning signs of potential ethical problems, you will have a chance to protect yourself and set the proper ethical tone of your workplace at the same time.

CODE OF CONDUCT

The Institute of Management Accountants has developed a code of conduct, called "Standards of Ethical Conduct for Management Accountants." We have reproduced it in the appendix to this chapter. The IMA code mandates that management accountants have a responsibility to maintain the highest levels of ethical conduct.[2] The IMA standards recommend that people faced with ethical conflicts take the following steps:

1. Follow the company's established procedures that deal with such conflicts. These procedures include talking to an ombudsman, who keeps the names of those involved confidential.
2. If step 1 does not resolve the conflict, accountants should consider discussing the matter with superiors, potentially as high as the audit committee or the board of directors.
3. In extreme cases, the accountant may have no alternative but to resign.

---

[2]See *Standards of Ethical Conduct for Management Accountants* (Montvale, N.J.: National Association of Accountants [now called the Institute of Management Accountants], June 1, 1983).

Most large organizations have a corporate code of conduct. If you are considering taking a job at a particular company, you should first read the company's code of conduct.[3] That code may tell you about the company's values. For example, the Johnson & Johnson code of conduct discusses the company's responsibilities to customers, to the medical profession, to employees, and to the community. Responsibility to shareholders comes after these primary responsibilities.

ACTIVITY-BASED MANAGEMENT

Activity-based management (ABM) is now one of the most important ways to be competitive. Many of the concepts discussed in this book are intended to support activity-based management.

UNDERSTANDING WHAT CAUSES COSTS

Effective cost control requires managers to understand how producing a product requires activities and how activities, in turn, generate costs. Activity-based management, which studies the need for activities and whether they are being undertaken efficiently, is essential for cost control.

Consider the activities of a manufacturer facing a financial crisis. In a system of managing by the numbers, each department is told to reduce costs in an amount equal to its share of the budget cut. The usual response by department heads is to reduce the number of people and supplies, as these are the only cost items that they can control in the short run. Asking everyone to work harder produces only temporary gains, however, as the pace cannot be sustained in the long run.

Under activity management, the manufacturer reduces costs by studying what activities it conducts and develops plans to eliminate nonvalue-added activities and to improve the efficiency of value-added activities. Eliminating activities that do not create customer value is a very effective way to cut costs. For example, spending $100 to train an employee to avoid common mistakes will repay itself many times over by reducing customer ill-will caused by those mistakes.

VALUE-ADDED AND NONVALUE-ADDED ACTIVITIES

A **value-added activity** is an activity that increases the product's service to the customer. For instance, purchasing the raw materials to make a product is a value-added activity. Without the purchase of raw materials, the organization would be unable to make the product. Sanding and varnishing a wooden chair are value-added activities because customers don't want splinters. Value-added activities are evaluated by how they contribute to the final product's service, quality, and cost.

Good management involves finding and, if possible, eliminating nonvalue-added activities. **Nonvalue-added activities** are activities that when eliminated reduce

---

[3]In some organizations, people take the code of conduct seriously. In others, the code goes quickly into the circular file.

Will L.A. Cut Costs by Eliminating Nonvalue-Added Activities?

Los Angeles Mayor Richard J. Riordan was determined to make L.A.'s motor pool maintenance operation more efficient and thereby reduce the $120 million spent annually on maintenance. By reducing the nonvalue-added activities associated with fleet operation, Mayor Riordan was able to increase efficiency and reduce costs.

One example of a nonvalue-added activity was the idling of workers who should have been using trucks for sanitation. However, trucks were being repaired during the daytime when they were needed for trash pickup. Trucks needing repairs were to be fixed during the night when they were idle, but many drivers did not do the end-of-shift inspections. As a result, trucks broke down during the day and idled workers.

Once drivers checked the trucks more closely and more regularly, the out-of-service rate dropped from 30 percent to 18 percent.

Source: Jeff Bailey, "How Can Government Save Money? Consider the L.A. Motor Pool," *The Wall Street Journal*, July 6, 1995, A1.

costs without reducing the product's service potential to the customer. In many organizations poor facility layout may require the work in process to be moved around or temporarily stored during production. For example, a Midwest steel company that we studied had more than 100 miles of railroad track to move things back and forth in a poorly designed facility. Moving work around a factory, an office, or a store is unlikely to add value for the customer.

Organizations must change the process that makes nonvalue-added activities necessary. Elimination of nonvalue-added activities requires organizations to improve the process so that the activities are no longer required. Organizations strive to reduce or eliminate nonvalue-added activities because, by doing so, they permanently reduce the costs they must incur to produce goods or services without affecting the value to the customer. The Managerial Application titled "Will L.A. Cut Costs by Eliminating Nonvalue-Added Activities?" presents a real example in an enterprise that is sorely in need of eliminating nonvalue-added activities—namely, government services.

Although managers should pay particular attention to nonvalue-added activities, they should also carefully evaluate the need for value-added activities. For example, in wine production, classifying storage as a value-added activity assumes the only way to make good-tasting wine is to allow it to age in storage. Think of the advantage that someone could have if he or she discovered a way to produce wine that tastes as good as conventionally aged wine but does not require long storage periods.

VALUE CHAIN

We use the value chain concept throughout the book to demonstrate how to use managerial accounting to add value to organizations. The **value chain** describes the linked set of activities that increase the usefulness (or value) of the products or services of an organization (value-added activities). Activities are evaluated by how they contribute to the final product's service, quality, and cost. In general, the business functions include the following (see Exhibit 1.3):

1. *Research and development:* the creation and development of ideas related to new products, services, or processes.
2. *Design:* the detailed development and engineering of products, services, or processes.
3. *Production:* the collection and assembly of resources to produce a product or deliver a service.
4. *Marketing:* the process that informs potential customers about the attributes of products or services, and leads to the purchase of those products or services.
5. *Distribution:* the process established to deliver products or services to customers.
6. *Customer service:* product or service support activities provided to customers.

Several administrative functions span all the business activities described. Human resource management, for example, potentially affects every step of the value chain.

STRATEGIC COST ANALYSIS

Companies can identify strategic advantages in the marketplace by analyzing the value chain and information about the costs of activities. A company that eliminates

EXHIBIT 1.3
The Value Chain

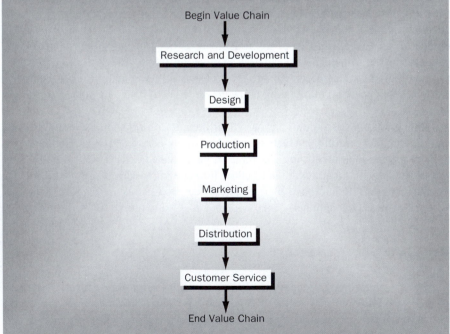

Begin Value Chain

Research and Development

Design

Production

Marketing

Distribution

Customer Service

End Value Chain

nonvalue-added activities reduces costs without reducing the value of the product to customers. With reduced costs, the company can reduce the price it charges customers, thus giving the company a cost advantage over its competitors. Or the company can use the resources saved from eliminating nonvalue-added activities to provide greater service to customers. For example, by eliminating nonvalue-added activities, Southwest Airlines has reduced airplane turnaround time at the gate. Reduced turnaround means that Southwest can fly more flights and passengers in a given time period, which increases the company's profitability.

The idea here is simple. Look for activities that are not on the value chain. If the company can safely eliminate nonvalue-added activities, then it should do so. By identifying and cutting them, you will save the company money and make it more competitive.

GLOBAL STRATEGIES

Another approach to gaining a cost advantage is to identify where on the value chain your company has a strategic advantage. Many software companies, for example, are looking at foreign markets as a way to capitalize on their investment in research and development. This reservoir of intellectual capital gives these firms an advantage over local competitors who have not yet developed this expertise. These competitors would face research and development costs already incurred by established companies, making it difficult for the newcomers to charge competitive prices and still make a profit.

MANAGERIAL ACCOUNTING IN THE NEW PRODUCTION ENVIRONMENT

Over the last two decades, new technologies and management philosophies have changed the face of managerial accounting. Following are the key developments that have reshaped the discipline. We will discuss these in more detail in upcoming chapters. For example, where robots and computer-assisted manufacturing methods have replaced people, labor costs have shrunk from between 20 and 40 percent of product costs to less than 5 percent. Accounting in traditional settings required more work to keep track of labor costs than do current systems. On the other hand, in highly automated environments, accountants have had to become more sophisticated in finding causes of costs because labor no longer drives many cost transactions.

JUST-IN-TIME AND LEAN PRODUCTION

Just-in-time (JIT) production is part of a "lean production" philosophy that has been credited for the success of many Japanese companies and such U.S. companies as General Electric, Lincoln Electric, and Harley-Davidson. Lean production eliminates inventory between production departments, making the quality and efficiency of production the highest priority. Lean production requires the flexibility to change quickly from one product to another. It emphasizes employee training and participation in decision making.

The development of just-in-time production and purchasing methods also affects cost-accounting systems. Firms using just-in-time methods keep inventories to a minimum. If inventories are low, accountants can spend less time on inventory valuation for external reporting.

For example, a Hewlett-Packard plant eliminated 100,000 journal entries per month after installing just-in-time production methods and adapting the cost-accounting system to this new production method. This freed accounting/finance people to work on managerial problems instead of recording accounting data.

QUALITY MANAGEMENT

One of the most successful and lasting of recent managerial fads is the concept of total quality management. **Total quality management (TQM)** means the organization is focused on excelling in all dimensions, and quality is ultimately defined by the customer. Customers determine the company's performance standards according to what is important to them (not necessarily what is important to product engineers, accountants, or marketing people). This exciting and sensible idea affects accounting performance measures. Under TQM, performance measures are likely to include product reliability and service delivery, as well as such traditional measures as profitability. Chapter 8 focuses on quality management.

THEORY OF CONSTRAINTS

Every profit-making enterprise must have at least one constraint. If not, according to the theory of constraints, then the enterprise would produce an infinite amount of whatever it strives for (for example, profits). The **theory of constraints (TOC)** views a business as a linked sequence of processes that transforms inputs into saleable outputs, like a chain. To improve the strength of the chain, a TOC company identifies the weakest link, which is the constraint. That link sets the pace for the rest of the process, so the company concentrates improvement efforts on that weakest link. When that link is no longer the weakest, or a constraint, the company changes focus to the new weakest link. TOC improves operations and has a lot of potential for helping certain kinds of companies, as discussed in Chapter 7.

BENCHMARKING AND CONTINUOUS IMPROVEMENT

Benchmarking and continuous improvements are recurring themes in modern management. **Benchmarking** is the continuous process of measuring one's own products, services, and activities against the best level of performance. These best levels of performance may be found either inside one's own organization or in other organizations.

Toyota Motor Company gets a lot of the credit for applying the concept of benchmarking and continuous improvement, but many other companies have joined this movement. These include Chrysler and Xerox, whose managers were shocked to find how poor its performance was compared to its Fuji-Xerox subsidiary in Japan. Benchmarking and continuous improvement is often called "the race with no finish" because managers and employees are not satisfied with a particular performance level but seek ongoing improvement. Organizations that adopt this philosophy find they are able to achieve performance levels previously thought to be unattainable.

FADS

This is an exciting time to be in management. There seems constantly to be a new book, management guru, or consulting firm prepared to save industry (or government) from great peril. Some of these fads are sensible old ideas that have been repackaged as new ideas. Some are frauds. Some are "useful frauds," in that they don't do what they claim but they get people thinking about the problem.[4] Generally, we find that (1) no matter how good an idea, there are places where it doesn't work; (2) there are things to be learned even from bad ideas; and (3) good common sense goes a long way in figuring out which ideas will work and which will not in your unique situation.

PROBLEM 1.2 FOR SELF-STUDY

How does the new production environment affect managerial accounting?

The solution to this self-study problem is at the end of this chapter on page 21.

COSTS AND BENEFITS OF ACCOUNTING

A steel company installed an accounting system that cost several million dollars. How did the managers justify such an expenditure? They believed better information would result in improved cost control and efficiency that would save the company enough to justify the cost of the system.

In practice, neither users of information nor accountants can independently assess both the costs and benefits of information. Users are more familiar with the benefits of information, whereas accountants are more familiar with its costs. Exhibit 1.4 shows that users identify their needs based on the decisions they make and then request data from accountants, who develop systems to supply information when a cost-benefit criterion justifies it. If accountants and users interact, they eventually settle on a cost-benefit-justified supply of accounting data that meets users' needs.

THE VALUE OF INFORMATION FOR PARTICULAR DECISIONS

The value of information is important in various managerial settings. For example, should the firm undertake an additional marketing study that involves customer sampling of a new product? Or should the company discontinue its marketing tests and

---

[4]Some of you may remember zero-base budgeting from the 1970s. Management gurus and President Jimmy Carter touted it as a way to improve efficiency and effectiveness in business and government. Zero-base budgeting could not realistically be implemented in complex organizations because of the time and effort it required. Nevertheless, zero-base budgeting was a fairly good concept that created opportunities to control costs. We expect to see it reinvented someday under a different name.

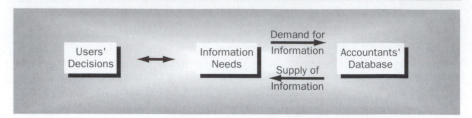

EXHIBIT 1.4

Supply of and Demand for Accounting Information

proceed immediately to full-scale production? Should a doctor order laboratory tests before taking action in an emergency situation? Should a production manager stop production to test a sample of products for defects, or allow production to continue? Managers solve such problems conceptually by comparing the cost of information with the benefits of better decisions.

Both users and accountants recognize that information is not free. Management must take into account the costs and benefits of information in deciding how much accounting is optimal.

THE MAKEUP OF THE BOOK

The book is organized into four sections:

1. Part One (Chapters 1 and 2) provides background concepts for later use.
2. Part Two (Chapters 3 through 9) discusses the use of accounting for managerial decision making and planning.
3. Part Three (Chapters 10 through 14) discusses managerial control and performance evaluation.
4. Part Four (Chapters 15 through 17) examines cost systems and considers key financial analysis topics.

We have designed the book so parts can be assigned in any order. Do not be alarmed if your instructor assigns later parts of the book before earlier parts.

SUMMARY

The following paragraphs correspond to the learning objectives presented at the beginning of the chapter.

1. **Distinguish between managerial and financial accounting.** Managerial accounting provides information that managers inside the organization will use. To that end, it need not comply with Generally Accepted Accounting Principles. It uses cost-benefit evaluation to determine the amount of detail presented, and uses estimates as well as historical data. Financial accounting prepares general purpose reports for people outside an organization to use and presents summary historical data in compliance with Generally Accepted Accounting Principles.

2. **Understand the use of accounting information for decision making, planning, control, and performance evaluation.** Accounting information is used to help project the consequences of various courses of action in the decision-making and planning process. Accounting information is also used to set standards or budgets and to measure actual results for control. Actual results are compared to expectations for performance evaluation.
3. **Identify the key financial players in the organization.** The top financial person is the financial vice-president, in charge of the entire accounting and finance function. The controller is the chief accounting officer who oversees providing information to managers. The corporate treasurer is the manager in charge of raising cash for operations and managing cash and near-cash assets. The internal audit department provides a variety of auditing and consulting services.
4. **Understand managerial accountants' professional environment and ethical responsibilities.** Companies hold managers accountable for achieving financial performance targets. Because compensation may be based on these targets, all managers have an ethical responsibility to report accurately whether or not such reports are favorable.
5. **Explain the benefits of activity-based management and application of the value chain.** Production activities create a demand for resources, and the acquisition and consumption of those resources create costs. Activity-based management is one method of controlling those costs. A value-added activity is an activity that increases the product's service to the customer in the long run. A nonvalue-added activity is any activity that does not increase a product's service potential to the customer.
6. **Describe how managerial accounting supports the new production environment.** Accountants have had to become more sophisticated in finding nonvalue-added activities.
7. **Understand the importance of effective communication between accountants and users of managerial accounting information.** The amount of accounting information generated for managerial purposes is determined by a cost-benefit analysis, which requires effective communication and cooperation between users and accountants. Clear communication is necessary to ensure the information is appropriate for its intended use.
8. **Understand the ethical standards that comprise the Institute of Management Accountants' Code of Ethics (Appendix 1.1)** Management accountants are responsible for maintaining competence, confidentiality, integrity, and objectivity.

KEY TERMS AND CONCEPTS

Financial accounting   The accounting for assets, equities, revenues, and expenses of a business. Primarily concerned with the historical reporting of the financial position and operations of an entity to external users on a regular, periodic basis.

Managerial accounting   Reporting designed to enhance the ability of management to do its job of decision making, planning, and control.

Cost-benefit criterion   Some measure of costs compared to some measure of benefits for a proposed undertaking. If the costs exceed the benefits, then the analyst judges the undertaking not worthwhile.

Financial vice-president   The person in charge of the entire accounting and finance function; typically one of the three most influential people in the company.

Controller   The person in charge of cost and managerial accounting; also involved in planning, decision making, designing information systems, designing incentive systems, helping managers make operating decisions, and a variety of other activities.

Treasurer   The person in charge of raising cash for operations and managing cash and near-cash assets.

Cost accountant   The internal accountant who records and analyzes costs and works on teams with other organization members for analysis and decision making.

Internal audit   An audit conducted by employees inside the organization to test whether internal control procedures are working and whether the company's policies are being carried out.

Generally Accepted Accounting Principles (GAAP)   As defined by the Financial Accounting Standards Board, the conventions, rules, and procedures necessary to define accepted accounting practice for external reporting at a particular time.

Institute of Management Accountants (IMA)   Organization of management accountants that oversees administration of the CMA examination.

Certified Management Accountant (CMA)   Designation awarded by the Institute of Management Accountants to those who pass a set of examinations and meet certain experience and continuing education requirements.

Certified Public Accountant (CPA)   An accountant who has satisfied the statutory and administrative requirements of his or her jurisdiction to be registered or licensed as a public accountant.

Cost Accounting Standards Board (CASB)   A board authorized by the U.S. Congress to promulgate standards designed to achieve uniformity and consistency in the cost-accounting principles followed by federal defense contractors and subcontractors.

Activity-based management (ABM)   The analysis and management of the activities that are needed to make a product. Focuses management's attention to enhance those activities that add value to the customer and eliminate those that do not add value. Also called **activity management.**

Value-added activity   Activity that increases the product's service to the customer.

Nonvalue-added activity   Any activity that when eliminated reduces costs without reducing the product's service potential to the customer.

Value chain   The business functions associated with increasing the usefulness (or value) of the products or services of an organization (value-added activities).

Just-in-time (JIT)   System of managing inventory in which a firm purchases or manufactures each component just before it is used. JIT systems have much smaller carrying costs for inventory, but run higher risks of incurring stockout costs than more traditional inventory management systems.

Total quality management (TQM)   Concept by which an organization is managed to excel on all dimensions, and quality is ultimately defined by the customer.

Theory of constraints   A system of improving operations by identifying and eliminating constraints within a process.

Benchmarking   The continuous process of measuring one's own products, services, and activities against the best levels of performance.

SOLUTIONS TO SELF-STUDY PROBLEMS

SUGGESTED SOLUTION TO PROBLEM 1.1 FOR SELF-STUDY

Managerial accounting is the preparation of accounting information for use by *managers inside organizations* in making decisions and evaluating performance. Financial accounting is the preparation of accounting information for use by *outsiders,* such as investors and creditors.

SUGGESTED SOLUTION TO PROBLEM 1.2 FOR SELF-STUDY

The new production environment has had the following effects on accounting:

- Accounting has become more computerized, thus reducing manual bookkeeping.
- Increased competition in many industries, including the automobile and electronic equipment industries, has increased management's interest in managing costs.
- Deregulation in industries like banking, air travel, and health care has also increased management's interest in managing costs.
- Development of more highly technical production processes has reduced emphasis on labor and increased emphasis on overhead cost control.
- Developments in new management techniques have affected accounting. For example, by reducing inventory levels, just-in-time (JIT) methods have reduced the need to compute costs of inventory. Total quality management (TQM), which strives for excellence in business, requires new measurements of performance as defined by the customers. Activity-based management (ABM) assigns indirect costs to products on the basis of the activities that caused the cost and the amount of the activity that the product consumed.

APPENDIX 1.1: STANDARDS OF ETHICAL CONDUCT FOR MANAGEMENT ACCOUNTANTS[5]

Management accountants have an obligation to the organizations they serve, their profession, the public, and themselves to maintain the highest standards of ethical conduct. In recognition of this obligation, the Institute of Management Accountants has promulgated the following standards of ethical conduct for management accountants. Adherence to these standards is integral to achieving the *Objectives of Management Accounting.* Management accountants shall not commit acts contrary to these standards nor shall they condone the commission of such acts by others within their organization.

COMPETENCE

Management accountants have a responsibility to do the following:

- Maintain an appropriate level of professional competence by ongoing development of their knowledge and skills.

---

[5]Source: Statement on Management Accounting Standards of Ethical Conduct for Management Accountants (Montvale, N.J.: Institute of Management Accountants, 1983).

- Perform their professional duties in accordance with relevant laws, regulations, and technical standards.
- Prepare complete and clear reports and recommendations after appropriate analyses of relevant and reliable information.

CONFIDENTIALITY

Management accountants have a responsibility to do the following:

- Refrain from disclosing confidential information acquired in the course of their work except when authorized, unless legally obligated to do so.
- Inform subordinates as appropriate regarding the confidentiality of information acquired in the course of their work and monitor their activities to assure the maintenance of that confidentiality.
- Refrain from using or appearing to use confidential information acquired in the course of their work for unethical or illegal advantage either personally or through third parties.

INTEGRITY

Management accountants have a responsibility to do the following:

- Avoid actual or apparent conflicts of interest and advise all appropriate parties of any potential conflict.
- Refrain from engaging in any activity that would prejudice their ability to carry out their duties ethically.
- Refuse any gift, favor, or hospitality that would influence or would appear to influence their actions.
- Refrain from either actively or passively subverting the attainment of the organization's legitimate and ethical objectives.
- Recognize and communicate professional limitations or other constraints that would preclude responsible judgment or successful performance of an activity.
- Communicate unfavorable as well as favorable information and professional judgments or opinions.
- Refrain from engaging in or supporting any activity that would discredit the profession.

OBJECTIVITY

Management accountants have a responsibility to do the following:

- Communicate information fairly and objectively.
- Disclose fully all relevant information that could reasonably be expected to influence an intended user's understanding of the reports, comments, and recommendations presented.

RESOLUTION OF ETHICAL CONFLICT

In applying the standards of ethical conduct, management accountants may encounter problems in identifying unethical behavior or in resolving an ethical conflict. When faced with significant ethical issues, management accountants should follow the established policies of the organization bearing on the resolution of such conflict. If these policies do not resolve the ethical conflict, management accountants should consider the following courses of action:

- Discuss such problems with the immediate superior except when it appears that the superior is involved, in which case the problem should be presented initially to the next higher managerial level. If satisfactory resolution cannot be achieved when the problem is initially presented, submit the issues to the next higher managerial level.
- If the immediate superior is the chief executive officer, or equivalent, the acceptable reviewing authority may be a group such as the audit committee, executive committee, board of directors, board of trustees, or owners. Contact with levels above the immediate superior should be initiated only with the superior's knowledge, assuming the superior is not involved.
- Clarify relevant concepts by confidential discussion with an objective advisor to obtain an understanding of possible courses of action.
- If the ethical conflict still exists after exhausting all levels of internal review, the management accountant may have no other recourse on significant matters than to resign from the organization and to submit an informative memorandum to an appropriate representative of the organization.

Except where legally prescribed, communication of such problems to authorities or individuals not employed or engaged by the organization is not considered appropriate.

QUESTIONS, PROBLEMS, AND CASES

REVIEW QUESTIONS

1. Review the meaning of the concepts and terms listed in Key Terms and Concepts.
2. What are the steps involved in the managerial decision-making and planning process? What role does accounting play in that process?
3. Who in the organization is generally in charge of managerial accounting?
4. What are the steps involved in the control and internal performance evaluation process? What role does accounting play in that process?
5. What are the two major uses of managerial accounting information?
6. What is meant by total quality management (TQM)? What performance measures are likely to be included under TQM?
7. (Appendix 1.1) An accounting employee notices that an employee in purchasing has been accepting tickets to sporting events from a company supplier, which is against company policy. According to the Institute of Management Accountants' code of conduct, what steps should the accounting employee take to stop the practice?
8. Financial accounting is primarily concerned with
   a. historical reporting of financial position.
   b. internal reporting of divisional performance.
   c. auditing internal controls.
   d. All of the above.

9. Managerial accounting is used for
   a. decision making.
   b. planning.
   c. control.
   d. All of the above.
10. The controller oversees
   a. financial reporting.
   b. reporting for tax purposes.
   c. the management of cash.
   d. **a** and **b**.

CRITICAL ANALYSIS AND DISCUSSION QUESTIONS

11. Generally accepted accounting principles are the methods of accounting publicly held firms use in preparing their financial statements. A principle in physics, such as the law of gravity, serves as a basis for developing theories and explaining the relations among physical objects. In what ways are generally accepted accounting principles similar to and different from principles in physics?
12. Distinguish between internal performance evaluation and external performance evaluation.
13. "It is important for managerial accountants to understand the uses of accounting data and for users of data to understand accounting. Only in this way can accountants provide the appropriate accounting data for the correct uses." Do you agree with this statement? Why or why not?
14. "The best management accounting system provides managers with all the information they would like to have." Do you agree with this statement? Why or why not?
15. What is just-in-time (JIT)? How does JIT help accountants serve managers better?
16. What is activity-based management (ABM)?
17. True or false? Benchmarking means you do the work properly the first time and don't worry about it after that.
18. Accounting may provide information for decision making in the form of
   a. historical data to be used as a basis for projections.
   b. projected costs of alternatives.
   c. external reports.
   d. **a** and **b**.
19. Incentives for managers to record sales early include
   a. an effective code of conduct.
   b. being held responsible for financial performance.
   c. compensation based on sales performance.
   d. **b** and **c**.
20. Activity-based management reduces costs by
   a. eliminating nonvalue-added activities.
   b. cutting budgets.
   c. improving efficiency of nonvalue-added activities.
   d. **a** and **c**.

21. "Managerial accounting is not important in nonprofit organizations, such as agencies of the federal government and nonprofit hospitals, because they do not have to earn a profit." Do you agree with this statement? Why or why not?
22. A student planning a career in marketing wondered why it was important to learn about accounting. How would you respond?
23. "Activity management reduces costs by cutting budgets." Do you agree with this statement? Why or why not?

PROBLEMS AND SHORT CASES

24. **Ethics and altering the books** (adapted from CMA exam). Alert, a closely held investment services group, has been successful for the past three years. Bonuses for top management have ranged from 50 percent to 100 percent of base salary. Top management, however, holds only 35 percent of the common stock, and recent industry news indicates that a major corporation may try to acquire Alert. Top management fears that they might lose their bonuses, not to mention their employment, if the takeover occurs. Management has told Roger Deerling, Alert's controller, to make a few changes to several accounting policies and practices, thus making Alert a much less attractive acquisition. Roger knows that these "changes" are not in accordance with Generally Accepted Accounting Principles. Roger has also been told not to mention these changes to anyone outside the top-management group.
    a. What are Roger Deerling's responsibilities?
    b. What steps should he take to resolve this problem?

25. **Identifying managers' information needs.** Identify the management accounting information needed by:
    a. the manager of a local Taco Bell outlet that serves customers who walk in or pick up at a drive-up window.
    b. the regional manager of Taco Bell who supervises the operations of 50 outlets in a region covering 10,000 square miles.
    c. senior management located at the PepsiCo corporate headquarters in Purchase, New York. (PepsiCo owns Taco Bell.)
    Be sure to address the following: content, frequency, and timeliness of information needed by these different managers. For each case, rate the information needs on the following scales:

FREQUENCY OF INFORMATION RECEIVED BY THE MANAGER:

Daily	Weekly	Monthly	Yearly

DEGREE OF DETAIL:

Detailed information on each employee's productivity	Report on performance of each outlet	Report on performance of each region

26. **Value chain.** Apple Computer Company incurs the following costs:
    a. transportation costs for shipping computers to retail stores
    b. utilities costs incurred by the facility assembling Apple computers
    c. salaries for personnel developing the next line of computers
    d. cost of Apple employee's visit to a major customer to illustrate computer capabilities
    e. cost of president's salary
    f. cost of advertising

    Assign each of these cost items to the appropriate part of the value chain shown in Exhibit 1.3.

27. **Value chain.** Johnson & Johnson, a pharmaceutical company, incurs the following costs:
    a. cost of redesigning blister packs to make drug containers more tamper-proof
    b. cost of videos sent to doctors to promote sales of a new drug
    c. equipment purchased by a scientist to conduct experiments on drugs yet to be approved by the government
    d. cost of fees paid to members of J&J's board of directors
    e. cost of Federal Express courier service to deliver drugs to hospitals

    Assign each of these cost items to the appropriate part of the value chain shown in Exhibit 1.3.

28. **Responsibility for ethical action** (adapted from CMA exam). Jorge Martinez recently joined GroChem, Inc., as assistant controller. GroChem processes chemicals for use in fertilizers. During his first month on the job, Jorge spent most of his time getting better acquainted with those responsible for plant operations. Jorge asked the plant supervisor what the procedure was for the disposal of chemicals. The response was that he (the plant supervisor) was not involved in the disposal of waste and that Jorge would be wise to ignore the issue. Of course, this just drove Jorge to investigate the matter further. Jorge soon discovered that GroChem was dumping toxic waste in a nearby public landfill late at night. Further, he discovered that several members of management were involved in arranging for this dumping. Jorge was, however, unable to determine whether his superior, the controller, was involved. Jorge considered three possible courses of action. He could discuss the matter with his controller, anonymously release the information to the local newspaper, or discuss the situation with an outside member of the board of directors whom he knows personally.
    a. Does Jorge have an ethical responsibility to take a course of action?
    b. Of the three possible courses of action, which are appropriate and which are inappropriate?

29. **Ethics and inventory obsolescence** (adapted from CMA exam). The external auditors of HHP (Heart Health Procedures) are currently performing their annual audit of the company with the help of assistant controller Linda Joyner. Several years ago Heart Health Procedures developed a unique balloon technique for opening obstructed arteries in the heart. The technique utilizes an expensive component that HHP produces. Until last year, HHP maintained a monopoly in this field.

    During the past year, however, a major competitor developed a technically superior product that uses an innovative, less costly component. The competitor was granted FDA approval, and it is expected that HHP will lose market share as a result. HHP currently has several years' worth of expensive components essential for the manufacture of its balloon product. Linda Joyner knows that these components will decrease in value due to the introduction of the competitor's product. She also knows that her boss, the controller, is aware of the situation. The controller, however, has informed the chief financial officer that there is no obsolete inventory nor any need for reductions of inventories to market values. Linda is aware that the chief financial officer's bonus plan is tied directly to the corporate profits which depend on ending inventory valuations.

In signing the auditor's representation letter, the chief financial officer acknowledges that all relevant information has been disclosed to the auditors and that all accounting procedures have been followed according to generally accepted accounting principles. Linda knows that the external auditors are unaware of the inventory problem, and she is unsure of what to do.

   a. Has the controller behaved unethically?

   b. How should Linda Joyner resolve this problem? Should she report this inventory overvaluation to the external auditors?

30. **Value-added and nonvalue-added activities.** Consider a plant producing widgets and dyes. The raw materials are purchased in bulk and delivered from the supplier to be placed in a warehouse until requested by the production departments. The warehouse has 24-hour security guards and one full-time maintenance person. The materials are then delivered to the departments three miles away by truck where they are used in the production of widgets and dyes. During the production the pieces are inspected twice. After production the finished product is stored in another warehouse until it is shipped to customers.

Identify the value-added and nonvalue-added activities.

31. **Value of information: nonbusiness setting.** Consider the value of the following information in a medical context.

Suppose that a patient visits a doctor's office and that the doctor decides on the basis of the signs that the patient's appendix should be removed immediately. Meanwhile, the doctor orders a white blood cell count. The doctor decides that the appendix must be removed no matter what the blood count happens to be.

   a. What is the value to the doctor of the information (in the cost-benefit sense discussed in this chapter) about the blood cell count?

   b. Why might the doctor order the test anyway?

CHAPTER 2

COST CONCEPTS FOR MANAGERIAL DECISION MAKING

LEARNING OBJECTIVES

1. Master the concept of cost.
2. Distinguish between direct and indirect costs.
3. Distinguish between manufacturing and nonmanufacturing costs.
4. Understand the nature of common, or indirect, costs.
5. Compare, contrast, and compute gross margin, contribution margin, and profit margin.
6. Compare and contrast income statements prepared for managerial use and those prepared for external reporting.
7. Understand the use of the value chain concept in preparing income statements for managerial use.

Chapter 1 indicated that managerial accounting deals with the information managers need for planning, for making decisions, and for evaluating performance. Accounting is the language of business. You need to know the concepts of accounting to communicate. This section defines and discusses those basic concepts.[1]

 Managers often require cost information to help them make decisions. The following are just a few examples:

- Compaq Computer Corporation managers evaluated market demand and product cost data for their personal computer models, as well as those of their competitors, before deciding to cut their prices in early 1992.
- General Motors' selection of plants that needed to be closed in the mid-1990s was based on a comparison of manufacturing costs at various facilities.

---

[1]A glossary of accounting terms and concepts appears at the back of this book to help you find definitions. See especially the cost definitions under *cost terminology*.

- In making periodic decisions about routes and fares, American Airlines weighs the costs of utilizing personnel and aircraft on a route against competitive market conditions that determine revenues.

Each of these examples focuses on costs of one type or another. The first step in studying accounting for managerial use is to understand the various types of costs incurred by organizations. This chapter presents the cost terms, concepts, and classifications routinely used by managerial accountants.

WHAT IS A COST?

In principle, a cost is a sacrifice of resources. For example, if you purchased an automobile for a cash payment of $12,000, the cost to purchase the automobile would be $12,000.

Although this concept is simple, it can be difficult to apply. For example, what are the relevant costs for an individual to obtain a college education? A student sacrifices cash to pay for tuition and books. What about cash paid for living costs? If these costs would have to be paid whether or not the student attended college, they should not be considered as costs of getting a college education.

Students sacrifice not only cash. They also sacrifice their time. Placing a value on that time is difficult; it depends on the best forgone alternative use of the time. For students who sacrifice high-paying jobs to attend college, the total cost of college is greater than for students who do not sacrifice high-paying jobs.

The term *cost* is meaningful only if it is used in some particular context. To say "the cost of this building is $1 million" is ambiguous unless the context of the cost is identified. Does cost mean the original price the current owner paid, the price that the owner would pay to replace it new, or the price to replace it today in its current condition? Is it the annual rental fee paid to occupy the building? Is it the cash forgone from not selling it? Is it the original price paid minus accumulated depreciation? You need to know the context in which the term *cost* is used to reduce its ambiguity.

Many disputes arise over the definition of cost. We devote much of this chapter to describing how different contexts affect the meaning of costs.

OPPORTUNITY COSTS

The definition of a cost as a "sacrifice" leads directly to the **opportunity cost** concept. An opportunity cost is the forgone income from using an asset in its best alternative. If a firm uses an asset for one purpose, the opportunity cost of using it for that purpose is the return forgone from its best alternative use.

The opportunity cost of a college education includes forgone earnings during the time in school. Some other illustrations of the meaning of opportunity cost follow:

1. The opportunity cost of funds invested in a government bond is the interest that an investor could earn on a bank certificate of deposit (adjusted for differences in risk).

2. Proprietors of small businesses often take a salary. But the opportunity cost of their time may be much higher than the nominal salary recorded on the books. A proprietor can work for someone else and earn a wage. The highest such wage (adjusting for differences in risk and nonpecuniary costs or benefits of being a proprietor) is the opportunity cost of being a proprietor. Entrepreneurs like Bill Gates at Microsoft and Phil Knight at Nike have become rich developing their enterprises. They might also have become wealthy as executives in established companies.

Example John Pavilla, a gas station attendant earning $11,000 a year, is trying to decide if he should go back to school to earn a B.S. degree in finance. He presently lives in an apartment for which he pays rent of $4,800 a year. John has already been accepted to State University and has determined that tuition, books, and supplies for four years could cost $9,600. Housing would cost the same as what he is paying now. In this example the opportunity costs to John are his forgone wages.

Behavioral scientists have shown that many people have a tendency to treat opportunity and outlay of costs differently. In one study people were asked if they would pay $1,000 for a ticket to the Super Bowl. Most people responded that they would not. However, many of the same people said that they would not sell the Super Bowl ticket for $1,000 if they were given the ticket free of charge. These people refused to incur the $1,000 out-of-pocket cost of buying the Super Bowl ticket, but they were willing to incur the $1,000 opportunity cost of keeping a ticket that they already had.

COSTS VERSUS EXPENSES

We distinguish *cost,* as used in managerial accounting, from *expense,* as used in financial accounting. A cost is a sacrifice of resources. An expense is the historical cost of the goods or services a firm uses in a particular accounting period.

Managerial accounting deals primarily with costs, not expenses. Generally accepted accounting principles and regulations such as the income tax laws specify when the firm can or must treat costs as expenses to be deducted from revenues. We reserve the term *expense* to refer to expenses for external reporting as defined by generally accepted accounting principles.

The main distinction is timing. For instance, a firm purchases goods for resale in the amount of $2,000, sells $1,000 of the goods during the first period, and sells the remaining $1,000 of goods during the next period. The cost during the first period is $2,000, while the expense is $1,000 for each of the two periods.

ACCOUNTING CONCEPTS AND DEFINITIONS

DIRECT AND INDIRECT COSTS

Costs that relate directly to a cost object are **direct costs.** Those that do not are **indirect costs.** A **cost object** is any item for which the manager wishes to measure cost. Departments, stores, divisions, product lines, or units produced are typical cost objects. The cost object establishes the context for labeling a cost as direct or indirect.

Example   Electron, Inc., produces calculators. It buys the components from outside suppliers, assembles the components, and inspects the product for defects in workmanship. The company leases the factory building. If the cost object is a calculator, the materials and labor that the firm traces directly to the production of each calculator are direct costs. Electron considers the components to be direct materials, and workers' time to assemble and inspect the calculator to be direct labor.

In this example, when the cost object is a calculator, the factory rent is indirect. Now suppose that the purpose of calculating costs is to evaluate the performance of the factory manager. In that case, the cost object is the entire factory, not a unit produced, so factory rent would be a direct cost. The lease cost for the factory building is direct to the factory but indirect to a calculator produced. The distinction between direct and indirect costs is meaningful only when applied to a particular cost object.

COMMON COSTS

The distinction between a direct cost and an indirect cost is in relation to a cost object. Indirect costs are also called **common costs.** A direct cost is one that firms can identify specifically with, or trace directly to, a particular product, department, or process. For example, direct materials and direct labor costs are direct with respect to products manufactured.

A common, or indirect, cost results from the shared use of a facility or a service by several products, departments, or processes. A department manager's salary is a direct cost of the department, but common to the units the department produces.

Examples of common costs include the following:

- The factory rent Electron, Inc., pays is common to departments within the factory.
- The maintenance costs of the business school building is common to each of the departments (accounting, finance, marketing, and others) of the school.

The allocation of indirect costs involves assigning a portion of these costs to each of the cost objects. Cost allocation is presented in both internal and external accounting reports. The subject of cost allocation will come up frequently in this text, where we discuss it in the context of managerial decision making and performance evaluation.

VARIABLE VERSUS FIXED COSTS

Variable costs are those costs that change in total as the level of activity changes. By contrast, **fixed costs** do not change in total with changes in total activity. Suppose you pay a monthly lease for an automobile. If the lease is a fixed amount regardless of the number of miles driven, then the lease is a fixed cost. If the lease required you to pay an amount per mile, then the lease would be a variable cost because the more miles you drive the more you pay.

Examples of variable costs include materials to make products and energy to run machines. Examples of fixed costs include rent on building space (assuming it is paid on a time basis not a volume-of-activity basis) and salaries of top company officials. Many costs do not fit neatly into fixed and variable categories. We try to be clear in our examples as to whether you should assume a cost is fixed or variable.

The distinction between fixed and variable costs is important for managerial decision making and is a recurrent theme throughout this book. You will see it discussed at length starting in Chapter 3.

MANUFACTURING COSTS

Manufacturing involves the transformation of materials into finished goods using labor and capital invested in machines and production facilities. **Manufacturing costs** comprise three elements: direct materials, direct labor, and manufacturing overhead.

Direct materials (also called *raw materials*) are those the firm can trace directly to a unit of output. They include iron ore to make steel, logs to make lumber, electronic chips used in making calculators, and plastics used in making toys. Direct materials are variable costs.

Indirect materials are materials that are not easily associated with production of a specific product. Examples of indirect materials include lubricants for machines, light bulbs, welding rods, and cleaning materials. Accounting classifies indirect materials as part of overhead, which we describe later in this section.

Direct labor represents the wages of workers who transform raw materials into finished products. Examples of direct labor costs are the wages of assembly-line workers who make automobiles and construction workers who build houses. Direct labor costs can be either variable or fixed. Assume they are variable unless we specifically state that they are fixed costs in particular examples.

Indirect labor is labor that is not easily associated with the production of a specific product. Examples include wages of maintenance personnel, supervisors, materials handlers, and inventory storekeepers. Like indirect materials, accounting classifies indirect labor costs as overhead.

Manufacturing overhead includes all manufacturing costs that the firm cannot trace to particular units of product as either direct materials or direct labor. These costs include indirect materials, indirect labor, utilities, property taxes, depreciation, insurance, rent, and other costs of operating the manufacturing facilities. Exhibit 2.1 diagrams the relation between the cost of producing a good and the materials, labor, and manufacturing overhead required to produce it. Overhead includes both fixed and variable components. Our examples will indicate how much overhead is fixed and how much is variable.

Although we use the term *manufacturing overhead,* accountants use many synonyms in practice, including *overhead, burden, factory burden, factory overhead,* and *factory expense.* The term *manufacturing overhead,* as we use it here, refers only to manufacturing costs, not to nonmanufacturing marketing and administrative costs.

EXHIBIT 2.1

The Cost of Producing a Good

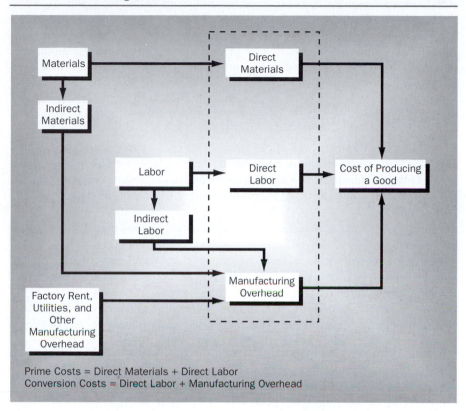

Prime Costs = Direct Materials + Direct Labor
Conversion Costs = Direct Labor + Manufacturing Overhead

Total manufacturing costs include direct material, direct labor, and manufacturing overhead. The primary inputs to the production of a product are the direct labor and the direct materials. The sum of direct materials and direct labor is called **prime cost.** Manufacturing overhead and direct labor are the costs of converting raw materials into final products. Thus accountants call them **conversion costs.**

SUMMARY OF MANUFACTURING COSTS

Prime Costs	Direct Materials	Directly traceable to a unit of output.
	Direct Labor	Directly traceable to a unit of output.
Conversion Costs	Manufacturing Overhead	
	Indirect Materials	Cannot be associated with a particular unit of output.
	Indirect Labor	Cannot be associated with a particular unit of output.
	Other Manufacturing Overhead	Cannot be associated with a particular unit of output.

Managers sometimes give prime costs a lot of attention because these costs represent 80 to 90 percent of total manufacturing costs. Just as Willie Sutton robbed banks because "that's where the money was," managers might focus nearly all their attention on prime costs because "that's where nearly all the costs are." Managers who focus on conversion costs use a controllability argument: "We can manage conversion costs. Direct materials costs are mostly outside of our control." Generally, companies with relatively low manufacturing overhead will focus on managing prime costs. Companies that have a lot of direct labor and/or manufacturing overhead tend to be more concerned about conversion costs. In practice, you should determine what cost information you need to manage effectively.

NONMANUFACTURING COSTS

Many other functional cost classifications are used in addition to those used to classify manufacturing costs. **Nonmanufacturing costs** include merchandise costs, marketing costs, administrative costs, and research and development costs. Merchandise costs are variable costs; the other nonmanufacturing costs include both fixed and variable components.

Merchandise costs are the costs of goods plus transportation costs incurred by the purchasers.

Marketing costs include salaries, commissions, and travel costs of sales personnel; the costs of advertising and promotion; and the costs of storing, handling, and shipping finished products.

Administrative costs refer to all costs of running the organization. The salaries of top-management personnel and the costs of the legal, accounting, and public relations activities are examples of administrative costs.

Research and development costs include all costs of developing new products and services. These include the costs of running laboratories, building prototypes of new products, and testing new products. Such costs are becoming increasingly important as more high-technology firms enter the economy and as international competition increases.

SERVICE ORGANIZATIONS' COSTS

How can we apply cost concepts to service organizations, both for-profit and not-for-profit, that are not engaged in manufacturing activities?

Most service organizations are not concerned with the financial reporting requirement of inventory valuation, because services produced cannot be inventoried for future sale. Alternative cost-accounting systems have been developed that operate parallel to the traditional financial reporting systems to facilitate managerial decision making.

Another characteristic distinguishes service organizations from manufacturing plants: a service organization's "product" is often less tangible and measurable than a product from a manufacturing operation. For example, how do we measure the output of a school, a women's crisis center, or a radio station? The answers are not straightforward or easy.

The difficulty of measuring output for service organizations raises special issues about designing product costing systems. Identifying direct material and direct labor costs is difficult when the output is indefinite. Therefore, many of the costs of service organizations are classified as indirect, and the concepts relating activity analysis to overhead costs become particularly important.

Computing categories of unit costs.   After the death of his Uncle Sven early this year, Peter Sorenson left his $40,000-a-year job at an electronics company to assume control of Klogs, Inc., a manufacturer of quality clogs. Klogs produced and sold 70,000 pairs of clogs last year. At capacity, Klogs could manufacture 100,000 pairs of clogs. Peter obtained the following breakdown of last year's costs.

Item	Cost
(a) Sandpaper and Manufacturing Supplies	$ 8,400
(b) Leather and Wood	210,000
(c) Factory Rent—10 Years Remaining on Lease	12,000
(d) Labor—Cutting and Assembling	385,000
(e) Supervisor's Salary	15,000
(f) Maintenance and Depreciation (fixed)	2,000
(g) Utilities—Factory (fixed)	6,000
(h) Sven's Salary	40,000
(i) Shipping Costs ($0.10 per unit)	7,000
(j) Office Supplies	100
(k) Advertising (fixed)	1,000

a. Ignoring any noneconomic value of self-employment, what is Peter Sorenson's opportunity cost of working for Klogs?
b. Identify the following costs, using last year's figures.
    (1) Unit direct materials costs.
    (2) Unit direct labor costs.
    (3) Unit manufacturing overhead.
    (4) Unit marketing costs.
    (5) Unit administrative costs.

The solution to this self-study problem is at the end of this chapter on page 46.

PERIOD AND PRODUCT COSTS

Firms eventually expense, for external financial reporting purposes, all costs that they incur. If a firm does not expense a cost immediately, but adds it to an inventory account on the balance sheet until it sells the goods, that cost is said to be "inventoriable." We call inventoriable costs **product costs.** We call those that are not inventoriable **period costs,** because the firm expenses them in the period incurred. These include research and development, marketing, and administrative costs.

Generally accepted accounting principles and income tax regulations require that firms treat all manufacturing costs as product costs for external financial reporting using full absorption costing (sometimes called absorption costing). Using **full absorption costing,** the firm assigns a unit's variable manufacturing cost plus a share of fixed manufacturing costs to each unit produced. Thus the total of units produced "fully absorbs" manufacturing costs.

For example, assume Campbell Soup Company, the large food producer, is making Swanson meals. Using full absorption costing, Campbell Soup Company would assign materials, labor, and manufacturing overhead to each Swanson meal produced. Each meal would be assigned a share of fixed manufacturing costs (for example, rent, building depreciation, plant administrative salaries) under full absorption costing.

By contrast, the **variable costing** method includes only each unit's variable manufacturing cost. Firms using variable costing treat fixed manufacturing costs as period costs. Using variable costing, Campbell Soup Company would not assign any of its fixed manufacturing costs to Swanson meals, but would expense fixed manufacturing costs as period costs.

Firms treat all nonmanufacturing costs as period costs, and therefore nonmanufacturing costs are not inventoried under either method.

PROBLEM 2.2 FOR SELF-STUDY

Match the concept with the definition.

Concept	Definition
Cost	**a.** Costs that are a part of inventory.
Opportunity cost	**b.** Costs directly related to a cost object.
Expense	**c.** A sacrifice of resources.
Product costs	**d.** Costs not directly related to a cost object.
Period costs	**e.** Any item for which the manager wishes to measure cost.
Cost object	**f.** The cost charged against revenue in a particular accounting period.
Direct costs	**g.** Costs shared by two or more cost objects.
Indirect costs.	**h.** Costs that firms can more easily attribute to time intervals.
Common costs	**i.** The return that one could realize from the best forgone alternative use of a resource.

The solution to this self-study problem is at the end of this chapter on page 47.

COMMON COST ALLOCATIONS

Many costs are common to different products manufactured by one firm. To develop product cost information, firms must allocate these common costs.

Firms allocate the costs of operating *service departments* (for example, computer services, maintenance departments) to production departments for several purposes, discussed below.

Common cost allocations pervade accounting reports, both internal and external. To understand accounting reports and make appropriate interpretations, you must be familiar with the alternative allocation methods used and their effects on the resulting reports.

MANAGERIAL PURPOSES OF COST ALLOCATION

Managers use allocated costs for several reasons, including the following:

1. *Pricing and Bidding.* Prices of products and services are often based, at least to some extent, on their costs. To determine the full cost of producing products or

Dispute over Indirect Costs between Stanford University and the U.S. Government

Stanford University and the Navy settled a fraud case involving research expenses, with the university repaying a small fraction of the Navy's original claim and the Navy saying that an inquiry had found no wrongdoing by the university. The issue surfaced when the Office of Naval Research representative at Stanford accused the university of overcharging the government about $230 million for so-called indirect costs in conducting government research.

The costs included items that the government deemed unallowable for purposes of government contract research, such as depreciation on the university's yacht and flowers for the president's house. To settle the dispute the university agreed to lower its overhead rate on government contracts.

Based on W. Celis III, "Navy Settles a Fraud Case on Stanford Research Costs," *New York Times*, October 19, 1994; and Steven Huddart, "Stanford University (A): Indirect Cost Recovery," Graduate School of Business, Stanford University, July 1991.

services, costs must be allocated. For example, part of the cost of providing lodging services at the Waikiki Hotel is the cost of hotel security, which is provided by the Grounds and Maintenance Department.

2. *Contract Cost Reimbursement.* Some organizations seek reimbursement for the costs of providing services. Examples include health-care facilities, which often are reimbursed by insurance companies or the federal government, and public utilities, which must justify rates on the basis of costs incurred. The Managerial Application about Stanford University demonstrates how cost allocation affects research contracts.

3. *Motivation.* Some organizations allocate costs to encourage desired behavior. For example, some manufacturers allocate part of their interest costs to inventories of raw materials and finished goods to encourage managers to minimize inventory levels.

COST ALLOCATION: A NOTE OF CAUTION

Organizations commonly use cost allocations. Although allocations often have a purpose, they can easily mislead users of accounting information because users often do not appreciate how arbitrarily some firms allocate most costs. We caution you to use allocated costs carefully.

Cost allocation is so prevalent that we often take it for granted. Companies must continually challenge the need for cost allocation and ask "Why allocate?" Research by Professors Fremgen and Liao provides some of the answers.[2] They found that:

■ 84 percent of the companies participating in the survey reported that they do allocate at least some corporate indirect costs for some purposes.

[2]J. M. Fremgen and S. S. Liao, *The Allocation of Corporate Indirect Costs* (Montvale, N.J.: National Association of Accountants, 1981); J. M. Fremgen and S. S. Liao, "The Allocation of Indirect Costs," *Management Accounting* (September 1981).

• the most widely cited reason for allocations for purposes of performance evaluation was "simply to remind (department) managers that the indirect costs exist and had to be recovered by the (department's) earnings."

COST AND MARGIN CONCEPTS

This section presents components of product costs and different measures of margins.

COSTS OF MAKING A PRODUCT

The diagram in Exhibit 2.2 illustrates components of a product cost for one unit using the facts for Electron, Inc. Because fixed costs occur per period (like rent), not per unit (like materials), we can compute fixed costs per unit only if we specify a particular volume. For this example, we assume a volume of 20,000 units for the month.

EXHIBIT 2.2

ELECTRON, INC.
What Makes Up a Product's Cost

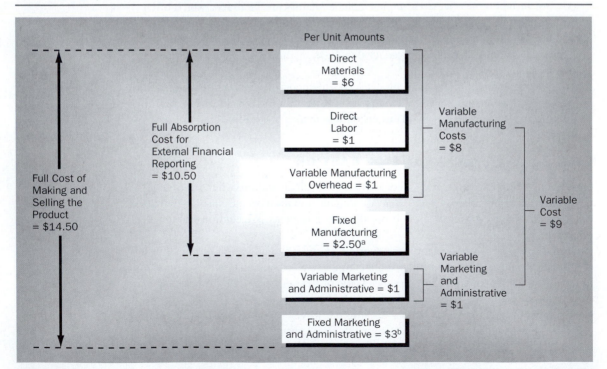

[a]Fixed manufacturing costs per unit = $50,000/20,000 units = $2.50.
[b]Fixed marketing and administrative costs per unit = $60,000/20,000 units = $3.00.

The diagram shows several important distinctions. First, note the difference between the full cost of making and selling the product and the full absorption cost inventory value. The full cost of making and selling the product includes marketing and administrative costs, but the full absorption cost inventory value does not. If you ask accountants for unit costs, you may be surprised to find the accountants have provided full absorption inventory costs when you wanted full costs.

Second, note the difference between unit variable costs, which include variable marketing and administrative costs, and unit variable manufacturing costs, which do not. Neither full absorption nor variable costing inventory values include marketing and administrative costs. Looking at Exhibit 2.2, what would be the full absorption cost if variable manufacturing costs were $10 per unit? (Answer: $12.50.)

MEASURES OF MARGINS

Exhibits 2.3 and 2.4 illustrate gross margin, contribution margin, and profit margin computations. Assume the unit selling price for Electron, Inc., is $20. Using the information from Exhibit 2.2, illustrated in Exhibits 2.3 and 2.4, we find:

$$\text{Unit } \mathbf{Profit\ Margin} = \frac{\text{Unit Selling}}{\text{Price}} - \frac{\text{Full Cost per Unit of Making}}{\text{and Selling the Product.}}$$

EXHIBIT 2.3

ELECTRON, INC.
Gross Margin

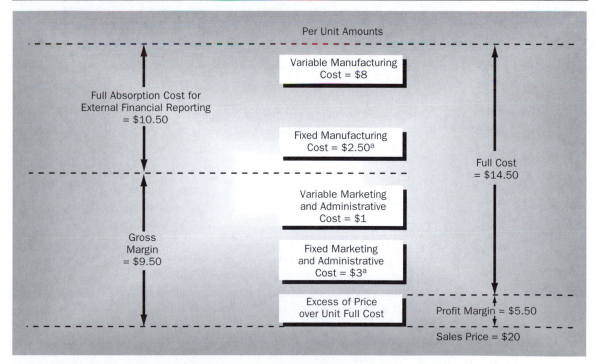

Per Unit Amounts

- Variable Manufacturing Cost = $8
- Fixed Manufacturing Cost = $2.50[a]
- Variable Marketing and Administrative Cost = $1
- Fixed Marketing and Administrative Cost = $3[a]
- Excess of Price over Unit Full Cost

Full Absorption Cost for External Financial Reporting = $10.50

Gross Margin = $9.50

Full Cost = $14.50

Profit Margin = $5.50

Sales Price = $20

[a]Unit fixed costs based on volume of 20,000 units.

EXHIBIT 2.4

ELECTRON, INC.
Contribution Margin

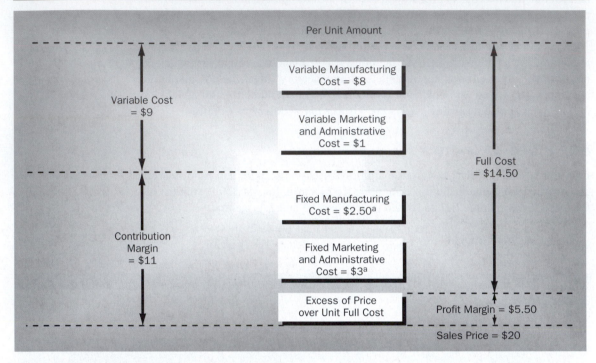

Per Unit Amount

Variable Cost = $9

Variable Manufacturing Cost = $8

Variable Marketing and Administrative Cost = $1

Full Cost = $14.50

Contribution Margin = $11

Fixed Manufacturing Cost = $2.50ª

Fixed Marketing and Administrative Cost = $3ª

Excess of Price over Unit Full Cost

Profit Margin = $5.50

Sales Price = $20

ªUnit fixed costs based on volume of 20,000 units. Unit fixed cost = total fixed costs ÷ volume. In this case, fixed manufacturing costs for the period were $50,000 and volume was 20,000 units. So fixed manufacturing costs per unit = $2.50 = $50,000/20,000 units. (You can go through the same calculations for fixed marketing and administrative cost per unit.)

For Electron, Inc., the unit profit margin is $5.50 = $20 − $14.50.

$$\text{Unit } \textbf{Gross Margin} = \frac{\text{Unit Selling}}{\text{Price}} - \frac{\text{Unit Full Absorption Cost of}}{\text{Making the Product.}}$$

For Electron, Inc., the unit gross margin is $9.50 = $20 − $10.50.

$$\text{Unit } \textbf{Contribution Margin} = \frac{\text{Unit Selling}}{\text{Price}} - \frac{\text{Unit Variable Cost of Making}}{\text{and Selling the Product.}}$$

For Electron, Inc., the unit contribution margin is $11 = $20 − $9.

Gross margin and contribution margin are different concepts despite their similar-sounding names. Firms routinely report total gross margins on external financial statements. Many internal decisions involve choosing among products based on those products' contribution to covering fixed costs and generating profits, which requires knowledge of contribution margins. Consequently, contribution margins are generally more useful than gross margins for internal decisions. Looking at Exhibits 2.3 and 2.4, what would the contribution and gross margins be if the sales price were $22 per unit? (Answer: contribution margin = $13, gross margin = $11.50.)

PROBLEM 2.3 FOR SELF-STUDY

Relation between Contribution Margin and Cost. Tori Adams makes exotic clocks. Tori has asked for your help in understanding the relation between contribution margin and costs. Complete the diagram for Tori by inserting amounts, given the data (after the diagram) about a particular clock:

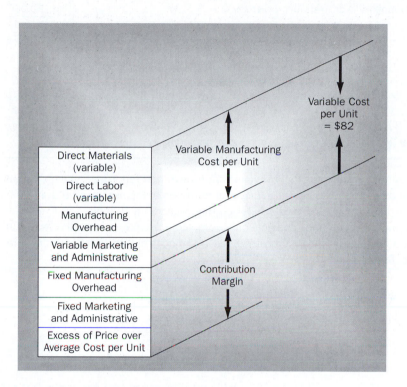

	$	
Price per Unit	$	100
Contribution Margin per Unit		18
Gross Margin for 1,000 Units		21,000
Variable Manufacturing Costs per Unit		70
Direct Materials per Unit		40
Direct Labor per Unit		20
Fixed Marketing and Administrative Costs per Unit		6

Complete the diagram for Tori by placing an amount beside each label. We have done one to help you get started.

The solution to this self-study problem is at the end of this chapter on page 47.

EXHIBIT 2.5

ELECTRON, INC.
Income Statement for External Financial Reporting
for the Month Ending February 28

Sales Revenue	$400,000[a]
Less Cost of Goods Sold	210,000[b]
Gross Margin	$190,000
Less Marketing and Administrative Expenses	80,000[c]
Net Income before Taxes	$110,000

[a]$400,000 = $20 × 20,000 Units.
[b]$210,000 = ($8 Variable Manufacturing Cost × 20,000 Units) + $50,000 Fixed Manufacturing Cost.
[c]$80,000 = ($1 Variable Marketing and Administrative Cost × 20,000 Units) + $60,000 Fixed Marketing and Administrative Costs.

INCOME STATEMENT FOR EXTERNAL REPORTING

This section presents the income statement for external reporting, which we compare with income statements for managerial purposes in the next two sections.

The income statement for external reporting appears in Exhibit 2.5. To comply with income tax regulations and generally accepted accounting principles using full absorption costing, Electron allocates fixed manufacturing costs to each unit produced, as follows:

$$\text{Fixed Manufacturing Cost per Unit} = \frac{\text{Fixed Manufacturing Costs}}{\text{Units Produced}}$$

$$= \frac{\$50,000}{20,000 \text{ Units}}$$

$$= \$2.50 \text{ per Unit.}$$

Adding this $2.50 per unit to the $8 variable manufacturing cost per unit makes the full absorption cost of manufacturing a unit $10.50. Hence, the cost of goods sold is $210,000 (= $10.50 × 20,000 units).

INCOME STATEMENT FOR MANAGERIAL DECISION MAKING

The income statement for external reporting does not show actual manufacturing cost behavior because it "unitizes" fixed manufacturing costs to assign a share of these costs to each unit produced. The income statement in Exhibit 2.6, as prepared for managerial use, will help management do its job because it represents cost behavior.

Note the difference between the *gross margin* and the *contribution margin,* as shown in Exhibits 2.5 and 2.6. The gross margin is the difference between revenue and cost of goods sold, whereas the contribution margin is the difference between revenue and variable costs, including variable marketing and administrative costs.

EXHIBIT 2.6

ELECTRON, INC.
Income Statement for Managerial Decision Making: Contribution Margin Format
for the Month Ending February 28

Sales Revenue		$400,000
Less Variable Costs:		
Variable Cost of Goods Sold	$160,000[a]	
Variable Marketing and Administrative Costs	20,000[b]	
Total Variable Costs		180,000
Contribution Margin		$220,000
Less Fixed Costs:		
Fixed Manufacturing Costs	$ 50,000	
Fixed Marketing and Administrative Costs	60,000	
Total Fixed Costs		110,000
Operating Profit		$110,000

[a]$160,000 = 20,000 Units $\times$ $8 Variable Cost.
[b]$20,000 = 20,000 Units $\times$ $1 Variable Cost.

We use the term *operating profit* at the bottom of income statements prepared for managerial use to distinguish it from net income used in external reporting.

USING THE VALUE CHAIN TO DEVELOP FINANCIAL STATEMENTS

In Chapter 1, we stated that the value chain is a linked set of activities that increases the usefulness of an organization's products or services.

Given the importance of the value chain, as described in Chapter 1, companies should consider developing financial statements that classify costs into value-added or nonvalue-added categories. By classifying activities as value-added or nonvalue-added, managers are better able to focus on which activities to reduce or eliminate and therefore reduce costs.

Suppose the president of Electron, Inc., wants to know which costs add value. The controller reviews value chain activity analyses provided by managers and related costs in detail, and prepares the value chain income statement shown in Exhibit 2.7. The controller uses past-year sales of 20,000 units and the same per-unit costs as outlined in the example. The controller's value chain income statement shows total nonvalue-added activities of $40,000. This information can be used by management to improve efficiency by reducing nonvalue-added activities.

Reducing nonvalue-added activities is not a simple task. For example, how should the production process be changed to reduce materials waste? Should higher-quality materials be purchased, resulting in higher direct materials costs? Or, should production personnel be trained and evaluated based on materials wasted? As you can see, the answer is not always clear. The value chain income statement is an important starting point for management, but it does not guarantee the reduction of nonvalue-added activities.

EXHIBIT 2.7

ELECTRON, INC.
Income Statement for Managerial Decision Making: Value Chain Format for the Month Ending February 28

	Nonvalue-added Activities	Value-added Activities	Total
Sales Revenue		$400,000	$400,000
Variable Manufacturing Costs:			
Materials used in production		100,000	100,000
Materials waste	$20,000		20,000
Labor used in production		18,000	18,000
Labor used to rework products	2,000		2,000
Manufacturing overhead used in production		18,000	18,000
Manufacturing overhead used to rework products	2,000		2,000
Variable Marketing and Administrative Costs:			
M&A services used to sell products		19,000	19,000
M&A services used to process returned products	1,000		1,000
Contribution Margin	(25,000)	245,000	220,000
Fixed Manufacturing Costs:			
Fixed manufacturing costs used in production		45,000	45,000
Fixed manufacturing costs used to rework products	5,000[a]		5,000
Fixed Marketing and Administrative Costs:			
M&A services used to sell products		50,000	50,000
M&A services used to process returned products	10,000[a]		10,000
Operating Profit	($40,000)	$150,000	$110,000

[a]These fixed costs probably will be eliminated in the long run but not in the short run if the nonvalue-added activity is eliminated.

SUMMARY

The following items correspond to the learning objectives presented at the beginning of the chapter.

1. **Master the concept of cost.** A cost is a sacrifice of resources. An expense is the historical cost of goods or services. An opportunity cost is the sacrifice of forgoing the return from the best alternative use of an asset.

2. **Distinguish between direct and indirect costs.** Costs that relate directly to a cost object are direct costs. Those that do not are indirect costs.

3. **Distinguish between manufacturing and nonmanufacturing costs.** Manufacturing costs comprise three elements: direct materials, direct labor, and manufacturing overhead. Nonmanufacturing costs include merchandise, marketing, administrative, and research and development costs.

4. **Understand the nature of common, or indirect, costs.**   A common, or indirect, cost results from the joint use of a facility or a service by several products, departments, or processes.

5. **Compare, contrast, and compute gross margin, contribution margin, and profit margin.** Gross margin, based on full absorption product costs, is reported on external financial statements. Many internal decisions involve choosing among products based on their contribution to covering fixed costs and generat-

ing profits—the contribution margin. Profit margin is the excess of selling price over the full costs, including nonmanufacturing costs, of the product.

Key Equations:

Unit Profit Margin   = Unit Selling Price −   Full Cost per Unit of Making and Selling the Product

Unit Gross Margin   = Unit Selling Price −   Unit Full Absorption Cost of Making the Product

Unit Contribution Margin   = Unit Selling Price −   Unit Variable Cost of Making and Selling the Product

6. **Compare and contrast income statements prepared for managerial use and those prepared for external reporting.** To comply with income tax regulations and generally accepted accounting principles, income statements for external reporting use full absorption costing. Income statements for managerial use, based on variable costs, show actual manufacturing cost behavior.

Key Equation:

$$\text{Fixed Manufacturing Cost per Unit} = \frac{\text{Fixed Manufacturing Costs}}{\text{Units Produced}}$$

7. **Understand the use of the value chain concept in preparing income statements for managerial use.** The value chain income statement separates all costs into value-added and nonvalue-added activities. This enables managers to concentrate their efforts on eliminating nonvalue-added activities and therefore lowering costs.

KEY TERMS AND CONCEPTS

Opportunity cost   The present value of the income (or costs) that a firm could earn (or save) from using an asset in its best alternative use to the one under consideration.

Direct costs   Cost of direct material and direct labor incurred in producing a product.

Indirect costs   Costs of production not easily associated with the production of specific goods and services, also called *overhead*.

Cost object   Any item for which to measure cost—for example, a facility, department, or product.

Common costs   Costs resulting from use of raw materials, a facility, or a service that benefits several products or departments.

Variable costs   Costs that change as activity levels change.

Fixed costs   Costs that do not vary with volume of activity in the short run.

Manufacturing costs   Costs of producing goods. Includes direct materials, direct labor, and manufacturing overhead.

Direct materials   Materials applied and assigned directly to a product.

Indirect materials   Materials not easily associated with a specific unit of product, such as supplies.

Direct labor   Cost of labor applied and assigned directly to a product.

Indirect labor   Labor not easily associated with a particular unit of product, such as a supervisor's salary.

Manufacturing overhead   General manufacturing costs incurred in providing a capacity to carry on productive activities not directly associated with identifiable units of product.

Prime cost   Sum of direct materials and direct labor.

Conversion costs   The costs to convert raw materials to finished products; includes direct labor and manufacturing overhead.

Nonmanufacturing costs   All costs incurred other than those to produce goods. Includes marketing, administrative, merchandise, and research and development costs.

Merchandise costs   Costs incurred to acquire merchandise for resale.

Marketing costs   Costs incurred to sell a product—for example, commissions and advertising.

Administrative costs   Costs incurred for operating the firm as a whole—the salary of the managerial accountant, for example.

Research and development costs   All costs of developing new products and services.

Product costs   Any manufacturing cost that can be inventoried. Includes direct materials, direct labor, and manufacturing overhead.

Period costs   Expenditures, usually based upon the passage of time, charged to operations of the accounting period. Includes nonmanufacturing costs, such as marketing and administrative.

Full absorption costing   The method of costing that assigns all types of manufacturing costs to units produced, required by GAAP.

Variable costing   Method of allocating costs that assigns only variable manufacturing costs to products and treats fixed manufacturing costs as period expenses.

Profit margin   Sales minus full cost of product.

Gross margin   Sales minus full absorption costs.

Contribution margin   Sales less all variable expenses.

SOLUTIONS TO SELF-STUDY PROBLEMS

SUGGESTED SOLUTION TO PROBLEM 2.1 FOR SELF-STUDY

a. Opportunity cost = $40,000.

b. (1) Item **(b):** $\dfrac{\$210,000}{70,000 \text{ units}} = \$3.00 \text{ per unit}$

   (2) Item **(d):** $\dfrac{\$385,000}{70,000 \text{ units}} = \$5.50 \text{ per unit}$

   (3) Items **(a), (c), (e), (f),** and **(g):**

$$\frac{\$8,400 + \$12,000 + \$15,000 + \$2,000 + \$6,000}{70,000 \text{ units}} = \$.62 \text{ per unit}$$

(4) Items **(i)** and **(k)**:

$$\frac{\$7,000 + \$1,000}{70,000 \text{ units}} = \$.114 \text{ (rounded) per unit}$$

(5) Items **(h)** and **(j)**:

$$\frac{\$40,000 + \$100}{70,000 \text{ units}} = .573 \text{ (rounded) per unit}$$

SUGGESTED SOLUTION TO PROBLEM 2.2 FOR SELF-STUDY

Concept	Definition
Cost	**c.** A sacrifice of resources.
Opportunity cost	**i.** The return that one could realize from the best forgone alternative use of a resource.
Expense	**f.** The cost charged against revenue in a particular accounting period.
Product costs	**a.** Costs that are a part of inventory.
Period costs	**h.** Costs that firms can more easily attribute to time intervals.
Cost object	**e.** Any item for which the manager wishes to measure cost.
Direct costs	**b.** Costs directly related to a cost object.
Indirect costs	**d.** Costs not directly related to a cost object.
Common costs	**g.** Costs shared by two or more cost objects.

SUGGESTED SOLUTION TO PROBLEM 2.3 FOR SELF-STUDY

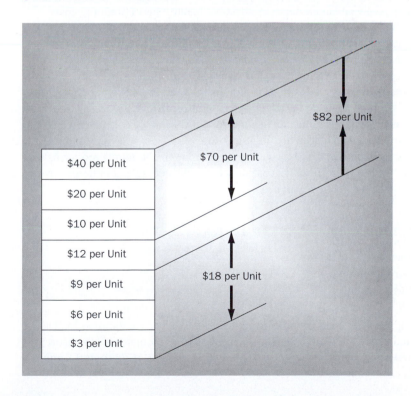

Variable Manufacturing Cost per Unit	$70 per Unit
Direct Materials	$40 per Unit
Direct Labor	$20 per Unit
Variable Manufacturing Overhead = $70 − ($40 + $20) = ...	$10 per Unit
Variable Costs per Unit = Price − Unit Contribution Margin = $100 − $18 = ...	$82 per Unit
Variable Marketing and Administrative Costs = $82 − $40 − $20 − $10 = ...	$12 per Unit

Fixed Manufacturing Costs per Unit = Manufacturing Costs per Unit
  − Variable Manufacturing Costs per Unit = (Price
  − Gross Margin per Unit) − Variable Manufacturing Costs per Unit
 	
  $= \$100 - \left(\dfrac{\$21{,}000}{1{,}000 \text{ Units}} \right) - \$70 =$ ....
	$ 9 per Unit

Fixed Marketing and Administrative Costs per Unit = ...	$ 6 per Unit
Excess of Price over Average Cost per Unit = $100 − ($40 + $20 + $10 + $12 + $9 + $6) = ...	$ 3 per Unit

QUESTIONS, EXERCISES, AND PROBLEMS

REVIEW QUESTIONS

1. Review the meaning of the concepts or terms listed in Key Terms and Concepts.
2. Zappa, a mechanic, left his $25,000-a-year job at Joe's Garage to start his own body shop. Zappa drew an annual salary of $15,000. Identify his opportunity costs.
3. People often use *expenses* and *costs* interchangeably, yet the terms do not always mean the same thing. Distinguish between the two terms.
4. Identify and describe the three elements that make up manufacturing costs.
5. Compare and contrast prime costs and conversion costs.
6. Firms usually classify nonmanufacturing costs as either marketing costs or administrative costs. How do these two types of costs differ?
7. What do managerial accountants mean when they speak of cost behavior? Why is it important in managerial decision making?
8. Match each of the items, **(a)** through **(c)**, with one of the numbered terms that *most specifically* identifies the cost concept indicated in parentheses. (Note: There are more terms than you need.)

   Terms
   (1) Fixed cost
   (2) Opportunity cost
   (3) Prime cost
   (4) Full absorption costing
   (5) Variable costing

   Items
   a. A company declined an offer to rent out one of its warehouses. Instead, it elected to use the warehouse for storage of extra raw materials to ensure uninterrupted production. What is *the monthly amount of the rental forgone?* (*This cost is known as ?*)

b. A manufacturing company excludes all "fixed" costs from its valuation of inventories, assigning to inventory only applicable portions of costs that vary with changes in volume. (*The term accounting employs for this costing procedure.*)

c. The "direct" production cost of a unit includes those portions of *labor* and *materials* obviously traceable directly to the unit. (*The term used to specify the sum of the two named components.*)

9. The equation for determining the contribution margin (CM) is (X = number of units per period; P = unit price; V = unit variable cost; F = fixed costs per period)

   a. CM = P − F/X

   b. CM = P − V

   c. CM = V − F/X

   d. CM = F − VX

CRITICAL ANALYSIS AND DISCUSSION QUESTIONS

10. "The cost of my trip to Hawaii was $3,000." Using the concept of cost developed in this chapter, explain why this statement is ambiguous.

11. In financial accounting, accountants always treat manufacturing costs as product costs, and nonmanufacturing costs as period costs. Is this hard-and-fast?

12. Give three examples of variable costs and three examples of fixed costs in a fast food restaurant.

13. "Fixed costs are really variable. The more you produce, the smaller the unit cost of production." Is this statement correct? Why or why not?

14. "Since fixed manufacturing overhead costs such as factory rent or property taxes are independent of the number of units produced, we should treat them as period costs rather than product costs." Comment.

15. Refer to the section "Cost Allocation: A Note of Caution," on page 37. Why do you think companies need to remind managers about administrative costs? Is it justified?

16. Refer to the section named in Question **15.** Comment on the statement, "Allocation may be good if it has the intended effect." When would this be true?

EXERCISES

Solutions to even-numbered exercises are at the end of this chapter after the problems.

17. Opportunity cost analysis. Cary Lewis owns an ice skating rink that accommodates 200 people. Cary charges $1.00 per hour to skate. Attendants are paid $5.00 per hour to staff the entrance booth at CL Skating. Utilities and other fixed costs average $2,000 per month.

  Recently, the manager of an out-of-town hockey team approached Cary concerning renting the rink for a full day of practice on an upcoming Sunday for the lump sum of $700. CL's normal operating hours on Sunday are 10 AM to 7 PM and the average attendance is 100 skaters per hour. What is the opportunity cost of accepting the offer?

18. Opportunity cost analysis. Geoff Parkhurst operates a covered parking structure that can accommodate up to 600 cars. Geoff charges $2.50 per hour for parking. Parking attendants are paid $6.00 an hour to staff the cashier's booth at Parkhurst Parking. Utilities and other fixed costs average $2,000 per month.

Recently, the manager of a nearby Marriott Hotel approached Geoff concerning the reservation of 100 spots over an upcoming weekend for a lump sum of $1,500. This particular weekend was a football weekend, and the structure would be full for six hours. Other than those six hours, the structure would have more than 100 empty spots available. What is the opportunity cost of accepting the offer?

19. **Manufacturing cost concepts.** Quinby's, a toy manufacturer, produces a variety of inflatable plastic toys. One day, the owner (Aussie, as he is affectionately known to his employees) decided to take a look at the manufacturing costs of Roo, a product the company introduced two years ago. Roo is an inflatable plastic kangaroo. During the last six months, Quinby's produced 10,000 Roos and incurred the following manufacturing costs:

Variable Costs:	
Plastic	$ 8,000
Labor—Cutting	4,000
Labor—Assembling	20,000
Supplies	2,000
Machine Cost	8,000
Fixed Costs:	
Rent	4,000
Plant Supervisor's Salary	3,000
Utilities	2,500
Depreciation—Machinery	2,500

Aussie wants to know the following costs of each Roo:
a. Direct materials cost
b. Direct labor cost
c. Variable manufacturing overhead
d. Fixed manufacturing overhead
e. Prime cost
f. Conversion cost
Calculate these costs per unit.

20. **Manufacturing costs.** Whizz Incorporated produced 3,000 Kiddy Kars in May. The Whizz plant incurred the following costs for that month:

Variable Costs						
Cutting		**Fabrication**		**Assembly**		
Wood	$6,000	Labor	$12,000	Paint and miscellaneous supplies	$ 1,800
Labor	9,000	Nails	1,000	Labor	15,000
		Sandpaper	200	Wheels	24,000
				Axles	12,000

Fixed Costs:	
Plant Supervisor's Salary	$6,000
Utilities (heat and light)	800
Depreciation—Machinery	2,000
Plant Rent	3,200

Management wants to know the following costs of each Kiddy Kar:

a. Direct materials cost

b. Direct labor cost

c. Variable manufacturing overhead

d. Fixed manufacturing overhead

e. Prime cost

f. Conversion cost

Calculate these costs per unit.

21. **Nonmanufacturing costs.** Trailblaster, a tent manufacturer, sold 10,000 tents last year and reported the following financial results:

Sales Revenue (10,000 units)		$1,500,000
Less Cost of Goods Sold		900,000
Gross Margin		$ 600,000
Less:		
Advertising (fixed costs)	$13,000	
Sales Commissions to Dealers	42,000	
Office Rent	14,400	
Office Supplies	600	
Depreciation—Office Equipment	3,000	
Sales Promotion (fixed cost)	18,000	91,000
Operating Profit		$ 509,000

Management asks you to determine costs other than Cost of Goods Sold of the following three categories:

a. Variable marketing costs

b. Fixed marketing costs

c. Administrative costs

22. **Product and period costs.** Refer to Trailblaster in Exercise **21.** Suppose that the Cost of Goods Sold could be broken down into the following costs:

Variable Costs:	
Direct Materials	$150,000
Direct Labor	300,000
Variable Overhead	240,000
Fixed Overhead	210,000

a. What would be the product costs and period costs using full absorption costing?

b. Management wants to make decisions requiring variable manufacturing costs to be product costs (that is, variable costing). What would be the product costs and period costs using variable costing?

23. **Components of full costs.** The following data apply to the cost of producing a particular model snowboard. Using these data, put amounts beside each label in Exhibit 2.2 in the text.

Price per Unit	$300
Fixed Costs:	
Marketing and Administrative	$48,000 per Period
Manufacturing Overhead	$80,000 per Period
Variable Costs:	
Variable Marketing and Administrative	$10 per Unit
Direct Materials	$60 per Unit
Direct Labor	$40 per Unit
Variable Manufacturing Overhead	$20 per Unit
Units Produced and Sold: 1,000 per Period	

24. **Margins.** Refer to the data in Exercise **23.** Compute the profit margin and gross margin.

25. **Product and period costs.** Berg's Ice Cream Factory, a small family-run factory in a historic town frequented by many tourists, has the following costs:

Variable Costs per Gallon:	
Direct Materials	$0.75
Direct Labor	0.30
Manufacturing Overhead	0.15
Marketing	0.25
Fixed Costs per Month:	
Rent	$500
Depreciation on Equipment	100
Administrative	300

If Berg's produces and sells 2,000 gallons in a month, what are the
- **a.** total product costs?
- **b.** total period costs?

PROBLEMS

26. **Cost and margin relations.** You and a friend are considering manufacturing a new type of roller blades. Based on industry publications and other research, you have collected the following data:

Sales Price	$100 per Unit
Fixed Costs:	
Marketing and Administrative	$15,000 per Period
Manufacturing Overhead	$16,800 per Period
Variable Costs:	
Marketing and Administrative	$3 per Unit
Manufacturing Overhead	$4 per Unit
Direct Labor	$15 per Unit
Direct Materials	$30 per Unit
Units Produced and Sold: 1,200 per Period	

a. How much are each of the following costs per unit (see Exhibit 2.2)?
  (1) variable manufacturing cost
  (2) variable cost
  (3) full absorption cost
  (4) full cost
b. How much *per unit* are each of the following margins (see Exhibits 2.3 and 2.4)?
  (1) profit margin
  (2) gross margin
  (3) contribution margin
c. How much *per unit* are each of the following costs (see Exhibit 2.1)?
  (1) prime costs
  (2) conversion costs

27 **Product and period costs.** Under full absorption costing, all costs of manufacturing the product are product costs (that is, they are inventoriable). Using the data from Problem **26,** what are the following?
  a. product cost *per unit,* using full absorption costing
  b. period costs for the *period,* using full absorption costing

28. **Costs and margins.** In one of your accounting classes the instructor decides to play Jeopardy. The subject is "Accounting." You are given the basic data as follows:

Sales Price	$190 per Unit
Fixed Costs:	
Marketing and Administrative	$10,000 per Period
Manufacturing Overhead	$8,000 per Period
Variable Costs per Unit:	
Marketing and Administrative	$6
Manufacturing Overhead	$18
Direct Labor	$20
Direct Materials	$30
Units Produced and Sold: 200 per Period	

Following are all the answers, including the question to answer **a.** Beside each answer write the question. Assume that the answer states an amount per unit.

Answer	Question	
a. $68	How much is variable manufacturing cost?	
b. $74	How much is _____	?
c. $108	How much is _____	?
d. $164	How much is _____	?
e. $78	How much is _____	?
f. $50	How much is _____	?
g. $82	How much is _____	?
h. $26	How much is _____	?
i. $116	How much is _____	?

29. **Costs and margins.** You've just been handed an exam in your Managerial Accounting class. Instead of giving answers, however, you're asked to make up the questions. Given the basic data as follows:

Sales Price	$95
Fixed Costs:	
Marketing and Administrative	$8,000 per Period
Manufacturing Overhead	$4,000 per Period
Variable Costs per Unit:	
Marketing and Administrative	$4
Manufacturing Overhead	$12
Direct Labor	$15
Direct Materials	$20
Units Produced and Sold: 400 per Period	

Following are all the answers, including the question to answer **a.** Beside each answer write the question. Assume that the answer states an amount per unit.

Answer	Question
a. $47	How much is variable manufacturing cost?
b. $81	How much is _____?
c. $57	How much is _____?
d. $51	How much is _____?
e. $37	How much is _____?
f. $35	How much is _____?
g. $14	How much is _____?
h. $38	How much is _____?
i. $44	How much is _____?

30. **Costs and margins.** In preparing for an examination, you discover that you have the answer but only part of the question from an old examination. You know the question asked the test taker to give the amounts per unit for several different accounting measures, but you don't know which measures were asked for (with one exception). You have the basic data used in the question, as follows:

Sales Price	$190 per Unit
Fixed Costs:	
Marketing and Administrative	$20,000 per Period
Manufacturing Overhead	$15,000 per Period
Variable Costs:	
Marketing and Administrative	$5 per Unit
Manufacturing Overhead	$15 per Unit
Direct Labor	$25 per Unit
Direct Materials	$35 per Unit
Units Produced and Sold: 500 per Period	

You recall that question a on the exam asked: How much is the variable manufacturing cost? The answer was $75.

   Following are all the answers, including the question to answer **a.** Beside
each answer, write the question. Assume that the answer states an amount
per unit.

Answer	Question
a. $75	How much is variable manufacturing cost?
b. $150	How much is _____?
c. $80	How much is _____?
d. $105	How much is _____?
e. $60	How much is _____?
f. $70	How much is _____?
g. $40	How much is _____?
h. $110	How much is _____?
i. $85	How much is _____?

31. **Fixed and variable cost analysis** (adapted from a problem by D. O. Green).
The sales representatives of Mathers Paper Products have secured two special
orders, *either* of which, in addition to regular orders, will keep the plant operating at capacity through the slack season. Hence, the company can accept one
order or the other, or neither. One order is for 20 million printed placemats and
the other is for 30 million sheets of engraved office stationery. The proposed
prices are $.0070 per mat for the placemats and $.0062 per sheet for the stationery. Cost estimates follow:

	Mats (cost per 100 mats)	Stationery (cost per 100 sheets)
Direct Materials	$0.3590	$0.2795
Labor Costs:		
Variable	0.1160	0.1073
Fixed	0.0300	0.0089
Manufacturing Overhead Costs:		
Variable	0.0430	0.0330
Fixed	0.0370	0.0523
Variable Marketing and Administrative Cost (already incurred to procure order)	0.0900	0.0912
Fixed Marketing and Administrative Cost (already incurred to procure order)	0.0950	0.0878
Total Cost per 100 items	$0.7700	$0.6600
Selling Price per 100 items	$0.7000	$0.6200

After reviewing these figures, management decides to reject the orders on the
basis that "we cannot make much money if it costs more than we can sell it for."

   Is management correct? Based on the data in the table, prepare a schedule to
show which alternative Mathers Paper Products should accept, if either.

32. **Cost data for multiple purposes** (contributed by J. Lim). Allen's Auto Accessories manufactures an automobile safety seat for children that it sells through several retail chains. Allen's makes its sales exclusively within its five-state region in the Midwest. The cost of manufacturing and marketing children's automobile safety seats at the company's normal volume of 15,000 units per month follows:

Variable Materials	$300,000	
Variable Labor	150,000	
Variable Overhead	30,000	
Fixed Overhead	180,200	
Total Manufacturing Costs		$660,200
Variable Nonmanufacturing Costs	$ 75,000	
Fixed Nonmanufacturing Costs	105,000	
Total Nonmanufacturing Costs		180,000
Total Costs		$840,200

The following questions refer only to the data given here. Unless otherwise stated, assume that the situations described in the questions are not connected; treat each independently. Unless otherwise stated, assume a regular selling price of $70 per unit. Ignore income taxes and other costs that we do not mention in the data or in the question itself.

a. In any normal month, what would be the inventory value per completed unit according to generally accepted accounting principles? (Hint: Full absorption.)

b. On April 1, a nonprofit charitable organization offers Allen's a special-order contract to supply 2,000 units to several orphanages for delivery by April 30. Production for April was initially planned for 15,000 units, and Allen's can easily accommodate this special order without any additional capacity costs. (Thus Allen's would produce a total of 17,000 units.) The special-order contract will reimburse Allen's for all manufacturing costs plus a fixed fee of $25,000. (Allen's would incur no variable marketing costs on the special order.) Write a short report to management indicating whether management should accept the special order.

SUGGESTED SOLUTIONS TO EVEN-NUMBERED EXERCISES

18. **Opportunity cost analysis.** On football weekends, the opportunity cost is

$$100 \text{ Spots for Cars} \times 6 \text{ Hours} \times \$2.50 = \underline{\$1,500}.$$

All other costs do not change. Geoff is indifferent between the Marriott manager's offer and the normal football crowd.

20. Manufacturing costs.

a. Direct materials cost:

Wood	$ 6,000
Wheels	24,000
Axles	12,000
	$42,000

Unit direct materials cost = $14.00.

b. Direct labor cost:

Labor—Cutting	$ 9,000
Labor—Fabrication	12,000
Labor—Assembly	15,000
	$36,000

Unit direct labor cost = $12.00.

c. Variable manufacturing overhead:

Nails	$1,000
Sandpaper	200
Paint and Miscellaneous Supplies	1,800
	$3,000

Unit variable overhead = $1.00.

d. Fixed manufacturing overhead:

Plant Supervisor's Salary	$ 6,000
Utilities	800
Depreciation	2,000
Plant Rent	3,200
	$12,000

Unit fixed overhead = $4.00.

e. Prime cost:

Direct Materials	$42,000
Direct Labor	36,000
	$78,000

Unit prime cost = $26.00.

f. Conversion cost:

Direct Labor	$36,000
Variable Manufacturing Overhead	3,000
Fixed Manufacturing Overhead	12,000
	$51,000

Unit conversion cost = $17.00.

22. Product and period costs.

a. Product costs are all manufacturing costs using full absorption costing. Therefore,

$$\text{Product Costs} = \$900,000.$$

Period costs are all nonmanufacturing costs. Therefore,

$$\text{Period Costs} = \$91,000.$$

b. Only *variable* manufacturing costs are treated as product costs using variable costing. Therefore,

$$\text{Product Costs} = \$150,000 + \$300,000 + \$240,000$$

$$= 690,000.$$

All nonmanufacturing costs and fixed manufacturing costs are treated as period costs. Therefore,

$$\text{Period Costs} = 210,000 + \$91,000$$

$$= \$301,000.$$

24. Margins.

$$\text{Profit Margin} = \text{Price} - \text{Full Cost}$$

$$= \$300 - \$258$$

$$= \$42.$$

$$\text{Gross Margin} = \text{Price} - \text{Full Absorption Cost}$$

$$= \$300 - \$200$$

$$= \$100.$$

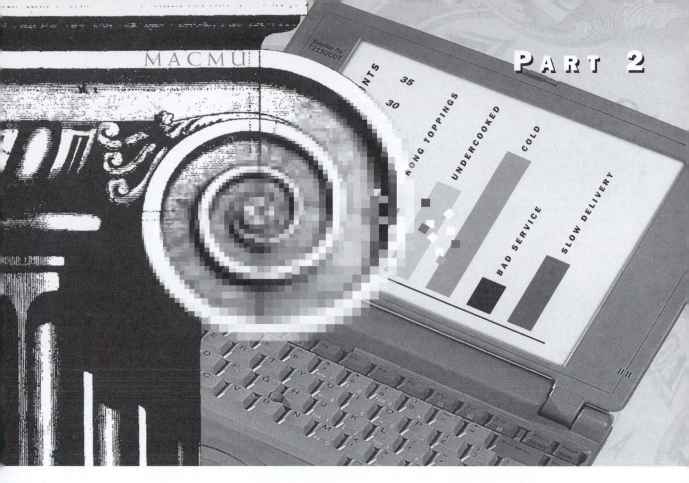

PART 2

MANAGERIAL DECISION MAKING

At the beginning of this book, we described two major uses of managerial accounting information: (1) managerial decision making and (2) managerial planning, control, and performance evaluation. This part of the book, Chapters 3 through 9, deals with *managerial decision making*. This use of accounting information addresses questions like the following:

- What costs will the university save if it cuts enrollment?
- What is the minimum price that a coffee shop should charge for a cup of espresso?
- Should a hospital build a new wing?
- Is it cheaper for Nike to make shoes or to buy them from factories in Southeast Asia?

All these decisions have one thing in common—they are future-oriented. Managers attempt to estimate the future costs and benefits of alternatives. The data in the accounting records are, of course, data about the past, but these data provide a potentially useful source of information about the future.

CHAPTER 3

ESTIMATING COST BEHAVIOR

LEARNING OBJECTIVES

1. Distinguish between variable costs and fixed costs, between short run and long run, and define the relevant range.
2. Identify capacity costs, committed costs, and discretionary costs.
3. Understand the nature of the various cost behavior patterns.
4. Describe how managers use cost behavior patterns.
5. Understand how analysts estimate cost behavior using engineering methods and account analysis.
6. Use historical data to estimate cost.
7. Explain the costs, benefits, and weaknesses of the various cost estimation methods.
8. (Appendix 3.1) Know how learning curves are derived.
9. (Appendix 3.2) Interpret the results of regression analyses.

Chapter 2 discussed the fundamental distinction between fixed and variable costs. This chapter discusses methods of *estimating* or deriving the breakdown of costs into fixed and variable components. Some costs, such as rent, usually have only a fixed portion, whereas others, such as direct materials, usually have only a variable portion. Many costs, however, have both fixed and variable components. For example, automobiles incur both fixed costs per year (for example, license fees) and variable costs per mile.

We express the total costs of an item as follows:

$$
\begin{pmatrix} \text{Total} \\ \text{Cost} \\ \text{during} \\ \text{Period} \end{pmatrix} = \begin{pmatrix} \text{Fixed} \\ \text{Cost} \\ \text{during} \\ \text{Period} \end{pmatrix} + \begin{pmatrix} \text{Variable} \\ \text{Cost per} \\ \text{Unit of} \\ \text{Activity} \end{pmatrix} \times \begin{pmatrix} \text{Units of} \\ \text{Activity} \\ \text{during} \\ \text{Period} \end{pmatrix}
$$

or, using briefer notation:

$$ TC = F + VX, $$

60

where *TC* refers to the total cost for a time period. *F* refers to the total fixed cost for the time period, *V* refers to the variable cost per unit, and *X* refers to the number of units of activity for the time period. Nearly all managerial decisions deal with choices among different activity levels; hence, the manager must estimate which costs will vary with the activity and by how much.

Cost estimation works like this: Suppose management expects a temporary reduction in customers at a particular restaurant during the summer. Some costs will not decline. Other costs will. Management would estimate the relation between costs and meals served to ascertain which costs would decline with the decline in number of meals.

Because many costs do not fall neatly into fixed and variable categories, managers use statistical and other techniques for estimating **cost behavior.** These techniques help managers identify underlying cost behavior patterns.

THE NATURE OF FIXED AND VARIABLE COSTS

SHORT RUN VERSUS LONG RUN

Variable costs, also known as **engineered costs,** change in total as the level of activity changes. An engineered cost bears a definitive physical relationship to the activity measure. Direct materials cost is an engineered cost. It is impossible to manufacture more products without incurring greater materials costs.

Fixed costs do not change with changes in activity levels. During short time periods, say, one year, the firm operates with a relatively fixed sales force, managerial staff, and set of production facilities. Consequently, many of its costs are fixed. Over long time spans—many years perhaps—no costs are fixed because staff size can be changed and facilities sold.

This fact provides the basis for the distinction drawn in economics between the long run and the short run and in accounting between fixed costs and variable costs. To the economist, the **short run** is a time period long enough to allow management to change the level of production or other activity within the constraints of current total productive capacity. Management can change total productive capacity only in the **long run.**

To the manager, costs that vary with activity levels in the short run are variable costs; costs that will not vary in the short run, no matter what the level of activity, are fixed costs. The accounting concepts of variable and fixed costs are, then, short-run concepts. They apply to a particular period of time and relate to a particular level of productive capacity.

Consider, for example, the total costs (both variable and fixed) for the firm appearing in Exhibit 3.1. The graph on the left shows the total costs in the long run. If the productive capacity of the firm is 10,000 units per year, total costs will vary as on line *AB*. If the firm acquires new production facilities to increase capacity to 20,000 units, total costs will be as on line *CD*. An increase in capacity to 30,000 units will increase the total costs as on line *EF*. These shifts in capacity represent long-run commitments. Of course, some overlap will occur; production of 10,000 units per year could be at the high-volume end of the *AB* line or at the low-volume end of the *CD* line.

EXHIBIT 3.1

Long-Run versus Short-Run Nature of Costs

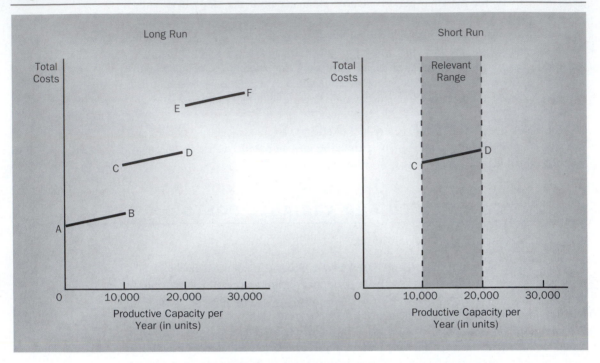

Why is there a gap between *D* and *E* in the diagram on the left? (Answer: To reflect the increase in fixed costs required to expand capacity from the 10,000 to 20,000 units range to the 20,000 to 30,000 units range.)

In the short run, a firm has only one capacity level: namely, the capacity of the existing plant. The total costs in the short run appear at the right side of the graph in Exhibit 3.1 on the assumption that the capacity of the existing plant is 20,000 units per year. Note that line CD represents costs for the production level of approximately 10,000 units to 20,000 units only. Production levels outside of this range require a different plant capacity, and the total cost line will shift up or down.

RELEVANT RANGE

Managers frequently use the notion of relevant range in estimating cost behavior. The **relevant range** is the range of activity over which the firm expects a set of cost behaviors to be consistent. For example, if the relevant range of activity shown in Exhibit 3.1 is between 10,000 and 20,000 units, the firm assumes that certain costs are fixed while others are variable within that range. The firm would not necessarily assume that costs fixed within the relevant range will stay fixed outside the relevant range. As Exhibit 3.1 shows, for example, costs step up from point *D* to point *E* when production increases from the right side of the 10,000 to 20,000 range to the left side of the 20,000 to 30,000 range.

Estimates of variable and fixed costs apply only if the contemplated level of activity lies within the relevant range. If the firm considers an alternative requiring a level of activity outside the relevant range, then the breakdown of costs into fixed and variable components requires a new computation.

Example Exotic Eats, a profitable restaurant, features a menu of Far Eastern dishes. Because it is located in the financial district of a city, management keeps it open only from 11:00 AM until 2:00 PM, Monday through Friday, for lunch business. Although the restaurant can serve a maximum of 210 customers per day, it has been serving a daily average of 200 customers. The daily costs and revenues of operations follow:

Revenues	$1,000
Less Variable Costs	400
Less Fixed Costs	350
Operating Profits	$ 250

   Based on this information, the restaurant's management considers doubling capacity. Cost behavior for doubling capacity is outside the relevant range. Initial calculations indicate that the number of customers would double. Management wants to know whether operating profits would double. A simple extrapolation indicates that the operating profits would *more* than double, as Exhibit 3.2 shows, because total revenues would double whereas total costs would not. Looking at Exhibit 3.2, what would profit be at 300 units? (Answer: $550.)

EXHIBIT 3.2

EXOTIC EATS
Analysis Ignoring Increase in Fixed Costs (which is incorrect)

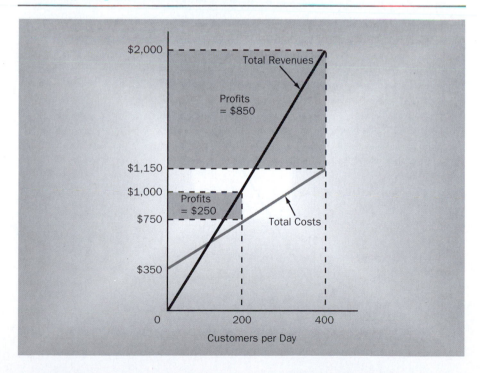

Why is the graph incorrect? (Answer: Because it ignores the increase in fixed costs required to increase capacity.)

This simple extrapolation assumes that the total revenues and total variable costs double to $2,000 and $800, respectively, whereas fixed costs remain constant at $350. When capacity changes, fixed costs are likely to increase also.

The management of Exotic Eats realizes that with additional capacity and increased customers, it must hire additional cooks, occupancy costs (for example, space rental) would increase, and other fixed costs would increase. The projected new volume is outside the relevant range of volume over which the originally assumed cost behavior pattern would hold. Therefore the original cost behavior pattern shown in Exhibit 3.2 would be invalid.

A revised, more realistic analysis of the cost behavior pattern estimates the unit variable cost of $2 per customer to be the same as before, but estimates fixed costs to increase from $350 to $550 per day. Fixed costs would not double because some fixed costs would not increase (for example, many of the administrative costs).

The revised cost behavior pattern appears in Exhibit 3.3. Looking at Exhibit 3.3, what would profit be at 300 units? (Answer: $350.) Exhibit 3.4 compares profits at the original activity level, 200 customers per day, with the projected increase to 400 per day. Management would use these cost estimates to decide whether to increase capacity. These decisions usually require discounted cash flow analysis in addition to the estimated change in cash flow discussed here. (Discounted cash flow analysis is discussed in Chapter 9.)

EXHIBIT 3.3

EXOTIC EATS
Increase in Fixed Costs Accompanying Expansion

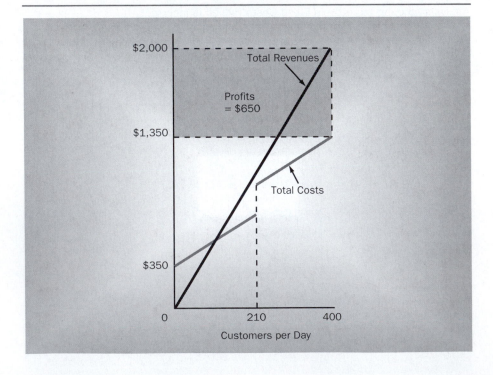

EXHIBIT 3.4

EXOTIC EATS
Comparison of Profits at Original and Projected Activity Levels

	Status Quo: 200 Customers per Day	Alternative: 400 Customers per Day	
		Incorrect Assumption That Fixed Costs Are Constant	Correct Assumption That Fixed Costs Will Change
Revenues	$1,000	$2,000	$2,000
Less Variable Costs	400	800	800
Total Contribution Margin	$ 600	$1,200	$1,200
Less Fixed Costs	350	350	550
Operating Profits	$ 250	$ 850	$ 650

TYPES OF FIXED COSTS

In practice, where the short run stops and the long run starts is fuzzy. The accountant divides fixed cost into subclassifications to explain the relation between particular types of fixed costs and current capacity.

CAPACITY COSTS

Certain fixed costs, called **capacity costs,** provide a firm with the capacity to produce or sell or both. A firm incurs some capacity costs, known as **committed costs,** even if it temporarily shuts down operations. Committed costs result from an organization's ownership of facilities and its basic organization structure. Examples include property taxes and some executive salaries.

Other capacity costs cease if the firm's operations shut down, but continue in fixed amounts if the firm carries out operations at any level. A firm can lay off a security force if production ceases, but once employed, the security force guards the plant no matter how little or how much activity goes on inside.

DISCRETIONARY COSTS

Productive or selling capacity requires fixed capacity costs. Companies also incur fixed **discretionary costs.** These costs are also called **programmed costs** or **managed costs.** Examples include research, development, and advertising to generate new business.

These costs are discretionary because the firm need not incur them in the short run to operate the business. They are, however, usually essential for achieving long-run goals. Imagine the long-run impact on Procter & Gamble of eliminating media advertising. Or consider the effects if Eastman Kodak were to drop research and development. Although these companies would survive for a time, after a while they would become different, and would most likely be less profitable companies.

Discretionary costs reflect top management's policies and commitments to particular programs. When General Motors started thinking about building the Saturn automobile, the company incurred discretionary costs for the Saturn program. Once General Motors committed to building the Saturn plant, the company began incurring fixed capacity costs.

OTHER COST BEHAVIOR PATTERNS

We have made the following distinction between fixed and variable costs: Total fixed costs remain constant for a period of time (the short run) over a range of activity level (the relevant range); total variable costs change as the volume of activity changes within the relevant range.

CURVED VARIABLE COSTS

The straightforward linear fixed and variable cost behavior patterns, shown in Exhibits 3.2 and 3.3, do not always arise in practice. Total variable cost behavior may be curvilinear as Exhibit 3.5 shows with three different examples of variable cost

EXHIBIT 3.5

Examples of Curvilinear Total Variable Cost Behavior

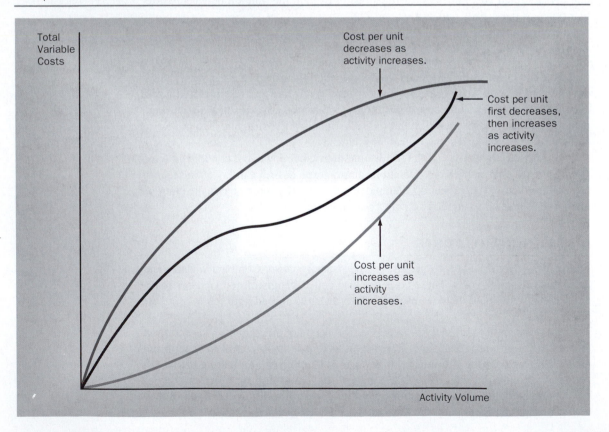

behavior. **Curvilinear variable cost** functions indicate that the costs vary with the volume of activity, but not in constant proportion. For example, as volume increases, the unit prices of some inputs, such as materials and power, may decrease, exhibiting decreasing marginal costs. The **marginal cost** is the cost of producing the next unit. Another example of curved cost behavior occurs when employees become more efficient with experience, as discussed in the following section.

LEARNING CURVES

Systematic learning from experience often occurs. As employees' experience increases, productivity improves and costs per unit decrease. This phenomenon frequently occurs when a firm initiates new products or processes or hires a group of new employees. Many high-tech companies, like National Semiconductor and Sun Microsystems, experience learning effects on costs. These companies compete by learning quickly so they can become low-cost producers and capture significant market share.

The effect of learning is often expressed as a **learning curve** (also known as an **experience curve**). The learning curve function shows how the amount of time required to perform a task goes down, per unit, as the number of units increases (see Exhibit 3.6).

Accountants model the nature of the learning phenomenon as a constant percentage reduction in the *average* direct labor input time required per unit as the *cumulative output* doubles. For example, assume a time reduction rate of 20 percent; that is, an 80-percent cumulative learning curve. Assume also that the first unit takes 125 hours. The *average* for two units should be 100 hours per unit (= .80 × 125 hours), a total of 200 hours for both units. Four units would take an average of 80 hours each (= .80 × 100 hours), or a total of 320 hours. Appendix 3.1 presents the mathematical formula for the learning curve.

The results in this example follow:

Quantity		Time in Hours	
Unit	Cumulative Units	Cumulative	Average per Unit
First	1	125	125
Second	2	200	100 (= .80 × 125)
Third and Fourth	4	320	80 (= .80 × 100)
Fifth through Eighth	8	512	64 (= .80 × 80)

Exhibit 3.6 shows the relation between volume and *average* labor hours in graph A. Note that four units require 80 hours per unit, on average. Eight units require only 64 hours per unit, on average. The relation between volume and *total* labor hours appears in graph B. The relation between volume and total labor costs appears in graph C. The labor cost is $20 per hour. Looking at Exhibit 3.6, what is the total labor cost of eight units? (Answer: $10,240.)

The possible consequences of learning on costs can affect decision making and performance evaluation. Suppose that you are trying to decide whether to make a new product that would be subject to the 80 percent cumulative learning curve.

EXHIBIT 3.6

Impact of Learning Curves on Time and Cost Behavior

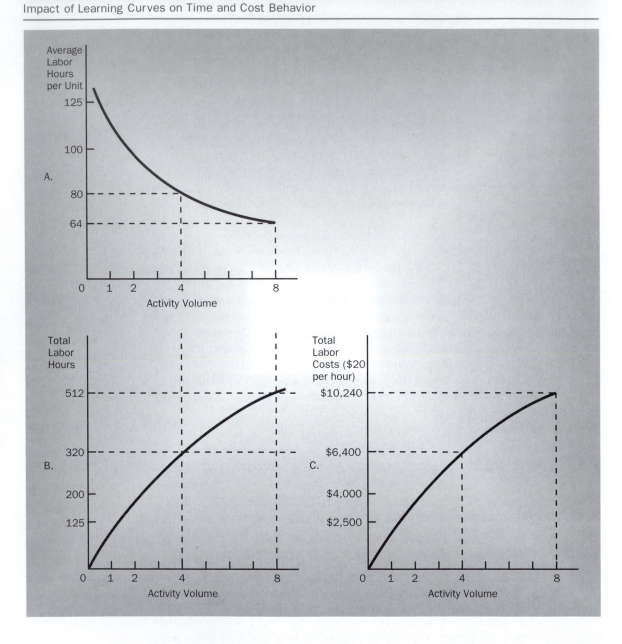

Using the data in Exhibit 3.6, if you assumed that the product would require labor costs of $2,500 (= $20 × 125 hours) per unit for the first eight units made, you would seriously overstate the costs for the eight units. If you used the $2,500 per unit as a standard for judging actual cost performance, you would set too loose a standard for all but the first unit.

To what costs do learning curves apply? The learning phenomenon results in savings of time; any labor-related costs could be affected. The learning phenomenon can also affect material costs, as in the semiconductor industry, if the cost of wasted materials decreases as experience increases.

PROBLEM 3.1 FOR SELF-STUDY

Computing cost decreases because of learning. Bounce Electronics recently recorded the following costs, which are subject to a 75 percent cumulative learning effect.

Cumulative Number of Units Produced	Average Labor Cost per Unit	Total Labor Costs
1	$1,333	$1,333
2	1,000	2,000
4	?	?
8	?	?
16	?	?

Complete the chart by filling in the cost amounts for volumes 4, 8, and 16 units.

The solution to this self-study problem is at the end of the chapter on page 88.

SEMIVARIABLE COSTS

Semivariable costs refer to costs that have both fixed and variable components such as those represented by lines *CD, CE,* and *CF* in Exhibit 3.7A. Repair and maintenance costs or utility costs exemplify semivariable cost behavior, like line *CE*.

EXHIBIT 3.7

Patterns of Cost Behavior: Semivariable and Semifixed Costs

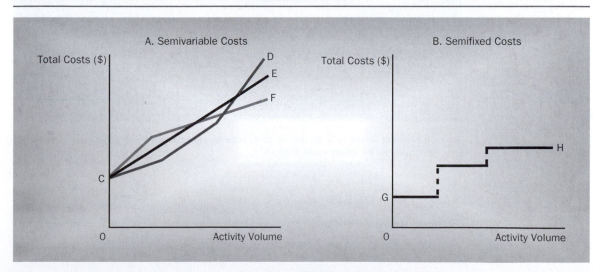

Minimum repair service capability within a plant requires a fixed cost (*C*) for providing service and an extra charge for uses of the service above some fixed amount. If the charge per unit of, say, electricity decreases at certain stages as consumption increases, the cost curve would look like line *CF*. If the per-unit charge increases at certain stages as usage increases, the costs would look like line *CD*. The term *mixed costs* often denotes semivariable costs.

Example Assume you purchase a cellular phone and service. You decide on a plan that provides you with up to one hour of airtime for a flat rate of $39.99 a month. You will pay this rate for the service even if you use only 20 minutes of airtime. The charge for any calls you make in excess of one hour is $0.15 per minute. The semivariable cost pattern would be as follows:

Minutes of Airtime Used		Charge
0–60		$39.99
61	[$39.99 + 0.15 (61 − 60)]	40.14
62	[$39.99 + 0.15 (62 − 60)]	40.29
63	[$39.99 + 0.15 (63 − 60)]	40.44
.		.
.		.
.		.

The cost would appear in a graph as follows:

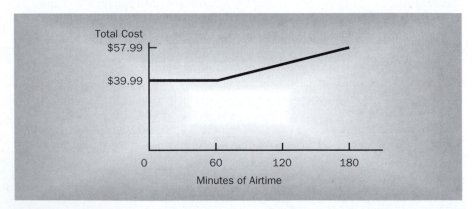

For each minute of airtime up to 60 minutes there is no incremental, or marginal, cost. For each minute over 60 minutes the incremental cost is $0.15.

SEMIFIXED COSTS

The term **semifixed costs** refers to costs that increase in steps, such as those shown by the broken line *GH* in Exhibit 3.7B. Accountants sometimes describe semifixed costs as *step fixed costs*. If a quality-control inspector can examine 1,000 units per day, inspection costs will be semifixed, with a step up for every 1,000 units per day.

Example   Radio House hires one quality-control inspector for each 25,000 toy robots produced per month. The annual salary is $30,000 per inspector. Production has been 65,000 units, so the company has three inspectors. If a special order increases volume from 65,000 to 75,000 units, the firm need hire no additional inspectors. If the special order increases production to a level greater than 75,000 units (say, to 85,000 units) the firm must hire a fourth inspector.

     The distinction between fixed and semifixed costs is subtle. A change in fixed costs (other than for inflation or other price changes) usually involves a change in long-term assets, whereas a change in semifixed costs often does not.

KEY THINGS YOU SHOULD KNOW

Costs vary with the volume of activity in several ways. Some costs do not vary in the short run over a relevant range—they are *fixed*. Others vary with volume—that is, they are *variable*. Some costs, neither strictly fixed nor strictly variable, contain both components.

     To simplify the analysis of cost behavior, decision makers usually assume that costs are either strictly fixed or linearly variable. They do this because the incremental cost of analyzing the more complex data often exceeds the incremental benefits of doing so. The assumed simple linear variable-fixed cost behavior usually sufficiently approximates the reality for decision-making purposes. Many cases require estimates and analysis of cost behavior with greater precision, however.

PROBLEM 3.2 FOR SELF-STUDY

     Sketching cost graphs. Draw graphs for the following cost behaviors.

   a. Costs of direct materials used in producing a firm's products.

   b. Wages of delivery truck drivers. The firm requires one driver, on average, for each $1 million of sales.

   c. Leasing costs of a delivery truck, which are $250 per month and $.18 per mile.

   d. Fixed fee paid to an independent firm of CPAs for auditing and attesting to financial statements.

   e. Compensation of sales staff with salary of $10,000 plus commission rates that increase as sales increase: 4 percent of the first $100,000 of annual sales, 6 percent of all sales from $100,000 to $200,000, and 8 percent for sales in excess of $200,000.

   f. Cost of electricity, where the electric utility charges a flat rate of $50 for the first 5,000 units, $.005 per unit for the next 45,000 units, and $.004 per unit for all units in excess of the first 50,000 units.

The solution to this self-study problem is at the end of the chapter on page 88.

USING COST BEHAVIOR PATTERNS TO PREDICT COSTS

Managers use the cost behavior patterns identified in cost studies to help in the budgeting process. First, a sales forecast is made for each month during the budget year. Then cost predictions for that level of sales are projected based on the cost behavior patterns identified earlier.

COST ESTIMATION METHODS

In **cost estimation,** analysts break down total costs *(TC)* into fixed and variable components:

$$TC = F + VX,$$

where F is total fixed costs during the period, V is variable cost per unit of activity, and X is the number of units of activity. For example, assume that analysts show the total cost of utilities per month to be $400 plus $.05 per kilowatt-hour used. If the firm expects to use 100,000 kilowatt-hours next month, it estimates utilities cost to be $5,400 [= $400 + ($.05 per kilowatt-hour × 100,000 kilowatt-hours)].

The activity represented by X is often called the **independent variable** and the amount of total costs is the **dependent variable.** In some analyses, more than one activity or independent variable influences total cost. If so, such a relation may be expressed as

$$TC = F + V_1X_1 + V_2X_2 + \cdots + V_nX_n,$$

where F is total fixed cost per period, V_1 is the variable cost per unit of activity X_1 carried out, V_2 is the variable cost per unit of activity X_2 carried out, and so on. X_1 might be the number of automobiles produced in the Nissan plant in Tennessee and X_2 might be the number of trucks produced in the same plant, for example.

Next we discuss the major methods of estimating cost behavior. Each method attempts to estimate the equation $TC = F + VX$ for the particular cost item we are analyzing.

ENGINEERING METHOD OF ESTIMATING COSTS

Engineering estimates indicate what costs *should be.* The **engineering method of cost estimation** probably got its name because managers first used it in estimating manufacturing cost from engineers' specifications of the inputs required to manufacture a unit of output. These costs are mostly variable costs, where there is a clear input/output relation. The method is not, however, confined to manufacturing. Banks, McDonald's, the U.S. Post Office, hospitals, and other nonmanufacturing enterprises use time-and-motion studies and similar engineering methods to estimate what costs "should be" to perform a particular service.

Engineers study the physical relation between the quantities of inputs and outputs. Analysts figure out the steps required to perform the task, the time needed to complete each step, the number and type of employees required, and the materials or other inputs needed. The accountant assigns costs to each of the inputs (wages, prices of material, insurance costs, etc.) to estimate the cost of outputs. Here are some examples of engineering study applications:

Company	Activity	Cost Driver
Bank of America	Processing loans	Applications processed
U.S. Postal Service	Sorting mail	Pieces of mail sorted
Department store	Billing customers	Invoices processed
Internal Revenue Service	Processing tax returns	Returns processed
Prudential Insurance	Settling claims	Claims settled
American Airlines	Ticketing passengers	Passengers ticketed

Let's look at the banking example. Analysts would first identify the steps required to process a loan application, most efficient order for those steps, and the average amount of time that should be needed for each step. Next they figure the cost of each step.

For example, suppose it takes an average of 30 minutes to verify that a loan application is completed properly, and the loan department employee's time costs $12 per hour, including fringe benefits. The cost of this loan processing step is $6:

$$\begin{array}{c}\text{Time required to verify} \\ \text{application is complete} \\ 1/2 \text{ hour}\end{array} \times \begin{array}{c}\text{Cost of compensating} \\ \text{employee for one hour} \\ (\$12 \text{ per hour})\end{array} = \$6$$

Analysts include other inputs, such as computer time and long-distance telephone calls, in the cost of processing the loan application.

Assume the bank institutes a new promotional program to refinance mortgages and wants to know what the costs of verifying the loan applications will be in the next month. The bank expects to process 600 loan applications next month. The analyst would estimate costs based on the $6 per loan application verification, already measured, and the number of applications processed as follows:

$$\begin{array}{c}\text{Verifying Cost} \\ \text{per Application} \\ \$6\end{array} \times \begin{array}{c}\text{Number of} \\ \text{Applications} \\ 600\end{array} = \$3,600$$

The bank can expect verification costs for the next month to be $3,600.

The engineering method is surprisingly costly to use. Analysis of time, motion, materials, operating characteristics of equipment, and the abilities of workers with varying skills requires experts. Expert engineers are expensive. Further, it is difficult to estimate indirect costs.

In short, the engineering method of estimating costs is most useful when input/output relations are well defined and fairly stable over time. For an aluminum manufacturer like ALCOA that has stable production methods over time, the engineering method results in good estimates of product costs, particularly for direct materials, direct labor, and certain overhead items like energy costs.

ACCOUNT ANALYSIS

In contrast to the engineering method, other methods of estimating cost behavior use actual accounting data. The **account analysis method** reviews each cost account and classifies it according to cost behavior. People familiar with the activities of the firm, and the way the firm's activities affect costs, do the classification.

Example   The administrators of the Chicago Hospital want to classify operating room overhead costs into fixed and variable components. They will use the information to estimate the effects of increases or decreases in the number of operations performed on operating room overhead costs.

Exhibit 3.8 shows operating room costs coded according to cost behavior. Virtually all organizations have a chart of accounts that presents the numerical codes assigned to accounts. Exhibit 3.8 codes variable costs as V and fixed costs as F. If management wants a more complex classification of cost behavior, such as classification into semivariable costs, semifixed costs, or discretionary fixed costs, the coding system can have additional symbols added. Looking at Exhibit 3.8, could the fixed costs be considered discretionary? (Answer: No.)

The accountant assigned a code to each operating room overhead account for Chicago Hospital to indicate whether it was fixed or variable. The following table shows the sum of the amounts in the respective fixed and variable categories for a year. During the year the operating room was in service for 5,700 hours of surgery.

Code	Cost Behavior	Amount
V	Variable	$3,990,000
F	Fixed	1,491,000
		$5,481,000

Dividing the fixed costs by 12 gives a monthly average of $124,250. Dividing the variable costs by the 5,700 operating room hours gives a variable cost rate per hour

---

EXHIBIT 3.8

CHICAGO HOSPITAL
Cost Behavior
Account Analysis

Account	Account Codes	
	Item[a]	Behavior[b]
Supplies Directly Assigned to Particular Operations	101	V
Labor (physicians and nurses)	102	V
Operating Room Overhead:		
Indirect Supplies	103	V
Indirect Labor (janitorial, supply room, personnel)	104	V
Utilities (heat, lights)	105	F

[a]Each account is assigned a different number.

[b]V = variable cost; F = fixed cost.

Note: Additional codes can be used to assign costs to departments or other responsibility centers.

of operating room use: $700 per operating room hour. The following monthly estimated cost equation results:

TC = \$124,250 + (\$700 × Operating Room Hours Used during Month).

Account analysis requires detailed examination of the data, presumably by accountants and managers who are familiar with the cost. Their expert judgments can uncover cost behavior patterns that other methods may overlook. Because account analysis is judgmental, different analysts are likely to provide different estimates of cost behavior.

PROBLEM 3.3 FOR SELF-STUDY

Estimating fixed and variable costs using the account analysis method. By the end of its second year of operations, Wonder Genetics had enough data for Naomi Ramos, the company's chief financial officer, to do a detailed analysis of its overhead cost behavior. Ms. Ramos accumulated monthly data that are summarized below as two-year totals.

Indirect Materials	$ 503,000
Indirect Labor	630,000
Lease	288,000
Utilities (heat, light, etc.)	206,000
Power to Run Machines	104,000
Insurance	24,000
Maintenance	200,000
Depreciation	72,000
Research and Development	171,000
Total Overhead	$2,198,000
Direct Labor Hours	815,800 hours
Direct Labor Costs	$4,997,400
Machine Hours	1,022,700 hours
Units Produced	202,500 units

Ms. Ramos has asked you to prepare an analysis that, using the account analysis method, calculates the *monthly average* fixed costs and the variable cost rate per:

1. direct labor hour.
2. machine hour.
3. unit of output.

You discuss operations with production managers, who inform you that three costs are variable—indirect labor, indirect materials, and power to run machines. All other costs are fixed.

The solution to this self-study problem is at the end of the chapter on page 89.

ESTIMATING COSTS USING HISTORICAL DATA

When a firm has been carrying out activities for some time and expects future activities to be similar to those of the past, the firm can analyze the historical data to estimate the variable and fixed components of total cost and to estimate likely future costs. The procedure for analyzing historical cost data requires two steps:

1. Make an estimate of the past relation for $TC = F + VX$.
2. Update this estimate so that it is appropriate for the present or future period for which management wants the estimate. This step requires adjusting costs for inflation and for changes that have occurred in the relation between costs and activity. For example, if a firm expects the production process to be more capital intensive in the future, the accountant should reduce variable costs and increase fixed costs.

Accountants use several methods to estimate costs from historical data; these range from simple "eyeball estimates" to sophisticated statistical methods. Before relying on cost estimates, the manager should take the following preliminary steps.

PRELIMINARY STEPS IN ANALYZING HISTORICAL COST DATA

Data analysts use the term "garbage-in, garbage-out" to indicate that the results of an analysis cannot be better than the input data. Before using cost estimates, the analyst should be confident that the estimates make sense and result from valid assumptions.

Keep in mind that we are trying to find fixed costs per period, F, and variable cost per unit, V, of some activity variable, X, in the relation

$$TC = F + VX.$$

Historical data comprise numerous observations. An observation is the total cost amount for a period and the level of activity carried out during that period. Thus we may have total labor costs by month (the dependent variable) and the number of units produced during each of the months, or the number of direct labor hours worked during each of the months (the independent variable). Exhibit 3.9 shows 12 observations, one for each month, for the suite of operating rooms at Chicago Hospital. Looking at Exhibit 3.9, what is the average monthly use of the operating room? (Answer: 475 hours = 5,700 hours/12 months)

We should take the following steps in analyzing cost data:

1. **Review Alternative Cost Drivers (Independent Variables)** A **cost driver** ideally measures the activity that *causes* costs. The cost drivers, if not the sole cause of costs, should directly influence cost incurrence. Operating room hours is an example of a cost driver in a hospital; machine hours is an example in a manufacturing firm; labor hours is an example in a service firm.
2. **Plot the Data** One simple procedure involves plotting each of the observations of total costs against cost driver activity levels. Plotting the data may make it clear that no relation or only a nonlinear relation exists between the chosen cost driver and actual costs.

EXHIBIT 3.9

CHICAGO HOSPITAL
Operating Room Overhead Cost Data by Month

Month	Total Overhead Costs Incurred during Month	Operating Room Hours[a]
January	$ 558,000	600
February	433,000	550
March	408,000	350
April	283,000	300
May	245,500	250
June	308,000	200
July	358,000	400
August	445,500	450
September	533,000	500
October	658,000	650
November	558,000	700
December	693,000	750
	$5,481,000	5,700

[a]An operating room hour is one hour that one operating room is being used for surgery.

3. **Examine the Data and Method of Accumulation** Do the time periods for the cost data and the activity correspond? Occasionally, accounting systems will record costs actually incurred late on a given day as occurring on the following day. Observations collected by the month may smooth over meaningful variations of the cost driver's activity level and cost that would appear if the accountant collected weekly data.

Be aware that a number of common recording procedures can make data appear to exhibit incorrect cost behavior patterns. Accounting systems often charge fixed overhead to production on a unit-by-unit basis. This unitizing of fixed costs makes these costs appear to be variable when they are not.

Sometimes an inverse relation seems to appear between activity and particular costs—when activity is high, costs are low; when activity is low, costs are high. An excellent example is maintenance. Firms sometimes purposefully do maintenance only when activity is slow. High maintenance levels often occur during plant shutdowns for automobile model changes, for example. The analyst would be naive to infer that low activity levels cause high maintenance costs.

These examples are a few of the data-recording methods that could lead the analyst astray. In general, we should investigate cost allocations, accruals, correcting and reversing entries, and relations between costs and activity levels to ensure that costs match activities in the appropriate time period for estimating costs.[1] Invalid relations between activity and costs will invalidate the analysis.

---

[1]For an extension of these remarks, see W. E. Wecker and R. L. Weil, "Statistical Estimation of Incremental Costs from Accounting Data," Chapter 43 in R. L. Weil et al., eds., *Litigation Services Handbook,* 2nd edition (New York: John Wiley & Sons, 1995).

METHODS OF ESTIMATING COSTS USING HISTORICAL DATA

Having taken the preliminary steps to analyze the historical data, we can use several methods to estimate the historical relations between total costs and cost driver activity levels—that is, to estimate $TC = F + VX$.

This section discusses the estimation of variable and fixed overhead for the Chicago Hospital operating rooms. Keep in mind that the concepts apply to any type of organization. Also, we assume all data have been adjusted for the effects of inflation.

The task is to estimate the relation between total overhead costs and activity. We expect that, of the possible activity bases, the number of operating room hours during the month primarily causes total overhead costs. Exhibit 3.9 shows total overhead costs and operating room hours each month.

The cost relation we will estimate is

$$
\begin{array}{c}
\text{Total Overhead} \\
\text{Costs per} \\
\text{Month}
\end{array}
=
\begin{array}{c}
\text{Fixed} \\
\text{Costs} \\
\text{per Month}
\end{array}
+
\left(
\begin{array}{c}
\text{Variable Overhead} \\
\text{Cost per} \\
\text{Operating} \\
\text{Room Hour}
\end{array}
\times
\begin{array}{c}
\text{Operating Room} \\
\text{Hours} \\
\text{Used during} \\
\text{Month}
\end{array}
\right)
$$

$$TC = F + VX.$$

REGRESSION ANALYSIS

With computers now widely available, the most cost-effective and accurate method for estimating cost relations is the statistical method known as **regression analysis.** Managers rely on regression analysis to estimate costs for decision making. The Managerial Application "United Airlines Uses Regression to Estimate Cost Behavior" (page 79) tells how United Airlines estimated the proportion of total costs that were variable.

The regression analysis "fits" a line to the data by the method of least squares. The method fits a line to the observations to minimize the sum of the squares of the vertical distance of the observation points from the point on the regression line. The statistical regression locates the line that best fits the data points using the least-squares criterion.

In our example, an observed actual value of total overhead cost is TC, and the line we fit by the least-squares regression will be of the form

$$\widehat{TC} = \hat{F} + \hat{V}X,$$

where the $\wedge$ on $\widehat{TC}$, $\hat{F}$ and $\hat{V}$ indicates that we have estimated the value of TC, F and V.

Standard terminology designates the vertical distance between the actual and the fitted values, $TC - \widehat{TC}$, as the *residual*. The method of least squares fits a line to the data to minimize the sum of all the squared residuals, which makes the line the "best fit" to the data.

Virtually every computer system and spreadsheet software package for personal computers can execute regression analysis. Furthermore, pocket calculators available for less than $50 will perform many of these calculations. Here we illustrate statistical methods and explain how to interpret the results. You should be aware, however, that entire books are needed to explain these methods fully.

MANAGERIAL APPLICATION

United Airlines Uses Regression to Estimate Cost Behavior[a]

In the 1970s, United Air Lines (UAL) developed Apollo, a computer reservation system costing several hundred million dollars. This system allows a travel agency to communicate directly with UAL and other airlines about reservations. UAL suspected that one benefit of having Apollo is that some passengers who might not otherwise fly on UAL would do so. The following question arose: What were the variable costs of those additional passengers?

UAL analysts specified the regression model by regressing the change in total costs each period against the changes in revenue passenger miles and systemwide takeoffs. The analysts concluded that about 70 percent of UAL's costs varied with passenger traffic and takeoffs; that is, about 70 percent of UAL's costs were variable.

This result surprised other analysts, who thought that UAL's costs must be mostly fixed. These skeptics observed that UAL averages 35 percent empty seats on its flights. They thought that when UAL carried a few extra passengers, these passengers would sit in the otherwise empty seats. Then, the only incremental costs would be about 25 percent of revenues for extra fuel, food, check-in agents, and baggage handling. The skeptics assumed UAL would not buy new airplanes and other major assets to handle the incremental passenger traffic.

The analysts who developed the regression estimates showed that the airline responded to an increase in demand for seats by expanding its total airline capacity, not just by putting the extra passengers in otherwise empty seats.

[a]Based on the authors' research.

Running the data for *TC* and *X* in Exhibit 3.9 through a computer least-squares regression program gives the following results, which we explain later.

Estimated
Total
Overhead = $100,168 + ($751 × Operating Room Hours Worked during Month)
Costs
per Month

Exhibit 3.10 presents the plotted data and the line implied by this equation.

Next we interpret the $100,168 and $751 amounts. The first—the intercept—estimates the fixed overhead cost per month, and the second estimates the variable overhead cost per unit of base activity—operating room hours worked during the month. The two numbers—$100,168 (for fixed costs) and $751 (for variable costs)—are the *coefficients* of the regression equation, sometimes called the regression coefficients. Looking at Exhibit 3.10, what is the deviation in April? (Answer: The vertical distance between the April dot and the regression line.)

USING THE REGRESSION TO ESTIMATE COSTS

The least-squares regression equation,

$$TC = \$100,168 + (\$751 \times \text{Operating Room Hours}),$$

appears as a heavy straight line in Exhibit 3.10 with the observations identified by month. The dashed line graphed on Exhibit 3.11 shows that these same data

EXHIBIT 3.10

CHICAGO HOSPITAL
Statistical (Least-Squares Regression) Method of Estimating
Fixed Overhead Costs per Month and Variable
Overhead Costs per Operating Room Hour

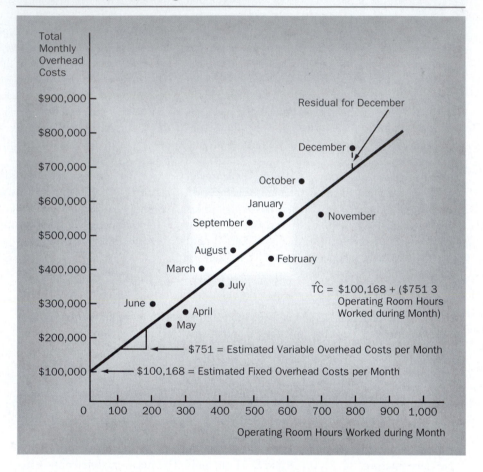

observations may result from a nonlinear relation between costs and activity that
appears to be linear in the range of observations. Assume the hospital is expecting
to use 600 hours of operating room time next month. The expected cost using the
regression results is $550,768 [= $100,168 + ($751 × 600 hours)].

We should be wary of predicting total costs for operating room hours worked outside the range of observations. Any activity less than about 200 hours per month or
more than about 800 hours per month is outside the range of observations.

We should also be wary of our estimate of fixed costs, because it is also outside
the range of observations. We can check the regression estimate of fixed costs with
the account analysis or other methods to be sure that it makes sense. If we made this
check here, for example, we might find that in Exhibit 3.11, the dashed line, not the
assumed straight line, represents the true relation between costs and activity. Look-

EXHIBIT 3.11

CHICAGO HOSPITAL
Comparison of Regression Estimate to Possible Nonlinear Relation

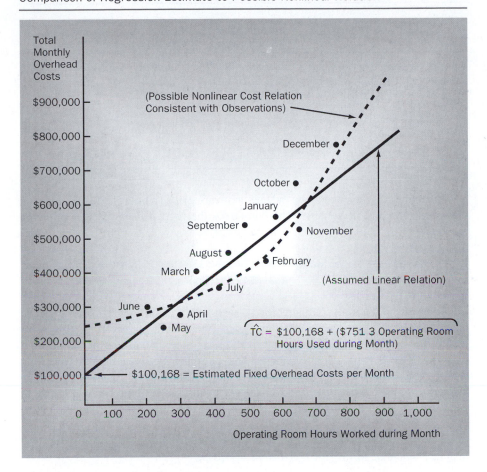

ing at Exhibit 3.11, what type of behavior does the dashed line represent? (Answer: Curvilinear, where cost per unit increases as activity increases.)

MULTIPLE REGRESSION

The preceding discussion dealt with only one independent variable. *Multiple regression* has more than one independent variable. Using the Chicago Hospital data, multiple regression can be utilized when operating room hours are divided by type of operating room. Operating Room Type A is set up with equipment and staffed for sophisticated operations; Operating Room Type B is equipped and staffed for outpatient operations.

We talked to nurses to get further information on the usage of the operating rooms per month. The nurses indicated that Operating Room Type B is used for routine cases (for example, biopsies) and Operating Room Type A for complicated cases (for example, open heart surgery). The following is the estimate we received on the operating hours per operating room.

Month	Total Overhead Costs Incurred	Operating Room A Hours Used	Operating Room B Hours Used
January	$ 558,000	400	200
February	433,000	400	150
.	.	.	.
.	.	.	.
.	.	.	.
December	693,000	500	250
Total	$5,481,000	4,055	1,645

The technique when using two independent variables is similar to that when using only one independent variable. The output for the regression gives the following results:

Total Overhead Costs per Month = $99,243 + ($891 × Operating Room A Hours)
+ ($412 × Operating Room B Hours)

The results of the multiple regression showed a marked difference in cost between Operating Room Type A and Operating Room Type B. Managers can use this information for billing insurance companies the appropriate amount per operation to at least cover costs. For instance, assume that during a particular month Operating Room Type A was used 450 hours and Operating Room Type B was used 150 hours. Using the single regression results, a manager would bill for both types of rooms at $751, for a total of $550,768, as projected in the preceding section. Using the multiple regression results, however, the manager would bill for $561,993 [= $99,243 + ($891 × 450 hours) + ($412 × 150 hours)]. Using the single regression results, the manager would be billing for less than actual costs.

DATA PROBLEMS

Whatever method is used to estimate costs, the results will only be as good as the data used. Collecting appropriate data is complicated by the following problems:

1. *Missing data.* Misplaced source documents or failure to record a transaction can result in missing data.
2. *Outliers.* Extreme observations of cost-activity relations may unduly affect cost estimates. For example, a hurricane affected operations in a Florida company in August, resulting in high overhead due to one-time costs that will not be incurred every month.
3. *Allocated and discretionary costs.* Fixed costs are often allocated on a volume basis and, as a result, may appear to be variable. Discretionary costs may also be

MANAGERIAL APPLICATION

Matching Time Period to Cost Estimation Needs

An old rule of thumb in the newspaper industry says that circulation revenues pay for the cost of newsprint while advertising revenues pay for all other costs and generate profits. During extended periods of stability, newspaper companies could use long time periods in regression analysis and the estimated revenue/cost behavior would be consistent with future trends. However, such estimates lose their credibility as advertising trends shift and newsprint prices change.

In the 1990s, increasing numbers of retailers began advertising by direct mail, which decreased newspaper advertising revenues. In addition, newsprint prices changed substantially. During this period of changing cost and revenue behavior, short time periods should be used for regression analysis—periods short enough that the cost and revenue behavior is very recent and close to what is expected in the future. However, the situation is expected to stabilize, making the old rule of thumb applicable once again. Analysts may return to using longer time periods for their estimates.

Source: "Newspaper Profits: A Delicate Balance," *Nieman Reports* 49, no. 2 (Spring 1995).

budgeted so that they appear variable (for example, advertising expense budgeted as a percentage of revenue).

4. *Inflation.* During periods of inflation, historical cost data do not accurately reflect future cost estimates.

5. *Mismatched time periods.* The time period for the dependent and independent variable may not match (for example, running a machine in February but receiving and recording the energy bill in March).

6. *Trade-offs in choosing the time period.* Short, recent time periods may give a more accurate estimate of what will happen in the future. However, longer time periods may be more accurate for matching costs and activities. For example, using a machine this month may cause maintenance costs to be incurred next month. The activity and cost would not match on a monthly basis, but would match on a yearly basis.

Managers should be aware of problems in the data. There is no substitute for experience when determining how costs and activities are related. The Managerial Application "Matching Time Period to Cost Estimation Needs" demonstrates this point.

STRENGTHS AND WEAKNESSES OF COST ESTIMATION METHODS

Each of the methods discussed has advantages and disadvantages. Probably the most informative estimate of cost behavior results from using several of the methods together, because each method has the potential to provide information not revealed by the others. Exhibit 3.12 summarizes the strengths and weaknesses of these methods. Looking at Exhibit 3.12, when would you most likely expect to see the engineering method used? (Answer: In manufacturing settings.)

We have discussed a variety of cost estimation methods ranging from the simple account analysis approach to sophisticated techniques involving regression or learning curves. Which of these methods is best? In general, the more sophisticated methods will yield more accurate cost estimates than the simpler methods. However, even a sophisticated method yields only an imperfect estimate of an unknown cost behavior pattern.

Analysts often simplify all cost estimation methods. The two most common simplifications are the following.

1. Analysts often assume that cost behavior depends on just one cost driver. (Multiple regression is an exception.) In reality, however, costs are affected by a host of factors, including the weather, the mood of the employees, and the quality of the raw materials used.
2. Analysts often assume that cost behavior patterns are linear within the relevant range. We know that costs actually follow curvilinear, step, semivariable, and other patterns.

You must consider on a case-by-case basis whether these assumptions are reasonable. You also must decide when it is important to use a more sophisticated, and more costly, estimation method and when it is acceptable to use a simpler approach. Like the rest of managerial accounting, you must evaluate the costs and benefits of various cost estimation techniques.

EXHIBIT 3.12

Strengths and Weaknesses of Cost Estimation Methods

Method	Strengths	Weaknesses
Engineering Method	Based on studies of what future costs should be rather than what past costs have been.	Not particularly useful when the physical relation between inputs and outputs is indirect.
		Can be costly to use.
Account Analysis	Provides a detailed expert analysis of the cost behavior in each account.	Subjective.
Regression Method	Uses all the observations of cost data.	The regression model requires that several relatively strict assumptions be satisfied for the results to be valid.
	The line is statistically fit to the observations.	
	Provides a measure of the goodness of fit of the line to the observations.	
	Relatively easy to use with computers and sophisticated calculators.	

PROBLEM 3.4 FOR SELF-STUDY

Plotting data and regression analysis output. Geoffrey Corporation, a manufacturer of stuffed animals, is interested in estimating its fixed and variable costs in the shipping department. Management has chosen the number of cartons packed as the cost driver and collected the following information for a year:

Total Overhead per Month	Total Cartons Packaged per Month
$20,500	500
22,300	650
22,300	625
23,000	700
21,000	550
21,400	570
24,500	725
21,000	525
21,500	600
23,200	675
21,400	560
22,500	640

A regression analysis shows the following:

$$TC = \$12{,}625 + (\$15.45 \times \text{Number of Cartons}).$$

a. Plot the data on a graph.
b. Draw the regression line.
c. What is the range of observations?

The solution to this self-study problem is at the end of the chapter on page 90.

SUMMARY

The following items correspond to the learning objectives presented at the beginning of the chapter.

1. **Distinguish between variable costs and fixed costs, and between short run and long run, and define the relevant range.** Variable costs change as the level of activity changes. Fixed costs do not change with changes in activity levels. The short run is a time period long enough to allow management to change the level of production or other activity within the constraints of current total productive capacity. Management can change total productive capacity only in the long run. The relevant range is the range of activity over which the firm expects a set of cost behaviors to be consistent.

2. **Identify capacity costs, committed costs, and discretionary costs.** Capacity costs are certain fixed costs that provide a firm with the capacity to produce or sell or both. Committed costs are costs that will continue regardless of production level. Discretionary costs need not be incurred in the short run to conduct business.

3. **Understand the nature of the various cost behavior patterns.** Curvilinear variable cost functions indicate that the costs vary with the volume of activity, but not in constant proportion. The learning curve function shows how the amount of time required to perform a task goes down, per unit, as the number of units increases. Semivariable costs have both fixed and variable components. Semifixed costs increase in steps. A change in fixed costs usually involves a change in long-term assets, whereas a change in semifixed costs often does not.

4. **Describe how managers use cost behavior patterns.** Managers use the cost behavior patterns identified in cost studies to help in the budgeting process.

5. **Understand how analysts estimate cost behavior using engineering methods and account analysis.** Cost estimation breaks down total costs into fixed and variable components. The activity represented by X is called the independent variable and the amount of total costs is the dependent variable.

    The engineering method of cost estimation studies the physical relation between the quantities of inputs and output. The accountant assigns costs to each of the inputs to estimate the cost of the outputs. The account analysis method reviews each cost account and classifies it according to cost behavior.

Key Equation:	$TC = F + VX$

6. **Use historical data to estimate cost.** Step one: Make an estimate of the past relation for $TC = F + VX$. Step two: Update this estimate so that it is appropriate for the present or future period for which management wants the estimate. In analyzing cost data, (1) review alternative cost drivers, (2) plot the data, and (3) examine the data and method of accumulation.

    The methods for cost estimation using historical data include regression analysis. Regression analysis is a statistical method whereby a line is fitted to the observations using the least-squares method. Collection of appropriate data for regression analysis can be complicated by missing data, outliers, allocated and discretionary costs, inflation, mismatched time periods, and the length of time period chosen.

7. **Explain the costs, benefits, and weaknesses of the various cost estimation methods.** Except for the multiple regression technique, all the methods assume that cost behavior depends on one activity variable. Another simplifying assumption is that cost behavior patterns are linear within the relevant range. The cost analyst must consider on a case-by-case basis whether these assumptions are reasonable. The analyst must also decide when it is important to use a more sophisticated, and more costly, method and when it is acceptable to use a simpler approach.

8. **(Appendix 3.1) Know how learning curves are derived.** The learning curve derivation in the appendix is known as the cumulative-average-time learning model.

Key Equation:	$Y = aX^b$
	$\log Y = \log a + b \log X$

9. **(Appendix 3.2) Interpret the results of regression analyses.** In regression analysis the standard errors of the coefficients measure their variation and give an idea of the confidence we can have in the fixed and variable cost coefficients. The ratio between an estimated regression coefficient and its standard error is known as the *t*-statistic. If the absolute value is 2 or more, we can be relatively confident that the actual coefficient differs from zero. The R^2 attempts to measure how well the line fits the data; a value of 1.0 denotes a perfect fit. Some statistical problems that may affect interpretation of regression output include multicollinearity, autocorrelation, and heteroscedasticity.

KEY TERMS AND CONCEPTS

Cost behavior   The functional relations between changes in activity and changes in cost.

Variable costs (engineered costs)   Costs that change as activity levels change.

Fixed costs   An expenditure or expense that does not vary with volume of activity, at least in the short run.

Short run   The time period during which total productive capacity cannot be changed.

Long run   A term denoting a time or time periods in the future, during which total productive capacity can be changed. For most managers, it means anything beyond the next year or two.

Relevant range   Activity levels over which costs are linear or for which flexible budget estimates and breakeven charts will remain valid.

Capacity costs   Fixed costs incurred to provide a firm with the capacity to produce or to sell.

Committed costs   Costs incurred for the acquisition of long-term activity capacity, usually as the result of strategic planning.

Discretionary costs (programmed costs, managed costs)   Fixed costs not essential for carrying out operations in the short run.

Curvilinear variable cost   A continuous, but not necessarily linear, functional relation between activity levels and costs.

Marginal cost   The incremental cost or differential cost of the last unit added to production or the first unit subtracted from production.

Learning curve (experience curve)   A mathematical expression of the phenomenon that incremental unit costs to produce decrease as managers and labor gain experience from practice.

Semivariable costs   Costs that have both fixed and variable cost components. Also called mixed costs.

Semifixed costs   Costs that increase with activity as a step function.

Cost estimation   The process of measuring the functional relation between changes in activity levels and changes in cost.

Independent variable   The variable used to estimate cost behavior in regression analysis.

Dependent variable   In cost estimation, the cost the regression analysis explains.

Engineering method of cost estimation   Estimates of unit costs of product derived from study of the materials, labor, and overhead components of the production process.

Account analysis method A method of separating fixed from variable costs involving the classification of the various product cost accounts.

Cost driver A factor that causes an activity's costs or indirectly measures the activity that causes costs.

Regression analysis A method of cost estimation based on statistical techniques for fitting a line to an observed series of data points, usually by minimizing the sum of squared deviations of the observed data from the fitted line.

Standard errors of the coefficients A measure of the uncertainty about the magnitude of the estimated parameters of an equation fit with a regression analysis.

***t*-statistic** For an estimated regression coefficient, the estimated coefficient divided by the standard error of the estimate.

R^2 The proportion of the statistical variance of a dependent variable explained by the equation fit to the independent variable in a regression analysis.

SOLUTIONS TO SELF-STUDY PROBLEMS

SUGGESTED SOLUTION TO PROBLEM 3.1 FOR SELF-STUDY

Cumulative Number of Units Produced	Average Labor Cost per Unit	Total Labor Costs
1	$1,333	$1,333
2	1,000 (= 75% × $1,333)	2,000
4	750 (= 75% × $1,000)	3,000
8	562.50 (= 75% × $750)	4,500
16	421.88 (= 75% × $562.50)	6,750

SUGGESTED SOLUTION TO PROBLEM 3.2 FOR SELF-STUDY

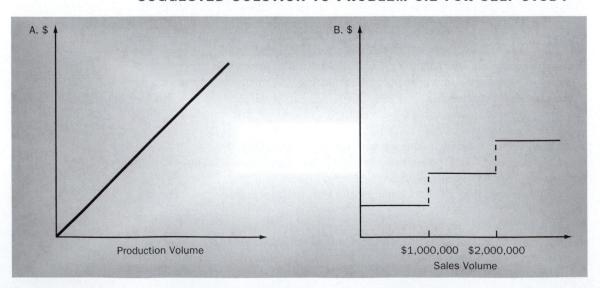

A. $ Production Volume

B. $ $1,000,000 $2,000,000   Sales Volume

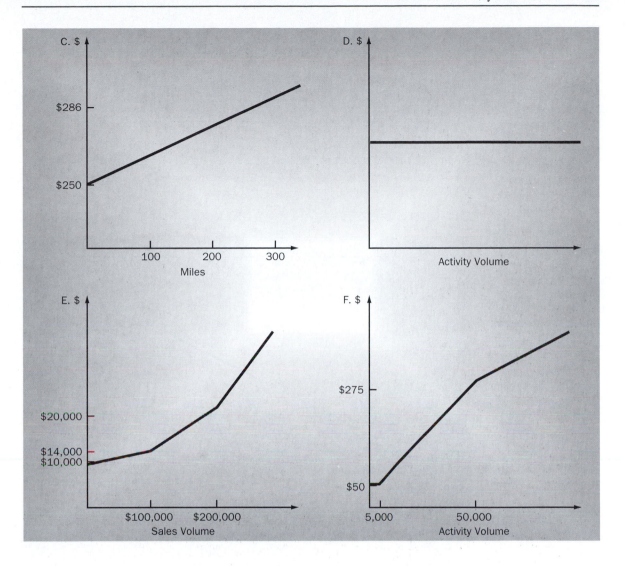

SUGGESTED SOLUTION TO PROBLEM 3.3 FOR SELF-STUDY

Indirect Materials	$ 503,000
Indirect Labor	630,000
Power	104,000
Total Variable Costs	$1,237,000
Lease	$ 288,000
Utilities	206,000
Insurance	24,000
Maintenance	200,000
Depreciation	72,000
Research and Development	171,000
Total Fixed Costs	$ 961,000

$$\text{Average monthly fixed costs} \quad = \frac{\$961,000}{24} = \underline{\underline{\$40,042}}$$

$$\text{Variable cost per DLH} \quad = \frac{\$1,237,000}{815,800} = \underline{\underline{\$1.516}}$$

$$\text{Variable cost per machine-hour} = \frac{\$1,237,000}{1,022,700} = \underline{\underline{\$1.210}}$$

$$\text{Variable cost per unit produced} = \frac{\$1,237,000}{202,500} = \underline{\underline{\$6.109}}$$

SUGGESTED SOLUTION TO PROBLEM 3.4 FOR SELF-STUDY

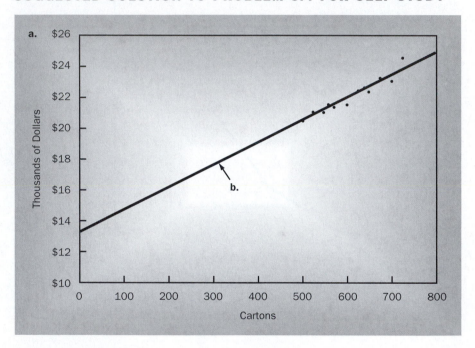

c. 500 to 725 cartons

APPENDIX 3.1: DERIVING LEARNING CURVES[2]

Mathematically, the learning curve effect is

$$Y = aX^b,$$

---

[2]The learning curve derivation in this appendix is known as the cumulative-average-time learning model.

where

> Y = average number of labor hours required per unit for X units
>
> a = number of labor hours required for the first unit
>
> X = cumulative number of units produced
>
> b = index of learning equal to the log of the learning rate divided by the log of 2.

For the 80 percent cumulative learning curve example in the text, $b = -.322$, which we derive as follows.

If the first unit takes a hours, then the average for 2 units is $.8a$ hours according to the model. Because $X = 2$, the equation gives $.8a = a2^b$. Taking logs,

$$\log 0.8 + \log a = \log a + b \log 2.$$

Simplifying,

$$b = \log 0.8/\log 2 = -.322.$$

Thus we can derive the average number of labor hours from the example in the text as follows:

X	Y	
1	125	
2	100	$Y = 125 \times (2^{-.322}) = 100$
3	88	$Y = 125 \times (3^{-.322}) = 88$
4	80	$Y = 125 \times (4^{-.322}) = 80$
.	.	
.	.	
.	.	
8	64	$Y = 125 \times (8^{-.322}) = 64$

The function

$$Y = aX^b$$

is curvilinear, as shown in the text. The function is linear when expressed in logs, because

$$\log Y = \log a + b \log X,$$

so the function is linear when plotted on log-log paper, as Exhibit 3.13 shows.

Operations management textbooks provide expanded discussions.

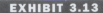

EXHIBIT 3.13

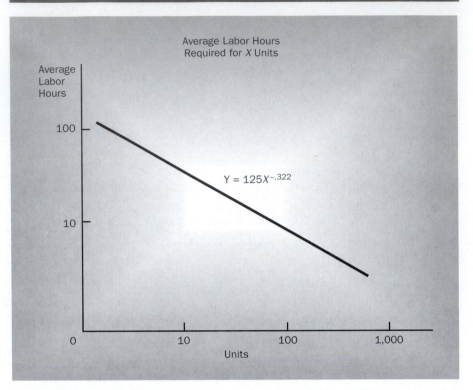

Average Labor Hours
Required for *X* Units

$Y = 125X^{-.322}$

APPENDIX 3.2:
REGRESSION ANALYSIS OUTPUT

This appendix expands the discussion in the text to help you understand and interpret regression output.

STANDARD ERRORS OF THE COEFFICIENTS AND *t*-STATISTICS

The **standard errors of the coefficients** give an idea of the confidence we can have in the fixed and variable cost coefficients. The smaller the standard error relative to its coefficient, the more precise the estimate. (Such computational precision does not necessarily indicate that the estimating procedure is *theoretically* correct, however.)

The ratio between an estimated regression coefficient and its standard error is known as the *t*-value or ***t*-statistic.** If the absolute value of the *t*-statistic is approximately 2 or larger, we can be relatively confident that the actual coefficient differs from zero.[3]

---

[3]Statistics books provide *t*-tables that make the analysis of *t*-statistics more precise.

If a variable cost coefficient has a small t-statistic, we may conclude that little, if any, relation exists between this particular activity (or independent variable) and changes in costs. If a fixed cost coefficient has a small t-statistic, we may conclude that these costs have little, if any, fixed cost component (which we would expect for operating room supplies or direct materials in manufacturing, for example).

R^2

The R^2 attempts to measure how well the line fits the data (that is, how closely the data points cluster about the fitted line). If all the data points were on the same straight line, the R^2 would be 1.00—a perfect fit. If the data points formed a circle or disk, the R^2 would be zero, indicating that no line passing through the center of the circle or disk fits the data better than any other. Technically, R^2 is a measure of the fraction of the total variance of the dependent variable about its mean that the fitted line explains. An R^2 of 1 means that the regression explains all of the variance; an R^2 of zero means that it explains none of the variance. R^2 is sometimes known as the "coefficient of determination."

Many users of statistical regression analysis believe that low R^2s indicate a weak relation between total costs (dependent variable) and the activity base (independent variable). A low standard error (or high t-statistic) for the estimated variable cost coefficient signals whether or not the activity base performs well as an explanatory variable for total costs. With a large number of data observations, both low R^2 and significant regression coefficients can occur. Exhibit 3.14 illustrates this possibility.

EXHIBIT 3.14

Relation between Statistical Significance of Variable Cost Coefficient and R^2

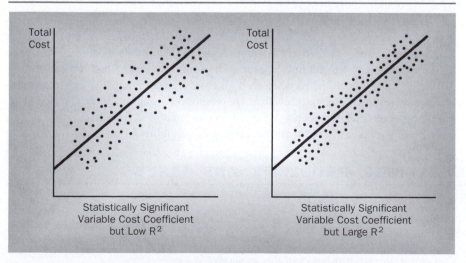

CAUTIONS WHEN USING REGRESSION

Computers easily perform statistical estimating techniques but often do not provide the necessary warnings. We conclude this section by providing several cautionary comments. A relation achieved in a regression analysis does not imply a causal relation; that is, a correlation between two variables does not imply that changes in one will cause changes in the other. An assertion of causality must be based on either *a priori* knowledge or some analysis other than a regression analysis.

Users of regression analysis should be wary of drawing too many inferences from the results unless they are familiar with such statistical estimation problems as *multicollinearity, autocorrelation,* and *heteroscedasticity* and how to deal with them. Statistics books deal with these statistical estimation problems.

Briefly, *multicollinearity* refers to the problem caused in multiple linear regression (more than one independent variable) when the independent variables are not independent of each other but are correlated. When severe multicollinearity occurs, the regression coefficients are unreliable. For example, direct labor hours worked during a month are likely to be highly correlated with direct labor costs during the month, even when wage rates change over time. If both direct labor hours and direct labor costs are used in a multiple linear regression, we would expect to have a problem of multicollinearity.

Autocorrelation problems arise when the data represent observations over time. Autocorrelation occurs when a linear regression is fit to data where a nonlinear relation exists between the dependent and independent variables. In such a case, the deviation of one observation from the fitted line can be predicted from the deviation of the prior observation(s). For example, if demand for a product is seasonal and production is also seasonal, a month of large total costs will more likely follow another month of large total costs than a month of small total costs. In such a case, we would have autocorrelation in the deviations of the data points from a fitted straight line.

Autocorrelation affects the estimates of standard errors of the regression estimates, and therefore it affects the *t*-statistics. If autocorrelation exists, the estimates of standard errors may be understated and the *t*-statistics may be overstated in the regression output.

Heteroscedasticity refers to the phenomenon that occurs when the average deviation of the dependent variable from the best-fitting linear relation is systematically larger in one part of the range of independent variable(s) than in others. For example, if the firm uses less reliable equipment and employs less skilled labor in months of large total production, variation in total costs during months of large total production is likely to be greater than in months of small total production. Heteroscedasticity affects the reliability of the estimates of standard errors of the regression coefficients (and therefore affects the reliability of the *t*-statistics).

QUESTIONS, EXERCISES, PROBLEMS, AND CASES

REVIEW QUESTIONS

1. Review the meaning of the concepts or terms given in Key Terms and Concepts.
2. Which method of cost estimation does not rely primarily on historical cost data? What are the drawbacks of this method?

3. Name three methods of cost estimation.

4. The simplifying assumptions that cost estimations are based on include which of the following?
   a. Cost behavior depends on one activity variable (except regression).
   b. Cost behavior patterns are not linear within the relevant range.
   c. Costs are only fixed.
   d. All of the above.

5. (Appendix 3.2) R^2
   a. measures how well the line fits the data.
   b. is a perfect fit when its value is 1.0.
   c. is the standard error of the coefficient.
   d. a. and **b.**

6. Multiple regression
   a. has one dependent variable.
   b. has more than one independent variable.
   c. has only one independent variable.
   d. a. and **b.**

CRITICAL ANALYSIS AND DISCUSSION QUESTIONS

7. "The concepts of short-run costs and long-run costs are relative—short run could mean a day, a month, a year, or even 10 years, depending on what you are looking at." Comment.

8. "My variable costs are $2 per unit. If I want to increase production from 100,000 units to 150,000 units, my costs should go up by only $100,000." Comment.

9. What methods of cost estimation rely primarily on historical data? Discuss the problems an unwary user may encounter with the use of historical cost data.

10. Why might the relevant range be limited to the range of observations in a data set?

11. If an analyst simply enters data into a program to compute regression estimates, what major problems might he or she encounter?

12. When estimating fixed and variable costs, it is possible to have an equation with a negative intercept. Does this mean that at zero production level the company has negative fixed costs?

13. Refer to the Managerial Application "United Airlines Uses Regression to Estimate Cost Behavior." What independent variables did the analysts use in the regression? What did the analysts who developed the regression conclude? Based on your experience, do you agree with their conclusions?

14. (Appendix 3.2) How is regression used to identify what cost drivers might be used in activity-based costing?

15. (Appendix 3.1) Describe the phenomenon that gives rise to learning curves. To what type of costs do learning curves apply?

16. "Simplification of all costs into just fixed and variable costs distorts the actual cost behavior pattern of a firm. Yet businesses rely on this method of cost classification." Comment.

17. "The account analysis method uses subjective judgment. So we cannot really consider it a valid method of cost estimation." Comment.
18. Suggest ways that one can compensate for the effects of inflation when preparing cost estimates.

EXERCISES

Solutions to even-numbered exercises are at the end of the chapter.

19. **Graphs of cost relations.** Sketch cost graphs for the following situations:
    a. A 20 percent increase in fixed costs will enable Twickenham Products to produce up to 50 percent more. Variable costs per unit will remain unchanged.
    b. Refer to part **a.** What if Twickenham Products' variable costs per unit double for the additional units it intends to produce?
    c. Aerodyne's variable marketing costs per unit decline as more units are sold.
    d. Richmond Paper pays a flat fixed charge per month for electricity plus an additional rate of $.15 per unit for all consumption over the first 2,000 units.
    e. Indirect labor costs at National Bank consist only of supervisors' salaries. The bank needs one supervisor for every 20 clerks.
    f. Petersham Plastics currently operates close to capacity. A short-run increase in production would result in increasing unit costs for every additional unit produced.

20. **Cost behavior in event of capacity change.** Muller's Gasthaus, a lodge located in a fast-growing ski resort, is planning to open its new wing this coming winter, increasing the number of beds by 40 percent. Although variable costs per guest-day will remain unchanged, fixed costs will increase by 25 percent. Last year's costs follow:

Variable Costs	$50,000
Fixed Costs	$30,000

    a. Sketch the cost function.
    b. Calculate the additional fixed operating costs that Muller's Gasthaus will incur next year.

21. **Cost behavior when costs are semivariable.** Data from the shipping department of Vaughn Company for the last two months follows:

	Number of Packages Shipped	Shipping Department Costs
November	6,000	$12,000
December	9,000	15,000

    a. Sketch a line describing these costs as a function of the number of packages shipped.
    b. What is the apparent variable cost per package shipped?
    c. The line should indicate that these shipping costs are semivariable. What is the apparent fixed cost per month of running the shipping department during November and December?

22. **Cost behavior when costs are semivariable.** Data from the shipping department of Pete's Coffee for the last four months follow:

	Number of Packages Shipped	Shipping Department Costs
May	0	$1,500
June	2,000	3,500
July	2,500	4,500
August	1,500	3,000

Are these costs fixed, semifixed, variable, or semivariable?

23. **Cost estimation using regression analysis.** The Vigil Accounting Company prepares tax returns for small businesses. Data on the company's total costs and output for the past six months appear in the table that follows. The results of regression analysis are also provided.

   a. Plot the data and the regression line on a graph. (See Problem 3.4 for Self-Study.)

   b. Estimate total monthly costs for a month when 250 tax returns are prepared, using the estimates of fixed and variable costs from the regression output.

VIGIL ACCOUNTING COMPANY

Month	Tax Returns Prepared	Total Costs
January	200	$160,000
February	280	192,000
March	300	198,000
April	260	180,000
May	260	186,000
June	240	170,000

Regression output: $TC = \$78,045 + (\$401 \times \text{Number of Tax Returns})$.

24. **Learning curve.** R&D Co. makes technical products for mysterious customers. To make Product RPE, the company recently recorded the following costs, which decline subject to a 75 percent cumulative learning curve.

Cumulative Number of Units Produced	Average Labor Costs per Unit
1	$1,333
2	1,000
4	?
8	?
16	?

Complete the chart by filling in the cost amounts for volumes of 4, 8, and 16 units.

25. **Average cost calculations.** Lawrence Lamps has the following cost equation:

$$\text{Total Costs} = \$13,266 + \$20n,$$

where n = units of output.
   a. Calculate Lawrence's average fixed cost per unit when output is 1,000 units.
   b. Calculate the average variable cost per unit when output is 1,000 units.
   c. Calculate the average cost per unit when output is 1,000 units.
26. **Repair cost behavior.** The Baiman Company analyzed repair costs by month using linear regression analysis. The equation fit took the following form:

$$\begin{matrix}\text{Total} \\ \text{Repair} \\ \text{Costs}\end{matrix} = \begin{matrix}\text{Fixed} \\ \text{Costs}\end{matrix} + \left(\begin{matrix}\text{Variable Repair Costs} \\ \text{per Machine Hour Used} \\ \text{during Month}\end{matrix} \times \begin{matrix}\text{Machine Hours} \\ \text{Actually Used} \\ \text{during Month}\end{matrix} \right)$$

$$TRC = a + bx.$$

The results were

$$TRC = \$20,000 - \$.75x$$

   Average monthly repair costs have been \$18,800, and machine hours used have averaged 1,600 hours per month. Management worries about the ability of the analyst who carried out this work because of the *negative* coefficient for variable cost.
   What is your evaluation of these results?
27. **Interpreting regression results.** The output of a regression of overhead costs on direct labor costs per month follows:

Regression Results
Equation:
   Intercept (F) \$22,500
   Slope (V) 1.45
Statistical Data:
   R^2 .... .85

The company plans to operate at a level that would call for direct labor costs of \$14,000 per month for the coming year.
   a. Use the regression output to write the overhead cost equation.
   b. Based on the cost equation, compute the estimated overhead cost per month for the coming year.
   c. (Appendix 3.2) How well does this regression explain the relation between direct labor and overhead?
28. **Interpreting regression data.** A marketing manager of a company used a pocket calculator to estimate the relation between sales dollars for the past 3 years and monthly advertising expenditures (the independent variable). The regression results indicated the following equation:

$$\text{Sales Dollars} = \$97,000 - (1.45 \times \text{Advertising Dollars})$$

Do these results imply that advertising hurts sales? Why would there appear to be a negative relation between advertising expenditures and sales?

29. **Cost estimation using regression analysis.** Lopez Beverages has observed the following overhead costs for the past 12 months:

Month	Overhead Costs	Gallons of Output
January	$22,800	9,000
February	31,200	22,000
March	33,600	24,000
April	24,000	11,000
May	28,200	18,000
June	31,200	21,000
July	26,400	15,000
August	24,600	10,000
September	31,200	23,000
October	25,800	12,000
November	28,800	17,000
December	30,000	20,000

The results of the regression analysis are:

$$TC = \$17,562 + (\$0.63 \times \text{Number of Gallons}).$$

a. Plot the data and the regression line (like Problem 3.4 for Self-Study).
b. Estimate total monthly costs for a month when 19,000 gallons are produced.

PROBLEMS

30. **Interpreting multiple regression results** (Appendix 3.2). To select the most appropriate activity base for allocating overhead, Kakimoto Manufacturing ran a multiple regression of several independent variables against its nonmaintenance overhead cost. The results were as follows for 24 observations:

Variable Name	Coefficient	Standard Error	t-Statistic
Direct Labor Hours	.876	2.686	.326
Units of Output	10.218	5.378	1.900
Maintenance Costs	$(12.786)	$1.113	(11.488)
Cost of Utilities	$ .766	$ .079	9.696
Intercept	12.768	6.359	2.008

R^2 for the Multiple Regression = 0.90

Discuss the appropriateness of each of these variables for use as an activity base. Which would you recommend selecting? Why?

31. **Interpreting regression results** (adapted from an example by G. Benston, *The Accounting Review* 41, pp. 657–672). The Benston Company manufactures widgets and digits. Benston assembles the widgets in batches, but makes digits one at a time. Benston believes that the cost of producing widgets is

independent of the number of digits produced in a week. The firm gathered cost data for 156 weeks. The following notation is used:

C = Total manufacturing costs per week

N = Number of widgets produced during a week

B = Average number of widgets in a batch during the week

D = Number of digits produced during the week

A multiple linear regression fit to the observations gave the following results:

$$C = \$265.80 + \$8.21N - \$7.83B + \$12.32D.$$

a. According to the regression results, how much are weekly costs expected to increase if the number of widgets increases by 1?
b. What are the expected costs for the week if Benston produces 500 widgets in batches of 20 each and produces 300 digits during the week?
c. Interpret the negative coefficient $\$(7.83)$ estimated for the variable B.

32. **Regression analysis, multiple choice.** Rainer Company estimated the behavior pattern of maintenance costs. Data regarding maintenance hours and costs for the previous year and the results of the regression analysis follow:

	Hours of Activity	Maintenance Costs
January	480	$ 4,200
February	320	3,000
March	400	3,600
April	300	2,820
May	500	4,350
June	310	2,960
July	320	3,030
August	520	4,470
September	490	4,260
October	470	4,050
November	350	3,300
December	340	3,160
Sum	4,800	43,200
Average	400	3,600

$$TC = F + VX$$
$$= \$684.65 + \$7.2884X$$

Intercept 684.65
V Coefficient 7.2884

a. In the equation $TC = F + VX$, the best description of the letter V is as the
   (1) independent variable.
   (2) dependent variable.
   (3) variable cost coefficient.
   (4) coefficient for the intercept.
b. The best description of TC in the preceding equation is as the
   (1) independent variable.

  (**2**) constant coefficient.
  (**3**) dependent variable.
  (**4**) variable coefficient.

c. The best description of the letter X in the preceding regression equation is as the
  (**1**) dependent variable.
  (**2**) coefficient for the intercept.
  (**3**) variable cost coefficient.
  (**4**) independent variable.

d. Based on the data derived from the regression analysis, 420 maintenance hours in a month mean that the maintenance costs would be estimated at
  (**1**) $3,780.
  (**2**) $3,746.
  (**3**) $3,461.
  (**4**) $3,797.
  (**5**) Some other amount.

33. Graphing costs and interpreting regression output (adapted from CMA exam). Management of Monahan's Pizza wants to estimate overhead costs accurately to plan the company's operations and its financial needs. A trade association publication reports that certain overhead costs tend to vary with pizzas made. Management gathered monthly data on pizzas and overhead costs for the past two years for 12 pizza restaurants. No major changes in operations were made over this time period. The data follow:

Month No.	Number of Pizzas	Overhead Costs
1	20,000	$84,000
2	25,000	99,000
3	22,000	89,500
4	23,000	90,000
5	20,000	81,500
6	19,000	75,500
7	14,000	70,500
8	10,000	64,500
9	12,000	69,000
10	17,000	75,000
11	16,000	71,500
12	19,000	78,000
13	21,000	86,000
14	24,000	93,000
15	23,000	93,000
16	22,000	87,000
17	20,000	80,000
18	18,000	76,500
19	12,000	67,500
20	13,000	71,000
21	15,000	73,500
22	17,000	72,500
23	15,000	71,000
24	18,000	75,000

An analyst entered these data into a computer regression program and obtained the following output:

Coefficients of the Equation:
Intercept $39,859
Independent Variable (slope) 2.1549

a. Prepare a graph showing the overhead costs plotted against pizzas.
b. Use the results of the regression analysis to prepare the cost estimation equation and to prepare a cost estimate for 22,500 pizzas for one month.
34. **Interpreting regression results** (adapted from CMA exam). Horizon Company is making plans for the introduction of a new product that it will sell for $6 a unit. The following estimates have been made for manufacturing costs on 100,000 units to be produced the first year:

Direct materials $50,000
Direct labor . . . . $80,000 (the labor rate is $8 an hour × 10,000 hours)

Manufacturing overhead costs have not yet been estimated for the new product, but monthly data on total production and overhead costs for the past 24 months have been analyzed using regression. The following results were derived from the regression and will provide the basis for overhead cost estimates for the new product.

Regression Analysis Results

Dependent variable—Factory overhead costs
Independent variable—Direct labor-hours
Computed values:
Intercept $55,000
Coefficient of independent variable . . . . $ 3.20
Coefficient of correlation 953
R^2 908

a. (Appendix 3.2) What percentage of the variation in overhead costs is explained by the independent variable?
(1) 90.8 percent
(2) 42 percent
(3) 48.8 percent
(4) 95.3 percent
(5) Some other amount.
b. The total overhead cost for an estimated activity level of 20,000 direct labor-hours would be:
(1) $55,000
(2) $64,000
(3) $82,000
(4) $119,000
(5) Some other amount.

c. What is the expected contribution margin per *unit* to be earned during the first year on 100,000 units of the new product? (Assume all marketing and administrative costs are fixed.)
   (1) $4.38
   (2) $4.89
   (3) $3.83
   (4) $5.10
   (5) Some other amount.

d. How much is the variable manufacturing cost per *unit,* using the variable overhead estimated by the regression (and assuming direct materials and direct labor are variable costs)?
   (1) $1.30
   (2) $1.11
   (3) $1.62
   (4) $3
   (5) Some other amount.

e. What is the manufacturing cost equation implied by these results, where x refers to *units* produced?
   (1) $TC = \$80,000 + \$1.11x$
   (2) $TC = \$55,000 + \$1.62x$
   (3) $TC = \$185,000 + \$3.20x$
   (4) Some other equation.

35. **Effect of learning on cost behavior.** Levenson Incorporated manufactures aircraft parts for various commercial airlines. One particular contract resulted in the following labor costs:

Cumulative Number of Units Produced, X	Average Labor Costs (in real dollars), Y
1	$1,333
2	1,000
3	845
4	750
5	684
6	634
7	594
8	562

a. Sketch the relation between X and Y.
b. If there is a learning phenomenon, estimate the constant percentage reduction in labor costs, that is, the percent cumulative learning curve.

CASES

36. **Estimating health-care cost behavior.** The health-care industry has been faced with increasing pressure to control costs. Health-care costs have increased substantially more rapidly than general inflation rates. At the same time, health-care facilities face price competition for services because insurance companies and government-funded health programs are limiting opportunities for cost reimbursement.

To control costs, one must first relate the costs of providing services to the volume of activity. The first step is often to estimate a cost model, $TC = F + VX$, where X refers to the volume of activity. Examples of activity bases include patient days to estimate nurse staff costs or number of tests to estimate costs in a laboratory.

Although it may appear simple to estimate the relation $TC = F + VX$, analysts often find a lack of good data to make the estimates. For example, the cost of medical supplies shown in the accounting records is often the cost of *purchases,* not the cost of supplies *used.* Consequently, large purchases in one month followed by no purchases in the next month make these costs appear to behave in unrealistic ways.

Although recent pressures on health-care facilities to reduce costs have increased the incentives for administrators and doctors to improve recordkeeping, our research indicates the information needed to control costs is lacking in many health-care organizations. For example, hospitals often keep track of *charges* to patients but not the *costs* of the items being charged.

How would information that makes it possible to estimate the equation $TC = F + VX$ help health-care managers control costs?

37. **Learning curves, managerial decisions** (adapted from CMA exam). The Xyon Company purchases 80,000 pumps annually from Kobec, Inc. The price has increased each year and reached $68 per unit last year. Because the purchase price has increased significantly, Xyon management has asked its analyst to estimate the cost to manufacture the pump in its own facilities. Xyon's products consist of stamping and castings. The company has little experience with products requiring assembly.

The engineering, manufacturing, and accounting departments have prepared a report for management that includes the following estimate for an assembly run of 10,000 units. The firm would hire additional production employees to manufacture the subassembly. It would not need extra equipment, space, or supervision.

The report estimates total costs for 10,000 units at $957,000, or $95.70 a unit. The current purchase price is $68 a unit, so the report recommends continued purchase of the product.

Components (outside purchases)	$120,000
Assembly Labor[a]	300,000
Factory Overhead[b]	450,000
General and Administrative Overhead[c]	87,000
Total Costs	$957,000
Fixed Overhead	50 Percent of Direct Labor Dollars
Variable Overhead	100 Percent of Direct Labor Dollars
Factory Overhead Rate	150 Percent of Direct Labor Dollars

[a]Assembly labor consists of hourly production workers.

[b]Factory overhead is applied to products on a direct labor dollar basis. Variable overhead costs vary closely with direct labor dollars.

[c]General and administrative overhead is applied at 10 percent of the total cost of material (or components), assembly labor, and factory overhead.

a. Was the analysis prepared by the engineering, manufacturing, and accounting departments of Xyon Company and the recommendation to continue purchasing the pumps that followed from the analysis correct? Explain your answer and include any supportive calculations you consider necessary.

b. Assume Xyon Company could experience labor cost improvements on the pump assembly consistent with an 80 percent learning curve. An assembly run of 10,000 units represents the initial lot or batch for measurement purposes. Should Xyon produce the 80,000 pumps in this situation? Explain your answer.

SUGGESTED SOLUTIONS TO EVEN-NUMBERED EXERCISES

20. Cost behavior in event of capacity change.

a.

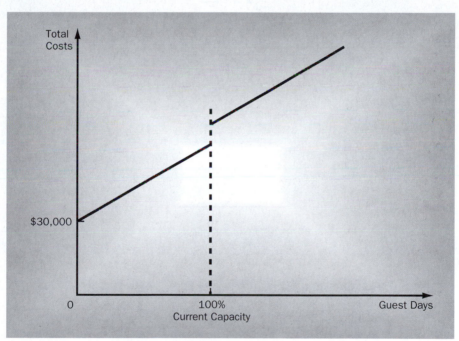

b. Additional fixed operating costs = 0.25(30,000)

$$= \$7,500.$$

22. Cost behavior when costs are semivariable. Plotting the data, these costs appear to be semivariable. The fixed-cost component estimate is $1,500, and the variable cost component is $1 per package up to 2,000 packages [$1 = ($3,500 − $1,500)/2,000 pkgs.]. With only four data points, you should view these estimates skeptically, however.

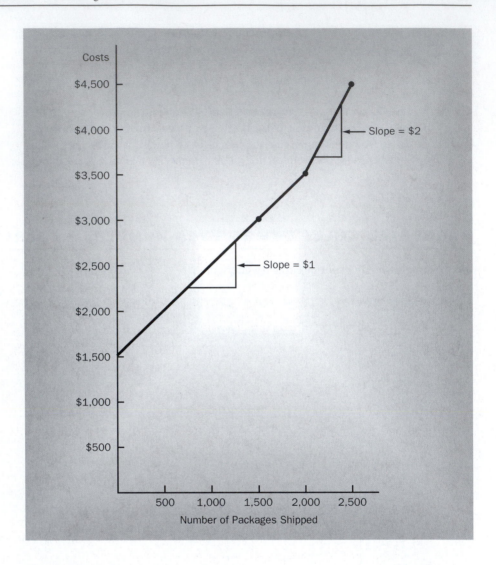

Costs

$4,500

$4,000 — Slope = $2

$3,500

$3,000

$2,500 — Slope = $1

$2,000

$1,500

$1,000

$500

500   1,000   1,500   2,000   2,500

Number of Packages Shipped

24. **Learning curve.**

Cumulative Number of Units Produced	Average Labor Costs per Unit
1	$1,333
2	1,000 ($1,333 × 75%)
4	750 ($1,000 × 75%)
8	562.50 ($750 × 75%)
16	421.88 ($562.50 × 75%)

26. **Repair cost behavior.** The most likely explanation for the inverse relation between production and repair costs is that the firm schedules repair work during slow, rather than busy, times. So repair costs increase when volume decreases.

28. **Interpreting regression data.** This problem frequently arises when applying analytical techniques to certain costs. Quite often the advertising expenditures result in sales being generated in the following month or later. In addition, many companies increase their advertising when sales are declining and cut back on advertising when manufacturing is at capacity. A better model might relate this month's sales to last month's advertising.

   Similar problems exit for repair and maintenance costs, because routine repairs and maintenance usually occur during slow periods. An inverse relation often exists between salespersons' travel expenses and sales, if the sales staff spends more time traveling when the sales are more difficult to make.

CHAPTER 4

COST-VOLUME-PROFIT ANALYSIS

1. Explain how costs, volume, and profits are interrelated.
2. List various applications of the cost-volume-profit model.
3. Describe the use of spreadsheets in cost-volume-profit analysis.
4. Identify the effects of cost structure and operating leverage on the sensitivity of profit to changes in volume.
5. Calculate breakeven using sales dollars as the measure of volume.
6. Use the cost-volume-profit model on an after-tax basis.
7. Calculate breakeven in a multiproduct setting.
8. Define the assumptions of the cost-volume-profit model.

Cost-volume-profit is a simple but appealing concept. At one level, it is a sweeping overview of an organization's financial activities. At another level, it is a useful tool for making specific decisions.

Here's an example. A student organization wants to show movies on campus. The organization can rent a particular movie for one weekend for $1,000. Rent for an auditorium, salaries to the ticket takers and other personnel, and other fixed costs would total $800 for the weekend. The organization would sell tickets for $4 per person. In addition, profits from the sale of soft drinks, popcorn, and candy are estimated to be $1 per ticket holder. How many people would have to buy tickets to break even, and therefore justify renting the movie? (The answer is 360.)

The analysis relies on concepts of fixed and variable cost behavior that was first discussed in Chapter 2 and continued through Chapter 3. This chapter presents the cost-volume-profit model and demonstrates how managers can use (or misuse) it in a number of decision-making situations.

After reading this chapter, you should understand how to use cost-volume-profit analysis as well as the model's limitations and assumptions.

THE COST-VOLUME-PROFIT MODEL

The **cost-volume-profit (CVP) model** states a relation among selling prices, unit costs, volume sold, and profits. It starts with the basic equation where profits are equal to total revenue minus total costs, or

$$\pi = TR - TC.$$

In the equation:

π = operating profit for the period,

TR = total revenues for the period, and

TC = total costs for the period.

The cost-volume-profit equation in more detail is

$$\pi = TR - TC$$
$$\pi = PX - (F + VX).$$

In the equation:

P = unit selling price,

X = number of units sold in the period,

F = fixed operating costs for the period, and

V = unit variable costs.

So $TR = PX$, or total revenues = price per unit $\times$ number of units sold in the period. Also, $TC = (F + VX)$, or total costs = fixed operating costs for the period + (unit variable costs $\times$ number of units sold in the period).

Profits in managerial models or on internal reports may differ from net income for external financial reporting under generally accepted accounting principles (GAAP). For example, the cost-volume-profit model treats fixed manufacturing overhead as a cost of the period (known as the variable costing method), not as a unit cost as required for external reporting under GAAP (known as the full absorption method).

Also, the cost-volume-profit model does not necessarily use data about the past. The model predicts the future, so it uses estimates of future costs and revenues.

HOW THE MODEL WORKS

We base much of our discussion in this chapter on illustrative data for The Little People's Place, a day-care center providing service from 7 AM to 6 PM, weekdays only. Service provided for one child for a month is considered one unit. These data appear in the top of Exhibit 4.1. The cost-volume-profit equation for The Little People's Place is

$$\pi = PX - (F + VX).$$
$$\pi = \$600X - (\$5{,}000 + \$200X).$$

The Little People's Place has a capacity of 20, after which more staff needs to be hired. The estimated variable costs include two snacks and lunch every day, various

EXHIBIT 4.1

The Little People's Place
Cost-Volume-Profit Data

Selling Price per Child per Month	$600
Variable Cost per Child per Month	$200
Fixed Costs per Month	$5,000

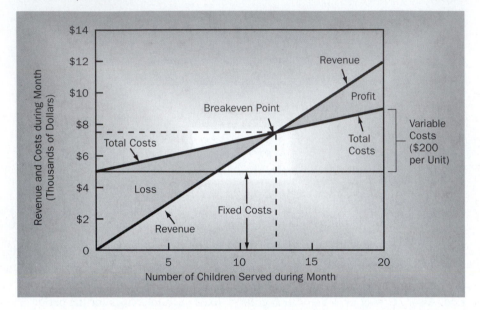

paper products and soap, a variable cost component of insurance, and toys, crayons, and other supplies. The fixed costs include rent, utilities, a fixed cost component of insurance, and minimum staffing requirements of three full-time "Big Friends," a part-time "Big Cook/Housekeeper," and some volunteers.

Exhibit 4.1 presents two linear relations as a function of the number of children served: total revenue, $TR = PX = \$600X$; and total cost, $TC = \$5,000 + \$200X$. Because the fixed costs are $5,000 per month, the total cost line goes through the vertical axis at $5,000. Because variable costs are $200 per unit, the total costs line increases $200 per unit for increases in units sold during the month. Looking at Exhibit 4.1, what is the loss if The Little People's Place serves no children? (Answer: $5,000.)

THE CONTRIBUTION CONCEPT

In general, each unit sold contributes to fixed costs and earning profits. The **contribution margin per unit** is the excess of unit selling price over unit variable cost:

$$\text{Contribution Margin per Unit} = P - V$$

For The Little People's Place, the contribution margin is

$400 = $600 selling price per unit − $200 variable cost per child served per month

USING THE CONTRIBUTION MARGIN IN PRODUCT CHOICE DECISIONS

The contribution margin plays an important role in making product choice decisions. Suppose that you have the opportunity to produce and sell one unit of either of the following products to a customer (not both):

	Price
Product A	$12
Product B	15

Which would you sell? Product B? Is it more profitable? We cannot tell which product is more profitable until we consider their variable costs. Suppose that we find out the following:

	Price	Variable Cost	Contribution Margin
Product A	$12	$ 7	$5
Product B	15	11	4

Although B's price is higher and it would provide more revenues, A's contribution to fixed costs and profits is higher. (This point raises an interesting incentive problem if sales personnel are paid a commission that is a percent of revenue. They would have an incentive to sell the higher-priced, but less profitable, product.)

BREAKEVEN POINT

The **breakeven point** is the point at which total costs equal total revenues. The monthly breakeven point in Exhibit 4.1 is 12.5 units because that's where total revenue equals total costs. The firm incurs a loss equal to the vertical distance between the total cost line and the revenue line, at sales volumes less than 12.5 units per month.

The breakeven point comes from the cost-volume-profit equation

$$\pi = PX - (F + VX).$$

The equation is set equal to zero, then solved for X.

Step 1. Set the cost-volume-profit equation equal to zero. At the breakeven point profits equal zero by definition.

Step 2. Remove the parentheses from the total cost portion of the equation. This will allow us to combine the X variables.

Step 3. Combine the X variables.

Step 4. Add fixed costs (F) to both sides. This will remove the fixed costs from the right side of the equation and allow us to isolate the X variable.

Step 5. Isolate the X variable by dividing both sides by the contribution margin $(P - V)$.

Step	Equation	The Little People's Place
1.	$0 = PX - (F + VX)$	$0 = \$600X - (\$5,000 + \$200X)$
2.	$0 = PX - F - VX$	$0 = \$600X - \$5,000 - \$200X$
3.	$0 = (P - V)X - F$	$0 = (\$600 - \$200)X - \$5,000$
4.	$F = (P - V)X$	$\$5,000 = (\$600 - \$200)X$
5.	$\dfrac{F}{(P - V)} = X$	$\dfrac{\$5,000}{(\$600 - \$200)} = X$
		$X = 12.5$ units

X is the number of units sold at which total revenues equal total costs. In the case of The Little People's Place, serving more than 12.5 children per month results in a profit.[1] In general, the breakeven equation is

$$\text{Breakeven Point in Units} = \frac{\text{Fixed Costs per Period}}{\text{Contribution Margin per Unit}}$$

or, in symbols,

$$X = \frac{F}{(P - V)}$$

FINDING TARGET PROFITS

Finding the breakeven point is just a special case of using the cost-volume-profit equation to find the unit sales necessary to achieve a specified profit, where the target profit is zero.

Suppose the owners of The Little People's Place desire a profit of $3,000. How many children will they have to serve per month to earn $3,000 profit? To answer this they will use the breakeven equation

$$\pi = PX - (F + VX),$$

setting π equal to target profits of $3,000:

$$\$3,000 = \$600X - (\$5,000 + \$200X)$$

$$\$3,000 = \$400X - \$5,000$$

$$\$8,000 = \$400X$$

$$20 \text{ units per month} = X.$$

Or based on the equation for breakeven in units

$$X = \frac{(F + \text{Target } \pi)}{(P - V)},$$

---

[1] Serving .5 child per month means providing services for one child for one-half of a month.

and adding target profits to fixed costs for the total contribution needed

$$X = \frac{(F + \$3{,}000)}{(P - V)}$$

$$X = \frac{(\$5{,}000 + \$3{,}000)}{(\$600 - \$200)}$$

$$X = \frac{\$8{,}000}{\$400}$$

$$X = 20 \text{ units per month.}$$

The Little People's Place must serve 20 children per month to reach the target profit of $3,000.

THE PROFIT-VOLUME MODEL

Some managers prefer to use the relation between profit and volume with the **profit-volume graph** shown in Exhibit 4.2. The profit-volume relation derives from the cost-volume-profit equation. Start with the cost-volume-profit equation

$$\pi = PX - (F + VX).$$

Rearrange terms to get

$$\pi = PX - F - VX \quad \text{and} \quad \pi = -F + (P - V)X,$$

EXHIBIT 4.2

The Little People's Place
Profit-Volume Graph

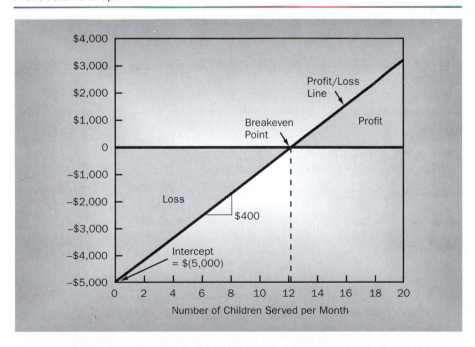

MANAGERIAL APPLICATION

Breaking Even in the Auto Industry[a]

During the past two decades, Chrysler, Ford, and General Motors found themselves, at various times, struggling to stay above the breakeven point. Chrysler was the first of the "Big Three" automobile companies to reach the brink of disaster. In the early 1980s, the company was forced to lay off thousands of employees to reduce fixed costs, as did IBM and AT&T in the 1990s. In the mid-1980s, Ford found its most successful cars were still costing thousands of dollars more to manufacture than comparable cars made by Japanese companies.

During the 1980s and early 1990s, Ford suffered losses, but retooled its manufacturing facilities, came out with new, popular designs, improved quality, and developed efficiencies that substantially cut costs.

Managers of large companies sometimes become complacent about the need to improve quality, provide new products, and reduce costs. The impact of this complacency is felt in the lives of the employees who lose their jobs so the companies can remain profitable.

[a]Based on the authors' research.

which is the **profit-volume equation**. F is the amount of fixed costs. The negative F represents the *intercept,* the amount of losses if no units are sold. The $(P - V)$ term is the contribution margin, the amount each unit sold adds to profits.

The vertical axis of the profit-volume graph shows the amount of profit or loss for the period—one month in our example. At zero sales, the loss equals the fixed costs of $5,000. At the breakeven point—12.5 children per month in our example—the profit is zero. The slope of the profit line is equal to $P - V$ (the contribution margin per unit sold) = $600 - $200 = $400. Looking at Exhibit 4.2, what is the profit level at sales of 14 units? (Answer: $-$5,000 + ($600 - $200) 14 units = $600.)

APPLICATIONS OF THE COST-VOLUME-PROFIT MODEL

In this section, we illustrate several uses of the cost-volume-profit model.

PRICING DECISIONS

Sometimes organizations may want to know the price they must charge for a product to earn a target profit for sales of a given number of units. We can solve for the required selling price by solving the cost-volume-profit equation for P, as follows:

$$\pi = PX - (F + VX)$$

$$\pi = PX - F - VX$$

$$\pi = (P - V)X - F$$

$$F + \pi = (P - V)X$$

$$\frac{(F + \pi)}{X} = P - V$$

$$\frac{(F + \pi)}{X} + V = P.$$

For instance, if in a particular month managers of The Little People's Place knew that they would serve 19 children and wanted target profits of $3,550, they would calculate the necessary price using the equation

$$\frac{(F + \pi)}{X} + V = P$$

$$\frac{(\$5,000 + \$3,550)}{19 \text{ units}} + \$200 = P$$

$$\$650 = P.$$

The price they must charge per child to earn profits of $3,550 is $650.

SENSITIVITY ANALYSIS AND SPREADSHEETS

Managers find cost-volume-profit particularly useful for sensitivity analysis in planning. **Sensitivity analysis** helps managers measure the impact of changes or variations in estimates of prices, costs, and volume. It allows managers to see what would happen in each situation they want to know about. For example, the managers of The Little People's Place are worried that demand for their service may drop during the summer months, while both the fixed and variable insurance may increase. They do have the option of increasing their price and want to know the impact of changing costs, prices, and volume on profits. Presently sales are 20 units, the price is $600 per unit, fixed costs are $5,000 per month, and variable costs are $200 per unit. Specifically, consider the following alternative cases:

Costs:

(1) No change
(2) 10 percent increase

Price and volume:

(1) No change
(2) 10 percent price increase and 5 percent volume decrease.

Setting this up in a spreadsheet would produce the results shown in Exhibit 4.3.

EXHIBIT 4.3

The Little People's Place
Sensitivity Analysis

Costs: No Change

Price and Volume		A	B	C	D	E
	1			Variable		
	2		Price	Cost	Units	Fixed
No Change	3	Profit	per Unit	per Unit	Sold	Costs
	4	$3,000	$600	$200	20	$5,000

Price and Volume		A	B	C	D	E
	1			Variable		
10 Percent Price Increase and 5 Percent Volume Decrease	2		Price	Cost	Units	Fixed
	3	Profit	per Unit	per Unit	Sold	Costs
	4	$3,740	$660	$200	19	$5,000

Costs: 10 percent increase

		A	B	C	D	E
	1			Variable		
	2		Price	Cost	Units	Fixed
	3	Profit	per Unit	per Unit	Sold	Costs
	4	$2,100	$600	$220	20	$5,500

		A	B	C	D	E
	1			Variable		
	2		Price	Cost	Units	Fixed
	3	Profit	per Unit	per Unit	Sold	Costs
	4	$2,860	$660	$220	19	$5,500

The results show the managers that, even with a 5 percent volume decrease, a 10 percent price increase will increase profits. Even if costs increase by 10 percent combined with the increase in price and decrease in volume, profits only decrease minimally. However, a cost increase without an increase in price will significantly decrease profits. Depending on how sure the managers are about the coming cost increase, they may start preparing their customers for an increase in price. You can easily perform a sensitivity analysis like this using your own personal computer spreadsheet.

Exhibit 4.3 shows one spreadsheet reproduced four times, once for each alternative. Notice that we have arranged the variables in the same sequence as the cost-volume-profit model,

$$\pi = (P - V)X - F.$$

This made it simple to set up the formula in cell A4, which is

$$[(B4 - C4) * D4] - E4.$$

Each time a new amount is entered in any of the variable cells, the profit is automatically recalculated.

COMPARISON OF ALTERNATIVES

The managers of The Little People's Place recently received a call from their insurance agent. Presently the center's insurance is a mixed cost—that is, there is a base fixed cost with a variable cost added per child. The agent suggested changing to an alternative insurance with the same coverage, but with a lower variable cost per child and a higher base fixed cost. Switching insurance would lower the center's variable cost per child from $200 to $160 and raise the fixed costs from $5,000 to $5,500.

Since we will analyze the impact on profits of the alternative using the cost-volume-profit model

$$\pi = (P - V)X - F,$$

we can use the spreadsheet we already have set up in Exhibit 4.3. The expected profit under the status quo is:

Profit	Price per Unit	Variable Cost per Unit	Units Sold	Fixed Costs
$3,000	= [($600	− $200)	× 20]	− $5,000

The expected profit under the proposed alternative is

Profit	Price per Unit	Variable Cost per Unit	Units Sold	Fixed Costs
$3,300	= [($600	− $160)	× 20]	− $5,500

The analysis indicates that the alternative insurance will increase expected profits if The Little People's Place has 20 children.

PROBLEM 4.1 FOR SELF-STUDY

Finding profits, breakeven point, and quantities. Given the following information for Sara's Ice Cream Company for April:

Sales (20,000 units)	$180,000
Fixed Manufacturing Costs	22,000
Fixed Marketing and Administrative Costs	14,000
Total Fixed Costs	36,000
Total Variable Costs	120,000
Unit Price	$9
Unit Variable Manufacturing Cost	5
Unit Variable Marketing Cost	1

Compute the following:
a. Operating profit when sales are $180,000 (as above).
b. Breakeven quantity in units.
c. Quantity of units that would produce an operating profit of $30,000.

The solution to this self-study problem is at the end of this chapter on page 130.

STEP COSTS

When the costs include step costs we have to consider a different amount of fixed costs for each step. Let's examine how to deal with step costs for The Little People's Place.

Assume the facility has been full, and management is considering expanding size. This would require getting more space and hiring more "Big Friends." Assume that each additional Big Friend would expand capacity by five children. Fixed costs would increase by $4,600, to $9,600, for the first step. The increased costs include leasing additional space, hiring an additional Big Friend, increasing insurance, and hiring another part-time cook. The second step would require hiring a second Big Friend, that would increase fixed costs by an additional $2,800, to $12,400. Variable costs would remain at $200 per child per month and selling price at $600 per child per month. Management calculates the breakeven point for each level of capacity as follows:

1. Status quo, 0–20 children:

$$X = \frac{F}{P - V}$$

$$X = \frac{\$5,000}{\$400}$$

$$X = 12.5 \text{ units}$$

2. First additional step, 21–25 children:

$$X = \frac{F}{P - V}$$

$$X = \frac{\$9,600}{\$400}$$

$$X = 24 \text{ units}$$

3. Second additional step, 26–30 children:

$$X = \frac{\$12,400}{\$400}$$

$$X = 31 \text{ units}$$

Notice that with one additional step the breakeven point is below capacity, so this is a viable alternative. However, with two additional steps the breakeven of 31 units exceeds full capacity of 30 units. Therefore, this alternative is not feasible.

From a profit-seeking perspective, adding the first step would not be wise. Although the facility would break even with 24 children, profits would be lower if the facility expanded from 20 to 25 children. This occurs because five additional children add $2,000 of contribution but require a step up in costs of $4,600.

MARGIN OF SAFETY

The **margin of safety** is the excess of projected (or actual) sales units over the breakeven unit sales level. The formula for margin of safety is

Sales Units − Breakeven Sales Units = Margin of Safety.

In our example, assume the level of activity is 20 units. The breakeven point is 12.5 units. Therefore, the margin of safety is 7.5 units. Sales volume can drop 37.5 percent (= 7.5/20) before the firm incurs a loss, other things held constant.

The margin of safety also relates to profits, as follows:

Margin of Safety × Unit Contribution Margin = Profits

In our example, the margin of safety is 7.5 units; multiplying this by $400 equals profits of $3,000, as we determined earlier.

When breakeven analysis has been conducted for alternatives, it makes comparison of profits easy. For instance, in the preceding section we found the breakeven for status quo and for hiring one or two more care givers. The following is a comparison of full capacity profits for the alternatives using the margin of safety concept. All the alternatives have a contribution margin of $400.

Alternative	Capacity	Breakeven	Margin of Safety	Contribution Margin per Unit	Possible Profits
Status Quo	20	12.5	7.5	$400	$3,000
One Additional Step	25	24	1	$400	$400
Two Additional Steps	30	31	(1)	$400	$(400)

This shows that the margin of safety decreases as The Little People's Place expands.

PROBLEM 4.2 FOR SELF-STUDY

Identifying CVP relations on a graph. The graph below contains cost-volume-profit and profit-volume graph elements. Identify the concept from the accompanying list that corresponds to the line segment or relation on the graph.

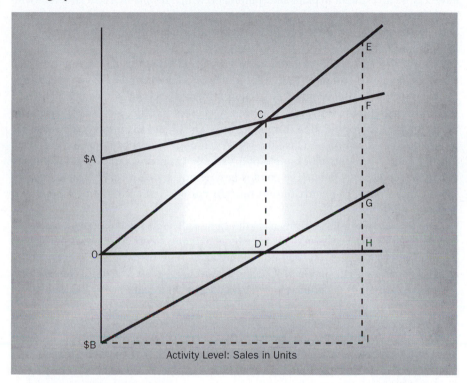

Activity Level: Sales in Units

Line Segment or Relation
- **a.** 0A
- **b.** IG
- **c.** 0D
- **d.** B0
- **e.** 0H − 0D
- **f.** B0/0D
- **g.** HF + HG

Concept
- (1) Variable Cost per Unit
- (2) Fixed Cost per Period
- (3) Revenue
- (4) Contribution Margin per Unit
- (5) Margin of Safety in Units
- (6) Breakeven Sales in Units
- (7) None of the above

Referring to the graph, answer each of the following as true or false (holding everything else constant).

- **h.** If revenue is CD, the margin of safety is zero.
- **i.** If revenue is HE, the margin of safety is D0.
- **j.** Total fixed costs could never be larger than total variable costs.
- **k.** If selling price increases, breakeven sales in units would decrease.
- **l.** If selling price increases, HF would increase.
- **m.** FE = HG.

The solution to this self-study problem is at the end of this chapter on page 131.

COST STRUCTURE AND OPERATING LEVERAGE

The **cost structure** of an organization refers to the proportion of fixed and variable costs to total costs. Cost structures differ widely among industries and among firms within an industry. Manufacturers using computer-integrated manufacturing systems have a large investment in plant and equipment, which results in a cost structure with high fixed costs. In contrast, for a builder of homes, a much higher proportion of costs are variable. The home builder has a cost structure with high variable costs relative to fixed costs.

An organization's cost structure has a significant effect on the sensitivity of its profit to changes in volume. The extent to which an organization's cost structure is made up of fixed costs is called **operating leverage**. Operating leverage is high in firms with a high proportion of fixed costs, a small proportion of variable costs, and the resulting high contribution margin per unit. The higher the firm's fixed costs, the higher the breakeven point. Once the breakeven point is reached, profit increases a lot. Exhibit 4.4 presents an example of a Variable Company and a Fixed Company that demonstrates this point. The point is best demonstrated by comparing contribution margin ratios. The **contribution margin ratio** is the contribution amount per dollar of sales.

Note that although these firms have the same sales revenue and operating profit, they have different cost structures. Variable Company's cost structure is dominated by variable costs with a lower contribution margin ratio of 0.25. So for every dollar of sales there is a contribution of 25 cents toward fixed costs and profit. Fixed Company's cost structure is dominated by fixed costs with a higher contribution margin of 0.75. So for every dollar of sales there is a contribution of 75 cents toward fixed costs and profit.

Suppose both companies experience a 10 percent increase in sales. Variable Company's profits would increase by $25,000 (= 0.25 × $100,000), while Fixed Company's profits would increase by $75,000 (= 0.75 × $100,000). Looking at Exhibit 4.4, if variable costs for both companies were $500,000 and fixed costs were $200,000, would there be any difference in operating leverage? (Answer: No. Both companies would have the same operating leverage.)

EXHIBIT 4.4

Comparison of Structures

	Variable Company (1,000,000 units)		Fixed Company (1,000,000 units)	
	Amount	%	Amount	%
Sales	$1,000,000	100	$1,000,000	100
Variable Costs	750,000	75	250,000	25
Contribution Margin	$ 250,000	25	$ 750,000	75
Fixed Costs	50,000	5	550,000	55
Operating Profit	$ 200,000	20	$ 200,000	20
Breakeven Point	200,000 units		733,334 units	
Contribution Margin Ratio	0.25		0.75	

USING SALES DOLLARS AS A MEASURE OF VOLUME

Firms that produce many different types of products find it convenient to measure volume in sales dollars instead of units. (Imagine defining a unit for a company like General Motors that makes cars, radios, batteries, and so forth.) The formula to calculate the breakeven sales dollars is

$$\text{Breakeven Sales Dollars} = \frac{\text{Fixed Costs}}{\text{Contribution Margin Ratio}}$$

With this measure, the cost-volume-profit equation remains the same as before, except that PX refers to total revenue, not "price times quantity," and VX refers to total variable costs, not "unit variable cost times quantity." Now we substitute sales dollars, or PX, for X when solving for volume of activity. With volume defined as PX, we multiply both sides of the breakeven, in units, formula by P to express volume in sales dollars. For instance, for The Little People's Place:

Equation	The Little People's Place
Breakeven in Units	
$X = \dfrac{F}{(P - V)}$	$X = \dfrac{\$5,000}{(\$600 - \$200)}$ $X = 12.5$ children served per month
Breakeven in Sales Dollars	
$PX = \dfrac{F}{[(P - V)/P]}$	$PX = \dfrac{\$5,000}{[(\$600 - \$200)/\$600]}$ $PX = \dfrac{\$5,000}{[\$400/\$600]}$ $PX = \dfrac{\$5,000}{.667}$ $PX = \$7,500$

Thus the breakeven volume expressed in sales dollars is $7,500.

The term $(P - V)/P$ in the denominator of the breakeven equation is the contribution margin ratio—that is, the ratio of the unit contribution margin to unit price.

This equation may also be used to determine target profit level of sales. For instance, if managers of The Little People's Place want profits of $2,000, they would calculate the target volume as:

Equation	The Little People's Place
$\dfrac{\text{Required}}{\text{Sales}} = \dfrac{\text{Fixed Costs} + \text{Target Profit}}{\text{Contribution Margin Ratio}}$	$\dfrac{\text{Required}}{\text{Sales}} = \dfrac{\$5,000 + \$2,000}{0.6667}$ $= \$10,500$

INCOME TAXES

You can solve cost-volume-profit problems on an after-tax basis by multiplying each dollar amount in the model by $(1 - t)$ where t is the tax rate. This multiplication converts each dollar amount to after-tax dollars. On an after-tax basis, the equation to find a target profit would be as follows:

$$\frac{\text{Required}}{\text{Volume}} = \frac{F(1 - t) + \text{Target After-Tax Profit}}{(P - V)(1 - t)}$$

Recall for The Little People's Place, the before-tax amounts were: $P = \$600$, $V = \$200$, and $F = \$5,000$. Assume the tax rate is 40 percent for this example. Assume management wants to know how many children per month must be served for The Little People's Place to generate an after-tax profit of $1,800 per month. Here are the calculations:

$$\frac{\text{Required}}{\text{Volume}} = \frac{F(1 - t) + \text{Target After-Tax Profit}}{(P - V)(1 - t)}$$

$$\frac{\text{Required}}{\text{Volume}} = \frac{\$5,000(1 - .40) + \$1,800}{(\$600 - \$200)(1 - .40)}$$

$$= \frac{\$3,000 + \$1,800}{\$240}$$

$$= 20 \text{ students per month.}$$

MULTIPRODUCT COST-VOLUME-PROFIT

Most companies produce and sell many products. Multiple products make using cost-volume-profit analysis more complex, as the following example shows.

Example Sport Autos, a sports car dealership, sells two models, Sleek and Powerful. The relevant prices and costs of each appear in Exhibit 4.5. Average monthly fixed costs of the new car department are $100,000. Looking at Exhibit 4.5, what is the average contribution margin ratio of each product? (Answer: Sleek = 25 percent = $5,000/$20,000. Powerful = 33 percent = $10,000/$30,000.)

We expand the cost-volume-profit equation presented earlier to consider the contribution of each product:

$$\pi = (P_s - V_s)X_s + (P_p - V_p)X_p - F,$$

where the subscript s designates the Sleek model, and the subscript p designates the Powerful model. Based on the information for Sport Autos, the company's profit equation is

$$\pi = (\$20,000 - \$15,000)X_s + (\$30,000 - \$20,000)X_p - \$100,000$$

$$\pi = \quad \$5,000X_s \quad + \quad \$10,000X_p \quad - \$100,000$$

EXHIBIT 4.5

SPORT AUTOS
Price and Cost Data

		Sleek		Powerful
Average Selling Price per Car		$20,000		$30,000
Less Average Variable Costs:				
Cost of Car	$11,000		$15,000	
Cost of Preparing Car for Sale	3,000		3,000	
Sales Commissions	1,000	15,000	2,000	20,000
Average Contribution Margin per Car . .		$ 5,000		$10,000

The chief executive of Sport Autos has been listening to a debate between two of the salespeople about the breakeven point for the company. According to one, "We have to sell 20 cars a month to break even." But the other one claims that 10 cars a month would be sufficient. The chief executive wonders how these two salespeople could hold such different views. (It turns out that both are right.)

The breakeven volume is the volume that provides a contribution that just covers all fixed costs. For Sport Autos, that is

$$\$5,000X_s + \$10,000X_p = \$100,000$$

The claim that 20 cars must be sold to break even is correct if the firm sells only the Sleek model, whereas the claim that only 10 cars need to be sold is correct if the firm sells only the Powerful model. In fact, Sport Autos has many possible product-mix combinations at which it would break even.

Exhibit 4.6 lists possible breakeven points for Sport Autos. Looking at Exhibit 4.6, how many Sleek models must be sold to break even if four Powerful models are sold? (Answer: 12.)

EXHIBIT 4.6

SPORT AUTOS
Combinations of Breakeven Quantities

Sleek Model		Powerful Model		Total	Fixed	
Quantity	Contribution	Quantity	Contribution	Contribution	Costs	Profit
20	$100,000	0	$ 0	$100,000	$100,000	$0
18	90,000	1	10,000	100,000	100,000	0
16	80,000	2	20,000	100,000	100,000	0
.	.	.	.	.	.	.
.	.	.	.	.	.	.
.	.	.	.	.	.	.
4	20,000	8	80,000	100,000	100,000	0
2	10,000	9	90,000	100,000	100,000	0
0	0	10	100,000	100,000	100,000	0

This simple example demonstrates how complex multiproduct cost-volume-profit analysis can become. In a company with many products, billions of combinations of product volumes can provide a specific target profit. To deal with this problem, managers and accountants have several alternatives:

1. Assume that all products have the same contribution margin.
2. Assume a weighted-average contribution margin.
3. Treat each product line as a separate entity.
4. Use sales dollars as a measure of volume.

In addition to these simplifications, firms can conduct multiproduct analyses with a mathematical method known as linear programming, discussed in Chapter 7. We now look at each of these alternatives.

ASSUME THE SAME CONTRIBUTION MARGIN

The analyst can often group products so they have equal or nearly equal contribution margins. It does not matter whether the firm sells a unit of Product A or a unit of Product B if both have the same contribution margin. (This approach won't work for Sport Autos, because Sleeks and Powerfuls have different contribution margins.)

ASSUME A WEIGHTED-AVERAGE CONTRIBUTION MARGIN

If we assume the product mix to be two Sleeks for every Powerful, the per-unit weighted average contribution margin is

Sleeks	Powerfuls
$(2/3 \times \$5,000) + (1/3 \times \$10,000) = \$6,667$	

The breakeven point is

$$X = \frac{\$100,000}{\$6,667}$$

$$X = 15 \text{ cars,}$$

of which 2/3, or 10, are Sleeks and 1/3, or 5, are Powerfuls, according to the preceding product-mix assumption.

What is the effect of incorrect assumptions in this analysis about product mix? If the actual mix is richer than assumed (more Powerfuls, in our example), the firm requires fewer units than predicted to break even. The firm requires more units than predicted to break even if the mix is poorer than assumed. The data in Exhibit 4.6 demonstrate this point. If only Powerfuls are sold, for example, then only 10 cars must be sold to break even. However, 20 cars must be sold to break even if only Sleeks are sold.

TREAT EACH PRODUCT LINE AS A SEPARATE ENTITY

This method requires allocating indirect costs to product lines. To illustrate, we must allocate part of Sport Autos' $100,000 monthly fixed costs that the two products share to Sleeks and Powerfuls. To do this, managers and accountants must find a rea-sonable method of allocating costs. Often the product lines share these costs, so any allocation method may be somewhat arbitrary.

Suppose that of the $100,000 common cost, Sport Autos allocates 40 percent to Sleeks and 60 percent to Powerfuls. We can then do breakeven analysis and other cost-volume-profit analyses by product line as follows:

For Sleeks:

$$\pi = (P - V)X - F$$

$$= (\$20,000 - \$15,000)X - \$40,000$$

$$X = \frac{\$40,000}{\$5,000}$$

$$X = 8 \text{ Units.}$$

For Powerfuls:

$$\pi = (P - V)X - F$$

$$= (\$30,000 - \$20,000)X - \$60,000$$

$$X = \frac{\$60,000}{\$10,000}$$

$$X = 6 \text{ Units.}$$

Allocating indirect cost to product lines makes it possible for managers to analyze each product line's cost-volume-profit relations. Be wary, however, of any analysis that relies on arbitrary cost allocations. It would be a mistake to believe that Sleeks cause fixed costs of $40,000 and Powerfuls cause fixed costs of $60,000. The two product lines combined cause fixed costs of $100,000; the breakdown of those costs between product lines is arbitrary. Further, note that a change in the arbitrary allo-cation method changes the breakeven volume.

For example, if we allocated the $100,000 as $20,000 to Sleeks and $80,000 to Powerfuls, breakeven requires the sale of 4 Sleeks (= $20,000/$5,000 per unit) and 8 Powerfuls (= $80,000/$10,000 per unit).

Cost Allocation   In many situations, companies often resort to allocating costs on the basis of relative sales dollars or on the basis of quantities of the product lines. Other allocation bases used include relative number of employees per product line (particularly to allocate labor-related costs) or relative square feet of space used by each product line (particularly to allocate space-related costs).

Cost allocation pervades managerial reports. The accuracy of the basis used to allocate costs will have an impact on the accuracy of cost-volume-profit analysis. In an effort to be more accurate, many companies try to identify cost drivers—the activities that cause costs—to be used as the basis of allocation. Cost allocation is discussed in detail in Chapter 16.

PROBLEM 4.3 FOR SELF-STUDY

Finding breakeven points in units sales and dollars. Triple X Company manufactures three different products with the following characteristics:

	Product I	Product II	Product III
Price per Unit	$5	$6	$7
Variable Cost per Unit	$3	$2	$4
Expected Sales (units)	100,000	150,000	250,000

Total fixed costs for the company are $1,240,000.

Assume that the product mix at the breakeven point would be the same as that for expected sales. Compute the breakeven point in

a. Units using weighted-average method.
b. Sales dollars using weighted-average method.

The solution to this self-study problem is at the end of this chapter on page 131.

USE SALES DOLLARS AS A MEASURE OF VOLUME

Earlier we referred to the sales dollars approach to find breakeven when a company has multiple products. This approach can be used for Sport Autos as follows.

Assume Sport Autos has been selling 20 Sleeks and 10 Powerfuls per month. Sales have been $700,000, as shown in Exhibit 4.7. The contribution margin has been $200,000. Therefore, the contribution margin ratio is as follows:

$$\text{Contribution Margin Ratio} = \frac{(P - V)}{P}$$

$$= \frac{\$200,000}{\$700,000}$$

$$= 0.286$$

EXHIBIT 4.7

SPORT AUTOS
Income Statement
Month Ended April 30

	Sleeks	Powerfuls	Total
Sales	$400,000	$300,000	$700,000
Variable Costs	300,000	200,000	500,000
Contribution Margin	$100,000	$100,000	$200,000

We now calculate breakeven in sales dollars assuming product mix is the same at breakeven as at past sales levels.

$$PX = \frac{F}{(P - V)/P} \quad \text{or} \quad BE \text{ sales dollars} = \frac{F}{\text{contribution margin ratio}}$$

$$PX = \frac{\$100,000}{0.286}$$

$$= \$350,000$$

SIMPLIFICATIONS AND ASSUMPTIONS

The cost-volume-profit model simplifies costs, revenues, and volume to make the analysis easier. It is possible to come up with a description of the economic relations that is more complete than the model gives, but to do so is costly. The careful user of cost-volume-profit analysis should be aware of the following common assumptions and be prepared to perform sensitivity analysis to see how the assumptions affect the model's results.

You can use the cost-volume-profit model most powerfully by analyzing how various alternatives affect operations. This analysis works because the model captures most of the important operating relationships of the firm in a single equation. We can analyze the effects of changes in any of the following variables on the remaining variables: selling price, number of units sold, variable cost, fixed cost, sales mix, and production mix.

Our illustrations in this chapter assumed a linear relation between revenues and volume and between cost and volume. You can, however, apply the model with non-linear revenue and cost functions. Practice usually assumes cost and revenue curves to be linear over some **relevant range** of activity, as discussed in Chapter 3.

We also implicitly assumed that the analyst can predict the variables in the model with certainty and that selling price per unit, total fixed costs, and variable costs per unit will not change as the level of activity changes. This assumption implies that prices paid and charged are constant, and workers' productivity does not change during the period. Finally, to derive a unique breakeven point for multiple products, we require that the production mix and sales mix will not change as the level of activity changes.

SUMMARY OF ASSUMPTIONS REQUIRED TO MAKE THE CVP MODEL WORK

1. We can divide total costs into fixed and variable components.
2. Cost and revenue behavior is linear throughout the relevant range of activity. This assumption implies the following:
   a. Total fixed costs do not change throughout the relevant range of activity.
   b. Variable costs per unit remain constant throughout the relevant range of activity.
   c. Selling price per unit remains constant throughout the relevant range of activity.
3. Product mix remains constant throughout the relevant range of activity.

Assumptions of the cost-volume-profit model make it easy to use, but they also make it unrealistic. Before criticizing the model for being unrealistic, however, consider the costs and benefits of relaxing those assumptions to create more realism. Often the cost of more realism exceeds the benefits from improved decision making.

One method of dealing with the assumptions is to perform some sensitivity analyses. For example, the mean or expected value of the variable costs for The Little People's Place is $200. But suppose that a reasonable range of values is from $175 to $225; that is, management estimates a very small probability that variable costs are less than $175 or greater than $225. Managers would probably want a sensitivity analysis performed to ascertain whether decisions would change if variable costs were, say, $175 or $225 instead of $200 per unit.

SUMMARY

The following items relate to the learning objectives listed at the beginning of the chapter.

1. **Explain how costs, volume, and profits are interrelated.** The cost-volume-profit model specifies a relation among selling prices, unit costs, volume sold, and profits. The contribution margin per unit is the amount each unit contributes to fixed costs and profit. The point where total costs equal total revenues is the breakeven point, which can be stated in units or sales dollars. The cost-volume-profit graph shows the breakeven point or provides a rough idea of profit or loss at various sales levels. The profit-volume equation is derived from the cost-volume-profit equation. The profit-volume graph shows the amount of profit or loss for a period.

Key Equations:

$$\pi = TR - TC$$

$$\pi = PX - (F + VX)$$

$$\text{Unit Contribution Margin} = P - V$$

$$X = \frac{F}{(P - V)}$$

$$X = \frac{(F + \text{Target } \pi)}{(P - V)},$$

2. **List various applications of the cost-volume-profit model.** The cost-volume-profit model can be used to calculate required selling price, find new breakeven points, conduct sensitivity analyses, compare alternatives, and calculate multiple breakeven points. The margin of safety is the excess of projected sales units over the breakeven unit sales level.

> **Key Equations:**
>
> Margin of Safety = Sales Units − Breakeven Sales Units
>
> Profits = Margin of Safety × Contribution Margin per Unit

3. **Describe the use of spreadsheets in cost-volume-profit analysis.** Spreadsheets can be used to conduct "what-if" analyses. Once you have set up the basic formula it is easy to determine the effect of changing price, costs, or volume amounts.

4. **Identify the effects of cost structure and operating leverage on the sensitivity of profit to changes in volume.** The cost structure of an organization is the proportion of fixed and variable costs to total costs. Operating leverage is high in firms with a high proportion of fixed costs, a small proportion of variable costs, and the resulting high contribution margin per unit. The higher the firm's leverage, the higher the degree of sensitivity of profits to volume changes.

5. **Calculate breakeven using sales dollars as the measure of volume.** The cost-volume-profit equation remains the same as before, except that *PX* is total revenue, not "price times quantity," and *VX* is total variable costs, not "unit variable cost times quantity." The contribution margin ratio is the ratio of the unit contribution margin to unit price.

> **Key Equation:**
>
> $$PX = \frac{F}{[(P - V)/P]}$$
>
> $$\text{Contribution Margin Ratio} = \frac{(P - V)}{P}$$

6. **Use the cost-volume-profit model on an after-tax basis.** To solve for after-tax cost-volume-profit, multiply each dollar amount by $(1 - t)$, where t is the tax rate.

> **Key Equation:**
>
> $$\text{Regional Volume} = \frac{F(1 - t + \text{Target After-Tax Profit})}{(P - V)(1 - t)}$$

7. **Calculate breakeven in a multiproduct setting.** Multiple products make using cost-volume-profit analysis more complex. To deal with it, managers can (1) assume that all products have the same contribution margin, (2) assume that a particular product mix does not change, (3) assume a weighted-average contribution margin, or (4) treat each product line as a separate entity.

> Key Equation:
>
> $$\pi = (P_s - V_s)X_s + (P_p - V_p)X_p - F$$

8. **Define the assumptions of the cost-volume-profit model.** The cost-volume-profit model approximates actual cost and revenue behavior. The assumptions of the cost-volume-profit model are: (1) costs can be divided into fixed and variable components, (2) cost and revenue behavior is linear throughout the relevant range of activity, and (3) product mix remains constant throughout the relevant range of activity.

KEY TERMS AND CONCEPTS

Cost-volume-profit model   A model that specifies a relation among selling prices, unit costs, volume sold, and profits.

Contribution margin per unit   Selling price less variable costs per unit. The amount each unit contributes to fixed costs and profits.

Breakeven point   The volume of sales required so that total revenues and total costs are equal.

Profit-volume graph   A graph that shows the relation between fixed costs, contribution per unit, breakeven point, and sales.

Profit-volume equation   An equation that analyses changes in volume, contribution margin per unit, or fixed costs on profit.

Sensitivity analysis   The study of how the outcome of a decision-making process changes as one or more of the assumptions change.

Margin of safety   The excess of actual, or budgeted, sales over breakeven sales, expressed in dollars or in units of product.

Cost structure   The proportion of fixed and variable costs to total costs.

Operating leverage   The tendency of net income to rise at a faster rate than sales when fixed costs are present.

Contribution margin ratio   Contribution margin divided by net sales.

Relevant range   Activity levels over which costs are linear.

SOLUTIONS TO SELF-STUDY PROBLEMS

SUGGESTED SOLUTION TO PROBLEM 4.1 FOR SELF-STUDY

a.   Operating profit:

$$\pi = PX - VX - F$$
$$\pi = \$180,000 - \$120,000 - \$36,000$$
$$= \$24,000$$

b.   Breakeven point:

$$X = \frac{F}{P - V} = \frac{\$36,000}{\$9 - \$6}$$
$$X = 12,000 \text{ units}$$

c. Target volume:

$$X = \frac{F + \text{Target } \pi}{P - V}$$

$$X = \frac{\$36{,}000 + \$30{,}000}{\$3}$$

$$= 22{,}000 \text{ units.}$$

SUGGESTED SOLUTION TO PROBLEM 4.2 FOR SELF-STUDY

a. $0A$ **(2)** Fixed Cost per Period

b. IG **(7)** None of the above

c. $0D$ **(6)** Breakeven Sales in Units

d. $B0$ **(2)** Fixed Cost per Period; also, Operating Loss When Sales Are Zero

e. $0H - 0D$ **(5)** Margin of Safety in Units

f. $B0/0D$ **(4)** Contribution Margin per Unit

g. $HF + HG$ **(3)** Revenue

h. True

i. False, if revenue is HE, the margin of safety is DH.

j. False

k. True

l. False

m. True

SUGGESTED SOLUTION TO PROBLEM 4.3 FOR SELF-STUDY

a. Compute weighted-average contribution margin:

	Product I	Product II	Product III
Product Mix	$\dfrac{100{,}000 \text{ Units}}{500{,}000 \text{ Units}}$	$\dfrac{150{,}000}{500{,}000}$	$\dfrac{250{,}000}{500{,}000}$
	= .20	= .30	= .50
Weighted-Average Contribution Margin $(P - V)$	.20($2) +	.30($4) + = $3.10	.50($3)

Or

$$\frac{(100{,}000 \text{ Units}) (\$2) + (150{,}000) (\$4) + (250{,}000) (\$3)}{500{,}000} = \$3.10$$

$$X = \frac{\$1{,}240{,}000}{\$3.10}$$

$$X = 400{,}000 \text{ Units.}$$

b. To compute breakeven sales dollars, find the weighted-average price and variable costs:

$$P = (.20)\ (\$5) + (.30)\ (\$6) + (.50)\ (\$7)$$

$$P = \$6.30$$

$$V = (.20)\ (\$3) + (.30)\ (\$2) + (.50)\ (\$4)$$

$$V = \$3.20$$

$$\text{Breakeven } PX = \frac{F}{\dfrac{P - V}{P}} = \frac{\$1,240,000}{\$3.10/\$6.30}$$

$$= \frac{\$1,240,000}{.492\ \text{(rounded)}}$$

$$= \$2,520,000$$

(Check: 400,000 units × $6.30 = $2,520,000.)

QUESTIONS, EXERCISES, PROBLEMS, AND CASES

REVIEW QUESTIONS

1. Review the meaning of the terms or concepts given in Key Terms and Concepts.
2. Define the profit equation.
3. Define the term *contribution margin*.
4. Name three common assumptions of a linear cost-volume-profit analysis.
5. What effect could the following changes, occurring independently, have on (1) the breakeven point, (2) the unit contribution margin, and (3) the expected total profit?
   a. An increase in fixed costs.
   b. A decrease in wage rates applicable to direct, strictly variable labor.
   c. An increase in the selling price of the product.
   d. An increase in production and sales volume.
   e. An increase in building insurance rates.

CRITICAL ANALYSIS AND DISCUSSION QUESTIONS

6. How does the total contribution margin (unit contribution margin times total number of units sold) differ from the gross margin often seen on companies' financial statements?

7. Compare cost-volume-profit analysis with profit-volume analysis. How do they differ?

8. How do spreadsheets assist cost-volume-profit analysis?

9. How does the profit equation change when the analyst uses the multiproduct cost-volume-profit model?

10. Refer to the Managerial Application, "Breaking Even in the Auto Industry." If companies cannot raise prices, what must they do to break even?

11. Fixed costs are often defined as "fixed over the short run." Does this mean that they are not fixed over the long run? Why or why not?

12. Why do accountants use a linear representation of cost and revenue behavior in cost-volume-profit analysis? Justify this use.

13. Assume the linear cost relation of the cost-volume-profit model for a single-product firm and use the following answer key:

    (1) more than double
    (2) double
    (3) increase, but less than double
    (4) remain the same
    (5) decrease

    Complete each of the following statements, assuming that all other things (such as quantities) remain constant.

    a. If price doubles, revenue will _____ .
    b. If price doubles, the total contribution margin (contribution margin per unit times number of units) will _____ .
    c. If price doubles, profit will _____ .
    d. If contribution margin per unit doubles, profit will _____ .
    e. If fixed costs double, the total contribution margin will _____ .
    f. If fixed costs double, profit will _____ .
    g. If fixed costs double, the breakeven point of units sold will

    _____ .

    h. If total sales of units double, profit will _____ .
    i. If total sales dollars double, the breakeven point will

    _____ .

    j. If the contribution margin per unit doubles, the breakeven point will

    _____ .

    k. If both variable costs per unit and selling price per unit double, profit will

    _____ .

14. Is a company really breaking even if it produces and sells at the breakeven point? What costs may not be covered?

15. Why does multiproduct cost-volume-profit analysis often assume a constant product mix?

16. When would the sum of the breakeven quantities for each of a company's products not be the breakeven point for the company as a whole?

17. If a company breaks even in terms of accounting profits, will it be giving its investors a return on investment that covers their opportunity cost of capital? Distinguish between economic *profits* and accounting *net income* or *operating profit.*

EXERCISES

Solutions to even-numbered exercises are at the end of the chapter.

18. **Breakeven and target profits.** Analysis of the operations of the Super Ski Wax Company shows the fixed costs to be $100,000 and the variable costs to be $4 per unit. Selling price is $8 per unit.
    a. Derive the breakeven point expressed in units.
    b. How many units must the firm sell to earn a profit of $140,000?
    c. What would profits be if revenue from sales was $1,000,000?

19. **Cost-volume-profit; volume defined in sales dollars.** An excerpt from the income statement of the P. J. Held Company follows.

    Estimated fixed costs in Year 1 are $1,320,000.

    P. J. HELD COMPANY
    Income Statement
    Year Ended December 31, Year 1

Sales		$6,000,000
Operating Expenses:		
Cost of Goods Sold	$2,850,000	
Selling Costs	900,000	
Administrative Costs	450,000	
Total Operating Costs		4,200,000
Profit		$1,800,000

    ---

    a. What percentage of sales revenue is variable cost?
    b. What is the breakeven point in sales dollars for P. J. Held Company?
    c. Prepare a cost-volume-profit graph for P. J. Held Company.
    d. If sales revenue falls to $5,600,000, what will be the estimated amount of profit?
    e. What volume of sales produces a profit of $2,240,000?

20. **Cost-volume-profit graph.** Identify each item on the graph at the top of page 135:
    a. the total cost line
    b. the total revenue line
    c. total variable costs
    d. variable cost per unit
    e. the total fixed costs
    f. the breakeven point
    g. the profit area (or volume)
    h. the loss area (or volume)

21. **Profit-volume graph.** Identify the places on the profit-volume graph (shown on the bottom of page 135) indicated by the letters:

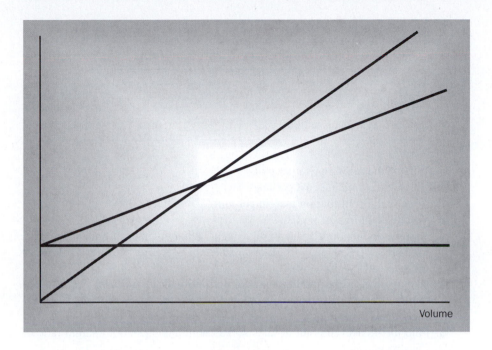

Graph for Exercise 20.

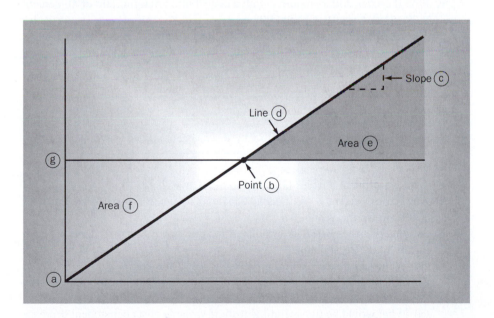

Graph for Exercise 21.

22. **Cost-volume-profit analysis.** Surf's Up Company produces one type of sunglasses with the following costs and revenues for the year:

Total Revenues	$5,000,000
Total Fixed Costs	$1,000,000
Total Variable Costs	$3,000,000
Total Quantity Produced and Sold	1,000,000 Units

   a. What is the selling price per unit?
   b. What is the variable cost per unit?
   c. What is the contribution margin per unit?
   d. What is the breakeven point?
   e. Assume an income tax rate of 40 percent. What quantity of units is required for Surf's Up Company to make an after-tax operating profit of $1,200,000 for the year?

23. **Breakeven and target profits; volume defined in sales dollars.** The manager of Padillo Company estimates operating costs for the year will total $225,000 for fixed costs.
   a. Find the breakeven point in sales dollars with a contribution margin ratio of 25 percent.
   b. Find the breakeven point in sales dollars with a contribution margin ratio of 40 percent.
   c. Find the sales dollars required with a contribution margin ratio of 40 percent to generate a profit of $150,000?

24. **CVP—sensitivity analysis.** Giovanni Kitchen Creations is considering introducing a new gourmet cooking seminar with the following price and cost characteristics:

Tuition	$100 per Student
Variable Costs (supplies, food, etc.)	$60 per Student
Fixed Costs (advertising, instructor's salary, insurance, etc.)	$200,000 per Year

   a. What enrollment enables Giovanni to break even?
   b. How many students will enable Giovanni to make an operating profit of $100,000 for the year?
   c. Assume that the projected enrollment for the year is 8,000 students for each of the following situations:
      (1) What will be the operating profit for 8,000 students?
      (2) What would be the operating profit if the tuition per student (that is, sales price) decreases by 10 percent? Increases by 20 percent?
      (3) What would be the operating profit if variable costs per student decrease by 10 percent? Increase by 20 percent?
      (4) Suppose that fixed costs for the year are 10 percent lower than projected, whereas variable costs per student are 10 percent higher than projected. What would be the operating profit for the year?

25. **Multiple product profit analysis.** Pat's Pizza Palace produces two products, thin crust and deep dish, with the following characteristics:

	Thin Crust	Deep Dish
Selling Price per Unit	$8	$12
Variable Cost per Unit	$4	$6
Expected Sales (Units)	100,000	150,000

The total fixed costs for the company are $600,000.
   a. What is the anticipated level of profits for the expected sales volumes?
   b. Assuming that the product mix would be the same at the breakeven point, compute the breakeven point.
   c. If the product sales mix were to change to four thin crusts for each deep dish, what would be the new breakeven volume?

26. **Multiple product profit analysis.** The Multiproduct Company produces and sells three different products. Operating data for the three products follow.

	Selling Price per Unit	Variable Cost per Unit	Fixed Cost per Month
Product P	$3	$2	—
Product Q	5	3	—
Product R	8	5	—
Entire Company	—	—	$48,000

Define a unit as the sum of one unit of product R sold, two units of product Q sold, and three units of product P sold.
   a. Draw a cost-volume-profit graph for the Multiproduct Company.
   b. At what number of units does the Multiproduct Company break even?
   c. Change the facts. Suppose a "unit" now consists of two units of product P for every two units of product Q and one unit of product R. At what does Multi-product break even?

PROBLEMS

27. **Explaining sales and cost changes.** You have acquired the following data for Years 1 and 2 for Half Moon Bay Aquarium.

	Year 1		Year 2		Dollar Increase
Revenue from Admissions ...	$750,000	100%	$840,000	100%	$90,000
Variable Costs of Operations	495,000	66	560,000	66 $\frac{2}{3}$	65,000
Contribution Margin	$255,000	34%	$280,000	33 $\frac{1}{3}$%	$25,000
Admission Price per Person	$5		$6		

Write a short report explaining the cause of the increase in contribution margin between Year 1 and Year 2. Your report should consider the effect of each of the following: admission price change, change in volume, and change in operating costs per admission.

28. **CVP—missing data.** Management of VanDeCarr Manufacturing has performed cost studies and projected the following annual costs based on 100,000 units of production and sales:

	Total Annual Costs (100,000 units)
Direct Material	$ 400,000
Direct Labor	360,000
Manufacturing Overhead	300,000
Selling, General, and Administrative	200,000
Total	$1,260,000

a. Compute VanDeCarr's unit selling price that will yield a profit of $100,000, given sales of 100,000 units.

b. Assume management selects a selling price of $12 per unit. Compute Van-DeCarr's dollar sales that will yield a projected 10 percent profit on sales, assuming variable costs per unit are 70 percent of the selling price per unit and fixed costs are $420,000.

29. **CVP—sensitivity analysis.** Assume last year's sales of a Music Land store were $1,200,000, fixed costs were $400,000, and variable costs were $600,000.

a. At what level of sales revenue will the store break even?

b. If sales revenue increases by 15 percent but unit prices, unit variable costs, and total annual fixed costs do not change, by how much will profit increase?

c. Ignoring the sales increase in **b**, if fixed costs decrease by 20 percent, by how much will profit increase?

d. Ignoring the facts in **b** and **c**, if variable costs decrease by 10 percent, by how much will profit increase?

30. **Solving for unknowns** (Problems 30 through 32 are adapted from problems by D. O. Green). When Britain's auto business slumped in 1921, William R. Morris (the "Henry Ford of Britain") gambled on cost saving from his new assembly lines and cut prices to a point where his expected loss per car in 1922 would be $240 if sales were the same as in 1921, or 1,500 cars. However, sales in 1922 rose to 60,000 cars, and profits for the year were $810,000. For 1922, calculate:

a. Contribution margin per car.

b. Total fixed costs.

c. Breakeven point in cars.

31. **Solving for unknowns.** During the third quarter of a recent year, a division of an automobile company sold 45,000 cars for $250 million and realized a loss for the quarter of $24 million. The breakeven point was 60,000 cars. Calculate for the quarter:

a. Contribution margin per car.

b. Total fixed costs.

c. Profits had sales been twice as large.

32. **Solving for unknowns.** *Time* magazine reported that the future of an automobile company seemed so shaky that its creditors, a consortium of banks headed by Chase Manhattan, examined the books every ten days. The new management trimmed fixed costs by $20 million to cut the breakeven point from 350,000 cars in one year to 250,000 cars for the next year. From this information, calculate:

   a. Contribution margin per car (assumed constant for both years).

   b. Fixed costs for each year.

   c. Losses in the first year, assuming sales of 300,000 cars.

   d. Profits in the second year, assuming sales of 400,000 cars.

33. **CVP—missing data; assumptions.** You are analyzing the financial performance of WGA Records based on limited data from a *BillBoard* article. The article says that despite an increase in sales revenue from $4,704,000 in Year 8 to $4,725,000 in Year 9, WGA recently reported a decline in net income of $129,500 from Year 8 to an amount equal to 2 percent of sales revenue in Year 9. The average total cost per unit increased from $2.200 in Year 8 to $2.205 in Year 9.

   a. Compute the changes, if any, in average selling price and sales in units from Year 8 to Year 9.

   b. Can you compute the total fixed costs and variable cost per unit during Year 9? If so, do so. If not, illustrate why with a graph and discuss any important assumptions of the cost-volume-profit model that this application violates.

34. **Alternatives to reduce breakeven sales.** The Hillsdale Dairy operated near the breakeven point of $2,250,000 during Year 1, while incurring fixed costs of $900,000. Management is considering two alternatives to reduce the breakeven level. Alternative A trims fixed costs by $200,000 annually with no change in variable cost per unit; doing so, however, will reduce the quality of the product and result in a 10 percent decrease in selling price, but no change in the number of gallons sold. Alternative B substitutes mechanical milking equipment for certain operations now performed manually. Alternative B will result in an annual increase of $300,000 in fixed costs, but a 5 percent decrease in variable costs per gallon produced, with no change in product quality, selling price, or sales volume.

   a. What was the total contribution margin (contribution margin per unit times number of units sold) during Year 1?

   b. What is the breakeven sales in dollars under alternative A?

   c. What is the breakeven sales in dollars under alternative B?

   d. What should the company do?

35. **Solving for cost-based selling price.** TriTec Medical Instruments Corporation follows a cost-based approach to pricing. Prices are 120 percent of cost. The annual cost of producing one of its products follows:

Variable Manufacturing Costs	$20 per Unit
Fixed Manufacturing Costs	$100,000 per Year
Variable Selling and Administrative Costs	$5 per Unit
Fixed Selling and Administrative Costs	$60,000 per Year

a. Assume that TriTec produces and sells 10,000 units. Calculate the selling price per unit.

b. Assume that TriTec produces and sells 20,000 units. Calculate the selling price per unit.

36. **Solving for cost-based selling price.** Total Body Spa follows a cost-based approach to pricing. It sets prices equal to 110 percent of cost. The spa has annual fixed costs of $300,000. The variable costs of the spa services follow:

Treatment Type	Variable Cost per Procedure
A	$10
B	20
C	30

The spa expects to provide 1,000 type A treatments, 4,000 type B treatments, and 1,000 type C treatments.

a. Compute the price of each treatment if the spa allocates fixed costs to services on the basis of the number of treatments.

b. Compute the selling price of each treatment if the spa allocates fixed costs to treatments on the basis of total variable costs.

37. **CVP analysis with semifixed (step) costs.** Adelita Co. has one product: dehydrated meals for backpacking. The sales price of $10 remains constant per unit regardless of volume, as does the variable cost of $6 per unit. The company is considering operating at one of the following three monthly levels of operations:

	Volume Range (production and sales)	Total Fixed Costs	Increase in Fixed Costs from Previous Level
Level 1	0–16,000	$60,000	—
Level 2	16,001–28,000	100,000	$40,000
Level 3	28,001–38,000	110,000	10,000

a. Calculate the breakeven point(s).

b. If the company can sell everything it makes, should it operate at level 1, level 2, or level 3? Support your answer.

38. **CVP analysis with semifixed costs and changing unit variable costs.** The Atkins Company manufactures and sells one product. The sales price, $50 per unit, remains constant regardless of volume. Last year's sales were 15,000 units and operating profits were $200,000. Fixed costs depend on production levels, as the following table shows. Variable costs per unit are 40 percent *higher* for level 2 (two shifts) than for level 1 (day shift only). The additional labor costs result primarily from higher wages required to employ workers for the night shift.

	Annual Production Range (in units)	Annual Total Fixed Costs
Level 1 (day shift)	0–20,000	$100,000
Level 2 (day and night shifts)	20,001–36,000	164,000

Atkins expects last year's cost structure and selling price not to change this year. Maximum plant capacity is 36,000. The company sells everything it produces.

a. Compute the contribution margin per unit for last year for each of the two production levels.

b. Compute the breakeven points for last year for each of the two production levels.

c. Compute the volume in units that will maximize operating profits. Defend your choice.

39. **CVP analysis with semifixed costs.** Beverly Miller, director and owner of the Discovery Day Care Center, has a master's degree in elementary education. In the seven years she has been running the Discovery Center, her salary has ranged from nothing to $20,000 per year. "The second year," she says, "I made 62 cents an hour." (Her salary is what's left over after meeting all other expenses.)

Could she run a more profitable center? She thinks perhaps she could if she increased the student-teacher ratio, which is currently five students to one teacher. (Government standards for a center such as this set a maximum of ten students per teacher.) She refuses to increase the ratio to more than six-to-one. "If you increase the ratio to more than 6:1, the children don't get enough attention. In addition, the demands on the teacher are far too great." She does not hire part-time teachers.

Beverly rents the space for her center in the basement of a church for $900 per month, including utilities. She estimates that supplies, snacks, and other nonpersonnel costs are $80 per student per month. She charges $380 per month per student. Teachers receive $1,200 per month, including fringe benefits. She has no other operating costs. At present, she cares for 30 students and employs six teachers.

a. What is the present operating profit per month of the Discovery Day Care Center before Ms. Miller's salary?

b. What is (are) the breakeven point(s), before Ms. Miller's salary, assuming a student-teacher ratio of 6:1?

c. What would be the breakeven point(s), before Ms. Miller's salary, if the student-teacher ratio increased to 10:1?

d. Ms. Miller has an opportunity to increase the student body by six students. She must take all six or none. Should she accept the six students, if she wants to maintain a maximum student-teacher ratio of 6:1?

e. (Continuation of part **d.**) Suppose that Ms. Miller accepts the six children. Now she has the opportunity to accept one more, which requires hiring one more teacher. What would happen to profit, before her salary, if she accepts one more student?

40. **CVP with taxes** (adapted from CMA exam). R. A. Ro and Company, maker of quality, handmade pipes, has experienced a steady growth in sales for the past

five years. However, increased competition has led Mr. Ro, the president, to believe that to maintain the company's present growth requires an aggressive advertising campaign next year. To prepare the next year's advertising campaign, the company's accountant has prepared and presented to Mr. Ro the following data for the current year, Year 1.

Cost Schedule

Variable Costs:

Direct Labor	$ 8.00 per Pipe
Direct Materials	3.25
Variable Overhead	2.50
Total Variable Costs	$13.75 per Pipe

Fixed Costs:

Manufacturing	$ 25,000
Selling	40,000
Administrative	70,000
Total Fixed Costs	$135,000
Selling Price, per Pipe	$25.00
Expected Sales, Year 1 (20,000 pipes)	$500,000.00

Tax Rate: 40 Percent

Mr. Ro has set the sales target for Year 2 at a level of $550,000 (or 22,000 pipes).

a. What is the projected after-tax operating profit for Year 1?

b. What is the breakeven point in units for Year 1?

c. Mr. Ro believes that to attain the sales target requires an additional selling expense of $11,250 for advertising in Year 2, with all other costs remaining constant. What will be the after-tax operating profit for Year 2 if the firm spends the additional $11,250?

d. What will be the breakeven point in dollar sales for Year 2 if the firm spends the additional $11,250 for advertising?

e. If the firm spends the additional $11,250 for advertising in Year 2, what is the sales level in dollars required to equal Year 1 after-tax operating profit?

f. At a sales level of 22,000 units, what is the maximum amount that the firm can spend on advertising to earn an after-tax operating profit of $60,000?

CASES

41. Breakeven analysis for management education. The dean of the Graduate School of Management at the University of California at Davis was considering whether to offer a particular seminar for executives. The tuition was $650 per person. Variable costs, which included meals, parking, and materials, were $80 per person. Certain costs of offering the seminar, including advertising the seminar, instructors' fees, room rent, and audiovisual equipment rent, would not be affected by the number of people attending (within a "relevant range"). Such costs, which could be thought of as step costs, amounted to $8,000 for the seminar.

In addition to these costs, a number of staff, including the dean of the school, worked on the program. Although the salaries paid to these staff were not affected by offering the seminar, working on the seminar took these people away from other duties, thus creating an opportunity cost, estimated to be $7,000 for this seminar.

Given this information, the school estimated the breakeven point to be ($8,000 + $7,000)/($650 − $80) = 26.3 students. If the school wanted to at least break even on this program, it should offer the program only if it expected at least 27 students to attend.

Write a report to the dean that evaluates the quality of this analysis. In particular, focus on concerns about the accuracy of the data and the limitations of cost-volume-profit analysis.

42. **Cost analysis for Chrysler Corporation.**[a] Cost-volume-profit analysis showed how much Chrysler had to improve just to break even in 1979. In that year, the breakeven point was 2.2 million units, but the company was selling considerably fewer than 2 million units. Faced with a severe recession in the automobile industry, Chrysler had virtually no chance to increase sales enough to break even. Meanwhile, the company had received loan guarantees from the U.S. government, which evoked considerable criticism that the federal government was supporting a "failing" company.

By 1982, Chrysler reduced its breakeven point to 1.1 million units, and the company reported a profit for the first time in several years. The headlines read, " 'We're in black,' Iacocca chortles."[b] The turnaround came despite continued low sales in the automobile industry; it resulted primarily from severe cost cutting, which reduced fixed costs in constant dollars from $4.5 billion in 1979 to $3.1 billion in 1982. In addition, the company made improvements in its production methods, which enabled it to maintain its volume of output despite the reduction in fixed costs.

a. If Chrysler's breakeven volume was 1.1 million units and its fixed costs were $3.1 billion, what was its average contribution margin per unit?

b. Why do you think Iacocca concentrated on reducing fixed costs to put Chrysler above its breakeven point?

c. As a shareholder of Chrysler, what concerns might you have about the company's massive cost cutting?

43. **CVP—partial data; special order.** Partial income statements of Ford Food Service for the first two quarters of Year 2 follow.

FORD FOOD SERVICE
Partial Income Statements for First and Second Quarters of Year 2

	First Quarter	Second Quarter
Sales at $3.50 per Meal (unit)	$ 36,000	$63,000
Total Costs	49,000	67,000
(Loss)	$(13,000)	$ (4,000)

---

[a]See R. S. Miller, "The Chrysler Story," *Management Accounting* (August 1983), pp. 22–27, and *Detroit Free Press*, June 6, 1982.

[b]*Detroit Free Press*, June 6, 1982.

Each dollar of variable cost per meal comprises 50 percent direct labor, 25 percent direct materials, and 25 percent variable overhead costs. Ford expects sales units, price per unit, variable cost per unit, and total fixed costs to remain at the same level during the third quarter as during the second quarter. Ford sold 17,500 meals in the second quarter.

a. What is the breakeven point in meals (units)?

b. The company has just received a special order from a government agency that provides meals for senior citizens for 7,500 meals at a price of $3.20 per meal (unit). If the company accepts the order, it will not affect the regular market for 17,500 meals in the third quarter. The company can produce the additional meals with existing capacity, but direct labor costs per meal will increase by 10 percent for *all* meals produced because of the need to hire and use new labor. Fixed costs will increase $3,000 per quarter if the company accepts the new order. Should it accept the government order?

c. Assume that the company accepts the order in part **b.** What level of sales to nongovernment customers provides third-quarter profit of $6,800? (The third quarter would be just like the second quarter if the company does not accept the government order.)

SUGGESTED SOLUTIONS TO EVEN-NUMBERED EXERCISES

18. **Breakeven and target profits.**

a.
$$X = \frac{F}{(P - V)}$$

$$= \frac{\$100,000}{(\$8 - \$4)}$$

$$= 25,000$$

b.
$$X = \frac{(\$100,000 + \$140,000)}{(\$8 - \$4)}$$

$$= 60,000$$

c.
$$\frac{\text{Contribution Margin}}{\text{Ratio}} = \frac{\text{Unit Selling Price} - \text{Unit Variable Cost}}{\text{Unit Selling Price}}$$

$$= \frac{\$8 - \$4}{\$8} = \frac{\$4}{\$8} = 50\%.$$

$$\text{Profit} = (.5 \times \$1,000,000) - \$100,000$$

$$= \$400,000.$$

20. Cost-volume-profit graph.

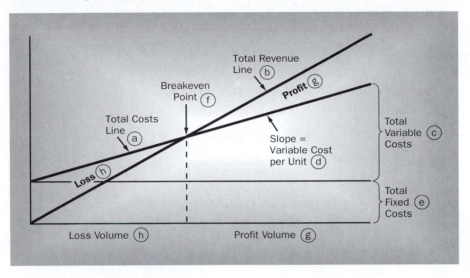

22. Cost-volume-profit analysis.

a. \$5,000,000/1,000,000 Units = \$5 per Unit.

b. \$3,000,000/1,000,000 Units = \$3 per Unit.

c. \$5 − \$3 = \$2 per Unit.

d. $\pi = (\$5 - \$3)X - \$1,000,000.$

$$X = \frac{\$1,000,000}{(\$5 - \$3)} = 500,000 \text{ Units.}$$

e. $X = \dfrac{\$1,000,000(1 - .40) + \$1,200,000}{(\$5 - \$3)(1 - .4)}$

$$= \frac{\$600,000 + \$1,200,000}{\$2 \times .6}$$

$$= \frac{\$1,800,000}{1.20}$$

$$= 1,500,000 \text{ Units.}$$

24. CVP—sensitivity analysis.

a. $X = \dfrac{\$200,000}{(\$100 - \$60)} = 5,000 \text{ Students.}$

b. $X = \dfrac{\$300,000}{(\$100 - \$60)} = 7,500 \text{ Students.}$

c. (1) $\pi = (\$100 - \$60)8,000 - \$200,000$

$$= \$120,000.$$

(2) *10 percent price decrease. Now*

$$P = \$90.$$

$$\pi = (\$90 - \$60)8{,}000 - \$200{,}000$$

$$= \$40{,}000.$$

20 percent price increase. Now

$$P = \$120.$$

$$\pi = (\$120 - \$60)8{,}000 - \$200{,}000$$

$$= \$280{,}000.$$

(3) *10 percent variable cost decrease. Now*

$$V = \$54.$$

$$\pi = (\$100 - \$54)8{,}000 - \$200{,}000$$

$$= \$168{,}000.$$

20 percent variable cost increase. Now

$$V = \$72.$$

$$\pi = (\$100 - \$72)8{,}000 - \$200{,}000$$

$$= \$24{,}000.$$

(4) $\pi = (\$100 - \$66)8{,}000 - \$180{,}000$

$$= \$92{,}000.$$

26. **Multiple product profit analysis.** (See graph on page 147.)

a.   A unit = production of one product R, two product Qs, and three product Ps.

Variable Cost per Unit = $(3 \times \$2) + (2 \times \$3) + (1 \times \$5) = \$17.$

Revenue per Unit = $(3 \times \$3) + (2 \times \$5) + (1 \times \$8) = \$27.$

b.   Contribution Margin = $\$27 - \$17 = \$10$

$$X = \frac{\$48{,}000}{10}$$

$$X = 4{,}800 \text{ Units.}$$

Product volume at breakeven point is

Product P = $3 \times 4{,}800 = 14{,}400$

Product Q = $2 \times 4{,}800 = 9{,}600$

Product R = $1 \times 4{,}800 = 4{,}800.$

(Note: Total Revenue at Breakeven Level = 4,800 Units × $27 = $129,600.)

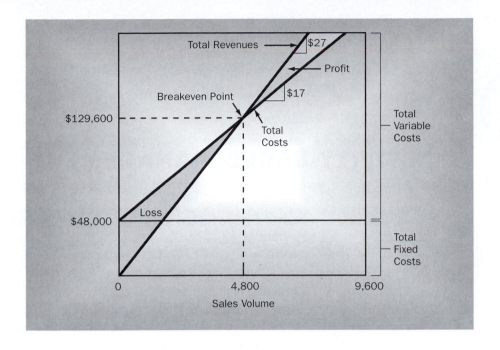

c. A unit = two product Ps, two product Qs, and one product R.

Variable Cost per Unit = (2 × $2) + (2 × $3) + (1 × $5) = $15.

Revenue per Unit = (2 × $3) + (2 × $5) + (1 × $8) = $24.

$$X = \frac{\$48,000}{9}$$

= 5,333.3 Units.

Sales at breakeven point are

Product P = 2 × 5,333.3 = 10,667

Product Q = 2 × 5,333.3 = 10,667

Product R = 1 × 5,333.3 = 5,333.

CHAPTER 5

ACTIVITY-BASED MANAGEMENT

1. Describe the basic premise of activity-based management.
2. Identify strategic uses of activity-based management.
3. Relate activity-based management to the value chain.
4. Explain how activity-based management can be used to reduce customer response time.
5. Understand the concept of activity-based costing.
6. Identify the steps in activity-based costing.
7. Differentiate among the methods used to allocate costs to products.
8. Identify how activity-based management and costing can be used for marketing.
9. Explain how the cost hierarchy affects activity-based costing and management.
10. Distinguish between resources used and resources supplied.
11. Identify the advantages of activity-based reporting for unused resources.
12. Summarize the issues involved in implementing advanced cost-management systems.

Many companies, like Hewlett-Packard, Procter & Gamble, Boeing, Caterpillar, and IBM, have recently implemented new methods to improve the way they manage costs. These new methods have revealed startling new information about product profitability. For example, Tektronix, Inc., found, to the surprise of management, that one of its products, a printed-circuit board, was generating negative margins of 46 percent.[1] In this chapter we will compare these new methods to traditional methods.

---

[1]"A Bean-Counter's Best Friend," *Business Week/Quality,* 1991, pp. 42–43.

This chapter deals with activity-based management (ABM), the allocation of indirect costs to products, and how ABM affects managerial decisions.

Indirect costs include overhead costs incurred to manufacture a good or provide a service, indirect costs to market a product, and indirect costs incurred to manage the company. Unlike direct materials and direct labor that accountants can trace directly to a product, accountants must *allocate* indirect costs to products.

In general, accountants group costs into either (1) plants, which are entire factories, stores, banks, and so forth, or (2) departments within plants, or (3) activity centers. This chapter discusses issues in establishing those groups of costs, which accountants call **cost pools,** and the allocation of costs from cost pools to products.

ACTIVITY-BASED MANAGEMENT

Activity-based management rests on this premise: *Products consume activities; activities consume resources.* If managers want their products to be competitive, they must know both (1) the activities that go into making the goods or providing the services, and (2) the cost of those activities. To reduce a product's costs, managers will likely have to change the activities the product consumes. A manager who announces, "I want across-the-board cuts—everyone reduce costs by 20 percent," rarely gets the desired results. To make significant cost reductions, people must first identify the activities that a product consumes. Then they must figure out how to rework those activities to improve production efficiency.

Due to the potential improvement resulting from improved activity management, many experts believe that organizations should develop activity data and then manage by using these activity data. Many organizations are developing activity information to evaluate and improve performance. Organizations are also developing information about activity costs to be used to identify costs of nonvalue-added activities and to focus on improvement efforts.

STRATEGIC USE OF ACTIVITY-BASED MANAGEMENT

Companies use activity-based management to plan their corporate strategies.[2] For example, some companies develop competitive advantages by becoming a low-cost producer or seller. Companies such as Wal-Mart in retailing, United Parcel in delivery services, and Southwest Airlines in the airline industry create a competitive advantage by managing activities to reduce costs. Some companies have learned to use information from their analysis of activities to make substantial price cuts to increase sales volume and market share.[3]

Activity-based management can help a company develop strategy, long-range plans, and subsequent competitive cost advantage by focusing attention on activities. To reduce costs generally requires changes in activities. Top management can beg or

---

[2]See J. Shank and V. Govindarajan, *Strategic Cost Analysis* (Homewood, Ill.: Irwin, 1989), for discussion of strategic uses of cost analysis.

[3]M. E. Porter, *Competitive Advantage* (New York: Free Press, 1985).

Cost Cutting Reduces Airline Quality

Competitive pressures from low-price airlines like Southwest have jolted major airlines into severe cost reductions. After a $1.6 billion in cost cutting at Delta Airlines, one mechanic scrambled among three planes to do the work formerly done by three mechanics. According to a senior maintenance supervisor, "When you have Southwest flying at seven cents a mile, you can't compete doing things like you used to do."

To meet customer expectations for low fares, Delta, United, Northwest, and USAir have taken several steps to reduce costs such as reducing cleaning costs, substituting smaller propeller planes for larger jets, reducing the number of flight attendants, and obtaining wage concessions from employees. These actions have lowered costs and turned Delta from an unprofitable airline into a profitable one. At the same time, customer complaints have increased substantially. Whether the cost cutting will be financially beneficial to these airlines in the long run depends on whether customers prefer lower fares or better service.

Source: M. Brannigan and E. de Lisser, "Cost Cutting at Delta Raises Stock Price But Lowers the Service," *The Wall Street Journal*, June 20, 1996, pp. A1 and A9.

command employees to reduce costs, but implementation requires changes in activities. Anyone can cut costs—just close down the operation. As the Managerial Application, "Cost Cutting Reduces Airline Quality" above indicates, cost cutting can be detrimental to the quality of services. Effective management cuts costs while maintaining quality and quantity of output.

ACTIVITY-BASED MANAGEMENT AND THE VALUE CHAIN

Activity analysis is a fundamental aspect of activity-based management. An activity is any discrete task that an organization performs to make or deliver a product or service. Activity analysis has four steps:

1. Chart, from start to finish, the activities employed to complete the product or service.
2. Classify activities as value-added or nonvalue-added.
3. Eliminate nonvalue-added activities.
4. Continuously improve and reevaluate the efficiency of value-added activities or replace them with more efficient activities.

The value-added activities in the chart make up the value chain. As shown in Exhibit 5.1, the **value chain** is a linked set of value-creating activities leading from raw material sources to the ultimate end use of the goods or services produced. Managers use the value chain as a way of breaking down a company's activities. Value chain analysis is an ongoing process, in which activities are constantly being classified, eliminated, and improved. The continuous analysis is shown in Exhibit 5.2.

Activity analysis is a systematic way for organizations to evaluate the processes that they use to produce products for their customers. Such an analysis can be used to identify and eliminate activities that add costs but not value to the product. Nonvalue-added costs are costs of activities that could be eliminated without reducing product

EXHIBIT 5.1

Value Chain

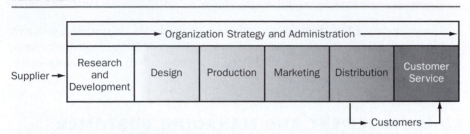

EXHIBIT 5.2

Analysis of Activities Cycle

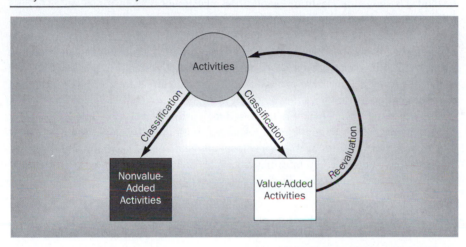

quality, performance, or value. For example, storing bicycle frames until needed for production does not add to the finished bicycles' value. If management can find ways to eliminate storing bicycle frames, say, by using just-in-time purchasing, the company could save money without reducing the quality of the finished product.

The following types of activities are candidates for elimination because they do not add value to the product.

1. *Storage.* Storage of materials, work-in-process, or finished goods inventories is an obvious nonvalue-added activity. Many companies have applied the just-in-time philosophy to purchasing and production to reduce or even eliminate storage.
2. *Moving items.* Moving parts, materials, and other items around the factory floor is another activity that does not add value to the finished product. A steel mill in Michigan once had hundreds of miles of railroad tracks just to move materials and partially finished products from one part of the factory to another. Eliminating a hundred miles or so of track reduced both labor and overhead costs, and even eliminated some spoilage because products were sometimes damaged by train accidents.
3. *Waiting for work.* Idle time does not add value to products. Reducing the amount of time people wait to work on something reduces the cost of idle time.

4. *Production process.* Managers should investigate the entire production process including purchasing, production, inspection, and shipping to identify activities that do not add value to the finished product.

These are only a few example of nonvalue-added activities. If you observe activities in universities, health-care organizations, fast-food restaurants, construction sites, government agencies, and many other organizations, you will see numerous examples of nonvalue-added activities.

ACTIVITY-BASED MANAGEMENT AND MANAGING CUSTOMER RESPONSE TIME

Exhibit 5.3 shows the chain of events from placement of a customer order to customer delivery.[4] Reducing that time can increase output, increase customer satisfaction, and increase profits. For example, suppose a loan officer at a mortgage company can process 30 loan applications per month. If the process can be improved so the loan officer can process 30 loan applications in one-half month, several good things happen. Customers are pleased that their applications are processed faster and the cost per application goes down.

Activity-based management helps to reduce customer response time by identifying activities that consume the most resources, both in dollars and time. For example, one of the holdups in mortgage loan applications is verifying credit, bank, employment, and other key information. Using computer networks could substantially reduce verification time. Further, many loan applicants can be easily classified

EXHIBIT 5.3

Elements of Customer Response Time

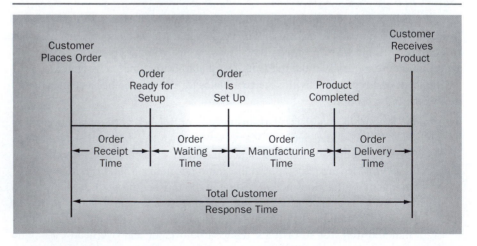

[4]For an example in a manufacturing setting, see R. Campbell, "Steeling Time with ABC or TOC," *Management Accounting,* January 1995.

as rejected or approved with limited financial information. Many universities use this approach with telephone or in-person acceptance before receiving the detailed transcripts, letters of recommendation, and so forth.

Activity-based management also helps reduce customer response time by identifying nonvalue-added activities. For example, if you apply to graduate or law school, you will find that many schools want transcripts from all the colleges you attended, even if you only took a few lower-division classes at a local college during the summer. Using activity-based management, admissions officers should consider whether obtaining these transcripts adds value to their universities. If not, why not eliminate this costly activity that slows down customer response time?

Many management accountants use customer response time as a measure of waste in the organization. Waiting, storing, moving, and inspecting add to customer response time and cost money. Nonvalue-added costs can be reduced by eliminating the causes of long customer response times.

As we improve the efficiency of value-added activities or eliminate nonvalue-added activities, both customer response time and cost will fall. Of course, customers also value a quick response to their orders, which is another important benefit of short customer response time.

ACTIVITY-BASED COSTING

Activity-based costing (ABC), a tool used in activity-based management, first assigns costs to activities, then to the products based on each product's use of activities. Activity-based management seeks to achieve continuous improvement. Activity-based costing provides information about activities and the resources required to perform them. Therefore, ABC is much more than a cost assignment process.

Is activity-based costing a new idea or an old idea whose time has come? Some accounting experts argue that activity-based costing simply extends departmental allocation methods. Just as departmental allocation provides more detailed cost information than plantwide allocation, activity-based costing provides more detailed cost information than department allocation. According to this view, activity-based costing simply extends allocation methods that companies have used for years.

Does it matter? Many proponents of activity-based costing argue that ABC does not simply extend traditional departmental allocation. Instead, they argue, activity-based costing changes the way managers do their jobs. These proponents argue that people manage activities, not costs. Activity-based costing focuses attention on the things that management can make more efficient or otherwise change. We believe that ABC *does* alter management focus in sensible ways.

DISTORTIONS CAUSED BY TRADITIONAL COST ALLOCATIONS

Cost allocation systems can distort product costs. Traditional cost allocation methods allocate overhead costs based on volume of production or sales. However,

MANAGERIAL APPLICATION

Traditional Cost Allocations Distorted Product Costs at Hewlett-Packard

After implementing activity-based costing at a Boise, Idaho, plant, Hewlett-Packard (HP) found that many of its product costs had been distorted under the traditional costing system.

Prior to adopting ABC, the plant applied overhead as a percent of direct materials cost, which is related to production volume. The ABC system used ten different cost pools and drivers. The plant compared the costs of its 57 products under the old and the new costing systems to evaluate the extent of cost distortion caused by the old system. Their findings are as follows:

Under the old costing system, HP had two types of problems. First, products with low material costs had low amounts of overhead assigned to them. Second, large-volume products that had high material costs were overcosted by the old system.

Distortion Caused by the Old System, Expressed as a Percent Difference from ABC Cost	Number of Products
Undercosted:	
Between 20% and 100%	12
Between 5% and 20%	23
Little Change:	
Less than 5% undercosted or overcosted	13
Overcosted:	
Between 5% and 20%	9
Total	57

Source: C. M. Merz and A. Hardy, "ABC Puts Accountants on Design Team at HP," *Management Accounting,* September 1993, pp. 22–27.

the demand for overhead activities is also driven by batch-related and product-sustaining activities, such as setups and engineering changes. These distortions can be lessened through the use of activity-based costing as demonstrated in the Managerial Application above, "Traditional Cost Allocations Distorted Product Costs at Hewlett-Packard."

ACTIVITY-BASED COSTING METHODS

Activity-based costing requires accountants to follow four steps.

1. Identify the activities that consume resources, and assign costs to those activities. Purchasing materials would be an activity, for example.
2. Identify the cost driver(s) associated with each activity. A **cost driver** is a factor that causes, or "drives," an activity's costs. For the activity "purchasing materials," the cost driver could be "number of orders." (Each activity could have multiple cost drivers.)
3. Compute a cost rate per cost driver unit. The cost driver rate could be the cost per purchase order, for example.
4. Assign costs to products by multiplying the cost driver rate times the volume of cost drivers consumed by the product. For example, the cost per purchase order times the number of orders required for Product X for the month of December would measure the cost of the purchasing activity for Product X for December.

IDENTIFYING THE ACTIVITIES THAT CONSUME RESOURCES (STEP 1)

This is often the most interesting and challenging part of the exercise because it requires people to understand all the activities required to make the product. Managers attempt to identify those activities that have the greatest impact on costs.

A Deere and Company plant identified eight major activities required to produce one of its products, for example. The company used one cost driver for each activity. Then it developed two cost rates for each cost driver, one for variable costs and one for fixed costs. For the materials handling activity, Deere used the number of loads required to move parts around the plant as the cost driver. Most of the materials handling costs were for labor. The company had very little fixed cost associated with materials handling.[5] To reduce materials handling costs, Deere and Company managers sought ways to reduce the number of loads required to move parts around the plant.

Complexity As an Activity That Consumes Resources

One of the lessons of activity-based costing has been that costs are a function not only of volume, but also of complexity.[6] Imagine you produce 100,000 gallons per month of vanilla ice cream and your friend produces 100,000 gallons per month of 39 different flavors of ice cream. Further, assume your ice cream is sold only in one-liter containers, while your friend sells ice cream in various sizes of containers. Your friend has more complicated systems for ordering, storage, packing in containers, and product testing (one of the more desirable jobs, nevertheless). Your friend has more machine setups, too. Presumably, you can set the machinery to one setting to obtain the desired product quality and taste; your friend has to reset the machines each time a new flavor is produced. Although both of you produce the same total volume of ice cream, you can easily imagine that your friend's overhead costs would be considerably higher.

Low-volume products often require more machine setups for a given level of production output because they are produced in smaller batches. In the ice cream example, one batch of 1,000 gallons of the low-volume 39th flavor might require as much overhead cost for machine setups, quality inspections, and purchase orders as one batch of 100,000 gallons of the highest-volume flavor. Further, the low-volume product adds complexity to the operation by disrupting the production flow of the high-volume items. (Consider this fact the next time you stand in line at the store, bank, fast-food restaurant, or student-aid line when someone ahead of you has a special, complex transaction.)

IDENTIFYING COST DRIVERS (STEP 2)

Exhibit 5.4 presents several examples of the kinds of cost drivers that companies use. Most cost drivers are related either to the volume of production or to the complexity

---

[5]See "John Deere Component Works," Harvard Business School, Case 187-107.

[6]R. D. Banker, G. Potter, and R. G. Schroeder, "An Empirical Analysis of Manufacturing Overhead Cost Drivers," *Journal of Accounting and Economics* 19, no. 1; G. Foster and M. Gupta, "Manufacturing Overhead Cost Driver Analysis," *Journal of Accounting and Economics* 12, no. 1–3; and E. Noreen and N. Soderstrom, "Are Overhead Costs Strictly Proportional to Activity?" *Journal of Accounting and Economics* 17, no. 1.

EXHIBIT 5.4

Examples of Cost Drivers

Machine Hours	Computer Time
Labor Hours or Cost	Items Produced or Sold
Pounds of Materials Handled	Customers Served
Pages Typed	Flight Hours
Machine Setups	Number of Surgeries
Purchase Orders	Scrap/Rework Orders
Quality Inspections	Hours of Testing Time
Number of Parts in a Product	Number of Different Customers
Miles Driven	

---

of the production or marketing process. Looking at Exhibit 5.4, which cost drivers on the list might be used in a law firm? (Answer: Labor hours, pages typed, miles driven, computer time, clients served, and number of different clients.)

How do managers decide which cost driver to use? The primary criteria for selecting a cost driver is *causal relation*. Choose a cost driver that *causes* the cost.

Other people recommend using the following two criteria for selecting cost drivers; however, we believe they are inferior to the causal criterion:

- *Benefits received.* Choose a cost driver so costs are assigned in proportion to benefits received. For example, if the Physics Department in a university benefits more from the university's supercomputer than does the History Department, the university should select a cost driver that recognizes the benefits to Physics. For example, the number of faculty and/or students in each department who use the computer would relate the costs of the supercomputer to the benefits.
- *Reasonableness.* Some costs cannot be linked to products based on causality or benefits received, so are assigned on the basis of fairness or reasonableness. We noted above that Deere and Company selected eight cost drivers for certain products. The cost of a ninth activity, general and administrative overhead, was allocated to products using the reasonableness approach; namely, these costs were allocated to products as a simple percentage of the costs of the other eight activities that had been allocated to products.

COMPUTING A COST RATE PER COST DRIVER UNIT (STEP 3)

In general, predetermined rates for allocating indirect costs to products are computed as follows:

$$\frac{\text{Predetermined}}{\text{indirect cost rate}} = \frac{\text{Estimated indirect cost}}{\text{Estimated volume of the allocation base}}.$$

This formula applies to all indirect costs, whether manufacturing overhead, administrative costs, distribution costs, selling costs, or any other indirect cost.

Companies using activity-based costing compute the rate for each cost driver in each activity center. For example, accountants assign the costs of setting up machines to the activity center that sets up machines. Each activity center has just one cost driver in many companies, but it is possible to have more than one cost driver in an activity center.

If inspecting products for quality is the cost driver, for example, then the company must be able to estimate the inspection costs before the period. Ideally, the company would also keep track of the actual cost of inspections as these costs are incurred during the period to compare actual and applied inspection costs.

ASSIGNING COSTS TO PRODUCTS (STEP 4)

Workers and machines perform activities on each product as it is produced. Costs are allocated to products by multiplying each cost driver's rate by the amount of cost driver activity used in making the product, as described in the illustration that follows.

ACTIVITY-BASED COSTING ILLUSTRATED

Assume the Ciudad Juarez factory makes two products—a mountain bike and a racing bike. The mountain bike is a high-volume product line in the plant, while the racing bike is a low-volume, specialized product.

The Ciudad Juarez factory allocated overhead to products at the rate of 500 percent of a product's direct labor costs. The direct materials costs were $100 and $200 per bike for the mountain and racing bikes, respectively; and the direct labor costs were $30 and $60 per bike for the mountain and racing bikes. Adding overhead at the rate of 500 percent of direct labor costs gave the following product costs per unit.

	Mountain Bikes	Racing Bikes
Direct Materials	$100	$200
Direct Labor	30	60
Manufacturing Overhead	150[a]	300[a]
Total	$280	$560

[a]Amount equals direct labor times 500 percent.

ASSIGNING COSTS USING ACTIVITY-BASED COSTING

Managers decided to experiment with activity-based costing at the Ciudad Juarez factory. First, they identified four activities that were important cost drivers. These activities were (1) purchasing materials, (2) setting up machines to produce a different product, (3) inspecting products, and (4) running machines.

The managers estimated the amount of overhead and the volume of activity events for each activity. For example, they estimated the company would purchase 10,000 frames that would require annual overhead costs of $200,000. Salaries of

158 CHAPTER 5 Activity-Based Management

people to purchase, inspect, and store materials are examples of these overhead costs. For purchasing overhead, they assigned a cost of $20 (= $200,000/10,000 frames) to each frame that the factory actually purchased. Machine operation requires energy and maintenance, which they estimated to cost $30 per machine hour. They estimated the rate for inspections to be $100 per hour in the inspection station and the machine setup rate to be $2,000 per setup. Exhibit 5.5 shows the predetermined annual rates computed for all four activities.

Picking the month of January for their study, the managers collected the following information about the actual number of cost driver units for each of the two products:

	Mountain Bikes	Racing Bikes
Purchasing materials	1,000 frames	200 frames
Machine setups	13 setups	30 setups
Inspections	200 hours	200 hours
Running machines	1,500 hours	500 hours

During January, the factory produced 1,000 mountain bikes and 200 racing bikes.

Multiplying the actual number of cost driver units for each product times the predetermined rates computed above resulted in the overhead allocated to the two products shown in Exhibit 5.6. Looking at Exhibit 5.5, what would be the rate for inspections if there were an estimated 5,000 hours per year? (Answer: $80 per hour.) Looking at Exhibit 5.6, what would be the inspection cost allocated to racing bikes? (Answer: $16,000.)

Unit Costs Recall the factory produced 1,000 mountain bikes and 200 racing bikes in January. The direct materials cost $100 per unit for mountain bike and $200 per unit for racing bikes. Direct labor costs were $30 per unit for mountain bikes and $60 per unit for racing bikes. Based on the overhead costs computed for the two product lines, which appear in Exhibit 5.6, overhead per unit was

EXHIBIT 5.5

Predetermined Annual Overhead Rates for Activity-Based Costing

(1) Activity	(2) Cost Driver	(3) Estimated Overhead Cost for the Activity	(4) Estimated Number of Cost Driver Units for Year 2	(5) Rate (Column 3/Column 4)
Purchasing materials	Number of frames purchased	$ 200,000	10,000 frames	$20 per frame
Machine setups	Number of machine setups	800,000	400 setups	$2,000 per setup
Inspections	Hours of inspections	400,000	4,000 hours	$100 per hour
Running machines	Machine hours	600,000	20,000 hours	$30 per hour
Total estimated overhead		$2,000,000		

EXHIBIT 5.6

Overhead Costs Assigned to Products Using Activity-Based Costing

		Mountain Bikes		Racing Bikes	
Activity	Rate	Actual Cost Driver Units	Cost Allocated to Mountain Bikes	Actual Cost Driver Units	Cost Allocated to Racing Bikes
Purchasing materials	$20 per frame	1,000 frames	$ 20,000	200 frames	$ 4,000
Machine setups	$2,000 per setup	13 setups	26,000	30 setups	60,000
Inspections	$100 per inspection hour	200 hours	20,000	200 hours	20,000
Running machines	$30 per hour	1,500 hours	45,000	500 hours	15,000
Total cost allocated to each product			$111,000		$99,000
Total overhead			→ $210,000 ←		

$111 (= $111,000/1,000 units) for mountain bikes and $495 (= $99,000/200 units) for racing bikes. After putting together the data shown in the top panel of Exhibit 5.7, the managers were surprised to find the product costs were a lot different using activity-based costing compared to the traditional approach. Using the traditional approach, they had computed numbers shown in the bottom panel of Exhibit 5.7. They had assigned *considerably* more overhead to racing bikes and less to mountain bikes using activity-based costing.

EXHIBIT 5.7

Product Costs Using Activity-Based Costing

Activity-Based Costing

	Mountain Bikes	Racing Bikes
Direct Materials	$100	$200
Direct Labor	30	60
Overhead	111[a]	495[b]
Total Cost	$241	$755

Traditional Approach

	Mountain Bikes	Racing Bikes
Direct Materials	$100	$200
Direct Labor	30	60
Overhead	150	300
Total Cost	$280	$560

[a]$111 = overhead cost allocation to products using activity-based costing divided by number of units produced = $111,000/1,000 units.

[b]$495 = overhead cost allocation to products using activity-based costing divided by number of units produced = $99,000/200 units.

Analysis In analyzing the results, the Ciudad Juarez managers realized the racing bikes were allocated considerably more overhead per unit than the mountain bikes because the factory performed more machine setups for the racing bikes. Also, the factory had as many total inspection hours for the lower-volume racing bike, meaning the inspection hours per bike were greater for the racing bike.

Activity-based costing revealed two important facts. First, the mountain bikes were cheaper to make and the racing bikes more expensive to make than the company had realized. Armed with this information, marketers lowered prices on the mountain bikes to make them more competitive. Second, management realized the Ciudad Juarez factory production methods were inefficient, so the company

PROBLEM 5.1 FOR SELF-STUDY

Compute product costs using activity-based costing. The following information is available for the month of December for the Ciudad Juarez factory:

Bikes Produced	
Mountain Bikes Produced	600
Racing Bikes Produced	200

	Cost Driver Units	
Activities	**Mountain Bikes**	**Racing Bikes**
Purchasing materials	600 frames	200 frames
Machine setups	7 setups	24 setups
Inspections	100 hours	200 hours
Running machines	800 hours	600 hours

Compute the costs (1) in total and (2) per unit for both products using the activity-based costing rates. The actual cost driver units for December are given in this self-study problem. You should use the rates presented in the text. Assume the direct materials costs are $100 and $200 per unit for mountain bikes and racing bikes, respectively; and direct labor costs are $30 and $60 per unit for mountain bikes and racing bikes, respectively. Round unit costs to the nearest dollar. Recall that overhead allocated to products equals the cost driver rate (for example, $20 per frame for materials handled according to the schedule of rates in Exhibit 5.5) times the cost driver units (for example, 600 frames for mountain bikes in December).

The solution to this self-study problem is at the end of the chapter on page 172.

reworked the production process to reduce the number of setups, particularly on racing bikes.

WHICH METHOD TO USE: A COST-BENEFIT DECISION

PLANTWIDE VERSUS DEPARTMENTAL VERSUS ACTIVITY CENTER (ABC)

The simplest allocation method, **plantwide allocation,** uses the entire plant as a cost pool. Although accountants call this method the plantwide method, in fact, the "plant" need not refer to a manufacturing facility but can mean store, hospital, or other multidepartment segment of a company. A bank, for example, could apply overhead to different customer accounts, to different types of loans, and to other products using just one overhead rate for the entire bank.

Simple organizations having only a few departments and not much variety in activities in different departments might justify using the plantwide method.

When companies use the **department allocation method,** they have a separate cost pool for each department. The company establishes a separate overhead allocation rate or set of rates for each department. Both plantwide and departmental methods are "traditional methods."

Many companies that use activity-based management philosophies, such as Hewlett-Packard, Procter & Gamble, Caterpillar, and Chrysler, use even more cost pools, one each for numerous activity centers. Each company defines its own activity centers as parts of the company that perform some easily described activity.

For example, a motorcycle plant that one of the authors studied defined the paint quality inspection activity in the paint department as an activity center. This activity center handled all paint-related quality inspections to see that the manufacturing had properly applied the paint, with no paint runs, splatters, splotches, oversprays, and the like. The detailed activity-based costing system in this motorcycle plant separated the paint inspection costs from the paint spraying costs. In contrast, a cost system based on department cost pools combines all paint department costs into a single pool, not separating paint spraying from the inspection of paint spraying. In contrast, the plantwide allocation method would have a single cost pool for the entire motorcycle factory. The plantwide allocation method thus compiles no separate costs for the paint department, much less the quality inspection activity.

Should managers use plantwide, departmental, or activity-center cost pools? The choice requires managers to make cost-benefit decisions. Plantwide methods cost least but provide the least information. Maintaining cost pools by activity center costs most but provides the most information. Do the benefits justify the costs?

If managers in the motorcycle plant have a use for information about which motorcycle types consume the most resources in paint quality inspection, they might prefer the more detailed activity-center information. The Managerial Application, "Contrasting Activity-Based Costing with the German/Dutch Cost Pool Method," on page 162 suggests that European managers see less benefit from ABC because they are less inclined to add or drop products frequently. Further, they rely more on market data for pricing than on prudent cost information.

Contrasting Activity-Based Costing with the German/Dutch Cost Pool Method

The continental European tradition in cost management is predominantly based on German management and cost accounting insights; it differs from American (Anglo-Saxon) theory and practice. The German/Dutch cost pool method does not support performing product cost calculations frequently, as adding or eliminating products is not a short-term decision.

"In general it is believed that it suffices to decide annually whether the present product mix or new products are desirable from a competitive point of view (p. 112). . . . Competitive market prices are thus far more important in guiding pricing decisions than internal full-cost allocations based on pure accounting data."

Source: A. Boons, H. Roberts, and F. Roozen, "Contrasting Activity-Based Costing with the German/Dutch Cost Pool Method," *Management Accounting Research*, vol. 3, no. 2, pp. 97–117.

ACTIVITY-BASED MANAGEMENT AND COSTING IN MARKETING

Marketing activities also consume resources; territories, customer groupings, and other segments require activities to maintain themselves. Activity-based costing (ABC) costs the marketing activities needed to service each customer. The variability in marketing costs across customer types and distribution channels requires attention by the costing system. ABC also supports activity-based management by encouraging the elimination of low-volume customers, for whom the activities to process are the same as for large-volume customers. ABC also provides cost analysis to support the addition of a surcharge on small orders.

The principles and methods are the same as discussed earlier:

1. Identify activities, such as warehousing, credit and collection, transportation, personal selling, and advertising.
2. Identify cost drivers. Some possible cost drivers are:

Detailed Activity	ABC Drivers
Transportation—Loading and unloading, gasoline, repairs, and supervision	Deliveries or shipments, truck miles, units or value shipped
Advertising and sales promotion—Newspaper advertising, radio and television ads, and product demonstrations	Newspaper inches, cost per thousand consumers reached, sales transactions, or product units sold

3. Compute the cost rate for each cost driver. Compute unit costs for each activity by dividing the budgeted activity cost by the cost driver selected. For example, assume advertising for a month in the *Chicago Tribune* is $30,000, including the newspaper ad and the company advertising and graphics employees'

salaries. The company has chosen column inches as the cost driver and runs a total of 300 inches per month. The cost per inch is $100.

4. Allocate indirect costs by multiplying the rate for each cost driver by the number of cost driver units.

COST HIERARCHIES

Some costs can be easily classified as either fixed or variable, but others cannot. For example, the costs of machine setups are generally batch-related costs. A machine setup is required for each new batch of products whether the batch contains 1 unit or 1,000 units. The setup cost is not affected by the number of units, but rather by the number of batches.

A hierarchy of costs like that shown in Exhibit 5.8 helps managers think about the major factors that drive costs.[7] The cost hierarchy includes strictly variable costs, such as energy costs to run machines. These appear at the bottom of the illustration as unit-level costs. Direct materials and piece-work labor costs are also unit-level costs.

At the other extreme, at the top of the illustration, are capacity-related costs. These costs are essentially fixed by management's decisions to have a particular size of store, factory, hospital, or other facility. Although they are fixed with respect to volume, it would be misleading to give the impression that these costs cannot be changed. Managers can make decisions that affect capacity costs; such decisions just require a longer time horizon to implement than do decisions to reduce unit-level costs.

EXHIBIT 5.8

Hierarchy of Product Costs

Activity Category	Examples
1. Capacity-Sustaining Activities	Plant Management
	Building Depreciation and Rent
	Heating and Lighting
2. Product- and Customer-Sustaining Activities	Customer Records and Files
	Product Specifications
	Customer Sevice
3. Batch Activities	Machine Setups
	Quality Inspections
4. Unit Activities	Energy to Run Machines
	Direct Materials

Source: Adapted from R. Cooper and R. S. Kaplan, "Profit Priorities from Activity-based Costing," *Harvard Business Review,* May–June 1991, p. 132.

---

[7]R. Cooper and R. S. Kaplan, "Profit Priorities from Activity-Based Costing," *Harvard Business Review,* May–June 1991, pp. 130–135.

The two middle categories of costs are affected by the way the company manages its activities. A company that makes products to order for a customer will have more product/customer-level costs than a company that provides limited choices. A company that schedules its work so that one product is made on Monday, a second product on Tuesday, and so on through Friday has lower batch-related costs than if it produced all five products on Monday, all five again on Tuesday, and so on through the week. In practice, many of the greatest opportunities for reducing costs are in these middle categories of product/customer-level and batch-related costs.

Using this hierarchy, if management makes decisions that affect units but not batches, products, customers, or capacity, management would analyze costs in category 4 (unit-level activities). If management makes decisions that affect capacity, however, all activities in categories 1 through 4 would probably be affected, and costs in all four categories would be analyzed.

PROBLEM 5.2 FOR SELF-STUDY

Identify which of the following items generate capacity-sustaining costs, product- or customer-sustaining costs, batch costs, or unit costs.

1. Piecework labor
2. Long-term lease on a building
3. Energy to run machines
4. Engineering drawings for a product
5. Purchase order
6. Movement of materials for products in production
7. Change order to meet new customer specifications

The solution to this self-study problem is at the end of this chapter on page 173.

DISTINGUISHING BETWEEN RESOURCES USED AND RESOURCES SUPPLIED

In some situations, costs go up and down proportionately with the cost driver. Materials, energy, and piecework labor are excellent examples. Suppose workers are paid $1.50 per crate to pick strawberries from a field. The cost driver would obviously be "crates of strawberries" and the cost driver rate would be $1.50 per crate.

Now suppose strawberry workers are hired by the day and paid $64 per day. Assume the cost driver is still "crates of strawberries." The cost driver rate would be computed as follows: estimated wages of strawberry workers for the day ÷ estimated number of crates of strawberries that workers can pick during the day. The grower estimates the workers will pick 32 crates per day which gives a rate of $2 per crate. In general, this cost driver rate could be higher, lower, or the same as the piecework rate. We assume the rate is $2 just to help you recognize there is a difference between the piecework rate and the cost driver rate when workers are paid in intervals such as hours, days, or months.

The grower employs five workers. Each has the capacity to pick 32 crates per day, or a total of 160 crates per day for five workers. But assume that on Tuesday, the workers pick only 140 crates. That means there are 20 crates, or $40 (= $2 cost driver rate $\times$ 20 crates), of unused capacity on Tuesday. The grower has costs of $480, computed either of two ways:

$$\$320 = 5 \text{ workers} \times \$64 \text{ per day}$$

$$\$320 = \$2 \text{ per crate} \times 160\text{-crate capacity}$$

The grower supplies resources of $320 to the strawberry-picking activity. However, on Tuesday, only $280 of strawberry-picking resources were used, leaving $40 of unused capacity ($280 = $2 \times 140 crates actually picked). The grower knows the five workers could have picked more strawberries without increasing the resources supplied to the activity.

In general, activity-based costing estimates the cost of resources used. In activity-based costing, **resources used** for an activity are measured by the cost driver rate times the cost driver volume. In the strawberry example, resources used were $280.

The **resources supplied** to an activity are the expenditures or the amounts spent on the activity. In the strawberry example, resources supplied were the $320 paid to the strawberry pickers. Financial statements show resources supplied. The difference between resources used and resources supplied is **unused capacity.**[8]

Activity-based management involves looking for ways to reduce unused capacity. For example, the strawberry grower may look for ways to reduce the $40 (or 20 crates) of unused capacity. Suppose the grower finds that the people checking each case for quantity and quality were not sufficiently trained. Consequently, the checkers were slowing the picking process. The activity-based management information signaled the existence of unused capacity, which helped the grower and workers improve the production flow.

Differences between resource usage and resource supply generally occur because managers have committed to supply a certain level of resources before they are used. In the strawberry example, the grower committed to the $8-per-hour wage in advance of the actual picking of the strawberries. In the Managerial Application, "Using Activity-Based Management to Control Health-Care Costs" on page 166, the resources supplied are nurses who are hired for an entire shift of four hours before patients arrive. Unused capacity occurs in the health-care setting when nurses are available to provide patient care but there are no patients requiring nursing services.

In cases where resources are supplied as they are used, the resource supply will generally equal the resource usage and there will be no unused capacity. Good examples are materials costs and piecework labor. If the grower had paid the piecework labor rate of $1.50 per crate, the resources supplied would have been $1.50 per crate of strawberries picked and the resource used would also have been $1.50 per crate picked. There would have been no unused capacity. The next section expands on these ideas by suggesting a new reporting format that presents managers with important information about resources used, resources supplied, and unused capacity.

---

[8] Failure to distinguish between resources used and resources supplied leads to suboptimal decisions. See E. Noreen, "Conditions under Which Activity-Based Costing Systems Provide Relevant Costs," *Journal of Management Accounting Research* 3, pp. 159–168.

MANAGERIAL APPLICATION

Using Activity-Based Management to Control Health-Care Costs

In the current era of managed competition, health maintenance organizations (HMOs) and capitation, health-care organizations are looking for ways to ways to reduce costs while improving the quality of care. Several health-care organizations recently experimented with a new anesthesia that would enable patients to leave the recovery room sooner. Managers hoped the new anesthesia would both reduce the costs of nurse staffing in the recovery room and increase customer satisfaction because patients would leave the surgery center earlier.

The managers faced the problem that resources used did not equal resources supplied. Resources used were patient minutes in the recovery room. Resources supplied were the expenditures to pay nurses to staff the recovery room. Researchers found that a particular new anesthesia reduced patient time in the recovery room by 33 percent. Although resources used in the recovery room were 33 percent less, would resources supplied also go down by 33 percent?

Researchers found the answer to be no in this case. By simulating the staffing of the recovery room assuming the new anesthesia was used, researchers found the resources supplied (that is, expenditures to pay nurses) went down by only 20 percent, despite the 33 percent decrease in patient time. Why? Primarily, the outpatient surgery center employed nurses in four-hour shifts. Once nurses started duty, the managers would not send them home even if the patient census dropped in the recovery room.

In the end, managers realized that the new anesthesia would have three desirable effects:

- Patients would go home sooner, which increased their satisfaction.
- Costs would be lower; even a 20 percent reduction is better than no reduction.
- Both patient care and nurse morale would be better. Reducing resource usage by 33 percent and reducing resource supply by only 20 percent creates unused capacity. Nurses could use this "unused capacity" for many desirable purposes, including spending more time with each patient, taking more time with patient follow-up, and doing unscheduled training.

Incidentally, turnover in other hospital departments provided ample jobs for nurses who would no longer be needed in outpatient surgery center recovery room.

Source: Based on research by M. L. Marais and M. W. Maher (for example, see "Process-Oriented Activity-based Costing," Graduate School of Management, University of California–Davis, November 1996).

ACTIVITY-BASED REPORTING OF UNUSED RESOURCES

We now discuss an important way for managers to add value in companies. The previous sections have demonstrated the importance of two key concepts: the cost hierarchy and the difference between resources used and resources supplied. Conventional management reports do not make those distinctions. Typical reports show costs as line items, as for Kaplan, Inc., shown in Exhibit 5.9. It is impossible for managers to distinguish resources used from resources supplied in such reports.

Here we present a new type of report that compares resources used with resources supplied, and classifies costs into cost hierarchies. This information is important if managers are to manage resources wisely.

EXHIBIT 5.9

KAPLAN, INC.
Traditional (Detailed) Income Statement
January

Sales		$180,000
Costs		
Materials	$ 30,000	
Energy	10,000	
Short-term Labor	4,000	
Outside Contracts	6,000	
Setups	20,000	
Parts Management	7,000	
Purchasing	10,000	
Marketing	15,000	
Customer Service	4,000	
Engineering Changes	6,000	
Long-term Labor	7,000	
Depreciation (buildings)	20,000	
Administrative	13,000	
Total Costs		$152,000
Operating Profits		$ 28,000

This new type of report appears in Exhibit 5.10. Note first that this report categorizes costs into the cost hierarchies discussed earlier in this chapter. Managers can look at the amount of costs in each hierarchy and figure out ways to manage those resources effectively. For example, managers see that $30,000 of resources are supplied to batch-related activities, such as setups. Now they investigate how much of that $30,000 can be saved by changing the production process—for example, by cutting the number of setups in half.

Perhaps of greater interest, the report shows managers how much of the resources for each type of cost are unused. Here's how it works. Take setup costs. Assume the cost driver is "hours of setup" and the cost driver rate is $100 per hour. Based on the information in the income statement, $20,000 was spent on setups. That represents 200 hours of setup capacity ($20,000/$100 per setup hour = 200 setup hours of available resource). However, only 140 hours were used during the month ($14,000 resources used/$100 cost driver rate = 140 hours of setup used). The report shows managers that $6,000 (or 60 hours) of unused setup resources are available.

All other things equal, perhaps as much as 60 additional hours of setup could have been done in January without increasing expenditures. In reality, managers know that some unused resources are a good thing. Having some unstructured time for ad hoc training, for leisure, or for thinking about ways to improve work and the work environment can be useful for morale and productivity.

Note that some costs have more unused resources than others. The costs listed under unit-related costs at the top of the report show little or no unused resources.

EXHIBIT 5.10

KAPLAN, INC.
Activity-Based Management Income Statement
January

	Resources Used	Unused Capacity	Resources Supplied	
Sales				$180,000
Costs				
Unit:				
Materials	$ 30,000	$ 0	$ 30,000	
Energy	10,000	0	10,000	
Short-term Labor	3,500	500	4,000	
Outside Contracts	6,000	0	6,000	
	$ 49,500	$ 500	$ 50,000	
Batch:				
Setups	$ 14,000	$ 6,000	$ 20,000	
Quality Inspections	9,000	1,000	10,000	
	$ 23,000	$ 7,000	$ 30,000	
Product- and Customer-Sustaining:				
Parts Management	$ 6,000	$ 1,000	$ 7,000	
Marketing	14,000	1,000	15,000	
Customer Service	2,000	2,000	4,000	
Engineering Changes	5,000	1,000	6,000	
	$ 27,000	$ 5,000	$ 32,000	
Capacity-Sustaining:				
Long-term Labor	$ 5,000	$ 2,000	$ 7,000	
Depreciation (buildings)	12,000	8,000	20,000	
Administrative	10,000	3,000	13,000	
	$ 27,000	$13,000	$ 40,000	
Total Costs	$126,500	$25,500		$152,000
Operating Profits				$ 28,000

Source: This statement is an extension of an idea presented in R. Cooper and R. Kaplan, "Activity-Based Systems: Measuring the Costs of Resource Usage," *Accounting Horizons* 6, no. 3, pp. 1–13.

These are costs that vary proportionately with output and will often have little or no unused resources. Short-term labor, for example, is the cost of piecework labor or temporary help that is employed on an "as needed" basis. In a college, a part-time lecturer hired for only one class is an example of short-term labor. Many of us have worked as short-term laborers during the summer in resorts, on farms, fighting forest fires, in retail stores, or providing delivery services.

Capacity-related costs will have unused resources unless the company is operating at full capacity. Long-term labor resources are the costs of employing people who are not laid off during temporary fluctuations in production. In colleges, permanent faculty and staff are examples of long-term labor.

IMPLEMENTING ADVANCED COST-MANAGEMENT SYSTEMS

Accountants cannot implement activity-based costing without becoming familiar with the operations of the company. Accountants become part of a team with management and people from production, engineering, marketing, and other parts of the company who all work to identify the activities that drive the company's costs. This often creates discomfort at first as accountants are forced to deal with unfamiliar areas, but in the long run their familiarity with the company's operating activities can improve their contribution to the company. Also, nonaccounting personnel feel a greater sense of ownership of the numbers reported by the accounting system as accounting improves its credibility among nonaccountants.

One problem encountered when implementing activity-based costing is the failure to get influential people in the organization to buy into the process. Accounting methods in companies are like rules in sports; people become accustomed to playing by one set of rules and oppose change to something unknown. In fact, specialists who advise companies about how to implement advanced cost-management systems believe that employee resistance is the single biggest obstacle to implementing activity-based management.[9] For example, analysts at one company spent several months of their time and hundreds of hours of computer time to develop an activity-based costing system. Their analysis revealed several hundred products that were clearly unprofitable and should be eliminated. However, the key managers who made product elimination decisions agreed to eliminate only about 20 products. Why? The analysts had failed to talk to these key managers early in the process. When presented with the results, these managers raised numerous objections that the analysts had not anticipated. The moral is: If you are involved in trying to make a change, get all the people who are important to that change involved in the process early.

SUMMARY

These items relate to the learning objectives stated at the beginning of the chapter.

1. **Describe the basic premise of activity-based management.** Products consume activities; activities consume resources. Managers must know (1) the activities that go into making the goods or providing the services, and (2) the cost of those activities.
2. **Identify strategic uses of activity-based management.** Activity-based management can help a company develop strategy, long-range plans, and subsequent competitive cost advantage by focusing attention on activities.
3. **Relate activity-based management to the value chain.** Activity analysis is a fundamental aspect of activity-based management. A value chain is a linked set of value-creating activities leading from raw material sources to the ultimate end use of the goods or services provided. Activity analysis is a systematic way for organizations to evaluate the processes that they use to produce products for

---

[9]J. Ness and T. Cucuzza "Tapping the Full Potential of ABC," *Harvard Business Review,* July–August 1995, pp. 130–138.

their customers and can be used to identify and eliminate activities that add costs but not value to the product.

4. **Explain how activity-based management can be used to reduce customer response time.** Customer response time can be reduced by identifying the activities that consume the most resources and making them more efficient, and by identifying nonvalue-added activities, which can be eliminated.

5. **Understand the concept of activity-based costing.** Activity-based costing first assigns costs to activities, then to the products based on each product's use of activities. Many believe that activity-based costing changes the way managers do their jobs. People manage activities, not costs. Activity-based costing thus focuses attention on the things that management can make more efficient or otherwise change. Traditional allocation systems can distort product costs. Although overhead costs are allocated on volume of production or sales, the demand for overhead activities is also driven by batch-related and product-sustaining activities.

6. **Identify the steps in activity-based costing.** Activity-based costing requires accountants to follow four steps: (1) identify the activities that consume resources and assign costs to those activities, (2) identify the cost drivers associated with each activity, (3) compute a cost rate per cost driver unit, and (4) assign cost to products by multiplying the cost driver rate times the volume of cost driver consumed by the product.

Key Equation:

$$\text{Predetermined indirect cost rate} = \frac{\text{Estimated indirect cost}}{\text{Estimated volume of the allocation base}}$$

7. **Differentiate among the methods used to allocate costs to products.** The simplest allocation method, plantwide allocation, considers the entire plant to be one cost pool. The department allocation method uses a separate cost pool for each department. Activity-based costing uses a cost pool for each activity center.

8. **Identify how activity-based management and costing can be used for marketing.** Activity-based costing identifies the marketing activities needed to service each customer or order more appropriately. The variability in marketing costs across customer types and distribution channels requires attention by the costing system. Activity-based costing also supports activity-based management by encouraging the elimination of accounts with high processing costs.

9. **Explain how the cost hierarchy affects activity-based costing and management.** Allocating all costs to units is misleading if some costs do not vary with the volume of units. To deal with this, management can set up a hierarchy of expenses—capacity-sustaining, product- and customer-sustaining, batch, and unit—and focus on the costs in the applicable category.

10. **Distinguish between resources used and resources supplied.** Resources used for an activity are measured by the cost driver rate times the cost driver volume. Resources supplied to an activity are the expenditures for the activity. Differences between resource usage and resources supply generally occur because managers have committed to supply a certain level of resources before they are

used. Activity-based management involves looking for ways to reduce unused capacity.

11. **Identify the advantages of activity-based reporting for unused resources.** Conventional management reports do not make the distinction between the hierarchy of costs and the difference between resources used and resources supplied. The activity-based report categorizes costs into cost hierarchies so managers can look at the amount of costs in each hierarchy and figure out ways to manage those resources effectively. The report also shows managers how much of the resources for each type of cost are unused, indicating activities that could have been undertaken without affecting costs. Unit-related costs vary proportionately with output and will often have little or no unused resources. Capacity-related costs will have unused resources unless the company is operating at full capacity.

12. **Summarize the issues involved in implementing advanced cost-management systems.** Accountants cannot implement activity-based costing without becoming familiar with the operations of the company. Accountants become part of a team with management and people from production, engineering, marketing, and other parts of the company who all work to identify the activities that drive the company's costs. One problem in implementing activity-based costing is the failure to get influential people in the organization to buy into the process.

KEY TERMS AND CONCEPTS

Cost pool   Grouping of costs.

Activity-based management (ABM)   The management process that uses the information provided by an activity-based costing (ABC) analysis to improve organizational profitability. Activity-based management includes performing activities more efficiently, eliminating the need to perform certain activities that do not add value for customers, improving the design of products, and developing better relationships with customers and suppliers. The goal of activity-based management is to satisfy customer needs while making fewer demands on organizational resources.

Value chain   A sequence of activities with the objective of providing a product or service to a customer or providing an intermediate good or service in another value chain.

Activity-based costing (ABC)   Method of assigning indirect costs, including non-manufacturing overhead, to products and services. ABC assumes that almost all overhead costs associate with activities within the firm and vary with respect to the drivers of those activities. The method first assigns costs to activities and then to products based on the products' usages of the activities.

Cost driver   A factor that causes an activity's costs.

Activity centers   Units of the organization that perform a set of tasks.

Plantwide allocation method   First, use one cost pool for the entire plant. Then, allocate all costs from that pool using a single overhead allocation rate, or one set of rates, to all the products of the plant, independent of the number of departments in the plant.

Department allocation method   First, accumulate costs as cost pools for each department. Then, using separate rates, or sets of rates, for each department, allocate from each cost pool to products produced in that department.

Resources used   Equal the cost driver rate times the cost driver volume.
Resources supplied   The expenditures or the amounts spent on the activity.
Unused capacity   The difference between resources supplied and resources used.

SOLUTIONS TO SELF-STUDY PROBLEMS

SUGGESTED SOLUTION TO PROBLEM 5.1 FOR SELF-STUDY

		Mountain Bikes		Racing Bikes	
Activity	**Rate**	**Actual Cost Driver Units**	**Costs Allocated to Mountain Bikes**	**Actual Cost Driver Units**	**Costs Allocated to Racing Bikes**
Purchasing materials	$20 per frame	600 frames	$12,000	200 frames	$ 4,000
Machine setups	$2,000 per setup	7 setups	$14,000	24 setups	$48,000
Inspections	$100 per inspection hour	100 hours	$10,000	200 hours	$20,000
Running machines	$30 per hour	800 hours	$24,000	600 hours	$18,000
Total cost allocated to each product:			$60,000		$90,000

The costs of producing 600 mountain bikes and 200 racing bikes are as follows:

	Mountain Bikes	Racing Bikes
Direct Materials	$ 60,000 ($100 each)	$ 40,000 ($200 each)
Direct Labor	18,000 ($30 each)	12,000 ($60 each)
Overhead	60,000 (see above)	90,000 (see above)
Total	$138,000	$142,000

	Unit Costs	
	Mountain Bikes	**Racing Bikes**
Direct Materials	$100	$200
Direct Labor	30	60
Overhead	100[a]	450[b]
Total	$230	$710

[a]$100 = total allocation to products divided by number of units produced = $60,000/600 units.
[b]$450 = total allocation to products divided by number of units produced = $90,000/200 units.

SUGGESTED SOLUTION TO PROBLEM 5.2 FOR SELF-STUDY

Activity	Category
1. Piecework labor	Unit
2. Long-term lease on building	Capacity sustaining
3. Energy to run machines	Unit
4. Engineering drawings for a product	Product sustaining
5. Purchase order	Batch
6. Movement of materials for products in production	Batch
7. Change order to meet new customer specifications	Customer sustaining

QUESTIONS, EXERCISES, AND PROBLEMS

REVIEW QUESTIONS

1. Review the meaning of the concepts and terms given in Key Terms and Concepts.
2. "Activity-based costing is great for manufacturing plants, but it doesn't really address the needs of the service sector." Do you agree? Explain.
3. If step 1 of ABC is to identify activities that consume resources, what is step 2?
4. What basis or cost driver does a company using a single plantwide rate typically select for the allocation of indirect costs?
5. What are the four basic steps required for activity-based costing?
6. Give the criterion for choosing cost drivers for allocating costs to products.
7. See the Managerial Application "Traditional Cost Allocations Distorted Product Costs at Hewlett-Packard." What were the two types of distortions the traditional costing system caused?

CRITICAL ANALYSIS AND DISCUSSION QUESTIONS

8. Explain the basic difference between plantwide and department allocation.
9. What exactly is a cost driver? Give three examples.
10. Activity-based costing requires more record keeping and extensive teamwork among all departments. What are the potential benefits of a more detailed product cost system?
11. "One of the lessons learned from activity-based costing is that all costs are really a function of volume." True, false, or uncertain? Explain.
12. Allocating overhead based on the volume of output, such as direct labor hours or machine hours, seems fair and equitable. Why, then, do many people claim that high-volume products "subsidize" low-volume products?
13. Give examples of two nonvalue-added activities that may be found in each of the following organizations: (1) a university, (2) a restaurant, and (3) a bicycle repair shop.

14. "The total estimated overhead for the year will differ depending on whether you use department allocation or activity-based costing." Do you agree? Explain.

15. Many companies have experienced great technological change resulting in potential for erroneous product cost figures, assuming traditional labor-based cost drivers are used to allocate overhead to products. What is that technological change?

16. "Activity-based costing is for accountants and production managers. I plan to be a marketing specialist, so ABC won't help me." Do you agree with this statement? Explain.

17. Refer to the Managerial Application, "Using Activity-Based Management to Control Health-Care Costs." If the new anesthesia reduces the number of minutes a patient stays in the recovery room after surgery, why wouldn't nursing costs necessarily be reduced proportional to the reduction in the number of minutes the patient stays in the recovery room?

18. Martha Clark, the vice-president of marketing, wonders how products can cost less under one cost system than under another: "Aren't costs cut-and-dried?" How would you respond?

19. According to a recent publication, "Activity-based costing is the wave of the future. Everyone should drop their existing cost systems and adopt ABC!" Do you agree? Explain.

20. What is the difference between a capacity-sustaining cost and a unit-level cost? How can managers use a hierarchy of overhead costs like the one presented in Exhibit 5.8?

21. Of the four categories of costs in the hierarchy, which one would you most expect to have unused resources? Why?

22. How are the used resources measured?

23. How does activity-based management use the hierarchy of costs?

24. How do the distinctions made in the activity-based reports help managers?

EXERCISES

Solutions to even-numbered exercises are at the end of the chapter after the problems.

25. **Activity-based costing.** Sandy O'Neal has just joined the Ciudad Juarez factory (text example) as the new production manager. He was pleased to see the company uses activity-based costing. O'Neal believes he can reduce production costs if he reduces the number of machine setups. He has spent the last month working with purchasing and sales to better coordinate raw material arrivals and the anticipated demand for the company's products. In March, he plans to produce 2,000 mountain bikes and 400 racing bikes. O'Neal believes that with his efficient production scheduling he can reduce the number of setups for both the mountain and racing bike products by 50 percent.

    a. Refer to Exhibit 5.5. Compute the amount of overhead allocated to each product line—mountain bikes and racing bikes—assuming a 50-percent annual reduction in setups. Assume all events are the same as in the text example except the number of machine setups in March are 13 setups for mountain bikes and 30 setups for racing bikes. Assume the overhead costs of setting up machines decrease proportionately with the reduction in the number of setups; thus, the setup rate remains at $2,000 per setup.

b. What information did activity-based costing provide that enabled Sandy O'Neal to pursue reducing overhead costs? In general, what are the advantages of activity-based costing over the traditional volume-based allocation methods? What are the disadvantages?

26. **Activity-based costing.** The manager of Wildwater Adventurers uses activity-based costing to compute the costs of her raft trips. Each raft holds six paying customers and a guide. The company offers two types of raft trips—3-day float trips for beginners and 3-day whitewater trips for seasoned rafters. The breakdown of the costs is as follows:

Activities (with cost drivers)	Float Trip Costs	Whitewater Trip Costs
Advertising (trips)	$215 per trip	$215 per trip
Permit to Use the River (trips)	30 per trip	50 per trip
Equipment Use (trips, people)	20 per trip + $5 per person	40 per trip + $8 per person
Insurance (trips)	75 per trip	127 per trip
Paying Guides (trips, guides)	300 per trip per guide	400 per trip per guide
Food (people)	60 per person	60 per person

a. Compute the cost of a four-raft, 28-person (including four guides) float trip.
b. Compute the cost of a four-raft, 28-person (including four guides) whitewater trip.
c. Recommend a minimum price per customer to the manager if she wants to cover her costs.

27. **ABC versus traditional costing.** Good Times Corporation produces two types of audiocassettes: standard and high-grade. The standard cassettes are used primarily in answering machines and are designed for durability rather than accurate sound reproduction. The company only recently began producing the higher-quality high-grade model to enter the lucrative music recording market. Since the new product was introduced, profits have been steadily declining, although sales of the high-grade tape have been growing rapidly. Management believes the accounting system may not be accurately allocating costs to products.

Management has asked you to investigate the cost allocation problem. You find that manufacturing overhead is currently assigned to products based on the direct labor costs in the products. Last year's manufacturing overhead was $880,000, based on production of 320,000 standard cassettes and 100,000 high-grade cassettes. Selling prices last year averaged $3.60 per standard tape and $5.80 per high-grade tape. Direct labor and direct materials costs for last year were as follows:

	Standard	High-Grade	Total
Direct Labor	$174,000	$ 66,000	$240,000
Materials	125,000	114,000	239,000

Management believes the following three activities cause overhead costs. The cost drivers and related costs are as follows:

	Costs Assigned	Activity Level		
		Standard	High-Grade	Total
Number of Production Runs	$400,000	40	10	50
Quality Tests Performed	360,000	12	18	30
Shipping Orders Processed	120,000	100	50	150
Total Overhead	$880,000			

a. How much of the overhead will be assigned to each product if the three cost drivers are used to allocate overhead? What would be the cost per unit produced for each product?

b. How much of the overhead would have been assigned to each product if direct labor cost had been used to allocate overhead? What would have been the total cost per unit produced for each product?

c. How might the results explain Good Times' declining profits?

28. **Activity-based costing in a nonmanufacturing environment.** Plantcare, Inc., is a garden care service. The company originally specialized in serving residential clients, but has recently started contracting for work with larger commercial clients. Ms. Plantcare, the owner, is considering reducing residential services and increasing commercial lawncare.

Five field employees worked a total of 10,000 hours last year—6,500 on residential jobs and 3,500 on commercial jobs. Wages were $9 per hour for all work done. Direct materials used were minimal and are included in overhead. All overhead is allocated on the basis of labor hours worked, which is also the basis for customer charges. Because of greater competition for commercial accounts, Ms. Plantcare can charge $22 per hour for residential work but only $19 per hour for commercial work.

a. If overhead for the year was $62,000, what were the profits of commercial and residential service using labor hours as the allocation base?

b. Overhead consists of office supplies, garden supplies, and depreciation and maintenance on equipment. These costs can be traced to the following activities:

Activity	Cost Driver	Cost	Activity Level	
			Commercial	Residential
Office Supplies	Number of Clients Serviced	$ 8,000	15	45
Equipment Depreciation and Maintenance	Equipment Hours	18,000	3,500	2,500
Garden Supplies	Area Covered (computed as number of square yards of garden times number of times garden is serviced per year)	36,000	65,000	35,000
Total Overhead		$62,000		

Recalculate profits for commercial and residential services based on these activity bases.

c. What recommendations do you have for management?

29. **ABC versus traditional costing.** Earthtec Corporation manufactures metal detectors and ore test kits. Overhead costs are currently allocated using direct labor hours, but the controller has recommended an activity-based costing system using the following data:

			Activity Level	
Activity	Cost Driver	Cost	Metal Detectors	Ore Test Kits
Production Setup	Number of Setups	$50,000	10	15
Material Handling and Requisition	Number of Parts	15,000	18	36
Packaging and Shipping	Number of Units Shipped	30,000	45,000	75,000
Total Overhead		$95,000		

a. Compute the amount of overhead allocated to each of the products under activity-based costing.
b. Compute the amount of overhead to be allocated to each product using labor hours as the allocation base. Assume 30,000 labor hours were used to assemble metal detectors and 90,00 labor hours were used to assemble ore test kits.
c. Should the company adopt an ABC system?

30. **ABC versus traditional costing.** Vicki Greenshade, CPA, provides consulting and tax preparation services to her clients. She charges a fee of $100 per hour for each service. Her revenues and expenses for the year are shown in the following income statement:

	Tax	Consulting	Total
Revenue	$80,000	$120,000	$200,000
Expenses:			
Filing, scheduling, and data entry	———	———	40,000
Supplies	———	———	36,000
Computer costs....................	———	———	20,000
Profit	———	———	$104,000

Vicki has kept records of the following data for cost allocation purposes:

		Activity Level	
Expenses	Cost Driver	Tax Preparation	Consulting
Filing, scheduling, and data entry	Number of Clients	72	48
Supplies	Number of Hours Billed	800	1,200
Computer costs	Computer Hours	1,000	600

a. Complete the income statement using Vicki's three cost drivers.
b. Recompute the income statement for using hours billed as the only allocation base.
c. How might Vicki's decisions be altered if she were to use only hours billed to allocate expenses?

31. **When do ABC and traditional methods yield similar results?** Refer to Exercise 30. In general, under what circumstances would the two allocation methods in parts **a** and **b** result in similar profit results?

32. **Resources used versus resources supplied.** Information about two activities for the Condor Corporation follows:

	Cost Driver Rate	Cost Driver Volume
Resources Used		
Energy	$6	500 machine hours
Marketing	25	200 sales calls
Resources Supplied		
Energy	$3,300	
Marketing	6,000	

Compute unused capacity for energy and marketing.

33. **Resources used versus resources supplied.** Information about resources for Sysmatic Publishing, which produces brochures, follows:

	Cost Driver Rate	Cost Driver Volume
Resources Used		
Setups	$175	50 runs
Administrative	300	20 jobs
Resources Supplied		
Setups	$8,925	
Administrative	6,300	

Compute unused capacity for these items.

PROBLEMS

34. **Comparative income statements and management analysis.** Comfort Plus, Inc., manufactures two types of mattresses: Dreamer and Sleeper. Dreamer has a complex design that uses gel-filled compartments to provide support. Sleeper is simpler to manufacture and uses conventional padding. Last year, Comfort Plus had the following revenues and costs:

Income Statement for Comfort Plus, Inc.

	Dreamer	Sleeper	Total
Revenue	$390,000	$368,000	$758,000
Direct Materials	110,000	100,000	210,000
Direct Labor	80,000	40,000	120,000
Indirect Costs:			
Administration	_____	_____	39,000
Production Setup	_____	_____	90,000
Quality Control	_____	_____	60,000
Sales and Marketing	_____	_____	120,000
Operating Profit	_____	_____	$119,000

Comfort Plus currently uses labor costs to allocate all overhead, but management is considering implementing an activity-based costing system. After interviewing the sales and production staff, management decides to allocate administrative costs on the basis of direct labor costs, but to use the following bases to allocate the remaining overhead:

Activity	Cost Driver	Activity Level	
		Dreamer	Sleeper
Production Setup	Number of Production Runs	15	15
Quality Control	Number of Inspections	30	50
Sales and Marketing	Number of Advertisements	20	40

a. Complete the income statement using the activity bases above.
b. Write a brief report indicating how management could use activity-based costing to reduce costs.
c. Restate the income statement for Comfort Plus, Inc., using direct labor costs as the only overhead allocation base.
d. Write a report to management stating why product line profits differ using activity-based costing compared to the traditional approach. Indicate whether activity-based costing provides more accurate information and why (if you believe it does provide more accurate information). Indicate in your report how the use of labor-based overhead allocation could result in Comfort Plus management making suboptimal decisions.

35. **Resources used versus resources supplied.** Selected information about resources for Falcon Footwear is as follows:

	Cost Driver Rate	Cost Driver Volume
Resources Used		
Materials	$ 3	4,000
Energy	12	170
Setups	75	40
Purchasing	60	40
Customer Service	40	25
Long-term Labor	50	160
Administrative	35	210
Resources Supplied		
Materials	$12,000	
Energy	2,280	
Setups	3,150	
Purchasing	2,580	
Customer Service	1,200	
Long-term Labor	10,000	
Administrative	8,750	

a. Compute unused capacity for these items.
b. Write a short report stating why managers should know the difference between resources used and resources supplied. Give examples of how managers could use the information on resources used and resources supplied.

36. **Comparative income statements and management analysis.** Fleetfoot, Inc., manufactures two types of shoes: Marathon and B-Ball. Last year, Fleetfoot had the following costs and revenues:

FLEETFOOT, INC.
Income Statement

	B-Ball	Marathon	Total
Revenue	$360,000	$400,000	$760,000
Direct Materials	50,000	50,000	100,000
Direct Labor	180,000	120,000	300,000
Indirect Costs:			
Administration			50,000
Production Setup			80,000
Quality Control			75,000
Sales and Marketing			30,000
Operating Profit			$125,000

Fleetfoot, Inc., currently uses labor costs to allocate all overhead, but management is considering implementing an activity-based costing system. After interviewing the sales and production staff, management decides to allocate administrative costs on the basis of direct labor costs, but to use the following cost drivers to allocate the remaining overhead:

Activity	Cost Driver	Activity Level B-Ball	Activity Level Marathon
Production Setup	Number of Production Runs	150	250
Quality Control	Number of Inspections	300	200
Sales and Marketing	Number of Advertisements	60	40

a. Complete the income statement using the cost drivers above.
b. Write a report indicating how management might use activity-based costing to reduce costs.
c. Restate the income statement for Fleetfoot using direct labor costs as the only overhead allocation base.
d. Write a report to management stating why product line profits differ using activity-based costing compared to the traditional approach. Indicate whether activity-based costing provides more accurate information and why (if you believe it does provide more accurate information). Indicate in your report how the use of labor-based overhead allocation could result in Fleetfoot management making suboptimal decisions.

37. **Implementing activity-based management.**[10] Robert Lutz, president and chief operating officer at Chrysler, was determined to replace the company's old cost-accounting system with a system that could report costs by process and that could separate value-added from nonvalue-added activities. After reading an article about activity-based costing, Lutz decided this was the system for Chrysler.

---

[10]Based on an article by J. A. Ness and T. G. Cucuzza, "Tapping the Full Potential of ABC," *Harvard Business Review*, July–August 1995, pp. 130–138.

As Chrysler introduced ABC, many employees at various levels resisted. The new system represented a threat by changing the existing power structure and revealing inefficient processes hidden by the old cost-accounting system.

Write a short report to Mr. Lutz explaining why you think the Chrysler employees opposed ABC. Recommend steps to take to mitigate the resistance of employees to the new activity-based costing system.

38. **ABC and predetermined overhead rates.** Camera Shy, Inc., makes three types of sunglasses: Nerds, Stars, and Fashions. Camera Shy, Inc., presently applies overhead using a predetermined rate based on direct labor hours. A consultant recommended that Camera Shy, Inc., switch to activity-based costing. Management decided to give ABC a try, and identified the following activities, cost drivers, and estimated costs for Year 2 for each activity center.

Activity	Recommended Cost Driver	Estimated	
		Costs	Cost Driver Units
Production Setup	Number of Production Runs	$ 30,000	100
Order Processing	Number of Orders	50,000	200
Materials Handling	Pounds of Materials Used	20,000	8,000
Equipment Depreciation and Maintenance	Machine Hours	60,000	10,000
Quality Management	Number of Inspections	50,000	440
Packing and Shipping	Number of Units Shipped	40,000	20,000
Total Estimated Overhead		$250,000	

The company estimated 5,000 labor hours would be worked in Year 2. Assume the following activities occurred in February of Year 2:

	Nerds	Stars	Fashions
Number of Units Produced	1,000	500	400
Direct Materials Costs	$4,000	$2,500	$2,000
Direct Labor Hours	200	150	87
Number of Orders	8	8	4
Number of Production Runs	1	2	6
Pounds of Material	400	200	200
Machine Hours	400	200	200
Number of Inspections	10	10	10
Units Shipped	1,000	500	300
Direct labor costs are $20 per hour.			

a. Compute an overhead allocation rate for each of the cost drivers recommended by the consultant and for direct labor.

b. Compute the production costs for each product for February using the cost drivers recommended by the consultant.

c. Management has seen your numbers and wants to know how you account for the discrepancy between the product costs using only direct labor hours as the allocation base and using activity-based costing. Write a brief response to management, including calculation of product costs using direct labor hours to allocate overhead.

39. **Choosing an ABC system.** Raleigh Corporation manufactures three bicycle models: a racing bike, a mountain bike, and a children's model. The racing model is made of a titanium-aluminum alloy and is called the Aerolight. The mountain bike is called the Summit and is made of aluminum. The steel-framed children's bike is called the Spinner. Because of the different materials used, production processes differ significantly between models in terms of machine types and time requirements. However, once parts are produced, assembly time per unit required for each type of bike is similar. For this reason, Raleigh had adopted the practice of allocating overhead on the basis of machine hours. Last year, the company produced 1,000 Aerolights, 2,000 Summits, and 5,000 Spinners and had the following revenues and expenses:

RALEIGH CORPORATION
Income Statement

	Aerolight	Summit	Spinner	Total
Sales	$380,000	$560,000	$475,000	$1,415,000
Direct Costs				
Direct Materials	150,000	240,000	200,000	590,000
Direct Labor	14,400	24,000	54,000	92,400
Variable Overhead				
Machine Setup	_____	_____	_____	26,000
Order Processing	_____	_____	_____	64,000
Warehousing Costs	_____	_____	_____	93,000
Depreciation of Machines . . .	_____	_____	_____	42,000
Shipping	_____	_____	_____	36,000
Contribution Margin	_____	_____	_____	$ 471,600
Fixed Overhead				
Plant Administration				88,000
Other Fixed Overhead				140,000
Operating Profit				$ 243,600

The CFO of Raleigh had heard about activity-based costing and hired a consultant to recommend cost allocation bases. The consultant recommended the following:

		Activity Level		
Activity	**Cost Driver**	**Aerolight**	**Summit**	**Spinner**
Machine Setup	Number of Production Runs	8	14	18
Order Processing	Number of Sales Orders Received	200	300	300
Warehousing Costs	Number of Units Held in Inventory	100	100	200
Depreciation	Machine Hours	5,000	8,000	12,000
Shipping	Number of Units Shipped	500	2,000	5,000

The consultant found no basis for allocating the plant administration and other fixed overhead costs and recommended that these not be applied to products.

a. Using machine hours to allocate variable overhead, complete the income statement for Raleigh Corporation. Do not attempt to allocate fixed overhead.

b. Complete the income statement using the cost drivers recommended by the consultant.

c. How might activity-based costing result in better decisions by Raleigh management?

d. After hearing the consultant's recommendations, the CFO decided to adopt activity-based costing, but expressed concern about not allocating some of the overhead (administration and other fixed overhead) to the products. In the CFO's view, "Products have to bear a fair share of all overhead or we won't be covering all our costs." How would you respond to this comment?

40. Resources used versus resources supplied. Selected information about resources for the Medallion China Company is as follows:

	Cost Driver Rate	Cost Driver Volume
Resources Used		
Materials	$4	2,000
Short-term Labor	35	215
Setups	120	20
Purchasing	40	50
Customer Service	40	25
Marketing	30	100
Administrative	20	150
Resources Supplied		
Materials	$8,000	
Short-term Labor	7,560	
Setups	3,000	
Purchasing	2,400	
Customer Service	1,280	
Marketing	3,600	
Administrative	4,000	

a. Compute unused capacity for these items.

b. Write a short report stating why managers should know the difference between resources used and resources supplied. Give examples of how managers could use information about resources used and resources supplied.

41. Activity-based reporting. The Beam Corporation manufactures airplane propellers. Information regarding resources for the month of March follows:

	Resources Used	Resources Supplied
Parts Management	$3,000	$3,500
Energy	5,000	5,000
Quality Inspections	4,500	5,000
Long-term Labor	2,500	3,500
Short-term Labor	2,000	2,400
Setups	7,000	10,000
Materials	15,000	15,000
Depreciation	6,000	10,000
Marketing	7,000	7,500
Customer Service	1,000	2,000
Administrative	5,000	7,000

In addition, $2,500 was spent on ten engineering changes with a cost driver of $250, and $3,000 was spent on four outside contracts with a cost driver rate of $750. There was no unused capacity for these two activities. Sales for March were $100,000. Management has requested that you:

a. prepare a traditional income statement (like Exhibit 5.9).
b. prepare an activity-based income statement (like Exhibit 5.10).
c. write a short report explaining why the activity-based income statement provides better information to managers. Use information for Beam Corporation in examples.

42. **Benefits of activity-based costing** (CMA adapted). Many companies recognize that their cost systems are inadequate for today's global market. Managers in companies selling multiple products are making important product decisions based on distorted cost information. Most systems of the past were designed to focus on inventory valuation. If management should decide to implement an activity-based costing system, what benefits should they expect?

43. **Benefits of activity-based costing** (CMA adapted). Moss Manufacturing has just completed a major change in the method it uses to inspect its products. Previously ten inspectors examined the product after each major process. The salaries of these inspectors were charged as direct labor to the operation or job. In an effort to improve efficiency, the Moss production manager recently bought a computerized quality control system consisting of a microcomputer, 15 video cameras, peripheral hardware, and software. The cameras are placed at key points in the production process, taking pictures of the product and comparing these pictures with a known "good" image supplied by a quality control engineer. This new system allowed Moss to replace the ten quality control inspectors with only two quality control engineers.

The president of the company is confused. She was told that the production process was now more efficient, yet she notices a large increase in the factory overhead rate. The computation of the rate before and after automation is as follows:

	Before	After
Budgeted Overhead	$1,900,000	$2,100,000
Budgeted Direct Labor	1,000,000	700,000
Budgeted Overhead Rate	190%	300%

How might an activity-based costing system benefit Moss Manufacturing and clear up the president's confusion?

44. **Activity-based reporting.** The Almay Corporation manufactures oxygen tanks for deep-sea divers. Information regarding resources for the month of March follows at the top of page 185.

In addition, $22,000 was spent on 800 quality inspections with a cost driver rate of $25, and $8,000 was spent on 200 customer service cost driver units with a cost driver rate of $30. Sales for March were $350,000. Management has requested that you:

a. prepare a traditional income statement (like Exhibit 5.9).

	Resources Used	Resources Supplied
Marketing	$28,000	$30,000
Depreciation	24,000	40,000
Outside Contracts	12,000	12,000
Materials	60,000	60,000
Setups	14,000	20,000
Energy	20,000	21,000
Parts Management	15,000	16,000
Engineering Changes	10,000	12,000
Short-term Labor	7,000	7,000
Long-term Labor	10,000	14,000
Administrative	20,000	26,000

    b. prepare an activity-based income statement (like Exhibit 5.10).

    c. write a short report explaining why the activity-based income statement provides better information to managers. Use information for Almay Corporation in examples.

45. **Customer response time.** The Farlain Corporation, which manufactures customer motorcycle racing equipment and parts, engages in the following activities (not in sequence):

    a. phone sales to motorcycle shops

    b. processing mail-in orders

    c. queuing orders to be shipped

    d. sending order to appropriate production department at the end of each day

    e. on-site salespeople call in orders at the end of each day

    f. shipping parts

    g. quality inspection during production

    h. catalog orders taken over the phone

    i. production department orders special materials for ordered parts

    j. queuing order in production department

    k. setup of machinery to produce part according to specifications

    l. production of part

    m. on-site sales to motorcycle shops

    n. classifying orders according to process required for production

    o. quality inspection after production

    p. sending part to shipping department

    q. on-site booths for taking orders at races

    r. holding parts until completion of other parts in order

Categorize these activities according to the elements of customer response time shown in Exhibit 5.3. Write a short report to management detailing what you think could be done to reduce customer response time.

SUGGESTED SOLUTIONS TO EVEN-NUMBERED EXERCISES

26. Activity-based costing.
a. and b. Cost per trip:

Activities	Float Trips (3-day)	Whitewater Trips (3-day)
Advertising	$ 215	$ 215
Permit to Use the River	$ 30	$ 50
Equipment Use	$ 160 [= ($5 × 28) + $20]	$ 264 [= ($8 × 28) + $40]
Insurance	$ 75	$ 127
Paying Guides	$1,200 (= $300 × 4 guides)	$1,600 (= $400 × 4 guides)
Food	$1,680 (= $60 × 28)	$1,680 (= $60 × 28)
Total	$3,360	$3,936

c. If the manager wants to cover her costs, she should charge $140 per customer for the 3-day float trip ($3,360/24 paying customers) and $164 per customer for the 3-day whitewater trip ($3,936/24) paying customers).

28. Activity-based costing in a nonmanufacturing environment.
a. *Using labor hours.*

	Commercial	Residential	Total
Revenue	$66,500[a]	$143,000[b]	$209,500
Direct Labor	31,500[c]	58,500[d]	90,000
Overhead	21,700[e]	40,300[f]	62,000
Profit	$13,300	$ 44,200	$ 57,500

[a]$66,500 = 3,500 hours × $19 per hour
[b]$143,000 = 6,500 hours × $22 per hour
[c]$31,500 = 3,500 hours × $9 per hour
[d]$58,500 = 6,500 hours × $9 per hour
[e]$21,700 = ($62,000/10,000 hours) × 3,500 hours
[f]$40,300 = ($62,000/10,000 hours) × 6,500 hours

b. *Using the three cost drivers.*

	Rate	Commercial	Residential	Total
Revenue[a]		$66,500	$143,000	$209,500
Direct Labor		31,500	58,500	90,000
Overhead				
Office Supplies	$133.33[b]	2,000[e]	6,000	8,000
Equipment	3.00[c]	10,500[f]	7,500	18,000
Garden Supplies	0.36[d]	23,400[g]	12,600	36,000
Total Overhead		35,900	26,100	62,000
Profit		$ (900)	$ 58,400	$ 57,500

[a]From part **a**
[b]$133.33 per client = $8,000/60 clients served
[c]$3.00 per hour = $18,000/6,000 equipment hours
[d]$0.36 per square yard = $36,000/100,000 square yards
[e]$2,000 = $133.33 × 15 commercial clients
[f]$10,500 = $3.00 × 3,500 equipment hours
[g]$23,400 = $0.36 × 65,000 square yards

c. Ms. Plantcare should reconsider reducing residential services in favor of the commercial business. From the results in part **b,** commercial work is losing money, while the residential business is making a profit. The cost driver analysis shows that commercial work, which provides only about 30 percent of the revenues, incurs most of the equipment and garden supplies overhead costs. Allocating overhead costs based on direct labor, as in part **a,** implies commercial business incurs about 35 percent of the total overhead whereas the cost driver analysis in part **b** shows commercial business incurs more than one-half of the total overhead.

30. ABC versus traditional costing.

a.

Account	Rate	Tax	Consulting	Total
Revenue		$80,000	$120,000	$200,000
Expenses				
Filing, scheduling, and data entry	$333.33[a]	24,000[d]	16,000	40,000
Supplies	18.00[b]	14,400[e]	21,600	36,000
Computer costs	12.50[c]	12,500[f]	7,500	20,000
Profit		$29,100	$74,900	$104,000

[a]$333.33 per client = $40,000/120 clients
[b]$18 per hour billed = $36,000/2,000 hours billed
[c]$12.50 per computer hour = $20,000/1,600 hours
[d]$24,000 = $333.33 per client × 72 clients
[e]$14,400 = $18 per hour × 800 hours
[f]$12,500 = $12.50 per computer hour × 1,000 hours

b.

Account	Rate	Tax	Consulting	Total
Revenue		$80,000	$120,000	$200,000
Expenses	$48[a]	38,400[b]	57,600	96,000
Profit		$41,600	$62,400	$104,000

[a]2,000 hours billed = $200,000 revenue/$100 per hour. $48 per hour = ($40,000 + $36,000 + $20,000)/2,000 hours.
[b]$38,400 = $48 per labor hour × 800 hours of labor

c. The cost driver approach shows consulting generates 62 percent profit-to-revenue whereas tax generates only about 36 percent. Consulting appears to be more profitable. However, under labor-based costing in **b** consulting work appears relatively less profitable. Believing that to be the case, Vicki might erroneously concentrate more heavily in tax work.

32. Resources used versus resources supplied.

	Supplied	− Used	= Unused
Energy	$3,300	− ($6 × 500)	= $300 or ($300/$6 = 50 hours)
Marketing	$6,000	− ($25 × 200)	= $1,000 or ($1,000/$25 = 40 sales calls)

CHAPTER 6

DIFFERENTIAL COST ANALYSIS: MARKETING DECISIONS

LEARNING OBJECTIVES

1. Understand the differential principle and know how to identify costs for differential analysis.
2. Describe the major influences on pricing.
3. Differentiate between short-run and long-run pricing decisions.
4. Know what costs must be covered by prices.
5. Understand how the value chain and product life cycle influence long-run pricing decisions.
6. Understand how to base target costs on target prices.
7. Understand how to use differential analysis to determine customer profitability.

Managers use accounting information to make marketing decisions, such as pricing, accepting special orders, and determining customer profitability. This chapter and Chapter 7 deal with several applications of one principle—**differential analysis,** the analysis of differences among particular alternative actions.[1] Owners typically judge management's performance on the basis of a firm's profitability. Thus managers want to know the differential effect of various alternative actions on profits. As you go through each application of differential analysis, we encourage you to keep the following questions in mind: What activities differ among the alternatives? How does that difference affect operating profits?

Virtually all managers use differential analysis. We see differential analysis used by professional sports teams, such as in the San Francisco Giants' acquisition of Barry Bonds and the Los Angeles Lakers' acquisition of Shaquille O'Neal.

---

[1]Differential analysis is also known as *incremental analysis* or, less accurately, *marginal analysis*. See Glossary for distinction.

THE DIFFERENTIAL PRINCIPLE

Managerial decision making is the process of choosing among alternatives. Each alternative represents a set of activities that will result in costs and revenues. The differential analysis model, shown in Exhibit 6.1, extends the cost-volume-profit model discussed in Chapter 4. The first column represents the alternative being considered. The second column presents the **status quo,** or what is expected if no change is made. The third column shows the difference between the status quo and the alternative. If the difference is such that $\pi_1 > \pi_0$, the alternative is more profitable than the status quo. If $\pi_0 > \pi_1$, the status quo is more profitable. A *differential cost* is a cost that changes (differs) as a result of changing activities or levels of activities.

The following example illustrates differential analysis. To provide continuity, we use the facts from this example throughout the chapter. We use a manufacturing firm in this illustration because it is the most comprehensive and complex of any type of organization. The concepts apply as well to service, financial, merchandising, and other organizations.

Example   Assume the following status quo data for Ullman Educational Videos, a company that produces tutorial videos for primary and preschool use.

Units Made and Sold	800 Units per Month
Maximum Production and Sales Capacity	1,200 Units per Month
Selling Price	$30

Activity Classification and Resulting Costs	Variable Cost (per unit)	Fixed Cost (per month)
Manufacturing	$17	$3,060
Marketing and Administrative	5	1,740
Total Costs	$22	$4,800

The management of the Ullman Company believes that it can increase volume from 800 units to 900 units per month by decreasing the selling price from $30 to $28 per unit. Would the price reduction be profitable given that the activities would be unaffected on a per-unit basis? The differential analysis for this example indicates that the alternative would not increase profits. Exhibit 6.2 shows the alternative's profit is only $600 whereas the status quo generates $1,600 in profits.

RELEVANT COSTS

Note in Exhibit 6.2 that this particular decision does not affect all costs. Specifically, fixed costs due to manufacturing, marketing, and administrative activities in this example do not change. Thus only revenues and *total* variable costs are relevant to the analysis; fixed costs are not. We sometimes call differential analysis **relevant cost analysis** as it identifies the costs (or revenues) relevant to the decision. A cost or revenue is *relevant* if an amount appears in the Difference column; all others are irrelevant. Thus we could ignore fixed costs in this example. (This is not true in general.

EXHIBIT 6.1

Differential Analysis Model[a]

	Alternative	–	Status Quo	=	Difference
Revenue	$P_1 X_1$	–	$P_0 X_0$	=	ΔPX
Less Variable Costs	$V_1 X_1$	–	$V_0 X_0$	=	ΔVX
Total Contribution Margin	$(P_1 - V_1)X_1$	–	$(P_0 - V_0)X_0$	=	$\Delta(P - V)X$
Less Fixed Costs	F_1	–	F_0	=	ΔF
Operating Profit	π_1	–	π_0	=	$\Delta \pi$

[a]P = price per unit; X = volume per period; V = variable cost per unit; $P - V$ = contribution margin per unit; F = fixed costs per period; π = operating profit per period; Δ = amount of difference.

Fixed costs nearly always differ in long-run decisions involving changes in capacity, and they sometimes differ in short-run operating decisions, as we shall see later in this chapter.)

As you become familiar with differential analysis, you will find shortcuts by ignoring irrelevant costs (and revenues) from the outset of your work. For instance, you needed to work only with revenues and total variable costs in the previous example to get the answer.

FOCUS ON CASH FLOWS

The emphasis on **cash flows** is fundamental for two reasons:

1. Cash is the medium of exchange.
2. Cash is a common, objective measure of the benefits and costs of alternatives.

EXHIBIT 6.2

ULLMAN EDUCATIONAL VIDEOS
Differential Analysis of a Price Reduction[a]

	Alternative $P = \$28$ $X = 900$	–	Status Quo $P = \$30$ $X = 800$	=	Difference
Revenue	$\$25,200$[b]	–	$\$24,000$[d]	=	$\$ 1,200$
Less Variable Costs	$19,800$[c]	–	$17,600$[e]	=	$2,200$
Total Contribution Margin	$\$ 5,400$	–	$\$ 6,400$	=	$\$(1,000)$
Less Fixed Costs	$4,800$	–	$4,800$	=	0
Operating Profit	$\$ \quad 600$	–	$\$ 1,600$	=	$\$(1,000)$

[a]Numbers within parentheses are losses; numbers with minus signs are the result of row operations.
[b]$\$25,200 = \$28 \times 900$ Units.
[c]$\$19,800 = \$22 \times 900$ Units.
[d]$\$24,000 = \$30 \times 800$ Units.
[e]$\$17,600 = \$22 \times 800$ Units.

Consequently, differential analysis focuses mostly on differential cash flows due to changes in activities. The previous example assumed both differential revenues and costs to be cash flows or near-cash flows (for example, it assumed that revenues and costs on account are cash flows).

UNCERTAINTY AND DIFFERENTIAL ANALYSIS

Cost and revenue estimates for the status quo are usually more certain than estimates for alternatives. The status quo represents something known, whereas estimates for alternatives may be little more than educated guesses. When considering an alternative, the types of activities, the level of activities, and the cost of activities are all estimates subject to error. Analysts may easily omit some critical aspect of the alternative.

Most managers are averse to risk and uncertainty unless they receive additional compensation to bear risk. They prefer the known to the unknown, all other things being equal. Consequently, we sometimes see managers rejecting, because of uncertainty, an alternative expected to be more profitable than the status quo. Managers often deal with uncertainty and differential analysis by setting high standards for the alternative. (For example, "The alternative must increase profits by 25 percent before we will accept it.") Some organizations set incentives for managers to take risks in these situations.

MAJOR INFLUENCES ON PRICING

Companies have become customer driven, focusing on delivering quality products at competitive prices. The three major influences on pricing decisions are customers, competitors, and costs:

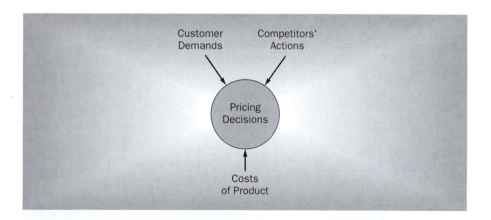

CUSTOMERS

Managers examine pricing problems through the eyes of their customers. Increasing prices may cause the loss of a customer to a competitor or it may cause a customer to choose a less expensive substitute product.

COMPETITORS

Competitors' reactions also influence pricing decisions. A competitor's aggressive pricing may force a business to lower its prices to be competitive. On the other hand, a business without a competitor can set higher prices. If a business has knowledge of its competitors' technology, plant capacity, and operating policies, it is able to estimate the competitors' costs, which is valuable in pricing decisions.

Increasingly, managers consider both their domestic and international competition in making pricing decisions. Firms with excess capacity because demand is low in domestic markets may price aggressively in their export markets. For instance, a software development company like Microsoft with high development costs and low variable costs may seek out foreign markets. In a foreign market the company can exploit the high development costs already incurred, while pricing lower than local competitors who must incur high development costs before they can produce anything.

COSTS

A product that is consistently priced below its cost can drain large amounts of resources from an organization. Cost-volume-profit analysis assists in determining the profits that result from different combinations of price and output sold for a particular product.

In making pricing decisions, companies weigh customers, competitors, and costs differently. Companies selling homogeneous products in highly competitive markets must accept the market price. Managers have some discretion in setting prices in markets with little competition, however. The pricing decision considers the value customers place on the product, the pricing strategies of competitors, and the costs of the product.

Pricing is an area where newly evolving themes, such as customer satisfaction, continuous improvement, and the dual internal/external focus, come together. For instance, lower prices for quality products are conducive to customer satisfaction—an external focus. However, when prices are lower, costs must be reduced as well. The internal focus on continuous improvement is the key to cutting costs.

SHORT-RUN VERSUS LONG-RUN PRICING DECISIONS

The time horizon of the decision is critical in computing the relevant costs in a pricing decision. The two ends of the time-horizon spectrum are:

Short-run decisions include pricing for a one-time-only special order with no long-term implications. The time horizon is typically six months or less. Long-run deci-

EXHIBIT 6.3

ULLMAN EDUCATIONAL VIDEOS
Differential Analysis of a Special Order

	Alternative	–	Status Quo	=	Difference
Revenue	$26,500[a]	–	$24,000	=	$2,500
Less Variable Costs	19,800[b]	–	17,600	=	2,200
Total Contribution	$ 6,700	–	$ 6,400	=	$ 300
Less Fixed Costs	4,800	–	4,800	=	0
Operating Profit	$ 1,900	–	$ 1,600	=	$ 300

[a] $26,500 = $24,000 + ($25 × 100 units).
[b] $19,800 = $17,600 + ($22 × 100 units).

sions include pricing a main product in a major market. For example, a special order to Nike for shoes for an athletic team would be a short-run pricing decision, whereas introducing a new type of running shoe to the market would be a long-run decision.

SHORT-RUN PRICING DECISIONS: SPECIAL ORDERS

The differential approach particularly helps in making special-order decisions. Assume Ullman Educational Videos has an opportunity to make a one-time sale of 100 units at $25 per unit to a state prison system. Exhibit 6.3 presents an analysis of the effects of not accepting and of accepting the special order. Assume the regular market is 800 units sold at a price of $30 a unit. Exhibit 6.3 demonstrates that Ullman should accept the special order at $25 per unit, because that price permits the firm to cover the differential costs of $22 per unit and provide a contribution of $3 per unit toward covering fixed costs and earning a profit.

DIFFERENTIAL APPROACH TO PRICING

The differential approach to pricing is useful for both short-run and long-run decisions. The differential approach to pricing presumes that the price must at least equal the **differential cost** of producing and selling the product. In the short run, this practice will result in a positive contribution to covering fixed costs and generating profit. In the long run, this practice will require covering all costs, *because both fixed and variable costs become differential costs in the long run.*

Consider the data for the Ullman Educational Videos in Exhibit 6.4. The minimum acceptable price in the short run is the differential cost of $22 per unit. In the long run, the minimum acceptable price is $28 per unit, because the firm must cover both variable and fixed costs. A more desirable long-run price is the current price, $30, which provides a profit. The firm may set a price slightly higher than the variable cost for a special order as long as excess capacity exists and doing so will not affect the firm's regular market.

EXHIBIT 6.4

ULLMAN EDUCATIONAL VIDEOS
Data for Pricing

Short-Run Differential Costs (variable costs)	$22	= Short-Run Minimum Price
Fixed Cost	6[a]	
Long-Run Incremental Costs	$28	= Long-Run Minimum Price
Expected Profits	2	
Target Selling Price	$30	= Long-Run Desired Price

---

[a]$6 = $4,800/800. This assumes a long-run volume of 800 units.

Suppose Ullman Educational Videos wants to price aggressively. It can set a price slightly higher than the $22 minimum. Managers hope to underprice competitors and to capture a larger share of the market. If the firm is the only supplier of this product, it can charge a price higher than $28. If the firm sets the price too high, however, its high profits may entice competitors into the market.

PROBLEM 6.1 FOR SELF-STUDY

Applying differential analysis. Boilermaker Technologies, Inc., produces a valve used in electric turbine systems. The costs of the valve at the company's normal volume of 5,000 units per month appear below. Unless otherwise specified, assume a selling price of $1,750.

Cost Data for Boilermaker Technologies

Unit Manufacturing Costs:		
Variable Materials	$250	
Variable Labor	175	
Variable Overhead	75	
Fixed Overhead	150	
Total Unit Manufacturing Costs		$ 650
Unit Nonmanufacturing Costs:		
Variable	$200	
Fixed	175	
Total Unit Nonmanufacturing Costs		375
Total Unit Costs		$1,025

Market research estimates that a price increase to $1,900 per unit would decrease monthly volume to 4,500 units. The accounting department estimates total variable costs would decrease proportionately with volume and total fixed costs would decrease from $1,625,000 to $1,617,500. Would you recommend that the firm take this action? What would be the impact on monthly revenues, costs, and profits?

The solution to this self-study problem is at the end of the chapter on page 201.

MANAGERIAL APPLICATION

Pricing Practices in Various Countries

Surveys indicate the use of cost-based pricing appears to be more prevalent in the United States than in Ireland, Japan, and the United Kingdom. Although a majority of Japanese companies in assembly-type operations (for example, electronics and automobiles) base prices on costs, cost-based pricing is far less prevalent in Japanese process-type industries (for example, chemicals, oil, and steel). When costs are used for pricing decisions, the pattern is consistent: Overwhelmingly, companies around the globe use full costs rather than variable costs. A later survey of United States industries supported these findings by showing that full-cost pricing dominated pricing practices (69.5 percent), while only 12.1 percent of the respondents used a variable-cost–based approach.[1]

Ranking of Factors That Are Primarily Used to Price Products (1 is most important)

	United States	Japan	Ireland	United Kingdom
Market-based	2	1	1	1
Cost-based	1	2	2	2

[1]Eunsup Shim and Ephraim Sudit, "How Manufacturers Price Products," *Management Accounting,* February 1995.

Sources: Grant Thornton, *Survey of American Manufacturers* (New York: Grant Thornton, 1992); M. Cornick, W. Cooper, and S. Wilson, "How Do Companies Analyze Overhead?" *Management Accounting* (June 1988); C. Drury, S. Braund, P. Osborne and M. Tayles, *A Survey of Management Accounting Practices in U.K. Manufacturing Companies* (London: Chartered Association of Certified Accountants, 1993); and authors' research.

LONG-RUN PRICING DECISIONS

Many firms rely on full cost information reports when setting prices, as discussed in the Managerial Application above, "Pricing Practices in Various Countries." *Full cost* is the total cost of producing and selling a unit, which includes all the costs incurred by the activities that make up the value chain, as shown in Exhibit 6.5.

Typically, the accounting department provides cost reports to the marketing department, which then adds appropriate markups to the costs to set benchmark or target prices for all products normally sold by the firm.

EXHIBIT 6.5

Value Chain Cost Buildup

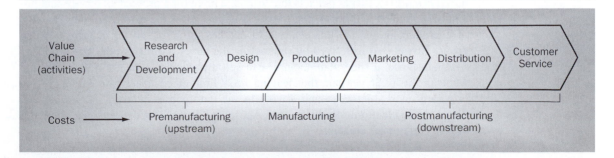

Using the full costs for pricing decisions can be justified in three circumstances:

1. When a firm enters into a long-term contractual relationship to supply a product, most activity costs will depend on the production decisions under the long-term contract. Therefore, full costs are relevant for the long-term pricing decision.
2. Many contracts for the development and production of customized products, and many contracts with governmental agencies specify prices as full costs plus a markup. Prices set in regulated industries such as electric utilities also are based on full costs.
3. Managers sometimes initially set prices based on full costs plus a profit then make short-term adjustments to prices to reflect market conditions. Conversely, when demand for their products is high, they recognize the greater likelihood that the existing capacity of activity resources is inadequate to satisfy all the demand. Accordingly, they adjust the prices upward based on the higher incremental costs when capacity is fully utilized.

LIFE-CYCLE PRODUCT COSTING AND PRICING

The **product life cycle** covers the time from initial research and development to the time at which support to the customer is withdrawn. For motor vehicles, like the Jeep Grand Cherokee, this time span may range from 10 to 20 years. For toys or fashion clothing products, the time span may be less than one year.

Managers estimate the revenues and costs for each product from its initial research and development to its final customer support. Life-cycle costing tracks costs attributable to each product from start to finish. The term *cradle-to-grave costing* conveys the sense of capturing all life-cycle costs associated with a product.

Life-cycle costs provide important information for pricing. For some products, particularly in electronics, the development period is relatively long. Many costs are incurred prior to manufacturing.

A product life-cycle budget highlights to managers the importance of setting prices that will cover costs in all the value-chain categories, as shown in Exhibit 6.5. To be profitable, companies must generate revenue to cover costs in all six categories.

USING TARGET PRICES TO SET TARGET COSTS

Simply stated, target costing is the concept of *price-based costing* (instead of *cost-based pricing*). A **target price** is the estimated price for a product or service that potential customers will be willing to pay. A target cost is the estimated long-run cost of a product or service that when sold enables the company to achieve targeted profit. **Target cost** is derived by subtracting the target profit from the target price.

For instance, a shoe manufacturer can sell a particular style for $33 a pair and wants profits of $6 per pair, thus leaving a $27 limit on costs per pair. Target costing is widely used. Mercedes and Toyota in the automobile industry, Panasonic and Sharp in the electronics industry, and Apple and Toshiba in the personal computer industry use target costing.

MANAGERIAL APPLICATION

A Target Costing Challenge in Forest Products

A forest products company was incurring losses on a particular product. The production people believed that the loss per ton was a price problem rather than a cost problem.

Sales management believed prices were given, based on market competition. To them, the losses were not a sales problem. Manufacturing believed costs were given, based on well-established production processes and materials requirements. To them, the losses were not a manufacturing problem.

Study of a competitor revealed that it was producing the product at a much lower cost. Once management accepted the fact that the product cost was too high, it decided to undertake "re-engineering" of the manufacturing process. Production management set about cutting costs by more than 60 percent.

The result of this project was a dramatic turnaround. The project started with a cost of $2,900 per unit versus a target cost of $1,075 per unit. After about 18 months of price-based costing initiatives, production was able to reduce costs to $1,162 per unit. When the target cost project started, the production management team had no idea that the results could be so dramatic.

Based on J. Shank, "Strategic Cost Management: A Target Costing Field Study," The Amos Tuck School of Business Administration, Dartmouth College, 1995.

Developing target prices and target costs requires the following four steps:

Step 1: Develop a product that satisfies the needs of potential customers.

Step 2: Choose a target price based on customers' perceived value for the product and the prices competitors charge.

Step 3: Derive a target cost by subtracting the desired profit margin from the target price.

Step 4: Perform value engineering to achieve target costs.

Value engineering is a systematic evaluation of all aspects of research and development, design of products and processes, production, marketing, distribution, and customer service, with the objective of reducing costs while satisfying customer needs. Value engineering can result in improvements in product designs, changes in materials specifications, or modifications in process methods.

Value engineering starts with an analysis of the value chain activities. An example of value chain analysis in conjunction with target costing is presented in the Managerial Application above, "A Target Costing Challenge in Forest Products."

LEGAL ISSUES RELATING COSTS TO PRICES

U.S. laws compel managers to consider costs when setting prices. For example, to comply with federal and many state laws, pricing must not be predatory. A business engages in **predatory pricing** when it deliberately prices below its costs in an effort to drive out competitors. Many legal jurisdictions define costs to be full costs. In other cases, courts have allowed companies to price as low as variable costs.

A related issue is "dumping." Under U.S. laws, **dumping** occurs when a foreign company sells a product in the United States at a price below the market value in the country of its creation, and this action materially injures (or threatens to materially injure) an industry in the United States. Dumping has occurred in the steel, semiconductor, and textile industries.

CUSTOMER PROFITABILITY AND DIFFERENTIAL ANALYSIS

You know that companies choose products based on profitability. They also choose customers based on profitability. Differential costing is useful for deciding which customers a firm should keep and which it should stop servicing.

Assume Harrison and Associates, an advertising firm, performs ongoing services for three clients—Sonora Community Hospital, Beairds Department Store, and Servinties Resort. Exhibit 6.6 presents Harrison's revenues and costs by customer and is typical for the last few years.

Exhibit 6.6 shows a loss of $18,000 on services to Servinties. Should Harrison discontinue the Servinties account? The key question is, What are the differential revenues and costs for this client? You learn the following information:

- Dropping the Servinties account will save the cost of services incurred on the account.
- Dropping the Servinties account will have no effect on Harrison's total salaries, rent, or general administration costs.
- Dropping the Servinties account will have no effect on the revenues or cost of services for the other accounts.

Exhibit 6.7 presents the computations. Harrison's operating profits will be $20,000 higher if it keeps the Servinties account. The last column in Exhibit 6.7 shows that the cost savings from dropping the Servinties account, $330,000, is not enough to offset the loss of $350,000 in revenue. This is true because depreciation, rent, and general administration costs will not decrease if the Servinties account is dropped.

EXHIBIT 6.6

HARRISON AND ASSOCIATES
Customer Profitability Analysis
(in thousands)

	Sonora Community Hospital	Beairds Department Store	Servinties Resort	Total
Revenue (fees charged)	$450	$270	$350	$1,070
Operating Costs				
Cost of Services (variable)	$370	$220	$330	$ 920
Salaries, Rent, and General Administration (fixed)	44	26	38	108
Total Operating Costs	$414	$246	$368	$1,028
Operating Profit	$ 36	$ 24	$(18)	$ 42

EXHIBIT 6.7

HARRISON AND ASSOCIATES
Computations for Decision on Dropping the Servinties Account
(in thousands)

	Drop Servinties (total minus Servinties)	Status Quo (total for company)	Difference
Revenue	$720	$1,070	$350 lower
Operating Costs			
Cost of Services (variable)	$590	$ 920	$330 lower
Salaries, Rent, and General Administration ..	108	108	0
Total Operating Costs	$698	$1,028	$330 lower
Operating Profit	$ 22	$ 42	$ 20 lower

The conclusion would be different if, after dropping the Servinties account, Harrison could utilize the extra capacity to generate profits of more than $20,000 per year from another client. Before coming to a final decision, however, Harrison should consider the possibility of changing Servinties into a profitable customer. Harrison should also consider the effect the decision might have on Harrison's reputation for developing stable, long-run relationships.

PROBLEM 6.2 FOR SELF-STUDY

Customer profitability. McKlintoff and Associates, an accounting firm, performs ongoing services for two clients, Jamoca Joe's and Levinon Industries. The following is information about McKlintoff's revenue and costs (in thousands) by customer, which is typical over the last few years.

	Jamoca Joe's	Levinon Industries	Total
Revenue (fees charged)	$460	$700	$1,160
Operating Costs			
Cost of Services (variable)	$425	$610	$1,035
Salaries, Rent, and General Administration (fixed)	40	60	100
Total Operating Costs	$465	$670	$1,135
Operating Profit	$ (5)	$ 30	$ 25

This shows a loss of $5,000 on services to Jamoca Joe's. Use differential analysis to determine if McKlintoff should discontinue the Jamoca Joe's account. Assume only the revenues and cost of services for Jamoca Joe's will be affected if Jamoca Joe's is dropped.

The solution to this self-study problem is at the end of the chapter on page 201.

SUMMARY

The following items correspond to the learning objectives presented at the beginning of the chapter.

1. **Understand the differential principle and know how to identify costs for differential analysis.** The differential analysis model extends the cost-volume-profit model. The relevant costs for differential analysis are the differential costs. The model focuses on cash flows, because cash is the medium of exchange and because cash serves as a common, objective measure of the benefits and costs of alternatives.

2. **Describe the major influences on pricing.** The three major influences on pricing decisions are customers, competitors, and costs.

3. **Differentiate between short-run and long-run pricing decisions.** Short-run decisions include pricing for a special order with no long-term implications. Typically the time horizon is six months or less. Long-run decisions include pricing a main product in a major market.

4. **Know what costs the differential approach requires to be covered.** The differential approach to pricing presumes that the price must at least equal the differential cost of producing and selling the product. In the short run, this practice will result in a positive contribution to covering fixed costs and generating profit. In the long run, this practice will cover all costs because both fixed and variable costs are differential in the long run.

5. **Understand how the value chain and product life cycle influence long-run pricing decisions.** Full cost is the total of all the costs incurred by the activities in the value chain. The product life cycle lasts from initial research and development through termination of customer support. Using full costs for pricing decisions can be justified in three circumstances: (1) when a firm enters into a long-term contractual relationship to supply a product, (2) for development and production of customized products and contracts with the government, and (3) when managers initially set prices to cover full costs plus a profit then adjust to reflect market conditions.

6. **Understand how to base target costs on target prices.** Target pricing is based on customers' perceived value for the product and the prices competitors charge. Target costs equal target prices minus target profits.

7. **Understand how to use differential analysis to determine customer profitability.** Customer profitability is determined using differential analysis with the customer as the cost object.

KEY TERMS AND CONCEPTS

Differential analysis Analysis of differential costs, revenues, profits, investment, cash flow, and the like.

Status quo Events or cost incurrences that will happen or that a firm expects to happen in the absence of taking some contemplated action.

Relevant cost analysis Differential cost analysis; identifies the cost (or revenues) relevant to the decision.

Cash flow Cash receipts minus disbursements from a given asset, or group of assets, for a given period.

Differential cost The amount of change in cost between two alternatives.

Product life cycle The time from initial research and development to the time at which support to the customer is withdrawn.

Target price Price based on customers' perceived value for the product and the prices competitors charge.

Target cost Equals the target price minus desired profit margin.

Value engineering A systematic evaluation of all aspects of research and development, design of products and processes, production, marketing, distribution, and customer service, with the objective of reducing costs while satisfying customer needs.

Predatory pricing Setting prices deliberately below costs in an effort to drive out competitors.

Dumping The practice of a foreign company selling a product in the United States at a price below the market value in the country of its creation, if this action materially injures (or threatens to materially injure) an industry in the United States.

SOLUTIONS TO SELF-STUDY PROBLEMS

SUGGESTED SOLUTION TO PROBLEM 6.1 FOR SELF-STUDY

a.

	Alternative	− Status Quo	=	Difference
Price	$ 1,900	$ 1,750		
Volume	4,500	5,000		
Revenue[a]	$8,550,000 −	$8,750,000	=	$ 200,000 lower
Variable Costs[b]	3,150,000 −	3,500,000	=	350,000 lower
Contribution Margin	$5,400,000 −	$5,250,000	=	$ 150,000 higher
Fixed Costs	1,617,500 −	1,625,000	=	7,500 lower
Operating Profit	$3,782,500 −	$3,625,000	=	$ 157,500 higher

[a]Number of units × sales price.
[b]Number of units × variable costs per unit. (Variable costs per unit = $700.)

Boilermaker Technologies should raise its prices to $1,900.

SUGGESTED SOLUTION TO PROBLEM 6.2 FOR SELF-STUDY

Computations for Decision on Dropping the Jamoca Joe's Account

	Alternative: Drop Jamoca Joe's	Status Quo: Total	Difference
Revenue (fees charged)	$700	$1,160	$460 lower
Operating Costs			
Costs of Services (variable)	610	1,035	425 lower
Salaries, Rent, and General Administration (fixed)	100	100	0
Total Operating Costs	$710	$1,135	$425 lower
Operating Profit	$ (10)	$ 25	$ 35 lower

McKlintoff should not drop Jamoca Joe's in the short run, as profits would drop by $35,000.

QUESTIONS, EXERCISES, AND PROBLEMS

REVIEW QUESTIONS

1. Review the meanings of the concepts or terms given in Key Terms and Concepts.
2. When, if ever, are fixed costs differential?
3. How is the evaluation of short-term pricing decisions different from the evaluation of long-term decisions?
4. Should facility-sustaining costs be considered in making a short-term pricing decision?
5. When is the use of full cost information appropriate for pricing decisions?
6. Production of a special order will increase operating profit when the additional revenue from the special order is greater than
   a. the direct material costs in producing the order.
   b. the fixed costs incurred in producing the order.
   c. the indirect costs of producing the order.
   d. the differential costs of producing the order.
7. In considering a special order situation that will enable a company to make use of idle capacity, which of the following costs would probably not be differential?
   a. materials   c. direct labor
   b. depreciation of buildings   d. variable overhead

CRITICAL ANALYSIS AND DISCUSSION QUESTIONS

8. State and explain the circumstances when using full costs for pricing decisions can be justified.
9. What is a common criticism made against the differential approach to product pricing based on variable cost? How can you refute this criticism?
10. How do you think a sports team uses differential analysis to estimate a player's economic value to the team?
11. "Prices must cover both variable and fixed costs of production." Under what circumstances would you agree or disagree with this statement?
12. What additional costs must be taken into account when making a short-term pricing decision where surplus capacity is not available, and overtime, additional shifts, or other means must be used to expand capacity?
13. Describe three situations in which the use of full costs for pricing decisions is appropriate.
14. Why is full cost information useful for long-term decisions?
15. "This whole subject of differential costing is easy—variable costs are the only costs that are relevant." Respond to this statement.

EXERCISES

Solutions to even-numbered exercises are at the end of the chapter after the problems.

16. **Product choice.** Yuppie Enterprises renovated an old train station into warehouse space, office space, restaurants, and specialty shops. If used all for warehouse space, the estimated revenue and variable costs per year to Yuppie would be $960,000 and $40,000, respectively. If used all for office space, the revenue and variable costs per year would be $982,800 and $70,000, respectively. If used

all for restaurants and specialty shops, the revenue and variable costs would be $1,101,100 and $95,000, respectively. Fixed costs per year would be $600,000 regardless of the alternative chosen.

To which use should Yuppie Enterprises put the old train station?

17. **Special order.** Anticipating unusually high sales for July, Tri-City, a lumber products company, plans to produce 40,000 linear feet of 2 × 4 studs, using all available capacity. Tri-City anticipates costs for July as follows:

Unit Manufacturing Costs per Foot:		
Variable Direct Materials Cost	$0.07	
Variable Labor	0.02	
Variable Overhead	0.01	
Fixed Overhead	0.06	
Total Manufacturing Costs per Foot		$0.16
Unit Marketing Costs per Foot:		
Variable	$0.02	
Fixed	0.11	
Total Marketing Costs per Foot		0.13
Total Unit Costs per Foot		$0.29
Selling Price per Foot		$0.51

On June 30, Tri-City received a contract offer from Housing and Urban Development (HUD), a government agency, to supply 10,000 feet of studs for delivery by July 31. The HUD offer would reimburse Tri-City's share of both variable and fixed manufacturing costs (that is, $0.16 per foot) plus a fixed fee of $2,000. Variable marketing costs would be zero for this order. None of the fixed costs would be affected by this order. Tri-City would lose 10,000 feet of sales to regular customers in July, but this order would not affect sales in any subsequent months.

Prepare a differential analysis comparing the status quo for July with the alternative case in which Tri-City accepts the special order from HUD. Write a brief report to Tri-City's management explaining why the company should or should not accept the special order.

18. **Finding most profitable price-quantity combination.** The Bulls Company is introducing a new product called Michael Dolls and must decide what price should be set. An estimated demand schedule for the product follows:

Price	Quantity Demanded (in units)
$10	40,000
12	36,000
14	28,000
16	24,000
18	18,000
20	15,000

Estimated costs follow:

Variable Manufacturing Costs	$4 per Unit
Fixed Manufacturing Costs	$40,000 per Year
Variable Selling and Administrative Costs	$2 per Unit
Fixed Selling and Administrative Costs	$10,000 per Year

   a. Prepare a schedule showing the total revenue, total cost, and total profit or loss for each selling price.

   b. Which price provides the most profits?

19. **Pricing decisions.** The marketing department of Roma Coffee estimates the following monthly demand for espresso in these five price-volume relations at one of its outlets:

1	5,000 cups at $1.50 per cup
2	4,000 cups at $1.80 per cup
3	3,000 cups at $2.00 per cup
4	2,000 cups at $2.50 per cup
5	1,000 cups at $3.00 per cup

   The fixed costs of $5,000 per month are the same for all of these volumes. Variable costs are $.50 per cup. Which of these prices should Roma charge for its espresso?

20. **Identify differential costs.** Assume Raichle Boot Company is considering making a specially designed snow boot just for the Winter Olympics. Which of the following costs or activities would probably be differential in developing, marketing, producing, and selling the special snow boot?

   a. Product design work to design the boot.

   b. The company president's salary.

   c. Advertising the boot.

   d. The lease of the building in which the boot is made. The building would be unused but the lease would be paid if it were not used to produce this special boot.

   e. Catering costs incurred to provide food at the monthly Board of Directors meeting.

   f. Sales commissions paid to sales personnel who attempt to get sporting goods stores to carry the special boot.

21. **Special order.** Sam's Sport Shop makes jerseys for athletic teams. The Diggers baseball club has offered to buy 80 jerseys for the teams in its league for $18 per jersey. The normal team price for such jerseys is $20. Sam's purchases the plain jerseys for $12 per jersey, then sews a name and number to each jersey at a variable cost of $3 per jersey. Sam's makes about 2,000 jerseys per year and has a capacity limit of 4,000 jerseys. The annual fixed cost of equipment used in the sewing process is $5,000 and other fixed costs allocated to jerseys are $2,000, bringing the total costs allocated to each jersey to $3.50.

   Compute the amount by which the operating profit of Sam's would change if the special order were accepted. Should Sam's accept the special order?

22. **Target costing and pricing.** Brown's Wheels makes wheels for a variety of toys and sports equipment. Brown's sells the wheels to manufacturers who assemble and sell the toys and equipment. The company's market research department has discovered a market for wheels for in-line skates, which Brown's presently does not produce. The market research department has indicated that a set of four wheels for in-line skates would likely sell for $6.

    Assume Brown's desires an operating profit of 20 percent. What is the highest acceptable manufacturing cost for Brown's to produce the sets of wheels?

23. **Target costing and pricing.** Durham Industries makes high-pressure lines for a variety of heavy road-improvement equipment. Durham sells the lines to manufacturers who manufacture and sell the equipment. The company's market research department has discovered a market for high-pressure lines used in automated manufacturing equipment, which Brown's presently does not produce. The market research department has indicated that lines would likely sell for $11 a foot.

    Assume Durham desires an operating profit of 10 percent. What is the highest acceptable manufacturing cost for which Durham would produce the lines?

PROBLEMS

24. **Special order.** Gates Furniture Company has a capacity of 100,000 tables per year. The company is currently producing and selling 80,000 tables per year at a selling price of $400 per table. The cost of producing and selling one table at the 80,000-unit level of activity follows:

Variable Manufacturing Costs	$160
Fixed Manufacturing Costs	40
Variable Selling and Administrative Costs	80
Fixed Selling and Administrative Costs	20
Total Costs	$300

The company has received a special order for 5,000 tables at a price of $260. Because it need not pay sales commission on the special order, the variable selling and administrative costs would be only $50 per table. The special order would have no effect on total fixed costs. The company has rejected the offer based on the following computations:

Selling Price per Table	$260
Variable Manufacturing Costs	160
Fixed Manufacturing Costs	40
Variable Selling and Administrative Costs	50
Fixed Selling and Administrative Costs	20
Net Loss per Table	$ (10)

Management is reviewing its decision and wants your advice. Should Gates have accepted the special order? Show your computations.

25. **Special order.** Southwestern Electronics Company produces precision instruments for airplanes. It currently operates at capacity. It has received an invitation to bid on a government contract for 1,000 specially designed precision instruments. The company has estimated its costs for the contract to be as follows:

Variable Manufacturing Costs	$30,000
Allocated Fixed Manufacturing Costs (not affected by the order)	15,000
Special Design and Production Setup Costs	5,000
Shipping Costs	6,000
Special Administrative Costs	3,000
Total Costs	$59,000
Cost per Precision Instrument ($59,000/1,000)	$ 59

If Southwestern accepts the government contract, it will have to forgo regular sales of 1,000 units. These 1,000 units would have a selling price for $100 each and variable costs of $60 each. The company's total fixed costs would not be affected by accepting the government contract offer. Management has asked your advice in answering the following questions:

a. What is the lowest per-unit price that Southwestern can bid on this contract without sacrificing profits?

b. Southwestern has learned that it will receive the contract if it bids $90 or less per unit. What action should Southwestern take?

26. **Accepting or rejecting an order.** The Austin Company produces a precision part for use in rockets, missiles, and a variety of other products. In the first half of the year, it operated at 80 percent of capacity and produced 160,000 units. Manufacturing costs in that period follow:

Direct Material	$430,000
Direct Labor	770,000
Other Variable Costs	150,000
Fixed Costs	450,000

The parts were all sold at a price of $14 per unit.

The Piper Aircraft Company offers to buy as many units of the part as the Austin Company can supply at a price of $9 per unit. Austin estimates that increasing operations to a 100 percent capacity level would increase office and administrative costs by $50,000 for a six-month period. Management believes that sales to Piper at this price will not affect the company's ability to reach the previous level of sales at the regular price. There are no legal restrictions on selling at the lower price.

Present a schedule indicating whether Austin should accept the Piper offer.

27. **Special order.** The Gilbert Company, a maker of a variety of rubber products, is in the midst of a business downturn and has many idle facilities. The Nationwide Tire Company has approached Gilbert to produce 300,000 oversized tire tubes. Nationwide will pay $2.40 for each tube.

Gilbert predicts that its variable costs will be $2.60 each. Its fixed costs, which had been averaging $2 per unit on a variety of products, will now be spread over twice as much volume, however. An executive commented, "Sure we'll lose $0.20 each on the variable costs, but we'll gain $1 per unit by spreading our fixed costs over more units. Therefore, we should take the offer, because it would gain us $0.80 per unit."

Gilbert currently has a volume of 300,000 units, sales of $1,200,000, variable costs of $780,000, and fixed costs of $600,000.

a. Compute the impact on operating profit if the special order is accepted.

b. Do you agree with the executive? Write a short report explaining why or why not.

28. **Target costing and pricing.** Marklee Industries makes electric motors for a variety of small appliances. Marklee sells the motors to manufacturers who assemble and sell the appliances. The company's market research department has discovered a market for electric motors used for trolling in small fishing boats. Marklee presently does not produce such motors.

The market research department has indicated that the motors would likely sell for $46 each. A similar motor currently being produced has the following manufacturing costs:

Direct Materials	$24
Direct Labor	10
Overhead	8
Total	$42

Assume Marklee desires an operating profit of 10 percent.

a. Suppose Marklee uses cost-plus pricing, setting the price 10 percent above the manufacturing cost. What price would be charged for the motor?

b. Suppose Marklee uses target costing. What is the highest acceptable manufacturing cost for which Marklee would produce the motor?

c. Would you produce such a motor if you were a manager at Marklee? Explain.

29. **Special order.** Marshall's Electronics, Inc., sells high-quality oversized printers for making blueprints. It manufactures two printers, the BP041 and the XBP400, for which the following information is available:

Costs per Unit	BP041	XBP400
Direct Materials	$ 450	$ 550
Direct Labor	600	750
Variable Overhead	750	900
Fixed Overhead	600	750
Total Cost per Unit	$2,400	$2,950
Price	$3,000	$3,900
Units Produced and Sold	400	200

The average wage rate is $20 per hour. The plant has a capacity of 21,000 direct labor hours, but current production uses only 19,500 direct labor hours.

a. A new customer has offered to buy 40 units of XBP400 if its price is lowered to $3,000 per unit. How many direct labor hours will be required to produce 40 units of XBP400? How much will the profit increase (or decrease) if Marshall's accepts this proposal? All other prices will remain the same.

b. Suppose the customer has offered instead to buy 60 units of XBP400 at $3,000 per unit. How much will the profits change if the order is accepted? Assume that the company cannot increase its production capacity to meet the extra demand.

c. Answer the question **b**, assuming instead that the plant can work overtime. Direct labor costs for the overtime production increase to $30 per hour. Variable overhead costs for overtime production are 50 percent more than for normal production.

30. **Pricing decisions.** Assume the marketing department of Holstein Cheeses estimates the following monthly demand for cheddar cheese in these four price-volume relations:

1	10,000 pounds at $2.00 per pound
2	8,000 pounds at $2.50 per pound
3	7,000 pounds at $3.00 per pound
4	5,000 pounds at $3.50 per pound

The fixed costs are $10,000 per month up to 7,500 pounds per month, then they increase to $13,000 per month for volumes over 7,500 pounds per month. Variable costs are $1.00 per pound. Which of these prices should Holstein Cheeses charge for its cheddar cheese?

31. **Pricing decisions.** Assume the marketing department of Allegheny Packs estimates the following annual demand for backpacks in these four price-volume relations:

1	20,000 units at $100 per unit
2	18,000 units at $120 per unit
3	15,000 units at $150 per unit
4	12,000 units at $170 per unit

The fixed costs are $100,000 per year up to 16,000 units, then they increase to $120,000 per year for volumes over 16,000 per year. Variable costs are $60 per unit. Which of these prices should Allegheny Packs charge for its backpacks?

SUGGESTED SOLUTIONS TO EVEN-NUMBERED EXERCISES

16. **Product choice.**
- Alternative 1: Warehouse.
- Alternative 2: Office space.
- Alternative 3: Restaurants and specialty shops.

	Alternative		
	1	**2**	**3**
Revenue	$960,000	$982,800	$1,101,100
Less Variable Costs	40,000	70,000	95,000
Total Contribution Margin	$920,000	$912,800	$1,006,100
Less Fixed Costs	600,000	600,000	600,000
Operating Profit	$320,000	$312,800	$ 406,100

Yuppie Enterprises should choose alternative 3.

18. Finding most profitable price-quantity combination.

a.

Price (1)	Quantity Demanded (2)	Revenues (3)	Total Variable Manufacturing Costsª (4)	Total Variable Selling and Administrative Costsᵇ (5)	Total Costsᶜ (6)	Total Profit (7)
$10	40,000	$400,000	$160,000	$80,000	$290,000	$110,000
12	36,000	432,000	144,000	72,000	266,000	166,000
14	28,000	392,000	112,000	56,000	218,000	174,000
16	24,000	384,000	96,000	48,000	194,000	190,000
18	18,000	324,000	72,000	36,000	158,000	166,000
20	15,000	300,000	60,000	30,000	140,000	160,000

ªQuantity demanded × $4.
ᵇQuantity demanded × $2.
ᶜColumns (4) + (5) + $50,000 (fixed costs).

b. Select a price of $16, because it results in the most profit.

20. Identify differential costs.

The following costs or activities would be differential:

a. Product design work.

c. Advertising the boot.

f. Sales commissions.

22. Target costing and pricing.

$$Price - (20\% \times Price) = \text{Highest Acceptable Cost}$$

$$.8\ Price = Cost$$

$$.8 \times \$6.00 = \$4.80$$

The highest acceptable manufacturing cost for which Brown's would be willing to produce the sets of wheels is $4.80.

CHAPTER 7

DIFFERENTIAL COST ANALYSIS: PRODUCTION

LEARNING OBJECTIVES

1. Apply differential analysis to product choice decisions.
2. Explain and apply the theory of constraints.
3. Identify the factors underlying make-or-buy decisions.
4. Identify the costs of producing joint products and the relevant costs for decisions to sell or process further.
5. Use differential analysis to determine when to add or drop parts of operations.
6. Identify the factors of inventory management decisions.
7. (Appendix 7.1) Use linear programming to optimize the use of scarce resources.
8. (Appendix 7.2) Understand the use of the economic order quantity model.

Managers use accounting information to make such decisions as making versus buying, choosing the optimal mix of products, and managing inventory. We emphasize short-run decisions in this chapter.

This chapter continues applying differential analysis to management problems. Managers must know the differential effect of various alternative actions on profits. As you go through each application of differential analysis, keep the following questions in mind: What activities differ among the alternatives? How does that difference affect operating profits?

PRODUCT CHOICE DECISIONS

One of a manager's most important decisions is which goods to make or services to provide. Firms must choose among alternatives just as students must choose how to allocate their limited study time between accounting and finance, or their time between Question 1 and Question 2 on a final exam. Team salary caps limit the amount professional basketball teams can pay and therefore the number of top players each team can have. In its Detroit Jeep plant, Chrysler must decide how many Limiteds to make, how many Laredos, and how many of the other models. The Gap must decide how many items of which size to carry in its limited retail space.

We normally think of these product choice problems as short-run decisions. With enough time, students can study for *both* accounting and finance. In the short run, however, capacity limitations require choices among options.

Example   The Cinadale Cookie Company has just purchased one machine that can make Plain Wafers, Chocolate-Covered Wafers, and Caramel-Filled Wafers that are also covered in chocolate. The market for these products will absorb all that Cinadale can produce in any combination. Management wants to pick the most profitable product, or combination of products, to produce. The firm has only 400 hours of time available on the machine each month.

The time requirements for each of the three products, their selling prices, and their variable costs appear in Exhibit 7.1. For this example, assume that all marketing and administrative costs are fixed. Also assume that fixed manufacturing, marketing, and administrative costs are the same (that is, are not differential) whichever product or combination of products the firm produces. One unit is one case of cookies.

EXHIBIT 7.1

Rationing Scarce Capacity
(Machine is available only 400 hours per month.)

	Product		
	Plain	**Chocolate-Covered**	**Caramel-Filled**
Time Required on the Machine per Unit Produced	0.5 Hour	2.0 Hours	4.0 Hours
Selling Price per Unit	$5.00	$12.00	$16.00
Less Variable Costs to Produce One Unit	3.00	5.00	6.00
Contribution Margin per Unit	$2.00	$7.00	$10.00
Contribution Margin per Hour on the Machine (contribution margin per unit/time requirement in hours)	$4.00 per Hour[a]	$3.50 per Hour[b]	$2.50 per Hour[c]
Total Contribution from Using 400 Hours on the Machine . . .	$1,600	$1,400	$1,000

[a]$4.00 per Hour = $2.00/0.5 Hour.

[b]$3.50 per Hour = $7.00/2.0 Hours.

[c]$2.50 per Hour = $10.00/4.0 Hours.

If the machine time were unlimited, the Cinadale Cookie Company should produce and sell all three products in the short run because all have a positive contribution margin. But with constrained machine time, the most profitable product is *the one that contributes the most per unit of time.* (Hint: If you face time constraints on an examination and must choose between Question 1 and Question 2, and if working on Question 1 will earn you 1 point per minute and Question 2 will earn you 2 points per minute, then work on Question 2.)

The Plain Wafers have a per-unit contribution of $2.00. The Caramel-Filled Wafers have a per-unit contribution of $10.00. Yet the Plain Wafers are still the best product to produce given the capacity constraint on the machine. The Plain Wafers contribute $4.00 per hour (= $2.00 per unit/0.5 hour per unit) of time on the machine, whereas the Caramel-Filled contribute only $2.50 per hour (= $10.00 per unit/4 hours per unit) of time on the machine. Differential analysis indicates that the total contribution margin from using the machine to produce Plain Wafers is $1,600, whereas the contribution from producing Chocolate-Covered is $1,400 and that from producing Caramel-Filled is $1,000.

When there is only one scarce resource, the decision is easy: *Choose the product that gives the largest contribution per unit of the scarce resource used.* When each product uses different proportions of several scarce resources, the computational problem becomes more difficult. Appendix 7.1 describes linear programming, a mathematical tool for solving such multiply-constrained decision problems. Textbooks on operations research and quantitative methods describe these techniques in more detail.

INCORRECT USE OF ACCOUNTING DATA

Many accounting systems routinely provide unit cost information that includes an *allocation* of fixed costs to each unit. This is the full absorption method of product costing. Full absorption unit costs for short-run decision making will lead to incorrect decisions, as the following example demonstrates.

Example   We have seen that production of Plain Wafers is optimal because the total monthly contribution is the highest of the three products. (Refer to Exhibit 7.1.) Suppose accountants have allocated fixed manufacturing costs in the amounts shown on line (7) of Exhibit 7.2. As line (10) of Exhibit 7.2 shows, full absorption cost may lead to an incorrect assessment that Chocolate-Covered Wafers are most profitable and Plain Wafers are least profitable per machine hour.

This example shows how the use of accounting data intended for one purpose may not be useful for other purposes. External reporting requires full absorption unit cost data. Most managerial decision models, on the other hand, require *variable* unit costs.

Unsophisticated users of accounting data often incorrectly assume that any calculated unit cost is a variable cost. You should not *assume* that the unit cost reported by an accounting system is a variable cost. Those unit costs often contain unitized fixed costs. When requesting data from the accounting department, be sure to specify what you need and how it will be used.

EXHIBIT 7.2

Rationing Scarce Capacity by Incorrectly Using Full Absorption Unit Costs

		Product	
	Plain	Chocolate-Covered	Caramel-Filled
(1) Time Required on the Machine per Unit Produced	0.5 Hour	2.0 Hours	4.0 Hours
(2) Selling Price per Unit	$5.00	$12.00	$16.00
(3) Direct Materials	$1.00	$ 2.00	$ 2.50
(4) Direct Labor	1.50	2.00	2.50
(5) Variable Manufacturing Overhead	.50	1.00	1.00
(6) Total Variable Costs per Unit	$3.00	$ 5.00	$ 6.00
(7) Allocation of Fixed Costs at 100 Percent of Direct Labor	1.50	2.00	2.50
(8) Full Absorption Cost per Unit	$4.50	$ 7.00	$ 8.50
(9) Gross Margin per Unit [line **(2)** minus line **(8)**]	$ .50	$ 5.00	$ 7.50
(10) Gross Margin per Hour	$1.00 per Hour	$ 2.50 per Hour	$1.875 per Hour

THEORY OF CONSTRAINTS AND THROUGHPUT CONTRIBUTION ANALYSIS

As noted in the previous section, organizations often have constraints, or limits, on what can be accomplished. The **theory of constraints** (**TOC**) is a newly developing management method for dealing with constraints.

The theory of constraints focuses on increasing the excess of differential revenue over differential costs when faced with bottlenecks. A **bottleneck** is an operation in which the work to be performed equals or exceeds the available capacity. With multiple parts of a production process, each operation is dependent on the preceding operations. An operation cannot be started until the previous operation has completed its work.

Inventory appears because items must wait in line until the bottleneck is free. For example, assume Pete's Pizza suddenly has orders at 7 PM for pizza to be delivered to 20 locations. Pete's has one delivery car that can deliver to 5 locations per delivery. With more than 5 locations, the pizzas are cold when delivered. Pete's can deliver all the pizzas eventually, but Pete's guarantees delivery in 30 minutes or the customer gets half off the price. As a result of the delivery time constraint, a bottleneck develops in the delivery process, which results in large numbers of customers getting a discount on their pizzas.

The theory of constraints focuses on such bottlenecks. It encourages managers to find ways to increase profits by relaxing constraints and increasing throughput. At Pete's Pizza, this means finding ways to get pizzas delivered quickly without giving customers a discount.

The theory of constraints focuses on three factors:

1. **Throughput contribution** Sales dollars minus short-run variable costs (for example, materials, energy and piecework labor).
2. **Investments** The assets required for production and sales.
3. **Other operating costs** All operating costs other than short-run variable costs. These costs are incurred to earn throughput contribution, and include salaries and wages that are fixed costs, rent, utilities, and depreciation.

The objective of the theory of constraints is to maximize throughput contribution while minimizing investments and operating costs. The theory of constraints assumes a short-run time horizon. Five key steps in managing bottleneck resources are outlined below:

1. Recognize that the bottleneck resource determines throughput contribution of the plant as a whole. For example, Pete's Pizza cannot deliver all the pizzas on time, which results in large discounts.
2. Search for and find the bottleneck resource by identifying resources with large quantities of inventory waiting to be worked on (lots of pizzas waiting over 30 minutes to be delivered).
3. Subordinate all nonbottleneck resources to the bottleneck resource. The needs of the bottleneck resource determine the production schedule of nonbottleneck resources. (A nonbottleneck process at Pete's is the preparation area, where the dough is made and appropriate toppings put on prior to cooking. The delivery rate should set the rate of preparation of pizzas for delivery.)
4. Increase bottleneck efficiency and capacity. The intent is to increase throughput contribution minus the differential costs of taking such actions (such as leasing another car and hiring another driver).
5. Repeat steps **1** through **4** for new bottleneck.

Let's look at an example of how to manage constraints. Pete's Pizza makes pizzas in three operations—preparing, cooking, and delivering. Pete's managers confront the delivery bottleneck during evening hours. In total, there is a bottleneck for 60 hours per month. Pertinent information for those 60 hours per month follows:

	Preparation	Cooking	Delivery
Hourly Capacity	15 Units	12 Units	10 Units
Monthly Capacity During the Pertinent 60 Hours ..	900 Units	720 Units	600 Units
Monthly Production Possible During the Pertinent 60 Hours	600 Units	600 Units	600 Units

Each unit (that is, each pizza) has an average variable cost of $6 and a selling price of $15. Pete's output is constrained by the 600 units on-time delivery capacity. Several options exist that can relieve the bottleneck at the delivery operation. It is necessary to consider differential costs associated with each option:

1. **Eliminate the idle time on the bottleneck operation.** Assume Pete's can increase bottleneck output by hiring one employee to organize the preparation and cooking

to ensure that pizzas are ready for delivery to five locations immediately upon arrival of the delivery car and to schedule pizza delivery so that the most efficient route is taken to deliver to the five locations. The additional cost for the employee time is $1,200 per month, and on-time delivery capacity is increased by 100 units per month. Thus, the throughput contribution increases by $900 [100 units $\times$ $9 (= $15 selling price − $6 variable costs)], which is less than the additional cost of $1,200. Pete's would not opt for this alternative.

2. **Shift parts that do not have to be made on the bottleneck machine to nonbottleneck machines or to outside facilities.** If Pete's can sell pizzas for pick-up instead of delivery, production would increase during the bottleneck hours to 720 units, which is the capacity of the cooking process. Assume the additional 120 units of pick-up pizzas will have a lower price of $12 and a lower variable cost of $5 per unit because delivery is not included. This option would increase throughput by $840 [120 $\times$ $7 (= $12 selling price − $5 variable costs)]. Assume Pete's would incur additional costs of $600 for the 60 pertinent hours per month for employees to sell pick-up pizzas. This alternative increases profits by $240 per month ($240 = $840 − $600).

3. **Increase the capacity of the bottleneck process.** Assume Pete's could hire another car and driver for the 60 bottleneck hours, increasing the delivery capacity to 720 units per month (which is the cooking constraint), costing an additional $900 for the 60 pertinent hours per month. This would increase throughput contribution by $1,080 [120 units $\times$ $9 (= $15 selling price − $6 variable costs)], which is $180 greater than the additional costs of $900. Although this alternative would increase profits, it would not increase profits by as much as alternative 2.

If Pete's management opts for alternative 2, it would then look for ways to increase the capacity of the new bottleneck, which is the cooking operation.

THEORY OF CONSTRAINTS AND COST ASSUMPTIONS

The theory of constraints assumes few costs are variable—generally only materials, purchased parts, piecework labor, and energy to run machines. Most direct labor and overhead costs are assumed to be fixed. This is consistent with the idea that the shorter the time period, the more costs are fixed, and the idea that the theory of constraints focuses on the short run. Generally, this assumption about cost behavior seems reasonable.

THEORY OF CONSTRAINTS, TOTAL QUALITY, AND JUST-IN-TIME

The theory of constraints identifies bottlenecks and possible disruptions that threaten throughput. For example, when disruptions are hard to pinpoint or eliminate, quality control techniques from total quality management (TQM) may be utilized. Total quality management stabilizes and improves processes to decrease variation; it is well suited to removing disruptions in the process. One manager summarized the relations among recent management techniques well by saying, "Essentially, JIT (just-in-time) improves lead times and due date performance, TQM (total quality management) improves people, and TOC (theory of constraints) provides focus for the entire improvement process."[1]

MAKE-OR-BUY DECISIONS

A firm facing a **make-or-buy decision** must decide whether to meet its needs internally or to acquire goods or services from external sources. If Pillsbury grows its own farm products for its frozen foods, then it "makes." If it buys products from other farmers, then it "buys." Housing contractors who do their own site preparation and foundation work "make," whereas those who hire subcontractors "buy." Professional baseball teams that rely on the draft and their minor league system "make," whereas those that trade for established players "buy."

Whether to make or to buy depends on cost factors and on nonquantitative factors such as dependability of suppliers and the quality of purchased materials.

Example The Ben & Jerry Cookie Company has an opportunity to buy part of its product for $12 per unit. This purchase would affect prices, volume, and costs as follows:

	Alternative: Buy	Status Quo: Make
Unit Selling Price	$30	$30
Volume	800 per Month	800 per Month
Unit Variable Costs	$11	$22
Purchased Parts, per Unit	$12	$0
Fixed Costs	$3,840	$4,800

Exhibit 7.3 shows that the alternative to buy is more profitable. The $9,600 cost to buy is more than offset by the fixed and variable cost savings.

EXHIBIT 7.3

BEN & JERRY COOKIE COMPANY
Differential Analysis of Make-or-Buy Decision

	Alternative: Buy	–	Status Quo: Make	=	Difference
Revenue	$24,000	–	$24,000	=	0
Less:					
Variable Costs to Produce and Sell	8,800[a]	–	17,600	=	$ 8,800 lower
Variable Costs of Goods Bought	9,600[b]	–	—	=	9,600 higher
Total Contribution Margin	$ 5,600	–	$ 6,400	=	$ 800 lower
Less Fixed Costs	3,840	–	4,800	=	960 lower
Operating Profit	$ 1,760	–	$ 1,600	=	$ 160 higher

[a]$8,800 = $11 × 800 Units.   [b]$9,600 = $12 × 800 Units.

---

[1] E. Noreen, D. Smith, and J. Mackey, *The Theory of Constraints and Its Implications for Managerial Accounting* (The North River Press, 1995) p. 42.

PROBLEM 7.1 FOR SELF-STUDY

Make-or-buy decision. Assume the Franklin Company, which manufactures wood stoves, has an opportunity to buy the handles for its stoves for $8.00 per unit. This purchase would affect prices, volume, and costs as follows:

	Buy	Make
Unit Selling Price	$ 340	$ 340
Volume (per month)	500	500
Unit Variable Costs	$ 88	$ 95
Purchased Parts (per unit)	$ 8	$ 0
Fixed Costs	$4,700	$5,500

Management wants you to decide whether the part should be made or bought.

The solution to this self-study problem is at the end of the chapter on page 227.

JOINT PRODUCTS: SELL OR PROCESS FURTHER

Suppose you get multiple products from a single production process. For example, Georgia-Pacific gets various wood products from its lumber mills. Dairy producers like Borden and Land O'Lakes get multiple products from raw milk.

Exhibit 7.4 presents the following information graphically. The firm initially introduces direct materials into processing. After incurring direct labor and manufacturing overhead costs, two identifiable products, Product A and Product B, emerge

EXHIBIT 7.4

Joint Production Process

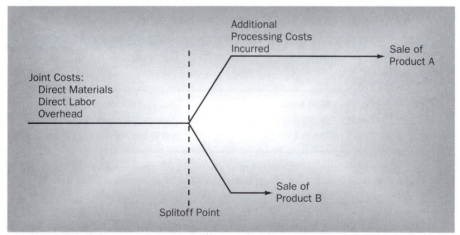

from the production process. The firm processes Product A further, but sells Product B immediately. We call the point at which the identifiable products emerge the **splitoff point.** Costs incurred up to the splitoff point are the **joint costs.** We call costs incurred after the splitoff point **additional processing costs.**

Companies producing joint products must decide at each splitoff point whether to sell the individual products as they are, or process further. Differential analysis is appropriate for these types of decisions.

Example   At Hanson Dairy the cows produce 10,000 gallons of raw milk a month. After milking, separating, and processing, which costs $11,000, the dairy has 7,000 gallons of whole milk and 3,000 gallons of cream. The milk could be sold at this point for $1.00 a gallon or processed further into 6,500 gallons of nonfat milk, with 500 gallons lost in the process. Further processing would cost $0.20 per gallon for the 6,500 gallons of output. The nonfat milk could then be sold for $1.25 per gallon. The cream could also be sold or processed further into sour cream, butter, and cheese.

The following is an analysis considering whether to process the milk further or sell now. The initial $11,000 is a joint cost and not differential for this decision. The differential costs are the additional processing costs of $0.20 per gallon.

	Alternative: Process Further	−	Status Quo: Sell	= Difference
Revenue	$8,125	−	$7,000	= $1,125
Less Additional Processing Costs	1,300	−	0	= 1,300
Contribution Margin before Costs Prior to Splitoff Are Considered	$6,825	−	$7,000	= $ (175)

Of the joint products milk and cream, the milk should not be processed further. It would cost more to process the milk further than revenues would increase. The company could perform the same analysis for the cream.

PROBLEM 7.2 FOR SELF-STUDY

Sell or process further. The Demi Company processes logs into 200,000 board feet of lumber and 50,000 board feet of scrap lumber per year. The scrap lumber can be sold at splitoff for $5 per board foot or processed further into plywood to be sold for $6 per board foot. Further processing would incur variable costs of $.50 per board foot. The equipment and space to process the scrap lumber would increase fixed costs by $25,000 a year.

Management wants you to determine if the scrap lumber should be sold or processed further.

The solution to this self-study problem is at the end of the chapter on page 227.

MANAGERIAL APPLICATION

Using Differential Costs to Estimate the Costs of the Baseball Strike

According to a differential cost study of the 1994 baseball strike conducted by the *New York Times,* the 28 major league baseball clubs lost more money in lost gate receipts, concessions, and parking ($300 million) than they saved in players' salaries ($260 million) for the season.

That loss increased when lost television and radio revenue and other revenues were considered. Further, after the strike ended, it took time for attendance to come up to the levels prior to the strike. The clubs may not have considered this lost fan loyalty in their decision to allow the players to strike. (Consider the marketing adage, "It's easier to keep an existing customer, than to gain a new one.")

Source: Based on Murray Chass, "Clubs Stand to Lose More Than They'll Save," *New York Times,* August 15, 1994.

ADDING AND DROPPING PARTS OF OPERATIONS

Managers must decide when to add or drop products from the product line and when to open or abandon sales territories. For example, Microsoft decided to drop certain networking products. Kmart decided to close certain stores. Sears decided to eliminate certain real estate and financial services operations.

These can be either long-run decisions involving a change in capacity or short-run decisions in which capacity does not change. This chapter deals with these as short-run decisions.

The differential principle implies the following rule: If the differential revenue from the sale of a product exceeds the differential costs required to provide the product for sale, then the product generates profits and the firm should continue its production. This decision is correct even though the product may show a loss in financial statements because of overhead costs allocated to it. If the product more than covers its differential costs, and if no other alternative use of the production and sales facilities exists, the firm should retain the product in the short run.

Example Suppose that the Baltimore Company had three products and used common facilities to produce and sell all three. No one product affects sales of the others. The relevant data for these three products follow:

	Product			
	A	**B**	**C**	**Total**
Sales Volume per Month	800	1,000	600	—
Unit Sales Price	$30	$20	$40	—
Sales Revenue	$24,000	$20,000	$24,000	$68,000
Unit Variable Cost	$22	$14	$35	—
Fixed Cost per Month	—	—	—	$13,600

Management has asked the accounting department to allocate fixed costs to each product so that it can evaluate how well each product is doing. Total fixed costs were 20 percent of total dollar sales, so the accountant charged fixed costs to each product at 20 percent of the product's sales. For example, Product C received $4,800 (= .20 × $24,000 sales) of fixed costs.

The product-line income statements in the top panel of Exhibit 7.5 show an apparent loss of $1,800 for Product C. One of Baltimore's managers argued, "We should drop Product C. It is losing $1,800 per month." A second manager suggested performing a differential analysis to see the costs saved and revenues lost. The bottom panel of Exhibit 7.5, the differential analysis, shows dropping Product C reduces the company's profits. The first manager incorrectly assumed that dropping the product would save fixed costs.

The firm should investigate more profitable uses of the facilities used to produce and sell Product C, because its contribution margin appears to be the weakest of the three products. Until such alternatives emerge, however, producing and selling Product C is profitable.

EXHIBIT 7.5

BALTIMORE COMPANY
Differential Analysis of Dropping a Product

Income Statement Analysis

	Product			Total
	A	**B**	**C**	
Sales	$24,000	$20,000	$24,000	$68,000
Less Variable Costs	17,600	14,000	21,000	52,600
Total Contribution Margin	$ 6,400	$ 6,000	$ 3,000	$15,400
Less Fixed Costs Allocated to Each Product	4,800[a]	4,000[a]	4,800[a]	13,600
Operating Profit (Loss)	$ 1,600	$ 2,000	$(1,800)	$ 1,800

Differential Analysis

	Alternative: Drop Product C	−	Status Quo	= Difference
Sales	$44,000	−	$68,000	= $ 24,000 lower
Less Variable Costs	31,600	−	52,600	= 21,000 lower
Total Contribution Margin	$12,400	−	$15,400	= $ 3,000 lower
Less Fixed Costs	13,600	−	13,600	= 0
Operating Profit (Loss)	$(1,200)	−	$ 1,800	= $ 3,000 lower

[a]Fixed costs of $13,600 allocated in proportion to sales.

PROBLEM 7.3 FOR SELF-STUDY

Product decisions. Assume Baltimore Company did not drop Product C, but Product B's revenue and variable costs dropped to 50 percent of the levels shown in Exhibit 7.5. Should Baltimore drop Product B?

The solution to this self-study problem is at the end of the chapter on page 228.

INVENTORY MANAGEMENT DECISIONS

Inventory management affects profits in merchandising, manufacturing, and other organizations with inventories. Having the correct type and amount of inventory can prevent a production shutdown in manufacturing. In merchandising, having the correct type of merchandise inventory may mean making a sale. Inventories are costly to maintain, however. The costs include storage costs, insurance, losses from damage and theft, property taxes, and the opportunity cost of funds tied up in inventory. Key inventory management questions include the following:

1. How many units of inventory should be on hand and available for use or sale?
2. How often should the firm order a particular item? What is the optimal size of the order?

DIFFERENTIAL COSTS FOR INVENTORY MANAGEMENT

Inventory management decisions involve two types of opposing costs. The firm incurs differential costs each time it places an order or makes a production run (for example, the cost of processing each purchase order or the cost of preparing machinery for each production run). These are **setup** or **order costs.** The firm could minimize them by minimizing the number of orders or production runs.

By ordering or producing less frequently, however, each order or production run must be for a larger number of units. The firm will carry a larger average inventory. Larger inventories imply larger **carrying costs** for these inventories (for example, the cost of maintaining warehouse facilities).

Management would like to find the optimal trade-off between these two types of opposing costs, carrying costs and order costs. Refer to Exhibit 7.6, based on the following example. (We refer to both order costs and setup costs as *order costs* for the rest of our discussion.) The problem is to calculate the optimal number of orders or production runs each year and the optimal number of units to order or produce. The optimal number of units to order or produce is the **economic order quantity (EOQ).**

Example Penn Merchandising sells 6,000 units of a product per year, spread evenly throughout the year. Each unit costs $2 to purchase. The differential cost of preparing and following up on an order is $100 per order. The cost of carrying a unit in inventory is 30 percent of the unit's cost. Thus, if the firm places one order for the

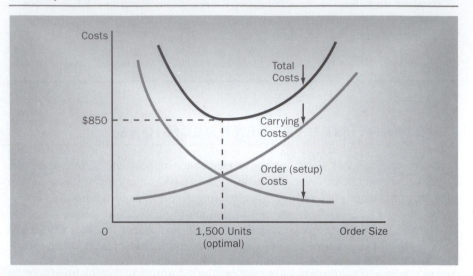

EXHIBIT 7.6

Inventory Costs

year, it will purchase 6,000 units and have, *on average,* 3,000 units ($6,000) in inventory during the year. The carrying cost would be $1,800 (= $6,000 × .30) for the year. Exhibit 7.7 presents the inventory carrying costs, order costs, and total costs of the inventory. Note the trade-off between carrying costs and order costs: As one decreases, the other increases. The optimal number of orders per year is four, which has the lowest total costs [see column (6) in Exhibit 7.7].

A formal model (called the EOQ model) for deriving the optimal number of orders (or setups or production runs) and the optimal number of items in an order (or in a production run) appears in Appendix 7.2.

ESTIMATING THE COSTS OF MAINTAINING INVENTORY

Managers, industrial engineers, analysts, and others who attempt to derive optimal solutions to inventory management problems typically use costs the accounting system provides. An important but difficult task for management accountants is estimating inventory order costs and carrying costs. Keep in mind that only *differential* costs matter. For example, suppose that the firm uses one purchasing agent whether customers place one order or twelve orders per year, and the number of orders made does not affect the agent's salary. Assume that the opportunity cost of the agent's time equals zero. Therefore, the agent's salary does not differ, and it would not be part of the order costs.

Order Costs   To estimate differential order costs, consider whether any salaries or wages differ because of the number of orders and whether there are opportunity costs of lost time. Production setups, in particular, usually result in lost time for production employees. Order costs should include differential costs of receiving and inspecting orders, costs of processing invoices from suppliers, and freight costs.

EXHIBIT 7.7

PENN MERCHANDISING
Economic Order Quantity Calculation

Differential costs per order are $100.
Annual requirement is 6,000 units.
Inventory carrying costs are 30 percent per year.
Purchase cost per unit is $2.00.

Orders (1)	Order Size[a] (2)	Average Number of Units in Inventory[b] (3)	Inventory Carrying Costs[c] (4)	Order Costs[d] (5)	Total Costs[e] (6)
1	6,000	3,000	$1,800	$ 100	$1,900
2	3,000	1,500	900	200	1,100
3	2,000	1,000	600	300	900
4	1,500	750	450	400	850[f]
5	1,200	600	360	500	860
6	1,000	500	300	600	900
12	500	250	150	1,200	1,350

[a]6,000 units/number of orders from column (1).

[b]Column (2)/2.

[c]Amount in column (3) $\times$ $2 cost per unit $\times$ .30.

[d]$100 $\times$ number of orders from column (1).

[e]Amount in column (4) + amount in column (5).

[f]Lowest total cost. Optimal number of orders is four per year.

Example   If freight costs are a constant amount (say, $.10) per unit, they do not differ as the number of orders varies. If the firm pays freight charges per *shipment,* however (say, $50 per shipment), costs increase as the number of shipments increases. In this case, freight is a differential cost.

Carrying Costs   Differential carrying costs include insurance, inventory taxes, the opportunity costs of funds invested in inventory, and other costs that differ with the number of units held in inventory. If the firm pays additional wages or leases additional warehouse space because inventory quantity increases, these costs are differential carrying costs. Carrying costs should not include an allocated portion of warehouse depreciation or rent if these costs do not vary with the number of units in inventory. Such depreciation and rent are not differential carrying costs.

INNOVATIONS IN INVENTORY MANAGEMENT AND FLEXIBLE MANUFACTURING

JUST-IN-TIME

Just-in-time (JIT) is a method of managing purchasing, production, and sales, by which (a) the firm attempts to produce each item only as needed for the next step in the production process, or (b) the firm attempts to time purchases so that items arrive just in time for production or sale. This practice can reduce inventory levels virtually to zero.

Just-in-time is a philosophy rather than a tool or set of tools. The objective is the elimination of all nonvalue-added activities and thus a reduction in cost and time. As with total quality management, JIT is an approach to improvement that is continuous and requires employee involvement.

Just-in-time is compatible with a total quality management philosophy, as it requires the production process to be laid out so that there is a continuous flow once production starts. Since products are produced only as needed, setup costs must be reduced to eliminate the need to produce in large batches.

Just-in-time requires that processing systems be reliable. Production must correct a process resulting in defective units immediately because the plan does not include accumulating defective units while they await reworking or scrapping. This turns out to be a major advantage of just-in-time and a major cost of carrying inventory. Economic order quantity models that omit this cost of carrying inventory overstate the optimal level of inventory. Manufacturing managers find that eliminating inventories can prevent production workers from hiding production problems.

All aspects of production, including developing the design, acquiring materials for production, producing the good or service, delivering the good or service to the customer, and providing service after the delivery, are encompassed by just-in-time, and all may be enhanced by total quality management. The performance measures used in a just-in-time system are inventory levels; failures, whether these are materials, people, or machine failures; moving; and storing. In a just-in-time system everyone works to keep these measures as close to zero as possible.

The use of just-in-time enables accountants to spend less time on inventory valuation for external reporting purposes and more time obtaining data for managerial decisions such as those discussed in this chapter.

FLEXIBLE MANUFACTURING

Another innovation that reduces both setup costs and inventory levels is flexible manufacturing. As this chapter discusses, reducing inventory levels means increasing the number of setups. Consider an automobile manufacturer that makes fenders for several models of cars. When it is time to change from left fenders to right fenders, or from fenders for cars to fenders for trucks, the production line stops while workers modify the machines to make the new fenders. Making only a few fenders of each type during a single production run requires many separate setups. So companies like Ford Motor Company use flexible manufacturing methods to make these changeovers quickly.

The use of flexible manufacturing practices to reduce setup costs enhances companies' abilities to use just-in-time. If setup costs are low, each production run can be small—perhaps just one unit. These innovations are likely to decrease the need for detailed record keeping for inventory valuation and to increase accountants' time spent on managerial activities.

PROBLEM 7.4 FOR SELF-STUDY

Inventory decisions. Compute the minimum total costs for JIT-not Incorporated, given the following facts:

Differential Costs per Order	$41
Total Units Purchased per Year	40,000 Units
Differential Carrying Costs per Unit of Inventory	$5.35 per Unit

Prepare a table like Exhibit 7.7, and find the minimum total costs of ordering and holding inventory. (Hint: Start with 50 annual orders.)

The solution to this self-study problem is at the end of the chapter on page 228.

SUMMARY

The following items correspond to the learning objectives presented at the beginning of the chapter.

1. **Apply differential analysis to product choice decisions.** Most firms can supply a number of different goods and services but manufacturing or distribution constraints limit what firms can do. In the short-run, capacity limitations require choices among alternatives.

2. **Explain and apply the theory of constraints.** The theory of constraints focuses on revenue and cost management when dealing with bottlenecks. The objective is to increase throughput contribution (sales dollars minus direct materials costs), minimize investments, and manage production by letting the bottleneck set the pace for the rest of operations.

3. **Identify the factors underlying make-or-buy decisions.** Whether to make-or-buy depends on cost factors and on nonquantitative factors, such as dependability of suppliers and the quality of purchased materials.

4. **Identify the costs of producing joint products and the relevant costs for decisions to sell or process further.** The point at which the identifiable products emerge is the splitoff point. Costs incurred up to the splitoff point are the joint costs. Additional processing costs—costs incurred after the splitoff point—are the relevant costs for decisions to sell or process further.

5. **Use differential analysis to determine when to add or drop parts of operations.** In the short-run, capacity does not change. If the differential revenue from the sale of a product exceeds the differential costs required to provide the product for sale, then the product generates profits and the firm should continue its production.

6. **Identify the factors underlying inventory management decisions.** The optimal number of units to order or produce is the *economic order quantity*, which is the optimal trade-off between setup (or order) costs and carrying costs. In estimating

order costs and carrying costs, only differential costs matter. Just-in-time inventory is a method of managing purchasing, production, and sales, by which (a) the firm attempts to produce each item only as needed for the next step in the production process, or (b) the firm attempts to time purchases so that items arrive just in time for sale or production. The use of total quality management and flexible manufacturing practices to reduce setup costs enhances companies' abilities to use just-in-time inventory.

7. **(Appendix 7.1) Use linear programming to optimize the use of scarce resources.** Linear programming (a) finds the product mix that will maximize profits given the constraints, (b) provides opportunity costs of constraints, and (c) allows for sensitivity analysis.

8. **(Appendix 7.2) Understand the use of the economic order quantity model.** The economic order quantity model derives the optimal number of orders or production runs.

KEY TERMS AND CONCEPTS

Theory of constraints (TOC)   Focuses on revenue and cost management when faced with bottlenecks.

Bottleneck   An operation in which the work to be performed equals or exceeds the available capacity.

Throughput contribution   Sales dollars minus short-run variable costs (for example, materials, energy costs, and piece-work labor).

TOC investments   The assets required for production and sales.

Make-or-buy decision   A managerial decision about whether the firm should produce a product internally or purchase it from others. Proper make-or-buy decisions in the short run result when a firm considers only differential costs in decision making.

Splitoff point   The point at which individual products emerge from a joint process.

Joint costs   Costs of simultaneously producing or otherwise acquiring two or more products, called *joint products,* that a firm must, by the nature of the process, produce or acquire together, such as the cost of beef and hides of cattle.

Additional processing costs   Costs incurred in processing joint products after the splitoff point.

Setup or order costs   The costs of preparing equipment and facilities so that they can be used for production, or the costs of placing or receiving an order.

Carrying costs   The costs of holding inventory (for example, insurance, storage space, and opportunity cost of idle capital).

Economic order quantity (EOQ)   In mathematical inventory analysis, the optimal amount of stock to order when demand reduces inventory to a level called the *reorder point.*

Just-in-time (JIT)   System in which a firm purchases or manufactures each component just before the firm uses or sells it.

Linear programming   (Appendix 7.1) A mathematical tool for finding profit maximizing (or cost minimizing) combinations of products to produce when a firm has several options but faces linear constraints either on the resources available in the production processes or on maximum and minimum production requirements.

Objective function   (Appendix 7.1) In linear programming, the name of the profit or cost criterion the analyst wants to optimize.

Shadow price   (Appendix 7.1) The potential value of having available more of scarce resource that constrains the production process; one output of linear programming analysis.

Economic order quantity (EOQ) model   (Appendix 7.2) The mathematical model used to determine the economic order quantity.

SOLUTIONS TO SELF-STUDY PROBLEMS

SUGGESTED SOLUTION TO PROBLEM 7.1 FOR SELF-STUDY

	Buy	−	Make	= Difference
Revenue	$170,000	−	$170,000	= $ 0
Less:				
Variable Costs to Produce and Sell	44,000	−	47,500	= 3,500 lower
Variable Costs of Goods Bought	4,000	−	0	= 4,000 higher
Total Contribution Margin	$122,000	−	$122,500	= $ 500 lower
Less Fixed Costs	4,700	−	5,500	= 800 lower
Operating Profit	$117,300	−	$117,000	= $ 300 higher

Operating profit for the Franklin Company increases by $300 if it purchases the handles rather than makes them.

SUGGESTED SOLUTION TO PROBLEM 7.2 FOR SELF-STUDY

	Process Further	−	Sell	= Difference
Revenue	$300,000	−	$250,000	= $50,000
Less Additional Processing Variable Costs	25,000	−	0	= 25,000
Total Contribution Margin before Considering Costs Prior to Splitoff Point	$275,000	−	$250,000	= $25,000
Less Additional Fixed Costs	25,000	−	0	= 25,000
Operating Profit	250,000	−	$250,000	= 0

Operating profit for the Demi Company will be the same whether it processes the scrap lumber into plywood or sells scrap lumber at split-off.

SUGGESTED SOLUTION TO PROBLEM 7.3 FOR SELF-STUDY

Baltimore should not drop Product B in the short run. It continues to have a positive contribution margin even if the revenue and variable costs drop by 50 percent.

SUGGESTED SOLUTION TO PROBLEM 7.4 FOR SELF-STUDY

Annual Orders	Order Size[a] in Units	Average Number of Units in Inventory	Inventory Carrying Costs[b]	Order Costs[c]	Total Costs
40	1,000	500	$2,675	$1,640	$4,315
.					
.					
.					
50	800	400	2,140	2,050	4,190
51	784	392	2,097	2,091	4,188
52	769	384.5	2,057	2,132	4,189
53	755	377.5	2,020	2,173	4,193
.					
.					
.					
60	667	333.5	1,784	2,460	4,244

[a]40,000 units/number of orders.
[b]Average units in inventory $\times$ $5.35.
[c]Number of orders $\times$ $41.

Minimum total costs are $4,188 at 51 orders per year.

APPENDIX 7.1: LINEAR PROGRAMMING

Factors such as factory capacity, personnel time, floor space, and so forth constrain most managerial decisions. If the firm has enough time before implementing a decision, it can relax constraints by increasing capacity. In the short run, however, decision makers face a constrained amount of resources available to them. **Linear programming** solves problems of this type. We refer to linear programming as a *constrained optimization* technique, because it solves for the optimal use of scarce (that is, constrained) resources.

Two simple examples demonstrate how linear programming works. We solve these using graphs and simple algebra. More complex problems require some systematic procedure like the *simplex method,* described in textbooks on operations research and quantitative methods. Most linear programming problem solutions result from computer implementation of the simplex method or variations of it.

PROFIT MAXIMIZATION

Example   Moline Company produces two products, 1 and 2. The contribution margins per unit of the two products follow:

Product	Contribution Margin per Unit
1	$3
2	4

Fixed costs are the same regardless of the combination of products 1 and 2 the firm produces; therefore, the firm wants to maximize the total contribution per period of these two products.

Both products have a positive contribution margin. If Moline Company faced no constraints, it should make (and sell) both products, eliminating our problem. When production of a unit of each product consumes the same quantity of a scare resource, managers solve the problem by making and selling only the highest contribution item. For our example, if Product 1 and Product 2 each require one hour of machine time, and the quantity of machine hours is finite, Moline would choose Product 2, all else being equal. Products usually do not consume equal amounts of scarce resources, however. So the problem is to find the optimal mix of products given the amount of a scarce resource each product consumes.

Moline Company uses two scarce resources to make the two products, labor time and machine time. Twenty-four hours of labor time and 20 hours of machine time are available each day. The amount of time required to make each product follows:

	Product	
	1	**2**
Labor Time	1 Hour per Unit	2 Hours per Unit
Machine Time	1 Hour per Unit	1 Hour per Unit

This problem formulation follows. (X_1 and X_2 refer to the quantity of Products 1 and 2 produced and sold.)

(1) Maximize: $\$3X_1 + \$4X_2 = $ Total Contribution
(2) Subject to: $X_1 + 2X_2 \leq 24$ Labor Hours
(3) $X_1 + X_2 \leq 20$ Machine Hours.

The first line, the **objective function,** states the objective of our problem as a linear equation. Here the objective is to maximize total contribution where each unit of Product 1 contributes $3 and each unit of Product 2 contributes $4. The lines that follow specify the parameters of the constraints. Line (2) is the labor time constraint, which states that each unit of Product 1 requires 1 labor hour and each unit of Product 2 requires 2 labor hours. Total labor hours cannot exceed 24 per period (that is, one day). Line (3) is the machine time constraint, which states that Product 1 and Product 2 each use 1 machine hour per unit, and total machine hours cannot exceed 20.

Exhibit 7.8 graphs the constraints. The shaded area shows feasible production; production does not use up more scarce resources than are available. The lowercase

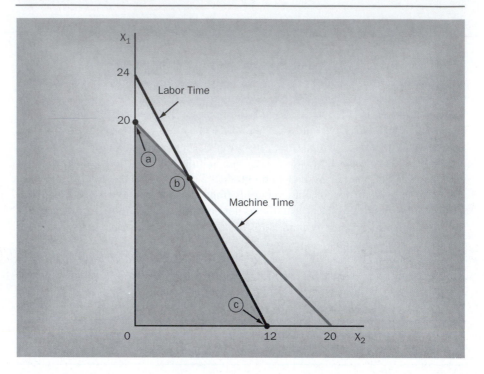

Linear Programming, Graphic Solution
Comparison of Corner and Noncorner Points

letters show the *corner points*. We find the optimal solution by deriving the total contribution margin at each point, using the following steps.

Step 1 Find the production level of Product 1 and Product 2 at each point. Points a and c are straightforward. At a, $X_1 = 20$ and $X_2 = 0$; at c, $X_2 = 12$ and $X_1 = 0$. Point b requires solving for two unknowns using the two constraint formulas:

$$\text{Labor Time:} \qquad X_1 + 2X_2 = 24$$
$$\text{Machine Time:} \quad X_1 + X_2 = 20.$$

Setting these two equations equal, we have

$$X_1 = 24 - 2X_2$$
$$X_1 = 20 - X_2,$$
$$24 - 2X_2 = 20 - X_2$$
$$4 = X_2.$$

If $X_2 = 4$, then

$$X_1 = 20 - X_2$$
$$= 20 - 4$$
$$= 16.$$

At point b, Moline produces 16 units of Product 1 and 4 units of Product 2.

EXHIBIT 7.9

Optimal Product Mix

Point	Production		Contribution		
	X_1	X_2	1	2	Total
a	20	0	$60	$ 0	$60
b	16	4	48	16	64
c	0	12	0	48	48

Step 2 Find the total contribution margin at each point. (Recall that the unit contribution margins of products 1 and 2 are $3 and $4.) Exhibit 7.9 shows the solution. It is optimal to produce at point b, where $X_1 = 16$ and $X_2 = 4$.

Why must the optimal solution be at a corner? If production moves away from the corner at point b in any feasible direction, total contribution will be lower. Exhibit 7.10 shows a movement away from point b in four feasible directions.

EXHIBIT 7.10

Linear Programming, Graphic Solution—Comparison of Corner and Noncorner Points

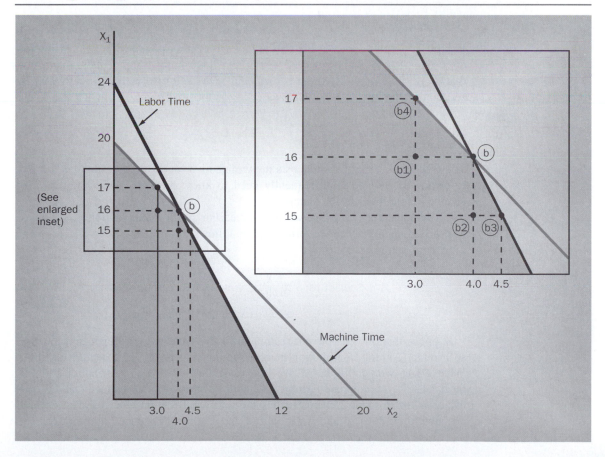

EXHIBIT 7.11

Comparison of Corner Point with Noncorner Points

Point	Production X$_1$	X$_2$	Contribution 1	2	Total
b	16	4	$48	$16	$64
b1	16	3	48	12	60
b2	15	4	45	16	61
b3[a]	15	4.5	45	18	63
b4[b]	17	3	51	12	63

---

[a]Let $X_1 = 15$ and find X_2 as follows:

$$X_1 = 24 - 2X_2$$
$$15 = 24 - 2X_2$$
$$2X_2 = 9$$
$$X_2 = 4.5.$$

[b]Let $X_2 = 3$ and find X_1 as follows:

$$X_1 = 20 - X_2$$
$$= 20 - 3$$
$$= 17.$$

Exhibit 7.11 compares contributions at those noncorner points with the contribution at corner point b. Although these examples show intuitively that the contribution margin declines away from the corner point, we can prove mathematically our assertion that the optimal solution always lies on a corner point.

SENSITIVITY ANALYSIS

The contribution margins and costs in the objective functions are estimates, subject to error. Decision makers frequently need to know how much the estimates can change before the decision changes.

To demonstrate our point, we use our earlier profit-maximization problem for Moline Company, which we formulated as follows:

$$\text{Maximize: } \$3X_1 + \$4X_2 = \text{Total Contribution}$$

$$\text{Subject to: } X_1 + 2X_2 \leq 24 \text{ Labor Hours}$$

$$X_1 + X_2 \leq 20 \text{ Machine Hours.}$$

Suppose that the variable cost estimate for Product 2 was $.50 per unit too low, so Product 2's unit contribution margin should have been $3.50 instead of $4.00. What effect would this have? We have calculated the new contributions in Exhibit 7.12. If you compare Exhibit 7.12 with Exhibit 7.9, you will see that the contribution for Product 2 changes; thus the total contribution changes. The optimal decision to produce 16 units of Product 1 and 4 units of Product 2 does not change,

EXHIBIT 7.12

Optimal Product Mix: Revised Cost Estimates

Point[a]	Production X_1	Production X_2	Contribution 1	Contribution 2	Contribution Total
a	20	0	$60	$ 0	$60
b	16	4	48	14[b]	62
c	0	12	0	42	42

[a]The graph in Exhibit 7.8 presents these points.
[b]Four units × $3.50 per unit.

however. In spite of the change in costs and thus in contributions, the *decision* does not change. In this example, the unit contribution margin of Product 2 would have to drop to less than $3 per unit before the optimal decision would change, assuming that all other things remained constant.

Most linear programming computer programs can provide this type of sensitivity analysis. With it, managers and accountants can ascertain how much a cost or contribution margin can change before the optimal decision will change.

OPPORTUNITY COSTS

Any constrained resource has an opportunity cost, which is the profit forgone by not having an additional unit of the resource. For example, suppose that Moline Company in our previous example could obtain one additional hour of machine time. With one more hour of machine time, the machine constraint would move out, as shown in Exhibit 7.13. We find the new production level at point b as follows:

$$X_1 = 24 - 2X_2$$

and

$$X_1 = 21 - X_2$$

$$24 - 2X_2 = 21 - X_2$$

$$X_2 = 3$$

$$X_1 = 18.$$

The new total contribution at point b would be $3(18) + $4(3) = $66, compared to $64 when machine time was constrained to 20 hours per day, as shown for point b in Exhibit 7.11. Thus the opportunity cost of not having an extra hour of machine time is $2 (= $66 − $64).

Linear programming computer programs regularly provide opportunity costs, called **shadow prices.** Opportunity cost data indicate the benefits of acquiring more units of a scarce resource. For example, if Moline Company could rent one more machine hour for less than $2 per hour, the company would profit by doing so, all other things being equal.

EXHIBIT 7.13

Linear Programming, Graphic Solution
Increase in Machine Time from 20 to 21 Hours

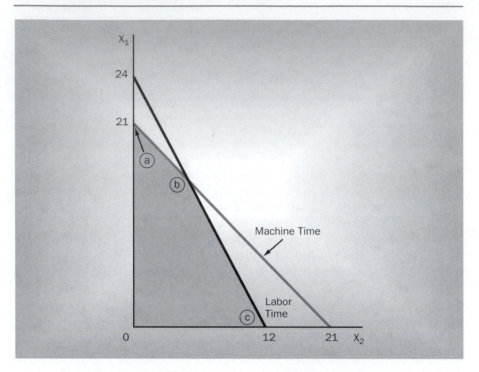

APPENDIX 7.2: ECONOMIC ORDER QUANTITY MODEL

In our discussion of inventory management, we derived the optimal number of orders or production runs by trial and error. We also could derive the optimal number of orders or production runs per period from the following formula:

$$N = \frac{D}{Q},$$

where

$$Q = \sqrt{\frac{2K_0 D}{K_c}}$$

N = the optimal number of orders or production runs for the period

Q = the economic order quantity, or the optimal number of items in an order or production run

D = the period demand in units

K_0 = the order or setup cost

K_c = the cost of carrying one unit in inventory for the period.

The formula $Q = \sqrt{2K_0 D/K_c}$ results from using calculus to minimize total cost with respect to Q. The total cost (TC) formula is

$$\begin{array}{c} \text{Total Cost} \\ \text{per Period} \end{array} = \begin{array}{c} \text{Carrying Costs} \\ \text{per Period} \end{array} + \begin{array}{c} \text{Order Costs} \\ \text{per Period} \end{array}$$

$$TC = K_c \frac{Q}{2} + K_0 \frac{D}{Q}.$$

Take the first derivative of TC with respect to Q, set it equal to zero, and solve for Q:

$$\frac{dTC}{dQ} = \frac{d}{dQ}\left(K_c \frac{Q}{2} + K_0 \frac{D}{Q} \right)$$

$$= \frac{K_c}{2} - \frac{K_0 D}{Q^2} = 0.$$

$$Q = \sqrt{\frac{2K_0 D}{K_c}}.$$

Example The following facts for the Penn Merchandising example appeared in the text:

D = period demand = 6,000 units per year

K_0 = order costs = \$100 per order

K_c = carrying cost = 30 percent of the cost of inventory or \$.60 per unit
  (\$.60 = 30 percent $\times$ \$2.00 per unit).

Solving for Q (the optimal number of items in an order), we have

$$Q = \sqrt{\frac{2K_0 D}{K_c}}$$

$$= \sqrt{\frac{2 \times \$100 \times 6,000 \text{ Units}}{\$.60}}$$

$$= \sqrt{2,000,000 \text{ Units}}$$

$$= 1,414 \text{ Units per Order.}$$

$$N = \frac{D}{Q}$$

$$= \frac{6,000 \text{ Units}}{1,414 \text{ Units}}$$

$$= 4.2 \text{ Orders per Year.}$$

From these equations, we derived the optimal order size 1,414 units, and the optimal number of orders per year, 4.2. This result is approximately the same one we derived by trial and error earlier. Using the economic order quantity model is usually more efficient for finding the least costly size and number of orders (or productions).

This is known as the **economic order quantity (EOQ) model.** Textbooks on operations research and quantitative methods present many variations and applications of this model.

QUESTIONS, EXERCISES, PROBLEMS, AND CASES

REVIEW QUESTIONS

1. Review the meaning of the terms and concepts given in Key Terms and Concepts.
2. Inventory management problems usually involve two types of opposing costs. Describe these costs and sketch a graph showing how they change as order size changes. (Put order size on the horizontal axis.)
3. Describe the relevant costs for make-or-buy decisions.
4. True or false: The objective of the theory of constraints is to increase through-put contribution.

CRITICAL ANALYSIS AND DISCUSSION QUESTIONS

5. "Users of differential analysis should use accrual-based revenues and expenses of a particular period rather than cash flows, because they better represent a firm's performance during a given period." Comment.
6. "A proper evaluation of any project using differential analysis requires the consideration of all relevant costs—past, present, and future." Comment.
7. Assume that there are no income taxes. How should each of the following costs enter into a decision to replace old equipment?
   a. book value of old equipment
   b. disposal value of old equipment
   c. cost of new equipment
8. You are asked to provide margin figures for a product choice decision. Do you give the gross margin per unit or contribution margin per unit? Why?
9. Explain why just-in-time requires reliable suppliers and production methods.
10. Explain how the theory of constraints is compatible with total quality management.
11. Interview the manager of a restaurant. Does the restaurant make or buy soups and desserts? Based on your interview, write a short report that explains why the restaurant makes or buys each of these two items.

EXERCISES

Solutions to even-numbered exercises are at the end of the chapter after the cases.

12. **Make or buy.** Ol'Salt Enterprises produces 1,000 sailboats per year. Although the company currently buys sails for the sailboats (one set of sails per boat), it is considering making sails in some space that it does not presently use. The company purchases each set of sails for $300. It could make the sails for variable costs of $250 per set, plus it would allocate $200,000 of fixed costs per year to the sail-making operation. However, this $200,000 is not a differential cost of making sails; it is part of the costs the company already incurs that it would allocate away from sailboat manufacture to sail making.
    a. Prepare a differential analysis to show whether Ol'Salt Enterprises should make or buy the sails. What do you recommend to management? Explain

why the $200,000 fixed costs allocated to sail making is or is not relevant to the decision.

b. If Ol'Salt buys the sails, then it would have unused factory space. Suppose Ol'Salt received an opportunity to rent out this unused factory space for $80,000 per year. Would that affect your recommendation in part **a**?

13. **Throughput contribution.** Harvey's Hair Caretakers styles hair in three operations—washing, cutting/setting, and drying—Harvey's charges $12 per styling. (Each styling is one "unit.") Harvey's styles hair on a walk-in basis and does not take appointments; customers who have to wait walk across the street to another salon. Harvey's managers find it has a cutting/setting bottleneck on Saturdays due to a limited number of stylists. The bottleneck exists for a total of eight hours each Saturday. Pertinent information follows:

	Washing	Cutting/Setting	Drying
Hourly Capacity	36 Units	10 Units	12 Units
Saturday Capacity (8 hours)	288 Units	80 Units	96 Units
Actual Saturday Production	80 Units	80 Units	80 Units
Fixed Operating Costs per Saturday ...	$ 20 Units	$60 Units	$120 Units

Each hair styling has variable costs of $7. Harvey's output is constrained by the 80 units of cutting/setting capacity. Two options exist that can relieve the bottleneck at the cutting/setting operation. Consider the differential costs associated with each of the following options to determine the impact on throughput.

Option a. Harvey's can increase bottleneck output by hiring one nonstylist employee to prepare customers for the cutting/setting by washing and combing their hair. This would increase the cutting/setting capacity to 90 each Saturday. The cost for this additional employee is $60 per Saturday.

Option b. Harvey's could hire another stylist for each Saturday increasing the cutting/setting capacity to 96 each Saturday and costing an additional $80 per Saturday. (Note that the drying operation has a capacity of 96.)

Should Harvey's managers go ahead with either of the above two options? Why or why not?

14. **Throughput contribution.** Polar Wear, Inc., produces extreme-weather parkas in three operations—cutting, assembling, and finishing. The parkas sell for $120 each. Polar Wear's managers find it has a cutting bottleneck due to limited layout space. Pertinent information per month follows:

	Cutting	Assembly	Finishing
Hourly Capacity	80 Units	100 Units	150 Units
Monthly Capacity (168 hours)	13,440 Units	16,800 Units	25,200 Units
Actual Monthly Production	13,440 Units	13,440 Units	13,440 Units
Fixed Operating Costs per Month ...	$11,200 Units	$15,500 Units	$12,000 Units

Each parka has variable costs of $65. Polar Wear's output is constrained by the 13,440 units of cutting capacity. Only one option exists that can relieve the bottleneck at the cutting operation. Consider the differential costs associated with the following option to determine the impact on throughput.

Polar Wear can increase bottleneck output by renting additional space for the cutting operation, increasing the monthly cutting capacity to 15,000. The additional cost of renting space and hiring additional cutters is $60,000.

Should Polar Wear go ahead with this option? Why or why not?

15. **Dropping a product line.** Waterwear Products currently operates at 75 percent capacity. Worried about the company's performance, the general manager segmented the company's income statement product by product and obtained the following picture:

	Product		
	A	**B**	**C**
Sales	$16,000	$21,000	$25,000
Less Variable Costs	11,000	19,000	20,000
Total Contribution Margin	$ 5,000	$ 2,000	$ 5,000
Less Fixed Costs	2,000	3,000	3,000
Net Operating Profit (Loss)	$ 3,000	$ (1,000)	$ 2,000

Should Waterwear Products drop Product B, if that would eliminate Product B's sales and variable costs and reduce the company's total fixed costs by $1,000?

16. **Dropping a product line.** Timeless Products, a clock manufacturer, operates at capacity. Constrained by machine time, the company decides to drop the most unprofitable of its three product lines. The accounting department came up with the following data from last year's operations:

	Manual	**Electric**	**Quartz**
Machine Time per Unit	0.4 Hour	2.5 Hours	5.0 Hours
Selling Price per Unit	$20	$30	$50
Less Variable Costs per Unit	10	14	28
Contribution Margin	$10	$16	$22

Which line should Timeless Products drop? (Hint: Compute the contribution per machine hour because machine time is the constraint.)

17. **Product choice using linear programming** (Appendix 7.1). Vigil Corporation manufacturers two products whose contribution margins follow:

Product	Contribution Margin
A	$10
B	13

Each month Vigil Corporation has only 12,000 hours of machine time and 14,400 hours of labor time available. The amount of time required to make Products A and B follows:

	Product A	Product B
Labor Time	4 Hours per Unit	2 Hours per Unit
Machine Time	2 Hours per Unit	3 Hours per Unit

The firm sells all units produced. Management wants to know the number of units of each product the company should make.

Set up the problem in the linear programming format and solve for the optimal production mix.

18. **Economic order quantity** (Appendix 7.2). The Magee Foundry regularly uses 2,500 axles per year. It can purchase axles for $100 each. Ordering costs are $10 per order, and the holding costs of items in inventory are 20 percent of cost per year. Prepare an analysis for management that answers the following question.

What are the economic order quantity and annual ordering costs, assuming that only lots of 1,000 items are available?

19. **Economic order quantity** (Appendix 7.2). The purchasing agent responsible for ordering boots estimates that Hanson's Footwear sells 5,000 pairs of boots evenly throughout each year, that each order costs $12.50 to place, and that holding a pair of boots in inventory for a year costs $.50 per pair.

a. How many pairs of boots should Hanson's Footwear request in each order?

b. How many times per year should Hanson's Footwear order boots?

20. **Product mix decisions** (Appendix 7.1; adapted from CPA exam). The Random Company manufactures two products, Zeta and Beta. Each product must pass through two processing operations. All materials enter production at the start of Process No. 1. Random has no work-in-process inventories. Random may produce either one product exclusively or various combinations of both products, subject to the following constraints:

	Process No. 1	Process No. 2	Contribution Margin per Unit
Hours Required to Produce One Unit of:			
Zeta	1	1	$4.25
Beta	2	3	5.25
Total Capacity per Day in Hours	1,000	1,275	

A shortage of technical labor has limited Beta production to 400 units per day. The firm has *no* constraints on the production of Zeta other than the hour constraints in the preceding schedule. Assume that all relations between capacity and production are linear.

What is the total contribution from the optimal product mix?

21. **Product mix decisions** (Appendix 7.1). Use the information for the Random Company in Exercise 20 and assume that the present Process No. 1 already costs

the company $1.65 for each unit of Zeta. What is the maximum price that Random would be willing to pay for additional Process No. 1 time to produce one more unit of Zeta?

22. **Dropping a product line.** Ascom Hasler is a public accounting firm that offers three types of services—audit, tax, and consulting. The firm is concerned about the profitability of its consulting business and is considering dropping that line. If the consulting business is dropped, more tax work would be done. If consulting is dropped, all consulting revenues would be lost, all of the variable costs associated with consulting would be saved, and 40 percent of the fixed costs associated with consulting would be saved. If consulting is dropped, tax revenues are expected to increase by 50 percent, the variable costs associated with tax would increase by 50 percent and the fixed costs associated with tax would increase 20 percent. Revenues and costs associated with auditing would not be affected.

Segmented income statements for these product lines appear as follows:

	Product		
	Consulting	**Tax**	**Auditing**
Revenue	$300,000	$400,000	$500,000
Variable Costs	250,000	300,000	350,000
Contribution Margin	$ 50,000	$100,000	$150,000
Fixed Costs	50,000	60,000	80,000
Operating Profit	$ –0–	$ 40,000	$ 70,000

Prepare a report to the management of Ascom Hasler advising whether to drop consulting and increase tax. Assume tax would not be increased if consulting were kept. Include a differential analysis like that in the bottom part of Exhibit 7.5.

23. **Differential costs.** Assume Nike Shoes has a plant capacity that can produce 5,000 units per week (each unit is a pair of shoes). Its predicted operations for the week follow:

Sales (4,000 units at $40 each)	$160,000
Manufacturing Costs:	
Variable	$25 per Unit
Fixed	$17,000
Marketing and Administrative Costs:	
Variable (sales commissions)	$2 per Unit
Fixed	$2,500

Should Nike accept a special order for 400 units at a selling price of $35 each? Assume these units are subject to half the usual sales commission rate per unit, and assume no effect on regular sales at regular prices. How will the decision affect the company's operating profit?

PROBLEMS

24. Dropping a machine from service. The Four Star Company has four large milling machines of approximately equal capacity. Each was run at close to its full capacity during Year 5. Each machine is depreciated separately using an accelerated method. Data for each machine follow (X0 refers to Year 0):

	No. 1	No. 2	No. 3	No. 4
Date Acquired	1/1/X0	1/1/X1	1/1/X3	1/1/X4
Cost	$50,000	$60,000	$75,000	$80,000
Operating Costs, Year 5:				
Labor	$20,000	$18,000	$22,000	$21,500
Materials	5,000	6,000	4,500	3,000
Maintenance	1,000	1,000	700	500
Depreciation (a fixed cost)	3,000	5,000	11,000	15,000
Total	$29,000	$30,000	$38,200	$40,000

Four Star expects activity in Year 6 to be less than in Year 5, so it will drop one machine from service. Management proposes that Four Star drop No. 4 on the grounds that it has the highest operating costs. Do you agree or disagree with this proposal? Why or why not?

25. Make or buy. Fisco, Inc., produces computer boards of which part no. 301 is a subassembly. Fisco, Inc., currently produces part no. 301 in its own shop. The Nordic Company offers to supply it at a cost of $400 per 500 units. An analysis of the costs of Fisco's producing part no. 301 reveals the following information:

	Cost Per 500 Units
Direct (Variable) Material	$160
Direct (Variable) Labor	180
Other Variable Costs	50
Fixed Costs[a]	100
Total	$490

[a]Fixed overhead comprises largely depreciation on general-purpose equipment and factory buildings.

Management of Fisco, Inc., needs your advice in answering the following questions:

a. Should Fisco, Inc., accept the offer from Nordic if Fisco's plant is operating well below capacity?

b. Should the offer be accepted if Nordic reduces the price to $360 per 500 units?

c. If Fisco can find other profitable uses for the facilities it now uses in turning out part no. 301, what maximum purchase price should Fisco pay for part no. 301?

26. Cost estimate for bidding: consulting firm. Anders and Benita Consultants (ABC) operates a management consulting firm. It has just received an inquiry from a prospective client about its prices for educational seminars for the prospective client's supervisors. The prospective client wants bids for three alternative activity levels: (1) one seminar with 20 participants, (2) four seminars with 20 participants each (80 participants total), or (3) eight seminars with 150 participants in total. The consulting firm's accountants have provided the following differential cost estimates:

Startup Costs for the Entire Job	$ 400
Materials Costs per Participant (brochures, handouts, etc.)	50
Differential Direct Labor Costs:	
One Seminar	900
Four Seminars	3,600
Eight Seminars	6,750

In addition to the preceding differential costs, ABC allocates fixed costs to jobs on a direct-labor-cost basis, at a rate of 80 percent of direct labor costs (excluding setup costs). For example, if direct labor costs are $100, ABC would also charge the job $80 for fixed costs. ABC seeks to make a profit of 10 percent of the bid price for each job. For this purpose, profit is revenue minus all costs assigned to the job, including allocated fixed costs. ABC has enough excess capacity to handle this job with ease.

    a. Assume ABC bases its bid on the average total cost, including fixed costs allocated to the job, plus the 10-percent profit margin. What should ABC bid for each of the three levels of activity?

    b. Compute the differential cost (including startup cost) and the contribution to profit for each of the three levels of activity.

    c. Assume the prospective client gives three options. It is willing to accept either of ABC's bids for the one-seminar or four-seminar activity levels, but the prospective client will pay only 90 percent of the bid price for the eight-seminar package. ABC's president responds, "Taking the order for 10 percent below our bid would wipe out our profit! Let's take the four-seminar option; we make the most profit on it." Do you agree? What would be the contribution to profit for each of the three options? The differential cost?

27. Differential cost analysis in a service organization (contributed by Robert H. Colson). Top-Dogs Search, Inc., is a "head-hunting" firm that provides information about candidates for executive and cabinet-level positions. Major customers include corporations and the federal government.

    The cost per billable hour of service at the company's normal volume of 8,000 billable hours per month follows. (A billable hour is one hour billed to a client.)

TOP-DOGS SEARCH, INC.
Cost per Billable Hour of Service

Average Cost per Hour Billed to Client:		
Variable Labor—Consultants	$100	
Variable Overhead, Including Supplies and Clerical Support	20	
Fixed Overhead, Including Allowance for Unbilled Hours	80	
		$200
Marketing and Administrative Costs per Billable Hour (all fixed) . . .		50
Total Hourly Cost		$250

Treat each question independently. Unless given otherwise, the regular fee per hour is $300.

a. How many hours must the firm bill per month to break even?

b. Market research estimates that a fee increase to $400 per hour would decrease monthly volume to 6,000 hours. The accounting department estimates that fixed costs would be $1,040,000 while variable costs per hour would remain unchanged. How would a fee increase affect profits?

c. Top-Dogs Search is operating at its normal volume. It has received a special request from a cabinet official to provide investigative services on a special-order basis. Because of the long-term nature of the contract (4 months) and the magnitude (1,000 hours per month), the customer believes a fee reduction is in order. Top-Dogs Search has a capacity limitation of 8,500 hours per month. Fixed costs will not change if the firm accepts the special order. What is the lowest fee Top-Dogs Search would be willing to charge?

28. Comprehensive differential costing problem. American Manufacturing, Inc., produces hydraulic hoists used by garages to move engines. The costs of manufacturing and marketing hydraulic hoists at the company's normal volume of 3,000 units per month follow:

AMERICAN MANUFACTURING
Costs per Unit for Hydraulic Hoists

Unit Manufacturing Costs:		
Variable Materials	$100	
Variable Labor	150	
Variable Overhead	50	
Fixed Overhead	200	
Total Unit Manufacturing Costs		$500
Unit Nonmanufacturing Costs:		
Variable	$100	
Fixed	100	
Total Unit Nonmanufacturing Costs		200
Total Unit Costs		$700

Unless otherwise stated, assume that the situations described in the questions are not connected; treat each independently. Unless otherwise stated, assume a regular selling price of $1,000 per unit and a volume of 3,000 hoists.

a. What is the breakeven volume in units? In sales dollars?

b. Market research estimates that volume could be increased to 3,500 units, which is well within hoist production capacity limitations, if the firm reduces the price from $1,000 to $900 per unit. Total fixed costs will not change. Do you recommend that the firm take this action? What would be the impact on monthly sales, costs, and income?

c. On March 1, American Manufacturing receives a contract offer from the federal government to supply 1,000 units to the Department of Defense for delivery by March 31. Because of an unusually large number of rush orders from its regular customers, American Manufacturing plans to produce 4,000 units during March, which will use all available capacity. If it accepts the government order, it will lose to a competitor 1,000 units normally sold to regular customers.

The contract offered by the government would reimburse the government's share of March manufacturing costs, plus pay a fixed fee (profit) of $100,000. The offer does not specify how to measure "manufacturing costs." The firm would not incur any variable nonmanufacturing costs on the government's units. Total fixed costs would not be affected by this order. What impact would accepting the government contract have on March income?

d. American Manufacturing can enter a foreign market in which price competition is keen. An attraction of the foreign market is that demand there is greatest when demand in the domestic market is low; thus the firm could use idle production facilities without affecting domestic business.

The firm received an order for 1,000 units at a below-normal price in this market. Shipping costs for this order will be $75 per unit; total costs of obtaining the contract (marketing costs) will be $8,000. This order will not affect domestic business. What is the minimum unit price American Manufacturing should consider for this order of 1,000 units?

e. An inventory of 230 units of an obsolete model of the hoist remains in the stockroom. If the firm does not sell these units through regular channels at reduced prices, the inventory will soon be worthless. What is the minimum acceptable price for selling these units?

29. **Make or buy with opportunity costs.** Refer to American Manufacturing in the previous problem.

a. American Manufacturing receives a proposal from an outside contractor who will make and ship 1,000 hydraulic hoist units per month directly to American Manufacturing's customers as American Manufacturing's sales force receives orders. The proposal would not affect American Manufacturing's fixed nonmanufacturing costs, but its variable nonmanufacturing costs would decline by 20 percent for these 1,000 units produced by the contractor. American Manufacturing's plant would operate at two-thirds of its normal level. Total fixed manufacturing costs would decline by 30 percent.

What in-house unit cost should the firm use to compare with the quotation received from the supplier? Should the firm accept the proposal for a price (that is, payment to the contractor) of $600 per unit?

b. Assume the same facts as in part **a**, except that the firm will use idle facilities to produce 800 modified hoists per month for ships. It can sell these modified hoists for $1,200 each, while the costs of production would be $700 per unit variable manufacturing cost. Variable nonmanufacturing costs would be $100 per unit. Fixed nonmanufacturing and manufacturing costs will not change whether the firm manufactures the original 3,000 regular hoists or the mix of 2,000 regular hoists plus 800 modified hoists. What is the maximum purchase price per unit that American Manufacturing should be willing to pay the outside contractor? Should it accept the proposal for a price of $600 per unit?

30. **Product mix decision.** Larato Company has one machine on which it can produce either of two products, Y or Z. Sales demand for both products is such that the machine could operate at full capacity on either of the products, and Larato can sell all output at current prices. Product Y requires 2 hours of machine time per unit of

output and Product Z requires 4 hours of machine time per unit of output. Larato charges depreciation of machines to products at the rate of $8 per hour.

The following information summarizes the per-unit cash inflows and costs of Products Y and Z.

	Per Unit	
	Product Y	Product Z
Selling Price	$60	$110
Materials	$ 8	$ 12
Labor	2	6
Machine Depreciation[a]	16	32
Allocated Portion of Fixed Factory Costs[b] ..	12	20
Total Cost of Unit Sold	$38	$ 70
Gross Margin per Unit	$22	$ 40

[a]This item under these circumstances could be referred to as "variable factory costs."
[b]Allocated in proportion to (direct) labor costs.

Selling costs are the same whether Larato produces Product Y or Z, or both. You may ignore them. Should Larato Company plan to produce Product Y, Product Z, or some mixture of both? Why?

31. **Alternative concepts of cost: George Jackson** (adapted from CMA exam). George Jackson operates a small machine shop. He manufactures one standard product available from many other similar businesses and he also manufactures products to customer order. His accountant prepared the following annual income statement:

	Custom Sales	Standard Sales	Total
Sales	$50,000	$25,000	$75,000
Material	$10,000	$ 8,000	$18,000
Labor	20,000	9,000	29,000
Depreciation	6,300	3,600	9,900
Power	700	400	1,100
Rent	6,000	1,000	7,000
Heat and Light	600	100	700
Other	400	900	1,300
Total Costs	$44,000	$23,000	$67,000
Operating Profit	$ 6,000	$ 2,000	$ 8,000

The depreciation charges are for machines used in the respective product lines. The rent is for the building space, which Mr. Jackson has leased for 10 years at $7,000 per year. The accountant apportions the rent and the heat and light to the product lines based on amount of floor space occupied. Material, labor, power, and other costs are variable costs that are directly related to the product line causing them.

A valued custom parts customer has asked Mr. Jackson to manufacture 2,500 special units. Mr. Jackson is working at capacity and would have to give up some other business in order to take this business. He must produce custom orders already agreed to, but he could reduce the output of his standard product by about one-half for 1 year and use the freed machine time normally used for the standard product to produce the specially requested customer part. The customer is willing to pay $9.00 for each part. The material cost will be about $3.00 per unit and the labor will be $3.60 per unit. Mr. Jackson will have to spend $2,000 for a special device that he will discard when the job is done. The new job will also require additional power costing $300.

a. Calculate and present the differential cash cost of filling the order, considering both the cost of the order and the costs saved by reducing work on standard products.

b. Should Mr. Jackson accept the order? Explain your answer.

CASES

32. **Department closing.** Prior to last year, Kahn Wholesalers Company had not kept departmental income statements. To achieve better management control, the company decided to install department-by-department accounts. At the end of last year, the new accounts showed that although the business as a whole was profitable, the Dry Goods Department had shown a substantial loss. The income statement for the Dry Goods Department, shown here, reports on operations for last year.

KAHN WHOLESALERS COMPANY
Dry Goods Department
Partial Income Statement

Sales	$500,000	
Cost of Goods Sold	375,000	
Gross Margin		$125,000
Costs:		
Payroll, Direct Labor, and Supervision	$ 33,000	
Commissions of Sales Staff[a]	30,000	
Rent[b]	26,000	
State Taxes[c]	3,000	
Insurance on Inventory	4,000	
Depreciation[d]	7,000	
Administration and General Office[e]	22,000	
Interest for Inventory Carrying Costs[f]	5,000	
Total Costs		(130,000)
Loss before Allocation of Income Taxes		$ (5,000)

Additional computations:

[a]All sales staff are compensated on straight commission, at a uniform 6 percent of all sales.

[b]Rent is charged to departments on a square-foot basis. The company rents an entire building, and the Dry Goods Department occupies 15 percent of the building.

[c]Assessed annually on the basis of average inventory on hand each month.

[d]Eight and one-half percent of cost of departmental equipment.

[e]Allocated on basis of departmental sales as a fraction of total company sales.

[f]Based on average inventory quantity multiplied by the company's borrowing rate for 3-month loans.

Analysis of these results has led management to suggest that it close the Dry Goods Department. Members of the management team agree that keeping the Dry Goods Department is not essential to maintaining good customer relations and supporting the rest of the company's business. In other words, eliminating the Dry Goods Department is not expected to affect the amount of business done by the other departments.

What action do you recommend to management of Kahn Wholesalers Company in the short run? Why?

33. **Product choice with constraints** (Appendix 7.1; adapted from CMA exam). Leastan Company manufactures a line of carpeting that includes a commercial carpet and a residential carpet. Both types of carpeting use two grades of fiber— heavy-duty and regular. The mix of the two grades of fiber differs in each type of carpeting, with the commercial grade using a greater amount of heavy-duty fiber.

Leaston will introduce a new line of carpeting in 2 months to replace the current line. The new line cannot use the fiber now in stock. Management wants to exhaust the present stock of regular and heavy-duty fiber during the last month of production.

Data regarding the current line of commercial and residential carpeting follow:

	Commercial	Residential
Selling Price per Roll	$1,000	$800
Production Specifications per Roll of Carpet:		
Heavy-Duty Fiber	80 Pounds	40 Pounds
Regular Fiber	20 Pounds	40 Pounds
Direct Labor Hours	15 Hours	15 Hours
Standard Cost per Roll of Carpet:		
Heavy-Duty Fiber ($3 per pound)	$240	$120
Regular Fiber ($2 per pound)	40	80
Direct Labor ($10 per direct labor hour)	150	150
Variable Manufacturing Overhead (60 percent of direct labor cost)	90	90
Fixed Manufacturing Overhead (120 percent of direct labor cost)	180	180
Total Standard Cost per Roll	$700	$620

Leaston has 42,000 pounds of heavy-duty fiber and 24,000 pounds of regular fiber in stock. Leaston will sell all fiber not used in the manufacture of the present types of carpeting during the last month of production for $.25 a pound.

A maximum of 10,500 direct labor hours are available during the month. The labor force can work on either type of carpeting.

Sufficient demand exists for the present line of carpeting so that the firm can sell all quantities produced.

a. Calculate the number of rolls of commercial carpet and residential carpet Leastan Company must manufacture during the last month of production to exhaust completely the heavy-duty and regular fiber still in stock.

b. Can Leastan Company manufacture these quantities of commercial and residential carpeting during the last month of production? Explain your answer.

34. **Sell or process further** (adapted from CMA exam). The management of Bay Company is considering a proposal to install a third production department within its existing factory building. With the company's present production setup, 200,000 pounds per year of direct materials are passed through Department I to produce Materials A and B in equal proportions. Material A is then passed through Department II to yield 100,000 pounds to Product C. One hundred thousand pounds of Material B is presently being sold "as is" at a price of $20.25 per pound.

The costs for Bay Company are as follows:

	Department I (Materials A and B)[a]	Department II (Product C)[a]	(Material B)[a]
Prior Department Costs	$ —	$33.25	$33.25
Direct Materials	20.00	—	—
Direct Labor	7.00	12.00	—
Variable Overhead	3.00	5.00	—
Fixed Overhead:			
Direct (Total = $675,000)	2.25	2.25	—
Allocated ($^2/_3$, $^1/_3$)	1.00	1.00	—
	$33.25	$53.50	$33.25

[a]Cost per pound.

Common fixed overhead costs of $300,000 are allocated to the two producing departments on the basis of the space used by the departments: $^2/_3$ to Dept. I and $^1/_3$ to Dept. II.

The proposed Department III would process Material B into Product D. One pound of Material B yields one pound of Product D. Any quantity of Product D can be sold for $30 per pound. Costs under this proposal are as follows:

	Department I (Materials A and B)	Department II (Product C)	Department III (Product D)
Prior Department Costs	$ —	$33.00	$33.00
Direct Materials	20.00	—	—
Direct Labor	7.00	12.00	5.50
Variable Overhead	3.00	5.00	2.00
Fixed Overhead:			
Direct (Total = $850,000) . . .	2.25	2.25	1.75
Allocated ($^1/_2$, $^1/_4$, $^1/_4$)	.75	.75	.75
	$33.00	$53.00	$43.00

If sales and production levels are expected to remain constant in the foreseeable future, if these cost estimates are expected to be true, and if there are no foreseeable alternative uses for the available factory space, should Bay Company produce Product D? Show calculations to support your answer.

SUGGESTED SOLUTIONS TO EVEN-NUMBERED EXERCISES

12. Make or buy.

a.

	Buy	−	Make	= Difference
Variable Costs	$300,000	−	$250,000	= $50,000

Ol'Salt should make the sails. The fixed costs are not relevant to the discussion.

b.

	Buy	−	Make	= Difference
Variable Costs	$300,000	−	$250,000	= $ 50,000
Revenue	(80,000)	−	0	= (80,000)
Net Effect	$220,000	−	250,000	= $(30,000)

Ol'Salt should buy. (The rental opportunity makes buying the sails more attractive.)

14. Throughput contribution.

The throughput contribution increases by $85,800 [= 1,560 units × ($120 selling price − $65 direct materials)], which exceeds the additional cost of $60,000 per month. Polar Wear should go ahead with this option because the differential throughput contribution exceeds the differential costs of relieving the bottleneck. (Then management should seek additional ways to further relieve the bottleneck.)

16. Dropping a product line.

	Manual	Electric	Quartz
Machine Time per Unit	0.4 Hours	2.5 Hours	5.0 Hours
Contribution Margin	$10.00	$16.00	$22.00
Contribution Margin per Machine Hour	$25.00[a]	$6.40[b]	$4.40[c]

[a]$25 = $10/0.4 hrs.
[b]$6.40 = $16/2.5 hrs.
[c]$4.40 = $22/5 hrs.

Timeless Products should drop the quartz line.

18. Economic order quantity.

$$D = 2{,}500 \text{ axles per year}$$

$$K_o = \$10$$

$$K_c = 0.20 \times \$100 = \$20$$

$$Q = \sqrt{\frac{2 \times \$10 \times 2{,}500}{\$20}} = \underline{\underline{50}}$$

$$N = \frac{D}{Q} = \frac{2{,}500}{50} = \underline{\underline{50}}$$

Annual ordering costs = $\underline{\underline{\$500}}$ (= 50 × \$10).

20. Product mix decisions.

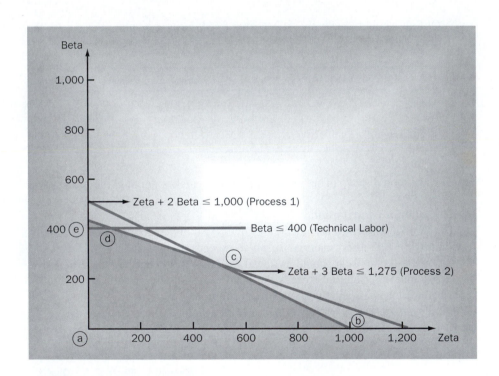

Problem Formulation:

Maximize Total Contribution Margin = 4.25 Zeta + 5.25 Beta.

Subject to:

Process 1 Constraint:	Zeta + 2 Beta ≤ 1,000
Process 2 Constraint:	Zeta + 3 Beta ≤ 1,275
Technical Labor Constraint:	Beta ≤ 400.

Critical Points	Produce and Sell		Total Contribution Margin[a]
	Zeta	Beta	
a	0	0	0
b	1,000	0	$4,250.00*
c	450[b]	275[b]	$3,356.25
d	75[c]	400[c]	$2,418.75
e	0	400	$2,100.00

*Optimal solution.

[a]Total Contribution Margin = $4.25 Zeta + $5.25 Beta.

[b]Zeta + 2 Beta = 1,000 (Process 1 Constraint).

Zeta + 3 Beta = 1,275 (Process 2 Constraint).

Solving simultaneously:

(1,000 − 2 Beta) + 3 Beta = 1,275

Beta = 275.

Zeta + 2(275) = 1,000

Zeta = 450.

[c]Zeta + 3 Beta = 1,275

Beta = 400.

Solving simultaneously:

Zeta + 3(400) = 1,275

Zeta = 75.

22. Dropping a product line.

	Alternative	− Status Quo	= Difference
Revenue	$1,100,000[a]	− $1,200,000[d]	= $ 100,000
Variable Costs	800,000[b]	− 900,000[e]	= 100,000
Contribution Margin	$ 300,000	− $ 300,000	= $ 0
Fixed Costs	182,000[c]	− (190,000)[f]	= 8,000
Operating Profit	$ 118,000	− $ 110,000	= $ 8,000

[a]$1,100,000 = (1.5 × $400,000) + $500,000.

[b]$800,000 = (1.5 × $300,000) + $350,000

[c]$182,000 = (1.2 × $60,000) + $80,000 + (0.6 × $50,000).

[d]$1,200,000 = $300,000 + $400,000 + $500,000.

[e]$900,000 = $250,000 + $300,000 + $350,000.

[f]$190,000 = $50,000 + $60,000 + $80,000.

Dropping consulting and increasing tax work would increase profits by $8,000.

MANAGING QUALITY AND TIME

1. Distinguish between the traditional view of quality and the quality-based view.
2. Define quality according to the customer.
3. Compare the costs of quality control to the costs of failing to control quality.
4. Explain why trade-offs in quality control and failure costs are made.
5. Describe the tools used to identify quality control problems.
6. Explain why just-in-time requires total quality management.
7. Explain why time is important in a competitive environment.
8. Explain how traditional managerial accounting systems must be modified to support total quality management.

WHY IS QUALITY IMPORTANT?

You may have decided never to deal with a company again because you experienced poor-quality service or purchased defective merchandise. That company lost you as a customer. This is why managers are concerned about providing quality products.

A recent survey asked chief financial officers to select the most important changes in their companies' strategies in recent years. The most frequently cited change was to improve customer satisfaction and product quality. In today's competitive environment, improving quality is clearly a high priority. The Managerial Application, "These People Take Quality Seriously," is a stark example of the emphasis placed on quality.

Several prestigious, internationally renowned awards are given to companies for quality. For example, the Baldrige Quality Award was created by Congress in 1987 to recognize U.S. firms with outstanding records of quality improvement and quality management. The Deming Prize was created in Japan long before the Baldrige Quality Award, and is also awarded to companies that focus on quality improvement.

Improving quality is one of the most important strategic factors affecting companies. Many companies require that their suppliers comply with international standards for quality management called ISO 9000. These suppliers' ability to win contracts depends on their complying with ISO. The ISO standards are guidelines for the design and development, production, final inspection and testing, installation, and servicing of products and processes. Guidelines also exist for determining the quality of services. To register, a company must document its quality systems and go through a third-party audit of its manufacturing and customer service processes. The growing importance of ISO 9000 provides clear evidence of a global movement toward quality improvement.

TRADITIONAL VERSUS NEW QUALITY-BASED VIEW

The traditional view assumes there is always a trade-off between the cost of improving quality and maintaining the status quo. According to the traditional view, it may be cheaper to produce lower quality goods and have a minimum level of defective goods. The quality-based view assumes quality can and should always be improved. Rather than waiting for inspections of finished products or reworking defective goods, the quality-based view states that quality must be established at the beginning of the process with zero defects being the goal.

Exhibit 8.1 compares the "traditional view" of managing quality with the new "quality-based view." The perspective of the Quality-Based View column is that high quality pays for the costs incurred to get it. Further, the quality-based view emphasizes continually improving systems and processes.

QUALITY ACCORDING TO THE CUSTOMER

Many organizations develop measures to assess performance based on their critical success factors. Critical success factors are the elements of performance that are required for success. The three critical success factors that relate to meeting customer requirements are service, quality, and cost.

EXHIBIT 8.1

Traditional versus Quality-based View

Traditional View	Quality-Based View
Quality is expensive to produce. The costs associated with producing quality products may be high.	*Quality lowers costs.* Reworking poor-quality parts and making warranty repairs can be costly.
Inspection. Product inspections are the primary way to ensure quality.	*Little need to inspect defect-free goods.* Quality must be established prior to inspections.
Workers cause most defects. Defects generally result from worker errors.	*System causes defects.* Defects generally result from production process deficiencies.
Standards, quotas, goals. Company must constantly strive to meet standards.	*Eliminate standards, quotas, goals.* The production process can always be improved.
Buy from lowest cost supplier. Minimize cost of production materials.	*Buy on basis of lowest total cost, including costs of inspection, rework, and bad customer relations.* Consider the consequences of purchasing poor-quality production materials (reworking, scrap, etc.).
Focus on short-run profits. Maximize short-run profits even if the result is poor quality.	*Loyal customers = higher profits.* High quality leads to loyal, repeat customers. This maximizes long-run profits.

SERVICE

Service refers to the product's tangible as well as intangible features. Tangible features include such qualities as performance and functionality. For example, a washing machine provides service by functioning to clean clothes. Intangible features include how customers are treated by salespeople. Service relates to the expectations the customer has about the product's purchase and use. Organizations can develop a profile of the type of service that customers expect by asking them.

QUALITY

Quality is related the organization's ability to deliver on its service commitments. It means different things to different people. We define quality as giving the customer what was promised; quality is how well the product conforms to specifications. For example, a high-quality washing machine continues to provide service without breaking down.

Quality is defined by the extent to which the customer is satisfied. If a customer expects a product life of three years and gets it, the quality is as high for that product as for a product purchased by a customer expecting a product life of five years and getting it.

Customers expect to get what they have paid for; therefore, quality is important. High quality means that the customer is rarely disappointed. As quality goes up, organizations get better at keeping promises to customers.

Many managers believe that quality and efficiency are related. A process that produces high-quality products usually has high efficiency ratings. When quality is poor, products either have to be reworked or destroyed and the cost per unit of good output increases. As quality goes up, scrap and rework fall, as do costs.

EXHIBIT 8.2	

Customer Satisfaction Measures

Factor	Examples of Performance Measures
Service	Number of customers
	Amount of purchases per customer
	Customer satisfaction surveys
Quality	Number of customer complaints per 1,000 orders filled
	Customer satisfaction surveys
Cost	Ratio of material in final product to material purchased
	Ratio of labor allowed for work done to total labor cost incurred
	Ratio of overhead allowed based on cost drivers used in production to total overhead cost incurred

COST

Cost is a function of the organization's ability to efficiently use resources to obtain its objectives. Accomplishing the same things using fewer resources and, therefore, creating lower costs, means that the organization is increasing efficiency.

Cost is important because of the relationship between product cost and price. In the long run, the price of a product must cover its costs or the organization will go out of the business of making that product. Since customers buy the product from the company with the lowest price, all other things being equal, keeping costs low is a priority for organizations in maintaining a strong competitive advantage.

In choosing among all the products that provide them with the quality and services they want, customers will buy the product that provides them with the preferred mix of quality, services, and price. If two products provide the same quality and services, the customer will choose the product with the lower price.

Customers value service, quality, and cost performance; therefore, the organization must measure these attributes to manage the performance of its activities. Exhibit 8.2 presents some basic examples of performance measures. For example, companies routinely measure service and product quality with customer satisfaction surveys. Managers also look at the ratio of materials in the final product to material purchased, to measure cost performance. If the ratio is high, say greater than 95 percent, that means few materials have been wasted, and the use of materials in production is efficient. If the ratio is only about 50 percent, then one-half of the materials purchased were wasted. This drives up the cost of the final product.

QUALITY CONTROL

In responding to customers' expectations for quality, managers often ask: "How do we improve quality?" and "How much will it cost?" Addressing the second question first, there are two costs of *controlling quality* and two costs of *failing to control quality*.

The two costs of controlling quality are prevention costs and appraisal costs:

1. **Prevention costs** are costs incurred to prevent defects in the products or services being produced. These include:

   - Procurement inspection—Inspecting production materials upon delivery.
   - Processing control (inspection)—Inspecting the production process.
   - Design—Designing production processes to be less susceptible to quality problems.
   - Quality training—Training employees to continually improve quality.
   - Machine inspection—Ensuring machines are operating properly within specifications.

2. **Appraisal costs** (also called **detection costs**) are costs incurred to detect individual units of products that do not conform to specifications. These include:

   - End-process sampling—Inspecting a sample of finished goods to ensure quality.
   - Field testing—Testing products in use at customer site.

Suppose you are the manager at Steve's Sushi, where sushi is made for delivery only. What costs of quality might be incurred? You may decide to have all ingredients inspected before accepting delivery to ensure they meet specifications to help prevent poor quality (prevention cost). You could also taste sample sushi for quality (appraisal cost).

FAILURE TO CONTROL QUALITY

The two costs of failing to control quality are internal failure costs and external failure costs:

1. **Internal failure costs** are costs incurred when nonconforming products and services are detected *before* being delivered to customers. These include:

   - Scrap—Materials wasted in the production process.
   - Rework—Correcting product defects after the product is finished.
   - Reinspection/retesting—Quality control testing after rework is performed.

2. **External failure costs** are costs incurred when nonconforming products and services are detected *after* being delivered to customers. These include:

   - Warranty repairs—Repairing defective products.
   - Product liability—Liability to company resulting from product failure.
   - Marketing costs—Marketing necessary to improve company image tarnished from poor product quality.
   - Lost sales—Decrease in sales resulting from poor-quality products (customers will go to competitors).

As a manager at Steve's, you would probably throw away any prepared sushi that does not meet the strict quality standards established by Steve's (internal failure cost). You might be concerned about lost customer loyalty (and thus, lost future sales) as a result of selling poor-quality sushi or failing to make delivery on time (external failure cost).

Measuring the Cost of Quality in a Nonmanufacturing Setting

A high technology company in the Midwest decided to measure the cost of internal failure in its order entry department, both to ascertain how much internal failure cost the company and to identify where it should direct efforts to improve quality (the idea being the company should direct quality improvement efforts where the costs were). Order entry starts immediately after an order is received. Some examples of internal failure included failure to obtain the customer's credit approval and payment terms for the order. The cost of internal failure, counting only the salary and fringe benefit costs for time spent correcting errors, was more than 4 percent of the order entry department's annual budget. This did not include customer dissatisfaction from delay in getting the order filled.

Collecting the cost information was not an end in itself, but it was an important first step in improving the order entry process. "The manager of the order entry department indicated that the changes would not have been pursued if cost information had not been presented."[a] However, the manager indicated that other information about the processes was actually more helpful in improving processes. "Therefore, [cost of quality] information functioned as a catalyst to accelerate the improvement effort."[b]

Source: S. S. Kalagnanam and E. M. Matsumura, "Cost of Quality in an Order Entry Department," *Journal of Cost Management,* Fall 1995.

[a] Ibid. p. 72.

[b] Ibid.

TRADING OFF QUALITY CONTROL AND FAILURE COSTS

The ultimate goal in implementing a quality improvement program is to achieve zero defects while incurring minimal costs of quality. Managers must make trade-offs among the four cost categories, and total costs of quality must be reduced over time.

How would Steve's Sushi estimate the cost of quality? One employee examines ingredients as part of her daily duties. Assume the cost of ingredient inspections (prevention cost) is $200 per week. The annual cost of quality for ingredient inspections totals $10,400. Assuming yearly sales of $1,000,000, this cost equates to 1.04 percent of sales.

Steve's must decide how much to spend on ingredient inspections versus finished product inspections. It may be cheaper to inspect the finished product rather than inspect all the ingredients delivered.

Costs of quality are often expressed as a percent of sales. An example of a cost of quality report prepared for Steve's appears in Exhibit 8.3. Managers of Steve's Sushi would use the information to ascertain where they could reduce the overall cost of quality. For example, suppose "scrap" occurs because ingredients get too old. Improving inventory management could reduce scrap costs. "Customer complaints" is the cost of dealing with customers, including managerial time and reimbursement to irate customers. Perhaps this cost could be reduced by finding the source of customer complaints and dealing with the problem before it becomes a customer complaint.

Note that external failure costs do not explicitly report the cost of lost business. That is generally true of accounting-based cost of quality reports. Such reports often

EXHIBIT 8.3

STEVE'S SUSHI
Cost of Quality Report
Year Ended December 31

Cost Categories		Costs of Quality	Percent of Sales (Sales = $1,000,000)
Prevention Costs:			
Quality training	$ 6,000		
Materials (ingredients) inspection	10,200	$16,200	1.62%
Appraisal Costs:			
End-of-process sampling		18,000	1.80
Internal Failure Costs:			
Scrap		14,400	1.44
External Failure Costs:			
Customer complaints		12,000	1.20
Total Costs of Quality		$60,600	6.06%

show the results of transactions but not the opportunity cost of lost business. To obtain qualitative measures of lost business, organizations often use customer satisfaction surveys and measures of repeat business.

PROBLEM 8.1 FOR SELF-STUDY

Costs of quality. Carom Company makes skateboards. The following presents financial information for one year.

	Year 1
Sales	$500,000
Costs:	
Materials inspection	6,000
Scrap	8,000
Employee training	13,000
Returned goods	3,000
Finished goods inspection	15,000
Customer complaints	8,000

a. Classify the above items into prevention, appraisal, internal failure, or external failure costs.
b. Create a cost of quality report for Year 1.

The solution to this self-study problem is at the end of the chapter on page 268.

IS THERE REALLY A COST FOR QUALITY?

As you already may understand, it is difficult to measure increased customer satisfaction resulting from additional spending on quality. It is also difficult to measure decreased customer satisfaction resulting from reduced quality costs. For example, if prevention costs are reduced, how do we measure lost sales as a result of this reduction? Conversely, how do we measure the increase in sales directly associated with an increase in prevention costs? It is difficult to accurately measure the change in sales specifically resulting from either scenario.

Although the "cost of quality" concept is prevalent among companies throughout the world, a current theme in business today is that "quality is free." The belief is that if quality is built into the product, the resulting benefits in customer satisfaction, reduced reworking and warranty costs, and other important factors far outweigh the costs of improving quality. Cost-benefit analyses are no longer the primary focus in improving quality. Instead, the emphasis is on improving quality with the understanding that quality is free in the long-run.

Those who subscribe to the quality is free concept believe that zero defects is the only acceptable goal. The production process should be continuously improved by eliminating as many nonvalue-added activities as possible and improving the process for all value-added activities. The result? Quality will improve, customers will be increasingly satisfied, and the cost of improving quality will pay for itself through increased sales and lower costs (providing for increased profit margins).

Although both approaches ("cost of quality" and "quality is free") strive for improved quality, the cost of quality approach assumes a cost-benefit trade-off when spending money on quality improvement. The quality is free approach assumes the long-run benefits will always outweigh the costs of improving quality. One thing is for certain: Quality is important to the success of any company.

IDENTIFYING QUALITY PROBLEMS

How does a company know if quality is a problem? Managers use several tools to identify quality problems. These tools — control charts, cause and effect analysis, and Pareto charts — provide signals about quality control.

A *signal* is information provided to a decision maker. Tools used to identify quality control problems provide two types of signals. The first type is a **warning signal** that indicates something is wrong, in the same way that an increase in your body temperature signals a problem. The warning signal triggers an investigation to find the cause of the problem. The second type is a **diagnostic signal** that suggests the cause of the problem and perhaps a way to solve it.

Managers need both warning and diagnostic information about activities to identify problems that require attention. However, most diagnostic information is expensive to collect, so managers use warning signals to trigger collection of diagnostic information.

Control charts provide warning signals. They help managers distinguish between random or routine variations in quality and variations that should be investigated. They show the results of statistical process-control measures for a sample, batch, or

EXHIBIT 8.4

EXHIBIT 8.4

Control Chart for Steve's Sushi

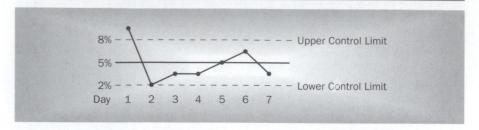

some other unit. These charts are used to study variation in a process and to analyze the variation over time. A specified level of variation may be acceptable, but deviation beyond this level is unacceptable.

Exhibit 8.4 shows an example of a control chart for Steve's Sushi of the amount of scrap ingredients each day. Management believes the scrap should range between 2 percent and 8 percent of total ingredients each day. If scrap is less than 2 percent, management worries that some poor quality ingredients may be included in the sushi. If scrap exceeds 8 percent, management worries about wasting ingredients.

Pareto charts, which provide warning signals, are used to prioritize efforts to improve the most out-of-control processes. Pareto charts are simple to construct, displaying the number of problems or defects as bars of varying lengths. Exhibit 8.5

EXHIBIT 8.5

Pareto Chart for Steve's Sushi for a One-Month Period

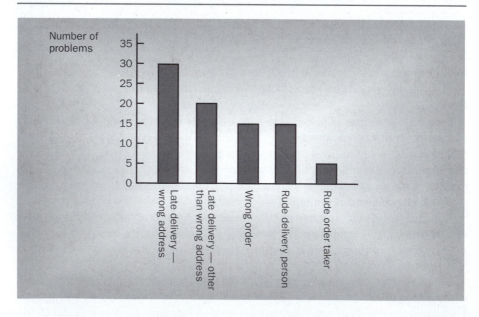

shows an example of a Pareto chart for Steve's Sushi. Based on this Pareto chart, Steve's management can take actions to correct important problems. For example, management can train order takers to triple-check addresses and it can develop a computer file of telephone numbers and addresses so the address automatically appears when the customer calls in the order.

Cause and effect analysis, which provides diagnostic signals, identifies potential causes of defects. To use this analysis, first define the effect (for example, wrong address for delivery) and then identify events that may contribute to the problem (causes). The potential causes can be classified into four categories: human factors, methods and design factors, machine-related factors, and materials and components factors. As the prevailing causes are identified, corrective measures are developed and implemented.

As companies increase their focus on quality in the face of intense global competition, quality control has become an essential element in competing effectively. Managers use the above tools to identify quality problems and find solutions.

JUST-IN-TIME AND TOTAL QUALITY MANAGEMENT

The just-in-time philosophy is closely linked to total quality management. The objective of the **just-in-time (JIT)** philosophy is to purchase and/or produce goods and services just when needed. Companies that apply JIT find it not only reduces, or potentially eliminates, inventory carrying costs, it also requires high quality standards. Processes, or people, making defective units must be corrected immediately because there is no inventory where defective units can be sent to await reworking or scrapping. Manufacturing managers find that JIT can prevent production problems from being hidden. But JIT also requires a smooth production flow without downtime to correct problems.

Think of JIT and quality requirements for a consulting job you have been hired to do. Suppose you schedule your time so you have just enough time to complete a project before the job is due. If all goes as planned, you will finish typing the report just in time.

Suppose your personal computer crashes in the midst of typing the report. This presents a major problem for you because of the combination of your JIT philosophy and the defective machine in your production process. JIT forces you to think through all the things that could go wrong and to correct them in advance of your project. If you use JIT for jobs, you need to be sure that your machine is reliable (or you have a backup) and that your means of delivering the product is reliable. In short, you need total quality management!

Companies using JIT find the following factors are essential for JIT to work:

- **Total quality.** All employees must be involved in quality.
- **Smooth production flow.** Fluctuations in production lead to delays.
- **Purchasing quality materials.** Defective materials disrupt the production flow. Suppliers must be reliable, providing on-time deliveries of high quality materials.

- **Well-trained, flexible workforce.** Workers must be well-trained and also be cross-trained to use various machines and work on various parts of the production process.
- **Short customer-response times.** Keeping the customer response time short enables companies to respond quickly to customer needs.
- **Backlog of orders.** A company needs to have a backlog of orders to keep the production line moving with a JIT system. If there is no backlog, production would stop when an order has been filled and remain idle until a new order is received. This could create chaos in the factory.

Companies have found that JIT essentially requires total quality management. JIT eliminates buffers of inventory and time where problems can be dealt with or even hidden. With no buffers, processes must work right the first time. In practice, few companies have zero buffers and processes do not always work perfectly the first time. Nevertheless, zero buffers and zero defects are useful targets.

THE IMPORTANCE OF TIME IN A COMPETITIVE ENVIRONMENT

Success in competitive markets increasingly demands shorter new-product development time and more rapid response to customers. Rapid response to customers can occur when work processes are designed to meet both quality and response goals. Response time improvement should be included as a major focus in quality improvement. Response time improvements often drive simultaneous improvements in quality and productivity. Hence it is beneficial to consider response time, quality, and customer satisfaction objectives together.

It's easiest to think of customer response time in two categories: (1) new-product development time, and (2) operational measures of time.

NEW-PRODUCT DEVELOPMENT TIME

New-product development time is the period between the first consideration of a product and its delivery to the customer. Firms that respond quickly to customer needs for new products may develop an advantage over competitors. For example, when Honda identified U.S. consumers' need for fuel-efficient cars, the firm's fast development capabilities gave it a competitive advantage for several years.

Not only is management interested in improving new-product development time, it is interested in how quickly a company can recover its investment in a new product. **Break-even time (BET)** is the length of time required to recover the investment made in new-product development.

It is important to identify the relevant cash flows in break-even time analysis. The relevant cash flows are the differential future cash inflows and outflows that change as a result of introducing the new product. Overhead costs are irrelevant if adding a new product only changes the way overhead is allocated without changing the total cash outflow for overhead costs. Break-even time analysis should also include both positive and negative cash-flow effects that the new product may have on sales of existing products.

Break-even time works as follows.

1. Break-even time begins when management approves a project, rather than when cash outflows first occur.
2. Break-even time considers the time value of money by discounting all cash flows.[1]

Although Hewlett-Packard and other successful companies utilize break-even time in assessing new-product development, this approach has several limitations:

1. Break-even time ignores all cash flows after the break-even time has been identified. Thus, projects with high profit potential in later years may be rejected in favor of less-profitable projects with higher cash inflows in the early years. As a result, managers may pursue short-term projects with lower profits rather than long-term innovative projects that may contribute more to the long-run viability of the company.
2. Break-even time does not consider strategic and nonfinancial reasons for product development. The focus is strictly on cash flows.
3. Break-even time varies greatly from one business to the next, depending on product life cycles and investment requirements. For example, an acceptable break-even time for the automobile industry may be five years, while the computer industry might demand a break-even time of two years or less.

For instance, Steve's Sushi just approved adding salad to its menu. This will require expanding the walk-in refrigerator at a cost of $3,000. Steve calculated the discounted cash flows per year as $11,600 in increased receipts and $10,100 for increased materials, labor, and energy consumption beginning in six months when the expansion is complete. The break-even time is calculated as

$$\frac{\text{Investment}}{\text{Net discounted cash flow}} + \text{Time period from approval to providing product}$$

$$\frac{\$3,000}{(\$11,600 - \$10,100)} + 0.5 \text{ years} = 2.5 \text{ years}$$

The break-even time for the salad product line is 2.5 years.

PROBLEM 8.2 FOR SELF-STUDY

Jammin' Company manufactures ice skates and roller skates, and has just approved production of a new line of roller blades scheduled to begin sales in nine months. The roller blades production will require investing $150,000 in new machinery and leasing an additional building. The manager has determined that expected production and sales of 200,000 units per year will generate $1,100,000 discounted cash flow in receipts and $800,000 discounted cash flow in expenditures. Calculate the break-even time for the roller blade line.

The solution to this self-study problem is at the end of the chapter on page 268.

---

[1] You do not need to know discounting techniques for this chapter.

EXHIBIT 8.6

Customer Response Time

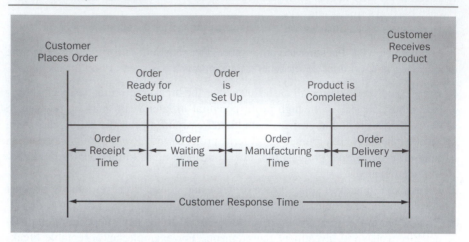

OPERATIONAL MEASURES OF TIME

Operational measures of time indicate the speed and reliability with which organizations supply products and services to customers. Companies generally use two operational measures of time: customer response time and on-time performance.

Customer response time is the amount of time that elapses from the moment a customer places an order for a product or requests service to the moment the product or service is delivered to the customer. The quicker the response time, the more competitive the company. Several components of customer response time appear in Exhibit 8.6. Order receipt time and order delivery time are typically minimal. Thus, improvement may be made within order waiting time and order manufacturing time.

For example, Steve's order receipt time is minimal—an employee answers the phone and takes the order. The time the order waits between being taken at the phone and being passed to the preparation area varies—during rush times the order taker cannot always transfer the order immediately as other calls are coming in. This time could be decreased by relocating the phone closer to the preparation area. Order preparation time might be decreased by arranging the ingredients in a more efficient order. Order delivery time is a function of distance, which Steve's cannot decrease, and efficient routing, which it can control.

On-time performance refers to situations in which the product or service is actually delivered at the time it is scheduled to be delivered. For example, Steve's keeps records of the time orders are taken, the stated delivery time, and the time the order is actually delivered, then measures performance as the ratio of on-time deliveries to total deliveries.

TRADITIONAL MANAGERIAL ACCOUNTING SYSTEMS CAN LIMIT THE IMPACT OF TOTAL QUALITY MANAGEMENT

A company that implements total quality management is likely to find it has little economic benefit unless the company's managerial accounting system supports it.

Many companies have found that managers respond to the managerial accounting system instead of the total quality management initiatives. For example, suppose total quality management requires expenditures on employee training that will improve quality but increase costs in the short-run. Suppose further that the company records and reports cost increases but does not record quality improvements. Given a choice between a recorded cost increase and an unrecorded quality improvement, the manager may choose not to increase cost to improve quality.

Effective implementation of total quality management requires five changes to traditional managerial accounting systems.[2]

First, the information should include problem solving information like that coming from control charts and Pareto diagrams, not just financial reports. Financial reports would indicate a decline in revenues, for example, but not the causes of the decline. Control charts could show an increase in customer complaints as the cause of the revenue decline. To carry this a step further, Pareto charts could indicate the cause of increased customer complaints.

Second, the workers themselves should collect the information and use it to get feedback and solve problems. The information should be "bottom up" in the organization, not just "top down." Traditional managerial accounting reports are based on data collected and aggregated by accountants who present reports to managers who then typically send some of the information down to the workers. These reports are likely to be meaningful to accountants and managers, but not necessarily to workers unfamiliar with accounting concepts.

Third, the information should be available quickly (for example, daily) so workers can get quick feedback. Frequent information accelerates identifying and correcting problems. Traditional managerial accounting systems often report weekly or monthly, which does not facilitate quick response to problems.

Fourth, information should be more detailed than that found in traditional managerial accounting systems. Instead of reporting just the cost of defects, for example, the information system should report the types and causes of defects in addition to the costs of defects.

Fifth, rewards should be based more on quality and customer satisfaction measures of performance. This is the idea that "you get what you reward." If companies do not reward quality, they probably won't get it.

SUMMARY

The following items correspond to the learning objectives presented at the beginning of the chapter.

1. Distinguish between the traditional view of quality and the quality-based view. Improving quality has become one of the most important strategic factors

---

[2] See C. Ittner and D. Larcker, "Total Quality Management and the Choice of Information and Reward Systems," *Journal of Accounting Research,* vol. 33 Supplement.

affecting most companies. Significant differences between the "traditional view" of quality and the emerging "quality-based view" relate to quality production, inspections, causes of defects, standards, purchasing, and customer focus.

2. **Define quality according to the customer.** The three critical success factors that relate to meeting customer requirements are service, quality, and cost. Service relates to the expectations the customer has about all the aspects, both tangible and intangible, of the product's purchase and use. Quality is giving the customer what was promised; it is the extent to which the customer is satisfied. Cost is important because of the relationship between product cost and price. In the long run, the price of a product must cover its costs or the organization will go out of the business of making that product.

3. **Compare the costs of quality control to the costs of failing to control quality.** The two costs of controlling quality are prevention costs (costs incurred to prevent defects in the products or services being produced) and appraisal costs (costs incurred to detect individual units of products that do not conform to specifications). The two costs of failing to control quality are internal failure costs (costs incurred when nonconforming products and services are detected *before* being delivered to customers), and external failure costs (costs incurred when nonconforming products and services are detected *after* being delivered to customers).

4. **Explain why trade-offs in quality control and failure costs are made.** Trade-offs must be made in and among the four cost categories to reduce total costs of quality over time. The company works to achieve an allowable level of defective units, which is often zero.

5. **Describe the tools used to identify quality control problems.** Control charts, cause and effect analyses, and Pareto charts are tools used to identify quality problems. Control charts show the results of statistical process-control measures for a sample, batch, or some other unit over time. The cause and effect analysis defines the effect and lists events that may contribute to the problem (cause). Pareto charts display the number of problems or defects in a product.

6. **Explain why just-in-time requires total quality management.** Companies using JIT find it requires high quality standards and smooth production flow with no downtime to correct problems.

7. **Explain why time is important in a competitive environment.** Success in competitive markets increasingly demands shorter new-product development time and more rapid customer response time. Response time improvements often drive simultaneous improvements in quality and productivity.

   Time is divided into (1) new-product development time, and (2) operational measures of time. New-product development time is important because firms that respond quickly to customer needs may develop a competitive advantage. Operational measures of time indicate the speed and reliability with which organizations supply products and services to customers. The shorter the customer response time, the more competitive the company.

8. **Explain how traditional managerial accounting systems must be modified to support total quality management.** First, information should include problem solving, not just financial, information. Second, workers themselves should collect the information and use it to get feedback and solve problems. Third, the in-

formation should be available quickly so workers get quick feedback. Fourth, information should be more detailed than that found in traditional managerial accounting systems. Fifth, rewards should be based more on quality and customer satisfaction measures of performance.

KEY TERMS AND CONCEPTS

Service   The product's tangible as well as intangible features.

Quality   Giving the customer what was promised; how well the product conforms to specifications.

Prevention costs   Costs incurred to prevent defects in the products or services being produced.

Appraisal costs (also called **detection costs**)   Costs incurred to detect individual units of products that do not conform to specifications.

Internal failure costs   Costs incurred when nonconforming products and services are detected *before* being delivered to customers.

External failure costs   Costs incurred when nonconforming products and services are detected *after* being delivered to customers.

Warning signal   First of two types of signals provided by tools used to identify quality control problems; warns that a problem exists.

Diagnostic signal   Second of two types of signals provided by tools used to identify quality control problems; suggests what the problem is and perhaps a path to follow to solve it.

Control charts   Show the results of statistical process-control measures for a sample, batch, or some other unit.

Pareto charts   Displays of the number of problems or defects in a product over time.

Cause and effect analysis   Defines the effect and lists events that may contribute to the problem (causes).

Just-in-time (JIT)   A system designed to produce or purchase goods or services just in time for the next step of the production process or just in time for sale.

New-product development time   The period between the first consideration of a product and its delivery to the customer.

Break-even time (BET)   The length of time required to recover the investment made in new-product development.

Operational measures of time   Indicate the speed and reliability with which organizations supply products and services to customers.

Customer response time   The amount of time from when a customer places an order for a product or requests service to when the product or service is delivered to the customer.

On-time performance   Refers to situations in which the product or service is actually delivered at the time it is scheduled to be delivered.

SOLUTIONS TO SELF-STUDY PROBLEMS

SUGGESTED SOLUTION TO PROBLEM 8.1 FOR SELF-STUDY

a. and **b.**

Carom Company
Cost of Quality Report
For the Year Ended December 31

Cost Categories	Costs of Quality		Percent of Sales (Sales = $500,000)
Prevention Costs:			
Employee training	$13,000		
Materials inspection	6,000	$19,000	3.8%
Appraisal Costs:			
Finished goods inspection		15,000	3.0
Internal Failure Costs:			
Scrap		8,000	1.6
External Failure Costs:			
Returned goods	3,000		
Customer complaints	8,000	11,000	2.2
Total Costs of Quality		$53,000	10.6%

SUGGESTED SOLUTION TO PROBLEM 8.2 FOR SELF-STUDY

The break-even time is calculated as

$$\frac{\text{Investment}}{\text{Net discounted cash flow}} + \text{Time period from approval to providing product}$$

$$\frac{\$150,000}{(\$1,100,000 - \$800,000)} + 0.75 \text{ years}^a = 1.25 \text{ years}$$

$$^a 0.75 = \frac{9 \text{ months}}{12 \text{ months}}$$

The break-even time for the roller blade line is 1.25 years.

QUESTIONS, EXERCISES, AND PROBLEMS

REVIEW QUESTIONS

1. Review the meaning of the terms and concepts listed in Key Terms and Concepts.
2. What are the three factors that relate to meeting customer requirements?
3. How does the quality-based view differ from the traditional approach of managing quality by inspections?
4. The quality-based management focuses on higher *long-run* profits. Why?
5. What are the two costs of controlling quality?
6. What are the two costs of failing to control quality?

CRITICAL ANALYSIS AND DISCUSSION QUESTIONS

7. How does service relate to the expectations of the customer?
8. Are there any products you can think of in which one or several of the elements of service, quality, and cost are not important to the customer? Explain.
9. Discuss how a restaurant might differ under a quality-based view versus the traditional view of managing quality.
10. For goods or services that you see produced, what are three examples of a warning signal, and the related diagnostic signal you would use to identify quality problems?
11. How could control charts be used? Give two examples.
12. Why does just-in-time require total quality management?
13. Why is time important in a competitive environment?
14. Why would improvements in response time drive improvements in quality and productivity? Use a specific example.
15. Southwest Airlines has particularly emphasized the importance of on-time flight arrivals. Why?
16. Allegiance Insurance Company sends a questionnaire to policy holders who have filed a claim. The questionnaire asks these claimants if they are satisfied with the way the claim has been handled. Why does Allegiance Insurance do this?
17. Course evaluations were introduced to the classrooms during the 1960s. Why were course evaluations introduced?
18. Give two examples of cases in which you think managers would respond to the accounting system instead of to total quality management initiatives.

EXERCISES

Solutions to even-numbered exercises are at the end of the chapter after the problems.

19. **Quality according to the customer.** What are the three most important elements of service for each of the following products?
    a. Tuxedo for bridegroom
    b. Microwave oven
    c. Accounting course at an university
    d. Cruise on a Princess ship
    e. Frozen dinner
20. **Quality according to the customer.** What are the three most important elements of service for each of the following products?
    a. Cowboy boots
    b. Television
    c. Meal in a fine restaurant
    d. Student study guide for managerial accounting
    e. Dishwasher
21. **Quality according to the customer.** What are the three most important elements of service for each of the following products?
    a. Personal computer keyboard

     b. Portable compact disc player

     c. Checking account

     d. Taxi cab ride through New York

     e. Sewing machine

22. **Costs of quality.** Ramirez Corporation manufactures refrigerators. The following presents financial information for two years.

	Year 1	Year 2
Sales	$2,450,000	$2,200,000
Quality Costs:		
Quality training	16,500	18,800
Scrap	18,500	19,300
Production process design	198,000	130,000
Repair of returned goods	43,000	48,000
Rework (goods spoiled during production)	170,000	185,000
Preventive maintenance	135,000	95,000
Materials inspection	65,000	48,000
Finished product testing	94,000	124,000

     a. Classify the above costs into prevention, appraisal, internal failure, or external failure costs.

     b. Calculate the percentage of the total prevention, appraisal, internal failure, and external failure costs to sales for Year 1 and Year 2.

23. **Costs of quality.** Verdal Industries manufactures computer printers. The following presents financial information for two years.

	Year 1	Year 2
Sales	$1,960,000	$1,760,000
Quality Costs:		
Scrap	14,800	15,500
Repair of returned goods	34,000	38,000
Dealing with customer complaints	22,500	27,200
Rework (goods spoiled during production)	136,000	148,000
Materials inspection	52,000	38,000

     a. Classify the above items into prevention, appraisal, internal failure, or external failure costs.

     b. Calculate the percentage of the total prevention, appraisal, internal failure, and external failure costs to sales for Year 1 and Year 2.

24. **Costs of quality.** Owenborrough Corporation manufactures air conditioners. The following presents financial information for two years.

	Year 1	Year 2
Sales	$3,920,000	$3,520,000
Quality Costs:		
Scrap	28,800	30,100
Warranty repairs	70,000	75,000
Rework (goods spoiled during production)	272,000	195,000
Preventive maintenance	220,000	152,000
Materials inspection	105,000	75,000
Product testing	150,000	200,000

a. Classify the above items into prevention, appraisal, internal failure, or external failure costs.

b. Calculate the percentage of the total prevention, appraisal, internal failure, and external failure costs to sales for Year 1 and Year 2.

25. **Reporting costs of quality.** Using the costs calculated in Exercise **22,** prepare a cost of quality report for Year 1 and Year 2.

26. **Cost of quality report.** Using the costs calculated in Exercise **23,** construct a cost of quality report for Year 1 and Year 2.

27. **Cost of quality report.** Using the costs calculated in Exercise **24,** construct a cost of quality report for Year 1 and Year 2.

28. **Quality versus costs.** Assume Clearly Canadian has discovered a problem involving the mix of flavor to the seltzer water that costs the company $3,000 in waste and $2,500 in lost business per period. There are two alternative solutions. The first is to lease a new mix regulator at a cost of $4,000 per period. The new regulator would save Clearly Canadian $2,000 in waste and $2,000 in lost business. The second alternative is to hire an additional employee to manually monitor the existing regulator at a cost of $2,500 per period. This would save Clearly Canadian $1,500 in waste and $800 in lost business per period.

Which alternative should Clearly Canadian choose?

29. **Quality versus costs.** Tylor Precast Manholes has discovered a problem involving the mix of lye to the dry concrete mix that costs the company $5,000 in waste and $3,500 in lost business per period. There are two alternative solutions. The first is to lease a new mix regulator at a cost of $3,500 per period. The new regulator would save Tylor $3,500 in waste and $2,000 in lost business. The second alternative is to hire an additional employee to manually monitor the existing regulator at a cost of $3,000 per period. This would save Tylor $2,500 in waste and $2,000 in lost business per period.

Which alternative should Tylor choose?

30. **Quality versus costs.** Hillsdale Bicycles has discovered a problem involving the welding of bicycle frames that costs the company $3,000 in waste and $1,500 in lost business per period. There are two alternative solutions. The first is to lease

a new automated welder at a cost of $3,500 per period. The new welder would save Hillsdale $1,500 in waste and $1,000 in lost business. The second alternative is to hire an additional employee to manually weld the frames at a cost of $3,000 per period. This would save Hillsdale $2,500 in waste and $1,000 in lost business per period.

Which alternative should Hillsdale choose?

31. **Break-even time.** The research and development department of Nugget Industries is presenting a proposal for new product research. The new product will require research, development, and design investments for three years. The following discounted cash flows (in millions) are presented to management for approval.

Year	1	2	3	4	5	6	7
Cash Outflows:							
Research & development ..	$40	$80	$ 10	$ 0	$ 0	$ 0	$ 0
Design	20	50	100	0	0	0	0
Manufacturing	0	0	0	50	600	400	90
Marketing	0	0	0	120	400	350	160
Cash Inflows:							
Sales	0	0	0	80	1,500	1,000	300

Calculate the break-even time of the new product.

32. **Break-even time.** The research and development department of Newport Oil Company is presenting a proposal for new product research. The new product will require research, development, and design investments for two years. The following discounted cash flows (in millions) are presented to management for approval.

Year	1	2	3	4	5
Cash Outflows:					
Research & development	$5	$20	$ 0	$ 0	$ 0
Design	5	15	0	0	0
Manufacturing	0	0	15	150	100
Marketing	0	0	30	100	60
Cash Inflows:					
Sales	0	0	20	400	250

Calculate the break-even time of the new product.

33. **Break-even time.** The research and development department of Lenox Manufacturing is presenting a proposal for new product research. The new product will require research, development, and design investments for two years. The following discounted cash flows (in millions) are presented to management for approval.

Year	1	2	3	4	5
Cash Outflows:					
Research & development	$2	$8	$ 0	$ 0	$ 0
Design	2	6	0	0	0
Manufacturing	0	0	6	60	40
Marketing	0	0	13	40	20
Cash Inflows:					
Sales	0	0	8	150	80

Calculate the break-even time of the new product.

PROBLEMS

34. **Just-in-time and quality.** Individually or as a group, interview the manager of a retail (or wholesale) store such as a music store, an automobile parts store, or the parts department of an appliance dealership. Ask the manager how items are ordered to replace those sold. For example, do they order based on observing inventory levels or do they place an order each time a customer buys an item? Do they appear to use just-in-time? If so, how important is total quality management to their just-in-time methods? Write a report to your instructor summarizing the results of your interview and analysis.

35. **Total quality management.** Individually or as a group, interview the manager of a fast food restaurant. Ask the manager how quality of service is measured and used to evaluate the manager's performance. Write a report to your instructor summarizing the results of your interview.

36. **Break-even time.** Refer to Exercise **31.** What steps might Nugget Industries take to reduce break-even time on the project?

37. **Break-even time.** Refer to Exercise **32.** What steps might Newport Oil Company take to reduce break-even time on the project?

38. **Quality control.** Alaskan Jumper operates daily round-trip flights between Anchorage and Seattle using a fleet of three planes: the Dove, the Owl, and the Robin.

The budgeted quantity of fuel for each round-trip is the average fuel usage, which over the last 12 months has been 150 gallons. Alaskan has set the upper control limit at 180 gallons and the lower control limit at 130 gallons. The operations manager received the following report for round-trip fuel usage for the period by the three planes.

Trip	Dove	Owl	Robin
1	156	155	146
2	141	141	156
3	146	144	167
4	152	161	156
5	156	138	183
6	161	170	177
7	167	149	189
8	186	159	171
9	173	152	176
10	179	140	185

a. Create quality control charts for round-trip fuel usage for each of the three planes for the period. What inferences can you draw from them?

b. Some managers propose that Alaskan present its quality control charts in monetary terms rather than in physical quantity (gallons) terms. What are the advantages and disadvantages of using monetary fuel costs rather than gallons in the quality control charts?

39. **Break-even time, working backward.** Assume Intel is considering manufacturing a new motherboard for personal computers, the M-Board. The new product development committee will not approve a new product proposal if it has a break-even time of greater than four years. If the project is approved, the investments to make the M-Board will begin on January 1, Year 0. The project discounted cash flows from sales of the M-Board are $5 million each year for Years 0 through 4. The discounted cash flows from costs of manufacturing, distribution, marketing, and customer service are expected to be $3 million each year.

a. What is the maximum cash investment that the new product development committee will agree to fund for the M-Board project?

b. Why might Intel specify a policy that it will not fund new product proposals with an estimated break-even time greater than four years?

40. **Quality improvement.** Quincy Manufacturing makes bicycle frames in two processes, tubing and welding. The tubing process has a capacity of 100,000 units per year; welding has a capacity of 150,000 units per year. Costs of quality information follows:

Design of product and process costs	$220,000
Inspection and testing costs	85,000
Scrap costs (all in the tubing dept.)	350,000

The demand is very strong. Quincy can sell whatever output it can produce at $50 per frame.

Quincy can start only 100,000 units into production in the tubing department because of capacity constraints on the tubing machines. Any defective units produced in the tubing department are scrapped. Of the 100,000 units started at the tubing operation, 10,000 units (10%) are scrapped. Scrap costs, based on total (fixed and variable) manufacturing costs incurred through the tubing operation, equal $35 per unit as follows:

Direct materials (variable)	$18
Direct manufacturing, setup, and materials handling labor (variable)	7
Depreciation, rent, and other overhead (fixed)	10
	$35

The good units from the tubing department are sent to the welding department. Variable manufacturing costs at the welding department are $3.50 per unit.

There is no scrap in the welding department. Therefore Quincy's total sales quantity equals the tubing department's output. Quincy incurs no other variable costs.

Quincy's designers have determined that adding a different type of material to the existing direct materials would reduce scrap to zero, but it would increase the variable costs per unit in the tubing department by $2.00. Recall that only 100,000 units can be started each year.

a. What is the additional direct materials cost of implementing the new method?

b. What is the additional benefit to Quincy from using the new material and improving quality?

c. Should Quincy use the new materials?

d. What other nonfinancial and qualitative factors should Quincy consider in making the decision?

SUGGESTED SOLUTIONS TO EVEN-NUMBERED EXERCISES

20. **Quality according to the customer.** Answers will vary but may include:
    a. fit, design, and cost
    b. size, channel capacity, and cost
    c. taste, friendly wait-persons, and atmosphere
    d. accuracy, cost, and comprehensiveness
    e. cost, quietness, and energy efficiency

22. **Ramirez Corporation costs of quality.**
    a. and **b.**

	Year 1	%	Year 2	%
Sales	$2,450,000		$2,200,000	
Costs of quality:				
Prevention:				
Preventive maintenance	135,000	5.5%	95,000	4.3%
Materials inspection	65,000	2.7	48,000	2.2
Quality training	16,500	0.7	18,800	0.9
Production process design	198,000	8.1	130,000	5.9
Appraisal:				
Finished product testing	94,000	3.8	124,000	5.6
Internal failure:				
Scrap	18,500	0.8	19,300	0.9
Rework	170,000	6.9	185,000	8.4
External failure:				
Repair of returned goods	43,000	1.8	48,000	2.2

24. **Costs of quality.**
    a. and b.

	Year 1	%	Year 2	%
Sales	$3,920,000		$3,520,000	
Costs of Quality:				
Prevention:				
Preventive maintenance	220,000	5.6%	152,000	4.3%
Materials inspection	105,000	2.7	75,000	2.1
Appraisal:				
Product testing	150,000	3.8	200,000	5.7
Internal failure:				
Scrap	28,800	0.7	30,100	0.9
Rework	272,000	6.9	195,000	5.5
External failure:				
Warranty repairs	70,000	1.8	75,000	2.1

26. **Trading off costs of quality.**

VERDAL INDUSTRIES
Cost of Quality Report

	Year 1	%	Year 2	%
Sales	$1,960,000		$1,760,000	
Costs of Quality:				
Prevention:				
Materials inspection	52,000		38,000	
Total prevention costs	$ 52,000	2.7%	$ 38,000	2.2%
Internal failure:				
Scrap	14,800		15,500	
Rework	136,000		148,000	
Total internal failure costs	$ 150,800	7.7	$ 163,500	9.3
External failure:				
Repair of returned goods	34,000		38,000	
Dealing with customer complaints	22,500		27,200	
Total external failure costs	$ 56,500	2.9	$ 65,200	3.7
Total Costs of Quality	$ 259,300	13.2%	$ 266,700	15.2%

28. Quality versus costs.

	Present	New Mix Regulator	Additional Employee
Costs:			
Waste	$3,000	$1,000	$1,500
Lost business	2,500	500	1,700
Lease		4,000	
Wages			2,500
Total	$5,500	$5,500	$5,700

Clearly Canadian is indifferent between leasing the new mix regulator or not because the costs would be the same. Clearly Canadian will not hire another employee as that would increase total quality costs.

30. Quality versus costs.

	Present	New Welder	Additional Employee
Costs:			
Waste	$3,000	$1,500	$ 500
Lost business	1,500	500	500
Lease		3,500	
Wages			3,000
Total	$4,500	$5,500	$4,000

Hillsdale should hire an additional employee as that is the alternative that incurs the least total quality costs.

32. Break-even time.

Year	1	2	3	4	5
Net cash flow (in millions)	$(10)	$(35)	$(25)	$150	$90

Newport Oil will have a cash outflow of $70 through year 3. The next year will recover $150. So the breakeven-time is 3.47 years. [3.47 = 3 years + ($70/$150)]

CHAPTER 9

CAPITAL EXPENDITURE DECISIONS

LEARNING OBJECTIVES

1. Note the separation of the investing and financing aspects of making long-term decisions.
2. Summarize the strategic benefits of capital investments.
3. Explain why audits are an important step in the capital investment process.
4. Identify the behavioral issues involved in capital budgeting.
5. Describe the steps of the net present value method for making long-term decisions using discounted cash flows. Analyze the effect of income taxes on cash flows.
6. Conduct sensitivity analyses of capital budgeting using spreadsheets.
7. Apply the internal rate of return method of assessing investment alternatives.
8. Explain why cash flow analysis is sometimes not enough to justify or reject an investment.

Earlier chapters applied the differential principle to several kinds of short-run operating decisions. In each case, the firm's capacity was fixed. The manager must decide how best to use that fixed capacity in the short run. For example, how many units should we produce this month? Should a management consulting firm accept a one-time consulting assignment?

This chapter shifts attention to the long run. We focus on decisions to change operating capacity—for example, should Weyerhaeuser build a larger plant to manufacture paper? Should Citibank open a new branch? Should Nordstrom's expand? Should Boston Consulting Group hire more staff consultants on long-term employment contracts? Should a job shop acquire new machinery to replace older, less efficient machinery? Should Track Auto acquire new technology that will perform

278

services currently performed by workers? No decision affects the long-run success of a firm more than deciding which capital investment projects to undertake.

Short-run operating decisions and long-run capacity decisions both rely on a differential analysis of cash inflows and cash outflows. Long-run capacity decisions involve cash flows over several future periods, whereas typical operating decisions involve only short-run cash flows. When the cash flows extend over several future periods, the analyst must use some technique to make the cash flows comparable, because the value of one dollar received now exceeds that of one dollar received in the future. Present value analysis, sometimes called discounted cash flow (or DCF) analysis, provides the technique. The appendix at the back of this book further illustrates present value techniques. You should be familiar with its contents before studying this chapter.

CAPITAL BUDGETING: INVESTMENT AND FINANCING DECISIONS

Capital budgeting involves deciding which long-term, or capital, investments to undertake and how to finance them. These decisions involve **capital assets**, or long-term assets. A firm considering acquiring a new plant or equipment must decide first whether to make the investment, and then how to raise the funds required for the investment.

The principle of separating investment decisions from financing decisions is based on the assumption that when a firm raises funds, the funds are used to support all the firm's assets, or the firm as a whole. Lenders and shareholders normally do not invest in specific assets but in the firm as a whole.

The capital budgeting decision involves estimating future cash flows, deciding on an appropriate interest rate for discounting those cash flows, and, finally, deciding on how to finance the project. This text focuses on estimating future cash flows and assumes the appropriate discount rate is given. Financing of projects is left to corporate finance courses. We also consider the sensitivity of capital investments to the estimates required to make those decisions.

STRATEGIC CONSIDERATIONS

The profits from, or the expected cost savings offered by, a capital asset are the most common benefits associated with acquiring capital assets, but the strategic benefits of capital assets are of increasing importance. Including the strategic benefits in capital budgeting is very controversial—they are risky to include because they are difficult to estimate. However, strategic benefits are not likely to be any more difficult to estimate than the expected profits or cost savings.

Strategic benefits reflect the increased profit potential derived from some attribute of a capital asset. The following are some common strategic benefits that may be provided by a capital asset:

1. Reducing the potential to make mistakes, thus improving the quality of the product (for instance, improving machine tolerance or reducing reliance on manual techniques).

2. Making goods or delivering a service that competitors cannot (for instance, developing a patented process to make a product that competitors cannot replicate).
3. Reducing the cycle time to make the product (for instance, making a custom-designed product on the spot).

AUDITS AND CAPITAL BUDGETING

The accuracy of a capital budgeting model relies heavily on the estimates used in the model, particularly the project's cash flows and its life span. These estimates come from past experience, judgment, or the experience of others, such as competitors.

Comparing the estimates made in the capital budgeting process with the actual results, called auditing in this context, provides several advantages. Among these are the following.

1. Audits identify which estimates were wrong so planners can incorporate that knowledge into future estimates to avoid making similar mistakes.
2. Audits can be used to identify and reward those planners who are good at making capital budgeting decisions, thus allowing decision makers to take into account the skill of the planner in making the capital investment decision.
3. Audits create an environment in which planners will not be tempted to inflate their estimates of the benefits associated with the project.

Audits bring an important discipline to a subjective judgmental process and provide many valuable insights for decision makers.

BEHAVIORAL ISSUES

Recognizing the behavioral implications behind the estimates is important in capital budgeting. Planners cannot help but be influenced by their environment. Such factors as a desire to implement a project or meet performance evaluation measures may influence their objectivity in making estimates. Therefore, it is important that organizational policies, procedures, and performance measures support accurate estimations and that the effect they have on planners be considered when evaluating capital investment projects.

As an example of how personal desire might influence a planner, a production manager who is anxious to have the latest equipment might, in order to promote its purchase, be overly optimistic in forecasting the benefits offered by the machine in terms of cost reduction, quality improvement, and cycle time reduction. A standard procedure of comparing the results after the equipment has been acquired to the claims that were made in support of its acquisition will help to curb this type of over-optimistic behavior.

A potential conflict may exist between the criteria used to evaluate individual projects and the criteria used to evaluate an organization's overall performance or the performance of a unit. An example of how performance measures influence a planner follows.

Suppose a manager of Desert Industries, a producer of microwave ovens, is considering acquiring machinery to produce another line of kitchen aids. The estimates of cash flows over the life of the equipment indicate that the acquisition should be undertaken. However, although the later years provide large positive cash flows, the first two years have negative cash flows due to low revenues. At Desert Industries, the manager's performance evaluation is based on the annual operating profits, which the acquisition would lower during the first two years. Thus, a conflict exists between the capital budgeting model and financial accounting performance measures. The possible result of this conflict is that a capital investment that would have a positive effect on the organization in the long run might be rejected because of its effect on short-run performance measures. Wise managers recognize these conflicts and make sure employees are rewarded for making the decision that is in the company's best long-run interests.

DISCOUNTED CASH FLOW

If you have an opportunity to invest $1 today in return for $2 in the future, your evaluation of the attractiveness of the opportunity depends, in part, on how long you have to wait for the $2. If you must wait only one week after making the initial investment, you are much more inclined to accept the offer than if you have to wait ten years to receive the $2. **Discounted cash flow (DCF) methods** aid in evaluating investments involving cash flows over time where there is a significant time difference between cash payment and receipt. The two discounted cash flow methods are the net present value (NPV) method and the internal rate of return (IRR) method.

THE DISCOUNT RATE

The **discount rate** is the interest rate used in computing the present value of future cash flows. The discount rate for an investment of average risk is the cost of capital of the firm. If an investment is of above-average risk, then the discount rate should be the cost of capital adjusted for the increased risk.

The appropriate discount rate has three separate elements:

1. A pure rate of interest reflecting the productive capability of capital assets. This is the interest rate in receipt/payment for loaning/borrowing the funds, like rent. (Economists debate the results of empirical research, but most would agree that the pure rate of interest generally lies between 0 and 5 percent.)
2. A risk factor reflecting the riskiness of the project. The greater a project's risk, the higher the discount rate. (For example, investing a company's money in a high-risk project compared to low-risk bonds. The federal government has the lowest probability of default, so government bonds usually have the lowest risk premiums.)
3. A premium reflecting inflation expected to occur over the life of the project.

The **risk free rate** includes the pure interest rate and a premium for expected inflation. Government bonds are often used as a measure of the current risk free rate.

The **real interest rate** includes the pure interest rate and a premium for the risk of the investment. The real interest rate does not include expected inflation. The **nominal interest rate** includes all three factors—pure interest, risk premium, and expected inflation.

In our experience, analysts typically forecast project cash flows in nominal dollars. Nominal dollars are the actual dollar amounts expected to be received in the future, including inflation. If we forecast project cash flow in nominal dollars, we use a nominal discount rate. In this chapter, all cash flow forecasts are in nominal dollars and discount rates are nominal discount rates.

THE NET PRESENT VALUE METHOD

The net present value method involves the following steps:

1. Estimate the amounts of future cash inflows and future cash outflows in each period for each alternative under consideration.
2. Discount the future cash flows to the present using the project's discount rate. The **net present value of cash flows** of a project is the present value of the cash inflows minus the present value of the cash outflows.
3. Accept or reject the proposed project or select one from a set of mutually exclusive projects.

If the present value of the future cash inflows exceeds the present value of the future cash outflows for a proposal, the firm should accept the alternative. If the net present value of the future cash flows is negative, the firm should reject the alternative. If the firm must choose one from a set of mutually exclusive alternatives with the same life span, it should select the one with the largest net present value of cash flows.

This three-step procedure summarizes a process involving many estimates and projections. We begin the discussion of the process with the first step of identifying the cash flows.

In practice, analysts consider a variety of cash flows. The cash flows associated with an investment project divide into the initial cash flows (at the beginning of the project), the periodic cash flows (during the life of the project), and the terminal cash flows (at the end of the project). A checklist of these cash flows is presented for your use in identifying cash flows. It is important to remember to identify the cash flows at the time of occurrence, not when they are recorded as revenues or expenses for financial accounting purposes.

Initial Cash Flows   Cash flows occurring at the beginning of the project often include:

1. Asset cost—outflow
2. Freight and installation costs—outflow
3. Salvage or other disposal value of existing asset being replaced—inflow
4. Income tax effect of gain (loss) on disposal of existing asset—outflow (inflow)
5. Investment tax credit, if any, on new asset—inflow

Periodic Cash Flows   Cash flows occurring during the life of the project often include:

1. Receipts from sales (cash, *not* revenues, which generally precede receipt of cash)—inflow
2. Opportunity costs (lost "other" inflows) of undertaking this particular project—outflow. (For example, the new equipment allows production of a new product that will decrease the sales of an existing product.)

MANAGERIAL APPLICATION

Environmental Investments

Environmental accounting will be a major challenge for management accountants in the twenty-first century. A national survey was conducted to benchmark the way U.S. manufacturing companies identify, allocate, and analyze environmental costs in the context of evaluating the profitability of potential environmental investments. An example would be the costs of installing a pollution control device versus the costs of not installing the device, such as fines and environmental impact.

The survey requested respondents to identify the costs they consider when preparing cash flow projections of environmental projects. The cash flows considered most frequently were waste management costs that motivate environmental projects in the first place. The table shows a sample of the cash flows included in environmental investments.

The survey authors conclude that, although many social benefits may result from improved

Cost Item	Percent Who Consider
On-site air/water/hazardous waste testing/monitoring	79
On-site hazardous waste handling (storage/labeling)	70
Employee safety/health compensation claims	69
Staff training for environmental compliance	59
Environmental penalties/fines	57
Legal staff labor time	28

investment in environmental projects, these investments may also be in the company's interest by eliminating fines, legal costs, and cleanups. For example, investing in safeguards in the Trans-Alaska Pipeline has probably saved oil companies billions of dollars by preventing oil spills.

Source: Based on A. White and D. Savage, "Budgeting for Environmental Projects: A Survey," *Management Accounting*, October 1995, pp. 48–54.

3. Expenditures for fixed and variable production costs—outflow
4. Savings for fixed and variable production costs—inflow
5. Selling, general, and administrative expenditures—outflow
6. Savings in selling, general, and administrative expenditures—inflows
7. Income tax effects of flows 1 through 6—opposite in sign to the cash flow that generates the tax consequences. The timing of the effect may be in a different period than the cash flow because the tax effect is based on financial accounting. (For instance, increased expenditures for production costs increase expenses, not necessarily during the same time period, which decrease taxes.)
8. Savings in taxes caused by deductibility of depreciation on tax return (sometimes called "depreciation tax shield")—inflow
9. Loss in tax savings from lost depreciation—outflow
10. Do *not* include noncash items, such as financial accounting depreciation expense (do include the tax effect, as stated in 8) or allocated items of overhead not requiring differential cash expenditures.

Terminal Cash Flows   Cash flows occuring at the end of a project often include:

1. Proceeds of salvage of equipment—inflow
2. Tax on gain (loss) on disposal—outflow (inflow)

BASIC EXAMPLE OF DISCOUNTED CASH FLOW ANALYSIS

The example in this section illustrates the steps of the net present value method. First we introduce the basics, then we make the example more realistic.

JEP Realty Syndicators, Inc., contemplates the acquisition of computer hardware that will allow it to bring a new variety of real estate investment partnerships to the market. Exhibit 9.1 shows the cash inflows and cash outflows expected for the life of the investment.

When a firm acquires an asset for a specific project, the asset's cost will be a cash outflow at the start of the project. At the end of the project, the firm will scrap or sell the asset. The firm must include in the analysis the cash flow impact of the disposal and any tax implications thereof.

The equipment JEP is considering purchasing will be obsolete for its intended purpose at the end of five years. However, it will have a scrap value of $5,000, which is equal to its book value at that time.

Often, when a firm undertakes a new investment, it already owns assets that it can sell or retire. The computer equipment JEP is considering acquiring would make its present system redundant. The market value of the present equipment, which is $10,000, is equal to the book value, so there will not be a tax effect due to gain or loss on equipment. Therefore, we include this disposal of the present equipment in the Year 0 column of Exhibit 9.2, as an initial cash flow.

Initial cash flows (Year 0):

1. Hardware and software purchase—$100,000 outflow.
2. Retirement of old equipment—$10,000 inflow.

Periodic cash flows (Years 1–5):

3. Receipt of commissions and underwriting fees—inflow. The decreasing pattern over the life of the investment is due to the expected entrance of competition into the market.
4. Expenditures for programmers, sales staff, and supplies—outflow.

EXHIBIT 9.1

JEP REALTY SYNDICATORS, INC.
Cash Flows Associated with New Real Estate Investment Products
(basic)

	Year					
	0	**1**	**2**	**3**	**4**	**5**
New Asset Acquisition	($100,000)					
Old Asset Retirement	10,000					
Commissions and Fees		$120,000	$80,000	$60,000	$50,000	$40,000
Expenditures		(70,000)	(40,000)	(30,000)	(25,000)	(25,000)
Salvage Value						5,000
Net Cash Inflow (Outflow)	($ 90,000)	$ 50,000	$40,000	$30,000	$25,000	$20,000

Terminal cash flows (Year 5):

5. Salvage value—$5,000.

EXPANDED EXAMPLE OF DISCOUNTED CASH FLOW ANALYSIS

We now expand the example to include depreciation and taxes. Although each topic is discussed separately, Exhibit 9.2 presents the cash flow analysis for the expanded example including these factors.

TAX EFFECTS

Depreciation   Although depreciation is not a cash flow, it affects the tax cash flow because it is a deductible expense that affects taxable income and, therefore, should be considered in the cash flow analysis. The equipment being purchased has a 5-year life. JEP has determined that the scrap value will be $5,000, and uses

EXHIBIT 9.2

JEP REALTY SYNDICATORS, INC.
Cash Flows Associated with New Real Estate Investment Products*
(expanded)

		Year				
	0	**1**	**2**	**3**	**4**	**5**
New Asset Acquisition	($100,000)					
Old Asset Retirement	10,000					
Commissions and Fees		$120,000	$80,000	$60,000	$50,000	$40,000
Expenditures		(70,000)	(40,000)	(30,000)	(25,000)	(25,000)
Salvage Value						5,000
Pretax Net Cash Inflow (Outflow)	($ 90,000)	$ 50,000	$40,000	$30,000	$25,000	$20,000
Depreciation		(19,000)	(19,000)	(19,000)	(19,000)	(19,000)
Taxable Income[a]		$ 31,000	$21,000	$11,000	$6,000	$1,000
Income Tax Payable[b]		(12,400)	(8,400)	(4,400)	(2,400)	(400)
Net Cash Inflow (Outflow)[c] . . .	($ 90,000)	$ 37,600	$31,600	$25,600	$22,600	$19,600
Present Value Factor at 12 Percent[d]	× 1.00000	× 0.89286	× 0.79719	× 0.71178	× 0.63552	× 0.56743
Present Value of Cash Flows . .	($ 90,000)	$ 33,572	$25,191	$18,222	$14,363	$11,122
Net Present Value[e]	$ 12,469					

*Discount rate is 12 percent.

[a]Pretax Net Cash Flow − Depreciation except Year 0 which has no taxable income for this project.

[b]Taxable Income × .40.

[c]Pretax Net Cash Flow − Income Tax Payable.

[d]Taken from Table 2 of the Compound Interest and Annuity Tables at the back of the book.

[e]Sum of Present Values for Years 0–5.

straight-line depreciation. The depreciation per year is equal to the purchase value of $100,000 less the scrap value of $5,000, divided by the 5-year life.

$$\text{Depreciation} = (\$100{,}000 - \$5{,}000)/5 \text{ years} = \$19{,}000$$

Income tax laws affect investment decisions through their effect on the type of depreciation method allowed. Tax laws change frequently and allow various approaches so the amount of depreciation allowed may be different, although we assume straight-line for this example. Analysts should check with their tax advisors at the time of the analysis. Although the method allowed may vary from time to time, the cash flow analysis is conducted in the same manner, adjusted for the amount of depreciation used and the time period in which the deductions fall. There is no taxable income or loss in Year 0. Although the cash flow is $(90,000), there is no tax effect because this is a cash flow, not a deduction for tax purposes.

JEP uses a discount rate of 12 percent for projects of this nature. The analysis shows that when all the factors are considered, the investment has a positive net present value and, therefore, should be undertaken.

Investment of Working Capital   Ordinarily, when a firm starts a new business, it expects to tie up cash in inventories and accounts receivable. Eventually it sells these inventories for cash and collects the accounts receivable. Cash flows out in the early periods and flows back in the later periods, usually much later. These factors require no special treatment because they are included in the analysis as cash flows at the time of occurrence. For example, the analyst should show cash outlay for materials in the period in which cash payments are made, and show cash received from sales when cash is collected. Of course, cash collected from a sale may differ from the period of sale.

The only time "working capital" may need to be recognized as a separate factor is when cash is sitting idle and inaccessible as a necessity of undertaking the investment. For instance, assume that a company wanting to conduct business in a foreign country is required by its bank to deposit funds in a noninterest-bearing account that are to be held idle as collateral for a line of credit and for the privilege of facilitating transactions through the bank. The cash would be recognized as a working capital cash outflow in the period of deposit and a cash inflow in the period of retrieval in the discounted cash flow analysis.

PROBLEM 9.1 FOR SELF-STUDY

Cash flow analysis. Kary Kinnard has an opportunity to open a franchised pizza outlet. He can lease the building, so he needs to invest only in equipment, which he estimates will cost $60,000. For tax purposes, assume he will depreciate the full amount for the equipment over 6 years using the straight-line method. For purposes of this analysis, assume the equipment will last for 6 years, after which Kinnard will sell it for $6,000. He will pay taxes at 40 percent on the taxable gain on the disposal at the end of Year 6.

Kinnard estimates the following revenues, variable costs, and fixed costs from operations for the 6-year period. He has included expected inflation in these estimates. Assume end-of-year cash flows.

	1	2	3	4	5	6
Revenues	$30,000	$36,000	$41,000	$45,000	$48,000	$50,000
Variable Costs	12,000	14,400	16,400	18,000	19,200	20,000
Fixed Costs (includes depreciation of $10,000 per year)	15,000	15,200	15,500	15,900	16,400	17,000

Use an after-tax cost of capital of 12 percent per year and an income tax rate of 40 percent for this analysis. The $60,000 outlay for the equipment will be made at the end of Year 0.

Prepare an analysis of all cash flows. Should Kinnard make the investment?

The solution to this self-study problem is at the end of the chapter on page 297.

SENSITIVITY OF NET PRESENT VALUE TO ESTIMATES

The calculation of the net present value of a proposed project requires three types of projections or estimates:

1. The amount of future cash flows.
2. The timing of future cash flows.
3. The discount rate.

Some error is likely in the amount predicted or estimated for each of these three items. The net present value model exhibits different degrees of sensitivity to such errors.

Errors in predicting the amounts of future cash flows will likely have the largest impact of the three items. Given the sensitivity of the net present value to errors in the projections of cash flows, the manager will want accurate projections. Statistical techniques have been developed for dealing with the uncertainty inherent in predictions of cash flows.[1]

The degree of sensitivity of the net present value model to shifts in the pattern, but not in the total amount, of cash flows depends on the extent of the shifting. However, such shifts tend not to be as serious as errors in predicting the amount of cash flows.

The difficulty in estimating returns to alternative uses of capital causes uncertainty in the discount rate used to determine net present value. Financial economists have not yet developed foolproof techniques for empirically verifying a firm's estimate of its cost of capital rate. In general, if a project appears marginally desirable for a given discount rate, it will ordinarily not be grossly undesirable for slightly higher rates. If a project is clearly worthwhile when analysts use a given discount rate, it is likely to be worthwhile even if they should have used a slightly higher discount rate.

---

[1] Interested readers might consult the following book for additional discussion of capital budgeting under uncertainty: Harold Bierman, Jr., and Seymour Smidt, *The Capital Budgeting Decision*, 7th ed. (New York: Macmillan, 1988). See also the computer spreadsheet add-on program, At Risk.

USING SPREADSHEETS FOR SENSITIVITY ANALYSIS

Personal computer spreadsheet programs, such as Lotus 1-2-3 and Microsoft Excel, have become the preferred tool for analysts carrying out DCF computations. A useful feature of the spreadsheet programs is that they help the user see the effect of changes in assumptions and estimates on the net present value. Thoughtful design of a computer spreadsheet enables the user to change assumptions (such as growth rates in sales, tax rates, or discount rates) with a few keystrokes. The net present value changes as the assumptions change, and the process takes only a few seconds.

For instance, Exhibit 9.3 presents a sensitivity analysis spreadsheet for the JEP Realty example. Panel A repeats the basic case on which we will perform a sensitivity analysis.

EXHIBIT 9.3

JEP REALTY SYNDICATORS, INC.
Sensitivity Analysis

Panel A: Basic Case (See Exhibit 9.2)

Discount Rate	12%					
Year	0	1	2	3	4	5
New Asset Acquisition	($100,000)					
Old Asset Retirement	10,000					
Commissions and Fees		$120,000	$80,000	$60,000	$50,000	$40,000
Expenditures		(70,000)	(40,000)	(30,000)	(25,000)	(25,000)
Salvage Value						5,000
Pretax Net Cash Inflow (Outflow) ..	($ 90,000)	$ 50,000	$40,000	$30,000	$25,000	$20,000
Depreciation		(19,000)	(19,000)	(19,000)	(19,000)	(19,000)
Taxable Income		$ 31,000	$21,000	$11,000	$ 6,000	$ 1,000
Income Tax Payable		(12,400)	(8,400)	(4,400)	(2,400)	(400)
Net Cash Inflow (Outflow)	($ 90,000)	$ 37,600	$31,600	$25,600	$22,600	$19,600
Net Present Value	$ 12,469					

Panel B: Cell Formulas

	A	B	C
1	Discount Rate	12%	
2	Year	0	1
3	New Asset Acquisition	−100000	
4	Old Asset Retirement	10000	
5	Commissions and Fees		120000
6	Expenditures		−70000
7	Salvage Value		
8			
9	Pretax Net Cash Inflow (Outflow)	@SUM(B3...B7)	@SUM(C3...C7)
10	Depreciation		−19000
11			
12	Taxable Income	0	@SUM(C9...C10)
13	Income Tax Payable	−(B12*.4)	−(C12*.4)
14			
15	Net Cash Inflow (Outflow)	+B9+B13	+C9+C13
16	Net Present Value	@NPV(B1,C15...G15)+B15	
17			

(*continued*)

EXHIBIT 9.3 CONTINUED

Panel C: Change in Amounts of Cash Flows

Discount Rate   12%

Year	0	1	2	3	4	5
New Asset Acquisition	($100,000)					
Old Asset Retirement	10,000					
Commissions and Fees		$118,000	$79,000	$59,000	$49,000	$39,000
Expenditures		(70,000)	(40,000)	(30,000)	(25,000)	(25,000)
Salvage Value						5,000
Pretax Net Cash Inflow (Outflow) ..	($ 90,000)	$ 48,000	$39,000	$29,000	$24,000	$19,000
Depreciation		(19,000)	(19,000)	(19,000)	(19,000)	(19,000)
Taxable Income		$ 29,000	$20,000	$10,000	$ 5,000	$ —
Income Tax Payable		(11,600)	(8,000)	(4,000)	(2,000)	—
Net Cash Inflow (Outflow)	($ 90,000)	$ 36,400	$31,000	$25,000	$22,000	$19,000
Net Present Value	$ 9,770					

Panel D: Change in Timing of Cash Flows

Discount Rate   12%

Year	0	1	2	3	4	5
New Asset Acquisition	($100,000)					
Old Asset Retirement	10,000					
Commissions and Fees		$115,000	$75,000	$63,000	$55,000	$42,000
Expenditures		(70,000)	(40,000)	(30,000)	(25,000)	(25,000)
Salvage Value						5,000
Pretax Net Cash Inflow (Outflow) ..	($ 90,000)	$ 45,000	$35,000	$33,000	$30,000	$22,000
Depreciation		(19,000)	(19,000)	(19,000)	(19,000)	(19,000)
Taxable Income		$ 26,000	$16,000	$14,000	$11,000	$ 3,000
Income Tax Payable		(10,400)	(6,400)	(5,600)	(4,400)	(1,200)
Net Cash Inflow (Outflow)	($ 90,000)	$ 34,600	$28,600	$27,400	$25,600	$20,800
Net Present Value	$ 11,267					

Panel E: Change in Discount Rate

Discount Rate   13%

Year	0	1	2	3	4	5
New Asset Acquisition	($100,000)					
Old Asset Retirement	10,000					
Commissions and Fees		$120,000	$80,000	$60,000	$50,000	$40,000
Expenditures		(70,000)	(40,000)	(30,000)	(25,000)	(25,000)
Salvage Value						5,000
Pretax Net Cash Inflow (Outflow) ..	($ 90,000)	$ 50,000	$40,000	$30,000	$25,000	$20,000
Depreciation		(19,000)	(19,000)	(19,000)	(19,000)	(19,000)
Taxable Income		$ 31,000	$21,000	$11,000	$ 6,000	$ 1,000
Income Tax Payable		(12,400)	(8,400)	(4,400)	(2,400)	(400)
Net Cash Inflow (Outflow)	($ 90,000)	$ 37,600	$31,600	$25,600	$22,600	$19,600
Net Present Value	$ 10,263					

Panel B shows the cell formulas to set up the spreadsheet. The formula in cell B9 sums the cash inflows and outflows in cells B3 through B7, as C9 sums the cash inflows and outflows in C3 through C7. The formula in cell B13 calculates the income tax payable based on a 40 percent tax rate. The formula in cell B16 uses the discount rate entered in cell B1 to discount the future cash flows of Years 1 through 5 to the present value of Year 0, then adds the present value of the Year 0 cash flow.

Panel C shows the impact of changing the amount of cash flows. Forecasting cash flows accurately is critical in a cash flow analysis because the net present value is very sensitive to the amount of cash flows, as shown in Panel C. Lowering the cash flows by $6,000 over Years 1 through 5 lowers the net present value by $2,699. The net present value isn't lowered by the full $6,000 that is a nominal amount not a discounted amount.

Panel D shows the impact of changing the timing of cash flows. While the total net cash flow is the same in both cases, moving cash flows to later periods impacts the net present value of the project. The net present value drops by $1,202 simply due to moving the cash flows to later periods.

Panel E presents the impact of changing the discount rate. Assume a manager at JEP thinks a slightly higher discount rate would be appropriate. Raising the discount rate by 1 percent only lowers the net present value to $10,263, still a good investment.

INTERNAL RATE OF RETURN

The **internal rate of return (IRR)**, sometimes called the *time-adjusted rate of return*, of a series of cash flows is the discount rate that equates the net present value of the series to zero. Stated another way, the IRR is the rate that discounts the future

EXHIBIT 9.4

JEP REALTY SYNDICATORS, INC.

				Year		
	0	1	2	3	4	5
New Asset Acquisition	($100,000)					
Old Asset Retirement	10,000					
Commissions and Fees		$120,000	$80,000	$60,000	$50,000	$40,000
Expenditures		(70,000)	(40,000)	(30,000)	(25,000)	(25,000)
Salvage Value						5,000
Pretax Net Cash Inflow (Outflow) ..	($ 90,000)	$ 50,000	$40,000	$30,000	$25,000	$20,000
Depreciation		(19,000)	(19,000)	(19,000)	(19,000)	(19,000)
Taxable Income		$ 31,000	$21,000	$11,000	$ 6,000	$ 1,000
Income Tax Payable		(12,400)	(8,400)	(4,400)	(2,400)	(400)
Net Cash Inflow (Outflow)	($ 90,000)	$ 37,600	$31,600	$25,600	$22,600	$19,600
Internal Rate of Return[a]	18%					

[a]Internal Rate of Return @IRR(0.12,B15...G15)

cash flows to a present value just equal to the initial investment. The IRR method is another discounted cash flow (DCF) method.

The calculation of the internal rate can be done with many calculators or with the use of a spreadsheet. Exhibit 9.4 presents the calculation using a spreadsheet for the JEP Realty basic example. The procedure is as follows: (1) insert cash flows, (2) use IRR function. The footnote to Exhibit 9.4 gives the formula for the calculation, beginning with .12 as a "best guess" starting point for the computer to search for the right answer. This formula uses data from the spreadsheet shown in Exhibit 9.3, Panel B. The internal rate of return for the example is 18 percent, or, at a discount rate of 18 percent, the net present value equals zero.

When using the internal rate of return to evaluate investment alternatives, analysts specify a **cutoff rate**, such as 12 percent for the JEP Realty Syndicators example. Generally, the analyst accepts a project if its internal rate of return exceeds the cutoff rate. The cutoff rate is sometimes called the *hurdle rate.*

NET PRESENT VALUE AND INTERNAL RATE OF RETURN: A COMPARISON

The decision to accept or reject an investment proposal can be made using either the internal rate of return method or the net present value method under most circumstances. A comparison of the methods is as follows:

Net Present Value Method	Internal Rate of Return Method
1. Compute the investment's net present value, using the organization's adjusted cost of capital as the discount rate (hurdle rate).	1. Compute the investment's internal rate of return.
2. Undertake the investment if its net present value is positive. Reject the investment if its net present value is negative.	2. Undertake the investment if its internal rate of return is equal to or greater than the organization's adjusted cost of capital (hurdle rate). If not, reject the investment.

PROBLEM 9.2 FOR SELF-STUDY

Internal rate of return. Using the data from Problem 9.1 for Self-Study, create a spreadsheet analysis to estimate the internal rate of return.

The solution to this self-study problem is at the end of the chapter on page 297.

JUSTIFICATION OF INVESTMENTS IN ADVANCED PRODUCTION SYSTEMS

Moving toward computer-integrated-manufacturing systems has changed manufacturing. Companies have found that these changes, along with revising management accounting systems, provide a competitive edge in the marketplace.

MANAGERIAL APPLICATION

Investing in Improved Technology

A small manufacturer in Medford, Massachusetts, considered buying a robot. The company controller calculated whether the $200,000 investment made financial sense. The controller found that net present value was negative. It wasn't even a close call.

The company bought the robot anyway, because the president wanted to inject new technology into the company's manufacturing operations. The investment has paid off. What standard procedures failed to see were intangibles like improved quality, greater flexibility, and lower inventories.

Many apparently worthwhile investments in improved technology do not show a positive net present value when management uses traditional investment analysis. Technological innovations usually have a high investment outlay and a long time period before the project returns cash inflows. It is not unusual for an investment in automated equipment to take three or four years (or more) before it is fully operational. In companies with high discount rates, cash flows received or cash savings several years in the future have low present values. Further, as noted for the Medford, Massachusetts, company, technological improvements usually provide benefits that are not easily quantified. Analysts often omit such benefits from the cash flow projections.

Source: Authors' research.

Successes with technologically advanced systems have other companies considering making the same investments. However, many of these investments project a negative net present value. Managers often believe that such an investment is justified, but they are confused when the discounted cash flow analysis indicates rejection of the investment.

Managers are often right that the company would benefit from advanced manufacturing technology. It is also difficult to find fault with the discounted cash flow model—it is economically and mathematically sound. The conflict lies in the difficulties of applying the discounted cash flow analysis to a computer-integrated-manufacturing system investment decision. Some of these difficulties are listed below.

1. **Hurdle rate is too high.** Sometimes analysts use hurdle rates that are too high. The appropriate hurdle rate for any investment decision is the cost of capital adjusted for risk. In many cases managers tend to overstate this risk. This is particularly a problem with investment in advanced technology because the acquisition cost of an advanced technology system can be large, and the benefits realized over a lengthy period of time. With high hurdle rates, analysts severely discount these cash flows that occur a long time in the future.

2. **Bias toward incremental projects.** Companies generally require that the larger the investment, the higher the authorization level. One result is an incentive for lower-level managers to request smaller, incremental projects to improve the manufacturing process rather than a large, comprehensive project. For example, if the investment limit for a plant manager is $50,000, the manager may institute a series of $45,000 improvements instead of requesting one investment in a

million-dollar advanced technology manufacturing system. A series of small, incremental improvements may not have the same improving effect that could be gained with a full commitment to advanced manufacturing technology.

3. **Uncertainty about operating cash flows.** Analysts are often uncertain about the cash flows that will result with the implementation of an advanced technology. This uncertainty, which is due to the complexity of the machinery and inexperience with such advanced technology, biases them against investing in advanced technology.

4. **Exclusion of benefits that are difficult to quantify**. The benefits of advanced technology systems are extensive and can be difficult to quantify. Some of these benefits are the following:

   - *Greater flexibility in the production process.* A flexible manufacturing process can produce batches of several distinct products in the same day. The machines can serve as backups for each other, which reduces machine downtime. Engineering changes can be made more easily as products are adapted to changing customer preferences.
   - *Shorter cycle times and reduced lead times.*
   - *Reduction of nonvalue-added costs.* These systems encourage employees to seek out activities that can be made more efficient or eliminated.

Because these benefits are difficult to quantify they are often excluded from the discounted cash flow analysis. Excluding these benefits from a discounted cash flow analysis means they are being valued at zero. It is better to make some estimate of these benefits, no matter how rough it is, than to exclude them. If it is impossible to make such an estimate, then the investment criteria should include these intangible benefits along with a proposal's net present value. For example, if the net present value of a project is $(45,000), management can then decide if the nonquantifiable factors are worth more than $45,000. If they are, then the investment is justified.

PROBLEM 9.3 FOR SELF-STUDY

Data analysis. This comprehensive problem illustrates the analysis of accounting data to derive cash flows for an investment decision and the choice among mutually exclusive alternatives. The last section of the answer to this problem presents a computer spreadsheet application.

PROBLEM DATA

Magee Company considers undertaking a new product line. If it does so, it must acquire new equipment with a purchase price of $140,000 at the beginning of Year 1. The equipment will last for 5 years and Magee expects to sell it at the end of the fifth year for its salvage value of $2,500 if there is no inflation. Magee forecasts equipment prices, including prices of used equipment of this sort, to rise at an annual rate of 12 percent, so the actual salvage expected to be realized at the end of the fifth year is $4,406 (= $2,500 \times 1.12^5$). Magee will pay taxes on any gain on disposal at 40 percent at the end of Year 6.

Magee Company owns old manufacturing equipment with both book and market value of $18,000 that it must retire, independent of whether it acquires the new machine.

Magee will depreciate any new equipment over 5 years for tax purposes using the following percentages: 20, 32, 19, 14.5, and 14.5.

Magee makes the following forecasts and projections:

1. Sales volume will be 15,000 units each year.
2. Sales price will be $7.00 per unit during Year 1, but will increase by 10 percent per year, to $7.70 in Year 2, $8.47 in Year 3, and so on.
3. Variable manufacturing costs are $3.00 per unit in Year 1, but will increase by 8 percent per year, to $3.24 in Year 2, and so on.
4. Selling costs are $5,000 per year plus $.50 per unit in Year 1. Variable selling costs per unit will increase by 10 percent per year to $.55 in Year 2, $.61 in Year 3, and so on.
5. Income tax rates will remain at 40 percent of taxable income each year.
6. The after-tax cost of capital is 15 percent per year.

Magee makes the following assumptions about the timing of cash flows:

7. It will pay all variable manufacturing costs in cash at the beginning of each year.
8. It will pay all selling costs, fixed and variable, in cash at the end of each year.
9. It will collect cash from customers at the end of each year.
10. It will pay income taxes for each year's operations at the end of the year.

Magee makes the following assumptions about its operations and accounting:

11. Although it may deduct selling costs on the tax return in the year incurred, it may not deduct manufacturing costs until it sells the goods.
12. It will have sufficient other taxable income that losses on this project in any period will offset that income, saving $.40 in income taxes for every $1.00 of operating loss.
13. It must produce enough each year to meet each year's sales, except that it must produce 20,000 units in Year 1 to provide a continuing supply of inventory of 5,000 units. It need produce only 10,000 units in Year 5, so that ending inventory will be zero.
14. It will use a LIFO cost flow assumption for inventories.
15. It will charge all depreciation for a year to the cost of units it produces that year.

Construct a schedule of cash flows for acquiring the new asset.

Analyze the alternative and suggest a decision to management of Magee Company.

The solution to this self-study problem is at the end of the chapter on page 297.

SUMMARY

The following items correspond to the learning objectives presented at the beginning of the chapter.

1. **Note the separation of the investing and financing aspects of making long-term decisions.** Capital budgeting involves deciding which long-term, or capital, investments to undertake and how to finance them. A firm considering acquiring a new plant or equipment must first decide whether to make the investment, then decide how to raise the funds required for the investment.

2. **Summarize the strategic benefits of capital investments.** Strategic benefits reflect the increased profit potential derived from some attribute of a capital asset. Some common strategic benefits that may be provided by a capital asset are (1) reducing the potential to make mistakes, (2) making goods or delivering a service that competitors cannot, and (3) reducing the cycle time to make the product.

3. **Explain why audits are an important step in the capital investment process.** Comparing the estimates made in the capital budgeting process with the actual results provides several advantages. Audits identify what estimates were wrong. Audits can be used to identify and reward good planners. Audits create an environment in which planners will not be tempted to inflate their estimates of the benefits associated with the project to get it approved.

4. **Identify the behavioral issues involved in capital budgeting.** Planners cannot help but be influenced by their environment. Factors such as desire to implement a project and performance evaluation measures may influence their objectivity in making estimates. Therefore, it is important that organizational policies, procedures, and performance measures support accurate estimations, and that the effect these factors have on planners be considered when evaluating capital investment projects.

5. **Describe the steps of the net present value method for making long-term decisions using discounted cash flows. Analyze the effect of income taxes on cash flows.** Discounted cash flow (DCF) methods aid in evaluating investments involving cash flows over time where there is a time difference between cash payment and receipt. Estimate the amounts of future cash inflows and future cash outflows in each period for each alternative under consideration. The discount rate is the interest rate used in computing the present value of future cash flows. If the present value of the future cash inflows exceeds the present value of the future cash outflows for a proposal, accept the alternative.

   Although depreciation is not a cash flow, it affects the tax cash flow because it is a deductible expense that affects taxable income and should be considered in the cash flow analysis. Income tax laws affect investment decisions through their effect on the type of depreciation method allowed.

6. **Conduct sensitivity analyses of capital budgeting using spreadsheets.** Some error is likely in the amount predicted or estimated for the amount or timing of cash flows or the discount rate. Errors in predicting the amounts of future cash flows will likely have the largest impact of the three items. In general, if a project appears marginally desirable for a given discount rate, it will ordinarily not be grossly undesirable for slightly higher rates. A useful feature of spreadsheet

programs is that they help the user see the effect on the net present value of changes in assumptions and estimates.

7. **Apply the internal rate of return method of assessing investment alternatives.** The internal rate of return (IRR), sometimes called the time-adjusted rate of return, of a series of cash flows is the discount rate that equates the net present value of the series to zero. The calculation of the internal rate can be done with many calculators or with the use of a spreadsheet. When using the internal rate of return to evaluate investment alternatives, analysts specify a cutoff rate.

8. **Explain why cash flow analysis is sometimes not enough to justify or reject an investment.** Justification of investments in advanced manufacturing systems is a difficult problem. Discounted cash flow analysis is the appropriate method for analyzing such an investment, but implementing the analysis presents a challenge. Managers should strive to make the best possible estimates of costs and benefits and ultimately make a judgment that recognizes the nonquantifiable benefits as well.

KEY TERMS AND CONCEPTS

Capital budgeting   Involves deciding which long-term, or capital, investments to undertake and how to finance them.

Capital assets   Long-term assets that create the fixed, or committed, costs referred to as batch-related, product-related, and process-sustaining costs.

Discounted cash flow (DCF) methods   Aid in evaluating investments involving cash flows over time where the time elapsing between cash payment and receipt is significant.

Cost of capital   The cost of acquiring resources for an organization through debt or equity.

Discount rate   The interest rate used in computing the present value of a cash flow; the risk adjusted cost of capital.

Risk free rate   Includes the pure interest rate and a premium for expected inflation. Government bonds are often used as a measure of the current risk free rate.

Real interest rate   Includes the pure interest rate and a premium for the risk of the investment; does not include expected inflation.

Nominal interest rate   Includes pure interest, risk premium, and expected inflation; used to discount nominal cash flows.

Net present value of cash flows   The present value of the cash inflows minus the present value of the cash outflows.

Initial cash flows   Cash flows occurring at the beginning of the project.

Periodic cash flows   Cash flows occurring during the life of the project.

Terminal cash flows   Cash flows occurring at the end of a project.

Internal rate of return (IRR)   The discount rate that equates the net present value of the series to zero; sometimes called the *time-adjusted rate of return*.

Cutoff rate   The risk-adjusted cost of capital; sometimes called the *hurdle rate*.

SOLUTIONS TO SELF-STUDY PROBLEMS

SUGGESTED SOLUTIONS TO PROBLEMS 9.1 AND 9.2 FOR SELF-STUDY

Year	0	1	2	3	4	5	6
Cash Inflows							
Revenues		$ 30,000	$36,000	$41,000	$45,000	$48,000	$ 50,000
Disposal of Machinery							6,000
Less Cash Outflows							
Purchase of Machinery . . .	(60,000)						
Variable Costs		(12,000)	(14,400)	(16,400)	(18,000)	(19,200)	(20,000)
Fixed Costs[a]		(5,000)	(5,200)	(5,500)	(5,900)	(6,400)	(7,000)
Cash flow before Taxes		$ 13,000	$16,400	$19,100	$21,100	$22,400	$ 29,000
Depreciation		(10,000)	(10,000)	(10,000)	(10,000)	(10,000)	(10,000)
Taxable Income[b]		$ 3,000	$ 6,400	$ 9,100	$11,100	$12,400	$ 19,000
Tax (40%)		(1,200)	(2,560)	(3,640)	(4,440)	(4,960)	(7,600)
Net Cash Flows[c]	($60,000)	$ 10,536	$13,840	$15,460	$16,660	$17,440	$ 21,400
Net Present Value (at 12%) . .	$ 3,899	$ 10,327					
Internal Rate of Return		14%					

[a]Fixed costs less depreciation.
[b]Revenues less variable costs, fixed costs, and depreciation, plus disposal in Year 6.
[c]Cash flow before taxes less taxes.

Kinnard should undertake the project, because it has a positive net present value and an internal rate of return exceeding the cutoff rate of 12 percent.

SUGGESTED SOLUTION TO PROBLEM 9.3 FOR SELF-STUDY

Acquiring the New Asset   Exhibit 9.5 derives the operating cash flows, including income tax effects. Exhibit 9.6, discussed later, combines operating and nonoperating cash flows. The calculations for the various lines of Exhibit 9.5 follow:

Line (1)   Magee sells 15,000 units each year and produces those amounts each year except in Year 1, when production is 20,000, or 5,000 units more than sales, and in Year 5, when production is 10,000, or 5,000 units fewer.

Line (2)   Variable cost per unit is $3.00 for Year 1 and $3.24 for Year 2 and increases at the rate of 8 percent per year thereafter to $3.50 in Year 3, $3.78 in Year 4, and $4.08 in Year 5.

EXHIBIT 9.5

MAGEE COMPANY
Analysis of Cash Flow Data by Year[a]
(Part b of Problem 9.3 for Self-Study)

	1	2	3	4	5
Production and Selling Costs during Year					
(1)[a] Number of Units Produced	20,000	15,000	15,000	15,000	10,000
(2) Variable Manufacturing Cost per Unit	$ 3.00	$ 3.24	$ 3.50	$ 3.78	$ 4.08
(3) Total Variable Costs (at the beginning of year) = (1) × (2) . . .	$ 60,000	$ 48,600	$ 52,500	$ 56,700	$ 40,800
(4) Depreciation Charge for Year for Taxes	28,000	44,800	26,600	20,300	20,300
(5) Total Manufacturing Costs for Taxes = (3) + (4)	$ 88,000	$ 93,400	$ 79,100	$ 77,000	$ 61,100
(6) Manufacturing Cost per Unit for Taxes = (5)/(1)	$ 4.40	$ 6.23	$ 5.27	$ 5.13	$ 6.11
(7) Variable Selling Cost per Unit	$ .50	$ .55	$ .61	$ .67	$ .73
Revenues, End of Year					
(8) Number of Units Sold	15,000	15,000	15,000	15,000	15,000
(9) Selling Price per Unit	$ 7.00	$ 7.70	$ 8.47	$ 9.32	$ 10.25
(10) Total Revenues = (8) × (9)	$105,000	$115,500	$127,050	$139,800	$153,750
Tax Return for Year					
(11) Revenues = (10)	$105,000	$115,500	$127,050	$139,800	$153,750
(12) Less Manufacturing Costs of Sales	66,000	93,400	79,100	77,000	83,100
(13) Less Selling Expenses	12,500	13,250	14,150	15,050	15,950
(14) Taxable Income = (11) − (12) − (13)	$ 26,500	$ 8,850	$ 33,800	$ 47,750	$ 54,700
(15) Income Taxes Payable = .40 × (14)	$ 10,600	$ 3,540	$ 13,520	$ 19,100	$ 21,880

Cash Flow at:						
End of Year	0	1	2	3	4	5
Beginning of Year	1	2	3	4	5	6
(16) Revenues = (10)	—	$105,000	$115,500	$127,050	$139,800	$153,750
(17) Less Variable Costs = (3)	$ 60,000	48,600	52,500	56,700	40,800	—
(18) Less Selling Expenses = (13), Lagged	—	12,500	13,250	14,150	15,050	15,950
(19) Less Income Taxes for Year = (15), Lagged	—	10,600	3,540	13,520	19,100	21,880
(20) Net Cash Inflow (Outflow) = (16) − (17) − (18) − (19) . . .	$(60,000)	$ 33,300	$ 46,210	$ 42,680	$ 64,850	$115,920
(21) Present Value at 15 Percent = $126,672	$(60,000)	$ 28,957	$ 34,941	$ 28,063	$ 37,078	$ 57,633

[a]See text for discussion of line-by-line derivation.

EXHIBIT 9.6

MAGEE COMPANY

Analysis of All Cash Flows from Sale of Old Equipment and Purchase of New Equipment

	Present Value at Beginning of Year 1	Undiscounted Cash Flows
Operating Cash Flows (Exhibit 9.5)	$126,672	$242,960
Cash Outlay for Equipment at Beginning of Year 1	(140,000)	(140,000)
Cash Proceeds from Selling Old Equipment	$ 18,000	18,000
Salvage Proceeds from Selling Equipment at End of Year 5 ($4,406 × .49718)	2,191	4,406
Taxes at 40 Percent on Salvage Proceeds of $4,406 Paid at the End of Year 6 ($4,406 × .40 × .43233)	(762)	(1,762)
Total	$ 6,101	$123,604

Line (3)   Total variable costs result from multiplying line (1) by line (2). Magee pays this amount in cash at the beginning of the year, so transfers it to line (17) as a cash outflow at the beginning of each year.

Line (4)   Depreciation charge for the year results from multiplying the taxable depreciable basis, $140,000, by the percentages: 20, 32, 19, 14.5, and 14.5. Tax depreciation is relevant only because of its impact on tax-deductible cost of goods sold, which affects taxable income and income tax payments.

Line (5)   Total manufacturing cost is the sum of the preceding two lines.

Line (6)   Manufacturing cost per unit is generally irrelevant for decision making in the absence of taxes. Because, however, inventory builds up in Year 1 for sale in Year 5, and because tax rules require full absorption costing, Magee must compute the full cost of the units put into inventory in Year 1. Any firm must compute such unit costs to derive tax effects whenever production volume differs from sales volume.

Line (7)   Variable selling costs of $.50 per unit per year increase at the rate of 10 percent per year. The figure affects total selling costs later on line (13) and cash outflow for selling costs on line (18).

Line (8)   Magee has forecast the number of units it will sell.

Line (9)   Selling price per unit increases at the rate of 10 percent per year. (The numbers here result from using this formula: Selling price at the end of Year $t = \$7.00 \times 1.10^{t-1}$. One might multiply each year's price by 1.10 to derive the next year's price. These two procedures do not differ significantly, but because of different rounding conventions, analysts may reach differing numbers by the fifth year.)

Line (10)   Total revenue results from multiplying the preceding two lines. The product appears on line **(11)** for tax purposes and to line **(16)** for cash flow calculations.

Line (11)   See discussion of line **(10).**

Line (12)   Manufacturing cost comes from line **(5)** except for Years 1 and 5. In Year 1, manufacturing cost is the product of manufacturing cost per unit, line **(6)**, times number of units sold, line **(8)**: $4.40 \times 15,000 = \$66,000$. Magee uses a LIFO cost flow assumption. In Year 5, 10,000 units carry Year 5 manufacturing costs and 5,000 units carry Year 1 manufacturing costs: $\$61,100 + (\$4.40 \times 5,000) = \$83,100$.

Line (13)   Selling expenses are variable costs per unit on line **(7)** multiplied by the number of units sold from line **(8)** plus $5,000.

Line (14)   Taxable income is revenues, line **(11)**, minus expenses on lines **(12)** and **(13)**.

Line (15)   Income taxes are 40 percent of the amount on line **(14)**. Magee pays the amounts at the end of the year of sale.

Line (16) through (20)   These lines show all cash flows. Be careful to align the timing of the cash flows. Note that the preceding lines show operations for a period. Magee assumes each cash flow occurs at a specific moment. Because the end of one year is also the beginning of the next, we find it convenient to label these moments with both their end-of-year and beginning-of-year designations to aid analysis. Note, for example, how the cash flows for variable manufacturing costs appear in one column, but the revenues from sale of the items produced appear in the next column.

Line (21)   The present values at the beginning of Year 1 result from multiplying the numbers on line **(20)** by the appropriate factor from the 15-percent column in Table 2 at the back of the book. The sum of the numbers on line **(21)** is $126,672.

Analysis of All Cash Flows   Exhibit 9.6 shows all the cash flows, operating and nonoperating, with present values at the beginning of Year 1. Magee pays taxes at the end of Year 6 on the salvage proceeds from the end of Year 5. Tax reporting often ignores salvage value in computing depreciation. The entire depreciable basis of $140,000 becomes deductible. Thus, the gain on sale is equal to all the salvage proceeds, $4,406 (= \$4,406 - \$0$).

The net present value of this project is positive, $6,101. Magee should not undertake it, however, without considering the net present value of the alternative—selling the old equipment and not purchasing the new equipment.

If Magee sells the old and quits, the cash flow is $18,000. If Magee acquires the new equipment, the net present value of the estimated cash flows is about $6,000. Because the new equipment does not generate substantial amounts of positive cash flows in the last few years and because the result is worse than selling the old equipment outright, we prefer the outright sale, assuming that is a realistic business alternative. We would not conclude, however, that these data indicate a clear-cut decision either way. Whatever Magee Company does is not likely to be too costly, as compared to the rejected alternative.

PERSONAL COMPUTER SPREADSHEET APPLICATION TO SOLVING SELF-STUDY PROBLEM 9.3

The text recommends personal computer spreadsheets such as Lotus 1-2-3 and Microsoft Excel for analyzing DCF problems. The discussion here does not teach spreadsheet use. To learn how to use spreadsheets, you need hands-on experience. We hope this short presentation persuades those who do not already know how to use computer spreadsheets to learn to use them. The exhibit may teach users some new techniques. Exhibit 9.7 shows part of the Lotus 1-2-3 file we used to construct Exhibits 9.5 and 9.6. Observe the following:

1. The exhibit shows only part of the spreadsheet for Exhibit 9.5, the assumptions, called *parameters,* at the top and the calculations at the bottom.
2. Think of a computer spreadsheet as a chess board, a rectangular grid of squares, called cells. Identify a cell with a column letter and a row number. Every item of data or text in a computer spreadsheet appears in a cell. For example, cell D5 contains the number $3.00, and cell B3 contains the caption "Parameter Section."
3. The parameters section gathers in one place all of the assumptions needed for Exhibit 9.5.
4. The calculation section shows the columns for Year 3 and Year 4 in numerical form. We rounded the numbers for Exhibit 9.5.
5. The calculation section shows also a column of formulas. These are the actual formulas appearing in the cells of the spreadsheet. For example, cell C35 contains the formula +C32*C33, not the number $52,488. When the computer multiplies the contents of cell C32 by the contents of cell C33, the number $52,488 results. Cell C35 shows the number. Cell F35 shows the formula as it would appear in column F.
6. The formulas in column F use Lotus 1-2-3 (almost identical to Excel) notation. We do not explain that notation.
7. The formulas in columns C, D, and F use the parameter cells. Observe that cell D5 contains the variable manufacturing cost per unit, $3 in our example. If you change cell D5 to $4, then the formula for cells C33 and D33 will automatically use the changed number. To see this, note that the formula in cell F33 shows $D$5, which means that the formula does not use $3 every time the program executes, but uses the contents of cell D5, whatever it may be at the time.

Good spreadsheet technique requires discipline and patience. Someone trying to rush through a solution might, for example, not parameterize cell D5. One could just insert the $3 number for variable manufacturing cost for Year 1 in the formula for cell C33. You can construct the spreadsheet faster this way and it will appear simpler. If you do so, you will be unable to test easily the sensitivity of the final result to the assumption about variable manufacturing cost per unit in Year 1.

EXHIBIT 9.7

PERSONAL COMPUTER SPREADSHEET EXCERPT
For Exhibit 9.5, Lines (1)–(15): All Parameters and Calculations for Years 3 and 4

	B	C	D/E	F	G
1					
2					
3	Parameter Section– – – – – – – – – –				
4					
5	Variable manufacturing cost in Year 1		$3.00	Tax Depreciation	
6	Growth rate in variable manufacturing costs per year . . .		8.0%	Rate by Year	
7	Variable selling cost in Year 1		$0.50	Year 1 =	20.0%
8	Growth rate in variable selling costs per year		10.0%	Year 2 =	32.0%
9	Fixed selling costs per year		$5,000	Year 3 =	19.0%
10	Selling price per unit in Year 1		$7.00	Year 4 =	14.5%
11	Growth rate in selling price per unit		10.0%	Year 5 =	14.5%
12	Income tax rate		40.0%		
13	New asset tax basis		$140,000		
14	Number of units sold each year		15,000		
15	Number of units produced in Year 1		20,000		
16	Number of units produced in Years 2, 3, and 4		15,000		
17	Number of units produced in Year 5		10,000		
18	Discount rate per year		15.0%		
19					
20	Net present value (calculations not shown here)		$126,672		
21					
22					
23					

	B	C	D	E	F	G
24						
25	Calculation Section – – – – – – – – – –					
26						
27		Calculations			Formulas	
28						
29	Year	– – 3 – –		– – 4 – –	Insert year number as column head	
30						
31	Production and Selling Costs during Year					
32	(1) Number of Units Produced	15,000	15,000		+$D$16	
33	(2) Variable Manufacturing Costs per Unit . . .	$3.50	$3.78		+$D$5*(1+$D$6)^(F29-1)	
34						
35	(3) Total Variable Manufacturing Costs	$ 52,488	$ 56,687		+F32*F33	
36	(4) Depreciation Charge for Year for Taxes . . .	26,600	20,300		+$G$9*$D$13	
37						
38	(5) Total Manufacturing Costs for Taxes	$ 79,088	$ 76,987		+F35+F36	
39						
40	(6) Manufacturing Costs per Unit for Taxes . . .	$5.27	$5.13		+F38/F32	
41						
42	(7) Variable Selling Costs per Unit	$0.61	$0.67		+$D$7*(1+$D$8)^(F29-1)	
43						
44	Revenues, End of Year					
45	(8) Number of Units Sold	15,000	15,000		+$D$14	
46	(9) Selling Price per Unit	$8.47	$9.32		+$D$10*(1+$D$11)^(F29-1)	
47						
48	(10) Total Revenues	$127,050	$139,755		+F45*F46	
49						
50	Tax Return for Year					
51	(11) Total Revenues	$127,050	$139,755		+F45*F46	
52	(12) Less: Manufacturing Cost of Sales	(79,088)	(76,987)		–F38	
53	(13) Less: Selling Expenses	(14,075)	(14,983)		–$D$9–F32*F42	
54						
55	(14) Taxable Income	$ 33,887	$ 47,785		@SUM(F51..F53)	
56						
57	(15) Income Taxes Payable	$ 13,555	$ 19,114		+F55*$D$12	
58						

QUESTIONS, EXERCISES, PROBLEMS, AND CASES

REVIEW QUESTIONS

1. Review the meaning of the concepts or terms given above in Key Terms and Concepts.
2. The capital budgeting process comprises two distinct decisions. Describe these.
3. Assume a margin of error of plus or minus 10 percent in estimating any number required as an input for a capital budgeting decision. Under ordinary conditions, the net present value of a project is most sensitive to the estimate of which of the following?
   (1) Amounts of future cash flows.
   (2) Timing of future cash flows.
   (3) Cost of capital.
4. Describe the factors that influence the market rate of interest a company must pay for borrowed funds.

CRITICAL ANALYSIS AND DISCUSSION QUESTIONS

5. "Under no conditions should the investment decision be made simultaneously with the financing decision."
   Comment.
6. Discuss the strategic benefits of acquiring capital assets.
7. What advantages do audits provide?
8. How, if at all, should the amount of inflation incorporated in the cost of capital influence projected future cash flows for a project?
9. In *measuring* the cost of capital, management often measures the cost of the individual equities. A firm has no contractual obligation to pay anything to common shareholders. How can the capital they provide be said to have a cost other than zero?
10. A firm has a choice of three alternative investments:
    (1) Short-term government note promising a return of 8 percent.
    (2) Short-term commercial paper (issued by a blue-chip corporation) promising a return of 10 percent.
    (3) Short-term, lower-grade commercial paper (issued by a less well-established corporation) promising a return of 15 percent.
    How can one define the opportunity cost of capital as the marginal investment available to the firm with at least three such alternatives, each with a different promised rate?
11. Explain how you might analyze a capital budgeting decision where the cash flow data are nominal (including expected inflation of, say, 3 percent per year) but the quoted cost of capital of 10 percent per year is real (excluding anticipated inflation).
12. Assume no change in marginal income tax rates over the life of new equipment about to be acquired. "Whenever the trade-in allowance for an already-owned asset is smaller than its book value for tax purposes, it will always pay to sell that asset rather than trade it in."
    Comment.

13. Describe the chain of influence, if any, between the rate of anticipated inflation in an economy and the opportunity cost of capital to a firm in that economy.

14. "But, Mr. Miller, you have said that the opportunity cost of capital is the rate of return on alternative investment projects available to the firm. So long as the firm has debt outstanding, one opportunity for idle funds will be to retire debt. Therefore, the cost of capital cannot be higher than the current cost of debt for any firm with debt outstanding."

     How should Mr. Miller reply?

15. Some people claim, "The internal rate of return is more difficult to compute than the net present value of a project. The internal rate of return method can never give a better answer than the net present value method." Why, then, do you suppose that so many people use the internal rate of return method?

EXERCISES

Solutions to even-numbered exercises appear at the end of the chapter after the cases.

16. **Computing net present value.** Compute the net present value of
    a. An investment of $15,000 that will yield $1,000 for 28 periods at 4 percent per period.
    b. An investment of $100,000 that will yield $250,000 8 years from now at 10 percent compounded semiannually.

17. **Computing net present value.** A firm has an after-tax cost of capital of 10 percent. Compute the net present value of each of the five projects listed in the following exhibit.

Project	After-Tax Cash Flow, End of Year			
	0	1	2	3
A	$(5,000)	$ 2,000	$2,000	$2,000
B	(5,000)	3,000	2,000	1,000
C	(5,000)	1,000	2,000	3,000
D	(5,000)	2,200	2,200	2,200
E	(5,000)	1,800	1,800	1,800

18. **Computing net present value.** Hammersmith Homes is considering four possible housing development projects, each requiring an initial investment of $5,000,000. The cash inflows from each of the projects follow:

Year	Project A	Project B	Project C	Project D
1	$2,000,000	$4,000,000	0	$1,000,000
2	2,000,000	2,000,000	0	2,500,000
3	2,000,000	2,000,000	0	3,000,000
4	2,000,000	1,000,000	0	2,500,000
5	2,000,000	1,000,000	$10,000,000	1,000,000

a. Compute the net present value of each of the projects. Hammersmith's cost of capital is 15 percent.

b. Hammersmith can take on only one project; which should it choose? Explain why this project is superior to the others.

19. **Computing net present value.** Eastern States Products is considering a project that requires an initial investment of $1,600,000 and that will generate the following cash inflows for the next 6 years:

Year	Cash Inflow at End of Year
1	$200,000
2	400,000
3	600,000
4	800,000
5	600,000
6	400,000

Calculate the net present value of this project if Eastern States' cost of capital is

a. 12 percent.

b. 20 percent.

20. **Computing net present value.** Megatech, a computer software developer, is considering a software development project that requires an initial investment of $200,000 and subsequent investments of $150,000 and $100,000 at the end of the first and second years. Megatech expects this project to yield annual after-tax cash inflows for 6 more years: $90,000 at the end of each year for the third through eighth years. Megatech's after-tax cost of capital is 10 percent.

Calculate the net present value of this project.

21. **Deriving cash flows and computing net present value.** The Westminster Railroad (WRR) is considering replacing its power jack tamper, used to maintain track and roadbed, with a new automatic-raising power tamper. WRR spent $18,000 5 years ago for the present power jack tamper and estimated it to have a total life of 12 years. If WRR keeps the old tamper, it must overhaul the old tamper 2 years from now at a cost of $5,000. WRR can sell the old tamper for $2,500 now; the tamper will be worthless 7 years from now.

A new automatic-raising tamper costs $23,000 delivered and has an estimated physical life of 12 years. WRR anticipates, however, that because of developments in maintenance machines, it should retire the new machine at the end of the seventh year for $5,000. Furthermore, the new machine will require an overhaul costing $7,000 at the end of the fourth year. The new equipment will reduce wages and fringe benefits by $4,000 per year.

Track maintenance work is seasonal, so WRR normally uses the equipment only from May 1 through October 31 of each year. WRR transfers track maintenance employees to other work but pays them at the same rate for the rest of the year.

The new machine will require $1,000 per year of maintenance, whereas the old machine requires $1,200 per year. Fuel consumption for the two machines is identical. WRR's cost of capital is 12 percent per year, and because of operating losses, WRR pays no income tax.

Should WRR purchase the new machine?

22. **Observing the effects of using different discount rates.** Refer to the data and analysis developed for the Magee Company in Exhibits 9.5 and 9.6. Evaluate the alternatives using a cost of capital of 12 percent.

23. **Net present value and mutually exclusive projects.** Assume Holiday Inns must choose between two mutually exclusive innovations for improving its computer reservation system—one offered by Digital Equipment (DEC) and the other by IBM. Holiday Inn's after-tax cost of capital is 10 percent.

   DEC's system costs $1 million and promises after-tax cash flows in personnel cost savings for 4 years: $400,000 at the end of Year 1 and Year 2, $300,000 at the end of Year 3, and $200,000 at the end of Year 4.

   IBM's system costs $1.5 million and promises after-tax cash flows for 3 years: $800,000 at the end of Year 1, $600,000 at the end of Year 2, and $400,000 at the end of Year 3.

   a. Compute the net present values of each of the alternatives.

   b. Compute the internal rate of return for each of the alternatives.

   c. Which alternative, if either, should Holiday Inns choose and why?

24. **Net present value and mutually exclusive projects.** The Larson Company must choose between two mutually exclusive projects. The cost of capital is 12 percent. Given the following data, which project should Larson choose, and why?

Project Label	After-Tax Cash Flows, End of Year			
	0	**1**	**2**	**3**
M	$(500,000)	$175,000	$287,500	$400,000
N	(450,000)	477,000	195,000	60,000

25. **Computing internal rate of return.** What is the internal rate of return on the following projects, each of which requires a $5,000 cash outlay now and returns the cash flows indicated?

   a. $2,803.84 at the end of Years 1 and 2.

   b. $799.10 at the end of Years 1 through 10.

   c. $855.82 at the end of Years 1 through 13.

   d. $934.10 at the end of Years 1 through 20.

   e. $2,099.46 at the end of Years 3 through 7.

   f. $904.70 at the end of Years 2 through 10.

   g. $8,811.71 at the end of Year 5 only.

26. **Computing internal rate of return.** Compute the internal rate of return for each of the following projects, each of which requires an initial investment of $100,000 and provides the periodic cash flows indicated.

   a. $23,098 per period for 5 periods.

   b. $20,336 per period for 6 periods.

    c. $17,401 per period for 8 periods.

    d. $16,144 per period for 12 periods.

    e. $17,102 per period for 15 periods.

27. **Working backward with net present value method.** A manager's favorite project requires an after-tax cash outflow on January 1 of $8,000 and promises to return $2,000 of after-tax cash inflows at the end of each of the next 5 years. The after-tax cost of capital is 10 percent per year.

    a. Use the net present value method to decide whether this favorite project is a good investment.

    b. How much would the projected cash inflow for the end of Year 5 have to increase for the project to be acceptable?

    c. How much would the projected cash inflow for the end of Year 5 have to increase for the project to have a net present value of $100?

28. **Computing internal rate of return.** Carlo Company is considering acquiring a machine that costs $40,000 and that promises to save $8,000 in cash outlays per year, after taxes, at the end of each of the next 12 years. Carlo expects the new machine to have no salvage value at the end of its useful life.

    a. Compute the internal rate of return for this project.

    b. Compute the internal rate of return, assuming that the cash savings were to last only 6, instead of 12, years.

    c. Compute the internal rate of return, assuming that the cash savings were to last 20, rather than 12, years.

    d. Compute the internal rate of return, assuming that the cash savings would be $6,000 rather than $8,000 per year for 12 years.

PROBLEMS

29. **Deriving cash flows and computing net present value.** The Biggart Corporation is contemplating selling a new product. Biggart can acquire the equipment necessary to distribute and sell the product for $100,000. The equipment has an estimated life of 10 years and has no salvage value. The following schedule shows the expected sales volume, selling price, and variable cost per unit of production:

Year	Sales Volume	Selling Price	Variable Cost of Production
1	10,000 Units	$5.00	$3.00
2	12,000	5.00	3.10
3	13,000	5.50	3.25
4	15,000	5.75	3.25
5	20,000	6.00	3.30
6	25,000	6.00	3.40
7	20,000	6.10	3.50
8	18,000	6.10	3.50
9	15,000	6.25	3.50
10	15,000	6.30	3.75

Production in each year must be sufficient to meet each year's sales. In addition, Biggart will purchase 5,000 extra units in Year 1 to provide a continuing inventory of 5,000 units. Thus production in Year 1 will be 15,000 units but in Year 10 will be only 10,000 units, so that at the end of Year 10, ending inventory will be zero. Biggart will use a LIFO (last-in, first-out) cost flow assumption. Biggart's income tax rate is 40 percent, and its after-tax cost of capital is 9 percent per year. It receives cash at the end of the year when it makes sales and spends cash at the end of the year when it incurs costs. Biggart estimates variable selling expenses at $1 per unit sold. Depreciation on the new distribution equipment is not a product cost but is an expense each period. For tax reporting, depreciation will follow these accelerated depreciation schedule percentages: 20 percent in the first year, 32 percent in the second, 19.2 percent in the third, 11.5 percent in the fourth, 11.5 percent in the fifth, 5.8 percent in the sixth, and zero thereafter. The Biggart Corporation generates sufficient cash flows from other operations so that it can use all depreciation deductions to reduce current taxes otherwise payable.

a. Prepare a schedule of cash flows for this project.

b. Compute the net present value of the project.

30. **Analyzing cash flows from alternatives.** Largay Company is considering replacing some machinery. The old machinery has book value and tax basis of $8,000. Its current market value is $3,000. Largay does not face the alternative of just selling the old machinery now. It must either use it for another year or replace it. Largay has been depreciating the old equipment on a straight-line basis at the rate of $8,000 per year. If Largay retains the machinery it will depreciate the remaining tax basis over 1 year and the financial book value over 3 years. The machinery will have no market value 1 year hence.

Largay can acquire new machinery for $30,000, which will produce $10,000 of cash savings at the end of the first year. The new machinery will produce cash savings at the end of Year 2 that is 5 percent greater than at the end of Year 1, and at the end of Year 3 the savings will be 5 percent greater than at the end of Year 2. The new machinery will have a 3-year life. Largay will depreciate the equipment on a straight-line basis over 3 years for both tax and financial reporting purposes. It will sell the machinery for $5,000 at the end of Year 3 but will ignore salvage value in tax depreciation computations.

Largay pays income taxes at the rate of 40 percent for both ordinary income and for capital gains. The cost of capital for the new machinery, after taxes, is 16 percent per year. Largay earns sufficient taxable income that it can deduct from its taxes payable at the beginning of Year 1 (= end of Year 0) the loss from disposition of the old machinery at the beginning of Year 1 (= end of Year 0).

Analyze the present value of the cash flows of the alternatives and made a recommendation to Largay Company.

31. **Analyzing cash flows from alternatives.** Fresno Steelworks is considering purchasing a new machine for $1 million at the end of Year 0 to be put into operation at the beginning of Year 1. The new machine will save $220,000, before taxes, per year from the cash outflows generated by using the old machine. For tax purposes, Fresno Steelworks will depreciate the new machine in the following amounts: $100,000 in Year 1, $300,000 in Year 2, and $200,000 per year

thereafter until fully depreciated or sold. The new machine will have no salvage value at the end of Year 5. Fresno Steelworks expects the new machine to have a market value of $400,000 at the end of 3 years.

If Fresno Steelworks acquires the new machine at the end of Year 0, it can sell the old one for $200,000 at that time. The old machine has a tax basis of $300,000 at the end of Year 0. If Fresno Steelworks keeps the old machine, Fresno Steelworks will depreciate it for tax purposes in the amount of $100,000 per year for 3 years, when it will have no market value.

Fresno Steelworks pays taxes at the rate of 40 percent of taxable income and uses a cost of capital of 12 percent in evaluating this possible acquisition. Fresno Steelworks has sufficient otherwise-taxable income in Year 0 to save income taxes for each dollar of loss it may incur if it sells the old machine at the end of Year 0.

a. Compute the net present value of cash flows from each of the alternatives facing Fresno Steelworks.

b. Make a recommendation to Fresno Steelworks.

c. Assume that the cash flows described in the problem for Years 2 through 5 are real, not nominal, amounts, but the 12-percent cost of capital includes an allowance for inflation of 6 percent. Describe how this will affect your analysis. You need not perform new computation.

32. **Net present value graph and indifference cost of capital.** The after-tax net cash flows associated with two mutually exclusive projects, Alpha and Beta, are as follows:

Project	Cash Flow, End of Year		
	0	1	2
Alpha	$(100)	$125	—
Beta	(100)	50	$84

a. Calculate the net present value for each project using discount rates of 0, .04, .08, .12, .15, .20, and .25.

b. Prepare a graph as follows. Label the vertical axis "Net Present Value in Dollars" and the horizontal axis "Discount Rate in percent per Year." Plot the net present value amounts calculated in part **a** for project Alpha and project Beta.

c. State the decision rule for choosing between projects Alpha and Beta as a function of the firm's cost of capital.

d. What generalizations can you draw from this exercise?

33. **Deriving cash flows for asset disposition.** The Michner Millworks Company (MMC) purchased a made-to-order machine tool for grinding machine parts. The machine costs $100,000 and MMC installed it yesterday. Today, a vendor offers a machine tool that will do exactly the same work but costs only $50,000. Assume that the cost of capital is 12 percent, that both machines will last for 5 years, that MMC will depreciate both machines on a straight-line basis for tax purposes with no salvage value, that the income tax rate is and will continue to be 40 percent, and that MMC earns sufficient income that it can offset any loss from disposing of or depreciating the "old" machine against other taxable income.

How much, at a minimum, must the "old" machine fetch upon resale at this time to make purchasing the new machine worthwhile?

34. **Deriving cash flows for abandonment decision.** The Humbolt Company must decide whether to continue selling a line of children's shoes manufactured on a machine that has no other purpose. The machine has a current book value of $12,000 and Humbolt can sell it today for $7,000. Humbolt depreciates the machine on a straight-line basis for tax purposes assuming no salvage value and could continue to use it for 4 more years. If Humbolt keeps the machine in use, it can sell it at the end of 4 years for $600, although this will not affect the depreciation charge for the next 4 years. The variable cost of producing a pair of shoes on the machine is less than the cash received from customers by $13,000 per year. To produce and sell the children's shoes requires cash outlays of $10,000 per year for administrative and overhead expenditures as well. Humbolt Company pays taxes at a rate of 40 percent. The rate applies to any gain or loss on disposal of the machine as well as to other income. From its other activities, Humbolt Company earns more income than any losses from the line of children's shoes or from disposal of the machine.

   a. Prepare a schedule showing all the cash and cost flows that Humbolt Company needs to consider in order to decide whether to keep the machine.

   b. Should Humbolt Company keep the machine if its cost of capital is 12 percent?

   c. Repeat part **b** assuming a cost of capital of 18 percent.

35. **Managerial incentives of performance evaluation based on accounting data.** A firm with an opportunity cost of capital of 20 percent faces two mutually exclusive investment projects:

   (1) Acquire goods at the start of the year, ship them to Japan, and sell them at the end of the year. The internal rate of return on this project is 25 percent, and it has positive net present value.

   (2) Making certain expenditures today that will cause reported earnings for the year to decline. This will result, however, in large cash flows at the ends of the second and third years. The internal rate of return on this project is 35 percent, and it has even larger net present value than the first project. Management observes that for the current year the second project will result in smaller earnings reported to its shareholders than the first.

   How might management's observation influence its choice between the two investment projects?

CASES

36. **Make-or-buy—Liquid Chemical Co.**[2] The Liquid Chemical Company manufactures and sells a range of high-grade products. Many of these products require careful packing. The company has a special patented lining made from a material known as GHL, and the firm operates a department to maintain its containers in good condition and to make new ones to replace those beyond repair.

   Mr. Walsh, the general manager, has for some time suspected that the firm might save money, and get equally good service, by buying its containers from

---

[2]Adapted from a case by Professor David Solomons, Wharton School, University of Pennsylvania.

an outside source. After careful inquiries, he approached a firm specializing in container production, Packages, Inc., and asked for a quotation from it. At the same time, he asked Mr. Dyer, his chief accountant, to let him have an up-to-date statement of the costs of operating the container department.

Within a few days, the quotation from Packages, Inc., arrived. The firm proposed to supply all the new containers required—at that time, running at the rate of 3,000 a year—for $1,250,000 a year, the contract to run for a guaranteed term of 5 years and thereafter to be renewable from year to year. If the number of containers required increased, the contract price would increase proportionally. Also, independent of this contract, Packages, Inc., proposed to carry out purely maintenance work on containers, short of replacement, for a sum of $375,000 a year, on the same contract terms.

Mr. Walsh compared these figures with Mr. Dyer's cost figures, which covered a year's operations of the container department of the Liquid Chemical Company and appear in Exhibit 9.8.

Walsh concluded that he should immediately close the department and sign the contracts offered by Packages, Inc. He felt bound, however, to give the manager of the department, Mr. Duffy, an opportunity to question this conclusion before acting on it. Walsh told Duffy that Duffy's own position was not in jeopardy: even if Walsh closed his department, another managerial position was becoming vacant to which Duffy could move without loss of pay or prospects. The manager Duffy would replace also earns $80,000 a year. Moreover, Walsh knew that he was paying $85,000 a year in rent for a warehouse a couple of miles away for other corporate purposes. If he closed Duffy's department, he'd have all the warehouse space he needed without renting.

Duffy gave Walsh a number of considerations to think about before closing the department. "For instance," he said, "what will you do with the machinery?

EXHIBIT 9.8

LIQUID CHEMICAL COMPANY
Container Department

Materials		$ 700,000
Labor:		
Supervisor		50,000
Workers		450,000
Department Overheads:		
Manager's Salary	$ 80,000	
Rent on Container Department	45,000	
Depreciation of Machinery	150,000	
Maintenance of Machinery	36,000	
Other Expenses	157,500	
		468,500
		$1,668,500
Proportion of General Administrative Overheads		225,000
Total Cost of Department for Year		$1,893,500

It cost $1,200,000 4 years ago, but you'd be lucky if you got $200,000 for it now, even though it's good for another 5 years. And then there's the stock of GHL (a special chemical) we bought a year ago. That cost us $1,000,000, and at the rate we're using it now, it'll last us another 4 years. We used up about one-fifth of it last year. Dyer's figure of $700,000 for materials includes $200,000 for GHL. But it'll be tricky stuff to handle if we don't use it up. We bought it for $5,000 a ton, and you couldn't buy it today for less than $6,000. But you'd get over $4,000 a ton if you sold it, after you'd covered all the handling expenses."

Walsh worried about the workers if he closed the department. "I don't think we can find room for any of them elsewhere in the firm. I could see whether Packages can take any of them. But some of them are getting on. Walters and Hines, for example, have been with us since they left school 40 years ago. I'd feel bound to give them a pension—$15,000 a year each for 5 years, say."

Duffy showed some relief at this. "But I still don't like Dyer's figures," he said. "What about this $225,000 for general administrative overheads? You surely don't expect to sack anyone in the general office if I'm closed, do you?" Walsh agreed.

"Well, I think we've thrashed this out pretty fully," said Walsh, "but I've been turning over in my mind the possibility of perhaps keeping on the maintenance work ourselves. What are your views on that, Duffy?"

"I don't know," said Duffy, "but it's worth looking into. We shouldn't need any machinery for that, and I could hand the supervision over to the current supervisor who earns $50,000 per year. You'd need only about one-fifth of the workers, but you could keep on the oldest and save the pension costs. You wouldn't save any space, so I suppose the rent would be the same. I don't think the other expenses would be more than $65,000 a year."

"What about materials?" asked Walsh.

'We use 10 percent of the total on maintenance," Duffy replied.

"Well, I've told Packages, Inc., that I'd give them my decision within a week," said Walsh. "I'll let you know what I decide to do before I write to them."

Assume the company has a cost of capital of 10 percent per year and uses an income tax rate of 40 percent for decisions such as these. Liquid Chemical would pay taxes on any gain or loss on the sale of machinery or the GHL at 40 percent. (Depreciation for book and tax purposes is straight-line over 8 years.) The tax basis of the machinery is $600,000.

Assume the company had a 5-year time horizon for this project. Also assume that any GHL needed for Year 5 is purchased during Year 5.

a. What are the four alternatives available to Liquid Chemical?

b. What action should Walsh take? Support your conclusion with a net present value analysis of all the mutually exclusive alternatives.

c. What, if any, additional information do you think Walsh needs to make a sound decision? Why?

37. **Merits of net present value.** A well-known university sponsors a continuing education program for engineers. One of its programs is called "Evaluating Project Alternatives by Rate of Return." The advertising copy for this program says, in part:

Why You Should Attend   Traditionally, a large percentage of business decisions have been based solely on payback, which is the amount of time before the cash inflows from a project equal the cash outflows. Although the payback method has the advantage of computational simplicity, it is not a true measure of life-cycle cost effectiveness and can lead to erroneous accept-reject decisions.

Why Use Net Present Value

(1) Takes into account:
Cash flows beyond the payback period.
Timing of cash flows within the payback period.

(2) Does not discriminate against long-lived projects.

(3) Does not ignore the time value of money.

(4) Provides for:
Return of and on debt and equity capital.
Income taxes, income tax write-offs.
Inflation.
Costs that escalate at a rate greater than the rate of inflation.

(5) Permits an accurate ranking of alternatives.

(6) Gives correct choice among independent alternatives.

(7) Maximizes return on investment.

Comment on the numbered points from the copy.

SUGGESTED SOLUTIONS TO EVEN-NUMBERED EXERCISES

16. **Computing net present value.**
   a. Net Present Value = −$15,000 + ($1,000 × 16.66306)
                            = $1,663.

   b. Net Present Value = −$100,000 + ($250,000 × 0.45811)
                            = $14,528.

18. **Computing net present value.**
   a.

Year	Present Value Factor	Discounted Cash Flows			
		Project A	**Project B**	**Project C**	**Project D**
0	1.00000	$(5,000,000)	$(5,000,000)	$(5,000,000)	$(5,000,000)
1	.86957	1,739,140	3,478,280	0	869,570
2	.75614	1,512,280	1,512,280	0	1,890,350
3	.65752	1,315,040	1,315,040	0	1,972,560
4	.57175	1,143,500	571,750	0	1,429,375
5	.49718	994,360	497,180	4,971,800	497,180
		$1,704,320	$2,374,530	$ (28,200)	$1,659,035

b. Hammersmith should take Project B, which has the largest net present value. Even though all four projects have similar undiscounted total cash flow streams—that is, $10,000,000—Project B is superior because the bulk of the cash returns come in the earlier years.

20. Computing net present value.

Year (1)	Net Cash Flow (2)	10% Present Value Factor (3)	Present Value (4)[a]
0	$(200,000)	1.00000	$(200,000)
1	(150,000)	.90909	(136,364)
2	(100,000)	.82645	(82,645)
3	90,000	.75131	67,618
4	90,000	.68301	61,471
5	90,000	.62092	55,883
6	90,000	.56447	50,802
7	90,000	.51316	46,184
8	90,000	.46651	41,986
			$ (95,065)

[a](4) = (2) × (3).

22. Observing the effects of using different discount rates.

MAGEE COMPANY
Operating Cash Flows, End of Year
(cost of capital, 12 percent)

End of Year (1)	Cash Flow (2)	Present Value Factor at 12 Percent (3)	Present Value at 12 Percent = (2) × (3) (4)
0	$ (60,000)	1.00000	$ (60,000)
1	33,300	.89286	29,732
2	46,210	.79719	36,838
3	42,680	.71178	30,379
4	64,850	.63552	41,213
5	115,920	.56743	65,776
Total			$143,938

Present Value of All Cash Flows from Sale of Old Equipment and Purchase of New Equipment

Operating Cash Flow	$143,938
Net Cash Outlay for Equipment (= $140,000 − $18,000)	(122,000)
Salvage Proceeds End of Year 5: $4,406 × .56743	2,500
Taxes on Salvage End of Year 6: $4,406 × .40 × .50663	(893)
Net Present Value	$ 23,545

Present Value of Outright Sale

Sale Proceeds	$ 18,000

24. **Net present value and mutually exclusive projects.** Choose Project N. See the following table:

End of Year	Discount Factors at 12 Percent	Cash Flows in Thousands		Present Value of Cash Flows in Thousands	
		M	N	M	N
0	1.00000	$(500)	$(450)	$(500.0)	$(450.0)
1	.89286	175	477	156.3	425.9
2	.79719	287.5	195	229.2	155.5
3	.71178	400	60	284.7	42.7
				$ 170.2	$174.1

Net present value of cash flows discounted at 12 percent is larger for N.

26. **Computing internal rate of return.**

	Internal Rate of Return
a.	5 percent
b.	6 percent
c.	8 percent
d.	12 percent
e.	15 percent

28. **Computing internal rate of return.**
Internal rate of return:
   a. 16.94%
   b. 5.47%
   c. 19.43%
   d. 10.45%

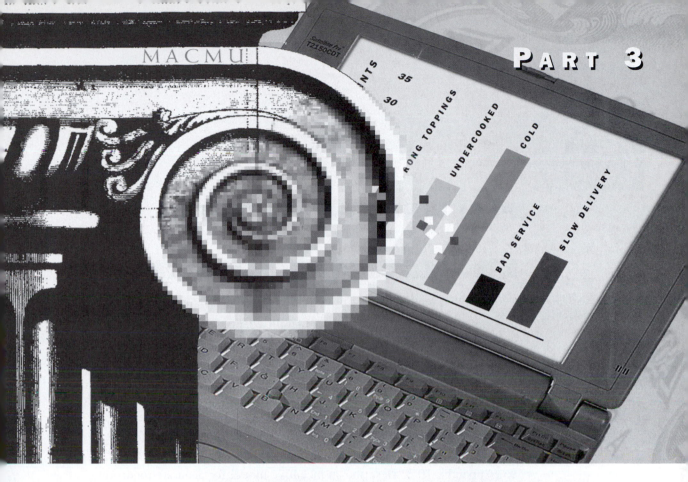

PART 3

MANAGERIAL PLANNING AND PERFORMANCE EVALUATION

This part of the book deals with the use of managerial accounting information for managerial planning and performance evaluation.

Managers use accounting information to address planning and performance evaluation questions such as these:

- What is our projected level of profits for the year?
- How much should budgeted costs go down if the number of customers drops by 10 percent?
- How do we measure the efficiency of production activities?
- How can we design performance measurement systems to encourage employees to act simultaneously in their own best interests and in the best interests of the organization?

Managerial accounting helps managers deal with these issues. Managers use accounting to assign responsibility for actions, primarily through the use of budgets and standards. The accounting system provides information about actual performance that managers can compare with these budgets and standards.

CHAPTER 10

PLANNING AND BUDGETING

LEARNING OBJECTIVES

1. Analyze a budget as a tool for planning and performance evaluation.
2. Compare the four types of responsibility centers.
3. Recognize how a budget can affect employee motivation.
4. Describe the master budget.
5. Know how to use the budget for performance evaluation.
6. Define the different types of variances between actual results and the flexible budget.
7. Describe ethical dilemmas in budgeting.
8. (Appendix 10.1) Develop a comprehensive master budget.
9. (Appendix 10.2) Describe an incentive model for accurate reporting.

Many of us use budgets in our daily lives. Managers rely on them extensively for planning and performance evaluation.

▪ Budgets help managers to plan. Budgets communicate what top management wants the organization to achieve.
▪ Budgets provide a target or standard against which to compare performance and motivate employees to achieve the budget.

Budgets are serious business. They are usually approved by the board of directors in private enterprises. In the public sector, legislative bodies approve budgets.

This chapter focuses on the **short-term operating budget.** This budget states management's plan of action for the coming year in quantitative terms.

TOOL FOR PLANNING AND PERFORMANCE EVALUATION

The budget is like an architect's set of drawings. It presents a comprehensive picture of the expected financial effects of management's decisions on the firm as a whole. Put another way, budgets are estimates of financial statements prepared before the actual transactions occur.

As *tools for planning,* budgets are generally static. The firm develops **static budgets** for a particular expected level of activity, such as sales or production in units.

Budgets provide estimates of expected performance. Comparing budgeted with actual results provides a basis for evaluating past performance and guiding future action. To be effective as *tools for performance evaluation,* budgets must initially be developed for individual responsibility centers.

RESPONSIBILITY CENTERS

A **responsibility center** is a division or department in a firm responsible for managing a particular group of activities in the organization. The sportswear manager at Macy's is responsible for the activities of the sportswear department, for example. Accountants classify responsibility centers according to the activities for which the manager is responsible, as follows:

1. **Cost centers,** where management is responsible for costs. Manufacturing departments are examples, because the managers are responsible for the costs of making products.
2. **Revenue centers,** where management is responsible primarily for revenues. Marketing departments are revenue centers if the managers are responsible for revenues.
3. **Profit centers,** where management is responsible for both revenues and costs.
4. **Investment centers,** where management is responsible for revenues, costs, and assets. Most corporate divisions are profit centers or investment centers.

There are two categories of cost centers, based on the types of costs incurred in the center.

- **Engineered cost centers** have input-output relations sufficiently well established so that a particular set of inputs will provide a predictable and measurable set of outputs. Most production departments are engineered cost centers.
- Responsibility centers in which input-output relations are not well specified are **discretionary cost centers.** Managers of such centers receive a cost budget that provides a ceiling on the center's costs. Most administrative, research, and staff activities are discretionary cost centers.

FLEXIBLE BUDGETS

A **flexible budget** has two components:

1. A fixed cost expected to be incurred regardless of the level of activity.
2. A variable cost per unit of activity. Total variable costs change *in total* as the level of activity changes.

Example   Assume that studies of past cost behavior indicate the video booth at a Great America amusement park should incur total fixed costs of $100,000 per year and variable costs of $10 per video made. For planning purposes, management estimates that it will make 50,000 videos per year. The static cost budget for planning purposes is therefore $600,000 [= $100,000 + ($10 × 50,000)].

Suppose, however, that due to unexpected demand during the year, the booth made 70,000 videos. Management will not wish to compare the actual cost of producing 70,000 units with the expected cost of producing 50,000 units for performance evaluation purposes. The underlying levels of activity differ. To evaluate actual performance, accounting must express the budget in terms of what costs *should have been* to produce 70,000 units. The flexible budget is useful in this situation. It indicates the costs should have been $800,000 [= $100,000 + ($10 × 70,000)] during the year. This is the more appropriate budget for performance evaluation.

MOTIVATING EMPLOYEES

When you assess the effect of budgets or any other part of a motivation system on people, ask the following two questions:

1. What types of behavior does the system motivate?
2. Is this the desired behavior?

Much of managerial accounting has developed to motivate people to behave in particular ways. Accounting reports allow superiors to make decisions about the subordinates' future employment prospects. (For example, should they be promoted? Fired?) In addition, employment contracts use accounting information, such as when an employee receives a bonus based on accounting performance measures.

Thus accounting affects motivation. Subordinates who know managers evaluate them with accounting measures have incentives to make themselves look good with those measures. (Analogously, consider how students may believe employers or graduate school admissions offices use grade-point averages without regard to difficulty of courses. Such students have incentives to take easy courses.)

GOAL CONGRUENCE

Goal congruence occurs if members of an organization have incentives to perform in the common interest. Although complete goal congruence is rare, we observe team efforts in many cases. Examples include some military units and athletic teams. Many companies attempt to achieve this *esprit de corps* by carefully selecting employees whom management believes will be loyal, for example. Observers of Japanese industry report that Japanese managers and owners have created team orientation with considerable goal congruence.

Complete goal congruence is, however, unlikely to occur in most business settings. For example, employees may prefer to work less hard than the firm would like. Consequently, firms design performance evaluation and incentive systems to increase goal congruence by encouraging employees to behave more in the firm's interest.

The classroom setting is a good example. Examinations, written assignments, indeed, the entire grading process, are part of a performance evaluation and incentive system to encourage students to learn. Sometimes the system encourages the wrong type of behavior, because students may select easy courses to improve their grades instead of difficult courses in which they will learn more.

Problems of this type occur in all organizations where employees acting in their own best interests do not take actions that serve the best interests of the organization. Consider the case of a plant manager who believes that a promotion and bonus will follow from high plant operating profits. Undertaking a needed maintenance program will cost money and reduce profits in the short run, but the company will benefit in the long run because its product quality will improve. The manager faces a classic trade-off between doing what *looks* good in the short run and doing what serves the best interests of the company. (This point is analogous to the problem faced by a student in deciding between an easy course that will bolster the grade-point average or a hard course that will have greater long-term benefits.)

THE MASTER BUDGET

The **master budget** is a complete blueprint of the planned operations of the firm for a period. It requires recognizing the interrelations among the various units of a firm. For IBM to prepare a master budget requires knowing how a projected increase in sales of laptop computers affects the producing departments; the selling, general, and administrative effort; and the financial position of the company.

Example We illustrate the budget preparation process for Victoria Corporation for a single period, assumed to be one month. The Victoria Corporation produces gourmet coffee blends with spice flavors. We continue this example in our discussion of performance evaluation in this chapter and in Chapter 11. An organization chart of Victoria Corporation appears in Exhibit 10.1. Each box in the organization chart is a responsibility center.

EXHIBIT 10.1

VICTORIA CORPORATION
Organization Chart

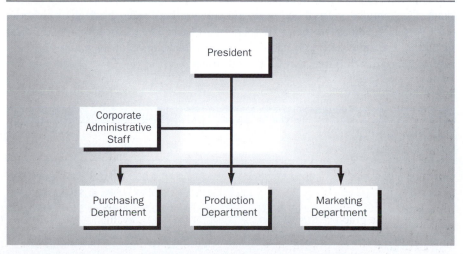

THE SALES BUDGET

The sales budget appears in Exhibit 10.2. The chief marketing executive of the firm usually is responsible for preparing the sales budget. The marketing executive relies on inputs from market research groups as well as from salespeople or district managers in the field. The discussions among sales groups in budget preparation frequently bring out problems in the firm's selling and advertising programs and broaden the participants' thinking about the firm's place in the market.

We use only the expected forecast in subsequent discussions to keep the example simple. According to a marketing vice-president that we interviewed, the market researchers and sales managers use two different databases:

> The market research group uses consumer studies, economic forecasts, and past data about the company. The group provides a good macro-level forecast of economic conditions and consumer preferences for our products, but it explains little about the day-to-day efforts of our sales personnel.

> This is where our sales managers' forecasts are most valuable. They know about potential customers, they know which of our present customers we are likely to lose, and they can forecast sales quite accurately for the first few months of the budget year. When I combine the forecasts of the market research group and the sales managers, I have a good idea of both the market conditions affecting the demand for our product and the immediate wishes of our customers.

Previous sales experience is usually the starting point for sales budget estimates. Managers modify these historical data to recognize relevant factors, such as market trends, anticipated changes in general economic conditions, and altered advertising plans. The marketing executive usually makes the final decision on the precise quantities and dollar amounts to appear in the sales budget for each product.

Example   Victoria Corporation produces one product, gourmet coffee blends. It expects to sell 70,000 units at $6 per unit (a unit is one can of coffee blend). Market researchers developed an initial sales forecast, estimating pessimistic, optimistic, and expected forecasts of total product sales in the market and Victoria's market share. The company defined optimistic as "probability of sales this high or higher is 0.2"; they defined pessimistic as "probability of sales this low or lower is 0.2." The marketing vice-president also had district sales managers prepare optimistic, pessimistic, and expected forecasts for their districts.

EXHIBIT 10.2

VICTORIA CORPORATION
Sales Budget for Period 1

Optimistic	90,000 Units at $7 = $630,000
Expected	70,000 Units at $6 = $420,000
Pessimistic	50,000 Units at $5 = $250,000

THE PRODUCTION BUDGET

The sales budget, combined with estimates of beginning inventories and estimates of desired ending inventories, forms the basis of the production budget for the Victoria Corporation shown in the top panel of Exhibit 10.3.

We compute the quantity of each product to be produced from the following equation:[1]

$$\text{Units to Be Produced} = \frac{\text{Number of Units}}{\text{to Be Sold}} + \frac{\text{Units in Ending}}{\text{Inventory}} - \frac{\text{Units in Beginning}}{\text{Inventory}}$$

The costs to be incurred in producing the desired number of units appear in the lower portion of Exhibit 10.3.

Direct Materials   Direct materials are materials traceable to individual units produced. Direct materials costs are almost always variable. Management estimates that each finished unit at Victoria will require 2 pounds of direct materials. The estimates of direct materials requirements result from engineering studies of material usage.

EXHIBIT 10.3

VICTORIA CORPORATION
Production Budget for Period 1

Units to Be Produced

Budgeted Sales, in Units (see sales budget)	70,000
Desired Ending Inventory (assumed)	8,000
Total Units Needed	78,000
Less Beginning Inventory (assumed)	(8,000)
Units to Be Produced	70,000

Cost Expected to Be Incurred

Direct Materials (2 pounds per unit at $.50 per pound)	$ 70,000
Direct Labor $\left(\frac{1}{8} \text{ hour per unit at } \$20 \text{ per hour}\right)$	175,000
Manufacturing Overhead:	
Indirect Labor ($.10 per unit)	7,000
Supplies ($.04 per unit)	2,800
Power ($1,000 per period plus $.03 per unit)	3,100
Maintenance ($13,840 per period)	13,840
Rent ($6,000 per period)	6,000
Insurance ($1,000 per period)	1,000
Depreciation ($10,360 per period)	10,360
Total Production Costs	$289,100

---

[1]Equation comes from the basic accounting equation:
  Beginning Balance + Transfers In = Transfers Out + Ending Balance
$$BB + TI = TO + EB$$
$$TI = TO + EB - BB$$

$$\text{Units to Be Produced} = \frac{\text{Number of Units}}{\text{to Be Sold}} + \frac{\text{Units in Ending}}{\text{Inventory}} - \frac{\text{Units in Beginning}}{\text{Inventory}}$$

The $.50 cost per pound of the direct materials comes from knowing projected prices of suppliers. Hence, the budgeted or standard direct materials cost per finished unit is $.50 × 2 pounds per finished unit = $1.00 per finished unit.[2]

Direct Labor   Direct labor is work traceable directly to particular units of product. Engineering time and motion studies and studies of past labor time usage indicate that one unit requires 1/8 hour of labor time. This estimate allows for normal, periodic rest periods, yet motivates employees to perform efficiently. The standard wage rate, including fringe benefits and payroll taxes (for example, employer's share of social security and unemployment taxes), for production workers in Victoria Corporation's plant is $20.00 per hour. The direct labor cost per unit is $2.50 (= $20 per labor hour × 1/8 hour per unit of output).

Direct labor could be fixed, as in high-tech companies having only a few workers, or variable. We assume direct labor is variable in this example.

Manufacturing Overhead   Variable manufacturing overhead costs vary with units produced. Fixed manufacturing overhead costs give a firm the capacity to produce. As Exhibit 10.3 shows, indirect labor and supplies are variable overhead costs. Power is a semivariable, or mixed, cost, having both variable and fixed components. Maintenance, rent, insurance, and depreciation are fixed overhead costs.

These estimates come from past experience. Managers should consider projected changes in costs and production methods to prepare estimates for the future. One can apply statistical regression methods to overhead to (1) separate fixed from variable overhead and (2) find the relations between variable overhead and a measure of activity (for example, direct labor hours or output).

Summary of Production Budget   The budget in Exhibit 10.3 shows planned production department activity for the period for 70,000 units and costs of $289,100.

Exhibit 10.3 shows the expected fixed costs to be the sum of the estimates for:

Power (fixed cost portion)	$ 1,000
Maintenance	13,840
Rent	6,000
Insurance	1,000
Depreciation	10,360
Total	$32,200

Exhibit 10.3 also shows the expected variable costs per unit to be the estimates for:

Direct Materials	$1.00
Direct Labor	2.50
Indirect Labor	0.10
Supplies	0.04
Power (variable cost portion)	0.03
Total	$3.67

[2]Managers and accountants often use the terms *budgets* and *standards* interchangeably.

If the level of production differs from the planned 70,000 units, we use the flexible budget to compute costs that the production department should have incurred for the actual units produced. The flexible budget for the production department is

$$\text{Total Budgeted Manufacturing Costs for Production Department} = \$32,200 + (\$3.67 \times \text{Actual Units Produced}).$$

Marketing and Administrative Costs   The budget for marketing costs for the Victoria Corporation's marketing department appears in Exhibit 10.4. Management expects all the items except commissions and shipping costs to be fixed. Commissions are 2 percent of sales dollars, or $.12 per unit at the budgeted price of $6 per unit ($.12 = .02 \times $6). Shipping costs are $.02 per unit shipped. Hence, the variable marketing cost is $.14 per unit sold. Note that variable marketing costs vary with units *sold*, whereas variable manufacturing costs vary with units *produced*.

Management estimates all the month's central corporate administrative costs in Exhibit 10.5 to be fixed.[3]

Discretionary Fixed Costs   Many of the so-called fixed costs in the production, marketing, and administrative budgets are *discretionary costs*. Maintenance, donations, and advertising are examples. Although management budgets them as fixed costs, managers realize that these costs are not committed costs, like rent on a factory building, that are required to run the firm.

When economic conditions make it doubtful that the firm will achieve its budgeted profit goals, management can cut discretionary costs. When managers state that they have reduced their fixed costs, or reduced their breakeven points, they have often cut discretionary costs, not committed costs. For example, IBM, AT&T, and General Motors recently made major cuts in expenses by laying off many

---

EXHIBIT 10.4

VICTORIA CORPORATION
Marketing Cost Budget for Period 1

Variable Costs

Commissions (2 percent of sales; see Exhibit 10.2, sales budget)	$ 8,400[a]	
Shipping Costs ($.02 per unit shipped; see Exhibit 10.2, sales budget)	1,400	
Total Variable Marketing Costs		$ 9,800

Fixed Costs

Salaries ($25,000 per period)	$25,000	
Advertising ($30,000 per period)	30,000	
Sales Office ($8,400 per period)	8,400	
Travel ($2,000 per period)	2,000	
Total Fixed Marketing Costs		65,400
Total Marketing Cost Budget		$75,200

[a]Also, $.12 per unit sold $\times$ 70,000 units sold = $8,400.

---

[3]In practice, administrative costs can be fixed or variable.

EXHIBIT 10.5

VICTORIA CORPORATION
Administrative Cost Budget for Period 1

President's Salary	$10,000
Salaries of Other Staff Personnel	17,000
Supplies	2,000
Heat and Light	1,400
Rent	4,000
Donations and Contributions	1,000
General Corporate Taxes	8,000
Depreciation—Staff Office Equipment	1,400
Total Administrative Cost Budget	$44,800

---

white-collar workers. Many executives believe those costs were discretionary because the firms continue to survive despite the cost cuts.

Discretionary costs are tempting cost-cutting targets because their reduction does not have serious short-term effects on production and marketing. The long-term consequences could be disastrous, however, if management cuts so-called discretionary functions like maintenance and advertising. Slashing the advertising budgets for companies like Nike, Miller Brewing Company, or Procter & Gamble would jeopardize those companies in the long run.

Profit Plan (Budgeted Income Statement) The *profit plan,* or *budgeted income statement,* appears in Exhibit 10.6 using a contribution margin format.

After compiling the budget, management projects an operating profit of $10,900. (Recall that this figure is *before taxes* and miscellaneous income and expenses.) If top management is satisfied with this budgeted result and can find adequate cash to carry out the operations, it will approve the master budget. If management considers the budgeted results unsatisfactory, it will look for ways to improve budget profits using cost reductions or sales increases.

EXHIBIT 10.6

VICTORIA CORPORATION
Master Budget Profit Plan (income statement)

Sales (70,000 units at $6)	$420,000
Variable Manufacturing Cost of Goods Sold (70,000 units at $3.67)	(256,900)
Variable Marketing Costs (70,000 units at $.14)	(9,800)
Contribution Margin	$153,300
Fixed Manufacturing Costs	(32,200)
Fixed Marketing and Administrative Costs	(110,200)
Operating Profits	$ 10,900

Budgeting for New Products at 3M

Several articles and books in the business press have heralded 3M for its product innovation and entrepreneurship. At the same time, good financial planning and tight cost control are very important to 3M. 3M accomplishes its objectives by using financial targets to set goals and measure performance. In particular, the company seeks to derive 25 percent of total sales each year from new products.

Many groups are involved in budgeting for new products. Marketing estimates market demand. People from research and development, manufacturing, and finance work out the budgeted costs and revenues. If new equipment is involved, manufacturing, engineering, and finance work out the cost of that equipment and how fast it will run.

Source: Based on the authors' research.

IMPLEMENTING THE MASTER BUDGET

The master budget includes a budgeted balance sheet, a cash flow budget, and other relevant budgets, as well as the profit plan developed in the preceding pages. Appendix 10.1 presents a comprehensive master budget including the profit plan, budgeted balance sheets, and the cash flow budget.

Preparing the master budget requires the participation of all managerial groups, as discussed in the Managerial Application "Budgeting for New Products at 3M." Once adopted, the budget becomes a major planning and control tool. Further, it becomes the authorization to produce and sell goods and services, to purchase materials, and to hire employees. In governmental units, the budget becomes the *legal* authorization for expenditure.

INCENTIVES FOR ACCURATE FORECASTS

You can see the importance of the sales forecast to the entire budget process from our Victoria Corporation example. If the sales forecast is too high and the company produces to meet the forecast, the company will have excess inventory. If the sales forecast is too low, the firm will likely lose sales opportunities because purchasing and production cannot meet demand. Rewarding managers only for accurate forecasting could create disincentives for better performance—managers would merely try to meet the forecast, not to beat it.

Companies use many different methods of providing incentives for both accurate forecasting *and* good performance. These methods include comparing sales forecasts from year to year and obtaining forecasts from multiple sources. Appendix 10.2 discusses formal incentive models that simultaneously motivate accurate forecasts and good performance.

USING THE BUDGET FOR PERFORMANCE EVALUATION

This section shows how accountants compare actual results achieved with budgets to derive **variances** for performance evaluation.

COMPARISON OF ACTUAL RESULTS WITH THE FLEXIBLE AND MASTER BUDGETS

The following discussion compares the master budget with the flexible budget and with actual results. This comparison ties the results of the planning process (which results in the master budget) with flexible budgeting, and forms the basis for analyzing differences between planned and actual results.

Flexible versus Master Budget   Exhibit 10.7 compares the flexible budget with the master budget profit plan for Victoria Corporation. The master budget results in the profit shown in Exhibit 10.6. To review, some of the important amounts follow:

Sales Price per Unit	$6.00
Sales Volume per Period	70,000 Units
Variable Manufacturing Costs per Unit	$3.67
Variable Marketing Costs per Unit (2 percent sales commission plus $.02 per-unit shipping costs)	$.14
Fixed Manufacturing Costs per Period	$32,200
Fixed Marketing Costs per Period	$65,400
Fixed Administrative Costs per Period	$44,800

EXHIBIT 10.7

VICTORIA CORPORATION
Flexible Budget and Sales Volume Variance

	Flexible Budget (based on actual sales volume of 80,000)	Sales Volume Variance	Master Budget (based on a prediction of 70,000 units sold)
Sales	$480,000[a]	$60,000 F	$420,000[d]
Less:			
Variable Manufacturing Costs	293,600[b]	36,700 U	256,900[e]
Variable Marketing Costs	11,200[c]	1,400 U	9,800[f]
Contribution Margin	$175,200	$21,900 F	$153,300
Less:			
Fixed Manufacturing Costs	32,200	—	32,200
Fixed Marketing Costs	65,400	—	65,400
Fixed Administrative Costs	44,800	—	44,800
Operating Profit	$ 32,800	$21,900 F	$ 10,900

[a]80,000 units sold at $6.00.   [e]70,000 units sold at $3.67.
[b]80,000 units sold at $3.67.   [f]70,000 units sold at $.14.
[c]80,000 units sold at $.14.   U denotes unfavorable variance.
[d]70,000 units sold at $6.00.   F denotes favorable variance.

We base the flexible budget in this case on the actual sales and production volume.[4] Variable costs and revenues should change as volume changes. The flexible budget indicates expected budgeted revenues and costs at the actual activity level, which is sales volume in this case. You can think of the flexible budget as the cost equation:

$$TC = F + VX,$$

where TC = total budgeted costs, F = budgeted fixed costs, V = budgeted variable cost per unit, and X = actual volume.

Although management predicted sales volume to be 70,000 units, Victoria produced and sold 80,000 units during the period. The **sales volume variance** is the difference in profits caused by the difference between the master budget sales volume and the actual sales volume. In this case, the difference of $21,900 between operating profits in the master budget and the flexible budget is a sales volume variance. It results from the 10,000 unit difference in sales volume from the sales plan of 70,000 units. We can also compute $21,900 by multiplying the 10,000 unit increase times the budgeted contribution margin per unit of $2.19 (= $6.00 − $3.67 − $.14).

What Is the Meaning of Favorable and Unfavorable?   Note the use of F (favorable) and U (unfavorable) beside each of the variances in Exhibit 10.7. These terms describe the impact of the variance on the budgeted operating profits. A **favorable variance** means that the variance would *increase* operating profits, holding all other things constant. An **unfavorable variance** would *decrease* operating profits, holding all other things constant.

We do not use these terms in a normative sense. A favorable variance is not *necessarily* good, and an unfavorable variance is not *necessarily* bad. Further note the variable cost variances—they are labeled unfavorable. Does this reflect unfavorable conditions in the company? Unlikely! These variable costs are *expected* to increase because the actual sales volume is higher than planned. In short, the labels *favorable* or *unfavorable* do not automatically indicate good or bad conditions. Rather, a favorable variance implies that actual profits are higher than budgeted, all other things (for example, other variances) being ignored; conversely, an unfavorable variance implies that actual profits are lower than budgeted, all other things being ignored. Ultimately, the accounting will credit favorable variances and debit unfavorable variances to income statement accounts.

Information Use   The information presented in Exhibit 10.7 has a number of uses. First, it shows that the increase in operating profits from the master budget results from the increase in sales volume over the level planned. Sales variances are usually the responsibility of the marketing department, so this information

---

[4]The relevant activity variable is *sales* volume because this is a profit plan (that is, an income statement). If the objective were to compare the flexible production budget with the master production budget, the relevant activity variable would be *production* volume. Sales and production volumes are assumed to be equal throughout this example so we can avoid allocating fixed manufacturing costs to inventories.

may be useful feedback to personnel in that department, and managers may find it informative for evaluating performance. Second, the resulting flexible budget shows budgeted sales, costs, and operating profits *after* taking into account the volume increase but *before* considering differences in unit selling prices, differences in unit variable costs, and differences in fixed costs from the master budgets.

PROBLEM 10.1 FOR SELF-STUDY

Comparing the master budget to the flexible budget. Computer Supply, Inc., budgeted production and sales of 40,000 laptop computer cases for the month of April at a selling price of $11 each. The company actually sold 50,000 cases for $10 each. The company budgeted the following costs:

Standard Manufacturing Variable Costs per Unit	$4.00
Fixed Manufacturing Overhead Cost: Monthly Budget	$80,000
Marketing and Administrative Costs:	
Variable (per unit)	$1.00
Fixed (monthly budget)	$100,000

Prepare a report for management like the one in Exhibit 10.7 showing the master budget, flexible budget, and sales volume variance.

The solution to this self-study problem is at the end of the chapter on page 346.

ACTUAL RESULTS VERSUS FLEXIBLE BUDGET

Assume that actual Victoria Corporation's results for period 1 follow:

Sales Price per Unit	$6.10
Sales Volume for the Period	80,000 Units
Variable Manufacturing Costs per Unit	$3.82
Variable Marketing Costs per Unit	$.16
Fixed Manufacturing Costs for the Period	$34,000
Fixed Marketing Costs for the Period	$64,400
Fixed Administrative Costs for the Period	$44,600

We can now compare these results with both the flexible budget and the master budget, as in Exhibit 10.8. We carry Columns (5), (6), and (7) forward from Exhibit 10.7. We calculate Column (1) in Exhibit 10.8 from the facts presented above.

EXHIBIT 10.8

VICTORIA CORPORATION
Profit Variance Analysis: A Comparison of Actual Results with the Profit Plan

	Actual (based on actual sales volume of 80,000 units) (1)	Purchasing and Production Variances (2)	Marketing and Administrative Cost Variances (3)	Sales Price Variance (4)	Flexible Budget (based on actual sales volume of 80,000 units)[f] (5)	Sales Volume Variance[f] (6)	Master Budget (based on a plan of 70,000 units sold)[f] (7)
Sales	$488,000[a]	—	—	$8,000 F	$480,000	$60,000 F	$420,000
Less:							
Variable Manufacturing							
Costs	305,600[b]	$12,000 U	—	—	293,600	36,700 U	256,900
Variable Marketing							
Costs	12,800[c]	—	$1,440 U[d]	160 U[e]	11,200	1,400 U	9,800
Contribution Margin	$169,600	$12,000 U	$1,440 U	$7,840 F	$175,200	$21,900 F	$153,300
Less:							
Fixed Manufacturing							
Costs	34,000	1,800 U	—	—	32,200	—	32,200
Fixed Marketing Costs	64,400	—	1,000 F	—	65,400	—	65,400
Fixed Administrative							
Costs	44,600	—	200 F	—	44,800	—	44,800
Operating Profits	$ 26,600	$13,800 U	$ 240 U	$7,840 F	$ 32,800	$21,900 F	$ 10,900

Total Profit Variance from Flexible Budget = $6,200 U

Total Profit Variance from Master Budget = $15,700 F

[a]80,000 units sold at $6.10 per unit.
[b]80,000 units sold at $3.82 per unit.
[c]80,000 units sold at $.16 per unit.
[d]$1,440 U = ($12,800 − $11,200) − $160.
[e]$160 U = .02 × $8,000 F Sales Price Variance.
[f]Amounts are from Exhibit 10.7.

U denotes unfavorable variance.
F denotes favorable variance.

OVERVIEW OF THE PROFIT VARIANCE

Exhibit 10.8 shows the source of the total variance from the profit plan, which is $15,700 favorable. The analysis of the causes of the total profit variance (that is, the $15,700 difference between the profit budgeted in the master budget and the profit earned for the period) is known as **profit variance analysis.**

Column (2) in Exhibit 10.8 summarizes purchasing and manufacturing variances, which Chapter 11 discusses in more detail. Columns (3) and (4) show marketing and administrative variances. The increased commissions of $160 (= 2% × $8,000) partly offset the favorable sales price variance of $8,000. The remaining $1,440U marketing and administrative cost variance is the residual: $12,800 actual − $11,200 flexible budget − $160 = $1,440.

Performance Appraisal   What is your overall assessment of Victoria Corporation's performance for the period? Clearly the company did better than expected, because sales prices and volume both exceeded expectations. However, costs also exceeded expectations, even after allowing for the increase in volume. The $12,000 unfavorable variable manufacturing cost variance could be of particular concern. Note that the flexible budget has increased the allowance for variable manufacturing costs from $256,900 in the master budget to $293,600 in the flexible budget. However, the actual costs were even higher—$305,600. This implies either that inefficiencies in manufacturing occurred or that the company paid more than expected for variable manufacturing inputs, such as direct materials, direct labor, or variable manufacturing overhead items.

Do Not Get Lost in Details   Variance computations and analysis can become detailed, and users of variances (as well as students) sometimes do not see how such detailed computations fit into the "big picture" comparison of achieved results with the master budget. Exhibit 10.8 presents the big picture. Chapter 11 goes into more detailed computations.

Exhibit 10.9 summarizes these results graphically. Note that the flexible budget line shows expected profits for various activity levels for a given level of fixed costs. Any change in fixed costs would *shift* the flexible budget line up or down.

KEY VARIANCES

Many top executives receive daily variance reports about a few key items. For example, airline officials receive variance reports on seats sold the previous day; officials in steel companies receive variance reports on the number of tons of steel produced; and officials of merchandising companies receive daily variance reports on sales. As these examples demonstrate, most of these key items deal with *output*. Input variances (that is, cost variances) usually require more detailed data collection. Accounting systems report these weekly or monthly. Accountants prepare "big picture" reports, such as Exhibit 10.8, less frequently, perhaps monthly, quarterly or yearly.

EXHIBIT 10.9

VICTORIA CORPORATION
Flexible Budget Line

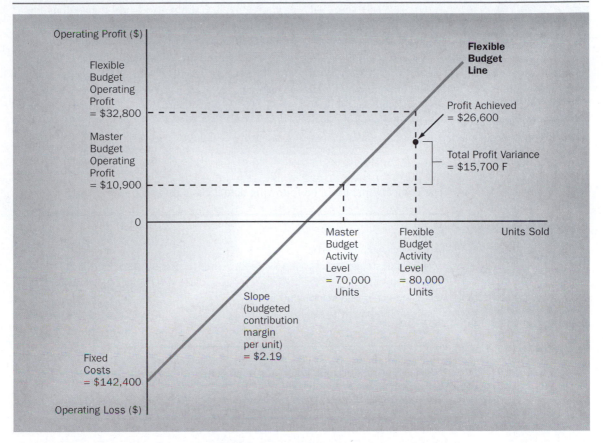

Preparing the profit variance analysis. This problem continues Problem 10.1 for self-study. Computer Supply, Inc., budgeted production and sales of 40,000 laptop computer cases for the month of April at a selling price of $11 each. The company actually sold 50,000 cases for $10 each. The company budgeted the following costs:

Budget

Standard Variable Manufacturing Costs per Unit	$ 4.00
Fixed Manufacturing Overhead for the Month	$ 80,000
Marketing and Administrative Costs:	
Variable (per unit)	$ 1.00
Fixed (monthly budget)	$100,000

The company incurred the following actual costs in April:

Actual

Actual Manufacturing Costs:

Variable Costs per Unit	$ 4.88
Fixed Overhead	$83,000

Actual Marketing and Administrative:

Variable (50,000 at $1.04)	$52,000
Fixed	$96,000

Prepare a profit variance report for management like the one in Exhibit 10.8.

The solution to this self-study problem is at the end of the chapter on page 347.

BUDGETING IN NONPROFIT ORGANIZATIONS

The master budget has added importance in nonprofit organizations because it is usually a document used as a basis for authorizing the expenditure of funds. In many governmental units, *the approved budget is a legal authorization for expenditure,* and the penalties for exceeding the authorized expenditures in the budget could be severe. This partially explains why a balanced budget takes on added importance in nonprofit organizations. The Managerial Application, "Using Toll-Free Hotlines to Solve Budget Problems," discusses attempts to balance the budget in California, where governmental organizations need to get serious about balancing their budgets.

ETHICAL ISSUES IN BUDGETING

Budgeting creates serious ethical issues for many people. Much of the information for the budget is provided by managers and employees whose performance is then

MANAGERIAL APPLICATION

Conflicts between Meeting Performance Standards and Behaving Ethically

According to employees at General Electric, "in the frenzy of meeting sales goals, there was little time to scrutinize phony transactions." In attempting to deal with conflicts between meeting performance standards and ethical behavior, General Electric has stated in its personnel manual, "If confronted with apparent conflicts between demands of their jobs and the highest standards of ethical conduct, employees should be guided by their sense of honor until the inconsistency has been resolved." According to a vice-president of the company's aerospace unit, when employees get the message to achieve their performance goals, they should also receive the message that they must comply with the company's standards for ethical behavior.

Source: Based on an article in *The Wall Street Journal,* July 22, 1992.

compared with the budget they helped develop. For example, as a manager, suppose you believe that, while it was possible to achieve a 10 percent increase in your department's sales, a 2 percent increase would be almost certain. If you tell upper management that a 10 percent increase is an appropriate budget, but you fall short of 10 percent, you will lose opportunities for merit pay increases and a promotion. Management may assume the reason you fell short of the 10 percent estimation was not because of market circumstances beyond your control, but because you did not perform well in making sales. On the other hand, if you report that only a 2 percent increase is possible, your performance is likely to exceed expectations, but the company will not provide for enough production capacity to fill the sales orders if the 10 percent increase comes through. What should you do? Should you prepare a budget that is in your best interest or one that presents your best estimate of reality?

People in companies face these dilemmas all the time. We hope companies provide incentives for people to report truthfully, which means the company must reward both the honest estimates and good performance. But the reality is that many companies put considerable pressure on employees to achieve continually more difficult targets. Fraudulent financial reporting often occurs because managers cannot meet continually more difficult budgets. The Managerial Application, "Conflicts between Meeting Performance Standards and Behaving Ethically," describes General Electric's attempts to instruct employees on ways to deal with conflicts between high standards of ethical conduct and the demands of their jobs.

SUMMARY

The following items correspond to the learning objectives presented at the beginning of the chapter.

1. **Analyze a budget as a tool for planning and performance evaluation.** A budget is an estimate of financial statements prepared before the actual transactions

occur. Budgets are generally developed for a particular expected level of activity. Budgets also provide estimates of expected performance and serve as standards for evaluating performance.

2. **Compare the four types of responsibility centers.** Managers are responsible for costs in cost centers. Managers are responsible for revenues in revenue centers. Managers are responsible for both costs and revenues in profit centers. Managers are responsible for revenues, costs, and assets in an investment center.

3. **Recognize how a budget can affect employee motivation.** Managers must determine what types of behavior the system motivates and if that is the desired behavior. Managers must try to promote goal congruence.

4. **Describe the master budget.** The master budget is a complete blueprint of the planned operations of a firm for a period. It begins with the sales budget, then adds the production budget, and finishes with the budgeted income statement.

5. **Know how to use the budget for performance evaluation.** Accountants compare actual results achieved with budgets to derive variances for performance evaluation. Comparison of actual results with the flexible and master budgets ties the results of the planning process with flexible budgeting, and forms the basis for analyzing differences between planned and actual results.

6. **Define the different types of variances between actual results and the flexible budget.** Variances include purchasing and production variances, marketing and administrative cost variances, sales price variance, and sales volume variance.

7. **Describe ethical dilemmas in budgeting.** Much of the information for the budget is provided by managers and employees whose performance is then compared with the budget they helped develop.

8. **(Appendix 10.1) Develop a comprehensive master budget.** A comprehensive master budget includes individual schedules for a materials purchases budget, a capital budget, a cash outlays budget, a receivables and collections budget, and a cash budget, all of which support the budgeted income and retained earnings statement. Finally the budgeted balance sheet is developed.

9. **(Appendix 10.2) Describe an incentive model for accurate reporting.** The incentive plan has three components: (1) It relates rewards positively to forecasted sales, (2) it provides incentives for the sales manager to increase sales beyond the forecast, and (3) it penalizes the sales manager when sales are less than forecasted.

KEY TERMS AND CONCEPTS

Short-term operating budget   Budget that states management's plan of action for the coming year in quantitative terms.

Static budget   Budget developed for a particular level of activity, such as production or sales.

Responsibility center   Part or segment of an organization that top management holds accountable for a specified set of activities.

Cost center   A responsibility center that is accountable for expenditures and expenses.

Revenue center   A responsibility center within a firm that is accountable only for revenues generated.

Profit center   A responsibility center that is accountable for both revenues and expenses.

Investment center   A responsibility center, with accountability for revenues, costs, and assets.

Engineered cost centers   Responsibility centers in which input-output relations are sufficiently well established that a particular set of inputs will provide a predictable and measurable set of outputs.

Discretionary cost centers   Responsibility centers in which input-output relations are not well specified.

Flexible budget   Budget that projects receipts and expenditures as a function of activity levels.

Goal congruence   All members of an organization have incentives to perform for a common interest, such as shareholder wealth maximization for a corporation.

Master budget   A budget projecting all financial statements and their components.

Variance   Differences between actual and standard costs or between budgeted and actual expenditures or, sometimes, expenses.

Sales volume variance   Budgeted contribution margin per unit $\times$ (planned sales volume $-$ actual sales volume).

Favorable variance   An excess of actual revenues over expected revenues; an excess of standard cost over actual cost.

Unfavorable variance   An excess of budgeted revenue over actual revenue or an excess of actual cost over standard cost.

Profit variance analysis   Analysis of the causes of the difference between budgeted profit in the master budget and the profits earned.

APPENDIX 10.1: COMPREHENSIVE MASTER BUDGET—VICTORIA CORPORATION

This appendix presents the comprehensive master budget for Victoria Corporation. First, we summarize the profit plan developed in the chapter. Second, we tie the profit plan into the other budgets, such as the cash budget and the capital budget. Finally, we present the budgeted balance sheet. The master budget ties together the financial activities of the firm for the budget period. Hence, it can aid both planning and coordination. For example, planning for cash needs requires knowing cash flows to and from operating activities and also knowing cash needs for the capital budget.

Exhibit 10.10 summarizes the information from the chapter about projected sales and production volumes, revenues, and costs. Exhibit 10.11 presents the master budget profit plan from the chapter.

EXHIBIT 10.10

VICTORIA CORPORATION
Summary of Sales, Production, and Cost Budgets for Period 1

Sales Budget[a]

70,000 Units at $6		$420,000

Production Budget[b]
Units to Be Produced

Budgeted Sales, in Units (see sales budget)	70,000 Units
Desired Ending Inventory (assumed)	8,000
Total Units Needed	78,000 Units
Beginning Inventory (assumed)	(8,000)
Units to Be Produced	70,000 Units

Cost Expected to Be Incurred

Direct Materials (2 pounds per unit at $.50 per pound)		$ 70,000
Direct Labor ($1/8$ hour per unit at $20 per hour)		175,000
Manufacturing Overhead:		
Indirect Labor ($.10 per unit)	$ 7,000	
Supplies ($.04 per unit)	2,800	
Power ($1,000 per period plus $.03 per unit)	3,100	
Maintenance ($13,840 per period)	13,840	
Rent ($6,000 per period)	6,000	
Insurance ($1,000 per period)	1,000	
Depreciation ($10,360 per period)	10,360	44,100
Total Production Costs		$289,100

Marketing Cost Budget[c]
Variable Costs

Commissions (2 percent of sales)	$ 8,400	
Shipping Costs ($.02 per unit shipped)	1,400	
Total Variable Marketing Costs		$ 9,800

Fixed Costs

Salaries ($25,000 per period)	$25,000	
Advertising ($30,000 per period)	30,000	
Sales Office ($8,400 per period)	8,400	
Travel ($2,000 per period)	2,000	
Total Fixed Marketing Costs		65,400
Total Marketing Cost Budget		$ 75,200

Administrative Cost Budget[d]

President's Salary	$ 10,000
Salaries of Other Staff Personnel	17,000
Supplies	2,000
Heat and Light	1,400
Rent	4,000
Donations and Contributions	1,000
General Corporate Taxes	8,000
Depreciation—Staff Office Equipment	1,400
Total Administrative Cost Budget	$ 44,800

[a]*Source:* Exhibit 10.2.   [b]*Source:* Exhibit 10.3.   [c]*Source:* Exhibit 10.4.   [d]*Source:* Exhibit 10.5.

EXHIBIT 10.11

VICTORIA CORPORATION
Master Budget Profit Plan for Period 1

Sales (70,000 units at $6)	$420,000
Less:	
Variable Manufacturing Cost of Goods Sold (70,000 units at $3.67)	(256,900)
Variable Marketing Costs (70,000 units at $.14)	(9,800)
Contribution Margin	$153,300
Less:	
Fixed Manufacturing Costs	(32,200)
Fixed Marketing and Administrative Costs	(110,200)
Operating Profits	$ 10,900

Source: Exhibit 10.6.

EXHIBIT 10.12

VICTORIA CORPORATION
Materials Purchases Budget

Quantities to Be Purchased (in pounds):

Units to be Produced (see Exhibit 10.10)	70,000 Units
Purchases Required at 2 Pounds per Unit	140,000 Pounds

There are no materials inventories.

MATERIALS PURCHASES BUDGET

The purchasing department is responsible for purchasing materials in Victoria Corporation. Exhibit 10.12 presents the materials purchases budget. The production budget is the basis for the materials purchases budget. For simplicity in presentation, we assume that payments to suppliers equal purchases each period.

CAPITAL BUDGET

The capital budget, Exhibit 10.13, shows Victoria Corporation's plan for acquisition of depreciable, long-term assets during the next period. Management plans to purchase major items of equipment, financing part of the cost by issuing notes payable to equipment suppliers. The capital budget deducts the expected proceeds of the note issuance from the cost of the acqusitions to estimate current cash outlays for equipment. An accepted alternative treatment would have viewed the note issuance as a cash inflow, with the entire cost of the equipment included in cash outflows.

CASH OUTLAYS BUDGET

Exhibit 10.14 presents a schedule of the planned cash outlays for the budget period. Each period, the Victoria Corporation pays the income taxes accrued in the previous

---

EXHIBIT 10.13

VICTORIA CORPORATION
Capital Budget for Period 1

	Period 1
Acquisition of New Factory Machinery	$12,000
Miscellaneous Capital Additions	2,000
Total Capital Budget	$14,000
Borrowings for New Machinery—Long-term Notes Payable	(6,000)
Current Cash Outlay	$ 8,000

EXHIBIT 10.14

VICTORIA CORPORATION
Cash Outflows Budget for Period 1

	Period 1
Materials (Exhibit 10.10)	$ 70,000
Labor (Exhibit 10.10)	175,000
Manufacturing Overhead (Exhibit 10.10)[a]	33,740
Marketing Costs (Exhibit 10.10)	75,200
Administrative Costs (Exhibit 10.10)[b]	43,400
Capital Expenditures (Exhibit 10.13)	8,000
Payments on Short-term Notes[c]	13,000
Interest[c]	3,000
Income Taxes[d]	6,200
Dividends[c]	5,000
Total Cash Outflows	$432,540

[a]Manufacturing Overhead Costs − Depreciation = $44,100 − $10,360 = $33,740.

[b]Administrative Costs −Depreciation = $44,800 − $1,400 = $43,400.

[c]Assumed for illustration.

[d]The firm pays income taxes on earnings of previous period in current period. We assume the amount in this case.

period. Income taxes payable at the start of the budget period appears as $6,200 on the beginning balance sheet (first column of Exhibit 10.18). The firm expects to declare and pay dividends of $5,000 in the budget period.

RECEIVABLES AND COLLECTIONS BUDGET

Victoria collects most of each period's sales in the period of sales, but there is a lag in some collections. The budget for cash collections from customers appears in Exhibit 10.15. Collecting for sales of a given period normally occur as follows: 85 percent in the period of sale and 15 percent in the next period. We could introduce sales discounts and estimates of uncollectible accounts into the illustration, but we omit them for simplicity. The estimated accounts receivable at the start of the budget

EXHIBIT 10.15

VICTORIA CORPORATION
Receivables and Collections Budget for Period 1

	Budget Period
Accounts Receivable, Start of Period:	
From the Period Immediately Preceding the Budget Period (15 percent of $476,000)	$ 71,400
Budget Period Sales	420,000
Total Receivables	$ 491,400
Less Collections:	
Current Period (85 percent of $420,000)	$(357,000)
Previous Period (15 percent of $476,000)	(71,400)
Total Collections	$(428,400)
Accounts Receivable, End of Period	$ 63,000

period of $71,400 appears on the beginning balance sheet (first column of Exhibit 10.18). The amount represents 15 percent of the previous period's sales of $476,000; $71,400 = .15 × $476,000. In the budget period, the firm expects to collect 85 percent of sales, leaving $63,000 in Accounts Receivable at the end of the budget period ($63,000 = 15 percent of budget period sales of $420,000).

CASH BUDGET

Cash flow is important. No budget is more important for financial planning than the cash budget, illustrated in Exhibit 10.16. This budget helps management plan to avoid unnecessary idle cash balances or unneeded, expensive borrowing. Almost all firms prepare a cash budget.

EXHIBIT 10.16

VICTORIA CORPORATION
Cash Budget for Period 1

	Budget Period
Cash Receipts:	
Collections from Customers (Exhibit 10.15)	$428,400
Other Income[a]	2,000
Total Receipts	$430,400
Cash Outflows (Exhibit 10.14)	(432,540)
Increase (Decrease) in Cash during Period	$ (2,140)
Cash Balance at Start of Period[a]	79,800
Cash Balance at End of Period	$ 77,660

[a]Assumed for illustration.

The budgeted amounts for cash outflows and collections from customers come from Exhibits 10.14 and 10.15, respectively. Management estimates the other income, interest, and miscellaneous revenues to be $2,000 for the period.

BUDGETED (PRO FORMA) INCOME AND RETAINED EARNINGS STATEMENT

The budgeted income and retained earnings statement and the budgeted balance sheet pull together all the preceding budget information. Exhibit 10.17 illustrates the budgeted income and retained earnings statement. At this stage in the budgeting process, management's attention switches from decision making, planning, and control to external reporting to shareholders. In other words, management becomes interested in how the income statement and balance sheet will reflect the results of its decisions. Accordingly, accountants prepare the budgeted income statement and balance sheet in accordance with generally accepted accounting principles. The statement in Exhibit 10.17 is an *income statement,* rather than a profit plan, and we present it using full absorption costing as required for external reporting.

Compilation of all the data for the period indicates a budgeted income of $6,039. If top management finds this budgeted result satisfactory, and has available cash adequate to carry out the operations as indicated by Exhibit 10.16, it will approve the master budget. If management does not consider the budgeted results satisfactory, it will consider ways to improve the budgeted results through cost reductions or altered sales plans.

EXHIBIT 10.17

VICTORIA CORPORATION
Budgeted (pro forma) Income and Retained Earnings Statement for Period 1

Sales (70,000 units at $6)	$ 420,000
Less Cost of Goods Sold (Exhibit 10.10)	(289,100)
Gross Margin	$ 130,900
Less Marketing Expenses (Exhibit 10.10)	(75,200)
Less Administrative Expenses (Exhibit 10.10)	(44,800)
Operating Profits (Exhibit 10.11)	$ 10,900
Other Income (Exhibit 10.16)	2,000
	$ 12,900
Less Interest Expense (Exhibit 10.14)	(3,000)
Pretax Income	$ 9,900
Less Income Taxes[a]	(3,861)
Net Income	$ 6,039
Less Dividends (Exhibit 10.14)	(5,000)
Increase in Retained Earnings	$ 1,039
Retained Earnings at Start of Period (Exhibit 10.18)	56,500
Retained Earnings at End of Period (Exhibit 10.18)	$ 57,539

---

[a]Income taxes average approximately 39 percent of pretax income. The amount $3,861 is shown as the end-of-period income taxes payable in Exhibit 10.18.

BUDGETED BALANCE SHEET

The final exhibit of this series, Exhibit 10.18, shows the budgeted balance sheets at the start and end of the period. (Accountants prepare the budget before the beginning of the budget period; hence, they must estimate the beginning balance sheet. For example, accountants would prepare a budget for the calendar year during the preceding September through November.)

Here, as in the budgeted income statement, management will have to decide if the budgeted overall results will be acceptable. Will cash balances be satisfactory? Do the receivables meet management's objectives? Will the final capital structure and

EXHIBIT 10.18

VICTORIA CORPORATION
Budgeted Balance Sheet for Period 1

	Start of Budget Period	End of Budget Period
Assets		
Current Assets		
Cash (Exhibit 10.16)	$ 79,800	$ 77,660
Accounts Receivable (Exhibit 10.15)	71,400	63,000
Finished Goods Inventory	33,040[a]	33,040[a]
Total Current Assets	$184,240	$173,700
Plant Assets		
Equipment	460,000[a]	474,000[a]
Less Accumulated Depreciation	(162,000)[a]	(173,760)[a]
Total Assets	$482,240	$473,940
Equities		
Current Liabilities		
Accounts Payable	$ 96,540[a]	$ 96,540[a]
Short-term Notes and Other Payables	41,000[a]	28,000[a]
Income Taxes Payable (Exhibit 10.14 and 10.17)	6,200	3,861
Total Current Liabilities	$143,740	$128,401
Long-term Liabilities		
Long-term Equipment Notes	82,000[a]	88,000[a]
Total Liabilities	$225,740	$216,401
Shareholders' Equity		
Capital Stock ($20 par value)	$200,000[a]	$200,000[a]
Retained Earnings (Exhibit 10.17)	56,500[a]	57,539[a]
Total Shareholders' Equity	$256,500	$257,539
Total Equities	$482,240	$473,940

[a]Assumed for purposes of illustration.

debt-equity ratio conform to management's desires? If the budgeted balance sheet and income statement are satisfactory, they will become the initial benchmarks against which management will check actual performance in the ensuing period.

SUMMARY OF THE MASTER BUDGET

The master budget summarizes management's plans for the period covered. Preparing the master budget requires the participation of all managerial groups, from local plant and sales managers to the top executives of the firm and the board of directors. Once management adopts the budget, it becomes the major planning and control instrument.

Master budgets are almost always static budgets; that is, they consider the likely results of the operations at the one level of operations specified in the budget. Computerizing the process makes it less costly to develop multiple master budgets that take into account various uncertainties facing the firm, such as market conditions, material prices, labor difficulties, and government regulations.

APPENDIX 10.2: INCENTIVE MODEL FOR ACCURATE REPORTING

How does management provide employees with incentives both for accurate reporting and for high performance?

Example   Assume that the Harris Raviv Company solicits sales forecasts from each of its district sales managers. These forecasts become budgets that management compares to actual sales to evaluate performance.

The firm's general manager of marketing wants to provide each district sales manager with a salary and a bonus. Previously sales managers earned a bonus by beating the budget. The sales managers, however, began to "low-ball" the forecasts. Management knew this was happening, but it did not know how high the forecasts *should* have been, because it did not have the information the managers had. The general manager of marketing explained:

> Managers could always counter our arguments with data that we could not audit. Their low estimates wreaked havoc with our production schedules, purchasing, and hiring decisions.
>
> Next we tried to give them incentives for accurate forecasts. We rewarded them if the actual sales were close to the forecasts, and penalized if actual and forecast deviated a lot. With this sytem, the managers forecast sales at a level that was sufficiently low to be achievable, then they "managed" their sales such that actual was almost right at the forecast. The consequences were that they had disincentives to beat the budget. Also, our internal auditors found numerous cases where managers had delayed sales orders until the following year and even turned down some orders because they did not want the current year's sales to overshoot the forecast.

The incentive plan to deal with this problem has three components:

1. Rewards are positively related to forecasted sales to give managers incentives to forecast high rather than low. If b_1 is a bonus coefficient that is a percent of forecasted sales, and forecasted sales are $\hat{Y}$, then this component of the bonus is

$$b_1\hat{Y}.$$

2. The plan provides incentives for the sales manager to increase sales beyond the forecast. If b_2 is the bonus coefficient for the excess of Y over $\hat{Y}$, forecast sales, then this component of the bonus is

$$b_2(Y - \hat{Y}), \quad \text{for } Y \geq \hat{Y}.$$

3. When actual sales, Y, are less than the forecast, $\hat{Y}$, the plan penalizes the sales manager. If b_3 is the bonus coefficient for the shortfall, $Y - \hat{Y}$, then this component of the bonus is

$$-b_3(\hat{Y} - Y), \quad \text{for } \hat{Y} > Y.$$

If B is the dollar bonus paid to the manager, the overall bonus plan is

$$B = \begin{cases} b_1\hat{Y} + b_2(Y - \hat{Y}), & \text{for } Y \geq \hat{Y} \text{ (actual sales meet or exceed the forecast);} \\ b_1\hat{Y} - b_3(\hat{Y} - Y), & \text{for } \hat{Y} > Y \text{ (the forecast exceeds actual sales).} \end{cases}$$

The coefficients are set such that

$$b_3 > b_1 > b_2 > 0,$$

and a rule of thumb is that b_3 should be at least 30 percent greater than b_1, and b_1 should be at least 20 percent greater than b_2. Management intends for this incentive plan to reward both accurate forecasts and outstanding performance.

Harris Raviv Company established an incentive system using the methods described here. Exhibit 10.19 shows the bonus that would result from various combinations of forecasted sales and actual sales. For example, if the forecast is

---

EXHIBIT 10.19

HARRIS RAVIV COMPANY
Incentives for Accurate Forecasting Bonus Paid to District Sales Managers
(thousands omitted from sales and bonus amounts)

Let b_1 = 5 percent, b_2 = 3 percent, and b_3 = 7 percent

$$B = \begin{cases} .05\hat{Y} + .03(Y - \hat{Y}), & \text{for } Y \geq \hat{Y}; \\ .05\hat{Y} - .07(\hat{Y} - Y), & \text{for } \hat{Y} > Y. \end{cases}$$

		Forecasted Sales, $\hat{Y}$		
		$1,000	$1,100	$1,200
Actual	**$1,000**	50[a]	48[d]	46[g]
Sales,	**$1,100**	53[b]	55[e]	53[h]
Y	**$1,200**	56[c]	58[f]	60[i]

---

[a]$50 = .05($1,000).

[b]$53 = .05($1,000) + .03($1,100 − $1,000).

[c]$56 = .05($1,000) + .03($1,200 − $1,000).

[d]$48 = .05($1,100) − .07($1,100 − $1,000).

[e]$55 = .05($1,100).

[f]$58 = .05($1,100) + .03($1,200 − $1,100).

[g]$46 = .05($1,200) − .07($1,200 − $1,000).

[h]$53 = .05($1,200) − .07($1,200 − $1,100).

[i]$60 = .05($1,200).

$1,100,000 and the actual sales are $1,000,000, the district sales manager receives a bonus of $48,000; if both the forecast and actual sales are $1,100,000, the sales manager receives a bonus of $55,000; and so forth.

IMPLICATIONS

What are the implications of this incentive system? If you read down a column in Exhibit 10.19, you will see that after making the forecast, the manager receives a larger reward for more sales even if an increase in sales makes the forecast inaccurate. Reading across the rows reveals that the manager receives the highest bonus when the forecast equals actual sales; hence, the manager has an incentive to make accurate forecasts.

This system provides incentives for accurate forecasting and sales output simultaneously. Although our example has dealt with sales forecasts, the method described applies to virtually any type of forecasting (for example, production levels, costs, productivity). At this point, we have little evidence about implementation difficulties. Whereas the method appears to be a clever innovation, we shall have to see it in operation before we pass judgment on it. (Note that top management can adjust the bonus coefficients, b_1, b_2, and b_3, to suit the needs of the particular situation.)

In summary, analysts have developed incentive methods that provide rewards for both accurate forecasts and good performance. Rewards are positively related to forecasted sales to give incentives to forecast high rather than low. Employees receive additional rewards for beating the forecast and penalties for results worse than forecast.

SOLUTIONS TO SELF-STUDY PROBLEMS

SUGGESTED SOLUTION TO PROBLEM 10.1 FOR SELF-STUDY

COMPUTER SUPPLY, INC.
Flexible Budget and Sales Volume Variance
April

	Flexible Budget (based on 50,000 units)	Sales Volume Variance	Master Budget (based on 40,000 units)
Sales Revenue	$550,000[a]	$110,000 F	$440,000
Less:			
Variable Manufacturing Costs	200,000	40,000 U	160,000
Variable Marketing and Administrative Costs	50,000	10,000 U	40,000
Contribution Margin	$300,000	$ 60,000 F	$240,000
Less:			
Fixed Manufacturing Costs	80,000	—	80,000
Fixed Marketing and Administrative Costs	100,000	—	100,000
Operating Profits	$120,000	$ 60,000 F	$60,000

[a]$550,000 = 50,000 × $11. Note the only change is volume, not sales price.

COMPUTER SUPPLY, INC.
Profit Variance Analysis
April

	Actual (based on 50,000 units)	Purchasing and Production Variances	Marketing and Administrative Variances	Sales Price Variances	Flexible Budget (based on 50,000 units)	Sales Volume Variance	Master Budget (based on 40,000 units)
Sales Revenue	$500,000	—	—	$50,000 U	$550,000	$110,000 F	$440,000
Less:							
Variable Manufacturing Costs	244,000	$44,000 U		—	200,000	40,000 U	160,000
Variable Marketing and Administrative Costs	52,000		$2,000 U		50,000	10,000 U	40,000
Contribution Margin	$204,000	$44,000 U	$2,000 U	$50,000 U	$300,000	$ 60,000 F	$240,000
Less:							
Fixed Manufacturing Costs	83,000	3,000 U		—	80,000	—	80,000
Fixed Marketing and Administrative Costs	96,000		4,000 F		100,000	—	100,000
Operating Profits	$ 25,000	$47,000 U	$2,000 F	$50,000 U	$120,000	$ 60,000 F	$ 60,000

Total Profit Variance from Flexible Budget = $95,000 U

Total Profit Variance from Master Budget = $35,000 U

QUESTIONS, EXERCISES, PROBLEMS, AND CASES

REVIEW QUESTIONS

1. Review the meaning of the concepts or terms listed in Key Terms and Concepts.
2. What is the difference between a cost center and a profit center?
3. What is the difference between a profit center and an investment center?
4. Why is it difficult to assess the effectiveness of discretionary cost centers?

CRITICAL ANALYSIS AND DISCUSSION QUESTIONS

5. Who, among university administrators, is most likely to be responsible for each of the following?
   a. Quantity of supplies used in executive education classes that the business school conducts.
   b. Electricity for equipment the university's printing operations use.
   c. Charge for classroom maintenance the business school uses.
   d. Finance professors' salaries.
6. A superior criticized a sales manager for selling high-revenue, low-profit items instead of lower-revenue but higher-profit items. The sales manager responded, "My income is based on commissions that are a percent of revenues. Why should I care about profits? I care about revenues!" Comment.
7. "The flexible budget is a poor benchmark. You should develop a budget and stay with it." Comment.
8. Why is the sales forecast so important in developing the master budget?
9. When would the master budget profit equal the flexible budget profit?
10. Managers in some companies claim that they do not use flexible budgeting, yet they compute a sales volume variance. How is that different from flexible budgeting?
11. Refer to the Managerial Application about 3M. What departments at 3M are involved in budgeting costs of new products? Why are people from so many different functions involved?

EXERCISES

Solutions to even-numbered exercises are at the end of the chapter after the cases.

12. **Solving for materials requirements.** Bala Company expects to sell 84,000 units of finished goods over the next 3-month period. The company currently has 44,000 units of finished goods on hand and wishes to have an inventory of 48,000 units at the end of the 3-month period. To produce 1 unit of finished goods requires 4 units of raw materials. The company currently has 200,000 units of raw materials on hand and wishes to have an inventory of 220,000 units of raw materials on hand at the end of the 3-month period. The company does not have, nor does it wish to have, work-in-process inventory.

    How many units of raw materials must the Bala Company purchase during the 3-month period?

13. **Solving for budgeted manufacturing costs.** Nguyen Company expects to sell 200,000 cases of paper towels during the current year. Budgeted costs per case are $12 for direct materials, $9 for direct labor, and $3 (all variable) for manu-facutring overhead. Nguyen began the period with 40,000 cases of finished goods on hand and wants to end the period with 10,000 cases of finished goods on hand.

   Compute the budgeted manufacturing costs of the Nguyen Company for the current period. Assume no beginning or ending inventory of work in process.

14. **Solving for cash collections.** (Appendix 10.1). Jones Corporation normally collects cash from credit customers as follows: 50 percent in the month of sale, 30 percent in the first month after sale, 18 percent in the second month after sale, and 2 percent never collected. Jones Corporation expects its sales, all on credit, to be as follows:

January	$500,000
February	600,000
March	400,000
April	500,000

   a. Calculate the amount of cash Jones Corporation expects to receive from customers during March.
   b. Calculate the amount of cash Jones Corporation expects to receive from customers during April.

15. **Solving for cash payments** (Appendix 10.1). Padillo Corporation purchases raw materials on account from various suppliers. It normally pays for 70 percent of these in the month purchased, 20 percent in the first month after purchase, and the remaining 10 percent in the second month after purchase. Raw materials purchases during the last 5 months of the year follow:

August	$1,400,000
September	1,800,000
October	2,500,000
November	3,500,000
December	1,500,000

   Compute the budgeted amount of cash payments to suppliers for the months of October, November, and December.

16. **Profit variance analysis.** Austin Company prepared a budget last period that called for sales of 7,000 units at a price of $12 each. Variable costs per unit were budgeted to be $5. Fixed costs were budgeted to be $21,000 for the period. During the period, production was exactly equal to actual sales of 7,100 units. The selling price was $12.15 per unit. Variable costs were $5.90 per unit. Fixed costs were $20,000.

   Prepare a profit variance report to show the difference between the master budget and the actual profits.

17. **Analyzing contribution margin changes.** The Lauper Center, which sells hard hats for construction, provided the following data for years 1 and 2:

	Year 1	Year 2
Sales Volume	14,000 Hats	10,000 Hats
Sales Revenue	$875,000	$750,000
Variable Costs	(735,000)	(525,000)
Contribution Margin	$140,000	$225,000

What impact did the changes in sales volume and in sales price have on the contribution margin? (Hint: Compare the actual, flexible budget, and master budget portion of the profit variance analysis. Use Year 1 as the "Master Budget.")

18. **Graphic comparison of budgeted and actual costs.**

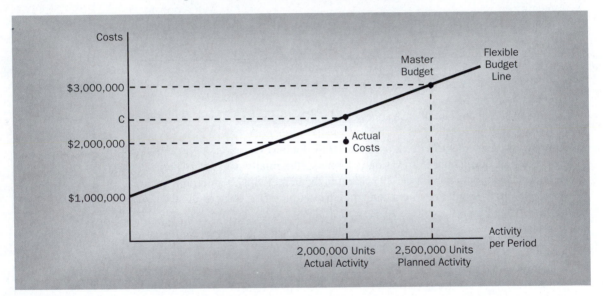

a. Given the data shown in the graph, what is the budgeted variable cost per unit?

b. What is the flexible budget cost for an activity level of 2,000,000 units (C on the graph)?

c. If the actual activity had been 4,000,000 units, what would have been the flexible budget cost amount?

19. **Preparing flexible budgets** (adapted from CPA exam). Exhibit 10.20 provides information concerning the operations of the Wallace Company for the current period. The firm has no inventories. Prepare a flexible budget for the company.

20. **Comparing master budget to actual results.** Using the data from Exhibit 10.20 and the flexible budget from Exercise **19,** prepare a profit variance report that will enable Wallace to identify the variances between the master budget and actual results.

EXHIBIT 10.20

WALLACE COMPANY

	Actual	Master Budget
Sales Volume	85 Units	100 Units
Sales Revenue	$9,200	$10,000
Manufacturing Cost of Goods Sold:		
Variable	3,440	3,900
Fixed	485	500
Cost of Goods Sold	$3,925	$ 4,400
Gross Profit	$5,275	$ 5,600
Operating Costs:		
Marketing Costs:		
Variable	$1,030	$ 1,100
Fixed	1,040	1,000
Administrative Costs, All Fixed	995	1,000
Total Operating Costs	$3,065	$ 3,100
Operating Profits	$2,210	$ 2,500

21. **Interpreting the flexible budget line.** The graph shows a flexible budget line with some missing data. Fill in the missing amounts for **(a)** and **(b)**.

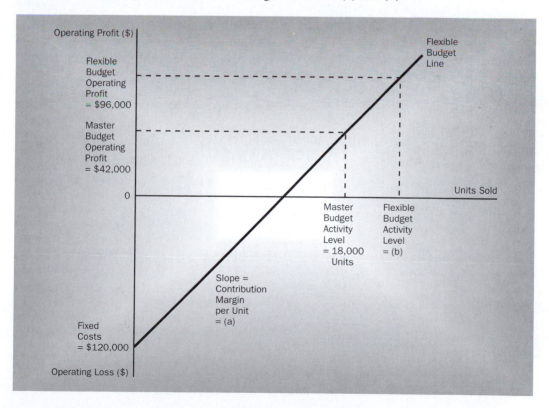

22. **Interpreting the flexible budget line.** Label **(a)** and **(b)** on the graph and give the number of units sold for each.

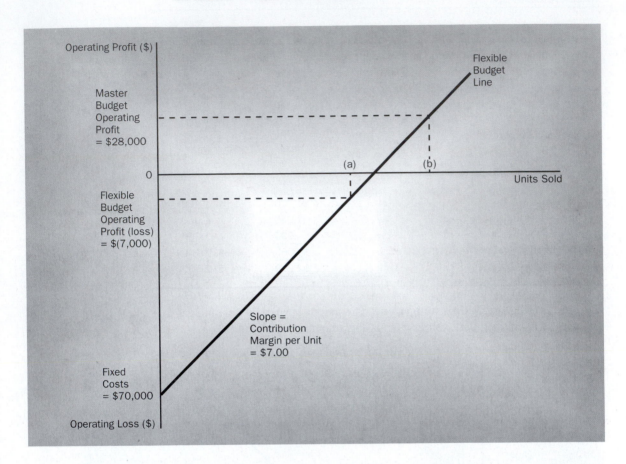

23. **Incentives for accurate forecasting** (Appendix 10.2). Compute the bonus, B, paid to a donut company's franchise managers using the following formulas:

$$B = b_1\hat{Y} + b_2(Y - \hat{Y}), \quad \text{for } Y \geq \hat{Y}$$

$$B = b_1\hat{Y} - b_3(\hat{Y} - Y), \quad \text{for } \hat{Y} > Y$$

where

$b_1 = 4\%$

$b_2 = 2\%$

$b_3 = 6\%$

$\hat{Y}$ = forecasted sales revenue

Y = actual sales revenue

Let Y and $\hat{Y}$ each have values of \$2,500, \$3,000, and \$3,500.

24. **Incentives for accurate forecasting** (Appendix 10.2). Compute the monthly bonus, B, paid to an automobile dealership using the following formulas:

$$B = b_1\hat{Y} + b_2(Y - \hat{Y}), \quad \text{for } Y \geq \hat{Y}$$
$$B = b_1\hat{Y} - b_3(\hat{Y} - Y), \quad \text{for } \hat{Y} > Y$$

where

$b_1 = \$100$ per car
$b_2 = \$70$ per car
$b_3 = \$150$ per car
$\hat{Y} = $ forecasted sales of cars (in units)
$Y = $ actual number of cars sold.

Let Y and $\hat{Y}$ each have values of 20 cars, 21 cars, 22 cars, 23 cars, and 24 cars.

25. **Flexible budgeting—manufacturing costs.** As a result of studying past cost behavior and adjusting for expected price increases in the future, Merricam Company estimates that its manufacturing costs will be as follows:

Direct materials	$4.00 per Unit
Direct Labor	$3.00 per Unit
Manufacturing Overhead:	
Variable	$1.50 per Unit
Fixed	$50,000 per Period

Merricam adopts these estimates for planning and control purposes.

a. Merricam expects to produce 20,000 units during the next period. Prepare a schedule of the expected manufacturing costs.

b. Suppose that Merricam produces only 16,000 units during the next period. Prepare a flexible budget of manfacturing costs for the 16,000-unit level of activity.

c. Suppose that Merricam produces 26,000 units during the next period. Prepare a flexible budget of manufacturing costs for the 26,000-unit level of activity.

26. **Marketing cost budget.** Refer to the marketing cost budget of the Victoria Corporation shown in Exhibit 10.4. Prepare a flexible marketing cost budget for the period, assuming the following levels of sales and shipments and a selling price of $6 per unit.

	Case 1	Case 2	Case 3
Units	60,000	75,000	64,000

27. **Administrative cost budget.** Refer to the central corporate administrative budget of the Victoria Corporation in Exhibit 10.5. Prepare a flexible central corporate administrative cost budget for the period, assuming that production and sales were 80,000 units. Is the term *flexible budget* a misnomer in this case? Explain.

28. **Computing sales price variances.** Budgeted sales of Holt Electronics Merchandisers for Year 0 were as follows:

Product X (5,000 units)	$100,000
Product Y (200 units)	20,000
Product Z (50,000 units)	250,000
Total Budgeted Sales	$370,000

Actual sales for the period were as follows:

Product X (5,300 units)	$111,300
Product Y (240 units)	23,040
Product Z (48,000 units)	192,000
Total Actual Sales	$326,340

Calculate the sales price variances for sales of the three products.

29. **Estimating flexible selling expense budget and computing variances.** Oxford Products estimates that it will incur the following selling expenses next period:

Salaries (fixed)	$ 20,000
Commissions (.05 of sales revenue)	17,875
Travel (.03 of sales revenue)	10,725
Advertising (fixed)	50,000
Sales Office Costs ($4,000 plus $.05 per unit sold)	7,250
Shipping Cost ($.10 per unit sold)	6,500
Total Selling Expenses	$112,350

a. Estimate the cost equation ($y = a + bx$) for selling expenses. (Hint: $y = a + bx + cy$.)

b. Assume that Oxford sells 50,000 units during the period at an average price of $6 per unit. The company had budgeted sales for the period to be: volume, 65,000 units; price, $5.50. Calculate the sales price and volume variance.

c. The actual selling expenses incurred during the period were $80,000 fixed and $30,000 variable. Prepare a profit variance analysis for sales revenue and selling expenses.

PROBLEMS

30. **Profit variance analysis in a service organization.** Kinser & Wolf (KW) is a CPA firm that gets a large portion of its revenue from tax services. Last year, KW's billable tax hours were up 20 percent from expected levels, but, as the following data show, profits from the tax department were lower than anticipated.

	Actual Results	Master Budget
Billable Hours[a]	60,000 Hours	50,000 Hours
Revenue	$3,300,000	$3,000,000
Production Costs:		
Professional Salaries (all variable)	1,850,000	1,500,000
Other Variable Costs (e.g., supplies,		
certain computer services)	470,000	400,000
General Administrative (all fixed)	680,000	700,000
Tax Department Profit	$ 300,000	$ 400,000

[a]These are hours billed to clients. Hours worked exceed this amount because of nonbillable time (e.g., slack periods, time in training sessions) and because KW does not charge all time worked for clients.

Prepare a comparison of the actual results to the master and flexible budgets. Adapt the approach shown in Exhibit 10.8 to this service organization.

31. Finding missing data. Find the values of the missing items **(a)** through **(q)**.

	Actual Results, 750 Units	Purchasing and Production Variances	Marketing and Administrative Variances	Sales Price Variance	Flexible Budget (a)	Variance	Master Budget, 800 Units
Sales Revenue	$1,890			(b)	$2,025	(c)	(d)
Variable Manufacturing Costs	(f)	$60 F			(e)	$38 F	(g)
Variable Marketing and Administrative Costs	(h)		(j)		(i)	(k)	$216
Contribution Margin	$1,180	(l)	(m)	(n)	(o)	(p)	(q)

32. Comprehensive problem. Scotch Products, which makes popcorn poppers, has the following master budget income statement for the month of May:

	Master Budget (based on 8,000 units)
Sales Revenue (8,000 units at $20)	160,000
Less:	
Variable Manufacturing Costs	88,000[a]
Variable Marketing and Administrative Costs	8,000[b]
Contribution Margin	$ 64,000
Less:	
Fixed Manufacturing Costs	20,000
Fixed Marketing and Administrative Costs	35,000
Operating Profit	$ 9,000

[a]8,000 budgeted units at $11 per unit.
[b]8,000 budgeted units at $1 per unit.

The company uses the following estimates to prepare the master budget:

Sales Price	$20 per Unit
Sales and Production Volume	8,000 Untis
Variable Manufacturing Costs	$11 per Unit
Variable Marketing and Administrative Costs	$1 per Unit
Fixed Manufacturing Costs	$20,000
Fixed Marketing and Administrative Costs	$35,000

Assume that the actual results for May were as follows:

	Actual
Sales Price	$19 per Unit
Sales and Production Volume	10,000 Units
Variable Manufacturing Costs	$115,440
Variable Marketing and Administrative Costs	$11,000
Fixed Manufacturing Costs	$21,000
Fixed Marketing and Administrative Costs	$34,000

Compare the master budget, flexible budget, and actual results for the month of May.

33. **Finding missing data.** Find the values of the missing items (**a**) and (**u**).

	Achieved Based on Actual Sales Volume	Cost and Sales Price Variances	Flexible Budget Based on Actual Sales Volume	Sales Volume Variance	Master Budget Based on Budgeted Sales Volume
Units	(b)		(a)	2,000 F	10,000
Sales Revenue	(i)	$18,000 F	(h)	(j)	$150,000
Less:					
Variable Manufacturing Costs	(n)	9,000 U	$96,000	(k)	80,000
Variable Marketing and Administrative Costs	$21,600	(o)	24,000	$4,000 U	(c)
Contribution Margin	(p)	(r)	$60,000	(l)	$ 50,000
Less:					
Fixed Manufacturing Costs	(q)	2,000 F	(d)		(e)
Fixed Marketing and Administrative Costs	$18,000	(t)	15,000		(f)
Operating Profits	(s)	(u)	$20,000	(m)	(g)

34. **Assigning responsibility.** King Bike Company is organized into two divisions. Assembling and Finishing. The Assembling Division combines raw materials into a semifinished product. The product then goes to the Finishing Divison for painting, polishing, and packing.

During May, the Assembling Division had significantly higher raw materials costs than expected because poor-quality raw materials required extensive re-work. As a result of the rework, Assembly transferred fewer units than expected to the Finishing Division. The Finishing Division incurred higher labor costs per unit of finished product because workers had substantial idle time. The president of the company is upset about these events.

a. Who should the firm hold responsible for the raw materials variance in the Assembling Division? Explain.

b. Who should the firm hold responsible for the labor (idle time) variance in the Finishing Division? Explain.

35. **Controls over planning function.** Keating Federal Bank set up an independent planning department at corporate headquarters. This department is responsible for most aspects of budgeting (revenue and expense forecasting, profit planning, capital investment). Planning department personnel are responsible to the vice-president for administration. The resulting budgets are incorporated into the control system that the controller's department designed and administered.

Outline an effective control system for the planning department's activities (that is, how the firm should evaluate the performance of the planning department.)

36. **Ethical issues** (adapted from CMA exam). Norton Company manufactures infant furniture and carriages. The accounting staff is currently preparing next year's budget. Michelle Jackson is new to the firm and is interested in learning how this process occurs. She has lunch with the sales manager and the production manager to discuss further the planning process. Over the course of lunch, Michelle discovers that the sales manager lowers sales projections 5 to 10 percent before submitting her figures, while the production manager increases cost estimates by 10 percent before submitting his figures. When Michelle asks about why this is done, the response is simply that everyone around here does it.

a. What do the sales and production managers hope to accomplish by their methods?

b. How might this backfire and work against them?

c. Are the actions of the sales and production managers unethical?

37. **Computing master budget given actual data.** TriSum Enterprises lost the only copy of the master budget for this period. Management wants to evaluate this period's performance but believes it needs the master budget to do so. Actual results for the period follow:

Sales Volume	12,000 Billable Hours
Sales Revenue	$672,000
Variable Costs	(208,600)
Contribution Margin	$463,400
Fixed Costs	(318,200)
Operating Profit	$145,200

The company planned on 10,000 billable hours at a price of $50 each. At that volume, the contribution margin would have been $350,000. Fixed costs were estimated to be $272,000 for the period. Management notes, "We budget an operating profit of $7.80 per billable hour."

a. Construct the master budget for the period.

b. Prepare a profit variance report comparing actual sales to the flexible budget and master budget.

CASES

38. Cost data for multiple purposes: Omega Auto Supplies. Omega Auto Supplies manufactures an automobile safety seat for children that it sells through several retail chains. Omega makes sales exclusively within its five-state region in the Midwest. The cost of manufacturing and marketing children's automobile safety seats at the company's forecasted volume of 15,000 units per month follows:

Variable Materials	$300,000
Variable Labor	150,000
Variable Overhead	30,000
Fixed Overhead	180,200
Total Manufacturing Costs	$660,200
Variable Nonmanufacturing Costs	$ 75,000
Fixed Nonmanufacturing Costs	105,000
Total Nonmanufacturing Costs	$180,000
Total Costs	$840,200

Unless otherwise stated, you should assume a regular selling price of $70 per unit. Ignore income taxes and other costs the problem does not mention.

Early in July, the senior management of Omega Auto Aupplies met to evaluate the firm on performance for the first half of the year. The following exchange ensued.

Bob Wilson (president): "Our performance for the first half of this year leaves much to be desired. Despite higher unit sales than forecast, our actual profits are lower than what we expected."

Sam Brown (sales manager): "I suspect production needs to shape up" (he said smugly). "We in sales have pursued an aggressive marketing strategy and the three-quarters of a million sales revenue higher than forecast is proof enough of our improved performance."

Linda Lampman (production manager): "Wait a minute, now! We managed to bring down unit costs from $44.00 to $43.00—with no help from sales, I must add! What's the use of production plans when sales can change them any time it likes? In February, Sam wanted a rush order for 4,000. In March, it was 8,000 units. Then in April he said to hold off on production; then in June he wanted 6,000. You know what I think . . ."

Wilson: "Hold on, now! I refuse to let this degenerate into a witch hunt. We have to examine this problem with more objectivity." (He turned to his assistant, who had been quietly taking notes.) "Do you have any ideas, Smith?"

Suppose you are Smith. Write a report to the president analyzing the company's performance. Include a comparison of the actual results to the flexible budget to the master budget. You know that planned production and sales for each month of the year is 15,000 units per month. You also know that 108,000 units were produced and sold in the first 6 months of this year, and the income statement was as follows:

Sales Revenue		$7,020,000
Manufacturing Costs:		
Variable Materials	$2,160,000	
Variable Labor	1,134,000	
Variable Overhead	324,000	
Fixed Overhead	1,026,000	4,644,000
Gross Margin		$2,376,000
Marketing Costs:		
Variable Marketing	$ 648,000	
Fixed Marketing	650,000	1,298,000
Operating Profit		$1,078,000

39. **Solving for unknowns; cost-volume-profit and budget analysis** (adapted from a problem by D. O. Green). A partial income statement of Baines Corporation for Year 0 follows. The company uses just-in-time inventory, so production each year equals sales. Each dollar of finished product produced in Year 0 contained $.50 of direct materials, $.33$\frac{1}{3}$ of direct labor, and $.16$\frac{2}{3}$ of overhead costs. During Year 0, fixed overhead costs were $40,000. No changes in production methods or credit policies are anticipated for Year 1.

BAINES CORPORATION
Partial Income Statement for Year 0

Sales (100,000 units at $10)		$1,000,000
Cost of Goods Sold		600,000
Gross Margin		$ 400,000
Selling Costs	$150,000	
Administrative Costs	100,000	250,000
Operating Profit		$ 150,000

Management has estimated the following changes for Year 1:

- 30 percent increase in number of units sold
- 20 percent increase in unit cost of materials
- 15 percent increase in direct labor cost per unit
- 10 percent increase in variable overhead cost per unit
- 5 percent increase in fixed overhead costs
- 8 percent increase in selling costs because of increased volume
- 6 percent increase in administrative costs arising solely because of increased wages

    There are no other changes.

a. What must the unit sales price be in Year 1 for Baines Corporation to earn a $200,000 operating profit?

b. What will be the Year 1 operating profit if selling prices are increased as before, but unit sales increase by 10 percent rather than 30 percent? (Selling costs would go up by only one-third of the amount projected previously.)

c. If selling price in Year 1 remains at $10 per unit, how many units must be sold in Year 1 for the operating profit to be $200,000?

40. **Incentive plans at McDonald's.** McDonald's Corporation is one of the world's largest and most successful food service companies. As in all service companies, the way the service employees perform their jobs affects the success of the company.

The performance of managers of McDonald's company-owned restaurants is critical to the quality and efficiency of service provided by McDonald's. Over the past two decades, McDonald's has tried several incentive compensation plans for its company-owned restaurant managers. We describe five of those plans here.

- *Plan 1:* Manager's bonus is a function of the restaurant's sales volume increase over the previous year.

- *Plan 2:* Manager's bonus is based on subjective evaluations by the manager's superiors. Bonuses are not tied explicitly to any quantitative performance measure.

- *Plan 3:* Manager's bonus comprises the following components:

    (1) A bonus of 10 percent of salary is paid if the manager meets the budgeted costs. This budget is based on sales volume and the standard allowed per unit.

    (2) Management visits each restaurant each month and evaluates its performance with regard to quality, cleanliness, and service. Founder Ray Kroc identified these three key success factors for the company. Managers in restaurants receiving an A get a bonus of 10 percent of salary, managers of restaurants receiving a B get a bonus of 5 percent of salary, and managers of restaurants receiving a C receive no bonus for this component of the plan.

    (3) An additional bonus up to 10 percent of salary is earned based on increases in sales volume over the previous year. (The manager can still receive the bonus if volume does not increase because of circumstances beyond the manager's control.)

- *Plan 4:* Superiors evaluate the manager as to the following six performance indicators: quality, service, cleanliness, training ability, volume, and profit. Each indicator is scored 0, 1, or 2. A manager receiving a score of 12 points receives a bonus of 40 percent of salary, a score of 11 points provides a bonus of 35 percent of salary, and so forth.

- *Plan 5:* The manager receives a bonus of 10 percent of the sales volume increase over the previous year plus 20 percent of the restaurant's profit.

Evaluate each of these incentive plans. Are there better alternatives? Be sure to consider the important things a manager and a restaurant should do to contribute to McDonald's overall company success.

41. Budgeting Case: River Beverages*

Overview   River Beverages is a food and soft drink company with worldwide operations. The company is organized into five regional divisions with each vice-president reporting directly to the CEO, Cindy Wilkins. Each vice-president has an R&D department, a controller, and three divisions—Carbonated Drinks, Non-Carbonated Drinks, and Food Products (see Exhibit 10.21). Management feels that the structure works well for River because different regions have different tastes and the divisions' products complement each other.

Industry   The beverage industry in the United States has become mature as it has grown in stride with population growth. Consumers drank about 47.2 billion gallons of fluids in 1993. Most of the industry growth has come from the nonalcoholic beverage market, which is growing by about 1.1 percent annually. In the

---

EXHIBIT 10.21

RIVER BEVERAGES
Organizational Chart

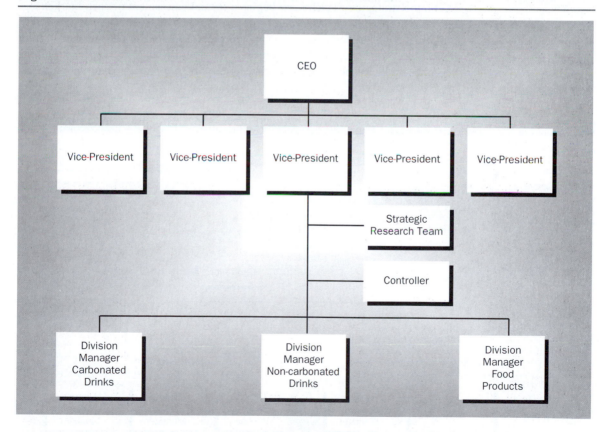

---

*Prepared by Thomas B. Rumzie under the direction of Michael W. Maher. Copyright Michael W. Maher 1996.

nonalcoholic arena, soft drinks are the largest segment, accounting for 53.4 percent of the beverages consumed. Americans consume about 25.8 billion gallons of soft drinks, ringing up retail sales of $50.2 billion every year. Water (bottled and tap) is the next largest segment representing 23.7 percent of the market. Juices represent about 12 percent of the beverages consumed. The smallest but fastest-growing segment is ready-to-drink tea, which is growing by over 91 percent in volume but accounts for less than 1 percent of the beverages consumed.

Sales Budgets   Susan Johnson, plant manager at River Beverage's Non-Carbonated Drink plant in St. Louis (see Exhibit 10.22), recently completed the annual budgeting process. According to Johnson, division managers have decision-making authority in their business units except for capital financing activities. Budgets are used to keep the division managers focused on corporate goals.

In the beginning of December, division managers submit a report to the vice-president for the region summarizing capital, sales, and income forecasts for the upcoming fiscal year, which begins July 1. Although the initial report is not prepared in much detail, it is prepared with care because it is used in the strategic planning process.

Next, the strategic research team begins a formal assessment of each market segment in its region. The team develops sales forecasts for each division and compiles them into a company forecast. The team considers economic conditions and current market share in each region. Management believes the strategic research team is effective because it is able to integrate division products and more accurately forecast

EXHIBIT 10.22

RIVER BEVERAGES
Organizational Chart of Non-Carbonated Drink Plant

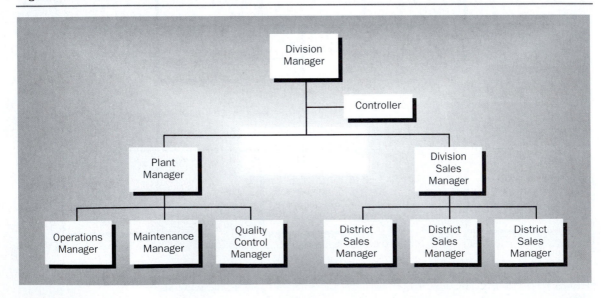

demand for complementary products. In addition, the team ensures continuity of assumptions and achievable sales goals.

Once the corporate forecast is completed, the district sales managers estimate sales for the upcoming budget year. The district sales managers are ultimately responsible for the forecasts they prepare. The district sales forecasts are then compiled and returned to the division manager. The division manager reviews the forecasts but cannot make any revisions without first consulting the district sales managers. Next, the district sales forecasts are reviewed by the strategic research team and the division controller. Finally, top management reviews each division's competitive position, including plans to increase market share, capital spending, and quality improvement plans.

Plant Budgets   After the sales budget is approved by top management, it is broken down to a sales budget for each plant. The budget is broken down further by price, volume, and product type. Plant managers budget contribution margins, fixed costs, and pretax income using information from the plant sales budget.

Budgeted profit is measured by subtracting standard variable costs and budgeted fixed costs from the sales forecast. If actual sales fall below forecasts, the plant manager is still responsible for budgeted profit. One of the most important aspects of the plant budgeting process is that plant managers break the plant budget down into various plant departments.

The operations and maintenance managers work together to develop cost standards and cost reduction targets for all departments. Budgeted cost reductions from productivity improvements, unfavorable variances, and fixed costs are developed for each department, operation, and cost center in the plant.

Before plant managers submit their budgets, a member of the strategic research team and the regional controller visit the plant. Visits are conducted to keep corporate in touch with what is happening at the plant level and to help corporate understand how plant managers determined their budgets. The visits also allow corporate to provide budget preparation guidance if necessary. The visits are especially important because they force plant managers to keep in touch with corporate-level managers.

The final budgets are submitted and consolidated by April 1. The vice-president reviews the budgets to ensure they are in line with corporate objectives. After all changes have been made by the vice-presidents and the CEO, the budgets are submitted to the board of directors for approval. The board votes on the final budget in early June.

Performance Measurement   Variance reports are generated monthly at the corporate office. River has a sophisticated information system that automatically generates reports based on input that is downloaded daily from each plant. The reports can also be generated manually by managers in the organization. Most managers generate variance reports several times during the month, allowing them to solve problems before things get out of control.

Corporate reviews the variance reports, looking closely at over-budget variance problems. Plant managers are only questioned about over-budget items. Management feels that this ensures the plant managers are staying on top of problem areas and keeping the plant operating as efficiently as possible. One week after the variance reports are generated, plant managers are required to submit a response outlining the causes of any variances and how they plan to prevent the problems in the future. If a plant manager has repeated problems, corporate may send a specialist to the plant to work with the plant manager to solve the problems.

Sales and Manufacturing Relations   "We are expected to meet our approved budget," remarked Kevin Greely, a division controller at River. Greely continued, "A couple years ago one of our major restaurant customers switched to another brand. Even though the restaurant sold over one million cases of our product annually, we were not allowed to make revisions to our budget."

Budgets are rarely adjusted after approval. However, if there is a decline in sales early in the year, plant managers may file an appeal to revise the budgeted profit for the year. If sales decline late in the year, management does not revise the budgeted amounts. Rather, plant managers are asked to cut costs wherever possible and delay any unnecessary expenditures until the following year. It is important to remember that River sets budgets so it is able to see where to make cuts or where it can find any operating efficiencies. Plant managers are not forced to meet their goals, but they are encouraged to cut costs below budget.

The sales department is primarily responsible for product price, sales mix, and delivery timing, while plant managers are responsible for plant operations. As you might imagine, problems occur between plant and regional sales managers from time to time. For example, rush orders may cause production costs to be higher than normal for some production runs. Another problem may occur when a sales manager runs a promotional campaign that causes margins to shrink. In both instances, a plant manager's profit budget will be affected negatively while a sales manager's forecasted sales budget will be affected positively. Such situations are often passed up to the division level for resolution; however, it is important to remember that the customer is always the primary concern.

Incentives   River Beverage management has devised what it thinks is an effective system to motivate plant managers. First, plant managers are promoted only when they have displayed outstanding performance in their current position. Next, River has monetary incentives in place that reward plant managers for reaching profit goals. Finally, charts are produced each month that display budgeted items versus actual results. Although not required to do so, most plant managers publicize the charts and use them as a motivational tool. The charts allow department supervisors and staff to compare activities in their department to similar activities in other plants around the world.

CEO's Message   Cindy Wilkins, CEO of River Beverages, looks to the future and comments, "Planning is an important aspect of budget preparation for every level of our organization. I would like to decrease the time spent on preparing the budget, but I feel that it keeps people thinking about the future. The negative aspect of the budgeting process is that sometimes it over controls our managers. We need to stay nimble enough to react to customer demands, while staying structured enough to achieve corporate objectives. For the most part, our budget process keeps our managers aware of sales goals and alerts them when sales or expenses are off track."

Required

1. Discuss the budgeting process at River Beverages. Begin with the division manager's initial reports and end with the board of directors' approval. Discuss the activities in each process and the reasoning for the activity.
2. Should the plants be profit centers or cost centers?

SUGGESTED SOLUTIONS TO EVEN-NUMBERED EXERCISES

12. Solving for materials requirements.

$$\frac{\text{Finished Units}}{\text{to Be Produced}} = \frac{\text{84,000 Units}}{\text{to Be Sold}} + \frac{\text{48,000 Units in}}{\text{Ending Inventory}} - \frac{\text{44,000 Units in}}{\text{Beginning Inventory}}$$

$$\frac{\text{Units to Be}}{\text{Produced}} = \underline{\underline{88,000.}}$$

$$\frac{\text{Units of Raw}}{\text{Materials to}} = \frac{\text{4 Units of Raw}}{\text{Materials per}} \times \text{88,000 Finished Units} = 352,000.$$
$$\text{Be Used} \qquad \text{Finished Unit}$$

$$\frac{\text{Units of Raw}}{\text{Materials to}} = \frac{\text{352,000 Units}}{\text{to Be Used}} + \frac{\text{220,000 Units}}{\text{Desired Ending}} - \frac{\text{200,000 Units}}{\text{in Beginning}}$$
$$\text{Be Purchased} \qquad\qquad\qquad \text{Inventory} \qquad \text{Inventory}$$

$$= \underline{\underline{372,000.}}$$

14. Solving for cash collections (Appendix 10.1).

  a. Budgeted cash collections in March:

From January Sales (.18 × $500,000)	$ 90,000
From February Sales (.30 × $600,000)	180,000
From March Sales (.50 × $400,000)	200,000
Total Budgeted Collections in March	$470,000

  b. Budgeted cash collections in April:

From February Sales (.18 × $600,000)	$108,000
From March Sales (.30 × $400,000)	120,000
From April Sales (.50 × $500,000)	250,000
Total Budgeted Collections in April	$478,000

16. **Profit variance analysis.**

	Actual (7,100 units)	Cost Variances	Sales Price Variance	Flexible Budget (7,100 units)	Sales Volume Variance	Master Budget (7,000 units)
Sales Revenue	$86,265[a]		$1,065 F	$85,200[c]	$1,200 F	$84,000[d]
Less Variable Costs	41,890[b]	$6,390 U		35,500	500 U	35,000
Contribution Margin	$44,375	$6,390 U	$1,065 F	$49,700	$700 F	$49,000
Fixed Costs	20,000	1,000 F	—	21,000	—	21,000
Operating Profits	$24,375	$5,390 U	$1,065 F	$28,700	$700 F	$28,000

[a]7,100 units × $12.15.   [b]7,100 units × $5.90.   [c]7,100 units × $12.   [d]7,000 units × $12.

18. **Graphic comparison of budgeted and actual costs.**
   a. $.80 per Unit

$$V = (TC - F) \div X$$

$$= (\$3,000,000 - \$1,000,000) \div 2,500,000$$

$$= \$.80.$$

   b. $2,600,000

$$TC = F + VX$$

$$= \$1,000,000 + (\$.8 \times 2,000,000)$$

$$= \$2,600,000.$$

   c. $4,200,000

$$TC = F + VX$$

$$= \$1,000,000 + (\$.8 \times 4,000,000)$$

$$= \$4,200,000.$$

20. **Comparing master budget to actual results.**

	Actual (85 units)	Manufacturing Variances	Marketing and Administrative Variances	Sales Price Variance	Flexible Budget (85 units)	Sales Volume Variance	Master Budget (100 units)
Sales Revenue	$9,200			$700 F	$8,500	$1,500 U	$10,000
Variable Costs:							
Manufacturing	3,440	$125 U			3,315	585 F	3,900
Marketing	1,030		$ 95 U		935	165 F	1,100
Contribution Margin ..	$4,730	$125 U	$ 95 U	$700 F	$4,250	$ 750 U	$ 5,000
Fixed Costs:							
Manufacturing	485	15 F			500	—	500
Marketing	1,040		40 U		1,000	—	1,000
Administrative	995		5 F		1,000	—	1,000
Operating Profit	$2,210	$110 U	$130 U	$700 F	$1,750	$ 750 U	$ 2,500

22. Interpreting the flexible budget line.

a. Actual Units Sold:

$$\text{Profit} = (P - V)X - F$$

$$\$(7,000) = \$7X - \$70,000$$

$$X = \frac{\$63,000}{\$7}$$

$$= 9,000 \text{ Units.}$$

b. Budgeted Units to Be Sold:

$$\$28,000 = \$7X - \$70,000$$

$$X = \frac{\$98,000}{\$7}$$

$$= 14,000 \text{ Units.}$$

24. Incentives for accurate forecasting (Appendix 10.2).

$$B = \begin{cases} \$100\hat{Y} + \$70(Y - \hat{Y}), & \text{for } Y \geq \hat{Y}; \\ \$100\hat{Y} - \$150(\hat{Y} - Y), & \text{for } \hat{Y} > Y. \end{cases}$$

		\multicolumn{5}{c	}{**Forecasted Sales, $\hat{Y}$**}
		20	**21**	**22**	**23**	**24**
	20	$2,000[a]	$1,950[f]	$1,900[i]	$1,850	$1,800
	21	2,070[b]	2,100[g]	2,050[j]	2,000	1,950
Actual Sales, Y	**22**	2,140[c]	2,170[h]	2,200	2,150	2,100
	23	2,210[d]	2,240	2,270	2,300	2,250
	24	2,280[e]	2,310	2,340	2,370	2,400

[a]$2,000 = \$100\,(20)$.

[b]$2,070 = \$2,000 + \$70\,(21 - 20)$.

[c]$2,140 = \$2,000 + \$70\,(22 - 20)$.

[d]$2,210 = \$2,000 + \$70\,(23 - 20)$.

[e]$2,280 = \$2,000 + \$70\,(24 - 20)$.

[f]$1,950 = \$100\,(21) - \$150\,(21 - 20)$.

[g]$2,100 = \$100\,(21)$.

[h]$2,170 = \$2,100 + \$70\,(22 - 21)$, etc.

[i]$1,900 = \$100\,(22) - \$150\,(22 - 20)$.

[j]$2,050 = \$2,200 - \$150\,(22 - 21)$, etc.

26. Marketing cost budget.

Fixed Costs:

Salaries	$25,000
Advertising	30,000
Sales Office Costs	8,400
Travel	2,000
Total	$65,400

Variable Costs:

Shipping Costs = $.02 per Unit Sold and Shipped.

Commissions = 2 Percent of Sales, or $.02 \times$ Units Sold $\times$ Selling Price per Unit.

$$\text{Variable Costs} = \left(\$.02 \times \frac{\text{Units}}{\text{Shipped}}\right) + \left(\$.02 \times \frac{\text{Unit } \$6}{\text{Selling}} \times \frac{\text{Units}}{\text{Sold}}\right).$$

Selling Expense Flexible Budget:

$$\$65,400 + \left(\$.02 \times \frac{\text{Units}}{\text{Shipped}}\right) + \left(\$.12 \times \frac{\text{Units}}{\text{Sold}}\right).$$

Case 1:

$\$65,400 + (\$.02 \times 60,000) + (\$.12 \times 60,000)$

$= \$65,400 + \$1,200 + \$7,200$

$= \underline{\underline{\$73,800.}}$

Case 2:

$\$65,400 + (\$.02 \times 75,000) + (\$.12 \times 75,000)$

$= \$65,400 + \$1,500 + \$9,000$

$= \underline{\underline{\$75,900.}}$

Case 3:

$\$65,400 + (\$.02 \times 64,000) + (\$.12 \times 64,000)$

$= \$65,400 + \$1,280 + \$7,680$

$= \underline{\underline{\$74,360.}}$

28. **Computing sales price variances.**

	Actual Sales	Sales Price Variance	Flexible Budget
Product X Sales	$111,300	$ 5,300 F	$106,000[a]
Product Y Sales	23,040	960 F	24,000[b]
Product Z Sales	192,000	48,000 U	240,000[c]
	$326,340	$43,660 U	$370,000

[a] $5,300 \text{ Units} \times \dfrac{\$100,000}{5,000 \text{ Units}} = \$106,000.$

[b] $240 \text{ Units} \times \dfrac{\$20,000}{200 \text{ Units}} = \$24,000.$

[c] $48,000 \text{ Units} \times \dfrac{\$250,000}{50,000 \text{ Units}} = \$240,000.$

CHAPTER 11

EVALUATING PERFORMANCE

LEARNING OBJECTIVES

1. Understand the reasons for conducting variance analyses.
2. Assign responsibility for variances.
3. Separate variances into price and efficiency components.
4. Analyze variances using the variable cost variance model.
5. Explain why variances occur.
6. Analyze overhead variances using the variable cost variance model.
7. Calculate fixed costs variances.
8. Describe the role of variance analysis in service organizations.
9. Summarize how activity-based costing relates to variance analysis.
10. Explain how target costing and kaizen costing change the focus of costing systems.
11. Understand the impact of technology on variance analyses.
12. Identify tools managers use to decide when to investigate variances.
13. (Appendix 11.1) Recognize the relation between actual, budgeted, and applied fixed manufacturing costs.
14. (Appendix 11.2) Calculate the mix variance portion of the efficiency variance.

Chapter 10 presented profit variance analysis, which compares the profits achieved with those budgeted. This chapter presents more detail in analyzing cost variances. As you encounter variance analysis in practice, remember that each organization calculates variances in a unique way, based on the nature of the organization and the needs of its decision makers. We present the fundamental variance analysis model that all types of organizations commonly use in one form or another. Organizations differ in their applications, but the basic concepts underlying the applications are generally the same in all organizations.

VARIANCE ANALYSIS

This chapter continues the Victoria Corporation example discussed in Chapter 10. For convenience, Exhibit 11.1 reproduces Exhibit 10.8, which compares actual results with the budget.

Exhibit 11.1 shows the total variance in operating profits from the original plan, $15,700 favorable. The next step investigates and analyzes the variance to find causes, to ascertain whether the firm needs to take corrective steps, and to reward or penalize employees, where appropriate. Looking at Exhibit 11.1, what is the sales price variance per unit? (Answer: $0.10F.)

RESPONSIBILITY FOR VARIANCES

This section describes variance calculations for each of the major groups responsible for variances in organizations: marketing, administration, purchasing, and production. We calculate each responsibility center's variances, *holding all other things constant.* Hence, we separate marketing variances from production, production variances from purchasing, and so forth. After accountants compute variances, managers investigate the causes of these variances and take corrective action if needed.

MARKETING

Management usually assigns responsibility for sales volume, sales price, and marketing cost variances to marketing. Thus the marketing department at Victoria Corporation would be responsible for the variances shown in Exhibit 11.2.

The $21,900 favorable sales volume variance measures the favorable impact on profits of higher-than-expected sales volume as the exhibit shows. The sales volume variance may be a function of factors outside the marketing department's influence, however, such as unexpected or unpredictable changes in the market. The sales volume variance is a contribution margin variance, which equals the budgeted contribution margin per unit times the difference between budgeted and actual sales volume. Chapter 10 stated that each unit sold generates $6.00 of revenue, each unit has a budgeted (or standard) variable manufacturing cost of $3.67, a budgeted shipping cost of $.02 per unit, and a budgeted sales commission of $.12 (= 2 percent × $6.00). Thus the contribution margin expected from each unit is $2.19 (= $6.00 − $3.67 − $.02 − $.12).

Why is the *standard* variable cost used to compute the contribution margin instead of the *actual* cost? Recall that we are calculating the effect of sales *volume* alone. By using standard variable cost in computing contribution margins, we avoid mixing cost variances with the effect of sales volume.

Marketing also may be responsible for the sales price variance. Note that the increase in sales commission (2 percent of $8,000 = $160), a result of the higher-than-budgeted selling price, partially offsets the favorable sales price variance of $8,000.

Investigation of the $1,440 (unfavorable) variable marketing cost variance should start with sales commissions. Did the firm inappropriately pay commissions—for example, on sales that customers returned? Did the commission rate exceed the

EXHIBIT 11.1

VICTORIA CORPORATION

Profit Variance Analysis: Comparison of Actual Results to Budgeted Profits

(This is Exhibit 10.8, repeated for the reader's convenience.)

	Actual (based on actual sales volume of 80,000 units) (1)	Purchasing and Production Variances (2)	Marketing and Administrative Cost Variances (3)	Sales Price Variance (4)	Flexible Budget (based on actual sales volume of 80,000 units) (5)	Sales Volume Variance (6)	Master Budget (based on a plan of 70,000 units sold) (7)
Sales	$488,000	—	—	$8,000 F	$480,000	$60,000 F	$420,000
Less:							
Variable Manufacturing Costs	305,600	$12,000 U	—	—	293,600	36,700 U	256,900
Variable Marketing Costs	12,800	—	$1,440 U	160 U	11,200	1,400 U	9,800
Contribution Margin	$169,600	$12,000 U	$1,440 U	$7,840 F	$175,200	$21,900 F	$153,300
Less:							
Fixed Manufacturing Costs	34,000	1,800 U	—	—	32,200	—	32,200
Fixed Marketing Costs	64,400	—	1,000 F	—	65,400	—	65,400
Fixed Administrative Costs	44,600	—	200 F	—	44,800	—	44,800
Operating Profits	$ 26,600	$13,800 U	$ 240 U	$7,840 F	$ 32,800	$21,900 F	$ 10,900

Total Profit Variance from Flexible Budget = $6,200 U

Total Profit Variance from Master Budget = $15,700 F

U denotes unfavorable variance.

F denotes favorable variance.

EXHIBIT 11.2

VICTORIA CORPORATION
Marketing Department Variances

Sales Volume	$21,900 F
Sales Price (net of commissions)	$ 7,840 F[a]
Variable Marketing Cost	$ 1,440 U
Fixed Marketing Cost	$ 1,000 F

---

[a]$8,000 F price variance − $160 U higher commissions associated with higher-than-expected price = $7,840.

2 percent budgeted? Did the sales staff earn commissions in previous periods reported in the current period? Managers would ask similar questions about shipping costs. Did rates increase, for example?

The accounting staff usually ascertains whether variances resulted from bookkeeping adjustments or errors, whereas marketing managers investigate marketing activities that may have caused the variances.

Fixed marketing costs are often discretionary. A favorable variance does not necessarily mean good performance. For example, the $1,000 favorable variance at Victoria Corporation could mean the company did less advertising than intended, which could have a negative effect on future sales.

ADMINISTRATION

The accounting process assigns a $200 favorable variance to administration. Administrative variances are often the hardest to manage because they are not engineered; that is, no well-defined causal relation exists between administrative input and administrative output.

Management usually budgets administrative costs with discretion, placing a ceiling on costs for a particular set of tasks. For example, suppose an organization's corporate internal audit staff received a budget of $2,000,000 for 40 people's salaries and an additional $400,000 for travel, supplies, and other costs. The internal audit department may not spend more than those limits without obtaining approvals, which would normally come from top executives (for example, the company president) or the board of directors.

Although discretionary budgets can provide a ceiling for expenditure, they do not provide a norm like a flexible manufacturing cost budget. If you cannot measure output, then you cannot measure the input-output relation, which makes ascertaining the "proper" levels of costs difficult. You should take these difficulties into account when you evaluate an administrative cost variance or any other discretionary cost variance.

PURCHASING

Purchasing departments are responsible for purchasing the materials to make products and provide services. Monitoring a purchasing department's success in getting a good value for the money is important because materials often make up 50 percent to 60 percent of a product's cost. Materials are not limited to manufacturing. They comprise a substantial portion of the cost of providing services in many nonmanufacturing businesses—for example, surgical, laboratory, and medical supplies in hospitals, and food in restaurants.

In our studies of purchasing departments, we have found virtually all managers using the *materials price variance* to evalute their purchasing department's performance. This variance measures the difference between the actual and standard prices paid for materials. To demonstrate how accountants compute the materials price variance, assume that Victoria Corporation actually purchased 162,000 pounds of direct materials at an average price of $.525 per pound. Recall that the standard cost was $.50 per pound. The process would charge purchasing with an unfavorable price variance of $4,050 [= ($.525 − $.50) × 162,000 pounds purchased].

PRODUCTION

The accounting process would charge production departments with the fixed manufacturing cost variance and with the remaining variable manufacturing cost variance that it did not assign to purchasing. For Victoria Corporation, the process would assign variances as follows:

	Total	− Purchasing	= Production
Variable Manufacturing Cost Variance	$12,000 U −	$4,050 U	= $7,950 U
Fixed Manufacturing Cost Variance	$1,800 U −	0	= $1,800 U

SEPARATING VARIANCES INTO PRICE AND EFFICIENCY COMPONENTS

Accountants generally split variable manufacturing cost variances into *price* and *efficiency* components. The price component is the difference between the budgeted (or standard) price and the actual price paid for each unit of input. The efficiency variance measures the efficiency with which the firm uses inputs to produce outputs. To demonstrate, suppose Victoria Corporation's $12,000 unfavorable variable manufacturing cost variance comprises the manufacturing cost variances shown in Exhibit 11.3. Assume that Victoria produced 80,000 units. Note that the total manufacturing variances also appear in column (2) of Exhibit 11.1.

At this point, you should calculate price and efficiency variances without looking ahead. We recommend this exercise because students often make variance calculations by memorizing formulas that they quickly forget. Most organizations incorporate these formulas into computer programs, so you need not memorize formulas.

A **price variance** measures the difference between the price set as the norm—that is, the standard or budgeted price—and the actual price.

An **efficiency variance** measures the difference between the actual quantity of inputs used and those allowed at standard to make a unit of output. Victoria Corporation allows 2 pounds of direct material for each unit produced. If it used

EXHIBIT 11.3

VICTORIA CORPORATION
Manufacturing Variances

	Actual	Standard Allowed Based on Actual Production Output of 80,000 Units	Variance
Variable Costs:			
Direct Materials	162,000 Pounds at $.525 = $85,050	160,000 Pounds at $.50 = $80,000	$ 5,050 U
Direct Labor	10,955 Hours at $18.90 = $207,050 (rounded to nearest dollar)	10,000 Hours (= 80,000 Units × $\frac{1}{8}$ Hour) at $20 = $200,000	7,050 U
Variable Manufacturing Overhead	$ 13,500	80,000 Units at $0.17 = $13,600	100 F
Total Variable Manufacturing Costs	$305,600	$293,600	$12,000 U

	Actual	Budget	Variance
Fixed Costs:			
Fixed Manufacturing Overhead	$34,000	$32,200	$ 1,800 U

162,000 pounds to produce 80,000 units, an unfavorable efficiency variance of 2,000 pounds in quantity, or $1,000 (= 2,000 pounds × $.50 standard price per pound), would result.

PROBLEM 11.1 FOR SELF-STUDY

Price and efficiency variances. Define price and efficiency variances. How might the manager of a coffeehouse that serves coffee and baked products use price and efficiency variances?

The solution to this self-study problem is at the end of the chapter on page 401.

VARIABLE COST VARIANCE MODEL

A general model for variance calculations appears in Exhibit 11.4. We have divided direct materials and direct labor variances into price and efficiency components. The terms *price* and *efficiency* variances are general categories. Although terminology

---

EXHIBIT 11.4

General Model for Variance Analysis: Variable Manufacturing Costs

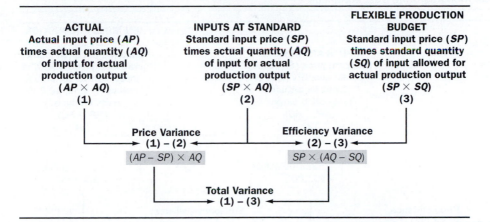

varies from company to company, the following specific variance titles are frequently used:

Input	Price Variance Category	Efficiency Variance Category
Direct Materials	Price (or Purchase Price) Variance	Usage or Quantity Variance
Direct Labor	Rate Variance	Efficiency Variance
Variable Overhead	Spending Variance	Efficiency Variance

We shall avoid unnecessary labeling by simply referring to these variances as either *price* or *efficiency* variances. Looking at Exhibit 11.4, what would the price variance be if the actual price were $5.50, the standard price were $5.10, and the actual quantity were 50,000? (Answer: $20,000 = ($5.50 − $5.10) × 50,000.)

We apply the cost variance model to the calculation of direct materials, direct labor, and variable manufacturing overhead variances for Victoria Corporation in Exhibit 11.5. Note that Exhibit 11.5 breaks down the total variable manufacturing cost variance in column (2) of Exhibit 11.1 into more detail. Think of Exhibit 11.1 as the "big picture" and of Exhibit 11.5 as a detailed supporting schedule.

Interpret the computations in column (3) of Exhibit 11.5 carefully. Note that the term *SQ* refers to the *standard quantity of input allowed to produce the actual output. SQ* is *not the expected* production volume. If each unit of output produced has a standard of $\frac{1}{8}$ hour of direct labor time, and if 80,000 units of output are *actually produced,* then $SQ = 10,000$ hours $(= \frac{1}{8}$ hour × 80,000 units). Note that column (3) is the flexible *production* budget.

Column (3) of Exhibits 11.4 and 11.5 shows the *standard cost allowed to produce the actual output,* whereas column (1) of Exhibits 11.4 and 11.5 shows the *actual*

EXHIBIT 11.5

VICTORIA CORPORATION
Calculation of Variable Manufacturing Cost Variances

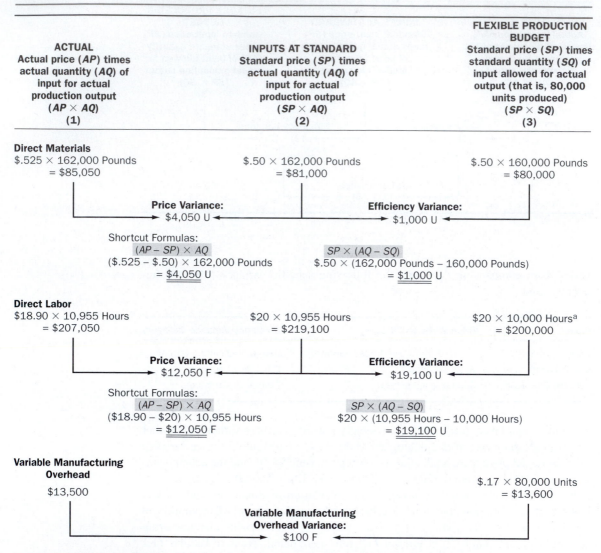

ACTUAL Actual price (*AP*) times actual quantity (*AQ*) of input for actual production output (*AP* × *AQ*) (1)	**INPUTS AT STANDARD** Standard price (*SP*) times actual quantity (*AQ*) of input for actual production output (*SP* × *AQ*) (2)	**FLEXIBLE PRODUCTION BUDGET** Standard price (*SP*) times standard quantity (*SQ*) of input allowed for actual output (that is, 80,000 units produced) (*SP* × *SQ*) (3)

Direct Materials

$.525 × 162,000 Pounds = $85,050 $.50 × 162,000 Pounds = $81,000 $.50 × 160,000 Pounds = $80,000

Price Variance: $4,050 U

Efficiency Variance: $1,000 U

Shortcut Formulas:
(*AP* − *SP*) × *AQ*
($.525 − $.50) × 162,000 Pounds
= $4,050 U

SP × (*AQ* − *SQ*)
$.50 × (162,000 Pounds − 160,000 Pounds)
= $1,000 U

Direct Labor

$18.90 × 10,955 Hours = $207,050 $20 × 10,955 Hours = $219,100 $20 × 10,000 Hours[a] = $200,000

Price Variance: $12,050 F

Efficiency Variance: $19,100 U

Shortcut Formulas:
(*AP* − *SP*) × *AQ*
($18.90 − $20) × 10,955 Hours
= $12,050 F

SP × (*AQ* − *SQ*)
$20 × (10,955 Hours − 10,000 Hours)
= $19,100 U

Variable Manufacturing Overhead

$13,500 $.17 × 80,000 Units = $13,600

Variable Manufacturing Overhead Variance: $100 F

[a]10,000 hours allowed = 80,000 units produced × $\frac{1}{8}$ hours per unit allowed.

Note: It is sometimes difficult to see intuitively which variances are favorable (F) and which are unfavorable (U). If the amount on the left (the actual) exceeds the amount on the right (the budget or standard), the variance is *unfavorable* because higher costs than budgeted mean lower profits than budgeted. The reverse is true for favorable cost variances: the amounts on the left (actuals) are lower than those on the right. We set up all the cost variance calculations in this book consistently, with actual costs on the left, standard or budget on the right.

costs incurred to produce the actual output. The differences between columns (1) and (3) are the variable manufacturing cost variances, which you can further separate into price and efficiency variances.

This overview of manufacturing variances provides the essential calculations for management use of variances. Most companies carry out this analysis in much greater detail. Most companies report variances for each type of material, for each category of labor, and for major cost components of variable overhead (for example, power to run machines, indirect materials and supplies, indirect labor).

PROBLEM 11.2 FOR SELF-STUDY

Computing variable cost variances. (This problem continues the problems for self-study that are in Chapter 10.) During the past month, the following events took place at Computer Supply, Inc.:

1. Produced and sold 50,000 laptop computer cases at a sales price of $10 each. (Budgeted sales were 40,000 units at $11.)
2. Standard variable costs per unit (that is, per case) were as follows:

Direct Materials: 2 Pounds at $1 per Pound	$2.00
Direct Labor: .10 Hours at $15 per Hour	1.50
Variable Manufacturing Overhead: .10 Labor Hours	
at $5 per Hour	.50
Total	$4.00 per Case

3. Actual production costs were as follows:

Direct Materials Purchased and Used: 110,000 Pounds at $1.20	$132,000
Direct Labor: 6,000 Hours at $14	84,000
Variable Overhead	28,000

Compute variable manufacturing cost variances in as much detail as possible.

The solution to this self-study problem is at the end of the chapter on page 401.

REASONS FOR MATERIALS AND LABOR VARIANCES

Variance reports include explanations for the variances. These explanations help managers to ascertain whether they should investigate variances and take corrective action, whether they should reward people responsible for variances, or whether they should take other managerial action.

Variances can occur for many reasons.

1. **A variance is simply the difference between a predetermined norm or standard and the actual results.** Some difference should be expected simply because one measure is expected and the other is actual. For example, if you and several of your friends were each to flip a coin ten times, not all of you would come up with five heads, even though five heads (= 50 percent of ten coin flips) may be the expected value. In short, even when standards are unbiased expected values, and no *systematic* reasons explain variances, some variances will occur anyway.

2. **The standards themselves may be biased.** Sometimes managers set standards intentionally loose or tight. Sometimes they are unintentionally biased, such as when the firm accidentally omits expected labor wage increases or an allowance for waste on direct material usage. The Managerial Application, "An Antidote to Biased Standards: How Workers Develop Their Own Standards at NUMMI," demonstrates how a particular plant management dealt with biased standards.

3. **Systematic reasons, as discussed next.**

REASONS FOR MATERIALS VARIANCES

Materials price variances occur for numerous reasons. They may result from failure to take purchase discounts, from using a better (or worse) grade of raw material than expected so that the price paid was higher (or lower) than expected, or from changes in the market supply or demand for the raw material that affected prices.

A number of factors cause **materials efficiency variances.** When management, industrial engineers, and others set standards for the amount of direct materials that a unit of output should use, they usually allow for material defects, inexperienced workers who ruin materials, improperly used materials, and so forth. If the firm uses materials more efficiently than these standards, favorable efficiency variances result; usage worse than these standards results in unfavorable variances.

Sometimes purchasing, not production, causes a materials efficiency variance. In an effort to reduce prices (and create a favorable price variance), purchasing departments may have bought inferior materials. Purchasing may also be responsible for ordering the wrong materials.

REASONS FOR LABOR VARIANCES

Direct labor price (or wage) variances can occur because managers do not correctly anticipate changes in wage rates. Wage rates established by a union contract may differ from the forecasted amount, for example. Also, a wage rate change may occur but the firm will not have adjusted standards to reflect it.

The **direct labor efficiency variance** measures labor productivity. Managers watch this variance because they can usually control it. Many of the things that create variances affect all competitors about the same. Labor wage rates going up dramatically because of a union contract settlement usually affects all companies in an industry, so little competitive advantage or disadvantage results. Labor efficiency is unique to a firm, however, and can lead to competitive advantages or disadvantages.

MANAGERIAL APPLICATION

An Antidote to Biased Standards: How Workers Develop Their Own Standards at NUMMI[a]

The Toyota-General Motors joint venture in Fremont, California, known as New United Motor Manufacturing, Inc. (NUMMI), has succeeded in allowing employees to set their own work standards. The NUMMI plant, which makes Toyota Corollas, Geo Prizms, and particular Toyota trucks, was once a General Motors plant notorious for poor quality, low productivity, and morale problems. One worker said he used to be ashamed of the product turned out by the GM Fremont plant, but when he recently saw one of the plant's cars parked at the Monterey Aquarium, he left a business card under the windshield wiper with a note that said, "I helped build this one."[b]

At the old GM Fremont plant, industrial engineers who had little, if any, work experience making cars would shut themselves in a room and ponder how to set standards. The industrial engineers ignored the workers, who in turn ignored the standards. The worker "did the job however he or she was able—except of course when one of [the supervisors or industrial engineers] was looking. If an industrial engineer was actually 'observing'—stopwatch and clipboard in hand—standard practice was to slow down and make the work look harder."[c]

Now, at NUMMI workers themselves hold the stopwatches and set the standards. Worker team members time each other, looking for the most efficient and safest way to do the work. They standardize each task so everyone on the team will do it the same way. The workers compare the standards across shifts and for different tasks, and then they prepare detailed written specifications for each task. The workers are more informed about how to do the work right than industrial engineers. They are more motivated to meet the standards they set, instead of those set by industrial engineers working in an ivory tower.

Involving the workers has had benefits in addition to improved motivation and standards. These include improved safety, higher quality, easier job rotation because tasks are standarized, and more flexibility because workers are both assembly-line workers and industrial engineers. For example, if orders for the product change, NUMMI can change the speed of the assembly line to respond. At the old GM Fremont plant, the assembly line ran at one speed, and responses to changes in orders came either from inventory or from adding or dropping entire shifts.

[a]Based on Paul S. Adler, "Time-and-Motion Regained," *Harvard Business Review* (January–February 1993), pp. 97–108.

[b]Ibid., p. 106.

[c]Ibid., p. 103.

A financial vice-president of a manufacturing company told us:

> Raw materials are 57 percent of our product cost; direct labor is only 22 percent. Yet we carry out the labor efficiency variance to the penny. We break it down by product line, by department, and sometimes by specific operation, while we give the raw materials variances only a passing glance. Why? Because there's not much we can do about some of our other variances, like materials price variances, but there's a lot we can do to keep our labor efficiency in line.

Labor efficiency variances have many causes. The cause may be the workers themselves—poorly motivated or poorly trained workers will be less productive, whereas highly motivated and well-trained workers may generate favorable efficiency variances. Other causes include poor materials, faulty equipment, poor supervision, and scheduling problems.

Although most firms hold production managers responsible for direct labor efficiency variances, they sometimes attribute responsibility to purchasing managers for buying faulty materials. Scheduling problems may result from upsteam production departments that have delayed production, from the personnel department that provided the wrong type of worker, or from numerous other sources.

Note the labor price variance in the Victoria Corporation example was favorable, whereas the labor efficiency variance was unfavorable. A manager would probably ask first: "Did we use workers who were lower paid and not as efficient as expected?" Although firms go to great lengths to break variances down into small components that they can easily understand and trace to particular responsibility centers, managers should not overlook the fact that variances are usually interrelated.

VARIABLE OVERHEAD PRICE AND EFFICIENCY VARIANCES

Separating variable overhead variances into price and efficiency components helps managers in their efforts to control overhead costs. For example, energy costs in many firms are both sufficiently large and controllable to warrant special attention.

The manager can use the same method to compute price and efficiency variances for variable overhead as for other variable manufacturing costs. The computation requires a measure of overhead input activity not yet presented in the Victoria Corporation example, however. Suppose the variable overhead at Victoria Corporation consisted of machines' operating costs, such as power and maintenance. The longer the machines ran, the more variable overhead cost is incurred. A **variable overhead price variance** results when the cost per machine hour is either more or less than the standard cost allowed per machine hour. A **variable overhead efficiency variance** results if the machine hours required to make the actual production output exceed the standard machine hours allowed to make that output. For example, suppose the firm makes a large batch of units that consumed several hundred machine hours. Subsequently, the firm found these units to be defective and destroyed them; thus the accounting system did not count them as part of the actual production output. (Managers implicitly assume only good units are counted as part of the actual production output.)

Assume the standard for machine usage was 40 units per machine hour at a standard cost allowed of $6.80 per hour. (This is equivalent to $.17 per unit of output, because $6.80/40 = $.17.) Also assume the actual production output of 80,000 units required 2,100 machine hours, so the efficiency variance was $680 U, as Exhibit 11.6 shows. The actual costs for variable overhead totaled only $13,500, so the favorable variable overhead price variance was $780 F.

The manager should interpret variable overhead price and efficiency variances with care. The accountant sometimes selects the input activity base (machine hours in our example) without regard to the cause of variable overhead costs. For example, if a company used direct labor hours to apply variable overhead, an unfavorable efficiency variance results when the company inefficiently uses direct labor hours. That variance means nothing if none of the variable overhead costs is associated with

EXHIBIT 11.6

VICTORIA CORPORATION
Variable Manufacturing Overhead Variances

ACTUAL Actual price (*AP*) times actual quantity (*AQ*) of input for actual production output (*AP* × *AQ*) (1)	**INPUTS AT STANDARD** Standard price (*SP*) times actual quantity (*AQ*) of input for actual production output (*SP* × *AQ*) (2)	**FLEXIBLE PRODUCTION BUDGET** Standard price (*SP*) times standard quantity (*SQ*) of input allowed for actual output (i.e., 80,000 units produced) (*SP* × *SQ*) (3)

$13,500[a] $6.80 × 2,100 Mach. Hrs. $6.80 × 2,000 Mach. Hrs.
                              = $14,280   = $.17 × 80,000 Units
                                                                = $13,600

Price Variance: Efficiency Variance:
     $780 F $680 U[b]

Variable Manufacturing Overhead Variance:
            $100 F

[a]Because the firm does not typically purchase overhead per machine hour or per unit of some other activity base, the total variable overhead does not contain an actual price (*AP*) component.

[b]Shortcut Formula:

$$SP \times (AQ - SQ)$$

$$\$6.80 \times (2{,}100 \text{ Hours} - 2{,}000 \text{ Hours}) = \$680 \text{ U}.$$

direct labor costs. This particular problem occurs in capital-intensive companies in which variable overhead mostly relates to machine usage.

In general, managers are wise to establish a detailed breakdown of variable overhead into cost categories that relate logically to the input activity base as is done with activity-based costing. For example, the following variable overhead costs could be applied on the following input activity bases:

Cost	Activity Base
Indirect Labor	Direct Labor Hours
Power to Run Machines	Machine Hours
Materials Inventory Carrying Costs	Materials Inventory

Later in this chapter, we apply these ideas using activity-based costing.

FIXED MANUFACTURING COST VARIANCES

The only fixed cost variances computed for managerial purposes are the price variances (also called spending or budget variances). A price variance is the difference between actual and budgeted fixed costs. Because fixed costs do not vary with the measure of activity (such as units), there are no efficiency variances for fixed costs.

OVERVIEW OF VARIANCES

Exhibit 11.7 presents an overview of variances for Chapters 10 and 11. The top panel reproduces columns 1 through 5 of the profit variance analysis discussed in Chapter 10 and presented in Exhibit 11.1. The bottom panel illustrates the breakdown of variable manufacturing costs into direct materials, direct labor, and variable overhead. This breakdown shows that the cost variance analysis discussed in this chapter simply extends the profit variance analysis discussed in Chapter 10.

Exhibit 11.8 diagrams all the variances discussed. It breaks down the $15,700 total favorable variance from Exhibit 11.1 into components and shows their assignment to responsibility centers. Generally, accounting systems report variances in much more detail than we show here. The analysis shows more detailed cost items—by type of direct material, labor, and overhead, for example.

VARIABLE OVERHEAD IN SERVICE ORGANIZATIONS

Variable overhead often makes up a large portion of the cost of providing services. Next we apply the overhead analysis model to a service organization.

Example American Parcel Delivery, a parcel service, competes with U.S. Postal Service and United Parcel Service. Each driver is responsible for picking up and delivering parcels in a particular geographic area. One major cost is fuel for the pickup and delivery vans. The firm uses a fuel efficiency variance to evaluate the performance of drivers. The firm calculates a standard amount of fuel consumption per parcel, whether delivered or picked up, for each territory. These allowances take the population density of the territory into account—allowing more fuel per parcel for sparsely populated territories, less for densely populated territories. Drivers control this variance primarily by scheduling trips to avoid unnecessary driving.

For a particular territory, the standard was .08 gallon of fuel per parcel. The driver assigned to this territory handled 1,100 parcels during March; hence, the budget allows 88 gallons (= 1,100 parcels × .08 gallons per parcel). In all, the driver actually used 93 gallons. Exhibit 11.9 (p. 385) shows the efficiency variance. Although the driver was not responsible for the fuel price variance, Exhibit 11.9 presents it to complete the comparison of actual with standard. Note the similarity between these calculations and the direct materials and direct labor calculations presented earlier.

ACTIVITY-BASED STANDARD COSTING

Activity-based costing is commonly used with standard costing. Hewlett-Packard, a pioneer in the development of activity-based costing, uses it to develop standard overhead costs. Using activity-based costing, a company has multiple cost drivers.

EXHIBIT 11.7

VICTORIA CORPORATION
Overview of Variance Analysis

Profit Variance Analysis

	Achieved Profit (based on actual sales volume of 80,000 units) (1)	Purchasing and Production Variances (2)	Marketing and Administrative Cost Variances (3)	Sales Price Variance (4)	Flexible Budget (based on actual sales volume of 80,000 units) (5)
Sales..........................	$488,000	—	—	$8,000 F	$480,000
Less:					
Variable Manufacturing Costs...	**305,600**	**$12,000 U**	—	—	**293,600**
Variable Marketing Costs........	12,800	—	$1,440 U	160 U	11,200
Contribution Margin	$169,600	$12,000 U	$1,440 U	$7,840 F	$175,200
Less:					
Fixed Manufacturing Costs	34,000	1,800 U	—	—	32,200
Fixed Marketing Costs..........	64,400	—	1,000 F	—	65,400
Fixed Administrative Costs	44,600	—	200 F	—	44,800
Operating Profits	$ 26,600	$13,800 U	$ 240 U	$7,840 F	$ 32,800

Total Profit Variance from
Flexible Budget = $6,200 U

Cost Variance Analysis

ACTUAL Actual price (AP) times actual quantity (AQ) of input for actual production output (AP × AQ) (1)	INPUTS AT STANDARD Standard price (SP) times actual quantity (AQ) of input for actual production output (SP × AQ) (2)	FLEXIBLE PRODUCTION BUDGET Standard price (SP) times standard quantity (SQ) of input allowed for actual output (that is, 80,000 units produced) (SP × SQ) (3)

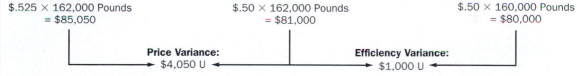

Direct Materials
$.525 × 162,000 Pounds = $85,050 $.50 × 162,000 Pounds = $81,000 $.50 × 160,000 Pounds = $80,000

    Price Variance: $4,050 U   Efficiency Variance: $1,000 U

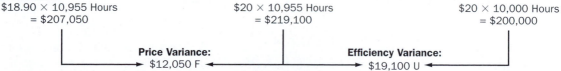

Direct Labor
$18.90 × 10,955 Hours = $207,050 $20 × 10,955 Hours = $219,100 $20 × 10,000 Hours = $200,000

    Price Variance: $12,050 F   Efficiency Variance: $19,100 U

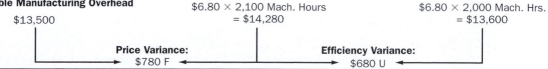

Variable Manufacturing Overhead
$13,500 $6.80 × 2,100 Mach. Hours = $14,280 $6.80 × 2,000 Mach. Hrs. = $13,600

    Price Variance: $780 F   Efficiency Variance: $680 U

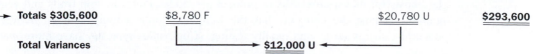

Totals $305,600 $8,780 F $20,780 U   **$293,600**

Total Variances   **$12,000 U**

EXHIBIT 11.8

VICTORIA CORPORATION
Variance Diagram

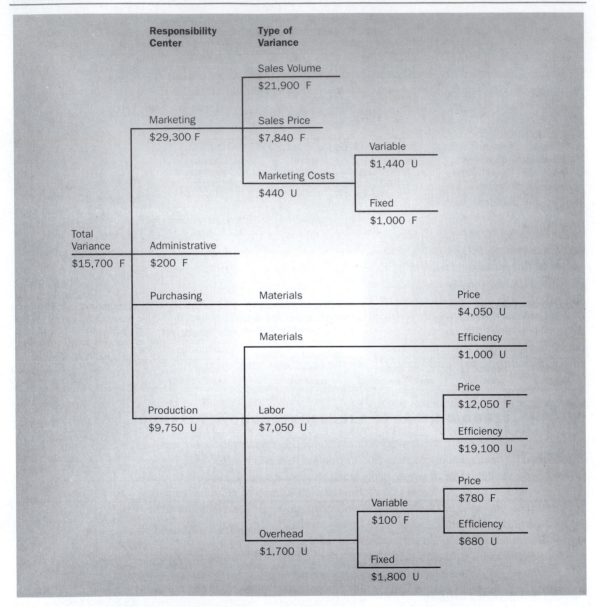

For example, assume Mesozoic Company uses activity-based costing to set standard costs for its variable costs of producing wooden crates to ship fruits and vegetables. Assume the company has the following three activity centers: indirect materials, energy costs, and quality testing. (Companies typically have more than

EXHIBIT 11.9

AMERICAN PARCEL DELIVERY
Example, Variable Overhead Efficiency Variance—Fuel Costs

Facts

Actual:

Output	1,100 Parcels Picked up or Delivered
Fuel Required	93 Gallons
Cost per Gallon	$1.58 per Gallon

Standard:

Fuel Allowed	.08 Gallon per Parcel Picked Up or Delivered
Cost per Gallon	$1.60 per Gallon

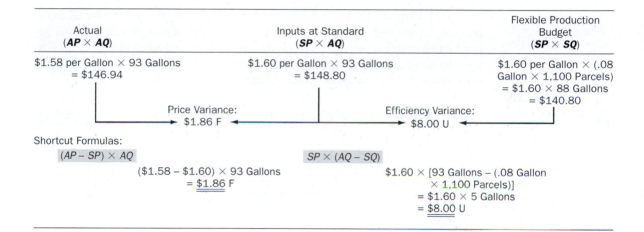

three activity centers, but we want to keep the example simple.) Management selects the following cost drivers for these activity centers:

Activity Center	Cost Driver
1. Indirect materials	Board feet of direct materials used
2. Energy	Machine hours
3. Quality testing	Minutes of test time

VARIANCE ANALYSIS FOR ACTIVITY-BASED COSTING

We use the same approach to variance analysis for activity-based costing as for traditional costing. The price variance is the difference between standard prices and actual prices for the actual quantity of input used for each cost driver. The efficiency variance measures the difference between the actual amount of input, or cost driver units used, and the standard allowed to make the output. We multiply this difference in quantities by the standard price per cost driver unit to get the dollar value of the variance.

To make this idea concrete, assume the following data for Mesozoic Company for the three activities for the month of June:

	Standard price per unit	Standard quantity of input allowed to produce 10,000 units of output	Actual cost	Actual quantity of input used
1. Indirect materials	$.05 per board foot	100,000 board feet	$ 5,180	110,000 board feet
2. Energy	$.02 per minute of machine time	250,000 minutes of machine time	$ 5,300	240,000 minutes
3. Quality testing	$.50 per test minute	30,000 minutes of test time	$16,000	34,000 test minutes

Exhibit 11.10 shows the results of the variance analysis. In effect, we have taken the principle underlying variance computations shown throughout this chapter and applied it to a situation having three activity centers. If a company had 40 activity centers, the computations would look like Exhibit 11.10, but with 40 computations of price and efficiency variances instead of only three.

EXHIBIT 11.10

Activity-Based Costing Variances

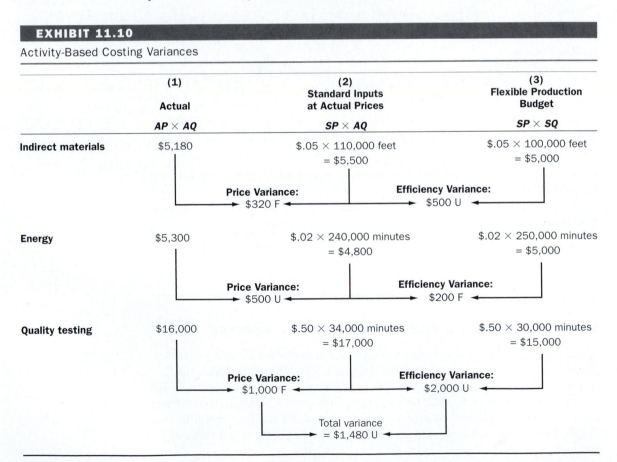

	(1) Actual	(2) Standard Inputs at Actual Prices	(3) Flexible Production Budget
	AP × AQ	SP × AQ	SP × SQ
Indirect materials	$5,180	$.05 × 110,000 feet = $5,500	$.05 × 100,000 feet = $5,000
		Price Variance: $320 F	Efficiency Variance: $500 U
Energy	$5,300	$.02 × 240,000 minutes = $4,800	$.02 × 250,000 minutes = $5,000
		Price Variance: $500 U	Efficiency Variance: $200 F
Quality testing	$16,000	$.50 × 34,000 minutes = $17,000	$.50 × 30,000 minutes = $15,000
		Price Variance: $1,000 F	Efficiency Variance: $2,000 U
		Total variance = $1,480 U	

Even with just three activity drivers, we think you can see the potential for managers to get a lot more information from activity-based costing than from the traditional approach. For example, the products required 34,000 minutes of quality test time instead of the 30,000 minutes allowed by the standard for 10,000 units produced in June. Does this "inefficiency" reflect poorer-quality materials than expected? Does it represent extra concern about putting out a quality product? Is the standard three minutes per crate too low? In short, activity-based costing raises numerous specific questions that managers can address to improve quality and productivity.

TARGET COSTING AND KAIZEN COSTING VERSUS TRADITIONAL COSTING

Two new approaches to costing—target costing and kaizen costing—have led managers to question the use of standard costing systems.

TARGET COSTING

Target costing is a systematic approach to establishing product cost goals based on market-driven standards. This approach is quite different from standard costing in that target costing begins with identifying customers' needs and calculating an acceptable sales price for the product. Working backward from the sales price, companies establish an acceptable target profit and calculate the target cost as follows:

$$\text{Target Sales Price} - \text{Target Profit} = \text{Target Cost.}$$

Target costs serve as goals for research and development, design, and production personnel (the first three areas in the value chain). If the target cost cannot be achieved, management takes a close look at the viability of making the proposed product.

While target costs are determined by market-driven standards (target sales price − target profit = target cost), standard costs are typically determined by design-driven standards with less emphasis on what the market will pay (engineered costs + desired markup = desired sales price).

KAIZEN COSTING

In contrast to the target costing approach, which supports the cost reduction process in the development and design phases of *new* products, **kaizen costing** supports the cost reduction process in the manufacturing phase of the value chain for *existing* products. *Kaizen* is a Japanese term referring to continuous improvement in relatively small activities rather than major innovative improvement.

The goal of kaizen costing is to reduce actual costs to manufacture a product below the standard cost. Standard cost systems generally focus on meeting the cost standard set by management, while kaizen costing systems are more concerned with reducing actual costs below standard costs. Under a kaizen costing system, cost reduction targets are established monthly and results are reviewed monthly. This allows management to identify problems and gains in cost reductions more regularly than under a standard costing system (typically reviewed annually or semiannually). Employees are expected to make changes to the production process throughout the life of the product to continually reduce production costs and increase efficiency.

VARIANCE ANALYSIS IN HIGH-TECHNOLOGY COMPANIES

The variance analysis model in Exhibit 11.4 generally applies to all types of organizations; however, high-technology firms apply the model somewhat differently. Most changes toward high technology involve substituting computerized equipment for direct labor. Examples include automatic teller machines in banks, robots in manufacturing plants, and word processors in various organizations. The result is less direct labor and more overhead.

The substitution of computerized equipment implies that the firm should treat labor more appropriately as a fixed cost than as a variable cost.[1] In high-technology manufacturing companies employees monitor and maintain machines rather than produce output. For these companies, labor efficiency variances may no longer be meaningful because direct labor is a capacity cost, not a cost expected to vary with output. Variable overhead may associate more with machine usage than labor hours. Some high-technology manufacturing organizations have found that the two largest variable costs involve materials and power to operate machines. The model in Exhibit 11.4 would apply to those costs.

QUALITY CONTROL AND VARIANCE INVESTIGATION

Managers may receive reports that contain hundreds or even thousands of variances. Managerial time is a scarce resource—following up and investigating variances is costly. When confronted with variance reports, managers ask: Which variances should we investigate?

Managers can deal with the decision of whether to investigate a variance like other decisions—on a cost-benefit basis. Hence they should investigate variances if they expect the benefits from investigation to exceed the costs of investigation. These benefits may include improvements from taking corrective action, such as repairing defective machinery, instructing workers who were performing their tasks incorrectly, or changing a standard purchase order so that the firm can purchase cheaper materials. Further, managers generally believe that periodically investigating or auditing employees improves performances. Because measuring the benefits and costs of investigation is often difficult, decisions about the value of investigating variances rely considerably on managerial judgments.

The major cost of **variance investigation** is the opportunity cost of employees' time. Investigators spend time as do those being investigated. Although measuring costs and benefits of variance investigation is difficult, in many cases the benefits are clearly too low or costs are clearly too high to make investigation worthwhile. In other cases variances are so large that obviously management must do something about them.

---

[1] In practice, many low-technology companies also treat direct labor as a fixed cost.

Managers use a variety of methods to help them ascertain which variances to investigate, including rules of thumb that have worked well in the past (for example, any variance greater than 10 percent of standard cost, any variance that has been unfavorable for 3 months in a row, and so on). Although we emphasize that managerial experience and good judgment are the most important ingredients for variance investigation decisions, accountants have developed some decision aids to assist managers.

TOLERANCE LIMITS

Quality control techniques have long relied on the use of *tolerance limits*. Quality is allowed to fluctuate within predetermined tolerance limits. Applying this concept to variances requires establishing predetermined limits within which variances may fluctuate. These limits may differ for various cost items. For example, managers usually allow greater tolerance for direct materials prices than for labor efficiency, because they have less control over the former due to market fluctuations. Some managers set tighter tolerance limits for unfavorable variances than for favorable variances.

Example   The manager of a kitchen that makes meals for a college cafeteria wants to set tolerance limits on labor efficiency variances so that variances fall outside the limits less than 5 percent of the time. Based on past experience, expected labor time is 58 minutes to prepare the lunch each day. Labor time to fix lunch is between 73.7 and 42.3 minutes 95 percent of the time.

Exhibit 11.11 presents a control chart of actual observations reported to the kitchen manager for 5 days. A time series of observations allows the manager to see trends and look for cumulative effects of variances. The manager gets this report at 9:00 AM each day for the 5 previous working days. The kitchen manager received

---

EXHIBIT 11.11

Labor Efficiency Variance Report: Friday through Thursday Control Chart

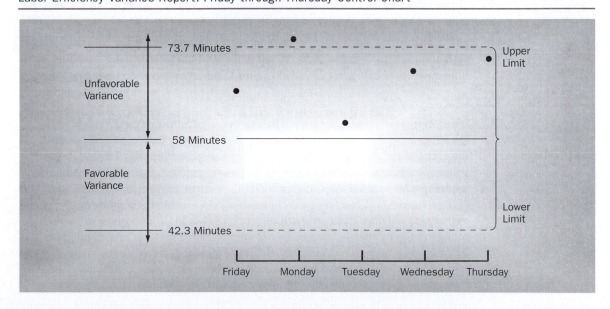

the report shown in Exhibit 11.11 at 9:00 AM Friday. The manager would have investigated the labor efficiency variance for Monday, presumably on Tuesday, because it fell outside the tolerance limits. In addition, the manager would probably investigate this labor variance after receiving the report on Friday because of the trend indicating a shift away from standard.

DECISION MODELS

Although control charts provide data about variances, they do not incorporate the costs and benefits of variance investigation. The simple decision model in the following example shows how to do this.

Example   Electromagnet, Inc., uses a stamping machine to make a product in 10,000-unit batches. An employee adjusts this machine at the beginning of a batch. During the production run, another employee calculates and reports the materials efficiency variances. If the machine is out of adjustment, it will use considerably more materials than needed. Hence, adjusting the machine during a production run could save materials costs.

Midway through a particular production batch, the stamping department manager receives a report indicating a large negative materials efficiency variance. Based on past experience, the manager estimates a 70 percent chance of the machine's running out of adjustment when the system reports a large negative materials efficiency variance.

The manager faces the decision of whether to investigate. Shutting down the machine would result in idle worker time, loss of materials, and lost managerial time. After computing the opportunity cost of lost time and the cost of lost materials, the department manager estimates the cost of variance investigation, C, to be $1,000. If the machine needs adjustment, making the adjustment will cost $1,200 but the firm will save $3,200 in materials cost. Given the costs, C, and the benefits, B, from investigation, and the probability, p, that the benefits can be obtained, the decision rule is to investigate when expected benefits exceed expected costs: $p \times B > C$.

Expected benefits equal the materials cost savings, $3,200, minus the cost of machine adjustments, $1,200, in this case. Investigating is worthwhile because

$$pB > C$$

$$.70(\$3,200 - \$1,200) > \$1,000$$

$$.70(\$2,000) > \$1,000$$

$$\$1,400 > \$1,000.$$

This simple example shows how to model the variance investigation decision by applying statistical decision theory tools.[2] Statistical analysis can provide decision aids to managers. Ultimately, these decision aids are just *aids;* they do not replace managerial judgment and good sense.

---

[2]We have assumed that decision makers are risk-neutral in this example.

MANAGERIAL APPLICATION

Quality Management and the Baldrige Award

Like many of the methods used in the success of the Japanese quality movement, the use of statistical controls in assessing processes originated in the United States. However, Japanese managers applied the concept and had much greater employee involvement in quality improvement than did U.S. companies. Although lagging in implementing quality management programs, many U.S. companies have jumped on the quality management bandwagon.

In 1987, the U.S. Congress created the Malcolm Baldrige National Quality Award in honor of the former secretary of commerce. This award is given to businesses that excel in major aspects of quality, such as quality planning, human resource development, and customer focus. Companies that have won this award include well-known manufacturing companies like Motorola, Westinghouse (Commercial Nuclear Fuel Division), IBM, Texas Instruments (Defense Systems and Electronics Group), and General Motors (Cadillac Division). The award has also been given to service organizations such as Ritz-Carlton Hotels, Federal Express, and AT&T (Network Systems Group) and to small businesses like Granite Rock Co. in Watsonville, California, and Globe Metallurgical in Cleveland. The Baldrige Award is intended to promote sharing of information about effective quality management programs and to identify companies with role-model quality management systems.

Source: Based on George S. Easton, "The 1993 State of U.S. Total Quality Management: A Baldrige Examiner's Perspective," *California Management Review,* vol. 35, no. 3 (spring 1993), pp. 32–54.

PROBLEM 11.3 FOR SELF-STUDY

Variance investigation. Pep Seco, the manager of a soft-drink bottling plant, watches the variance reports like a hawk because Pep knows the consequences of the machinery being out of adjustment. Pep just received a variance report indicating a possible problem. Based on years of experience, Pep figures the probability that the machinery is out of adjustment is .40 in light of the variance report. Investigation to learn whether the machinery is out of adjustment would cost $10,000 (mostly Pep's time, which has a high opportunity cost). If the machinery is out of adjustment, it would cost $20,000 to correct the problem but the company would save $50,000. Should Pep investigate? Why or why not?

The solution to this self-study problem is at the end of the chapter on page 401.

SUMMARY

The following items correspond to the learning objectives presented at the beginning of the chapter.

  1. **Understand the reasons for conducting variance analyses.** Variance analysis investigates and analyzes the variance to find causes, to ascertain whether the

firm needs to take corrective steps, and to reward or penalize employees, when appropriate.

2. **Assign responsibility for variances.** Variances for each responsibility center are separated from those for other centers and calculated holding all other things constant. Sales volume, sales price, and marketing cost variances are the responsibility of marketing. Administrative variances are often the hardest to manage because they are not engineered; management usually budgets administrative costs with discretion. Although discretionary budgets can provide a ceiling for expenditure, they do not provide a norm like a flexible manufacturing cost budget. Purchasing departments are responsible for materials price variances as they purchase the materials to make products and provide services. The production department is responsible for the fixed manufacturing cost variance and the remaining variable manufacturing cost variances not assigned to purchasing. These include materials efficiency variances, labor price and efficiency variances, and variable overhead price and efficiency variances.

3. **Separate variances into price and efficiency components.** The price component is the difference between the budgeted (or standard) price and the actual price paid for each unit of input. The efficiency variance measures the efficiency with which the firm uses inputs to produce outputs.

4. **Analyze variances using the variable cost variance model.** The cost variance model is applied to the calculation of direct materials, direct labor, and variable manufacturing overhead price and efficiency variances. The model uses the flexible production budget to analyze differences between actual and budgeted profits.

Key Equation:

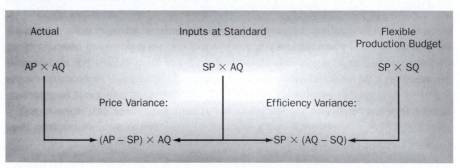

5. **Explain why variances occur.** Variances occur most often for one of the following reasons: random variation of actual around the standard, bias in setting the standard, or systematic variance not due to bias in the standard. Of these reasons, only the third may require investigation and correction. Materials price variances may be the result of failing to take purchase discounts, using a better (or worse) grade of raw material, or changes in the market supply or demand for the raw material that affected prices. Materials efficiency variances may arise due to more (or less) efficient use of materials than the standard or the purchase of inferior raw materials. Direct labor price variances can occur because managers do not correctly anticipate changes in wage rates. Direct labor efficiency variances may be caused by the workers themselves, poor materials, faulty

equipment, poor supervision, and scheduling problems. Direct labor efficiency is unique to a firm and can lead to competitive advantages or disadvantages.

6. **Analyze overhead variances using the variable cost variance model.** Separating variable overhead variances into price and efficiency components helps managers in their effort to control overhead costs. The manager can use the same method to compute price and efficiency variances for variable overhead as for other variable manufacturing costs using an appropriate input activity measure.

7. **Calculate fixed costs variances.** The only fixed cost variances computed for managerial purposes are the price variances, the difference between actual and budgeted fixed costs. Because fixed costs do not vary with the measure of activity, there are no efficiency variances for fixed costs.

8. **Describe the role of variance analysis in service organizations.** Variable overhead often makes up a large portion of the cost of providing services. Managers often calculate variances for particularly important, controllable overhead items, such as power or fuel costs. Computing price and efficiency variances for variable overhead as a total is more difficult. Sometimes managers perform this computation when variable overhead correlates highly with another production input.

9. **Summarize how activity-based costing relates to variance analysis.** Activity-based costing is commonly used with standard costing. Using activity-based costing, a company has multiple cost drivers. The same approach is used for variance analysis as for traditional costing. Using more activity drivers increases the potential for managers to get a lot more information from activity-based costing than from the traditional approach. Activity-based costing raises numerous specific questions that managers can address to improve quality and productivity.

10. **Explain how target costing and kaizen costing change the focus of costing systems.** Including target costing would create a total cost management system that supports the cost reduction process in the development and design phases of new models, while including kaizen costing would support the cost reduction process in the manufacturing phase of existing products.

Key Equation:

$$\text{Target Cost} = \text{Target Price} - \text{Target Profit}$$

11. **Understand the impact of technology on variance analyses.** Most changes toward high technology involve substituting computerized equipment for direct labor. The result is less direct labor and more overhead. This implies that the firm should treat labor as a fixed, or capacity, cost, and variable overhead may be associated more with machine usage than labor hours.

12. **Identify tools managers use to decide when to investigate variances.** Managers can deal with the decision of whether to investigate a variance like other decisions—on a cost-benefit basis. Hence, they should investigate variances if they expect the benefits from investigation to exceed the costs of investigation.

One method of identification where the benefit might be greater than the cost is the use of tolerance limits; the other is a decision model.

> Key Equation:
>
> $$pB > C$$
>
> p(Savings − Cost of Correction) > Cost of Investigation

13. **(Appendix 11.1) Recognize the relation between actual, budgeted, and applied fixed manufacturing costs.** Companies frequently use a predetermined overhead rate to apply fixed overhead to units produced. The production volume variance is the difference between the budgeted and applied fixed costs. The price variance is the difference between the actual costs and the budgeted costs. There is no efficiency variance as fixed costs are assumed not to vary with volume.

14. **(Appendix 11.2) Calculate the mix variance portion of the efficiency variance.** When multiple inputs are used to produce the output, the efficiency variance can be broken down into mix and yield variances. The mix variance shows the impact on profits of using something other than the budgeted mix of inputs. The yield variance is the portion of the efficiency variance that is not mix variance.

> Key Equation:
>
> Mix Variance = (Standard Price of the Inputs × Actual Proportions of the Actual Total Quantity × Actual Total Quantity of Inputs) − (Standard Price of the Inputs × Standard Proportions of the Actual Total Quantity × Actual Total Quantity of Inputs)

KEY TERMS AND CONCEPTS

Price variance   In accounting for standard costs, the difference between actual cost per unit of output (actual price times number of units of input per one unit of output) and standard cost per unit of output, times actual quantity of output.

Efficiency variance   A term used for the quantity variance for materials, labor, or variable overhead in a standard costing system; the difference between actual quantity and standard quantity of inputs, times standard price.

Materials price variance   The difference between actual cost and standard cost of materials, times actual quantity.

Materials efficiency variance   The difference between actual quantity and standard quantity of materials used, times standard price.

Direct labor price (or wage) variance   The difference between actual cost and standard cost of labor, times actual quantity.

Direct labor efficiency variance   The difference between actual quantity and standard quantity of labor used, times standard price.

Variable overhead price variance   The difference between actual cost and standard cost of overhead, times actual quantity.

Variable overhead efficiency variance   The difference between actual quantity and standard quantity of overhead used, times standard price.

Target costing   Establishing the target cost equal to target sales price (market price), minus target margin.

Kaizen costing   A costing system that emphasizes continuous improvement in small activities by seeking to reduce costs of production below standard costs.

Variance investigation   Standard cost systems produce variance numbers of various sorts. Management must decide when a variance differs sufficiently from zero to study its cause. This term refers to the process of studying the cause.

Production volume variance   Standard fixed overhead rate per unit of estimated volume times (budgeted units minus actual units).

Price variance (spending variance) for fixed manufacturing costs   Actual cost per unit minus standard cost per unit, times actual quantity.

Mix variance   The cost difference caused by changing the combination of inputs.

Yield variance   The part of the efficiency variance that is not a mix variance.

APPENDIX 11.1: FIXED MANUFACTURING COST VARIANCES

The chapter treated fixed costs as lump-sum, period costs in comparing budgeted and actual costs. This practice is appropriate for controlling fixed cost expenditures for managerial purposes. Manufacturing companies, however, use *full absorption costing* to value inventory. Full absorption costing unitizes fixed manufacturing costs and adds these unit fixed costs to unit variable manufacturing costs to compute the cost of a unit of inventory produced.

Companies frequently use a predetermined overhead rate to apply fixed overhead to units produced. For example, assume the following facts for Victoria Corporation:

Estimated (budgeted) Fixed Manufacturing Costs	$32,200
Estimated Production Volume	70,000 Units
Actual Production Volume	80,000 Units
Actual Fixed Manufacturing Costs	$34,000

If Victoria Corporation used full absorption, standard costing, it would apply its fixed manufacturing costs to units as follows:

$$\frac{\text{Applied Fixed Manufacturing}}{\text{Cost per Unit}} = \frac{\text{Estimated Fixed Manufacturing Cost per Period}}{\text{Estimated Production Volume per Period}}$$

$$= \frac{\$32,200}{70,000 \text{ Units Planned}}$$

$$= \$.46 \text{ per Unit.}$$

Note that we use production, not sales, volumes to unitize fixed manufacturing costs. If you were to unitize fixed marketing costs, you would divide the estimated cost by estimated sales volume.

During the period, the firm produced 80,000 units, so 80,000 units times $.46 per unit equals $36,800 applied to Work-in-Process Inventory. The amount "applied" is the amount of fixed manufacturing overhead debited to Work-in-Process Inventory. The firm could apply fixed manufacturing costs using an input basis such as machine hours. Assume the standard is 40 units per machine hour, or $\frac{1}{40}$ hour per unit. Then you would compute the rate per hour as follows:

$$\frac{\text{Fixed Manufacturing Cost}}{\text{Rate per Hour}} = \frac{\$32,200}{70,000 \text{ Units} \times \frac{1}{40}} = \frac{\$32,200}{1,750 \text{ Hours}}$$

$$= \$18.40 \text{ per Hour.}$$

The amount applied would still be $36,800 (= $18.40 per Hour $\times \frac{1}{40}$ Hour per Unit $\times$ 80,000 Units = $18.40 per Hour $\times$ 2,000 Hours).

PRODUCTION VOLUME VARIANCE

The **production volume variance** is the difference between the budgeted and applied fixed costs. For Victoria Corporation, the production volume variance is:

$$\begin{array}{ccc} \text{Production Volume} & \text{Budgeted Fixed} & \text{Applied Fixed} \\ \text{Variance} & = \text{Manufacturing Costs} & - \text{Manufacturing Costs} \end{array}$$

$$\$4,600 \text{ F} \quad = \quad \$32,200 \quad - \quad \$36,800.$$

This variance is favorable, as indicated by the F, as explained later.

If management had accurately estimated the production volume to be 80,000 units, the estimated unit cost would have been

$$\frac{\$32,200}{80,000 \text{ Units}} = \$.4025 \text{ per Unit.}$$

Applied fixed manufacturing overhead would have been $32,200 (= $.4025 per unit $\times$ 80,000 units actually produced), which equals the budget amount. Thus, if management correctly estimated the production volume, no production volume variance would occur.

The production volume variance applies only to fixed costs, and it emerges because we allocate a fixed period cost to products on a predetermined basis. The production volume variance appears to have little or no benefit for managerial purposes. Some accountants argue that this variance signals a difference between expected and actual production levels, but so does a simple production report comparing actual and planned production volumes.

The production volume variance comes from the use of predetermined fixed-cost rates in full absorption costing, unlike other cost variances that accountants compute to help managers manage the business. Manufacturing firms use predetermined rates and full absorption costing for external reporting, so you will probably encounter production volume variances during your career. Do not assume the production volume variance is useful just because companies compute it, however.

PRICE (SPENDING) VARIANCE

Recall from the chapter that the **price variance** (sometimes called the **spending variance**) **for fixed manufacturing costs** is the difference between the actual costs and the budgeted costs. Compute the fixed manufacturing price variance for Victoria Corporation as follows:

$$\begin{array}{ccc} \text{Price} & & \text{Actual Fixed} & \text{Budgeted Fixed} \\ \text{Variance} & = & \text{Manufacturing Costs} & - & \text{Manufacturing Costs} \end{array}$$

$$\$1{,}800\ U\ =\quad\quad \$34{,}000\quad\quad -\quad\quad \$32{,}200.$$

Although we use manufacturing costs for this example, you can compute the price variance this way for any fixed cost.

The fixed manufacturing cost variance used for management and control of fixed manufacturing costs is the price variance, whereas the fixed manufacturing cost production volume variance occurs only when we compute inventory values using full absorption costing and predetermined overhead rates.

RELATION OF ACTUAL, BUDGETED, AND APPLIED FIXED MANUFACTURING COSTS

We summarize the fixed manufacturing cost variances and the relation among actual, budget, and applied fixed manufacturing costs in Exhibit 11.12. Note the price variance is unfavorable because the actual exceeds the budget, but the production volume variance is favorable because the budget is less than the applied. Note that the master and flexible budgets for fixed costs do not differ here because we assume fixed costs do not vary with volume. If fixed costs differed in the flexible budget from the master budget, you would use the flexible budget fixed costs to compute these variances, because we use the flexible budget for performance evaluation and control purposes.

EXHIBIT 11.12

VICTORIA CORPORATION
Fixed Manufacturing Cost Variances

Actual	Budget	Budget	Applied
			$.46 × 80,000 Units of Output
			= $18.40 × 2,000 Hours
$34,000	$32,200	$32,200	= $36,800
Price Variance: $1,800 U		Efficiency Variance: Not Applicable	Production Volume Variance: $4,600 F

PROBLEM 11.4 FOR SELF-STUDY

Fixed cost variances. During the past month, the following events took place at Computer Supply, Inc.

(1) The company produced 50,000 computer cases. Actual fixed manufacturing cost was $83,000.

(2) Budgeted fixed manufacturing cost was $80,000. Budgeted direct labor hours worked were 4,000 hours for budgeted production of 40,000 cases. Full absorption costing, if used, applies fixed manufacturing costs to units produced on the basis of direct labor hours. Five thousand standard labor hours were allowed to make 50,000 computer cases.

Compute the fixed manufacturing price and production volume variances.

The solution to this self-study problem is at the end of the chapter on page 402.

APPENDIX 11.2: MIX VARIANCES

Most organizations use multiple inputs to produce their output. Massachusetts General Hospital uses a combination of registered nurses, licensed practical nurses, and nurse's aides to provide nursing care to patients. Bethlehem Steel Company uses a combination of iron ore, coke, and other raw materials to make its product. A **mix variance** shows the impact on profits of using something other than the budgeted mix of inputs.

Example   Engineering Associates, a consulting firm, has bid on a particular job assuming 1,000 hours of partner time at a cost of $100 per hour and 2,000 hours of staff time at $40 per hour. It it gets the job, these hour and cost assumptions become the flexible budget. During the job, scheduling problems arise—the partner spends 2,000 hours because the staff member spends only 1,000 hours. If the cost is actually $100 and $40 for partner and staff time, respectively, no labor price variance occurs. Further, the 3,000 hours required is exactly what was expected. Nevertheless, the job is $60,000 over the flexible budget, as shown in the following calculation:

$$\text{Actual Cost} = (2{,}000 \text{ Hours} \times \$100) + (1{,}000 \text{ Hours} \times \$40)$$

$$= \$200{,}000 + \$40{,}000$$

$$= \$240{,}000.$$

$$\text{Budgeted Cost} = (1{,}000 \text{ Hours} \times \$100) + (2{,}000 \text{ Hours} \times \$40)$$

$$= \$100{,}000 + \$80{,}000$$

$$= \$180{,}000.$$

$$\text{Actual Cost} - \text{Budgeted Cost}$$

$$= \$240{,}000 - \$180{,}000$$

$$= \$60{,}000.$$

The $60,000 unfavorable efficiency variance results from a mix variance: the substitution of 1,000 hours (= 2,000 hours actual − 1,000 hours budgeted) of partner time at $100 for 1,000 hours of staff time at $40. The mix variance is the difference in labor costs per hour of $60 (= $100 − $40) times the 1,000 hours substituted.

The general model for a mix variance is as follows:

Standard Price of the Inputs × **Actual Proportions** of the Actual Total Quantity × Actual Total Quantity of Inputs	−	Standard Price of the Inputs × **Standard Proportions** of the Actual Total Quantity × Actual Total Quantity of Inputs

Exhibit 11.13 shows the model for computing a mix variance. Columns (2) and (3) in the bottom part of Exhibit 11.13 show the mix variance that we computed above.

EXHIBIT 11.13

ENGINEERING ASSOCIATES
Mix Variance

Cost Variances Ignoring Mix Variance

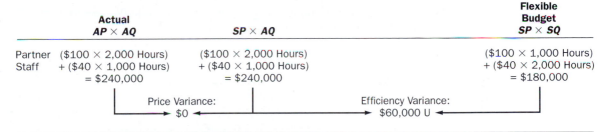

Cost Variances Considering Mix Variance

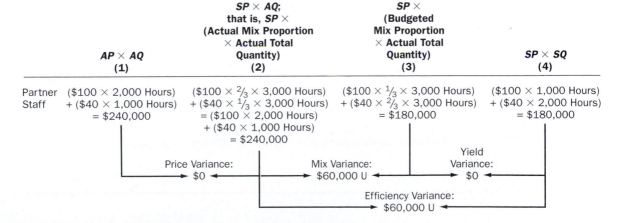

This example demonstrates the general concept of a mix variance. You should note two factors always present in a mix variance. First, we assumed that partner time was *substitutable* for staff time. Second, the prices must be different. If the cost per hour were the same for both partner and staff, the substitution of hours would not affect the total cost of the job.

Note that Exhibit 11.13 would have called the mix variance an efficiency variance if we had not calculated a separate mix variance. We call the portion of the efficiency variance that is not a mix variance a **yield variance**. The yield variance measures the input-output relation holding the standard mix of inputs constant.

In this example, we purposefully make the yield variance equal to zero to show that the entire variance results from the mix. Problem 11.5 for Self-Study presents a case in which there is a yield variance.

Managers use mix variances not only to measure performance when inputs are substitutes, as in the preceding example, but also to measure marketing performance with respect to sales mix. Companies with multiple products assume a particular sales mix in constructing their sales budget. If the actual mix of products sold differs from the budgeted mix, and if the products are substitutes, managers often compute a mix variance to measure the impact of the change in mix from the budget.

PROBLEM 11.5 FOR SELF-STUDY

Mix variance. Alexis Company makes a product, AL, from two materials, ST and EE. The standard prices and quantities follow:

	ST	EE
Price per Pound	$2	$3
Pounds per Unit of AL	10	5

In May, Alexis Company produced 7,000 units of AL, with the following actual prices and quantities of materials used:

	ST	EE
Price per Pound	$1.90	$2.80
Pounds Used	72,000	38,000

Compute materials price, mix, yield, and efficiency variances.

The solution to this self-study problem is at the end of the chapter on page 402.

SOLUTIONS TO SELF-STUDY PROBLEMS

SUGGESTED SOLUTION TO PROBLEM 11.1 FOR SELF-STUDY

Definitions. The price variance measures the difference between the actual and standard price per unit, times the number of units. This variance measures how well the company is controlling the cost of items purchased. The efficiency variance measures the difference between the actual quantity of inputs and the standard quantity allowed to make the actual output.

Uses. The manager of a coffee shop should monitor the price variance carefully. One can never tell when a revolution or natural disaster might break out in a coffee-producing country that would lead to an increase in the price of coffee beans. Coffeehouses are in a competitive business with low margins, in general, so failure to pass on the materials (that is, coffee beans) price increase to customers could take the company right out of business. Efficiency variances are more difficult to control because a certain level of staff is needed whether business volume is high or low. If the company has several employees, the manager can use efficiency measures to compare the efficiency of various employees.

SUGGESTED SOLUTION TO PROBLEM 11.2 FOR SELF-STUDY

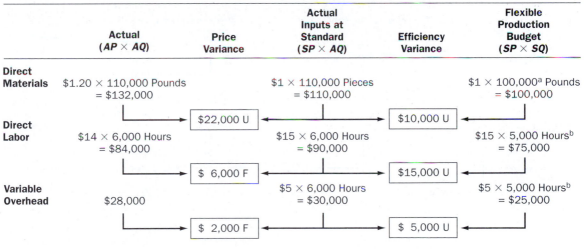

All based on 50,000 units produced

	Actual (AP × AQ)	Price Variance	Actual Inputs at Standard (SP × AQ)	Efficiency Variance	Flexible Production Budget (SP × SQ)
Direct Materials	$1.20 × 110,000 Pounds = $132,000		$1 × 110,000 Pieces = $110,000		$1 × 100,000[a] Pounds = $100,000
		$22,000 U		$10,000 U	
Direct Labor	$14 × 6,000 Hours = $84,000		$15 × 6,000 Hours = $90,000		$15 × 5,000 Hours[b] = $75,000
		$ 6,000 F		$15,000 U	
Variable Overhead	$28,000		$5 × 6,000 Hours = $30,000		$5 × 5,000 Hours[b] = $25,000
		$ 2,000 F		$ 5,000 U	

[a]Standard direct materials pounds allowed in production per unit times actual units produced (2 pounds × 50,000 units).

[b].10 hours × 50,000 units produced.

SUGGESTED SOLUTION TO PROBLEM 11.3 FOR SELF-STUDY

Pep should figure out whether $pB > C$. In this case, $p = .40$, $B = \$50,000 - \$20,000 = \$30,000$, and $C = \$10,000$. We find that $.40 × \$30,000 > \$10,000$, so Pep should investigate.

SUGGESTED SOLUTION TO PROBLEM 11.4 FOR SELF-STUDY

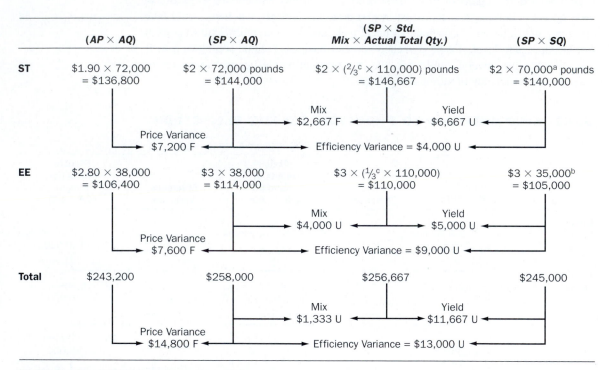

	Actual	Price Variance	Budget	Efficiency Variance	Budget	Production Volume Variance	Applied
Fixed Overhead	$83,000	$3,000 U	$80,000	Not Applicable	$80,000	$20,000 F	$100,000[a]

[a]Fixed overhead rate = $80,000/4,000 = $20 per standard labor hour; 5,000 standard labor hours allowed × $20 = $100,000.

SUGGESTED SOLUTION TO PROBLEM 11.5 FOR SELF-STUDY

	(AP × AQ)	(SP × AQ)	(SP × Std. Mix × Actual Total Qty.)	(SP × SQ)
ST	$1.90 × 72,000 = $136,800	$2 × 72,000 pounds = $144,000	$2 × ($2/3$[c] × 110,000) pounds = $146,667	$2 × 70,000[a] pounds = $140,000
		Price Variance $7,200 F	Mix $2,667 F ← Yield $6,667 U	
			Efficiency Variance = $4,000 U	
EE	$2.80 × 38,000 = $106,400	$3 × 38,000 = $114,000	$3 × ($1/3$[c] × 110,000) = $110,000	$3 × 35,000[b] = $105,000
		Price Variance $7,600 F	Mix $4,000 U ← Yield $5,000 U	
			Efficiency Variance = $9,000 U	
Total	$243,200	$258,000	$256,667	$245,000
		Price Variance $14,800 F	Mix $1,333 U ← Yield $11,667 U	
			Efficiency Variance = $13,000 U	

[a]70,000 Pounds = 7,000 Units × 10 Pounds per Unit.

[b]35,000 Pounds = 7,000 Units × 5 Pounds per Unit.

[c]Mix percentage ratio of ST pounds to total and EE pounds to total. For ST, $\frac{10}{10 + 5} = \frac{2}{3}$. For EE, $\frac{5}{10 + 5} = \frac{1}{3}$. 110,000 total = 72,000 ST plus 38,000 EE.

QUESTIONS, EXERCISES, PROBLEMS, AND CASES

REVIEW QUESTIONS

1. Review the meaning of the concepts or terms given in Key Terms and Concepts.

2. For control purposes, why is an efficiency variance not calculated for fixed manufacturing overhead?

3. An important point in variance analysis is that
   a. every variance must be investigated.
   b. a responsibility center's variances are calculated holding all other things constant.
   c. often price and usage variances cannot be separated.
   d. all of the above

4. Which function is normally responsible for sale price variances?
   a. marketing
   b. adminstration
   c. production
   d. top management

5. The price variance is calculated as follows:
   a. $AQ \times (AP - SP)$
   b. $SQ \times (AP - SP)$
   c. $AP \times (AQ - SQ)$
   d. $SP \times (AQ - SQ)$

6. (Appendix 11.1) A firm incurred fixed manufacturing overhead costs of $500,000 for the year. Fixed overhead applied to units produced during the year totaled $600,000. What are some of the reasons for this difference?

7. Describe the basic decision that management must make when considering whether to investigate a variance.

CRITICAL ANALYSIS AND DISCUSSION QUESTIONS

8. Why is a materials efficiency variance typically not calculated for the purchasing activity?

9. An airline is considering changing its flight and seat reservation system, enabling customers to make reservations directly using push-button telephones and computer terminals. This innovation would increase the airline's use of computers and almost eliminate the use of reservations agents. What impact would this change have on variances for the department responsible for reservations?

10. Why might the total variable manufacturing overhead variance not be divided into price and efficiency components?

11. How would you compute price and efficiency variances for taxicab drivers where the major variable costs are drivers' wages and automobile costs?

12. Refer to the Managerial Application, "An Antidote to Biased Standards: How Workers Develop Their Own Standards at NUMMI." What were the benefits of worker involvement in setting the standards at NUMMI?

13. How would you set labor and materials standards in a restaurant such as Denny's or Bakers Square?

14. How would a coffee shop use labor and materials variance information?

15. (Appendix 11.2) How could a CPA firm use mix variances to evaluate performance?

16. Refer to the Managerial Application, "Quality Management and the Baldrige Award." What purpose do you think is served by providing an award limited to only a few companies each year?

EXERCISES

Solutions to even-numbered exercises are at the end of the chapter after the cases.

17. **Materials and labor variances.** FreeRunning, Inc., produces sneakers. Recently established standard costs are as follows: materials, 10 pieces per unit, or pair, at $.50 per piece; labor, 1.50 hours per unit at $4.50 per hour. In November, 58,000 pieces of material were purchased for $29,580. These 58,000 pieces of material were used in producing 5,000 units of finished product. Labor costs were $37,750 for 8,500 hours worked.
    a. Compute the materials price variance.
    b. Compute the materials efficiency variance.
    c. Compute the labor price variance.
    d. Compute the labor efficiency variance.

18. **Materials and labor variances.** The Space Invader Company's budget contains these standards for materials and direct labor for a unit:

Material—2 Pounds at $.50 per Pound	$1.00
Direct Labor—1 Hour at $9.00	9.00

Although the firm budgeted 100,000 units of output for September, it produced only 97,810. It purchased and used 200,000 pounds of materials for $105,500. Direct labor costs were $905,000 for 99,200 hours.
    a. Compute the materials price variance.
    b. Compute the materials efficiency variance.
    c. Compute the labor price variance.
    d. Compute the labor efficiency variance.

19. **Materials and labor variances.** The City Carmel Company presents the following data for October:

	Standards per Batch	**Actual**
Materials	2 Pounds at $2.50 per Pound	98,000 Pounds
Labor	3 Hours at $3 per Hour	140,000 Hours
Units Produced		48,000 Batches

During the month, the firm purchased 98,000 pounds of materials for $255,000. Wages earned were $428,000. Compute all labor and material variances.

20. **Solving for materials quantities and costs.** Crystal Clear Pool Services uses from one to three chemicals to clean swimming pools. Variance data for the month follow (F indicates favorable variance; U indicates unfavorable variance):

	Chemical A	Chemical B	Chemical C
Materials Price Variance	$ 42,000 F	$ 25,000 F	$ 21,000 U
Materials Efficiency Variance	40,000 U	30,000 U	48,000 U
Net Materials Variance	$ 2,000 F	$ 5,000 U	$ 69,000 U
Pools Cleaned Requiring This Chemical	100,000	110,000	125,000

The budget allowed two pounds of each kind of chemical for each pool cleaning requiring that kind of chemical. For chemical A, the average price paid was $.20 per pound less than standard; for chemical B, $.10 less; for chemical C, $.07 greater. The firm purchased and used all chemicals during the month.

For each of the three types of chemicals, calculate the following:

a. Number of pounds of material purchased.

b. Standard price per pound of material.

21. **Nonmanufacturing variances.** Pete's Sales uses standard costs and variances for controlling costs. As a result of studying past cost data, it has established standards as follows: variable costs, $3 per sales call; 9 sales calls per unit sold. Actual data for May, June, and July follow:

	Sales Calls	Units Sold	Actual Costs
May	290,000	30,000	$940,000
June	310,000	40,000	920,000
July	260,000	20,000	790,000

Compute the variable cost price and efficiency variances for each month.

22. **Labor and overhead variances** (adapted from CPA exam). The following data relate to the current month's activities of Offshore Video Productions:

Actual Total Direct Labor	$43,400
Actual Hours Worked	14,000
Standard Hours Allowed for Actual Output (flexible budget)	15,000
Actual Total Overhead	$32,000
Standard Variable Overhead Rate per Direct Labor Hour	$1.50
Standard Direct Labor Wages per Hour	$3.00

Compute the following variances:

a. Labor and variable overhead price variances.

b. Labor and variable overhead efficiency variances.

23. **Materials variances.** Information on Glenn Company's direct materials costs is as follows:

Actual Quantities of Direct Materials Used	19,000
Actual Costs of Direct Materials Used	$80,000
Standard Price per Unit of Direct Materials	$ 4.10
Flexible Budget for Direct Materials	$82,000

   a. What was Glenn Company's direct materials price variance?
   b. What was the company's direct materials efficiency variance?

24. **Overhead variances.** Hyperspace, Inc., which uses standard costing, shows the following overhead information for the current period:

Actual Overhead incurred	$12,600, of which $3,500 is Fixed
Budgeted Fixed Overhead	$3,300
Variable Overhead Rate per Machine Hour	$3
Standard Hours Allowed for Actual Production	3,500
Actual Machine Hours Used	3,200

   What are the variable overhead price and efficiency variances and the fixed overhead price variance?

25. **Solving for labor hours.** Northern California Insurance Claims reports the following direct labor information for clerical staff in its claims department:

Month: April	
Standard Rate	$10.00 per Hour
Actual Rate Paid	$10.25 per Hour
Standard Hours Allowed for Actual Production Hours	1,500 Hours
Labor Efficiency Variance	$680 U

   What are the actual hours worked?

26. **Finding purchase price.** Information on Gretzky Softball Company's direct materials cost is as follows:

Standard Price per Materials Unit	$3.60
Actual Quantity Used	1,600
Materials Price Variance	$240 F

   What was the actual purchase price per unit, rounded to the nearest cent?

27. **Overhead variances.** (Appendix 11.1) Mario Corporation estimated its overhead costs for Year 0 to be as follows: fixed, $225,000; variable, $3.50 per unit. Mario expected to produce 50,000 units during the year.
   a. Compute the rate to be used to apply overhead costs to products.

b. During Year 0, Mario incurred overhead costs of $345,000 and produced 45,000 units. Compute overhead costs applied to units produced.

c. Refer to part **b.** Compute the amount of underapplied or overapplied overhead for the year.

28. **Overhead variances.** (Appendix 11.1) Wyman Company uses a predetermined rate for applying overhead costs to production. The rates for Year 0 follow: variable, $2 per unit; fixed, $1 per unit. Actual overhead costs incurred follow: variable, $95,000; fixed, $45,000. Wyman expected to produce 45,000 units during the year but produced only 40,000 units.

   a. What was the amount of budgeted fixed overhead costs for the year?

   b. What was the total underapplied or overapplied overhead for the year?

   c. Compute all possible fixed overhead variances.

29. **Variances from activity-based costs.** Assume Casio uses activity-based costing for variable overhead costs. For May, it has three cost drivers with the following standard and actual amounts for 5,000 units of output.

Activity Center	Cost Driver	Standard Rate per Cost Driver Unit	Standard Input for 5,000 Units of Output	Actual Costs	Actual Number of Inputs Used
Quality testing	Test minutes	$.50	20,000 test minutes	$10,000	19,000 test minutes
Energy	Machine hours	$1.00	20,000 machine hours	$20,000	21,000 machine hours
Indirect labor	Direct labor hours	$.50	30,000 labor hours	$14,200	28,000 hours

Prepare an analysis of the variances like that in Exhibit 11.10.

30. **Hospital supply variances.** (Appendix 11.2) Refer to Problem **37.** Compute mix and yield variances for the surgical supplies.

31. **Labor variances.** (Appendix 11.2) Refer to Problem **38.** Compute mix and yield variances for the labor costs.

32. **Variance investigation.** Manhatten Company's production manager is considering whether to investigate a computer-integrated manufacturing process. The investigation costs $7,000. If the manager finds that the process is out of control, correcting it costs $20,000. If the process is out of control and is corrected, the company saves $45,000 until the next scheduled investigation. The probability of the process being in control is .65, and the probability of the process being out of control is .35, given recent variance reports.

   Should management investigate the process? Why or why not?

33. **Variance investigation.** The accounting system has reported a large unfavorable variance for Tri-Dye Company's production process. Conducting an investigation costs $3,500. If the process is actually out of control, the benefit of correction will be $15,000. The probability is .22 that the large negative variance indicates the process is out of control.

   Should management investigate the process?

PROBLEMS

34. **Analysis of cost reports** (CMA adapted). Marcia is the production manager of the Bridgton Plant, a division of the larger corporation, Dartmoor, Inc. Marcia has complained several times to the corporate office that their cost reports used to evaluate her plant are misleading. Marcia states, "I know how to get good quality product out. Over a number of years, I've even cut raw materials used to do it. The cost reports don't show any of this; they're always negative, no matter what I do. There's no way you can win with accounting or the people at headquarters who use these reports."

    A copy of the latest report is shown below.

Bridgton Plant Cost Report
Month of November (in thousands)

	Master Budget	Actual Cost	Excess Cost
Raw Material	$400	$437	$37
Direct Labor	$560	$540	$(20)
Overhead	$100	$134	$34
Total	$1,060	$1,111	$51

Identify and explain changes to the report that would make the cost information more meaningful to the production managers.

35. **Change of policy to improve productivity** (CMA adapted). Brock Toy Company has been experiencing declining profit margins and has been looking for ways to increase operating income. It cannot raise selling prices for fear of losing business to its competitors. It must either cut costs or improve productivity.

    Brock uses a standard cost system to evaluate the performance of the assembly department. All negative variances at the end of the month are investigated. The assembly department rarely completes the operations in less time than the standard allows (which would result in a positive variance). Most months the variance is zero or slightly negative. Reasoning that the application of lower standard costs to the products manufactured will result in improved profit margins, the production manager had recommended that all standard times for assembly operations be drastically reduced. The production manager has informed the assembly personnel that she expects them to meet these new standards.

    Will the lowering of the standard costs (by reducing the time of the assembly operations) result in improved profit margins and increased productivity?

36. **Ethics and standard costs** (CMA adapted). Quincy Farms is a producer of items made from local farm products that are distributed to supermarkets. Over the years price competition has become increasingly important, so Doug Gilbert, the company's controller, is planning to implement a standard cost system for Quincy Farms. He asked his cost accountant, Joe Adams, to gather cost information on the production of strawberry jam (Quincy Farms' most popular product). Joe reported that strawberries cost $.80 per quart, the price he intends to pay to his good friend who has been operating a strawberry farm in the red for the last couple of years. Due to an oversupply in the market, the prices for strawberries have dropped to $.50 per quart. Joe is sure that the $.80 price will be enough to pull his friend's strawberry farm out of the red and into the black.

Is Joe Adams's behavior regarding the cost information he provided to Doug Gilbert unethical? Explain your answer.

37. Hospital supply variances. Assume Sonora Community Hospital had the following supplies costs for two products used in its operating room. Standard costs for one surgery: Item A, 10 pieces at $100 each; Item B, 20 pieces at $150 each. During August the following data apply to the hospital:

Surgeries Performed	2,000
Supplies Purchased and Used:	
Item A	22,000 Pieces at $90
Item B	39,000 Pieces at $152

Compute materials price and efficiency variances.

38. Labor variances. Assume In-n-Out Burger has two categories of direct labor: unskilled, which costs $8 per hour, and skilled, which costs $12 per hour. Management had established standards per "equivalent meal," which it has defined as a typical meal consisting of a sandwich, a drink, and a side order. Managers set standards as follows: skilled labor, 4 minutes per equivalent meal; unskilled labor, 10 minutes per equivalent meal. During May, In-n-Out Burger sold 15,000 equivalent meals and incurred the following labor costs:

Skilled Labor: 800 Hours	$ 9,500
Unskilled Labor: 2,100 Hours	18,500

Compute labor price and efficiency variances.

39. Comprehensive cost variance. Here are budget and standard cost data for May for Betty's Homestyle Pizza:

Budgeted sales	5,000 pizzas at $10 per pizza
Budgeted production	5,000 pizzas
(Betty's uses just-in-time production methods.)	
Budgeted marketing and administrative costs	$5,000 per month (all fixed)
Standard costs to make one pizza:	
Dough	1/2 pound at $2 per pound
Labor	1/4 hour per pizza at $10 per hour
Production overhead	$10,000 per month (fixed) plus $1 per pizza for toppings, paste, cheese, and the like.

For May, the results were as follows:

6,000 pizzas made and sold; revenue was $55,000.
3,050 pounds of dough used at $2.10 per pound.
1,600 labor hours used at $10 per hour.
Production overhead costs were $11,000 fixed and $7,500 variable.
Marketing and administrative costs were $6,500.

   a. Prepare a variable cost variance analysis.
   b. Write a brief report to the management of Betty's that gives your evaluation of performance and suggests ways management might improve the company's performance.

40. **Labor and overhead variances.** Sonny Company is a producer of handpainted china tea sets. Direct labor and variable overhead standards per finished unit are as follows: direct labor, 10 hours at $6.00 per hour; variable overhead, 10 hours at $1.00 per hour. During July, the firm produced 5,000 finished units. Direct labor costs were $293,000 (52,000 hours). Actual variable overhead costs were $53,000.
   a. Compute the price and efficiency variances for direct labor.
   b. Compute the price and efficiency variances for variable overhead.
   c. What similar factors might cause both the direct labor price variance and the variable overhead price variance?
   d. What factors might cause both the direct labor efficiency variance and the variable overhead efficiency variance?

41. **Performance evaluation in a service industry.** American Insurance Company estimates that its overhead costs for policy administration should be $72 for each new policy obtained and $2 per year for each $1,000 face amount of insurance outstanding. The company set a budget of 5,000 new policies for the coming period. In addition, the company estimated that the total face amount of insurance outstanding for the period would equal $10,800,000.

   During the period, actual costs related to new policies amounted to $358,400. A total of 4,800 new policies were obtained.

   The cost of maintaining existing policies was $23,200. Had the firm incurred these costs at the same prices as were in effect when it prepared the budget, the costs would have amounted to $25,900. However, $12,100,000 in policies were outstanding during the period.

   Prepare a schedule to indicate the differences between a master production budget and actual costs for this operation.

42. **Manufacturing variances.** Medina Company manufactures lamp shades. The company makes two types of shades, traditional and modern, from the same material. The company has no fixed overhead. The following are the standards and production data for November:

	Traditional	Modern
Standard Costs		
Raw Materials	$.25	$.50
	(.05 pounds at $5.00)	(.10 pounds at $5.00)
Labor	.40	.45
	(6 minutes at $4.00)	(6 minutes at $4.50)
Overhead	1.60 per	1.50 per
	Direct Labor Hour	Direct Labor Hour
Production Data for November		
Units	5,000	3,000
Pounds of Raw Materials Used . . .	250	305
Direct Labor Hours Used	500	298
Labor Costs Incurred	$2,060	$1,330

Total actual overhead was $1,238. The firm has decided to allocate this amount proportionately to the total costs of the two products on the basis of total standard direct labor hours. The firm purchased one thousand pounds of raw materials for $5,020. The labor efficiency variance for the traditional shade was zero.

   a. Compute the raw materials efficiency variance for the traditional and for the modern shades.

   b. Compute the direct labor price and efficiency variances for the traditional and for the modern shades.

   c. Compute the variable overhead price and efficiency variances for the traditional and for the modern shades.

43. **Solving for materials and labor.** Seasonal Company makes fireplace screens. Under the flexible budget, when the firm uses 60,000 direct labor hours, budgeted variable overhead is $60,000 whereas budgeted direct labor costs are $300,000. All data apply to the month of February.

   The following are some of the variances for February (F denotes favorable; U denotes unfavorable):

Variable Overhead Price Variance	$12,000 U
Variable Overhead Efficiency Variance	$10,000 U
Materials Price Variance	$15,000 F
Materials Efficiency Variance	$10,000 U

   During February, the firm incurred $325,500 of direct labor costs. According to the standards, each fireplace screen uses one pound of materials at a standard price of $2.00 per pound. The firm produced 100,000 units in February. The materials price variance was $.15 per pound, whereas the average wage rate exceeded the standard average rate by $.25 per hour.

   Compute the following for February, assuming there are beginning inventories but no ending inventories of materials:

   a. Pounds of materials purchased.

   b. Pounds of material usage over standard.

   c. Standard hourly wage rate.

   d. Standard direct labor hours for the total February production.

44. **Manufacturing variances.** The Tyler Company mass-produces oak file cabinets. The standard costs follow:

Wood	25 Pounds at $5.20 per Pound
Trim	8 Pounds at $5.00 per Pound
Direct Labor	5 Hours at $6.00 per Hour
Variable Overhead	$10 per Unit
Fixed Overhead	$62,000 per Period

Transactions during February follow:

(1) The firm purchased 160,000 pounds of wood at $4.95 per pound and issued 160,000 pounds to production.

(2) The firm purchased 25 tons (50,000 pounds) of trim at $5.05 per pound and issued 50,000 pounds to production.

(3) The direct labor payroll was 31,000 hours at $5.75.

(4) Overhead costs were $122,000, of which $60,500 were fixed.

(5) The firm produced 6,000 file cabinets during February.

Calculate all variances to the extent permitted by the data.

45. **Manufacturing cost variances.** The Ruby Paper Company makes place mats. The firm budgets fixed overhead at $6,000 per month. The firm expects variable overhead of $9,500 when it uses 10,000 direct labor hours per month.

The following data are available for April (F denotes favorable; U denotes unfavorable):

Materials Purchased and Used	20,000 Units
Direct Labor Costs Incurred	$36,000
Total Direct Labor Variance	$500 F
Average Actual Wage Rate ($.20 less than the standard wage rate)	$4.80
Variable Overhead Costs Incurred	$6,675
Materials Price Variance	$200 F
Standard Materials Allowed for Actual Output for the Month	$12,810
Price of Purchased Materials	$.60 per Unit
Actual Fixed Overhead	$7,200

Using these data, identify and present computations for all cost variances possible.

46. **Comprehensive variance computations.** (Appendix 11.1) The following information will assist you in evaluating the performance of the manufacturing operations of the Ukiah Company:

United Produced (actual)	21,000
Estimated Units Produced	20,000
Budgeted Fixed Overhead	$100,000
Standard Costs per Unit:	
Direct Materials	$1.65 × 5 Pounds per Unit of Output
Direct Labor	$14 per Hour × 1/2 Hour per Unit
Variable Overhead	$14 per Direct Labor Hour
Actual Costs:	
Direct Materials Purchased and Used . . .	$188,700 (102,000 Pounds)
Direct Labor	$140,000 (10,700 Hours)
Overhead	$255,000 (61% is Variable)

The company applied variable overhead on the basis of direct labor hours.

Prepare a cost variance analysis to show all variable manufacturing cost price and efficiency variances and fixed manufacturing cost price and production volume variances.

47. **Controlling labor costs.** Valley Convalescent Home has a contract with its full-time nurses that guarantees a minimum of $2,000 per month to each nurse with at least 12 years of service. One hundred employees currently qualify for coverage. All nurses receive $20 per hour.

    The direct labor budget for Year 1 anticipates an annual usage of 400,000 hours at $20 per hour, or a total of $8,000,000. Management believes that, of this amount, $200,000 (100 nurses × $2,000) per month (or $2,400,000 for the year) was fixed. Thus the budgeted labor costs for any given month resulted from the formula Budgeted Labor Costs = $200,000 + $14.00 × direct labor hours worked.

    Data on performance for the first 3 months of Year 1 follow:

	January	February	March
Nursing Hours Worked	22,000	32,000	42,000
Nursing Costs Budgeted	$508,000	$648,000	$788,000
Nursing Costs Incurred	440,000	640,000	840,000
Variance	68,000 F	8,000 F	52,000 U

    The results, which show favorable variances when hours worked were low and unfavorable variances when hours worked were high, perplex a hospital administrator. This administrator had believed the control over nursing costs was consistently good.

    a. Why did the variances arise? Explain and illustrate, using amounts and diagrams as necessary.

    b. Does this budget provide a basis for controlling nursing costs? Explain, indicating changes that management may make to improve control over nursing costs and to facilitate performance evaluation of nurses.

48. **Computing nonmanufacturing cost variances.** National Insurance Company estimates that its overhead costs for policy administration should amount to $80 for each new policy obtained and $2 per year for each $1,000 face amount of insurance outstanding. The company set a budget of selling 6,000 new policies during the coming period. In addition, the company estimated that the total face amount of insurance outstanding for the period would equal $12,000,000.

    During the period, actual costs related to new policies amounted to $430,000. The firm sold a total of 6,200 new policies.

    The cost of maintaining existing policies was $27,000. Had the firm incurred these costs at the same prices as were in effect when it prepared the budget, the costs would have been $26,000. However, some costs changed. Policies worth $13,000,000 were outstanding during the period.

    Prepare a schedule to show the variances between the flexible budget and actual costs for this operation.

49. **Computing variances for marketing costs.** Direct Marketing, Inc., uses telephone solicitation to sell products. The company has set standards that call for $450 of sales per hour of telephone time. Telephone solicitors receive a

commission of 10 percent of dollar sales. The firm expects other variable costs, including costs of sales in the operation, to be 45 percent of sales revenue. It budgets fixed costs at $411,500 per month. The firm computes the number of sales hours per month based on the number of days in a month minus an allowance for idle time, scheduling, and other inefficiencies. This month the firm expected 180 hours of telephone calling time for each of 40 callers.

During the month, the firm earned $2,700,000 of revenues. Marketing and administrative cost data for the period follow:

	Actual	Master Budget
Cost of Sales	$810,000	$972,000
Telephone Time Charges	32,200	32,400
Delivery Services	161,100	194,400
Uncollectible Accounts	121,500	145,800
Other Variable Costs	112,700	113,400
Fixed Costs	409,000	411,500

Using sales dollars as a basis for analysis, compute the variances between actual, flexible budget, and master budget for all costs including cost of sales. (*Hint:* Consider sales volume as an output measure.)

CASES

50. Behavioral impact of implementing standard cost system (CMA adapted). Windsor Healthcare, Inc., a manufacturer of custom-designed home health-care equipment, has been in business for 15 years. Last year, in an effort to better control the costs of their products, the controller implemented a standard cost system. Reports are issued monthly for tracking performance, and any negative variances are further investigated.

The production manager complained that the standards are unrealistic, stifle motivation by concentrating only on negative variances, and are out of date too quickly. He noted that his recent switch to titanium for the wheelchairs has resulted in higher material costs but decreased labor times. The net result was no increase in the total cost of producing the wheelchair. The monthly reports continue to show a negative material variance and a positive labor variance, despite the fact that there are indications that the workers are slowing down.

a. Describe several ways that a standard cost system strengthens management cost control.

b. Describe at least two reasons why a standard cost system may negatively impact the motivation of production employees.

51. Comprehensive problem: Tondamakers, Inc. Tondamakers produced and sold 1,000 Tonda riding lawnmowers in Year 1, its first year of operation. Actual costs of production are as follows:

Actual Results for the Year:	
Direct Materials: 11,000 Pounds at $19	$209,000
Direct Labor: 2,050 Hours at $31	$63,550
Manufacturing Overhead ($205,000 fixed)	$245,000
Actual Marketing and Administrative Costs ($320,000 fixed)	$380,000
Total Revenue: 1,000 Units at $940	$940,000
Actual Machine Hours Worked	550 Hours
Standard Variable Costs:	
Materials: 10 Pounds at $20	$200
Labor: 2 Hours at $30	$60
Variable Overhead: .5 Machine Hours at $80	$40
Budget Information:	
Budgeted Fixed Manufacturing Costs	$200,000 for Year 1
Master Budget Sales Volume	900 Tondas
Budgeted Marketing and Administrative Costs	$350,000 + $50 per Unit Sold
Budgeted Sales Price	$1,000 per Unit

Prepare profit and cost variance analyses such as those in Exhibit 11.7.

SUGGESTED SOLUTIONS TO EVEN-NUMBERED EXERCISES

18. **Materials and labor variances.**
   a. Materials Price Variance = $105,500 − (200,000 pounds × $.50) = $105,000 − $100,000 = $5,500 U.
   b. Materials Efficiency Variance = $.50(200,000 pounds actual − 2 standard pounds × 97,810 units produced) = $.50 × (200,000 − 195,620) = $2,190 U.
   c. Labor Price Variance = $905,000 − ($9 × 99,200) = $12,200 U.
   d. Labor Efficiency Variance = (99,200 − 97,810) × $9.00 = $12,510 U.
20. **Solving for materials quantities and costs.**
   Chemical A:
   a. Price Variance = $.20 F per Pound.
      Total Price Variance = $42,000 F.

      Pounds Purchased and Used = $\dfrac{\$42,000}{\$.20}$ = 210,000.
   b. Standard Pounds Allowed for 100,000 Units = 200,000.
      Pounds Used over Standard = 210,000 − 200,000 = 10,000.
      Efficiency Variance = $40,000 U.

      Standard Unit Price = $\dfrac{\$40,000}{10,000}$ = $4.00.

Chemical B:

a. Pounds Purchased and Used $= \dfrac{\$25,000}{\$.10} = 250,000.$

b. Standard Unit Price $= \dfrac{\$30,000}{(250,000 - 220,000)} = \dfrac{\$30,000}{30,000} = \$1.00.$

Chemical C:

a. Pounds Purchased and Used $= \dfrac{\$21,000}{\$.07} = 300,000.$

b. Standard Unit Price $= \dfrac{\$48,000}{(300,000 - 250,000)} = \$.96.$

22. Labor and overhead variances.

	Actual Costs	Price Variance	Inputs at Standard Prices	Efficiency Variance	Flexible Production Budget
Direct Labor	$43,400		$3.00 × 15,000 = $42,000		$3.00 × 15,000 = $45,000
		→ $1,400 U ←		→ $3,000 F ←	
Variable Overhead..........	$32,000 – $9,100 = $22,900		$1.50 × 14,000 = $21,000		$1.50 × 15,000 = $22,500
		→ $1,900 U ←		→ $1,500 F ←	

24. Overhead variances.

	Actual Costs	Price Variance	Inputs at Standard Prices	Efficiency Variance	Flexible Budget
Variable Overhead..........	$12,600 – $3,500 = $9,100		$3 × 3,200 Hours = $9,600		$3 × 3,500 Hours = $10,500
		→ $500 F ←		→ $900 F ←	
Fixed Overhead.............	$3,500				$3,300
		→ $200 U ←			

26. Finding purchase price.

Actual Costs	Price Variance	Inputs at Standard Prices
1,600 × *AP*		1,600 × $3.60 = $5,760
	→ $240 F ←	

$$1,600 \times AP = \$5,760 - \$240$$
$$AP = \$3.45$$

28. Overhead variances.

a. Budgeted Fixed Costs $= \$1.00$ per Unit $\times 45,000$ Units $= \$45,000.$

b. Applied Overhead = ($1.00 × 40,000) + ($2.00 × 40,000) = $120,000.
$140,000 − $120,000 = $20,000 Underapplied.

c. Fixed overhead variance analysis:

Actual	Price Variance	Budget	Production Volume Variance	Applied
$45,000		$45,000		$40,000
	→ $0 ←		→ $5,000 U ←	

30. Hospital supply variances. Review price and efficiency variances as given below.

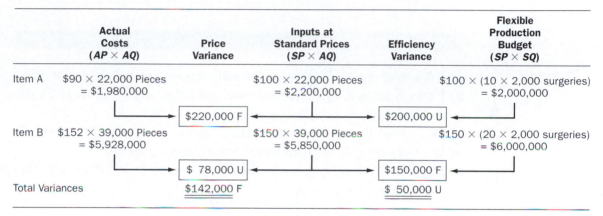

	Actual Costs ($AP \times AQ$)	Price Variance	Inputs at Standard Prices ($SP \times AQ$)	Efficiency Variance	Flexible Production Budget ($SP \times SQ$)
Item A	$90 × 22,000 Pieces = $1,980,000		$100 × 22,000 Pieces = $2,200,000		$100 × (10 × 2,000 surgeries) = $2,000,000
		$220,000 F		$200,000 U	
Item B	$152 × 39,000 Pieces = $5,928,000		$150 × 39,000 Pieces = $5,850,000		$150 × (20 × 2,000 surgeries) = $6,000,000
		$ 78,000 U		$150,000 F	
Total Variances		$142,000 F		$ 50,000 U	

Now extend the analysis to compute mix and yield variances.

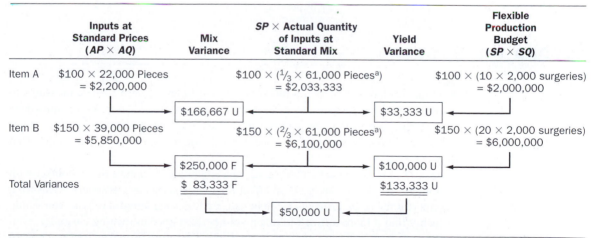

	Inputs at Standard Prices ($AP \times AQ$)	Mix Variance	$SP \times$ Actual Quantity of Inputs at Standard Mix	Yield Variance	Flexible Production Budget ($SP \times SQ$)
Item A	$100 × 22,000 Pieces = $2,200,000		$100 × (⅓ × 61,000 Pieces[a]) = $2,033,333		$100 × (10 × 2,000 surgeries) = $2,000,000
		$166,667 U		$33,333 U	
Item B	$150 × 39,000 Pieces = $5,850,000		$150 × (⅔ × 61,000 Pieces[a]) = $6,100,000		$150 × (20 × 2,000 surgeries) = $6,000,000
		$250,000 F		$100,000 U	
Total Variances		$ 83,333 F		$133,333 U	
			$50,000 U		

[a]61,000 = Total Pieces Used = 22,000 + 39,000.

32. Variance investigation. Is $p(B) > C$? $p = .35$, $B = ($45,000 − $20,000)$, and $C = $7,000$. We find that $.35 × ($45,000 − $20,000) = .35 × $25,000 = $8,750$. $8,750 > $7,000$; therefore, investigate.

CHAPTER 12

NONFINANCIAL PERFORMANCE MEASURES

LEARNING OBJECTIVES

1. Know how organizations recognize and communicate their responsibilities.
2. Understand how the balanced scorecard helps organizations recognize and deal with opposing responsibilities.
3. Know how the process of performance improvement works.
4. Identify examples of nonfinancial performance measures.
5. Explain why employee involvement is important in an effective performance measurement system.

BEYOND THE NUMBERS

Companies have traditionally relied heavily on financial performance measures to evaluate employee performance. In recent years, more and more companies have begun using nonfinancial measures, such as customer satisfaction and product quality, because nonfinancial performance measures direct employees' attention to what they can control.

For example, if you are a food server in a restaurant, you have direct contact with customers. You know that you can affect their satisfaction as customers. Measuring your performance in terms of customer satisfaction is meaningful to you. You would probably find it more difficult to relate your performance in treating customers well to the restaurant's future increases in revenues. Therefore, it makes sense to reward you for creating customer satisfaction rather than for increasing revenues.

418

This chapter discusses innovative ways to evaluate performance "beyond the numbers." Performance evaluation begins with an understanding of the organization's goals. For example, does the firm want to be a low-cost producer or an innovator? What markets will it compete in? The organization evaluates performance by first defining what it wants to accomplish. Then it develops measures that help it evaluate its performance in achieving those goals.

VALUES OF THE ORGANIZATION

A mission statement describes the organization's values, makes specific commitments to those who have an interest in the organization (such as shareholders) and identifies the major strategies the organization plans to use to achieve its goals.

Mission statements should answer the following questions:

1. Who are the organization's stakeholders? Who matters to the organization?
2. How will the organization add value to each stakeholder group? This identifies the **critical success factors** which are those factors important for the organization's success.

ETHICAL BEHAVIOR

The organization's mission statement communicates its guiding principles, beliefs, and values. It helps people in the organization identify priorities. This guides employees as they make decisions that help the organization achieve its goals.

For instance, General Motors' code of conduct includes a reference to employees conducting themselves so they would not be embarrassed to have their family watch a film of their activities. Johnson & Johnson's code of conduct, shown in Exhibit 12.1, sets forth the company's values in order of priority, stating its responsibilities to customers, employees, the community, and stockholders. Note Johnson & Johnson's code of conduct states the company's responsibility to many stakeholders, including those who use its products, its employees, and its communities. **Stakeholders** are individuals or groups who have a stake in what the organization does. Communicating what the organization stands for and what it needs to do to be successful is the foundation of organizational performance.

BALANCED SCORECARD

The balanced scorecard is a management method that focuses attention on achieving organizational objectives. It recognizes that organizations are responsible to different stakeholder groups, such as employees, suppliers, customers, business partners, the community, and shareholders. The **balanced scorecard** is a set of performance targets and results that show an organization's performance in meeting its objectives relating to its stakeholders.

Sometimes different stakeholders have different wants. For example, employees depend on an organization for their employment. Shareholders depend on an organization to maintain their investment. The organization must balance those competing wants. Hence, the concept of a balanced scorecard is to measure how well the organization is doing in view of competing stakeholder wants.

EXHIBIT 12.1

Johnson & Johnson Code of Conduct

Our Credo

We believe our first responsibility is to the doctors, nurses and patients,
to mothers and all others who use our products and services.
In meeting their needs everything we do must be of high quality.
We must constantly strive to reduce our costs
in order to maintain reasonable prices.
Customers' orders must be serviced promptly and accurately.
Our suppliers and distributors must have an opportunity
to make a fair profit.

We are responsible to our employees,
the men and women who work with us throughout the world.
Everyone must be considered as an individual.
We must respect their dignity and recognize their merit.
They must have a sense of security in their jobs.
Compensation must be fair and adequate,
and working conditions clean, orderly and safe.
Employees must feel free to make suggestions and complaints.
There must be equal opportunity for employment, development
and advancement for those qualified.
We must provide competent management,
and their actions must be just and ethical.

We are responsible to the communities in which we live and work
and to the world community as well.
We must be good citizens—support good works and charities
and bear our fair share of taxes.
We must encourage civic improvements and better health and education.
We must maintain in good order
the property we are privileged to use,
protecting the environment and natural resources.

Our final responsibility is to our stockholders.
Business must make a sound profit.
We must experiment with new ideas.
Research must be carried on, innovative programs developed
and mistakes paid for.
New equipment must be purchased, new facilities provided
and new products launched.
Reserves must be created to provide for adverse times.
When we operate according to these principles,
the stockholders should realize a fair return.

For many years, organizations focused only on financial results, which reflected mainly the shareholders' interests. In recent years, organizations have shifted attention to customer issues, such as quality and service, to employees, and to the community. For example, Ben & Jerry's Ice Cream measures its social performance along with financial performance and has a social audit next to its financial audit in its annual report.

An example of a balanced scorecard appears in Exhibit 12.2. As you can see, it balances the efforts of the organization among the financial, customer, process, and innovative responsibilities.

The balanced scorecard has been developed and used in many companies. Mostly, it has been used at the top management level where it supports the company's strategic management system. For example, Kaplan and Norton describe the development of the balanced scorecard at an insurance company as follows.[1]

Step 1: Ten of the company's top executives formed a team to clarify the company's goals and strategy.

Step 2: The top three layers of the company's management (100 people) were brought together to discuss the new strategy and to develop performance measures for each part of the company. These performance measures became the scorecards for each part of the business and reflected the company's desired balance in satisfying different stake-holders.

Step 3: Managers began eliminating programs that were not contributing to the company's goals.

Step 4: Top management reviewed the scorecards for each part of the organization.

Step 5: Based on its reviews in step 4, top management went back to step 1 to refine and further clarify the company's goals and strategy.

The balanced scorecard concept has been helpful for top and middle management to shape and clarify organizational goals and strategy. It has been useful at the worker level, when the complex trade-offs implied by the balanced scorecard are translated into simple performance measures.

PERFORMANCE EVALUATION: THE PROCESS

This section discusses key aspects of the process of improving performance. We focus on recent management innovations in that process; namely, use of continuous improvement and benchmarking.

CONTINUOUS IMPROVEMENT AND BENCHMARKING

Continuous improvement means continuously reevaluating and improving the efficiency of activities. It is the search to (1) improve the activities in which the organization engages through documentation and understanding, (2) eliminate activities that do not add value, and (3) improve the efficiency of activities that do add value.

---

[1]Based on R. S. Kaplan and D. P. Norton, "Using the Balanced Scorecard as a Strategic Management System," *Harvard Business Review,* January–February 1996.

EXHIBIT 12.2

Balanced Scorecard

Financial

"To succeed financially, how should we appear to our shareholders?"

Objectives	Measures	Targets	Initiatives

Internal Business Process

"To satisfy our shareholders and customers, at what business processes must we excel?"

Objectives	Measures	Targets	Initiatives

VISION AND STRATEGY

Customer

"To achieve our mission, how should we appear to our customers?"

Objectives	Measures	Targets	Initiatives

Learning and Growth

"To achieve our mission, how will we sustain our ability to change and improve?"

Objectives	Measures	Targets	Initiatives

Source: R. S. Kaplan and D. P. Norton, "Using the Balanced Scorecard as a Strategic Management System," *Harvard Business Review*, Jan-Feb, 1996.

EXHIBIT 12.3

Common Benchmark Categories

Product performance: How does the performance of our products (for example, cars, dish-washers, and printers) compare to others?

Customer service performance: How well do we serve our customers compared to others? How quickly do we serve them?

New product/service development and innovation performance: Are we as innovative as others?

Cost performance: How well do we manage costs compared to others?

Competitive benchmarking involves the search for, and implementation of, the best way to do something as practiced elsewhere in one's own organization or in other organizations. Benchmarking identifies an activity that needs to be improved, finds an organization that is the most efficient at that activity, studies its process, and then utilizes that process. Companies also use benchmarking to make dramatic one-time breakthroughs. For example, Xerox studied the inventory handling and shipping practices at L. L. Bean, a mail-order retailer, to make dramatic improvements in its own practices.

Following are some important benchmarking guidelines:

1. Don't benchmark *everything* at the best-in-the-business level. No company can be the best at everything.
2. Benchmark only best-in-class processes and activities that are the most important strategically.
3. Look for internal, regional, or industry benchmarks for less important activities.

Exhibit 12.3 presents four common types of benchmarking.

PERFORMANCE MEASUREMENT: THE MEASURES

VALUE CHAIN ANALYSIS

There is no single set of right performance measures that can be espoused in a text-book. Performance measures must be based on the organization's goals and strategy, which are likely to be different for each organization. Having said that, here are some examples of performance measures that you are likely to use or see used in organizations.

The value chain provides a good place to begin identifying the most useful factors to measure. Recall that the value chain is the linked set of activities that an organization undertakes to produce a good or service, as shown in Exhibit 12.4. Use the value chain activities that, if measured, would give managers and workers the best incentives to achieve the organization's goals.

EXHIBIT 12.4

Value Chain

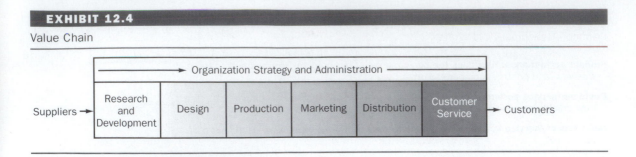

CUSTOMER SATISFACTION PERFORMANCE MEASURES

Customer satisfaction measures reflect the performance of the organization on quality control and delivery performance. Examples of such measures include the number of customer complaints and the percentage of deliveries that are on time.

> *Quality Control* The objective is to increase customer satisfaction with the product, reduce the costs of dealing with customer complaints, and reduce the costs of repairing products or providing a new service.
>
> *Delivery Performance* The objective is to deliver goods and services when promised so customers will continue to buy goods and services from you and provide positive word-of-mouth advertising.

FUNCTIONAL PERFORMANCE MEASURES

An organization must do internal functional performance evaluation. Many activities are performed throughout the product life cycle. The efficiency level of these activities affects the overall performance of the organization in attaining its goals for other stakeholders, such as stockholders and employees. Exhibit 12.5 presents several internal functional performance measures used by organizations.

For example, the accounting quality measures attempt to assess how well accountants perform their work by:

> measuring the percent of reports that are late.
>
> measuring the percent of errors in reports.
>
> measuring manager satisfaction with accounting reports.

TIME MEASURES

The total time it takes to produce a good or service is called **production cycle time.** The cycle time includes processing, moving, storing, and inspecting. It is commonly believed that a product's service, quality, and cost are all related to cycle time. As cycle time increases, so do the costs of processing, inspection, moving, and storage, while service and quality decrease.

MANAGERIAL APPLICATION

Does Effective Total Quality Management Require Nontraditional Performance Measures?

Critics of management accounting contend that innovative management methods, such as the importance of customers in the identification of new products and processes, and the use of employee suggestion programs, require new approaches to management accounting and control. According to these critics, traditional financial performance measures are obstacles to effective implementation of innovative management methods.

Two professors at the Wharton School, Chris Ittner and David Larcker, investigated this idea in a study of companies in the automotive and computer industries. They found that, in general, companies that adopted total quality management also used nontraditional management performance measures. Examples of nontraditional performance measures included use of quality and other nonfinancial measures, and the importance of team relative to individual performance measures.

Ittner and Larcker also noted that companies that are innovative in management methods like TQM are also innovative in management evaluation.

Source: Based on C. Ittner and D. Larcker, "Total Quality Management and the Choice of Information and Reward Systems," *Journal of Accounting Research* 33 (Supplement, 1995), pp. 1–40.

EXHIBIT 12.5

Functional Measures of Performance

Accounting Quality

Percent of late reports
Percent of errors in reports
Manager satisfaction with accounting reports

Clerical Quality

Errors per typed page
Number of times messages are not delivered

Forecasting Quality

Percent error in sales forecasts
Usefulness of forecasts to decision makers

Procurement/Purchasing Quality

Percent of supplies received on schedule
Average time to fill emergency orders

Production Control Quality

Time required to incorporate engineering changes
Time that line is down due to shortage of materials

Sources: Some of these measures are drawn from longer lists in G. Fellers, *The Deming Vision: SPC/TQM for Administrators* (ASQC Quality Press, 1992); and D. Talley, *Total Quality Management* (ASQC Quality Press, 1991). Other measures were developed by the authors.

Organizations may also find value in knowing the amount of time it takes to complete a sequence of activities. Many believe that by eliminating long cycle times, the costs of nonproduction personnel, equipment, and supplies would be reduced. Also, customers value a prompt response and a short processing time.

Production Cycle Efficiency   **Production cycle efficiency** measures the efficiency of the total production cycle. Production cycle efficiency is calculated as follows:

Production cycle efficiency = Processing time/(Processing time + Moving time
                                                                                      + Storing time + Inspection time)

This formula produces a percentage that represents the time that is actually spent processing the unit. The higher the percentage, the less the time—and costs—spent on nonvalue-added activities, such as moving and storage. For example, higher quality control of the process and inputs means less time is spent on inspections.

Just-in-time production requires that processing systems be reliable with a continuous flow. You can think of just-in-time production as trying to make the manufacturing cycle efficiency equal $1.00.

ENVIRONMENTAL PERFORMANCE[2]

Many companies are concerned about environmental issues and attempt to measure their performance and provide incentives for good performance. Companies such as 3M and Dow Chemical include environmental performance measures in evaluating employee and managerial performance.

For example, increasing environmental regulation prompted the 3M Corporation to develop its first comprehensive environmental policy in 1975. Management initiated a companywide pollution prevention program to change the thinking at 3M from "end-of-the-pipe" controls to reduction of pollution at the source.

Waste minimization is a goal for 3M. The performance measure to track waste minimization is:

$$\text{Waste Ratio (\%)} = \frac{\text{Waste (Pounds)}}{\text{Total Output (Pounds)}}$$

Total output is defined as the total weight of "Good Output" plus the total weight of "Waste." Waste includes chemical waste, trash, and discarded water waste, among others.

The waste minimization program at 3M represents an attempt to add environmental performance to other performance measures, such as efficiency variances and customer satisfaction. By measuring environmental performance and rewarding good performance, companies hope to provide incentives for their employees to create a clean environment. Good environmental performance is also in companies' best interests because it reduces governmental regulation, fines, litigation costs

---

[2]This discussion is based on W. N. Lanen, "Waste Minimization at 3M Corporation: A Case Study in Performance Measurement," University of Michigan Business School Working Paper, July 1995.

(such as those experienced by Exxon in the *Exxon Valdez* oil spill) and ill will from the community.

EMPLOYEE INVOLVEMENT

Many organizations involve workers in creating ideas for improving performance. In some Japanese companies that we have studied, every worker is expected to submit an idea for improvement at least once a week. Competent managers know that workers have good ideas for improving the operations of a company. After all, the workers are much closer than the managers to an organization's production and sales activities.

Worker involvement is important for three reasons:

1. Many managers believe that when workers take on real decision-making authority, their commitment to the organization and its goals increases.
2. When decision-making responsibility lies with workers closer to the customer, decision making becomes more responsive and informed.
3. Giving decision-making responsibility to workers uses their skills and knowledge and provides them with motivation to further develop their skills and knowledge in an effort to improve the organization's performance.

Effective worker involvement decentralizes decision-making authority and empowers workers.

How do companies evaluate their own performance in getting workers involved and committed? Exhibit 12.6 shows performance measures that organizations can use to assess how well they are doing in terms of worker involvement and commitment. Increasing the percentages on these performance measures demonstrates increasing worker involvement and commitment to the organization.

Effective worker involvement presents three challenges for management.

1. Management must create a system that conveys the organization's goals and critical success factors to all members. Information, training sessions, and the

---

EXHIBIT 12.6

Performance Measures of Worker Involvement and Commitment

1. Worker Development: Measured by percentage of workers in mentor programs

2. Worker Empowerment: Measured by percentage of workers authorized to issue credit

3. Worker Recognition: Measured by percentage of workers recognized by awards

4. Worker Recruitment: Measured by percentage of employment offers accepted

5. Worker Promotion: Measured by percentage of positions filled from within the company

6. Worker Succession Planning: Measured by percentage of eligible positions filled through succession planning

performance indicators themselves will determine the extent to which employees understand what behavior is desired of them.

2. The measures the organization uses to judge individual performance will determine the success of the system in promoting goal congruence. Management must analyze the performance measures chosen by each organizational unit to make sure that they (a) promote the desired behavior, (b) are comprehensive, (c) support the achievement of organizational goals, and (d) reflect the unit's role in the organization.

3. Management must ensure that the performance measures are applied consistently and accurately. The measures used to evaluate performance reflect each unit's understanding of its contribution to the organization.

SUMMARY

This chapter discussed innovative ways to evaluate performance "beyond the numbers." The following items correspond to the learning objectives presented at the beginning of the chapter.

1. **Know how organizations recognize and communicate their responsibilities.** Mission statements describe the organization's values, make specific commitments to stakeholders, and identify the major strategies the organization plans to use to meet its commitments. Codes of conduct communicate the organization's guiding principles, beliefs, and values.

2. **Understand how the balanced scorecard helps organizations recognize and deal with opposing responsibilities.** The balanced scorecard concept recognizes that organizations are responsible to different stakeholder groups and must perform well on several dimensions, such as financial, customers, process, and innovation.

3. **Know how the process of performance improvement works.** The main purpose of performance measurement is to assess operations and provide direction for improvement. Continuous improvement and benchmarking are effective methods of improving performance. Continuous improvement is the search to eliminate nonvalue-added activities and improve the efficiency of activities that add value. Competitive benchmarking is the search for, and implementation of, the best methods practiced in other organizations or in other parts of one's own organization.

4. **Identify examples of nonfinancial performance measures.** Customer satisfaction performance measures are directed at quality and delivery performance. Functional measures attempt to assess how well internal processes function. Production cycle efficiency measures the ratio of processing time to total time, the goal being a measurement of one. By measuring environmental performance and rewarding good performance, companies hope to motivate their employees to create a clean environment and reduce governmental regulation, fines, litigation, and ill will from the community.

5. **Explain why employee involvement is important in an effective performance measurement system.** Worker involvement is important for three reasons: (1) It increases commitment to the organization and its goals, (2) it leads to more re-

sponsive and informed decision making, and (3) it utilizes worker skills and knowledge.

KEY TERMS AND CONCEPTS

Critical success factors   The factors important for the organization's success.

Stakeholders   Groups or individuals, such as employees, suppliers, customers, shareholders, and the community, who have a stake in what the organization does.

Balanced scorecard   A set of performance targets and results that show an organization's performance in meeting its responsibilities to various stakeholders.

Continuous improvement   The continuous reevaluation and improvement of the efficiency of activities.

Benchmarking   Identifying an activity that needs to be improved, finding an organization that is the most efficient at that activity, studying its process, and then utilizing that process.

Production cycle time   The time involved in processing, moving, storing, and inspecting products and materials.

Production cycle efficiency   A measure of the efficiency of the total manufacturing cycle. It equals processing time divided by the manufacturing cycle time.

QUESTIONS, EXERCISES, AND PROBLEMS

REVIEW QUESTIONS

1. Review the meaning of the concepts or terms given in Key Terms and Concepts.
2. Why are companies using nonfinancial measures like customer satisfaction and product quality?
3. What technique do many companies use to focus attention on organizational objectives concerning various stakeholders?
4. Who are the stakeholders of an organization?
5. Describe a balanced scorecard.
6. What is competitive benchmarking?
7. How is competitive benchmarking used?
8. Which performance factors are customer satisfaction measures aimed at?
9. Why should management measure delivery performance?
10. Refer to Exhibit 12.5 on page 425. Why is each of the performance measures under the heading "Clerical Quality" important?
11. Refer to Exhibit 12.5 on page 425. Why is "manager satisfaction with accounting reports" an important functional measure of accounting quality?
12. How does production cycle efficiency relate to nonvalue-added activities?
13. Why is good environmental performance in a company's interest?
14. Refer to Exhibit 12.6 on page 427. How does "percentage of positions filled from within the company" measure worker involvement and commitment?

CRITICAL ANALYSIS AND DISCUSSION QUESTIONS

15. Refer to the Managerial Application "Does Effective Total Quality Management Require Nontraditional Performance Measures?" on page 425. Why do critics of

conventional management accounting systems contend that new approaches to management accounting and control are required?

16. Consider your campus bookstore. Who do you think are the stakeholders? What do you think are the critical success factors?

17. What are three specific measures of customer satisfaction for McDonald's?

18. What are three companies that should be particularly concerned with environmental performance measures? Why?

EXERCISES

Solutions to even-numbered exercises are at the end of this chapter after the problems.

19. **Balanced scorecard.** Write a report to the manager of a manufacturing company indicating why you think the use of a balanced scorecard for production-level employees will not work.

20. **Benchmarks.** Match the following specific measurement to its benchmark category.
    a. On-time delivery to customer   1. Employee performance
    b. Percentage of defective raw materials 2. Product performance
    c. Number of employee sick days   3. Supplier performance
    d. Maintenance response time   4. Support performance

21. **Benchmarks.** Match the following specific measurement to its benchmark category.
    a. On-time delivery of materials   1. Employee performance
    b. Percentage defective in process units 2. Product performance
    c. Employee turnover   3. Supplier performance
    d. Account report generation time   4. Support performance

22. **Performance measures.** Observe the operations of a retail clothing or sporting goods store. What is an important nonfinancial performance measure for the store?

23. **Functional measures.** Refer to Exhibit 12.5 on page 425. For each category of functional measures, such as "accounting quality" and "forecasting quality," give one more specific measurement that is not already listed.

24. **Production cycle time and efficiency.** A manufacturing company has the following average times:

Transporting products	2 hrs.
Product production	6 hrs.
Inspection	1 hr.
Inventory	24 hrs.

Calculate the production cycle efficiency.

25. **Production cycle time and efficiency.** A manufacturing company has the following average times:

Transporting products	.5 days
Product production	2 days
Inspection	.25 days
Inventory	5 days

Calculate the production cycle efficiency.

PROBLEMS

26. **Worker involvement.** Refer to Exhibit 12.6 on page 427. List three more measures of worker involvement and commitment. How would you use the information provided by the measures to improve worker involvement?

27. **Mission statement.** Write a report to the manager of a hospital indicating what factors you believe should be included in the mission statement.

28. **Benchmarks.** Write a report to the CEO recommending specific benchmark measurements for the Jeep motor vehicle division. Include specific competitors against whom to measure.

29. **Functional measures.** Write a report to the president of a bank recommending the use of functional measures of performance. Give specific examples of how they can be used to improve performance.

30. **Performance measures.** Individually or in groups, interview the manager of any organization that has employees. Does the manager use financial and/or nonfinancial measures? Why did the manager choose those particular performance measures?

31. **Performance measures.** Individually or in groups, interview a manager of a local retail store, for example, a store that sells sporting goods or clothing. Ask the manager what nonfinancial performance measures (such as measures of customer satisfaction) are used for the store. How is the measurement process done? By questionnaire? By measuring repeat business? By keeping track of complaints? Write a report to your instructor summarizing the results of your interview.

32. **Worker involvement.** Individually or in groups, interview a manager in any organization that has employees. Ask the manager how involved the organization's employees are in creating ideas for improving performance. Would the manager like the employees to be more involved than they currently are? Why or why not? Write a report to your instructor summarizing the results of your interview.

33. **Performance measures.** Monterey Corporation makes decorative clocks set in stained glass. Each month the controller prepares a report that is sent to corporate headquarters. Here are data compiled in these reports for the first six months of the year.

Performance Report
Monterey Corporation

	Jan	Feb	Mar	Apr	May	June
Units sold	110	120	160	140	190	210
Percentage of orders filled	100%	100%	100%	100%	100%	96%
Number of defective units, in process	5	15	17	20	30	30
Number of units returned because of defects	0	0	0	1	2	3
Number of late deliveries	0	0	2	0	15	2

a. Write a report to the company president evaluating the plant's performance.

    b. If you identify any problems in your report, indicate possible actions to correct the problems.

34. **Performance measures.** Miami Corporation produces weather gauges. Every week, the controller prepares a production efficiency report for management. The data compiled for the past six weeks follow:

Production Efficiency Report
Miami Corporation

	Week					
	1	**2**	**3**	**4**	**5**	**6**
Units sold	1,100	1,200	1,000	1,200	1,400	1,500
Production cycle efficiency	92%	90%	94%	88%	85%	85%
Percentage of on-time deliveries	99%	97%	98%	100%	94%	91%
Number of defective units returned	50	52	60	50	60	90

    a. Write a memo to the company president evaluating performance.

    b. If you identify any problems in your report, suggest ways to improve performance.

SUGGESTED SOLUTIONS TO EVEN-NUMBERED EXERCISES

20. **Benchmarks.**
   a. On-time delivery to customer.   2. Product performance.
   b. Percentage defective raw materials.   3. Supplier performance.
   c. Number of employee sick days.   1. Employee performance.
   d. Maintenance response time.   4. Support performance.

22. **Performance measures.**

Answers will vary, but may include any of the performance measures listed in the illustrations.

24. **Production cycle time and efficiency.**

$$\text{Production Cycle Efficiency} = \frac{6 \text{ hrs.}}{2 \text{ hrs.} + 6 \text{ hrs.} + 1 \text{ hr.} + 24 \text{ hrs.}}$$

$$= \frac{6 \text{ hrs.}}{33 \text{ hrs.}}$$

$$= .18$$

CHAPTER 13

DIVISIONAL PERFORMANCE MEASURES AND INCENTIVES

1. Identify the benefits and disadvantages of decentralization.
2. Know the complexities of using return on investment as a divisional performance measure.
3. Apply differential analysis to make-or-buy decisions with different transfer prices.
4. Discuss transfer pricing issues and methods.
5. Discuss multinational transfer prices.
6. Identify types of costs to be considered in measuring division operating costs.
7. Identify issues in measuring the investment base for return on investment calculation.
8. Know the contribution approach alternative to return on investment for division performance measurement.
9. Calculate return on investment and identify shortcomings of the measure.
10. Calculate residual income.

Companies like Coca-Cola, McDonald's, and IBM have multiple divisions. Central corporate management sets broad corporate policies, establishes long-range plans, raises capital, and conducts other coordinating activities. But corporate management must oversee hundreds of corporate affiliates and divisions. How do companies like these measure and control the performance of their divisions in such widely diverse and geographically dispersed operating environments?

433

Such firms rely heavily on their accounting systems to measure performance and to help control and coordinate their activities. This chapter discusses concepts and methods of measuring performance and controlling activities in multidivision companies. These concepts and methods are used extensively in both manufacturing and nonmanufacturing organizations.

DIVISIONAL ORGANIZATION AND PERFORMANCE

The term *division* means different things in different companies. Some companies use the term when referring to segments organized according to product groupings, whereas other companies use it when referring to geographic areas served. We use the term **division** to refer to a segment that conducts both production and marketing activities.

A division may be either a **profit center,** responsible for both revenues and operating costs, or an **investment center,** responsible for assets in addition to revenues and operating costs. Many companies treat the division almost as an autonomous company. Headquarters provides funds for its divisions, much as shareholders and bondholders provide funds for the company.

A partial organization chart for Honeywell, Incorporated, appears in Exhibit 13.1. This chart shows how the company's divisions fit into the entire organization.

EXHIBIT 13.1

HONEYWELL, INCORPORATED
Partial Organization Chart

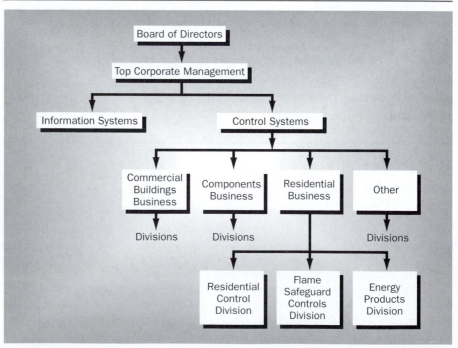

Source: Honeywell annual report.

The organization chart in Exhibit 13.1 presents only a small part of this complex organization. Corporate executives hold managers of divisions responsible for revenues, costs, and assets invested in the divisions and groups. Corporate management holds most operating units below the division level responsible for either revenues or costs alone. Performance measures often are calculated based on profit, revenues minus costs, and return on investment, which are affected by management policies regarding transfer pricing, measurement of costs, and measurement of investment base.

THE NATURE OF DIVISIONALIZED ORGANIZATIONS

Top managers delegate or **decentralize** authority and responsibility. The major advantages of decentralization follow:

1. Decentralization allows local personnel to respond quickly to a changing environment.
2. Decentralization frees top management from detailed operating decisions.
3. Decentralization divides large, complex problems into manageable pieces.
4. Decentralization helps train managers and provides a basis for evaluating their decision-making performance.
5. Decentralization motivates: Ambitious managers will be frustrated if they implement only the decisions of others. Delegation allows managers to make their own decisions.

Decentralization has disadvantages, however. Local managers may not act to achieve the overall goals of the organization. For example, a division manager may decide to purchase materials from an outside supplier even though another division of the firm could produce the materials at a lower incremental cost using currently idle facilities. Top management must be alert to situations where the benefits of decentralized authority and the possible conflicts between the goals of a division and those of the organization as a whole require trade-offs. Thus, divisional planning and control systems attempt to create **behavioral congruence** (or **goal congruence**) to encourage division managers to act in ways consistent with organizational goals.[1]

Consider the following interdivisional conflict. Assume a division purchased materials externally rather than from a division inside the company with idle capacity. By purchasing from an outside source, the company earned lower combined profits from the two divisions than if it purchased the materials from the division inside the company. Should the performance measure for each division reflect the results of its actual transactions? Or should the cost of idle capacity in the one division be charged against the profits of the other division? These questions are not easy to answer. The accounting system needs to inform top management of situations in which actions of individual divisions hurt overall company performance.

---

[1]For an expanded discussion of these points, see the classic book by David Solomons, *Divisional Performance Measurement and Control* (Homewood, Ill.: Irwin, 1968), or the book by Ken Merchant, *Reward Results: Motivating Profit Center Managers* (Boston, Mass.: Harvard Business School Press, 1989).

SEPARATING A MANAGER'S PERFORMANCE EVALUATION FROM DIVISIONAL PERFORMANCE EVALUATION

In general, top management should distinguish between the measure of an organizational division's performance and that of the division manager's performance. Managers often perform well despite the division's poor performance because of factors outside the manager's control.

For example, if a natural disaster occurred that affected the cost of materials, this would be outside the control of the manager. During the same period the manager improved efficiency in the use of the materials, cutting waste by 5 percent. However, if this is not enough to compensate for the higher price of the materials, it will still negatively affect the performance measurement of the division and hence the manager, even though efficiency was improved. Many measures used to evaluate divisions can be adjusted to account for the controllability of the revenues, costs, and investments by the manager.

RETURN ON INVESTMENT AS THE PERFORMANCE MEASURE

Because management expects each division to contribute to the company's profits, managers commonly use divisional operating profit to measure performance. Divisional operating profit by itself, however, does not provide a basis for measuring a division's performance in generating a return on the funds invested in the division. For example, the fact that Division A reported an operating profit of $50,000 does not necessarily mean that it was more successful than Division B, which had an operating profit of $40,000. The difference between these profit levels could be entirely attributable to a difference in the size of the divisions. Management must therefore use some means to relate the division profit measure to the amount of capital invested in the division. Management commonly achieves a comparable statistic by measuring the division **return on investment,** or **ROI,** calculated as follows:

$$\text{Division Return on Investment (ROI)} = \frac{\text{Division Operating Profit}}{\text{Division Investment}}$$

$$= \frac{\text{Division Revenue} - \text{Division Operating Costs}}{\text{Division Investment}}$$

In the preceding example if management invested $500,000 and $250,000 in Division A and Division B, respectively, the ROIs would be 10 percent (= $50,000/$500,000) and 16 percent (= $40,000/$250,000). Thus Division B earned a higher profit given its investment base than Division A, even though Division A generated a larger absolute amount of profit.

The manager must answer several important questions before applying ROI as a control measure:

1. How does the firm measure revenues, particularly when it transfers part of a division's output to another division rather than selling it externally?
2. Which costs does the firm deduct in measuring divisional operating costs—only those that the division can control, or also a portion of allocated central corporate administration and staff costs?

3. How does the firm measure investment: total assets or net assets; at historical cost or some measure of current cost?

We consider these questions in the following sections.

TRANSFER PRICING: MEASURING DIVISIONAL REVENUE AND COSTS FOR TRANSACTIONS INSIDE THE ORGANIZATION

When goods or services are transferred from one unit of an organization to another, the transaction is recorded in the accounting records. The value assigned to the transaction is called the *transfer price*. Considerable discretion can be used in putting a value on the transaction because this exchange takes place inside the organization. Transfer prices are widely used for decision making, product costing, and performance evaluation; hence, it is important to consider alternative transfer pricing methods and their advantages and disadvantages.

APPLYING DIFFERENTIAL ANALYSIS TO TRANSFER PRICING

To help you understand the issues involved with transfer pricing, we present two applications of differential analysis to transfer pricing. We provide these examples before discussing alternative ways that managers "solve" transfer pricing problems both to inform you about the nature of the problem and to develop examples for use in our later case.

Assume E-Z Computing has two decentralized divisions, Hardware and Marketing. Marketing (the buying division) has always purchased a particular mouse from Hardware at $50 per unit. Hardware (the selling division) is considering raising the price to $60 per unit. For now, don't worry about how the transfer price is set, just take it as a given. Later we discuss methods of setting the transfer price.

Assume the Hardware Division's costs are as follows:

Variable costs per unit: $50

Annual fixed costs: $10,000

Marketing handles the promotion and distribution of the mouse it purchases from Hardware and sells the items for $100 each. No additional variable costs are incurred by Marketing. Marketing's annual fixed costs total $5,000. Annual sales of these units is 1,500.

Each of the following situations is a type of make-or-buy decision, where either Hardware makes the mouse or Marketing buys the mouse from outside suppliers.

Case 1: Transfer Pricing When Outside Suppliers Are Available and Hardware Division *Below Capacity*.

Case 2: Transfer Pricing When Outside Suppliers Are Available and Hardware Division *At Capacity*.

Case 1: Transfer Pricing When Hardware Division Is Below Capacity
Use the data for E-Z Computing and assume Marketing can purchase units from an

outside supplier for $60 per unit. *If Marketing buys from an outside supplier, the facilities Hardware uses to manufacture these units would remain idle.* Which option yields the highest total company operating profit for E-Z Computing: transfer from Hardware or purchase from an outside supplier?

As shown in Exhibit 13.2, the result of purchasing units from an outside supplier is a loss in companywide operating profit of $15,000. A loss occurs because the differential cost to make the units is $50 per unit. The differential cost to buy is $60 per unit. The cost savings for making over buying is $15,000 [= ($60 − $50) × 1,500 units].

Case 2: Transfer Pricing When Hardware Division Is At Capacity   Using the same data as above for E-Z Computing, let's make one change in our assumptions. Assume Hardware does not have idle capacity if Marketing buys from an outside supplier. Instead, *if Marketing buys from an outside supplier, Hardware can sell all its units to outside customers at $60 per unit (i.e., Hardware is operating at capacity).* Which option yields the highest total company operating profit for E-Z Computing: transfer from Hardware or purchase from outside supplier?

As shown in Exhibit 13.3, it doesn't matter whether Marketing buys from Hardware or from the outside. All parties are indifferent to purchasing inside or outside

---

EXHIBIT 13.2

Case 1: Outside Suppliers Available and Hardware Division *Below* Capacity

Transfer price of $50 per unit	Hardware	Marketing
Sales:		
$50 × 1,500 (sales to Marketing)	$75,000	
$100 × 1,500 (sales to outsiders)		$150,000
Variable Costs:		
$50 × 1,500 (Hardware's costs)	75,000	
$50 × 1,500 (transfer from Hardware)		75,000
Fixed Costs	10,000	5,000
Operating Profit	($10,000)	$ 70,000
Total Company Operating Profit	$60,000	

Purchase externally for $60 per unit	Hardware	Marketing
Sales:		
$100 × 1,500		$150,000
Variable Costs:		
$60 × 1,500		90,000
Fixed Costs	$10,000	5,000
Operating Profit	($10,000)	$ 55,000
Total Company Operating Profit	$45,000	

EXHIBIT 13.3

Case with Outside Suppliers Available and Selling Division *At* Capacity

Transfer price of $60 per unit	Hardware		Marketing
Sales:			
$60 × 1,500 (sales to Marketing)	$90,000		
$100 × 1,500			$150,000
Variable Costs:			
$50 × 1,500	75,000		
$60 × 1,500 (transfer from Hardware)			90,000
Fixed Costs	10,000		5,000
Operating Profit	$ 5,000		$ 55,000
Total Company Operating Profit		$60,000	

Purchase externally for $60 per unit	Hardware		Marketing
Sales:			
$60 × 1,500 (sales to outsiders)	$90,000		
$100 × 1,500			$150,000
Variable Costs:			
$50 × 1,500	75,000		
$60 × 1,500 (purchase from outsiders)			90,000
Fixed Costs	10,000		5,000
Operating Profit	$ 5,000		$ 55,000
Total Company Operating Profit		$60,000	

the organization. Hardware's profits are $5,000 either way, Marketing's profits are $55,000 either way, and E-Z's profits are $60,000 either way.

ALTERNATIVE WAYS TO SET TRANSFER PRICES

Management's problem is to set transfer prices so the buyer and seller have goal congruence with respect to the organization's goals. Although there is no easy solution to the transfer pricing problem, there are three general alternative ways to set transfer prices:

1. Top management intervenes to set the transfer price for each transaction between divisions.
2. Top management establishes transfer price policies that divisions follow.
3. Division managers negotiate transfer prices among themselves.

Each of these approaches has advantages and disadvantages. We discuss these alternatives in the next sections.

TOP MANAGEMENT INTERVENTION

The disadvantage of top management intervention is that top management may become swamped with pricing disputes, and division managers will lose the flexibility and other advantages of autonomous decision making. Thus, direct intervention may give the right transfer price for a particular transaction, but it reduces the benefits from decentralization.

As long as transactions between divisions are infrequent, the benefits of direct intervention may outweigh the costs. However, if transfer transactions are common, direct intervention can be costly by requiring substantial top-management involvement in decisions that should be made at the divisional level.

CENTRALLY ESTABLISHED TRANSFER PRICE POLICIES

A transfer pricing policy should allow divisional autonomy yet encourage managers to pursue corporate goals consistent with their own personal goals. Additionally, the use of transfer prices to set the selling division's revenue and the buying division's cost should be compatible with the company's performance evaluation system.

The Economic Transfer Pricing Rule

General Rule: Differential Outlay Cost plus Opportunity Cost

The **economic transfer pricing rule** for making transfers to maximize a company's profits is to *transfer at the differential outlay cost to the selling division (typically variable costs) plus the opportunity cost to the company of making the internal transfers ($0 if the seller has idle capacity, or selling price minus variable costs if the seller is operating at capacity).*

Consider the E-Z Computing example to demonstrate the economic transfer pricing rule. The seller, the Hardware Division, could sell in outside markets to Computer Warehouse, a discount store, for $60 per mouse and has a variable cost of $50 per mouse, which we shall assume is its differential cost.

Now recall Case 1 discussed earlier in this chapter. The seller (Hardware Division) is operating below capacity, and has no opportunity cost of the internal transfer because no outside sale is forgone. In this case the transfer price should be $50 per mouse. If the seller is operating below capacity, then the seller is indifferent between providing the product and receiving a transfer price equal to the seller's differential outlay cost or not providing the product at all.

If the Hardware Division received a price of $50 for the product, then it would be indifferent between producing and selling it or not. The buyer, the Marketing Division, pays $50, which is the seller's differential cost of producing the mouse. It is in E-Z's interest for the Marketing Division to pay the Hardware Division's cost of producing the mouse and not more.

Charging a transfer price above the differential cost plus opportunity cost when the selling division is under capacity can lead to incorrect decisions as demonstrated now. Assume the Hardware Division insists on a transfer price of $58 per mouse, because they see no reason to produce at a transfer price of $50 as it will not increase their profits. An outside company offers to place an order for a few units of the mouse with the Marketing Department at a price of $57. Hardware would still be under capacity even with this special order. The Marketing Division will turn down the order because this is less than the differential cost to the Marketing Division of $58 (the transfer price). The correct decision is to accept the order because the $57 price is more than the differential cost which is only $50. Had the transfer price been set correctly at the $50 differential cost the Marketing Division would have made the correct decision.

Now recall Case 2. The seller is operating at capacity and would have to give up one unit of outside sales for every unit transferred internally. In Case 2, the opportunity cost of transferring the product to a division inside the company is the forgone contribution of selling the unit in an outside market. Consequently, the optimal transfer price would be $60 for the at-capacity case. Exhibit 13.4 summarizes these cases.

If the selling division (the Hardware Division in our example) is operating at capacity, then it is indifferent between selling in the outside market for $60 or transferring internally at $60. Consequently, as a rule of thumb, the economic transfer pricing rule can be implemented as follows:

1. If the selling division is operating below capacity, it should transfer at the differential cost of production (variable cost).
2. If the selling division is operating at capacity, it should transfer at market price.

In both the below-capacity and at-capacity cases, the selling division is no worse off if the internal transfer is made.

The selling division does not earn a contribution on the transaction in the below-capacity case, however. Further, it earns only the same contribution for the internal transfer as it would for a sale to the outside market in the at-capacity case. Thus, the general rule stated above is optimal for the company but does not benefit the selling division for an internal transfer. (For practical purposes, we assume that the selling division will transfer internally if it is indifferent between an internal transfer and an external sale.)

TRANSFER PRICES BASED ON MARKET PRICE

Externally based **market price-based transfer pricing** is generally considered the best basis when there is a competitive market for the product and market prices are

EXHIBIT 13.4			
Application of the Economic Transfer Pricing Rule			
	Differential Outlay Cost	+ Opportunity Cost of Transferring Internally	= Transfer Price
If the seller (that is, Hardware Division) has idle capacity	$50	+ -0-	= $50
If the seller has no idle capacity	$50	+ $10 ($60 selling price − $50 variable cost)	= $60

readily available. It is considered a good estimation of differential cost plus opportunity cost, as opportunity cost is based on what can be earned from selling to external markets. An advantage of using market prices in a competitive market is that both the buying and selling divisions can buy and sell as many units as they want at the market price. Managers of both buying and selling divisions are indifferent between trading with each other or with outsiders. From the company's perspective, this is fine as long as the selling division (the Hardware Division in our example) is operating at capacity.

TRANSFER PRICES BASED ON COSTS

Full-absorption costs   Although the rule "transfer at differential outlay cost to the selling division plus the opportunity cost to the company of making the internal transfer" assumes the company has a measure of differential or variable cost. This is not always the case. Consequently, full-absorption costs are sometimes used in manufacturing firms.

Activity-based costing   Many companies are implementing activity-based costing to improve the accuracy of costs in cost-based transfer pricing. One of the primary motives for Deere and Co., maker of John Deere equipment, to develop activity-based costing was to improve the accuracy of cost numbers used for transfer pricing.

Cost-plus transfers   We also find companies using **cost-plus transfer pricing** based on either variable costs or full-absorption costs. These methods generally apply a normal markup to costs as a surrogate for market prices when intermediate market prices are not available.

Standard costs or actual costs   If actual costs are used as a basis for the transfer, any variances or inefficiencies in the selling division are passed along to the buying division. The problem of isolating the variances that have been transferred to subsequent buyer divisions becomes extremely complex. To promote responsibility in the selling division, standard costs, not actual costs are usually used as a basis for transfer pricing in cost-based systems.

For example, suppose E-Z Computers transferred based on variable costs. The standard variable cost of producing the mouse is $50, but the actual cost of producing it turns out to be $52 because of inefficiencies in the Hardware Division. Should this inefficiency be passed on to the buying division? The answer is usually *no* to give the Hardware Division incentives to be efficient. In these cases, companies will use standard costs for the transfer price. If standards are out of date or otherwise do not reflect reasonable estimates of costs, then the actual cost may be a better measure to use in the transfer price.

OTHER MOTIVATIONAL ASPECTS
OF TRANSFER PRICING POLICIES

When the transfer pricing rule does not give the supplier a profit on the transaction, motivational problems can arise. For example, if transfers are made at differential cost, the supplier earns no contribution toward profits on the transferred goods. Then, the transfer policy does not motivate the supplier to transfer internally because there is no likely profit from internal transfers. This situation can be remedied in several ways.

A supplier whose transfers are almost all internal is usually organized as a cost center. The center manager is normally held responsible for costs, not for revenues. Hence, the transfer price does not affect the manager's performance measures. In companies where such a supplier is a profit center, the artificial nature of the transfer price should be taken into consideration when evaluating the results of that center's operations.

A supplying center that does business with both internal and external customers could be set up as a profit center for external business when the manager has price-setting power, and as a cost center for internal transfers when the manager does not have price-setting power. Performance on external business could be measured as if the center were a profit center, while performance on internal business could be measured as if the center were a cost center.

Dual transfer prices   A **dual transfer pricing** system could be installed to provide the selling division with a profit but charge the buying division with costs only. That is, the buyer could be charged the cost of the unit, however cost might be determined, and the selling division could be credited with cost plus some profit allowance. The difference could be accounted for by a special centralized account. This system would preserve cost data for subsequent buyer divisions, and it would encourage internal transfers by providing a profit on such transfers for the selling divisions.

Other incentives for internal transfers   We have seen a few companies using dual transfer prices to encourage internal transfers. However, there are other ways to encourage internal transfers. For example, many companies recognize internal transfers and incorporate them explicitly in their reward systems. Other companies base part of a supplying manager's bonus on the purchasing center's profits. These are ways of creating incentives for managers to transfer internally in organizational settings.

DIVISION MANAGERS NEGOTIATE TRANSFER PRICES

An alternative to a centrally administered transfer pricing policy is to permit managers to negotiate the price for internally transferred goods and services. Under this system, the managers involved act much the same as the managers of independent companies. The major advantage to **negotiated transfer pricing** is that it preserves the autonomy of the division managers. However, the two primary disadvantages are that a great deal of management effort may be consumed in the negotiating process, and the final price and its implications for performance measurement may depend more on the manager's ability to negotiate than on what's best for the company.

In the E-Z Computers case, the two managers have room to negotiate the price between $50 and $60. The two managers may choose to "split the difference" or develop some other negotiating strategy.

PROBLEM 13.1 FOR SELF-STUDY

Transfer pricing. The Nykee Shoe Company has two divisions: Production and Marketing. Production manufactures Nykee shoes, which it sells to both the Marketing Division and to other retailers (the latter under a different brand name). Marketing operates several small shoe stores in shopping centers. Marketing sells both Nykee and other brands. Relevant facts for Production are as follows:

Production is operating far below its capacity.

Sales price to outsiders	$	28.50 per pair
Variable cost to produce	$	18.00 per pair
Fixed costs	$100,000.00 per month	

The following data pertain to the sale of Nykee shoes by Marketing: Marketing is operating far below its capacity.

Sales price	$40 per pair
Variable marketing costs	$1 per pair

The company's variable manufacturing and marketing costs are differential to this decision, while fixed manufacturing and marketing costs are not.

a. What is the minimum price that can be charged by the Marketing Division for the shoes and still cover the company's differential manufacturing and marketing costs?

b. What is the appropriate transfer price for this decision?

c. If the transfer price was set at $28.50, what effect would this have on the minimum price set by the Marketing manager?

d. How would your answer to **b** change if the Production Division was operating at full capacity?

The solution to this self-study problem is at the end of the chapter on page 456.

GLOBAL TRANSFER PRICING PRACTICES

In a survey of corporate practices, shown in Exhibit 13.5, the author reported that 45 percent of the U.S. companies surveyed used a cost-based transfer pricing system. Thirty-three percent used a market price-based system, and 22 percent used a negotiated system. Similar results were found for companies in Canada and Japan.

Generally, we find that when negotiated prices are used, the prices negotiated are between the market price at the upper limit and some measure of cost at the lower limit.

Is there an optimal transfer pricing policy that dominates all others? The answer is no. An established policy will, most likely, be imperfect in the sense that it will not always work to induce the economically optimal outcome. However, as

EXHIBIT 13.5

Survey of Corporate Transfer-price Practices

Method Used	United States[a]	Canada[b]	Japan[c]
Cost based	45%	47%	47%
Market based	33	35	34
Negotiated transfer prices	22	18	19
Total	100%	100%	100%

Note: Companies using other methods were omitted from this illustration. These companies were 2 percent or less of the total.

[a]Source: S. Borkowski, "Environmental and Organizational Factors Affecting Transfer Pricing: A Survey," *Journal of Management Accounting Research,* Fall 1990.

[b]Source: R. Tang, "Canadian Transfer Pricing Practices," *CA Magazine,* March 1980.

[c]Source: R. Tang, C. Walter, and R. Raymond, "Transfer Pricing—Japanese vs. American Style," *Management Accounting,* January 1979.

with other management decisions, the cost of any system must be weighed against the benefits of the system. Improving a transfer pricing policy beyond some point (say, to obtain better measures of variable costs and market prices) will result in the costs of the system exceeding the benefits. As a result, management tends to settle for a system that seems to work reasonably well rather than devise a "textbook" perfect system.

MULTINATIONAL AND MULTISTATE TRANSFER PRICING

In international transactions, transfer prices may affect tax liabilities, royalties, and other payments because of different laws in different countries (or states). Since tax rates are different in different countries, companies have incentives to set transfer prices that will increase revenues (and profits) in low-tax countries and increase costs (thereby reducing profits) in high-tax countries.

These same issues apply to interstate transactions. Companies have incentives to transfer profits from high-tax states like Massachusetts and California to low-tax states like New Hampshire and Nevada.

Tax avoidance by foreign companies using inflated transfer prices has been a major political issue in the United States. Foreign companies who sell goods to their U.S. subsidiaries at inflated transfer prices artificially reduce the profit of the U.S. subsidiaries. According to some political observers, the United States could collect as much as $9 billion to $13 billion per year in additional taxes if transfer pricing was calculated according to U.S. tax laws. (Many foreign companies dispute this claim.)

To understand the effects of transfer pricing on taxes, consider the case of the Nehru Jacket Corp. The Nehru Jacket Corp.'s facility in Country N imports materials from the company's Country I facility. The tax rate in Country N is 70 percent, while the tax rate in Country I is 40 percent.

During the current year, Nehru incurred production costs of $2 million in Country I. Costs incurred in Country N, aside from the cost of the jackets, amounted to

$6 million. Sales revenues in Country N were $24 million. Similar goods imported by other companies in Country N would have cost an equivalent of $3 million. However, Nehru Jacket Corp. points out that because of its special control over its operations in Country I and the special approach it uses to manufacture its goods, the appropriate transfer price is $10 million. What would Nehru Jacket Corp.'s total tax liability in both jurisdictions be if it used the $3 million transfer price? What would the liability be if it used the $10 million transfer price?

Assuming the $3 million transfer price, the tax liabilities are computed as follows:

	Country I	Country N
Revenues	$3,000,000	$24,000,000
Third-Party Costs	2,000,000	6,000,000
Transferred Goods Costs		3,000,000
Taxable Income	1,000,000	15,000,000
Tax Rate	× 40%	× 70%
Tax Liability	$ 400,000	$10,500,000
Total Tax Liability	$10,900,000	

Assuming the $10 million transfer price, the liabilities are computed as follows:

	Country I	Country N
Revenues	$10,000,000	$24,000,000
Third-Party Costs	2,000,000	6,000,000
Transferred Goods Costs		10,000,000
Taxable Income	8,000,000	8,000,000
Tax Rate	× 40%	× 70%
Tax Liability	$ 3,200,000	$ 5,600,000
Total Tax Liability	$8,800,000	

Nehru Jacket Corp. can save $2,100,000 in taxes simply by changing its transfer price!

To say the least, international (and state) taxing authorities look closely at transfer prices when examining the tax returns of companies engaged in related-party transactions that cross national (and state) borders. Companies must frequently have adequate support for the use of the transfer price that they have chosen for such a situation, as discussed in the Managerial Application feature on page 447.

PROBLEM 13.2 FOR SELF-STUDY

Multinational transfer pricing. Refer to the information for Nehru Jacket Corp. in the text. Assume the tax rate for both Country I and Country N is 40 percent. What would the tax liability be for Nehru Jacket Corp. if the transfer price were set at $3 million? At $10 million?

The solution to this self-study problem is at the end of the chapter on page 456.

MANAGERIAL APPLICATION

Just-in-Time Production in Japan and the Internal Revenue Service in the United States

A Japanese motorcycle manufacturer that used just-in-time production methods for its manufacturing facility in Japan sold its motorcycles to its U.S. subsidiary using full-cost as the transfer price. During a recent period, demand in the United States for motorcycles dropped. At one point the U.S. subsidiary found itself with more than a year's supply of motorcycles on hand. Meanwhile, the Japanese manufacturing plant was reluctant to reduce production below its efficient operating level, and, because it followed the just-in-time philosophy, it did not stockpile finished goods inventory in Japan.

As inventories grew at the U.S. subsidiary, so did expenses to store and sell the mounting inventory of products. The U.S. subsidiary showed declining profits and eventually incurred losses. The U.S. Internal Revenue Service claimed the Japanese manufacturer should have lowered its transfer price and/or stopped shipping motorcycles to the U.S. subsidiary. According to the IRS, the Japanese manufacturer should bear some of the costs of the U.S. subsidiary's high inventory levels. The Japanese manufacturer disagreed. The case was settled out of court.

Source: Based on the authors' research.

MEASURING DIVISION OPERATING COSTS

In measuring divisional operating costs, management must decide how to treat the following costs: (1) controllable, direct operating costs; (2) noncontrollable, direct operating costs; (3) controllable, indirect operating costs; and (4) noncontrollable, indirect operating costs. Direct versus indirect refers to whether the cost associates directly with the division; controllable versus noncontrollable refers to whether the division manager can affect the cost. Exhibit 13.6 shows examples of each. In each case it must be decided whether or not to include costs as costs to the division in calculating division operating profit for performance evaluation of the division and of the division manager.

EXHIBIT 13.6

Examples of Direct (Indirect) and Controllable (Noncontrollable) Costs

	Direct	Indirect
Controllable	Labor used in the division's production	Costs of providing centralized services, such as data processing and employee training, which the division's use partially affects
Noncontrollable	Salary of the division manager (controlled by top management)	Company president's salary

DIRECT COSTS

Management virtually always deducts a division's direct operating costs from divisional revenues in measuring divisional operating profits. From top management's perspective, any cost necessary for that division to operate is a direct cost, even if the division manager cannot control the cost. If top management believes that division managers should not be held responsible for things outside their control, it can separate the measure of costs assigned to a *division* from the costs assigned to a division *manager*—the latter measure could exclude direct costs of the division that the division manager cannot control (for example, the division manager's salary).

INDIRECT, CONTROLLABLE OPERATING COSTS

Divisions can at least partially control indirect, controllable costs. Firms usually centralize particular services because of economies of scale. In some companies, costs would exceed benefits if each division had its own legal staff, research department, data-processing department, and so forth.

For example, many companies have centralized employee training departments. Should management charge divisions for sending their people to these centralized departments? As you may expect, the experiences in most companies follow fundamental laws of economics: The use of centralized services and the price charged for those services are inversely related. When companies charge a high price for employee training, people's attendance from the divisions drops, and vice versa.

Top management can use this experience to decide on the desired usage and set the price accordingly. Some companies treat centralized service departments as profit or investment centers; if so, the transfer pricing issues discussed earlier are relevant.

INDIRECT, NONCONTROLLABLE OPERATING COSTS

Indirect, noncontrollable operating costs may be necessary costs to the company (for example, the salaries and staff support of corporate top management). The most frequent arguments against allocating these costs down to divisions are based on the divisions' inability to control the amount of costs incurred.

One argument advanced for allocation is that, unless the company allocates these costs to the divisions, the divisions will underprice their products and cause the company as a whole to operate at a loss. In other words, the revenues the divisions generate would be insufficient to cover both the direct operating costs of the divisions and the indirect operating costs incurred at central headquarters.

A top manager of a retail company told us that central headquarters' costs were allocated to the stores to keep them aware of these costs. "We want out store managers to recognize that it's not enough for stores to make a profit for the company to be profitable." The corporate manager went on to say that part of a store manager's bonus was based on the store's profit after central headquarters' costs had been allocated to stores. "This makes them very aware of central headquarters' costs, and it makes us [top management] sensitive to their criticisms about administrative costs" (that is, central headquarters' costs).

MEASURING THE INVESTMENT IN DIVISIONS

Most companies use some measure of capital employed or invested in each division when calculating return on investment (ROI). In this section we discuss (1) what assets firms include in the investment base and (2) what valuation basis firms use.

ASSETS INCLUDED IN THE INVESTMENT BASE

Management obviously should include assets physically located in a division and used only in the division's operations in the investment base. More difficult problems arise with assets shared among divisions and assets that centralized services departments acquire (for example, buildings and equipment used in personnel training). Management often allocates the cost of a shared manufacturing plant between divisions.

VALUATION OF ASSETS IN THE INVESTMENT BASE

Once the firm chooses the assets in the investment base, it must assign them a monetary value. Most firms use acquisition cost as the valuation basis. Management can obtain the necessary amounts directly from the company's accounts.

The use of book values of assets, particularly fixed assets, in the ROI denominator can have undesirable results. The manager of a division with old, low-cost, and almost fully depreciated assets may be reluctant to replace the assets with newer, more efficient, but more costly assets. Replacing old assets with new, more costly ones decreases the numerator—operating profits—of the ROI calculation because of increased depreciation charges. It also increases the denominator—cost of total assets—of the ROI calculation. Each of these effects reduces calculated ROI.

If use of book values in the investment base affects divisional investment behavior this way, management may deal with the problem in two possible ways. One, they may state all assets at gross book value rather than at net book value. This approach states assets at full acquisition cost regardless of age. Another approach is to state assets at their current replacement cost or net realizable value.

In general, the older the assets, the higher the ROI under net book value compared to gross book value. If replacement cost increases over time, ROI is higher under historical cost compared to current replacement cost.

CONTRIBUTION APPROACH TO DIVISION REPORTING

In previous sections, we discussed some of the factors you should consider in calculating ROI. In this section, we discuss several additional considerations in using and interpreting ROI as a basis for evaluating divisional performance.

We suggest that a firm should decide how it is going to calculate ROI and then use it consistently. Exhibit 13.7 presents a divisional performance report in a format that facilitates a variety of uses. For example, management could use the report to evaluate the division and its manager's performance without regard to costs allocated to

EXHIBIT 13.7

The Contribution Approach to Division Reporting (all dollar amounts in thousands)

	Company as a Whole	Company Breakdown into Two Divisions	
		Division A	Division B
Revenues	$6,500	$2,500	$4,000
Variable Manufacturing Cost of Goods Sold	2,300	800	1,500
Manufacturing Contribution Margin	$4,200	$1,700	$2,500
Variable Selling and Administrative Costs	600	200	400
Contribution Margin	$3,600	$1,500	$2,100
Fixed Costs Directly Attributable to the Division	2,400	900	1,500
Division Contribution to Unallocated Costs and Profit	$1,200	$ 600	$ 600
Unallocated Costs	800[a]		
Operating Profit	$ 400		

	Division A	Further Breakdown of Division A into Two Product Lines	
		Product 1	Product 2
Revenues	$2,500	$1,300	$1,200
Variable Manufacturing Cost of Goods Sold	800	500	300
Manufacturing Contribution Margin	$1,700	$ 800	$ 900
Variable Selling and Administrative Costs	200	100	100
Contribution Margin	$1,500	$ 700	$ 800
Fixed Costs Directly Attributable to the Division	475	275	200
Division Contribution to Unallocated Costs and Profit	$1,025	$ 425	$ 600
Unallocated Costs	425[a]		
Operating Profit	$ 600		

[a]These costs are not direct costs of the division or product line and could be allocated only by an arbitrary allocation method.

divisions or to product lines. Further, the report provides data about the division's performance after the firm allocates all central administrative costs. Some corporate managers like to see a bottom line that takes into account all costs, even indirect costs that accounting has allocated to divisions.

COMPONENTS OF RETURN ON INVESTMENT

The rate of return on investment has two components: profit margin percentage and investment (or asset) turnover ratio.

Return on Investment = Profit Margin Percentage $\times$ Investment Turnover Ratio

$$\frac{\text{Profit Margin}}{\text{Divisional Investment}} = \frac{\text{Profit Margin}}{\text{Divisional Revenues}} \times \frac{\text{Divisional Revenues}}{\text{Divisional Investment}}.$$

To illustrate the usefulness of dividing ROI into its components, assume the following information about Division A:

Year	Sales	Profit	Investment
1	$1,000,000	$100,000	$ 500,000
2	2,000,000	160,000	1,000,000
3	4,000,000	400,000	2,500,000

The following table shows the ROI for each of the 3 years and the associated profit margin percentages and investment turnover ratios.

Year	ROI	=	Profit Margin Percentage	×	Investment Turnover Ratio
1	20%	=	10%	×	2.0
2	16	=	8	×	2.0
3	16	=	10	×	1.6

The **profit margin percentage** indicates the portion of each dollar of revenue that is profit. Management often uses it as a measure for assessing efficiency in producing and selling goods and services. The profit margin percentage for Division A in this example decreased from 10 percent to 8 percent between Year 1 and Year 2.

The **investment turnover ratio** is the ratio of divisional sales to the investment in divisional assets. It indicates potentially useful information on how effectively the management used the capital invested in the division. Returning to the preceding example, Division A could not increase its ROI between Year 2 and Year 3, despite an increase in its profit margin percentage, because its investment turnover ratio decreased. The division could not generate $2 of revenue for each dollar invested in Year 3, as it had done in previous years.

Studying profit margin percentages and investment turnover ratios for a given division over several periods will provide more useful information than comparing these ratios for all divisions in a particular period. Some divisions, due to the nature of their activities, require more capital than others; some have higher profit margins than others.

SETTING MINIMUM DESIRED ROIs

If the ROI is to measure divisional performance effectively, management must set a standard or desired rate each period. Management usually specifies a minimum desired ROI for each division, given its particular operating characteristics. Some divisions are in more risky businesses than others; hence, management may have higher expectations for them. Some divisions have a very low investment base (for example, professional services, consulting); thus, ROI is sometimes quite high. In short, management should recognize the particular characteristics of a division in setting minimum ROIs.

RESIDUAL INCOME

Critics of ROI argue that managers may turn down investment opportunities that are above the minimum acceptable rate but below the ROI currently being earned. For example, suppose that the division currently earns

$$ROI = \frac{\$1,000,000}{\$4,000,000} = 25\%.$$

Suppose the manager has an opportunity to make an additional investment. This investment would return $400,000 per year for 5 years for a $2 million investment. At the end of 5 years, the $2 million investment would be returned. Assume that there is no inflation. The ROI each year is

$$ROI = \frac{\$400,000}{\$2,000,000} = 20\%.$$

The company desires an ROI of at least 15 percent. This investment clearly qualifies, but it would lower the investment center ROI to 23.3 percent:

$$ROI = \frac{\$1,000,000 + \$400,000}{\$4,000,000 + \$2,000,000} = 23.3\%.$$

A comparison of the old (25 percent) and new (23.3 percent) returns would imply performance has worsened; consequently a manager might decide not to make such an investment.

An alternative to ROI is **residual income (RI).** Residual income is defined as

$$\begin{matrix} \text{Residual} \\ \text{Income} \end{matrix} = \begin{matrix} \text{Division} \\ \text{Profit} \\ \text{Margin} \end{matrix} - \left(\begin{matrix} \text{Percent} \\ \text{Capital} \\ \text{Charge} \end{matrix} \times \begin{matrix} \text{Division} \\ \text{Investment} \end{matrix} \right),$$

where the percent capital charge is the minimum acceptable rate of return. The terms *division profit margin* and *division investment* are defined the same for residual income as for ROI. Residual income is similar in concept to economists' definition of profits. If the firm encourages managers to maximize RI, they have incentives to accept all projects above the minimum acceptable rate of return.

Using data from the example just discussed, we find the following:

Before the investment, the residual income is $400,000.

$$RI = \$1,000,000 - (.15 \times \$4,000,000)$$

$$= \$1,000,000 - \$600,000$$

$$= \$400,000.$$

The residual income from the additional investment is $100,000.

$$RI = \$400,000 - (.15 \times \$2,000,000)$$

$$= \$400,000 - \$300,000$$

$$= \$100,000.$$

Hence, *after the additional investment,* the residual income of the division increases to $500,000.

$$RI = (\$1,000,000 + \$400,000) - [.15 \times (\$4,000,000 + \$2,000,000)]$$

$$= \$1,400,000 - (.15 \times \$6,000,000)$$

$$= \$1,400,000 - \$900,000$$

$$= \$500,000.$$

The additional investment *increases* residual income, appropriately improving the measure of performance, whereas the use of ROI worsened the measure of performance.

Managers generally recognize this problem with ROI, and they may take it into account when a new investment lowers the ROI. This practice may explain why residual income does not dominate ROI in practice as a performance measure. Further, ROI is expressed as a percentage that managers can intuitively compare with related percentages—like the cost of capital, the prime interest rate, and the Treasury Bill rate. Most companies use ROI, but many use a combination of RI and ROI.

PROBLEM 13.3 FOR SELF-STUDY

Return on investment and residual income. The Venus Division of Hyperspace Company has assets of $2.4 billion, operating profits of $.60 billion, and a cost of capital of 20 percent.

Compute return on investment and residual income.

The solution to this self-study problem is at the end of the chapter on page 456.

SUMMARY

The following items correspond to the learning objectives presented at the beginning of the chapter.

1. **Identify the benefits and disadvantages of decentralization.** Decentralization allows local personnel to respond quickly to a changing environment, frees top management from detailed operating decisions, divides complex problems into manageable pieces, helps train managers and provide a basis for evaluating performance, and motivates managers. The disadvantage is that it may promote non-goal congruent behavior.

2. **Know the complexities of using return on investment as a divisional performance measure.** Several questions must be addressed before applying return on investment as a control measure: How does the firm measure revenues? Which costs does the firm deduct in measuring divisional operating costs? How does the firm measure investment?

3. **Apply differential analysis.** See Exhibits 13.2 through 13.4 for examples applying differential analysis to make-or-buy decisions involving transfer prices.

4. **Discuss transfer pricing rules issues and methods.** Two general rules exist when establishing a transfer price: (1) If the selling division is *operating at capacity,* the transfer price should be the market price; and (2) if the selling division *has idle capacity,* and the idle facilities cannot be used for other purposes, the transfer price should be at least the variable costs incurred to produce the goods.

5. **Discuss multinational transfer prices.** Since tax rates are different in different countries, companies have incentives to set transfer prices that will increase revenues (and profits) in low-tax countries and increase costs (thereby reducing profits) in high-tax countries.

6. **Identify types of costs to be considered in measuring division operating costs.** In measuring divisional operating costs, management must decide how to treat the following costs: (1) controllable, direct operating costs; (2) noncontrollable, direct operating costs; (3) controllable, indirect operating costs; and (4) noncontrollable, indirect operating costs. Direct versus indirect refers to whether the cost associates directly with the division; controllable versus noncontrollable refers to whether the division manager can affect the cost.

7. **Identify issues in measuring the investment base for return on investment calculation.** Two issues arise when measuring the investment base: (1) how to allocate the cost of shared assets; and (2) what value to use for the assets.

8. **Know the contribution approach alternative to return on investment for division performance measurement.** The contribution approach allows management to evaluate the division and its manager's performance without regard to costs arbitrarily allocated to divisions or to product lines. The report also provides data about the division's performance after the firm allocates all central administrative costs.

9. **Calculate return on investment and identify shortcomings of the measure.** The rate of return on investment has two components: profit margin and investment turnover. A shortcoming of return on investment is that it may not lead managers to accept good investment opportunities if the ROI of the investment is lower than the present ROI of the division.

Key Equation:

$$\text{Return on Investment} = \text{Profit Margin Percentage} \times \text{Investment Turnover Ratio}$$

$$\frac{\text{Profit Margin}}{\text{Divisional Investment}} = \frac{\text{Profit Margin}}{\text{Divisional Revenues}} \times \frac{\text{Divisional Revenues}}{\text{Divisional Investment}}$$

---

10. **Calculate residual income.** The calculation of residual income alleviates the shortcoming of the return on investment measurement.

Key Equation:

$$\text{Residual Income} = \frac{\text{Division Profit}}{\text{Margin}} - \left(\text{Percent Capital Charge} \times \frac{\text{Division}}{\text{Investment}} \right)$$

KEY TERMS AND CONCEPTS

Division   A more or less self-contained business unit that is part of a larger family of business units under common control.

Profit center   A responsibility center for which a firm accumulates both revenue and expenses.

Investment center   A responsibility center with control over revenues, costs, and assets.

Decentralize   To give a manager of a business unit responsibility for that unit's revenues and costs, freeing the manager to make decisions about prices, sources of supply, and the like, as though the unit were a separate business that the manager owns.

Behavioral (goal) congruence   All members of an organization have incentives to perform for a common interest, such as shareholder wealth maximization for a corporation.

Division return on investment (ROI)   Equal to division operating profit divided by division investment.

Economic transfer pricing rule   Transfer at differential outlay cost plus opportunity cost.

Market price-based transfer pricing   Transfer pricing policy where the transfer price is set at the market price or at a small discount from the market price.

Cost-plus transfer pricing   Transfer pricing policy based on full costing or variable costing and actual cost or standard cost plus an allowance for profit.

Dual transfer pricing   Transfer pricing system where the buying division is charged with costs only, and the selling division is credited with cost plus some profit allowance.

Negotiated transfer pricing   System whereby the transfer prices are arrived at through negotiation between managers of buying and selling divisions.

Profit margin percentage   Indicates the portion of each dollar of revenue that is profit.

Investment turnover ratio   The ratio of divisional sales to the investment in divisional assets.

Residual income (RI)   The excess of division operating profits over the dollar cost of capital invested in the division. The dollar cost of capital equals the percent capital charge (minimum acceptable rate of return) times the investment in divisional assets.

SOLUTIONS TO SELF-STUDY PROBLEMS

SUGGESTED SOLUTION TO PROBLEM 13.1 FOR SELF-STUDY

a. From a company's perspective, the minimum price would be the variable cost of producing and marketing the goods, $19. If the company was centralized, we would expect this information would be conveyed to the manager of Marketing, who would be instructed not to set a price below $19.

b. The transfer price that correctly informs the Marketing manager about the differential costs of manufacturing is $18.

c. If the Production manager set the price at $28.50, the Marketing manager would set the minimum price at $29.50 (= $28.50 + $1.00). In fact, prices of $28, $25, or anything greater than $19 would have generated a positive contribution margin from the production and sale of shoes.

d. If the Production Division had been operating at capacity, there would have been an implicit opportunity cost of internal transfers. The implicit opportunity cost to the company is the lost contribution margin ($28.50 − $19 = $9.50) from not selling in the wholesale market.

The transfer price should have been:

$$\begin{matrix} \text{Differential cost} \\ \text{of production} \end{matrix} \quad + \quad \begin{matrix} \text{Implicit opportunity cost to company} \\ \text{if goods are transferred internally} \end{matrix}$$

$$= \$19 + \$9.50$$

$$= \$28.50$$

Marketing would have appropriately treated the $28.50 as part of its differential cost of buying and selling the shoes.

SUGGESTED SOLUTION TO PROBLEM 13.2 FOR SELF-STUDY

For the $3 million transfer, the total tax is (40% × $1,000,000) + (40% × $15,000,000) = $6,400,000. For $10 million, the total tax is (40% × $8,000,000) + (40% × $8,000,000) = $6,400,000. With equal tax rates, there is no advantage to inflating the transfer price.

SUGGESTED SOLUTION TO PROBLEM 13.3 FOR SELF-STUDY

$$\text{ROI} = \frac{\$.60 \text{ Billion}}{\$2.4 \text{ Billion}} = \underline{\underline{25\%}}.$$

$$\text{Residual Income} = \$.60 \text{ Billion} - (.20 \times \$2.4 \text{ Billion})$$

$$= \$.60 \text{ Billion} - \$.48 \text{ Billion}$$

$$= \underline{\underline{\$.12 \text{ Billion}}} \text{ (that is, residual income of } \$120 \text{ million)}.$$

QUESTIONS, EXERCISES, PROBLEMS, AND CASES

REVIEW QUESTIONS

1. Review the meaning of the concepts or terms given in Key Terms and Concepts.
2. Why may transfer prices exist even in highly centralized organizations?

3. Why do some consider market-based transfer prices optimal under many circumstances?

4. What are the limitations to market price-based transfer prices?

5. What are the advantages of a centrally administered transfer price (that is, direct intervention)? What are the disadvantages of such a transfer price?

6. Why do companies often use prices other than market prices for interdivisional transfers?

7. What are the disadvantages of a negotiated transfer price system?

CRITICAL ANALYSIS AND DISCUSSION QUESTIONS

8. "An action that is optimal for a division may not be optimal for the company as a whole." Explain.

9. Why are transfer prices necessary?

10. In what sense is the word "price" in the term *transfer price* a misnomer?

11. Refer to this chapter's Managerial Application, "Just-in-Time Production in Japan and the Internal Revenue Service in the United States." Why did the Internal Revenue Service dispute the transfer prices? Did the IRS want the prices set higher or lower? Why?

12. What factors should companies consider when setting transfer prices for products sold from a division in one country to a division in another country?

13. Division A has no external markets. It produces a product that Division B uses. Division B cannot purchase this product from any other source. What transfer pricing system would you recommend for the interdivisional sale of the product? Why?

14. Describe the economic basis for transfer pricing systems.

15. "It may be desirable to use a different ROI measure for evaluating the performance of a division and the performance of the division's manager." Explain.

16. "The return on investment measure may be biased in favor of divisions with older plant and equipment." Explain.

17. What are the advantages of using the ROI measure rather than the value of division profits as a performance evaluation technique?

18. Under what conditions would the use of ROI measures inhibit goal-congruent decision making by a division manager?

19. What are the advantages of using residual income instead of ROI?

20. Describe why the "general transfer pricing rule" will lead to the decision that benefits the company as a whole in the case where the selling division is under capacity.

EXERCISES

Solutions to even-numbered exercises are at the end of this chapter after the cases.

21. **Transfer pricing.** Crown Cola, Inc., produces bottled drinks. The New England Division acquires the water, adds carbonation, and sells it in bulk quantities to

the California Division of Crown Cola and to outside buyers. The California Division buys carbonated water in bulk, adds flavoring, bottles it, and sells it.

Last year, the New England Division produced 1,500,000 gallons, of which it sold 1,300,000 gallons to the California Division and the remaining 200,000 gallons to outsiders for $.30 per gallon. The California Division processed the 1,300,000 gallons, which it sold for $1,500,000. New England's variable costs were $440,000 and its fixed costs were $80,000. The California Division incurred an additional variable cost of $320,000 and $160,000 fixed costs. Both divisions operated below capacity.

a. Prepare division income statements assuming the transfer price is at the external market price of $.40 per gallon.

b. Repeat part **a** assuming a negotiated transfer price of $.30 per gallon is used.

c. Respond to the statement: "The choice of a particular transfer price is immaterial to the company as a whole."

22. **Return on investment computations.** The following information relates to the operating performance of three divisions of Langston Retail Corporation for last year.

	New York Division	Philadelphia Division	Los Angeles Division
Divisional Profit Margin before Allocating Central Corporate Expenses to Divisions	$ 500,000	$ 500,000	$ 500,000
Divisional Investment	$ 4,000,000	$ 5,000,000	$ 6,000,000
Divisional Sales	$24,000,000	$20,000,000	$16,000,000
Divisional Employees	22,500	12,000	10,500

Langston evaluates divisional performance using rate of return on investment (ROI) after allocating a portion of the central corporate expenses to each division. Central corporate expenses for last year were $900,000.

a. Compute the ROI of each division before allocation of central corporate expenses.

b. Compute the ROI of each division assuming central corporate expenses are allocated based on divisional investments (that is, allocate 4/15 to the New York Division, 5/15 to the Philadelphia Division, and 6/15 to the Los Angeles Division).

c. Repeat part **b**, allocating central corporate expenses based on divisional sales.

d. Repeat part **b**, assuming that management allocates central corporate expenses based on the number of employees.

23. **ROI computations with a capital charge.** The following information relates to the operating performance of three divisions of Temecula, Inc., for last year.

	Local Division	Intercity Division	Interstate Division
Operating Profit	$ 375,000	$1,500,000	$ 2,625,000
Investment	3,750,000	6,000,000	17,500,000

a. Compute the rate of return on investment (ROI) of each division for last year.

b. Assume that the firm levies a charge on each division for the use of capital. The charge is 11 percent on investment, and the accounting system deducts it in measuring divisional net income. Recalculate ROI using divisional net income after deduction of the use-of-capital charge in the numerator.

c. Which of these two measures do you think gives the better indication of operating performance? Explain your reasoning.

24. ROI computations with replacement costs. The following information relates to the operating performance of two divisions of Pratt Electronics Corporation of last year.

	Boston Division	Mexico City Division
Operating Profit	$ 400,000	$ 600,000
Total Assets (based on acquisition cost)	4,000,000	7,500,000
Total Assets (based on current replacement costs)	6,000,000	8,000,000

a. Compute the return on investment (ROI) of each division, using total assets stated at acquisition cost as the investment base.

b. Compute the ROI of each division, using total assets based on current replacement cost as the investment base.

c. Which of the two measures do you think gives the better indication of operating performance? Explain your reasoning.

25. ROI computations comparing net and gross book value. The following information relates to the operating performance of two divisions of Thomas Trucking for last year.

	Eastern Division	Western Division
Operating Profit	$ 1,200,000	$ 1,800,000
Total Assets (at gross acquisition cost)	15,000,000	36,000,000
Total Assets (net of accumulated depreciation)	10,000,000	9,000,000

a. Compute the return on investment (ROI) of each division, using total assets at gross book value as the investment base.

b. Compute the ROI of each division, using total assets net of accumulated depreciation (net book value) as the investment base.

c. Which of the two measures do you think gives the better indication of operating performance? Explain your reasoning.

26. Comparing profit margin and ROI as performance measures. Cafe Italia operates coffeehouses on college campuses in three districts. The operating performance for each district follows.

	District		
	New Hampshire	Illinois	California
Sales	$3,800,000	$17,000,000	$20,000,000
Operating Profit	200,000	500,000	1,000,000
Investment	2,000,000	6,250,000	8,000,000

a. Using the operating profit margin percentage as the criterion, which is the most profitable district?

b. Using the rate of return on investment as the criterion, which is the most profitable district?

c. Which of the two measures better indicates operating performance? Explain your reasoning.

27. **Profit margin and investment turnover ratio computations.** The Ruffles Division of the Chip'n'Dip Company had a rate of return on investment (ROI) of 12 percent (= $600,000/$5,000,000) during 19X0, based on sales of $10,000,000. In an effort to improve its performance during 19X1, the company instituted several cost-saving programs, including the substitution of automatic equipment for work previously done by workers and the purchase of raw materials in large quantities to obtain quantity discounts. Despite these cost-saving programs, the company's ROI for 19X1 was 10 percent (= $550,000/$5,500,000), based on sales of $10,000,000.

a. Break down the ROI for 19X0 and 19X1 into profit margin and investment turnover ratios.

b. Explain the reason for the decrease in ROI between the 2 years, using results from part **a**.

28. **ROI and residual income computations.** A bank considers acquiring new computer equipment. The computer will cost $160,000 and result in a cash savings of $70,000 per year (excluding depreciation) for each of the 5 years of the asset's life. It will have no salvage value after 5 years. Assume straight-line depreciation (depreciation expensed evenly over the life of the asset).

a. What is the ROI for each year of the asset's life if the division uses beginning-of-year net book value asset balances for the computation?

b. What is the residual income each year if the capital costs 25 percent?

29. **Transfer pricing (adapted from CPA exam).** Jenkin's Building Supplies has two decentralized divisions, Hardware and Pre-Fab. Pre-Fab has always purchased certain units from Hardware at $110 per unit. Because Hardware plans to raise the price to $140 per unit, Pre-Fab desires to purchase these units from outside suppliers for $110 per unit. Hardware's costs follow: variable costs per unit, $100; annual fixed costs, $15,000. Annual production of these units for Pre-Fab is 1,500 units.

If Pre-Fab buys from an outside supplier, the facilities Hardware uses to manufacture these units would remain idle. What would be the result if Jenkin's Building Supplies management enforces a transfer price of $140 per unit between Hardware and Pre-Fab?

30. **Transfer pricing.** The consulting group in an accounting firm offers its products to outside clients at a price of $200 per hour. Last month, the consultants billed 10,000 hours to outside clients, incurred variable costs of $70 per hour billed to outside clients, and incurred $500,000 in fixed costs.

The firm's auditing group can acquire consulting services from outsiders or from the firm's own consultants. If it acquires the services from outsiders, it must pay $180 per hour. It would pay $200 for consulting services from the internal group.

a. What are the costs and benefits of the alternatives available to these two groups, the consultants and the auditors, and to the accounting firm as a whole, with respect to consulting services? Assume the consulting group operates at capacity.

b. How would your answer change if the accounting firm's consulting group had sufficient idle capacity to handle all the auditors' needs?

PROBLEMS

31. **Transfer pricing.** E-Z Computing Company produces computers and computer components. The company is organized into several divisions that operate essentially as autonomous companies. The firm permits division managers to make capital investment and production-level decisions. The division managers can also decide whether to sell to other divisions or to outside customers.

Networks Division produces a critical component for computers manufactured by Computers Division. It has been selling this component to Computers for $1,500 per unit. Networks recently purchased new equipment for producing the component. To offset its higher depreciation charges, Networks increased its price to $1,600 per unit. The manager of Networks has asked the president to instruct Computers to purchase the component for the $1,600 price rather than to permit Computers to purchase externally for $1,500 per unit. The following information is obtained from the company's records: Computers' annual purchases of the component, 200 units; Networks' variable costs per unit, $1,200; Networks' fixed costs per unit, $300.

a. Assume that the firm has no alternative uses for Networks' idle capacity. Will the company as a whole benefit if Computers purchases the component externally for $1,500? Explain.

b. Assume that the firm can use the idle capacity of Networks for other purposes, resulting in cash operating savings of $20,000. Will the company as a whole benefit if Computers purchases the component externally for $1,500? Explain.

c. Assume the same facts as in part **b** except that the outside market price drops to $1,350 per unit. Will the company as a whole benefit if Computers purchases the component externally for $1,350? Explain.

d. As president, how would you respond to the manager of Networks? Discuss each scenario described in parts **a**, **b**, and **c**.

32. **Biases in ROI computations.** Lincoln Products uses rate of return on investment (ROI) as a basis for determining the annual bonus of divisional managers. The firm allocates central corporate expenses to the divisions based on total sales. The calculation of ROI for 19X0 for two of its divisions follows:

	Tennis Products Division	Golf Products Division
Division Contribution to Central Corporate Expenses and Operating Profit	$100,000	$ 500,000
Share of Central Corporate Expenses	(10,000)	(25,000)
Divisional Operating Profit	$ 90,000	$ 475,000
Divisional Investment (assets)	$600,000	$4,750,000
ROI	15 Percent	10 Percent

Indicate several factors that, if present, would bias the ROI measure as Lincoln has calculated it and lead to possible inequities in determining the annual bonus.

33. **Issues in designing ROI measures.** The Champion Corporation manufacturers and sells a patented electronic device for detecting burglaries. The firm uses return on investment as a measure for the control of operations for each of its sixteen U.S. divisions.

    Recently the firm has organized a new division in Brazil. Champion contributed the necessary capital for the construction of manufacturing and sales facilities in Brazil, whereas it obtained debt financing locally for working capital requirements. The new division will remit annually the following amounts to the U.S. central corporate office: (1) a royalty of $10 for each burglary device sold in Brazil, (2) a fee of $40 per hour plus traveling expenses for central corporate engineering services used by the division, and (3) a dividend equal to 10 percent of the capital Champion committed. The division will retain for its own use the remaining funds that operation generates. The division will receive the right to produce and market in Brazil any future electronic devices the central corporate research and development staff develops.

    List some of the questions that the firm must address in designing an ROI measure for this division.

34. **Evaluating profit impact of alternative transfer decisions** (adapted from CMA exam). A. R. Oma, Inc., manufactures a line of men's colognes and aftershave lotions. The firm manufactures the products through a series of mixing operations with the addition of certain aromatic and coloring ingredients; the firm packages the finished product in a company-produced glass bottle and packs it in cases containing six bottles.

    Management of A. R. Oma believes appearance of the bottle heavily influences the sale of its product. Management has developed a unique bottle of which it is quite proud.

    Cologne production and bottle manufacturing have evolved over the years in an almost independent manner; in fact, a rivalry has developed between management personnel as to which division is the more important to A. R. Oma. This attitude is probably intensified because the bottle manufacturing plant was purchased intact 10 years ago, and no real interchange of management personnel or ideas (except at the top corporate level) has taken place.

    Since the acquisition, the cologne manufacturing plant has absorbed all bottle production. Management considers each area a separate profit center and evaluates each area as a separate profit center. As the new corporate controller, you are responsible for the definition of a proper transfer value to use in crediting the bottle production profit center and in debiting the packaging profit center.

    At your request, the bottle division general manager has asked certain other bottle manufacturers to quote a price for the quantity and sizes the cologne division demands. These competitive prices follow:

Volume	Total Price	Price per Case
2,000,000 Cases	$ 4,000,000	$2.00
4,000,000 Cases	7,000,000	1.75
6,000,000 Cases	10,000,000	1.67 (rounded)

A cost analysis of the internal bottle plant indicates that it can produce bottles at these costs:

Volume	Total Cost	Cost per Case
2,000,000 Cases	$3,200,000	$1.60
4,000,000 Cases	5,200,000	1.30
6,000,000 Cases	7,200,000	1.20

These costs include fixed costs of $1,200,000 and variable costs of $1 per case.

These figures resulted in discussion about the proper value to use in the transfer of bottles to the cologne division. Corporate executives are interested because a significant portion of a division manager's income is an incentive bonus based on profit center results.

The cologne production division incurred the following costs in addition to the bottle costs:

Volume	Total Cost	Cost per Case
2,000,000 Cases	$16,400,000	$8.20
4,000,000 Cases	32,400,000	8.10
6,000,000 Cases	48,400,000	8.07

After considerable analysis, the marketing research department furnishes you with the following price-demand relation for the finished product:

Sales Volume	Total Sales Revenue	Sales Price per Case
2,000,000 Cases	$25,000,000	$12.50
4,000,000 Cases	45,600,000	11.40
6,000,000 Cases	63,900,000	10.65

a. The A. R. Oma Company has used market-based transfer prices in the past. Using the current market prices and costs, and assuming a volume of 6,000,000 cases, calculate the income for
  (1) The bottle division.
  (2) The cologne division.
  (3) The corporation.
b. Is this production and sales level the most profitable volume for
  (1) The bottle division?
  (2) The cologne division?
  (3) The corporation?
Explain your answer.

CASES

35. **Transfer pricing and organizational structure.**[2] "If I were to price these boxes any lower than $480 a thousand, I'd be countermanding my order of last month for our salespeople to stop shaving their bids and to bid full cost quotations. I've been trying for weeks to improve the quality of our business, and if I turn around now and accept this job at $430 or $450 or something less than $480, I'll be tearing down this program I've been working so hard to build up. The division can't very well show a profit by putting in bids that don't even cover a fair share of overhead costs, let alone give us a profit."

James Brunner, Manager of Thompson Division

Birch Paper Company was a medium-sized, partly integrated paper company, producing white and kraft papers and paperboard. A portion of its paperboard output was converted into corrugated boxes by the Thompson division, which also printed and colored the outside surface of the boxes. Including Thompson, the company had four producing divisions and a timberland division, which supplied part of the company's pulp requirements.

For several years, each division had been judged independently on the basis of its profit and return on investment. Top management had been working to gain effective results from a policy of decentralizing responsibility and authority for all decisions except those relating to overall company policy. The company's top officials believed that in the past few years they had applied the concept of decentralization successfully and that the company's profits and competitive position had definitely improved.

Early in 1975 the Northern division designed a special display box for one of its papers in conjunction with the Thompson division, which was equipped to make the box. Thompson's staff for package design and development spent several months perfecting the design, production methods, and materials that were to be used. Because of the box's unusual color and shape, these were far from standard. According to an agreement between the two divisions, the Thompson division was reimbursed by the Northern division for the cost of its design and development work.

When the specifications were all prepared, the Northern division asked for bids on the box from the Thompson division and from two outside companies, West Paper Company and Erie Papers, Ltd. Each division manager normally was free to buy from whichever supplier he or she wished; on intercompany sales, divisions selling to other divisions were expected to meet the going market price.

In 1975, the profit margins of converters such as the Thompson division were being squeezed. Thompson, as did many other similar converters, bought its board, liner, or paper, and its function was to print, cut, and shape the material

[2]Copyright © 1957, 1985 by the President and Fellows of Harvard College. W. Rotch prepared this case under the direction of Neil E. Harlan as the basis for class discussion rather than to illustrate either effective or ineffective handling of an administrative situation. Reprinted by permission of Harvard Business School. From Harvard Business School case 158-001.

into boxes.[3] Though it bought most of its materials from other Birch divisions, most of its sales were made to outside customers. If Thompson got the order from Northern, it probably would buy its liner board and corrugating medium from the Southern division of Birch. Thus, before giving its bid to Northern, Thompson got a quote for materials from the Southern division.

Though Southern division had been running below capacity and had excess inventory, it quoted the market price, which had not noticeably weakened as a result of the oversupply. Its out-of-pocket costs on both liner and corrugating medium were about 60 percent of the selling price. About 70 percent of Thompson's out-of-pocket cost of $400 a thousand for the order represented the cost of linerboard and corrugating medium.

The Northern division received bids on the boxes of $480 a thousand from the Thompson division, $430 a thousand from West Paper Company, and $432 a thousand from Erie Papers, Ltd. Erie Papers offered to buy from Birch the outside linerboard with the special printing already on it, but it would supply its own liner and corrugating medium. The outside liner would be supplied by the Southern division at a price equivalent to $90 a thousand boxes, and the Thompson division would print it for $30 a thousand. Of the $30, about $25 would be out-of-pocket costs.

Since the bidding results appeared to be a little unusual, William Kenton, manager of the Northern Division, discussed the wide discrepancy of bids with Birch's commercial vice-president. He told the commercial vice-president, "We sell in a very competitive market, where higher costs cannot be passed on. How can we be expected to show a decent profit and return on investment if we have to buy our supplies at more than 10 percent over the going market?"

Knowing that Mr. Brunner had been unable to operate the Thompson division at capacity on occasion in the past few months, it seemed odd to the vice-president that Mr. Brunner would add the full 20 percent overhead and profit charge to his out-of-pocket costs. When he asked Mr. Brunner about this over the telephone, his answer was the statement that appears at the beginning of the case. Mr. Brunner continued saying that since they did the developmental work on the box and received no profit on that, he felt entitled to a good markup on the production of the box itself.

The vice-president explored further the cost structures of the various divisions. He remembered a comment the controller had made at a meeting the week before to the effect that costs that for one division were variable could be largely fixed for the company as a whole. He knew that in the absence of specific orders from top management, Mr. Kenton would accept the lowest bid, which was that of the West Paper Company, for $430. However, it would be possible for top management to order the acceptance of another bid if the situation warranted such action. And although the volume represented by the transactions in question was less than 5 percent of the volume of any of the divisions involved, future transactions could conceivably raise similar problems.

---

[3]The walls of a corrugated box consist of outside and inside sheets of linerboard and a center layer of fluted corrugating medium.

a. Does the system motivate Mr. Brunner in such a way that actions he takes in the best interest of the Thompson division are also in the best interest of the Birch Paper Company? If your answer is no, give some specific instances related as closely as possible to the type of situation described in the case. Would the system correctly motivate managers of *other* divisions?

b. What should the vice-president do?

36. **Impact of division performance measures on management incentives.** The home office staff of The Nomram Group evaluates managers of the Nomram divisions by keeping track of the rate of return each division earns on the average level of assets invested at the division. The home office staff considers 20 percent, which is The Nomram Group's after-tax cost of capital, to be the minimum acceptable annual rate of return on average investment. When a division's rate of return drops below 20 percent, division management can expect an unpleasant investigation by the home office and perhaps some firings. When the rate of return exceeds 20 percent and grows through time, the home office staff is invariably pleased and rewards division management. When the rate of return exceeds 20 percent but declines over time, the home office staff sends out unpleasant memorandums and cuts the profit-sharing bonuses of the division managers.

In Division A, average assets employed during the year amount to $60,000. Division A has been earning 40 percent per year on its average investment for several years. Management of Division A is proud of its extraordinary record—earning a steady 40 percent per year.

In Division B, average assets employed during the year also amount to $60,000. Division B has been earning 25 percent per year on its average investment. In the preceding 3 years, the rate of return on investment was 20 percent, 22 percent, and 23 percent, respectively. Management of Division B is proud of its record of steadily boosting earnings.

New investment opportunities have arisen at both Division A and Division B. In both cases, the new investment opportunity will require a cash outlay today of $30,000 and will provide a rate of return on investment of 30 percent for each of the next 8 years. The average amount of assets invested in the project will be $30,000 for each of the next 8 years. Both new investment opportunities have positive net present value when the discount rate is 20 percent per year (the after-tax cost of capital of The Nomram Group).

When word of the new opportunities reached the home office staff, the prospects of the two new investments pleased the staff, because both investments would yield a better-than-average return for The Nomram Group.

Management of Division A computed its rate of return on investment both with and without the new investment project and decided not to undertake the project. Management of Division B computed its rate of return on investment both with and without the new investment project and decided to undertake it.

When word of the two divisions' actions reached the home office staff, it was perplexed. Why did Division A's management turn down such a good opportunity? What in the behavior of the home office staff induced Division A's management to reject the new project? Is management of Division B doing a better job than management of Division A? What may the home office do to give

Division A an incentive to act in a way more consistent with the well-being of The Nomram Group?

37. **Capital investment analysis and decentralized performance measurement—a comprehensive case.**[4] The following exchange occurred just after Diversified Electronics rejected a capital investment proposal.

Ralph Browning (Product Development): I just don't understand why you have rejected my proposal. This new investment is going to be a sure money maker for the Residential Products division. No matter how we price this new product, we can expect to make $230,000 on it before tax.

Sue Gold (Finance): I am sorry that you are upset with our decision, but this product proposal just does not meet our short-term ROI target of 15 percent after tax.

Browning: I'm not so sure about the ROI target, but it goes a long way toward meeting our earnings-per-share growth target of 20 cents per share after tax.

Phil Carlson (Executive Vice-President): Ralph, you are right, of course, about the importance of earnings per share. However, we view our three divisions as investment centers. Proposals like yours must meet our ROI targets. It is not enough that you show an earnings-per-share increase.

Gold: We believe that a company like Diversified Electronics should have a return on investment of 12 percent after tax, especially given the interest rates we have had to pay recently. This is why we have targeted 12 percent as the appropriate minimum ROI for each division to earn next year.

Carlson: If it were not for the high interest rates and poor current economic outlook, Ralph, we would not be taking such a conservative position in evaluating new projects. This past year has been particularly rough for our industry. Our two major competitors had ROIs of 10.8 percent and 12.3 percent. Though our ROI of about 9 percent after tax was reasonable (see Exhibit 13.10), performance varied from division to division. Professional Services did very well with 15 percent ROI, while the Residential Products division managed just 10 percent. The performance of the Aerospace Products division was especially dismal, with an ROI of only 6 percent. We expect divisions in the future to carry their share of the load.

Chris McGregor (Aerospace Products): My division would be showing much higher ROI if we had a lot of old equipment like the Residential Products or relied heavily on human labor like Professional Services.

Carlson: I don't really see the point you are trying to make, Chris.

Diversified Electronics, a growing company in the electronics industry, had grown to its present size of more than $140 million in sales. (See Exhibits 13.8, 13.9, and 13.10 for financial data.) Diversified Electronics has three divisions, Residential Products, Aerospace Products, and Professional Services, each of which accounts for about one-third of Diversified Electronics' sales. Residential Products, the oldest division, produces furnace thermostats and similar products. The Aerospace Products division is a large job shop that builds electronic

---

[4]This case requires knowledge of discounted cash flow methods.

EXHIBIT 13.8

DIVERSIFIED ELECTRONICS
Income Statement for 1995 and 1996
(all dollar amounts in thousands, except earnings-per-share figures)

	Year Ended December 31	
	1995	1996
Sales	$141,462	$148,220
Cost of Goods Sold	108,118	113,115
Gross Margin	$ 33,344	$ 35,105
Selling and General	13,014	13,692
Profit before Taxes and Interest	$ 20,330	$ 21,413
Interest Expense	1,190	1,952
Profit before Taxes	$ 19,140	$ 19,461
Income Tax Expense	7,886	7,454
Net Income	$ 11,254	$ 12,007
Earnings per Share (2,000 shares outstanding in 1995 and 1996)	$5.63	$6.00

devices to customer specifications. A typical job or batch takes several months to complete. About one-half of Aerospace Products' sales are to the U.S. Defense Department. The newest of the three divisions, Professional Services, provides consulting engineering services. This division has grown tremendously since Diversified Electronics acquired it 7 years ago.

EXHIBIT 13.9

DIVERSIFIED ELECTRONICS
Balance Sheets for 1995 and 1996
(all dollar amounts in thousands)

	December 31	
	1995	1996
Assets		
Cash and Temporary Investments	$ 1,404	$ 1,469
Accounts Receivable	13,688	15,607
Inventories	42,162	45,467
Total Current Assets	$ 57,254	$ 62,543
Plant and Equipment:		
Original Cost	107,326	115,736
Accumulated Depreciation	42,691	45,979
Net	$ 64,635	$ 69,757
Investments and Other Assets	3,143	3,119
Total Assets	$125,032	$135,419

continued

EXHIBIT 13.9 (*continued*)

	December 31	
	1995	1996
Liabilities and Owner's Equity		
Accounts Payable	$ 10,720	$ 12,286
Taxes Payable	1,210	1,045
Current Portion of Long-Term Debt	—	1,634
Total Current Liabilities	$ 11,930	$ 14,965
Deferred Income Taxes	559	985
Long-Term Debt	12,622	15,448
Total Liabilities	$ 25,111	$ 31,398
Common Stock	47,368	47,368
Retained Earnings	52,553	56,653
Total Owners' Equity	$ 99,921	$104,021
Total Liabilities and Owners' Equity	$125,032	$135,419

Each division operates independently of the others and corporate management treats each as a separate entity. Division managers make many of the operating decisions. Corporate management coordinates the activities of the various divisions, which includes review of all investment proposals over $400,000.

Diversified Electronics measures return on investment as the division's Net Income divided by total assets. Each division's expenses includes the allocated portion of corporate administrative expenses.

Since each of Diversified Electronics' divisions is located in a separate facility, management can easily attribute most assets, including receivables, to specific divisions. Management allocates the corporate office assets, including the centrally controlled cash account, to the divisions on the basis of divisional revenues.

Exhibit 13.11 shows the details of Ralph Browning's rejected product proposal.

a. Why did corporate headquarters reject Ralph Browning's product proposal? Was their decision the right one? If top management used the discounted cash flow (DCF) method instead, what would the results be? The company uses a 15 percent cost of capital (i.e., hurdle rate) in evaluating projects such as these.

EXHIBIT 13.10

DIVERSIFIED ELECTRONICS
Ratio Analysis

	1995	1996
ROI = Net Income/Total Assets	$\frac{\$11,254}{\$125,032} = 9.0\%$	$\frac{\$12,007}{\$135,419} = 8.9\%$

> **EXHIBIT 13.11**
>
> DIVERSIFIED ELECTRONICS
> Financial Data for New Product Proposal
>
> ---
>
> 1. Projected Asset Investment:[a]
>
> | | |
> |---|---:|
> | Land Purchase | $ 200,000 |
> | Plant and Equipment[b] | 800,000 |
> | Total | $1,000,000 |
>
> 2. Cost Data, before Taxes (first year):
>
> | | |
> |---|---:|
> | Variable Cost per Unit | $3.00 |
> | Differential Fixed Costs[c] | $170,000 |
>
> 3. Price/Market Estimate (first year):
>
> | | |
> |---|---:|
> | Unit Price | $7.00 |
> | Sales | 100,000 Units |
>
> 4. Taxes: The company assumes a 40 percent tax rate for investment analyses. Depreciation of plant and equipment according to tax law is as follows: Year 1, 20 percent; Year 2, 32 percent; Year 3, 19 percent; Year 4, 14.5 percent; Year 5, 14.5 percent. Taxes are paid for taxable income in Year 1 at the end of Year 1, taxes for Year 2 at the end of Year 2, etc.
>
> 5. Inflation is assumed to be 10 percent per year and applies to revenues and all costs except depreciation.
>
> 6. The project has an 8-year life. Land will be sold at the end of Year 8. The nominal land price is expected to increase with inflation.
>
> ---
>
> [a]Assumes sales of 100,000 units.
>
> [b]Annual capacity of 120,000 units.
>
> [c]Includes straight-line depreciation on new plant and equipment, depreciated for 8 years with no net salvage value at the end of 8 years.

    b. Evaluate the manner in which Diversified Electronics has implemented the investment center concept. What pitfalls did they apparently not anticipate? What, if anything, should be done with regard to the investment center approach and the use of ROI as a measure of performance?

    c. What conflicting incentives for managers can occur between the use of a yearly ROI performance measure and DCF for capital budgeting?

38. **Honeywell, Inc.: relative performance evaluation.**[5] A major issue in divisional performance evaluation is the process companies use to separate performance results that division managers can control from those that outside environmental factors cause. For instance, firms could hold division managers accountable for achieving a fixed target, independent of the performance of other divisions operating in similar product markets, or evaluate their performance relative to the performance of other divisions. The latter approach, known as *relative performance evaluation,* is analogous to "grading on the curve."

The Aerospace and Defense Business at Honeywell, Inc., experimented with relative performance evaluation. Honeywell is a technology-oriented company, particularly in the Aerospace and Defense Business. They historically emphasize growth, customer satisfaction, and new product development. As the Aero-

---

[5]Based on the authors' research.

space and Defense Business has become more cost competitive, with less cost-plus contracting, in recent years top management has become more interested in providing incentives to reduce costs. Honeywell has also increased its emphasis on financial measures of performance. The firm changed incentive contracts for top management and division managers to emphasize return on investment. Aerospace and Defense, in particular, experimented with a "peer company analysis" to create self-reassessment of the status quo.

The strategic planning group that performed the peer group analysis first identified the business segments of 22 competitors in the aerospace and defense industry. Of these 22 competitors, 9 are prime contractors (e.g., Boeing and Lockheed), who are in aerospace and defense but do not face the same market environment. Of the remaining 13 competitors, public data were not available for two competitors, leaving 11 competitors that Aerospace and Defense managers believed faced the same market environment as they did.

Honeywell used these results initially to identify highly ranked competitors and to examine their characteristics to see what Aerospace and Defense could do to improve its financial performance. Over time, the firm will incorporate these comparisons with peer companies into the evaluation of division managers' performance.

a. What are the advantages to Honeywell of using relative performance evaluation?

b. As a division manager, would you rather have your performance evaluated using relative performance evaluation ("grading on the curve") or without regard to your competitors?

39. **Transfer Pricing: Custom Freight Systems (A)**[6] "We can't drop our prices below $210 per hundred pounds," exclaimed Greg Berman, manager of Forwarders, a division of Custom Freight Systems. "Our margins are already razor thin. Our costs just won't allow us to go any lower. Corporate rewards our division based on our profitability and I won't lower my prices below $210."

Customer Freight Systems is organized into three divisions; Air Cargo provides air cargo services; Logistics Services operates distribution centers and provides truck cargo services; and Forwarders provides international freight forwarding services. Freight forwarders typically buy space on planes from international air cargo companies. This is analogous to a charter company that books seats on passenger planes and resells them to passengers. In many cases freight forwarders will hire trucking companies to transport the cargo from the plane to the domestic destination.

Management believes that the three divisions integrate well together and are able to provide customers with one-stop transportation services. For example, a Forwarders branch in Singapore would receive cargo from a shipper, prepare the necessary documentation, and then ship the cargo on Air Cargo to the San Francisco Forwarders station. The San Francisco Forwarders station would ensure the cargo passes through customs and ship it to the final destination with Logistics Services (see Exhibit 13.12).

---

[6]Prepared by Thomas B. Rumzie under the direction of Michael W. Maher. Copyright Michael W. Maher 1996.

EXHIBIT 13.12

Custom Freight Systems Operations

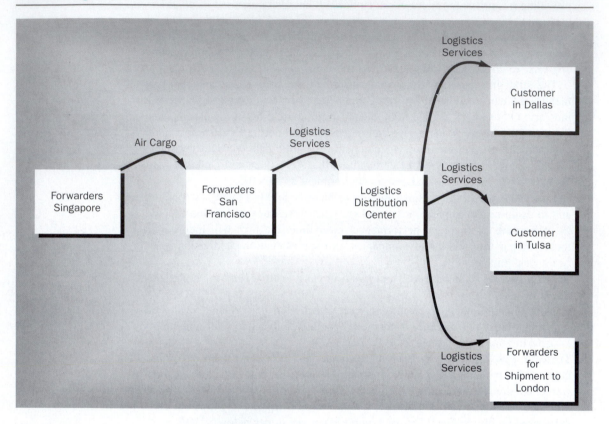

Management evaluates each division separately and rewards division managers based on return on investment (ROI). Responsibility and decision-making authority are decentralized. Each division has a sales and marketing organization. Division sales people report to the Vice-President of Sales for Custom Freight Systems as well as a division sales manager. Custom Freight Systems feels that it has been successful motivating division managers by paying bonuses for high division profits.

Recently, the Logistics division was completing a bid for a customer. The customer had freight to import from an overseas supplier and wanted Logistics to submit a bid for a distribution package that included air freight from the supplier, receiving the freight and providing customs clearance services at the airport, warehousing, and distributing to customers.

Because this was a contract for international shipping, Logistics needed to contact different freight forwarders for shipping quotes. Logistics requested quotes from the Forwarders division and United Systems, a competing freight forwarder. Divisions of Custom Freight Systems are free to use the most appropriate and cost-effective suppliers.

Logistics received bids of $210 per hundred pounds from Forwarders and $185 per hundred from United Systems. Forwarders specified in its bid that it will use Air Cargo, a division of Custom Freight Systems. Forwarder's variable costs were $175 per hundred, which included the cost of subcontracting air transportation. Air Cargo, which was experiencing a period of excess capacity, quoted Forwarders the market rate of $155. Typically, Air's variable costs are 60 percent of the market rate.

The price difference between the two different bids alarmed Susan Burns, a contract manager at Logistics. Burns knows this is a competitive business and is concerned because the total difference between the high and low bids was a lot of money for the contract estimated at 4,160,000 pounds during the first year. Burns contacted Greg Berman, the manager of Forwarders, and discussed the quote. "Don't you think full markup is unwarranted due to the fact that you and the airlines have so much excess capacity?" Burns complained.

Burns soon realized that Berman was not going to drop the price quote. "You know how small margins are in this business. Why should I cut my margins even smaller just to make you look good?" Berman asked.

Burns went to Bennie Espinosa, vice-president of Custom Freight Systems and chairperson for the corporate strategy committee. "That does sound strange," said Espinosa. "I need to examine the overall cost structure and talk to Berman. I'll get back to you by noon Monday."

  a. Which bid should the Logistics division accept: the internal bid from the Forwarders division or the external bid from United Systems?
  b. What should the transfer price be on this transaction?
  c. What should Bennie Espinosa do?
  d. Do the reward systems for the division managers support the best interests of the Forwarders division and the best interests of Custom Freight Systems? Give examples that support your conclusion.

40. **Transfer Pricing: Custom Freight Systems (B)** Assume all the information is the same as in Custom Freight Systems (A), but instead of receiving one outside bid, Logistics receives two. The new bid is from World Services for $195 per hundred. World offered to use Air Cargo for air cargo. Air Cargo will charge World $155 per hundred pounds. The bids from Forwarders and United Systems remain the same as in part A, $210 and $185, respectively.

  Which bid should Logistics Services take? Why?

SUGGESTED SOLUTIONS TO EVEN-NUMBERED EXERCISES

22. **Return on investment computations.**

  a. New York Division: $\dfrac{\$500,000}{\$4,000,000} = 12.5\%$

  Philadelphia Division: $\dfrac{\$500,000}{\$5,000,000} = 10\%$

  Los Angeles Division: $\dfrac{\$500,000}{\$6,000,000} = 8.33\%$

b. New York Division:

$$\frac{\$500,000 - (\$4,000,000/\$15,000,000)(\$900,000)}{\$4,000,000} = 6.5\%$$

Philadelphia Division:

$$\frac{\$500,000 - (\$5,000,000/\$15,000,000)(\$900,000)}{\$5,000,000} = 4.0\%$$

Los Angeles Division:

$$\frac{\$500,000 - (\$6,000,000/\$15,000,000)(\$900,000)}{\$6,000,000} = 2.33\%$$

c. New York Division:

$$\frac{\$500,000 - (\$24,000,000/\$60,000,000)(\$900,000)}{\$4,000,000} = 3.5\%$$

Philadelphia Division:

$$\frac{\$500,000 - (\$20,000,000/\$60,000,000)(\$900,000)}{\$5,000,000} = 4.0\%$$

Los Angeles Division:

$$\frac{\$500,000 - (\$16,000,000/\$60,000,000)(\$900,000)}{\$6,000,000} = 4.33\%$$

d. New York Division:

$$\frac{\$500,000 - (22,500/45,000)(\$900,000)}{\$4,000,000} = 1.25\%$$

Philadelphia Division:

$$\frac{\$500,000 - (12,000/45,000)(\$900,000)}{\$5,000,000} = 5.2\%$$

Los Angeles Division:

$$\frac{\$500,000 - (10,500/45,000)(\$900,000)}{\$6,000,000} = 4.83\%.$$

24. ROI computations with replacement costs.

a. Boston Division: $\dfrac{\$400,000}{\$4,000,000} = 10\%$;   Mexico City Division: $\dfrac{\$600,000}{\$7,500,000} = 8\%$.

b. Boston Division: $\dfrac{\$400,000}{\$6,000,000} = 6.67\%$;   Mexico City Division: $\dfrac{\$600,000}{\$8,000,000} = 7.5\%$.

c. Analysts make two principal arguments for using acquisition cost in the denominator as in part **a**. First, firms can easily obtain it from their records and it does not require estimates of current replacement costs. Second, it is consistent with the measurement of net income in the numerator (that is, depreciation expense is based on acquisition cost, and unrealized holding gains are excluded). Analysts also make two principal arguments for using current replacement cost in the denominator as in part **b**. First, it eliminates the effects of price changes and permits the division that can use the depreciable assets most efficiently to show a better ROI. Second, as discussed in the chapter, it may lead division managers to make better equipment-replacement decisions. If firms use acquisition cost as the valuation basis in calculating ROI, divisions with older, more fully depreciated assets may be reluctant to replace them and thereby introduce higher, current amounts in the denominator. If firms use current replacement cost in the denominator, the asset base will be the same regardless of whether or not the assets are replaced. Thus the replacement decision can be made properly (that is, based on net present value), independent of any effects on ROI.

26. **Comparing profit margin and ROI as performance measures.** The return on investment (ROI), profit margin percentage, and asset turnover ratio of the three divisions follow. (Asset turnover is not required, but we include it to show the relation between ROI and its components.)

$$\frac{\text{Return on}}{\text{Investment}} = \frac{\text{Profit Margin}}{\text{Percentage}} \times \frac{\text{Asset Turnover}}{\text{Ratio}}$$

New Hampshire District:
$$\frac{\$200,000}{\$2,000,000} = \frac{\$200,000}{\$3,800,000} \times \frac{\$3,800,000}{\$2,000,000}$$

$$10\% = 5.26\% \times 1.9$$

Illinois District:
$$\frac{\$500,000}{\$6,250,000} = \frac{\$500,000}{\$17,000,000} \times \frac{\$17,000,000}{\$6,250,000}$$

$$8\% = 2.94\% \times 2.72$$

California District:
$$\frac{\$1,000,000}{\$8,000,000} = \frac{\$1,000,000}{\$20,000,000} \times \frac{\$20,000,000}{\$8,000,000}$$

$$12.5\% = 5\% \times 2.5$$

a. Using the profit margin percentage, the ranking of the divisions is (1) New Hampshire, (2) California, and (3) Illinois.

b. Using ROI, the ranking of divisions is (1) California, (2) New Hampshire, and (3) Illinois.

c. The ROI is a better measure of overall performance because it relates profits to the investment, or capital, required to generate those profits. New Hampshire had the largest profit margin percentage. However, it required more capital to generate a dollar of sales than did California. Thus its overall profitability is less. Illinois had the largest asset turnover ratio. However, it generated the smallest amount of net income per dollar of sales, resulting in the lowest ROI of the three divisions.

28. **ROI and residual income computations.**

$$\text{Annual Income} = \$70,000 - \frac{\$160,000}{5 \text{ years}} = \$38,000.$$

Year	Investment Base	a. ROI $38,000/Base	b. Residual Income $38,000 − 25% × Base
1	$160,000	23.8%	$(2,000)
2	128,000[a]	29.7	6,000
3	96,000	39.6	14,000
4	64,000	59.4	22,000
5	32,000	118.8	30,000

[a]Base decreases by annual depreciation of $32,000.

30. Transfer pricing.

a.

	Auditors	Consultants		Accounting Firm	
Transfer Internally	Pay $200	Receive	$200	Pays	$ 0
		Pay	$ 70	Pays	$70
				Pays	$70
Transfer Externally	Pay $180	Receive	$200	Receives	$20 (net)
		Pay	$ 70	Pays	$70
				Pays	$50

It is advantageous to transfer externally.

b.

	Auditors	Consultants		Accounting Firm
Transfer Internally	Pay $200	Receive	$200	Pays $ 0
		Pay	$ 70	Pays $ 70
				Pays $ 70
Transfer Externally	Pay $180	Receive and Pay	$ 0	Pays $180

It is advantageous to transfer internally.

CHAPTER 14

INCENTIVE ISSUES

1. Describe key characteristics of divisional incentive compensation plans.
2. Know how incentive plans can affect the development phase of the product life cycle.
3. Know how the concept of economic value added (EVA) affects management incentive systems.
4. Explain what constitutes fraudulent financial reporting.
5. Define the two most common types of fraud and demonstrate their impact on financial statements.
6. Recognize the incentives for committing financial fraud.
7. Explain how environmental conditions influence fraudulent conduct.
8. Identify controls that can be instituted to prevent financial fraud.

This chapter discusses issues in the design and use of management performance evaluation and incentive plans. Ideally, these plans motivate managers to act in the organization's best interests. As self-interested utility-maximizers, managers may prefer to act in ways that are in their own best interests but not in those of the organization. Good performance evaluation and incentive plans induce "win-win" results such that managers are motivated to behave in ways that are mutually beneficial to their organizations and to themselves.

DIVISIONAL INCENTIVE COMPENSATION PLANS

Alfred Sloan, one of the first advocates of incentive compensation plans for management, instituted the General Motors bonus plan in 1918 to increase the alignment of interests between managers and the stockholders of the firm. General Motors had decentralized operating decisions, and before instituting the bonus plan, the managers had little incentive to think of the overall welfare of the organization. Instead, they tended to focus on their own performance measurements, sometimes at the expense of the corporation's welfare. Once the bonus plan was installed, the executives were more attentive to how their individual efforts affected the welfare of the entire organization.

Today, nearly all managers of decentralized profit centers in large corporations are eligible for a bonus and other nonsalary incentives that often make up 25-50 percent of salary. The form of bonus plans varies across corporations. Payments can be made in cash, in the stock of the company, in stock options, in performance shares, in stock appreciation rights, and in participating units. The bonus can be made contingent on corporate results or on divisional profits. It may be based on annual performance or on performance over a several-year period. It may be paid out immediately, deferred, or spread out over several years.

Management can evaluate a company's performance using both accounting numbers and returns to stockholders, the latter reflecting a market assessment of how well the company is doing. Divisions normally do not have their own shares trading in capital markets, and the impact of one division's performance on the total company's share value could be small. Consequently, stock market assessments of performance are less useful at the divisional level than at the company level.

A study of divisional incentive compensation plans found that most of these plans have the following characteristics.[1]

1. Cash bonuses and profit sharing plans reward managers for short-term performance.
2. Deferred compensation, such as stock and stock options, is available to managers several years after they earn the compensation.[2] Deferring receipt of proceeds from stock gives managers incentives to take actions that increase long-run share value.
3. Firms give special awards for particular actions or extraordinary performance. For example, Johnson & Johnson presents a special stock award to employees responsible for developing new products. Top management and the board of directors believe new product development is critical to the future success of the company.

When designing incentive systems, management must ascertain two things: (1) the behavior the system motivates, and (2) the behavior management desires. Although incentive plans universally attempt to motivate good performance, each organization has its own particular set of problems that affect incentive system design.

---

[1] See S. Butler and M. Maher, *Management Incentive Compensation Plans,* Montvale, N. J.: Institute of Management Accountants.

[2] Stock options give an individual the right to purchase a specified number of shares of the company's stock at a specified price within a specified time period.

Conflicts in an Incentive Compensation Plan

A large, multidivision manufacturer of industrial and consumer electrical products is organized into divisional profit centers. The firm rewards each division manager, at least in part, on the basis of the accounting profits and rate of return on assets that the division earned. Each division has its own controller, who reports directly to the central corporate controller. This direct reporting line, bypassing the division president, gives division controllers a feeling of independence from the division presidents, who would otherwise be their bosses. Central corporate management wants independent scorekeepers providing unbiased reports about ongoing operations.

In spite of this organizational design, the division controllers' compensation results in part from the same formula as that of the division presidents—a function of accounting profits and the rate of return on assets. Thus, division controllers have a financial stake in the reported profits of their divisions, giving them an incentive, at the margin, to boost reported profits.

The division controllers are aware of the potential conflict between their charge from central corporate management and their compensation packages. They feel conflict. At periodic meetings of controllers, they express their dissatisfaction to top management but so far have not been able to persuade top management to change the compensation plan.

Source: This example comes from a study by the authors. We do not reveal the company's name at management's request.

For example, when Pillsbury acquired Burger King, Pillsbury's manager had little experience in managing fast-food restaurants. The company wanted to provide incentives for Burger King's managers to remain with the company. Consequently, the incentive system provided for lucrative deferred compensation that the hamburger chain's managers would forgo if they quit. Each company's top management and board of directors must match its incentive system to its particular set of circumstances in deciding what type of behavior is desired.

Some critics point out that rewarding managers for performance reflected in annual accounting numbers gives managers incentives to take actions that make the numbers look good but not actions that benefit organizations in the long run. A classic example would be a division's failure to develop new production methods and new products that may substantially increase expenses in the short run but provide more value for shareholders in the long run. Using accounting numbers in performance measurement may also give managers incentives to make accounting choices and otherwise manipulate accounting data to put their performance in the most favorable light, as discussed later in this chapter in the section on fraudulent financial reporting.

INCENTIVES AND THE PRODUCT LIFE CYCLE

One of the major problems with short-run incentive plans is that managers are penalized in the current period for developing products that might produce long-run benefits. That is because accountants have traditionally written off the costs of developing new products as overhead.

A product's life cycle generally has four stages:

1. Design and development: low sales volume; research, design, and development costs are high.
2. Growth: sales increase.
3. Maturity: profits decline due to high competition.
4. Decline: market for product contracts.

The cost of a new product over its life cycle is 80 percent to 90 percent determined in the design phase. Manufacturing can influence only about 10 percent to 15 percent of the costs once a product has been designed. The development stage of the life cycle is where the design and production techniques can be honed to be the most efficient. Investment at this stage can improve efficiency and lower costs throughout the life cycle of the product.

When these costs are written off in the current period, managers are penalized for developing products that could produce long-term profits. Managers who invest little in new-product development may thus appear to have more efficient performance in the short run. But in the long run, the company will suffer. Therefore, an incentive plan should create incentives for managers to incur design and development costs now that are good investments for the future. One successful method of accomplishing this objective is to defer writing off new product design and development costs until the product has reached the growth and maturity stages.

ECONOMIC VALUE ADDED

Many companies are addressing the issues of aligning division managers' incentives with those of the company by using an approach called *economic value added analysis*. Economic value added analysis encourages managers to focus on increasing the value of the company to shareholders.

At the most fundamental level, management control systems should provide incentives for managers in the private sector to add economic value to their company. **Economic value added (EVA)** is the value created by a company in excess of the cost of capital for the investment base.

Economic value added indicates how much shareholder wealth is being created by company managers. As explained by Roberto Goizueta, CEO at Coca-Cola, the company raised capital to make concentrate and sold it at a profit. Then the company paid the cost of that capital. EVA measures the difference pocketed by shareholders.

Here is a simple example. Assume a company has invested $10 million of capital in a particular product line. If the company's cost of capital is 14 percent, then the product line must return more than $1.4 million (14 percent) to add economic value.

If a project's economic value added is negative, then shareholder wealth is being reduced and management should consider how to improve economic value added. Improving economic value added can be accomplished in three ways:

1. Increase profit without using more capital (cost cutting is the current trend).
2. Use less capital (e.g., less-expensive equipment).
3. Invest capital in high-return projects (high growth is typically an important factor).

Companies' interest in EVA reflects an increased awareness by corporate managers that their task is to create value for shareholders. Many institutional investors, such as TIAA-CREF, the giant teachers' retirement plan, and CALPERS, the State of California employees' retirement plan, have challenged company executives for failing to create sufficient value for shareholders. Companies that employ EVA include Coca-Cola, Quaker Oats, Georgia Pacific, AT&T, and Eli Lily.[3]

PROBLEM 14.1 FOR SELF-STUDY

Divisional incentive systems.

a. What two key questions must management answer in designing incentive systems?

b. What incentives are given to managers when accountants write off design and development costs as overhead in the period when these costs are incurred?

c. What are the three ways to improve economic value according to the EVA concept?

The solution to this self-study problem is at the end of the chapter on page 490.

INCENTIVE PROBLEMS

This section of the chapter deals with ethical issues in financial reporting. We focus on motives and opportunities for committing fraud by managers and employees in companies. We have added this discussion for a simple reason. An increasing number of former students have come to us stressing the importance of discussing real ethical dilemmas people face on the job. This discussion should take place in a variety of classes, they say, and not be limited to classes on ethics. We agree.

Many managers and other employees are often placed under enormous pressure to meet high performance short-term financial standards like profits and return on investment. Consequently, managers and other employees may be tempted to "cook the books" by carrying obsolete inventory on the books, overstating revenues, understating costs, or by other methods.

All of you are likely to encounter some form of pressure to fudge the numbers. Some of you will design systems to detect and deter fraudulent or other unethical behavior, or you will work in the growing field of forensic accounting in which you might assist attorneys as expert witnesses or as consultants. All of you will benefit from an understanding of the conditions conducive to fraudulent financial reporting.

The purpose of this discussion is to help you understand conditions conducive to fraudulent financial reporting. Before continuing, we want to emphasize that the

---

[3]See "Creating Stockholder Wealth," *Fortune,* December 1995, pp. 105–114; and K. Lehn and A. K. Makija, "EVA & MVA," *Strategy and Leadership,* May/June 1996, pp. 34–38.

vast majority of people in business organizations behave ethically, in our view. Even people who behave ethically find that they, or people they know, sometimes find themselves in situations that create pressure to behave unethically.

FRAUDULENT FINANCIAL REPORTING

Fraudulent financial reporting is intentional conduct resulting in materially misleading financial statements. Common examples of fraudulent financial reporting occur when companies recognize revenue before making the sale and when companies do not write down obsolete inventory. Stealing is not the same as financial fraud, but falsifying financial reports to cover up a theft could be financial fraud. Unintentional errors in preparing financial statements do not constitute fraudulent financial reporting.

For financial reporting to be fraudulent,

(1) it must result from intentional or reckless conduct, and

(2) the resulting misstatements must be material to the financial statements.

To be *material,* the misstatement must be large enough to affect the judgment of a responsible person relying on the information. Simply stated, to be *material,* the misstatement must be important.

For a law enforcement agency, such as the Securities and Exchange Commission (SEC), to prove fraud requires the agency to prove either intent to commit fraud or reckless conduct, a difficult task. Consequently, when the SEC brings charges against people for violating the antifraud provisions of the securities laws, it often settles the cases by having the accused sign "consent" documents. The signer of a consent decree says, in effect, "Maybe I did or maybe I didn't commit fraud, but I promise not to do it again." The cases we discuss in the following sections involve *alleged* fraud because the SEC has generally not proven financial fraud.

WHO COMMITS FRAUD?

Employees at all levels in the organization, from top management to low-level employees, might participate in fraudulent financial reporting. Enforcement agencies sometimes find the company's external auditors responsible for their clients' fraudulent financial reporting.

We focus on the use of accounting information by managers inside organizations. Department and division managers may commit fraud when reporting to their superiors. For example, managers at certain PepsiCo bottling plants misled their superiors at corporate headquarters in Purchase, New York, by failing to write off obsolete or unusable bottle inventories.

Fraudulent reporting inside a company misleads top management and the board of directors as well as stockholders and other outsiders who rely on the company's financial information. Top managers sometimes commit fraud by misleading outsiders. Most cases reported by the media involve top management.

In many cases, management or the board of directors cure the problem involving potential fraud before financial reporting occurs and the firm files fraudulent financial statements with the Securities and Exchange Commission. In many cases, people started out bending the rules a little, only to find themselves in deep trouble after bending the rules for a long time.

TYPES OF FRAUD

People have tried many types of fraud, including omitting liabilities from financial statements, overstating assets on the balance sheet, and preparing false appraisals or other documents to support loans. Subsequent investigation showed that many of the savings and loan companies that failed in the 1980s had relied on fraudulent loan documentation. Our research indicates the two most common types of fraud involve improper revenue recognition and overstating inventory.

IMPROPER REVENUE RECOGNITION

Over long-enough time spans, total revenue will equal total cash (or other assets) received from customers. Improper revenue recognition occurs when the firm reports the profit-increasing effects of revenue in the wrong accounting period—typically, but not always, too early. Improper revenue recognition results if a firm backdates sales to report revenue on December 30, Year 1, when the firm should have reported the sales as having occurred in January of Year 2. Such a firm shows both the revenue and the cost of goods sold in Year 1 instead of Year 2.

For example, MiniScribe, a Denver-based computer disk drive manufacturer, backdated invoices for sales made on the first day of the year to the last day of the previous year.[4] The company also had shipped bricks to distributors and booked them as sales of disk drives. The early recognition of revenue and booking of nonexistent revenues increased profits reported to shareholders. In other cases, companies have shipped products to company-owned warehouses but claimed the shipments were sales.

To compensate for the effects of previous fraud, perpetrators must continue to commit fraud. Note that early revenue recognition, resulting from backdating invoices or prematurely recording a sale, has only a temporary effect on reported revenues and profits. Pulling a sale out of Period 2 to report it in Period 1 improves profits for Period 1, but reduces sales to be reported in Period 2. Now Period 2 does not look as good as it should, so the perpetrator moves sales from Period 3 back to Period 2 to cover for the sales previously moved from Period 2 to Period 1. The perpetrator must continue this practice or else the current period will show a revenue shortfall.

---

[4]"How MiniScribe Got Its Auditor's Blessing on Questionable Sales," *The Wall Street Journal,* May 14, 1992, p. A5.

Example

The following example shows how one can get deeper and deeper into trouble with premature revenue recognition.

Financial Fraud: The Early Revenue Recognition Problem

Year I: December 28, 1996

    Buyer: "We really want your product, but we can't process the paperwork until January 3, 1997."

    Salesperson thinks: "No problem. We'll date everything December 28, 1996, so I'll get credit for the sale in 1996."

Year II: December 28, 1997

    Salesperson thinks: "I haven't heard from the buyer yet. I know they normally purchase an order about now. I'll just ship their normal order and date everything December 28, 1997."

Year III: December 28, 1998

    Salesperson thinks: "I'm under a lot of pressure to make my sales budget. I know *someone* will want this stuff. I'll ship it to some customers and record the sale on December 28, 1998. If the customers return the merchandise, I'll just say it's a mistake."

The salesperson started in Year I with a minor indiscretion. By Year III, the salesperson has committed a major fraud.

OVERSTATING INVENTORY

Overstated ending inventory leads to overstated earnings. Recall the inventory equation:

Cost of Goods Sold = Beginning Inventory + Purchases − Ending Inventory

The higher Ending Inventory, the lower Cost of Goods Sold, and the higher reported earnings. Overstated inventory results, for example, when managers or accountants fail to write down obsolete inventory. Department or division managers may not want to "take a hit" (reduce reported earnings) on the financial reports in the current period, so they postpone the write-off until later. In other cases, people falsify the ending inventory numbers during physical inventory counts or on audit papers.

For example, investigators of the MiniScribe case said that senior company officials "apparently broke into locked trunks containing the auditors' workpapers" during the audit and inflated inventory values by approximately $1 million. In addition, employees created a computer program they called "Cook Book" to inflate inventory figures.[5]

Overstating ending inventory will increase reported earnings in the period of overstatement, but in the absence of continuing overstatement must result in reduced earnings reported in the next period. Refer again to the inventory equation. Higher Beginning Inventory increases Cost of Goods Sold and decreases reported earnings.

---

[5]"Coopers & Lybrand Agrees to Payment of $95 Million in the MiniScribe Case," *The Wall Street Journal,* October 30, 1992, p. A2.

To continue to appear successful, the perpetrator of frauds must continue to overstate ending inventory, just to keep reported earnings from decreasing.

Example

Financial Fraud: The Overstated Inventory Problem

Year I: December 31, 1996

    Manager thinks: "About 20 percent of my inventory is obsolete. But if I write it off this year, my profits will be lower than budget. Maybe next year, profits will be higher (or I'll have a new job somewhere else in the company)."

Year II: December 31, 1997

    Manager thinks: "I'm still in the same job as last year and even more of my inventory is obsolete. Now I'll look *really* bad if I write off the inventory."

Effect on Taxes   Fraudulent financial reporting that results in higher reported earnings sometimes also overstates taxable income. Because over long-enough time spans, reported earnings must equal operating cash inflows less operating cash outflows, lower taxable income in some future period must offset any overstated taxable income in earlier periods. Nevertheless, overstating taxable income in early periods likely increases the present value of a company's tax payments. Financial fraud might not affect the total taxes paid, but does change the timing of tax payments and, therefore, their present value.

CAUSES OF FINANCIAL FRAUD

SHORT-TERM ORIENTATION

Many firms use accounting numbers to grade, or evaluate, managers. Bonuses, merit pay increases, and promotions often depend on reported accounting numbers.

Why would a manager backdate sales from one year to an earlier year, which merely shifts profits, but does not create them? Managers given a short-term perspective by their employment and pay arrangements will have an incentive to "manage earnings" this way. Department and division managers may believe they have an opportunity to be promoted to a new position or transferred to another part of the company if they perform well in the current year. If so, they have incentives to look good in their current year, not caring about the subsequent shortfall on their unit's reported performance.

Some companies reward managers for achieving a performance threshold, providing large and discontinuous, or lumpy, rewards for meeting specified targets. For example, a company may offer a bonus of 50 percent of salary if the manager's division achieves its target return on investment (ROI), but only 25 percent of the manager's salary if the division achieves 95 percent to 100 percent of the target ROI, and no bonus if the division reports an ROI less than 95 percent of the target. A manager who finds the ROI just below the threshold, say, just under 95 percent of the target ROI, has a personal financial stake on reporting ROI at the 95 percent level. The manager may hope that moving a few sales forward from next year to this year will not hurt next year's rewards as much as it helps this year's rewards.

DO PERFORMANCE EVALUATION SYSTEMS
CREATE INCENTIVES TO COMMIT FRAUD?

Management sometimes correctly believes that high-pressure performance evaluation systems effectively motivate employees. If so, management must also realize that putting pressure on people to perform well also creates incentives to commit fraud. The pressure to perform can affect top executives as well as middle managers and employees. Top executives in a company often feel pressured to perform because of the demands of stockholders, the expectations of financial analysts, or simply their own egos.

In 1987, the Treadway Commission, a federal commission on fraudulent financial reporting, reported the results of its study of financial fraud involving top management and fraudulent reporting to stockholders. The Commission concluded that fraudulent financial reporting occurred because of a combination of pressures, incentives, opportunities, and environment. According to the Commission, the forces that seemed to give rise to financial fraud "are present to some degree in all companies. If the right combustible mixture of forces and opportunities is present, fraudulent financial reporting may occur."[6]

The Commission went on to say fraud in financial reporting sometimes results from a manager's wish to improve a company's financial appearance to obtain a higher stock price or to escape penalty for poor performance. The Commission listed examples of pressures to perform that may lead to financial fraud, including the following:

- Unrealistic budget pressures, particularly for short-term results. These pressures occur when headquarters arbitrarily determines profit objectives and budgets without taking actual conditions into account.
- Financial pressure resulting from bonus plans that depend on short-term economic performance. This pressure is particularly acute when the bonus is a significant component of the individual's total compensation.[7]

Note the Treadway Commission's reference to companies' emphasis on *short-term* performance. Most cases of financial fraud involve a timing adjustment. Management will take chances on the future to make the current period look good. One department manager told us, "Of course I'm more concerned about the short run than the long run. If I don't look good now, I won't be around in the long run."

The Treadway Commission concluded that unrealistic profit objectives in budgets can cause financial fraud. Top management in large and widely dispersed companies have difficulty setting reasonable expectations for their far-flung divisions. That companies decentralize their operations reflects the reality that top management of large and dispersed companies cannot involve themselves in the details of local operations. Consequently, top management may mistakenly expect unrealistically good performance.

---

[6]*Report of the National Commission on Fraudulent Financial Reporting* (Treadway Commission) (Washington, D.C: National Commission on Fraudulent Financial Reporting, 1987), p. 23.

[7] Ibid., p. 24.

The MiniScribe case involved pressure from top management. According to investigators of the fraud at MiniScribe, MiniScribe's chief executive's unrealistic sales targets and abusive management style created pressure that drove managers to cook the books or perish. "And cook they did—booking shipments as sales, manipulating reserves, and simply fabricating figures—to maintain the illusion of unbounded growth even after the computer industry was hit by a severe slump."[8]

ENVIRONMENTAL CONDITIONS

In our opinion, the tone at the top most strongly influences fraudulent financial reporting. The tone at the top refers to the environment top management sets for dealing with ethical issues. No matter how extensive management's list of rules, no matter the clarity of a company code of conduct that employees must read and sign, top management's own behavior sends the most important signal about how to do things. Just looking the other way when subordinates act unethically sets a tone that encourages fraudulent reporting.

During your career, you will almost certainly sense the tone at the top in companies you work with or for. If top management looks away from unethical behavior, the chances increase that employees will commit fraud. You will less likely find financial fraud when top managers set firm guidelines and follow those guidelines themselves.

CONTROLS TO PREVENT FRAUD

Enough clever people working together to commit fraud will probably succeed. Companies establish internal controls to help prevent fraud. **Internal controls** are policies and procedures designed to provide top management with reasonable assurances that actions undertaken by employees will meet organizational goals. Internal controls help assure top management that the data it relies on for decision making do not result from fraudulent reports by lower-level employees. Because top management can override internal controls, such controls do not necessarily assure stockholders and other readers of companies' financial statements that top management reports accurately.

A fundamental principle of internal control to prevent fraud separates duties when a single person carrying out a series of tasks could commit fraud and take steps to hide it. For example, separation of duties in a department store requires that the person making the sale be different from the person who records it in the financial records. For the sale to be fraudulently reported, the sales clerk and the recorder would have to work together, or collude. **Collusion** is the cooperative effort of employees to commit fraud or other unethical acts.

---

[8]"How Pressure to Raise Sales Led MiniScribe to Falsify Numbers," *The Wall Street Journal,* September 11, 1989, p. A1.

Internal controls that separate duties make fraud more difficult because with separation of duties, fraud requires collusion. As the number of people colluding increases, so does the chance of whistle blowing to higher authorities, such as auditors, the Securities and Exchange Commission, and the media. Thus, the separation-of-duties doctrine of internal control prefers more, rather than fewer, people to handle a series of functions.

INTERNAL AUDITING

Firms hire internal auditors to help management or the board of directors, or both. They often report to the audit committee of a company's board of directors. Internal auditors can both deter and detect fraud. They can deter fraud by reviewing and testing internal controls and ensuring controls are in place and working well.

INDEPENDENT AUDITORS

Firms hire independent auditors primarily to express an opinion on published financial statements, not to detect fraud. Nevertheless, the presence of the independent auditors and their review of a company's internal controls help to prevent fraud. Further, independent auditors increasingly attempt to detect fraud, which should help deter it. The board of directors, management, or stockholders can also hire independent auditors to do examinations for fraud.

INCENTIVE PROBLEMS IN INTERNATIONAL MARKETS

There are many cultural differences between countries that affect business practices. For example, in some countries, payments to government officials (for example, bribes or gifts) are an acceptable form of obtaining government contracts. In 1977 Congress addressed this issue by passing the Foreign Corrupt Practices Act (FCPA), which makes it illegal for any U.S. citizen or company to make these types of payments to foreign government officials in the course of business.[9] Since the act applies only to U.S. firms, this may put them at a competitive disadvantage in the international market when firms from other countries are not subject to the same limitation.

The FCPA affects U.S. companies doing business in foreign countries where bribery is the norm in negotiating for government contracts. Subsidiaries of U.S. companies in foreign countries hire native employees who may not even realize that it is illegal for U.S. companies to conduct business in this manner. For instance, re-

---

[9]The act addresses questionable payments to foreign officials, record-keeping, and internal accounting control. The FCPA makes it unlawful for virtually any officer, director, employee, or agent acting for any company to use the mails or interstate commerce corruptly for the purpose of paying foreign officials to obtain or retain business. "Grease payments" paid to low-level government employees to expedite routine matters are excluded. The act requires all companies registered with the SEC to make and keep accurate books and records, and to devise and maintain a system of internal accounting controls adequate enough that managers of a company will know if a bribe is paid.

cently the SEC and the U.S. Justice Department investigated allegations that officials of IBM's subsidiary in Argentina made illegal payments in order to receive a $250 million contract to modernize the National Bank of Argentina.[10] So, when incentives are present for managers to act aggressively in securing contracts, the incentives and the company policies must support the company upholding the act or it may be ignored.

PROBLEM 14.2 FOR SELF-STUDY

Fraudulent financial reporting. Why is the "tone at the top" of a company important in preventing fraudulent financial reporting?

The solution to this self-study problem is at the end of the chapter on page 491.

SUMMARY

The following items correspond to the learning objectives presented at the beginning of the chapter.

1. **Describe key characteristics of divisional incentive compensation plans.** Effective incentive compensation plans must induce individual behavior compatible with increasing the firm's wealth. Three common characteristics are: cash bonuses and profit sharing for short-term performance, deferred compensation for long-term incentive, and special awards for particular actions or extraordinary performance.

2. **Know how incentive plans can affect the development phase of the product life cycle.** Incentive plans based on short-term accounting performance may deter managers from investing in product development at a point in the product life cycle when the investment can do the most to ensure the most cost-effective method of production through the product's life.

3. **Know how the concept of economic value added affects management incentive systems.** Management control systems should provide incentives for managers in the private sector to add economic value to their company. Economic value added (EVA) is defined as annual after-tax operating profit minus the total annual cost of capital. Economic value added indicates how much shareholder wealth is being created by company managers.

4. **Explain what constitutes fraudulent financial reporting.** Fraudulent financial reporting results from intentional or reckless conduct, and the resulting misstatements are material to the financial statements.

5. **Define the two most common types of fraud and demonstrate their impact on financial statements.** The two most common types of fraud involve improper revenue recognition and overstating inventory. Improper revenue recognition

---

[10]J. Friedland, *The Wall Street Journal,* January 18, 1996, pp. A10, A11.

occurs when the firm reports the profit-increasing effects of revenue in the wrong accounting period, usually early. Overstated ending inventory leads to overstated earnings, by understating Cost of Goods Sold.

6. **Recognize the incentives for committing financial fraud.** Bonuses, merit pay increases, and promotions often depend on reported accounting numbers. Managers given a short-term perspective by their employment and pay arrangements will have an incentive to "manage earnings." High-pressure performance evaluation systems not only put pressure on people to perform well but also create incentives to commit fraud.

7. **Explain how environmental conditions influence fraudulent conduct.** The tone at the top—the environment top management sets for dealing with ethical issues—most strongly influences fraudulent financial reporting. Regardless of policies and rules, looking the other way when subordinates act unethically sets a tone that encourages fraudulent reporting.

8. **Identify controls that can be instituted to prevent financial fraud.** A fundamental principle of internal control to prevent fraud separates duties where a single person carrying out a series of tasks could commit fraud and take steps to hide it. Separation of duties makes fraud more difficult because fraud then requires collusion. Internal auditors can both deter and detect fraud. The presence of the independent auditors and their review of a company's internal controls help to prevent fraud.

KEY TERMS AND CONCEPTS

Economic value added (EVA)   Annual after-tax operating profit minus the total annual cost of capital.

Fraudulent financial reporting   Intentional or reckless conduct that results in materially misleading financial statements.

Internal controls   Policies and procedures designed to provide management with reasonable assurance that employees behave in a way that enables the firm to meet its organizational goals.

Collusion   Cooperative effort by employees to commit fraud or other unethical acts.

SOLUTIONS TO SELF-STUDY PROBLEMS

SUGGESTED SOLUTION TO PROBLEM 14.1 FOR SELF-STUDY

a. First, what behavior does the incentive system motivate?
   Second, what behavior does management desire?

b. Managers have incentives to reduce expenditures on design and development even if the expenditures would be justified in terms of future cost savings.

c. EVA recommends:
   (1) increase profit without using more capital (e.g., cost cutting);

(2) use less capital;

(3) invest capital in high-return projects.

SUGGESTED SOLUTION TO PROBLEM 14.2 FOR SELF-STUDY

The "tone at the top" is important because top management influences the morale and behavior of all employees. Top management can override or circumvent an internal control system, and can circumvent the formal performance evaluation and reward system, to encourage fraudulent reporting.

QUESTIONS, EXERCISES, PROBLEMS, AND CASES

REVIEW QUESTIONS

1. Review the meaning of the concepts or terms discussed in Key Terms and Concepts.
2. What are the major characteristics of divisional incentive compensation plans?
3. How does economic value added (EVA) increase shareholder value?
4. What are the ways economic value added encourages increasing shareholder wealth?
5. What is fraudulent financial reporting? What are the two key concepts in the definition of fraudulent financial reporting?
6. What are common types of fraudulent financial reporting?
7. How does the separation of duties help prevent financial fraud?
8. How do internal auditors deter or detect financial fraud?

CRITICAL ANALYSIS AND DISCUSSION QUESTIONS

9. Refer to the Managerial Application, "Conflicts in an Incentive Compensation Plan." What were the conflicting incentives facing the divisional controllers?
10. How does the accounting write off of design and development costs as current period expenses affect managers' incentives to incur these costs?
11. What is the underlying philosophy of economic value added (EVA) incentive plans?
12. Do shareholders get much attention in economic value added incentive plans? Explain.
13. A large company hired your friend. She confides in you about a problem with her boss. Her boss is asking customers to sign a sales agreement just before the end of the year, which indicates a sale has been made. Her boss then tells these customers that he will give them 30 days, which is well into next year, to change their minds. If they do not change their minds, then he sends the merchandise to them. If they change their minds, her boss agrees to cancel the orders, take back the merchandise, and cancel the invoices. Her boss gives the sales agreements to the accounting department, which prepares an invoice and records the sale. One of the people in accounting keeps the invoices and shipping documents for these customers in a desk drawer until the customers either change their minds, in

which case the sale is canceled, or until the merchandise is sent at the end of the 30-day waiting period.

Your friend likes the company, and she wants to keep her job. What would you advise her to do?

14. The Treadway Commission indicated that bonus plans based on achieving short-run financial results have been a factor in financial frauds, particularly when the bonus is a large component of an individual's compensation. Why do these bonus plans affect fraud?

15. An employee has been stealing some of the company's merchandise and selling it. Is this behavior financial fraud?

16. Suppose the employee in question **15** covers up the theft by accounting for it as spoilage. Would accounting for the stolen items as spoilage be financial fraud?

17. Suppose an accounting clerk who knows nothing about the theft in question **15** erroneously records the "lost" parts as spoilage. Would that be fraudulent financial reporting?

18. Suppose an accounting clerk fails to write off $5 million of obsolete inventory at a large department store. The amount is material. Suppose the Securities and Exchange Commission filed a charge against the clerk alleging financial fraud. Do you believe the clerk's failure to write off the inventory, which resulted in misstated financial statements, could be considered unintentional? Explain your answer.

EXERCISES

Solutions to even-numbered exercises are at the end of this chapter after the cases.

19. **Economic value added.** Managers of Lebond Manufacturing have provided you with the following information about a project:

Capital employed:	
Equipment	$ 500,000
Land	350,000
Building	1,000,000
After-tax cash flow	400,000
Cost of capital: 15%	

Calculate the economic value added.

20. **Economic value added**. Patrina Products is considering the following project:

Capital employed:	
Equipment	$1,000,000
Land	850,000
Building	1,500,000
After-tax cash flow	500,000
Cost of capital: 14%	

Calculate the economic value added.

21. **Economic value added.** SRW Industries is considering the following project:

Capital employed:	
Equipment	$2,000,000
Land	1,250,000
Building	1,500,000
After-tax cash flow	600,000
Cost of capital: 13%	

 a. Calculate the economic value added.
 b. What would the economic value added be if an additional investment of $200,000 was made in equipment which increased productivity and therefore increased after-tax cash flow to $800,000?

PROBLEMS

22. **Accounting and decision making.** Equilibrium, Inc., uses a cost of capital rate of 12 percent in making investment decisions. It currently is considering two mutually exclusive projects, each requiring an initial investment of $10 million. The first project has a net present value of $21 million and an internal rate of return of 20 percent. The firm will complete this project within 1 year. It will raise accounting income and earnings per share almost immediately thereafter. The second project has a net present value of $51 million and an internal rate of return of 30 percent. The second project requires incurring large, noncapitalizable expenses over the next few years before net cash inflows from sales revenue result. Thus accounting income and earnings per share for the next few years will not only be lower than if the first project is accepted but will also be lower than earnings currently reported.
 a. Should the short-run effects on accounting income and earnings per share influence the decision about the choice of projects? Explain.
 b. Should either of the projects be accepted? If so, which one? Why?

23. **Accounting for advertising.** Biogenetics, Inc. spends $60,000 advertising the company's brand names and trademarks. Gross margin on sales after taxes is up $66,000 each year because of these advertising expenditures. For the purposes of this problem, assume that the firm makes all advertising expenditures on the first day of each year and that the $66,000 extra after-tax gross margin on sales occurs on the first day of the next year. Excluding any advertising assets or profits, Biogenetics, Inc. has $200,000 of other assets that have produced an after-tax income of $20,000 per year. Biogenetics, Inc. follows a policy of declaring dividends each year equal to net income, and it has a cost of capital of 10 percent per year.
 a. Is the advertising policy a sensible one? Explain.
 b. How should accounting report the expenditures for advertising in Biogenetics' financial statements to reflect accurately the managerial decision of advertising at the rate of $60,000 per year? In other words, how can the firm account for the advertising expenditures in such a way that the accounting rate of return for the advertising project and the rate of return on assets for the firm reflect the 10-percent return from advertising?

24. **Management incentives and accounting for research and development.** The Peltier Division has $300,000 of total assets, earns $45,000 per year, and generates $45,000 per year of cash flow. The cost of capital is 15 percent. Each year, Peltier pays cash of $45,000 to its parent company, Ramos, Inc. Peltier's management has discovered a project requiring research and development costs now that will lead to new products. The anticipated cash flows for this project follow: beginning of Year 1, outflow of $24,000; beginning of Years 2, 3, and 4, inflows of $10,000 each.

    Assume that Ramos undertakes the project, that cash flows are as planned, and Peltier pays $45,000 to Ramos at the end of the first year and $47,000 at the end of each of the next 3 years.

    a. Compute Peltier's rate of return on assets for each year of the project, assuming that accounting expenses R&D expenditures as they occur. Use the year-end balance of total assets in the denominator.

    b. Compute Peltier's rate of return on assets for each year of the project, assuming that accounting capitalizes and then amortizes R&D costs on a straight-line basis over the last 3 years of the project. Use the year-end balance of total assets in the denominator.

    c. Compute the new project's accounting rate of return, independent of the other assets and of the income of Peltier assuming that accounting capitalizes and then amortizes R&D costs on a straight-line basis over the entire 4 years of the project.

    d. How well has the management of the Peltier Division carried out its responsibility to its owners? On what basis do you make this judgment?

25. **Explain premature revenue recognition.** You have been asked to advise a manufacturing company how to detect fraudulent financial reporting. Management does not understand how early revenue recognition by backdating invoices from next year to this year would affect financial statements. Further, management wants to know which accounts could be audited for evidence of fraud in the case of early revenue recognition.

    a. Using your own numbers, make up an example to show management the effect of early revenue recognition.

    b. Prepare a short report to management explaining the accounts that early revenue recognition would affect. Suggest some ways management could find errors in those accounts.

26. **Explain inventory overstatement.** A merchandising company has asked you to advise it how to detect fraudulent financial reporting. Management wants your help in detecting inventory overstatement. Further, management wants to know how to find evidence of inventory overstatement.

    a. Using your own numbers, make up an example to show management the effect of overstating inventory. Show how inventory overstatement at the end of Year 1 carries through to the beginning inventory overstatement.

    b. Prepare a brief report to management suggesting ways management could detect inventory overstatement.

27. **Top management's awareness of fraud.** The chief executive of Leslie Fay, a dressmaking company charged with committing financial fraud, was dismayed that the controller and other employees had committed fraud. He said the company could have taken steps to improve the situation if senior management had

known the poor financial results. Financial analysts who follow the company had noted, however, that the company had marked down its clothing line in sales to retail stores such as May Department Stores and Federated Department Stores.

After the company cut prices 20 percent across the board, retail executives who were customers of Leslie Fay wondered how Leslie Fay could continue to be profitable. One analyst wondered how top management could not have known about the company's financial difficulties in view of the 20-percent markdown.

For your information, top management is located in New York City, and the fraud occurred at the financial offices in Wilkes-Barre, Pennsylvania. The line of reporting is as follows: the controller reports to the chief financial officer and the chief financial officer reports to the chief executive of the company. Both the controller and chief financial officer work in Wilkes-Barre. The chief financial officer reportedly has considerable autonomy.

Write a short report indicating whether you think top management of the company is responsible for the fraud and state why (or why not).

CASES

28. **Motives and opportunities for fraud.** A report on the "income transferal" activities at the H. J. Heinz Company made the following statements.[11] First, decentralized authority is a central principle of the company's operations. Second, the company expected its divisions to generate an annual growth in profits of approximately 10 to 12 percent per year. Third, it was neither unusual nor undesirable for management to put pressure on the division managers and employees to produce improved results.

The report noted that putting pressure on the divisions to produce improved results, coupled with the company's philosophy of autonomy, which it extended to financial and accounting controls, provided both an incentive and opportunity for division managers to misstate financial results. The report further stated, "The autonomous nature of the [divisions] combined with the relatively small World Headquarters financial staff permitted the conception of what at best can be described as a communications gap . . . In its simplest form, there seems to have been a tendency to issue an order or set a standard with respect to achieving a financial result without regard to whether complete attainment was possible."[12] "In the managements of certain of the [divisions], there was a feeling of 'us versus them' towards World Headquarters."[13]

The report indicated there was an effort in certain divisions to transfer income from one fiscal period to another to provide a "financial cushion" for achieving the goal for the succeeding year. For example, divisions would overpay expenses so they could get a credit or refund in a subsequent year. Or they would pay an expense such as insurance or advertising early, but instead of charging the amount to a prepaid expense account, they would charge the amount to expense.

[11]This case is based on the "Report of Audit Committee to the Board of Directors, Income Transferal and Other Practices," H. J. Heinz Company, May 6, 1980.

[12]Ibid., p. 9.

[13]Ibid., p. 14.

In good years, this practice would keep profits down and provide a cushion to meet the company's target for constantly increasing profits.

    a. Using your own numbers, construct an example to demonstrate the kind of income transferal that was done at H. J. Heinz.

    b. What was the motive to transfer income from one period to the other? What were the opportunities to transfer income?

    c. Comment on how the communications gap and the "us versus them" attitude contributed to the fraud.

    d. Refer to **c.** Have you seen communications gaps in organizations that have resulted in an "us versus them" attitude on the part of employees? If so, briefly describe the circumstances and the cause of the "us versus them" attitude. What could have been done (or could be done) to change the "us versus them" attitude in your example?

29. **Measuring managerial performance: new challenges.** Many commentators about North American business have argued that the relative deterioration in manufacturing productivity compared to Japanese manufacturers results from a preoccupation with short-term financial performance measures. Many firms base bonus plans for senior executives on annual accounting income. This method provides incentives to take actions that enhance short-term earnings performance that may not serve the best long-term interests of the firm. By contrast, Japanese firms give executives incentives to ensure the long-run viability of their companies. Consequently, they are more concerned than their North American counterparts with long-run productivity, quality control, and managing the company's physical assets.

    Not everyone agrees with the observation that North American business executives are preoccupied with short-term financial performance to the extent that they would take actions contrary to the best long-run economic interests of the organization just to make themselves look good on the performance measures. But suppose that an executive faces a choice between an action with a positive short-run effect on performance measures and another that has better long-run consequences for the organization but that will not affect short-run performance measures positively. We cannot fault a rational executive for taking the action that looks good in the short run. As the saying goes, "You have to look good in the short run to be around in the long run."

    How would you design a control system that encourages top-level managers to be concerned about long-run productivity, quality of products, and the long-run economic well-being of the company? Assume that these managers have previously focused on maximizing quarterly and annual earnings numbers to the detriment of these other factors.

30. **Management decisions and external financial reports.** "Squeezing oranges in your idle time is not a by-product," said the Big Six partner in charge of the audit of Regent Company, disapprovingly.

    "But," replied the president of Regent, "squeezing oranges is not our usual business, and your accounting plan will make us show a substantial decline in income. We all know that our decision this year to squeeze oranges was a good one that is paying off handsomely."

    The argument concerned the accounting for income during the year 1993 by Regent Company.

Background   The Alcoholic Control Board (ACB) of Georgia, a state not known for its production of grapes and wines, wanted to encourage the production of wine within the state. The executives formed the Regent Company in response to the encouragement of the ACB. The production process for wine involves aging the product. The company commenced production in 1987, but did not sell its first batch of wine until 1989. At the start of 1987, Regent made a cash investment of $4,400,000 in grape-pressing equipment and a facility to house that equipment. The ACB has promised to buy Regent Company's output for 10 years, starting with the first batch in 1989. Regent Company decided to account for its operations by including in the cost of the wine all depreciation on the grape-pressing equipment and on the facility to house it. The firm judged the economic life of the equipment to be 10 years, the life of the contract with the ACB. Regent Company reported general and administrative expenses of $100,000 per year in external financial reports for both 1987 and 1988.

Regent Company's contract with the ACB promised payments of $1.8 million per year. The direct costs of labor and materials for each year's batch of wine were $130,000 each year. Accounting charges depreciation on a straight-line bases over a 10-year life. The income taxes were 40 percent of pretax income.

The wine sales began in 1989 and operations proceeded as planned. The income statements for the years 1989 through 1992 appear in Exhibit 14.1.

Management of Regent Company was delighted with the offer from a manufacturer of frozen orange juice to put its idle capacity to work. It contracted with the manufacturer to perform the services. At the end of 1993, it compiled the income statement shown in Exhibit 14.1 as "Management's View."

The Accounting Issue   Management of Regent Company suggested that the revenues from squeezing oranges are an incremental by-product of owning the wine-making machinery. The wine-making process was undertaken on its own merits and has paid off according to schedule. The revenues from squeezing oranges are a by-product of the main purpose of the business. Ordinarily, the accounting for by-products assigns to them costs equal to their net realizable value; that is, accounting assigns costs in exactly the amount that will make the sale of the by-products show neither gain nor loss. In this case, because the incremental revenue of squeezing oranges was $100,000, Regent Company assigned $100,000 of the overhead to this process, reducing from $440,000 to $340,000 the overhead assigned to the main product. This will make the main product appear more profitable when it is sold.

Management of Regent Company was aware that its income for 1993 would appear no different from that of the preceding year. Management knew that the benefits from squeezing oranges began to occur in 1993 but allowed the benefits to appear on the financial statements later.

The Big Six auditor who saw management's proposed income statement disapproved. The partner in charge of the audit spoke as quoted at the beginning of this case.

The auditor argued that squeezing oranges under these circumstances was not a by-product and that by-product accounting was inappropriate. Regent Company must allocate the overhead costs between the two processes of grape pressing and orange squeezing according to some reasonable basis. The most

EXHIBIT 14.1

REGENT COMPANY
Income Statements
(all dollar amounts in thousands)

	1989 to 1992 Each Year, Actual	For 1993	
		Management's View	Auditor's View
Revenues:			
From Wine Put into Production 2 Years Previously	$1,800	$1,800	$1,800
From Orange Juice Squeezed in Current Year	—	100[a]	100[a]
Total Revenues	$1,800	$1,900	$1,900
Cost of Goods Sold:			
Direct Costs of Wine Put into Production 2 Years Previously	$ 300	$ 300	$ 300
Depreciation of Buildings and Equipment:			
From 2 Years Prior, Carried in Inventory until Wine Is Sold	440	440	440
From Current Year, Allocated to Orange Juice	—	100	352
Selling, General, and Administrative Expenses	130	130	130
Income Taxes at 40 Percent	372	372	271
Total Expenses	$1,242	$1,342	$1,493
Net Income	$ 558	$ 558	$ 407

[a]Manufacturer of orange juice pays out-of-pocket costs directly. These items are not shown here.

reasonable basis, the auditor thought, was the time devoted to each of the processes. Because grape pressing used about 20 percent of the year, whereas orange squeezing used 80 percent of the year, the auditor assigned $352,000, or 80 percent, of the overhead costs to orange squeezing and $88,000, or 20 percent, to the wine production. Exhibit 14.1 shows the auditor's income statement.

This statement upset the president of Regent Company. Reported net income in 1993 is down almost 30 percent from 1992, yet things have improved. The president fears the reaction of the board of directors and the shareholders. The president wonders what has happened and what to do.

a. Assuming that the Regent Company faces an after-tax cost of capital of 10 percent, did the company in fact make a good decision in 1986 to enter into an agreement with the state to produce wine? Explain.

b. Did the company in fact make a good decision in 1992 to enter into the agreement with the manufacturer of frozen orange juice?

c. Using management's view of the proper accounting practices, construct financial statements for the years 1994, 1995, and 1996, assuming that events occur as planned and in the same way as in 1993. Generalize these statements to later years.

d. Are management's statements correct given its interpretation of by-product accounting? If not, construct an income statement for 1993 that is consistent with by-product accounting.

e. Is management correct in its interpretation that the orange juice is a by-product?

f. Using the auditor's view of the situation and assuming the same facts as in part **c,** construct income statements for the years 1994, 1995, and 1996. Generalize these statements to later years.

g. Assuming that the auditor is right, what may management of Regent Company do to solve its problem?

SUGGESTED SOLUTIONS TO EVEN-NUMBERED EXERCISES

20. Economic value added.

Capital employed:	
Equipment	$1,000,000
Land	850,000
Building	1,500,000
Total capital employed	$3,350,000
After-tax cash flow	$ 500,000
Cost of capital: 14% × $3,350,000	469,000
Economic value added	$ 31,000

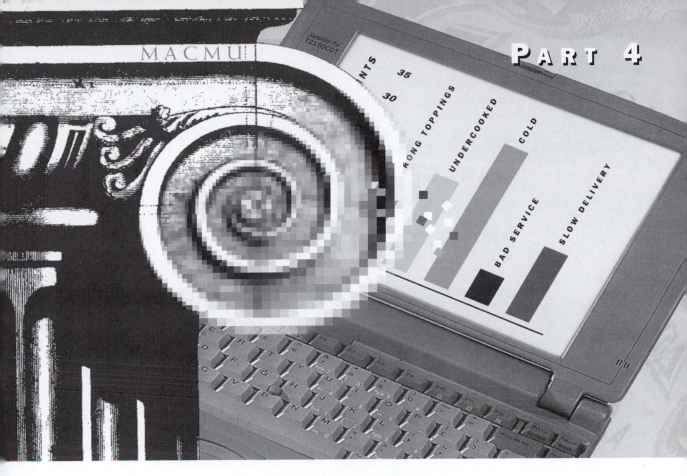

COST SYSTEMS

Chapter 15 presents an overview of cost systems in alternative production settings, including jobs, processes, and service companies. Chapter 15 also contrasts normal and actual costing, and contrasts backflush to traditional costing. Chapter 16 discusses departmental cost allocation.

MANAGERIAL ACCOUNTING SYSTEMS IN ALTERNATIVE PRODUCTION SETTINGS

LEARNING OBJECTIVES

1. Explain the need for recording costs by department and assigning costs to products.
2. Understand how the Work-in-Process account both describes the transformation of inputs into outputs in a company and accounts for the costs incurred in the process.
3. Compare and contrast normal costing and actual costing.
4. Know various production methods and the different accounting systems each requires.
5. Compare and contrast job costing and process costing systems.
6. Compare and contrast product costing in service organizations to that in manufacturing companies.
7. Identify ethical issues in job costing.
8. Recognize components of just-in-time (JIT) production methods and understand how accountants adapt costing systems to them.
9. (Appendix) Know how to compute end-of-period inventory value using equivalent units of production.

This chapter shows how the accounting system records and reports the flow of costs in organizations. The accounting system records costs to help managers answer questions such as these:

- What is the cost of a job at Kinko's copy shop or at the Deloitte & Touche public accounting firm?
- How much does it cost Levi Strauss to make a denim jacket? How does that cost compare to management's expectations?
- How much does it cost Chrysler Corporation to make the Jeep Grand Cherokee?

- How much does it cost the state of New York to provide an undergraduate education at one of the state universities of New York?

This chapter provides an overview of the ways different types of organizations account for their production costs.

RECORDING COSTS BY DEPARTMENT AND ASSIGNING COSTS TO PRODUCTS

As discussed in earlier chapters, experts must design a managerial accounting system to serve several purposes. For purposes of planning and performance evaluation, accountants record costs by departments or other *responsibility centers.* (A responsibility center is simply an organizational unit.) One or more managers are responsible for the activities in each responsibility center in a company. Divisions, territories, plants, and departments are all examples of responsibility centers.

Exhibit 15.1 shows the relation between recording costs by departments and assigning costs to products for a firm with two manufacturing departments, Assembling and Finishing. The accounting system records the costs of direct materials, direct labor, and manufacturing overhead incurred in production in separate accounts for the manufacturing departments, Assembly and Finishing. Management then compares these costs with the standard or budgeted amounts and investigates significant variances. In recording costs by departments, the accounting system has served its function of providing data for departmental performance evaluation. The accounting system also assigns costs to products for managerial decision making, such as evaluating a product's profitability.

NONMANUFACTURING APPLICATIONS

You will also find this relation between recording costs by departments and assigning costs to products in nonmanufacturing settings. For example, accountants record the costs of performing surgery on a patient by department (for example, Surgery), then assigns these costs to a particular patient. In general, for the accounting system

EXHIBIT 15.1

Relation between Departmental and Product Costing

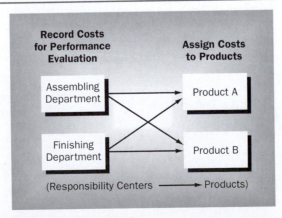

to provide product cost information, it must assign cost to products from responsibility centers.

FUNDAMENTAL ACCOUNTING MODEL OF COST FLOWS

Exhibit 15.2 shows how firms transform materials into finished goods. Note that Work-in-Process is the account that both *describes* the transformation of inputs into outputs in a company and *accounts for* the costs incurred in the process.

EXHIBIT 15.2

Flow of Costs through the Accounts and Departments

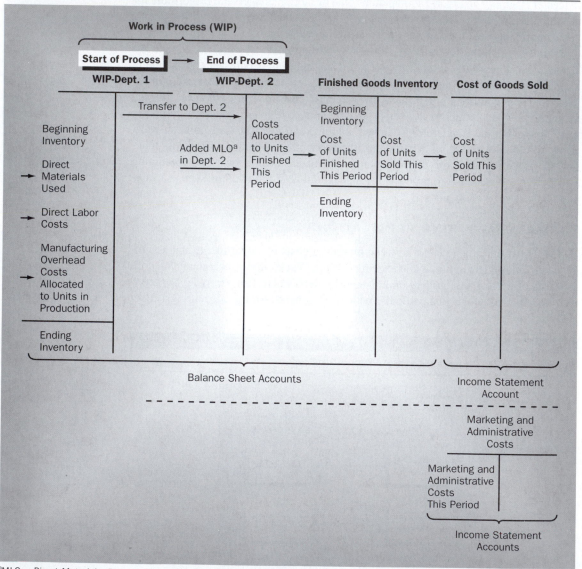

^aMLO = Direct Materials, Direct Labor, and Manufacturing Overhead.

In most companies, each department controls its costs (for example, the Assembly Department or the Finishing Department). Thus each department has a separate Work-in-Process account, as Exhibit 15.2 shows, which accumulates departmental costs. Management holds department managers accountable for the costs accumulated in their departments.

Companies that operate in competitive markets have little direct control over prices paid for materials or prices received for finished goods. Thus a key factor in a company's success is how well it controls the conversion costs (that is, direct labor and overhead). Companies closely monitor those costs in the Work-in-Process Inventory account.

In short, the accounting system serves two purposes in manufacturing and service companies: (1) to record costs by responsibility center (department) for performance evaluation and cost control and (2) to assign manufacturing costs to units produced for product costing.

BASIC COST FLOW EQUATION

Accounting systems are based on the following basic **cost flow equation:**

Beginning Balance + Transfers In = Transfers Out + Ending Balance.

Or in symbols:

$$BB + TI = TO + EB.$$

This equation is a fundamental equality in accounting. Transfers in to work in process represent the materials, labor, and overhead used in production. In merchandising, transfers in to the inventory accounts represent the goods purchased.

PROBLEM 15.1 FOR SELF-STUDY

Using the basic cost flow equation. Fill in the missing item for each of the following inventory accounts:

	A	B	C
Beginning Balance	$40,000	?	$35,000
Ending Balance	32,000	$16,000	27,000
Transferred In	?	8,000	8,000
Transferred Out	61,000	11,000	?

The solution to this self-study problem is at the end of this chapter on page 527.

MANAGERIAL APPLICATION

Using the Basic Cost Flow Equation to Detect Fraud

A top manager at Doughties Foods became curious about the high levels of inventory reported on the divisional financial statements of the Gravins Division. The amount of ending inventory at the Gravins Division seemed high compared to those of other divisions in the company. When asked about the high inventory levels, the division manager confessed that he had overstated the inventory numbers to overstate his divisional profits.

Overstating the ending balance of inventory understates cost of goods sold, which overstates gross margin and profits. In equation form,

$$BB + TI - (EB + F) = TO - F,$$

where F refers to the amount of overstatement from the financial fraud, EB is the correct ending inventory amount, and TO is the correct transfer out of inventory, which is also the correct Cost of Goods Sold. Thus, the reported Cost of Goods Sold was understated by the amount F. As the manager of the Gravins Division discovered to his dismay, the ending inventory for Period 1 is the beginning inventory for Period 2. Thus, the be-ginning inventory on the books carried an over-stated amount, which had to be matched by an equal amount of overstatement at the end of Period 2.

The Gravins Division was a food distributor that kept some of its food inventory in freezers. The company's independent auditors were reluctant to go into the freezer, so the manager of the Gravins Division overstated his inventory by overstating the number of items in the freezer. As time passed, the Gravins Division manager continued to overstate inventory to continue looking good to his bosses. When confronted with the high inventory numbers, the Gravins Division manager confessed to the inventory overstatement, and handed over a notebook containing records of the overstated amounts. Then he resigned.

The Securities and Exchange Commission filed charges alleging financial fraud against the (former) manager of the Gravins Division and filed charges against the auditors for not complying with Generally Accepted Auditing Standards in conducting their audit.

Source: Based on the authors' research.

COST MEASURE: ACTUAL OR NORMAL COSTING

NORMAL COSTING

This section describes a commonly used method known as **normal costing.** Normal costing assigns *actual* direct material and direct labor costs to products, plus an amount representing "normal" manufacturing overhead.

Under normal costing, a firm derives a rate for applying overhead to units produced before the production period, which is often a year in length. The firm uses this rate in applying overhead to each unit as the firm produces it throughout the year. We first discuss the rationale for using normal manufacturing overhead costs; then we show how normal costing works.

An alternative to assigning "normal" overhead to products is to assign the actual overhead costs incurred. Assigning normal overhead costs to products has advantages over assigning actual costs. Actual total manufacturing overhead costs may fluctuate because of seasonality (the cost of utilities, for example) or other reasons that are not related directly to activity levels. Also, if production is seasonal and total overhead costs remain unchanged, the per-unit costs in low-volume months will exceed the per-unit costs in high-volume months, as the following example shows:

	Production	Total Monthly Fixed Manufacturing Overhead	Per-Unit Overhead Cost
January	1,000 Units	$20,000	$20
July	2,000 Units	20,000	10

Normal costs enable companies to smooth, or normalize, these fluctuations. Accountants could even make the *per-unit* overhead cost the same throughout the year, regardless of month-to-month fluctuations in actual costs and activity levels.

Accounting systems can provide actual direct material and direct labor cost information quickly. In contrast, it may take a month or more to learn about the actual overhead costs for the same units. For example, often two weeks to a month will elapse after the end of an accounting period before the firm receives invoices for utilities. To get data quicker, firms frequently use a **predetermined overhead rate** to estimate the cost before the actual cost is known. For our discussion, we assume firms using normal costing use a predetermined rate for the entire year.

APPLYING OVERHEAD COSTS TO PRODUCTION

Here is how normal costing works. Accountants apply overhead costs to production using these four steps:

1. Select a **cost driver,** or **allocation base,** for applying overhead to production. Cost drivers are factors that cause an activity's costs. For example, machine hours could be the factor that causes energy and maintenance costs for a machine. For an automobile, miles driven would be a cost driver.
2. Estimate the amount of overhead and the level of activity for the period (for example, one year).
3. Compute the predetermined (that is, normal) overhead rate from the following formula:

$$\text{Predetermined Manufacturing Overhead Rate} = \frac{\text{Estimated Manufacturing Overhead}}{\text{Normal (or Estimated) Activity Level}}.$$

4. Apply overhead to production by multiplying the predetermined rate, computed in step **3,** times the actual activity (for example, the actual machine hours used to produce a product).

The first three steps take place before the beginning of the period. For example, a firm could complete these steps in November of Year 1 if it plans to use the predetermined rate for Year 2. Step **4** is done during Year 2.

Next we discuss these steps in more detail and show how a firm would apply them.

Example   Plantimum Builders builds mobile homes. In the previous year, Plantimum's total variable manufacturing overhead cost was $100,000 and the activity level was 50,000 direct labor hours. The company expects the same level of activity for this year. Therefore, the company's accountants compute the predetermined rate to be $2.00 per labor hour, as follows:

$$\frac{\text{Predetermined Variable}}{\text{Manufacturing Overhead Rate}} = \frac{\$100{,}000}{50{,}000 \text{ Labor Hours}} = \frac{\$2.00 \text{ per}}{\text{Labor Hour.}}$$

We compute the fixed manufacturing overhead rate in a similar fashion. Plantimum estimates fixed manufacturing overhead costs to be $50,000 for this year and the activity level to be 50,000 machine hours. The company's accountants computed the following rate:

$$\frac{\text{Predetermined Fixed}}{\text{Manufacturing Overhead Rate}} = \frac{\$50{,}000}{50{,}000 \text{ Labor Hours}} = \frac{\$1.00 \text{ per}}{\text{Labor Hour.}}$$

The predetermined overhead rates mean that for each direct labor hour, the accountants charge the houses with $2.00 for variable manufacturing overhead cost and $1.00 for fixed manufacturing overhead.

Assume that Plantimum actually used 4,500 direct labor hours for the month. Plantimum applied the following overhead to production:

Variable Manufacturing Overhead: 4,500 Hours at $2.00	$9,000
Fixed Manufacturing Overhead: 4,500 Hours at $1.00	4,500

PROBLEM 15.2 FOR SELF-STUDY

Normal costing. Pete Petezah, manager of the local Pizza Shack, has asked for your advice about product costs. Pete wants you to compute predetermined overhead rates for the Pizza Shack. Pete provides the following information to you.

Late last year, Pete made the following estimates for the Pizza Shack for this year:

(1) Estimated Variable Overhead	$108,000
(2) Estimated Fixed Overhead	$120,000
(3) Estimated Labor Hours	12,000 hours
(4) Estimated Labor Dollars per Hour	$20
(5) Estimated Output	120,000 pizzas

Compute the predetermined overhead rate for (1) variable overhead and (2) fixed overhead using each of the following cost drivers:

- Labor hours
- Labor dollars
- Output

The solution to this self-study problem is at the end of this chapter on page 528.

CHOOSING THE RIGHT COST SYSTEM

A good cost system has the following three characteristics:

- *Decision focus.* It meets the needs of decision makers.
- *Different costs for different purposes.* It is adaptable enough to provide different cost information for different purposes. For example, it provides variable costs for decision making and full absorption costs for external reporting.
- *Cost-benefit test.* It must meet a cost-benefit test. The benefits from the cost system must exceed its costs.

Exhibit 15.3 shows how production methods vary across organizations, depending on the type of product. Companies that produce **jobs** include print shops, like Kinko's and R. R. Donnelly; custom construction companies, like Morrison-Knudsen; defense contractors, such as General Dynamics; and computerized machine manufactures, like Cincinnati Milacron. These companies all produce customized products, which we call jobs. Companies producing customized products use **job costing** to record the cost of their products.

Many professional service organizations also use job costing, including public accounting and consulting firms, like Price Waterhouse and Andersen Consulting, and law firms, like Baker and McKenzie. The firms use job costing to keep track of costs for each client. Health-care organizations, like Kaiser and the Mayo Clinic, record the costs of each patient's care using job costing. Looking at Exhibit 15.3, which type of production and accounting system do you think NASA uses for the space shuttle program? (Answer: Job and job costing.)

Continuous flow processing is at the opposite end of the continuum from job shops. Companies using continuous flow processing mass-produce homogeneous products in a continuous flow. Companies with continuous flow processes use **process costing** to account for product costs. Coca-Cola and PepsiCo use process costing to track costs of making soft drink syrup. Dow Chemical uses process costing to record the costs of chemical production. AMOCO uses process costing for its oil refining, and Merck uses process costing to record costs of pharmaceutical manufacturing.

Many organizations use job systems for some products and process systems for others. A home builder might use process costing for standardized homes with a particular floor plan. The same builder might use job costing when building a custom-

---

EXHIBIT 15.3

Production Methods and Accounting Systems

Type of Production	Accounting System	Type of Product
Job (health-care services, custom homes, CPA firm)	Job Costing	Customized
Operations (computer terminals, automobiles, clothing)	Operation Costing	Mostly Standardized
Continuous Flow Processing (oil refinery, soft drinks)	Process Costing	Standardized

designed house for a single customer. Honeywell, Inc., a high-tech company, uses process costing for most of its furnace thermostats and job costing for customized aerospace contracting products.

Many companies use a hybrid of job and process costing, called operation costing. **Operations** are a standardized method of making a product that are performed repeatedly in production. Companies using **operation costing** produce products using standardized production methods, like process costing. Materials can be different for each product or batch of products like job costing. Companies in the apparel industry, such as Liz Claiborne and Levi Strauss, computer companies, such as Compaq, and furniture manufacturers, such as Herman Miller, use operation costing.

JOB AND PROCESS COSTING SYSTEMS

This section compares job and process costing. We continue the Plantimum Builders example, using normal costing.

In job costing, firms collect costs for each "unit" produced. Often each department collects costs for evaluating the performance of departmental personnel. For instance, in April, Plantimum Builders started and completed three custom mobile home jobs (no beginning inventories). The data and costs follow:

	Direct Labor	Direct Materials	Direct Labor Hours × Predetermined Overhead Rate	Total Cost of Job
Job No. 1001	$ 8,000	$20,800	(400 × $3) = $1,200	$30,000
Job No. 1002	6,000	18,100	(300 × $3) = 900	25,000
Job No. 1003	5,000	11,250	(250 × $3) = 750	17,000
Total	$19,000	$50,150	$2,850	$72,000

In process costing, firms accumulate costs in a department or production process during an accounting period (for example, one month), then spread those costs evenly over the units produced that month, computing an average unit cost. The formula follows:

$$\text{Unit Cost} = \frac{\text{Total Manufacturing Cost Incurred during the Period}}{\text{Total Units Produced during the Period}}$$

Assume Plantimum Builders had used process costing for the three jobs started and completed in April. The average cost per job would be computed as follows:

$$\frac{\overset{\text{Direct Labor}}{\$19,000} + \overset{\text{Direct Materials}}{\$50,150} + \overset{\text{Applied Overhead}}{\$2,850}}{3 \text{ jobs}} = \$24,000 \text{ per job}$$

Process costing does not require as much record keeping as job costing because it does not require keeping track of the cost of each job. However, process costing only informs decision makers about the average cost of the units, not the cost of *each particular* unit or job.

We have presented an overview of job and process costing. Next, we examine managerial issues in choosing between job and process costing.

JOB VERSUS PROCESS COSTING: COST-BENEFIT CONSIDERATIONS

Why do firms prefer one accounting system to another? Cost-benefit analysis provides the answer. In general, the costs of record keeping under job costing systems exceed those under process costing. Consider the house builder. Under job costing, the house builder must accumulate costs for each house. If a truck delivers lumber to several houses, it is not sufficient to record the total lumber issued. The driver must keep records of the amount delivered to, and subsequently returned from, each house. If laborers work on several houses, they must keep track of the time spent on *each* house.

Process costing, however, requires simply recording the total cost. For the house builder, process costing would report the average cost of all houses built. (In practice, house builders generally use job costing for custom-built houses and process costing for houses having a particular model type or floor plan.)

Under process costing, a firm does not report the direct cost incurred for a particular unit. If all units are homogeneous, this loss of information is probably minimal. Is it important for Kellogg's to know whether the cost of the 1,001st box of Raisin Bran differs from the 1,002nd box's cost? Not likely. The additional benefits from tracing costs to each box of Raisin Bran would not justify the additional record-keeping costs.

Although job costing provides more detailed information than process costing, it is a more expensive accounting system. Thus management and accountants must examine the costs and benefits of information and pick the method that best fits the organization's production operations.

Example   In this example, a custom house builder explains the benefits of job costing for companies that make heterogeneous products.

> We estimate the costs of each house for pricing purposes. Unless we know the actual costs of each house, we cannot evaluate our estimation methods. We use the information for performance evaluation and cost control, too. We assign a manager to each house who is responsible for seeing that actual costs don't exceed the estimate. If the actual costs come in under the estimate, the manager gets a bonus.
>
> We need a job system to help us charge customers for the cost of customer changes, too. Usually, customers make changes as we build. If the changes have a small impact on costs, we absorb them. But if these changes add significant costs, we go to the customer with our computation of the cost of changes, and get an adjustment in the price of the house. Sometimes, we build on a cost-plus basis, which means customers pay us an amount equal to the cost of the job plus a profit. In this case we *must* know and document costs for each house so we can collect from the customer.

Management generally finds that the comparative costs and benefits of job and process costing indicate matching the cost system to the production methods as follows:

Nature of Production	Costing System Used
Heterogeneous Units, Each Unit Large	Job Costing
Homogeneous Units, Continuous Process, Many Small Units	Process Costing

Classifying production as jobs or processes. Classify each of the following products as either a job or coming from a process:

- Work for a client on a lawsuit by lawyers in a law firm.
- Diet cola.
- Patient care in an emergency room for a college basketball player.
- House painting by a company called Student Painters.
- Paint.

The solution to this self-study problem is at the end of this chapter on page 528.

SERVICE ORGANIZATIONS

QUALITY AND SERVICE ISSUES

Service organizations, like manufacturing companies, need good managerial accounting information. Service organizations must be especially sensitive to the timeliness and the quality of the service they provide to their customers. Service organizations do not produce inventory in advance of the customer's need but generally deliver services in real time. Inspectors in manufacturing companies can check the quality of products before they are shipped to customers so that manufacturing errors can be detected and corrected. Service organizations deliver the service directly to the customers, so "defects" are harder to catch before being noticed by the customer.

FLOW OF COSTS IN SERVICE ORGANIZATIONS

The flow of costs in service organizations is similar to that in manufacturing. The service provided requires labor, overhead and, sometimes materials. Service organizations often collect costs by departments for performance evaluation.

In consulting, public accounting, and similar service organizations, the firm also collects costs by job or client. The accounting method is similar to that used in manufacturing job shops. As in manufacturing, the firm collects costs by job for performance evaluation, to provide information for cost control, and to compare actual with estimated costs for pricing of future jobs.

Service organizations differ from manufacturing or merchandising organizations in that service organizations do not show inventories (other than supplies) on the financial statements for external reporting. Service organizations often maintain "Work-in-Process" in their internal records. The account shows the cost of services performed for a client but not yet billed, similar to the accumulation of unbilled costs for a special contract or job in a manufacturing job shop.

Example   For the month of July, Strategic Action Group (SAG) has the following activity:

- Client A: 400 hours.
- Client B: 600 hours.

- Billing rate to client: $200 per hour.
- Labor costs (all consulting staff): $80 per hour.
- Total consulting hours worked in July: 1,200 hours. (SAG did not charge 200 hours to a client. The firm calls that time "direct labor—unbillable.")
- Actual overhead costs for July: $22,000. (Overhead includes travel, secretarial services, telephone, copying, supplies, and postage.)
- Accounting charges overhead to jobs based on labor hours worked using a predetermined rate of $20 per labor hour.
- Marketing and administrative costs: $12,000.
- All transactions are on account.
- Both jobs were billed to clients and the costs transferred from Work-in-Process to Cost of Services.

The entries to record these transactions are as follows:

(1)	Work in Process: Client A	32,000	
	Work in Process: Client B	48,000	
	Direct Labor—Unbillable	16,000	
	Wages Payable		96,000
	(Client A: 400 hours @ $80 = $32,000; Client B: 600 hours @ $80 = $48,000; Unbillable: 200 hours @ $80 = $16,000.)		
(2)	Work in Process: Client A	8,000	
	Work in Process: Client B	12,000	
	Overhead (applied)		20,000
	(Overhead applied to jobs at the rate of $20 per labor hour.)		
(3)	Overhead	22,000	
	Wages and Accounts Payable		22,000
	(Actual overhead: $22,000)		
(4)	Marketing and Administrative Costs	12,000	
	Wages and Accounts Payable		12,000
	(Actual cost: $12,000)		
(5a)	Accounts Receivable	200,000	
	Revenue		200,000
	(To record revenue at $200 per hour: 400 hours for Client A, 600 hours for Client B.)		
(5b)	Cost of Services Billed	100,000	
	Work in Process: Client A		40,000
	Work in Process: Client B		60,000
	(To record the cost of services billed to clients.)		

Note that 5a and 5b are really two parts of the same entry.

Exhibit 15.4 shows the flow of costs through T-accounts. Exhibit 15.5 presents an income statement. Note that the unbilled labor and unassigned overhead are expensed with marketing and administrative costs. We use the traditional (full absorption costing) format for demonstration purposes because some overhead is probably a fixed cost. The contribution margin format would work just as well.

EXHIBIT 15.4

STRATEGIC ACTION GROUP
Flow of Costs in a Service Organization for July

Accounts and Wages Payable		Work in Process: Client A		Cost of Services Billed	
	96,000 **(1)**	**(1)** 32,000		**(5b)** 100,000	
			40,000 **(5b)**		
		(2) 8,000			
	22,000 **(3)**				
	12,000 **(4)**				

	Work in Process: Client B		Marketing and Administrative Costs	
	(1) 48,000		**(4)** 12,000	
		60,000 **(5b)**		
	(2) 12,000			

Accounts Receivable		Overhead		Direct Labor— Unbillable		Revenue	
(5a) 200,000		**(3)** 22,000	20,000 **(2)**	**(1)** 16,000			200,000 **(5a)**

Note: Numbers in parentheses correspond to journal entries in text.

(See Chapter 2 for a comparison and contrast of the traditional and contribution margin formats.) Looking at Exhibit 15.4, what would the Cost of Services Billed and Revenue account balances be if SAG worked 200 instead of 400 hours for Client A? (Answer: Cost of Services Billed = $80,000, Revenue = $160,000.) Looking at Exhibit 15.5, what would the gross margin be? (Answer: $80,000.)

EXHIBIT 15.5

STRATEGIC ACTION GROUP
Income Statement for the Month Ending July 31

Revenue from Services	$200,000
Less Cost of Services Billed	100,000
Gross Margin	100,000
Less:	
Direct Labor—Unbillable	16,000
Overhead (underapplied)	2,000[a]
Marketing and Administrative Costs	12,000
Operating Profit	$ 70,000

---

[a]$2,000 = $22,000 incurred − $20,000 applied to jobs and expensed as part of cost of services billed.

PROBLEM 15.4 FOR SELF-STUDY

Cost flows in a service organization. For the month of September, Touche Andersen & Company, an accounting firm, worked 200 hours for Client A and 700 hours for Client B. Touche Andersen bills clients at the rate of $80 per hour, whereas the audit staff costs $30 per hour. The audit staff worked 1,000 total hours in September (100 hours were not billable to clients), and overhead costs were $10,000. (Examples of unbillable hours are hours spent in professional training and meetings unrelated to particular clients.) Accounting assigned overhead as follows: Client A $2,000, Client B $7,000, and $1,000 unassigned. In addition, Touche Andersen & Company spent $5,000 in marketing and administrative costs. All transactions are on account. The work done in September was billed to the clients.

a. Using T-accounts, show costs and revenue flows.
b. Prepare an income statement for the company for September.

The solution to this self-study problem is at the end of this chapter on page 528.

ETHICAL ISSUES IN JOB COSTING

Many organizations have been called to task for improprieties in the way they assign costs to jobs. For example, major defense contractors have come under fire for overstating the costs of jobs. Numerous universities have been accused of overstating the costs of research projects. Improprieties in job costing generally are caused by one or more of the following actions: misstating the stage of completion of jobs, charging costs to the wrong jobs or categories (for example, charging the cost of university yachts to research projects), or simply misrepresenting the costs of jobs.

To avoid the appearance of cost overruns on jobs, job supervisors sometimes ask employees to charge costs to the wrong jobs. If you work in consulting or auditing, you may encounter cases where supervisors ask you to allocate the time that you actually spent on old jobs that are in danger of exceeding their cost estimates to other jobs that are in less danger of cost overruns. At minimum, this practice misleads managers who rely on accurate cost information for pricing, cost control, and other decisions. At worst, it also cheats people who may be paying for a job on a cost plus fee basis, where that job has not really cost as much as the producer claims.

People who supply the money for jobs often insist on audits of financial records to avoid such deception. Government auditors generally work on the site of defense contractors, universities, and other organizations that have contracts with the government for large jobs.

JUST-IN-TIME (JIT) METHODS

Many companies (Toyota, Hewlett-Packard, and Yamaha, to name a few) have adopted just-in-time methods for parts of their production process. Management uses **just-in-time (JIT) methods** to obtain materials just in time for production and to provide finished goods just in time for sale. This practice reduces, or potentially eliminates, inventories and the cost of carrying them. Of particular importance, just-in-time requires that workers immediately correct a process making defective units because they have no inventory where they can hide defective units. Eliminating inventories exposes production problems. With no inventory to draw from for delivery to customers, just-in-time relies on high-quality materials and production.

Using a just-in-time system, production does not begin on an item until the firm receives an order. When an order is received for a finished product, people in production order raw materials. As soon as production fills the order, production ends. In theory, a JIT system eliminates the need for inventories because no production takes place until the firm knows that it will sell the item. As a practical matter, companies using just-in-time inventory usually have a backlog of orders or stable demand for their products to assure continued production.

Since just-in-time production responds to an order receipt, JIT accounting can charge all costs directly to cost of goods sold. If inventories remain at the end of an accounting period, accountants "back out" the inventory amounts from the cost of goods sold account and charge them to inventory accounts.

COMPARING JIT AND TRADITIONAL SEQUENTIAL COST FLOWS AT HEWLETT-PACKARD

After installing a new production process, a Hewlett-Packard plant that makes printed circuit boards found that (1) it was able to reduce inventory levels significantly, (2) direct labor was only 3 percent to 5 percent of total production costs, and (3) most labor and overhead costs were fixed.[1] Consequently, H-P was able to use production methods that were almost "just-in-time," which dramatically affected the plant's accounting methods.

The net result of these changes is that Hewlett-Packard realized significant savings in administrative staff time and costs without any significant changes in the quality of information reported in their financial statements. Production line managers understand the simpler reports provided by the accounting department and actually used the information in those reports.[2]

BACKFLUSH COSTING

What if a company's accountants record all manufacturing costs directly in Cost of Goods Sold, but at the end of the accounting period, the accountants learn that the company has some inventory? (Despite using just-in-time production, companies often find they have at least some inventory.) Companies that record costs directly in Cost of Goods Sold can use a method called **backflush costing** to transfer any costs back to the inventory accounts, if necessary.

---

[1]R. Hunt, L. Garrett, and C. M. Merz, "Direct Labor Cost Not Always Relevant at H.P.," *Management Accounting,* February 1985, pp. 58–62.
[2]Ibid., p. 61.

Backflush costing is a method that works backward from the output to assign manufacturing costs to work-in-process inventories. Companies have probably used the term *backflush* because costs are "flushed back" through the production process to the points at which inventories remain. Exhibit 15.6 compares the traditional method of sequential costing with the backflush approach. Costs are initially recorded at the end of the production process, either in Finished Goods Inventory or in Cost of Goods Sold, on the grounds that the company has little or no work-in-process inventory. If the company has inventories at the end of a period, the accountants can credit Cost of Goods Sold, as shown in Exhibit 15.6, and debit the inventory accounts for the amount of inventory. (Backflush costing *looks* more complicated than traditional sequential costing, but it is simpler in practice.) Looking at Exhibit 15.6 for a Nissan plant that makes trucks, to what account would finished trucks that have not been sold be backflushed? (Answer: Finished Goods Inventory.)

EXHIBIT 15.6

Comparison of Backflush Costing with Traditional Sequential Tracking of Costs

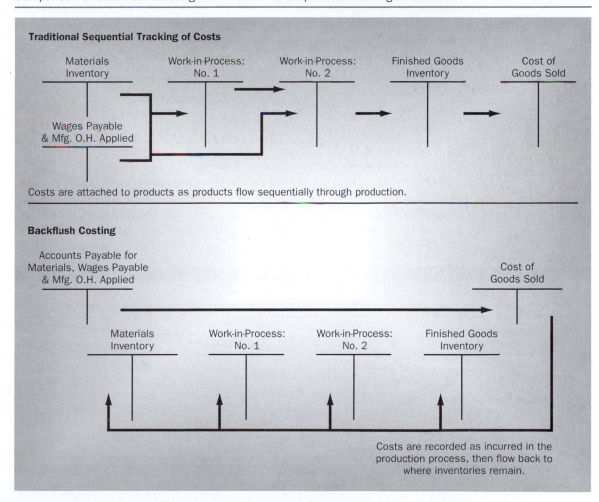

Example For example, Biotech Corporation uses JIT. Direct materials cost $1.50 per unit, and other manufacturing costs (including labor) are $.80 per unit. The company received an order for 10,000 units. Biotech incurred materials costs of $15,000 and other manufacturing costs of $8,000. The journal entries to record these events follow:

Cost of Goods Sold	15,000	
Accounts Payable		15,000
To record materials.		
Cost of Goods Sold	8,000	
Wages Payable and Manufacturing Overhead Applied		8,000
To record the other manufacturing costs.		

Accounting debits all of these costs directly to Cost of Goods Sold.

Assume 1,000 completed units are left in Finished Goods Inventory when accounting prepares the financial statements. Accounting backs out 1,000 units from Cost of Goods Sold based on a unit cost of $2.30, which is $1.50 for materials and $.80 for other manufacturing costs, for a total of $2,300 (= 1,000 units × $2.30 per unit). The journal entry to back out the inventory from Cost of Goods Sold follows:

Finished Goods Inventory	2,300	
Cost of Goods Sold		2,300
To record inventory.		

Exhibit 15.7 shows these transactions in T-accounts.

If accounting charged the costs of these units to production using traditional costing methods, it would need to debit the materials costs to a direct materials account. As production used the materials, accounting would transfer their costs to Work-in-Process Inventory. Accounting would charge other manufacturing costs to Work-

EXHIBIT 15.7

Just-in-Time Cost Flows

in-Process. As production completed goods, accounting would transfer their costs into Finished Goods and finally into Cost of Goods Sold. Looking at Exhibit 15.7, what would be the transaction for recording inventory if 9,500 units were sold? (Answer: Credit Cost of Goods Sold $1,150 and debit Finished Goods Inventory $1,150.)

SPOILAGE AND QUALITY OF PRODUCTION

Accountants typically include the cost of normal waste in the cost of work done this period. If Biotech Corporation incurs some normal wastage on a job, accountants would typically include that cost of materials in the cost of work done for the period. If the waste is not normal, accounting would remove it from the costs included in these computations and debit it to an account called "Abnormal Spoilage."

Companies concerned about quality production do not treat waste or spoiled goods as normal. Instead they remove waste and spoilage costs to avoid having waste costs buried in product costs. Some companies have been surprised to discover that, when they removed their waste and spoilage costs from other product costs, waste and spoilage costs were 20 percent to 30 percent of their total product costs.

PROBLEM 15.5 FOR SELF-STUDY

Traditional versus backflush cost flows. Influence "R" Us uses JIT production methods in making television commercials. For the month of January, the company incurred costs of $200,000 in making commercials. Twenty percent of January's costs was assigned to one commercial for a clothing store that was finished but not yet delivered or recorded in Cost of Goods Sold. Influence "R" Us has one materials account for film, one Work-in-Process account, one Finished Goods account, and one Cost of Goods Sold account.

Show the flow of costs through T-accounts using **(a)** traditional costing and **(b)** backflush costing. Assume that the credit entries for these costs when they were recorded were $10,000 to Accounts Payable for film, $90,000 to Accounts Payable for overhead, and $100,000 to Wages Payable for labor. The company had no beginning inventory on January 1.

The solution to this self-study problem is at the end of this chapter on page 529.

INTERNATIONAL APPLICATIONS OF JIT

Toyota gets credit as the first large company to install JIT (although we suspect JIT has been used in some form for many decades, perhaps centuries, in various parts of the world). We now find JIT used in companies around the world. Countries like Japan that have a well-defined network of suppliers and manufacturers are particularly well suited to JIT. JIT is more difficult to implement in countries like the United States that have dispersed suppliers and manufacturers. Efforts to increase international trade may increase the dispersion of suppliers, making JIT more difficult to implement.

SUMMARY

The following items correspond to the learning objectives presented at the beginning of the chapter.

1. **Explain the need for recording costs by department and assigning costs to products.** In recording costs by departments, the accounting system has served its function of providing data for departmental performance evaluation. The accounting system also assigns costs to products for managerial decision making, such as evaluating a product's profitability.

2. **Understand how the Work-in-Process account both describes the transformation of inputs into outputs in a company and accounts for the costs incurred in the process.** A key factor in a company's success is how well it controls the conversion costs (direct labor and overhead). Companies closely monitor those costs in the Work-in-Process Inventory account.

> Key Equation:
>
> $$BB + TI = TO + EB$$

3. **Compare and contrast normal costing and actual costing.** Actual costing measures product costs using actual costs incurred. Normal costing uses actual direct material and direct labor costs, plus an amount representing "normal" manufacturing overhead. Under normal costing, a firm derives a rate for applying overhead to units produced before the production period, then uses this "predetermined rate" in applying overhead to each unit as the firm produces it.

> Key Equations:
>
> $$\frac{\text{Predetermined Manufacturing}}{\text{Overhead Rate}} = \frac{\text{Estimated Manufacturing Overhead}}{\text{Normal (or Estimated) Activity Level}}$$

4. **Know various production methods and the different accounting systems each requires.** Companies that produce customized products—jobs—use job costing. Companies that mass-produce homogeneous products—continuous flow processing—use process costing. Companies that produce batches of products using standardized methods—operations—use operation costing. Operation costing is a hybrid of job and process costing, where the materials vary by batch but labor and overhead are the same.

5. **Compare and contrast job costing and process costing systems.** In job costing, firms collect costs for each unit produced. In process costing, firms accumu-

late costs in a department or production process during an accounting period, then spread those costs evenly over the units produced during that period, to determine an average cost per unit. Job costing provides more detailed information than process costing and the costs of record keeping under job costing systems exceed those under process costing.

Key Equation:

$$\text{Unit Cost} = \frac{\text{Total Manufacturing Cost Incurred during the Period}}{\text{Total Units Produced during the Period}}$$

6. **Compare and contrast product costing in service organizations to that in manufacturing companies.** Service companies, like manufacturing companies, need accurate, relevant, and timely management accounting information. Service organizations often collect costs by departments for performance evaluation, and also by job or client. Service organizations differ in that they do not show inventories on the financial statements.

7. **Identify ethical issues in job costing.** Many organizations have been called to task for improprieties in the way they assign costs to jobs. To avoid the appearance of cost overruns on jobs, job supervisors sometimes ask employees to charge costs to the wrong jobs.

8. **Recognize components of just-in-time (JIT) production methods and understand how accountants adapt costing systems to them.** Management uses JIT methods to obtain materials just in time for production and to provide finished goods just in time for sale. JIT requires that workers immediately correct a process making defective units because there is no inventory where defective units can be hidden. Accounting in a JIT environment charges all costs directly to Cost of Goods Sold, creating a significant savings in administrative time and costs, and charges them to Inventory accounts, when needed, using backflush costing.

9. **(Appendix) Know how to compute end-of-period inventory value using equivalent units of production.** The five steps to compute inventory value are: (1) summarize the flow of physical units, (2) compute equivalent units, (3) summarize cost to be accounted for, (4) compute unit costs for the current period, and (5) compute the cost of goods completed and transferred out of work-in-process inventory.

KEY TERMS AND CONCEPTS

Cost flow equation   Beginning Balance + Transfers In = Transfers Out + Ending Balance; BB + TI = TO + EB.

Normal costing   Method of allocating costs to products using actual direct materials, actual direct labor, and predetermined overhead rates.

Predetermined overhead rate Rate used in applying overhead to products or departments and developed at the start of a period by dividing estimated overhead cost by the estimated number of units of the overhead allocation base.

Cost driver A factor that causes an activity's costs.

Allocation base A cost driver used for applying overhead to production.

Job A customized product.

Job costing Accumulation of costs for a particular identifiable product, known as a job, as it moves through production.

Continuous flow processing Mass production of homogeneous products in a continuous flow.

Process costing A method of cost accounting based on average costs (total cost divided by the equivalent units of work done in a period). Typically used for assembly lines or for products that are produced in a series of steps that are more continuous than discrete.

Operations Standardized methods of making a product that are performed repeatedly in production of identifiable batches of products. Materials can be different for each product or batch of products, like job costing.

Operation costing A costing system that uses job costing to assign materials costs and process costing to assign conversion costs.

Just-in-time (JIT) method System of managing inventory for manufacturing in which a firm purchases or manufactures each component just before the firm uses it. JIT systems have much smaller—ideally no—carrying costs for inventory.

Backflush costing A method that works backward from the output to assign manufacturing costs to work-in-process inventories.

Equivalent units (E.U.) The number of units of completed output that would require the same costs as a firm would actually incur for production of completed and partially completed units during a period.

APPENDIX 15.1: COMPUTING COSTS OF EQUIVALENT PRODUCTION

This appendix describes product costing methods when a firm has only partially completed work on a product at the beginning or end of a period. For example, assume Davis Contractors, a house builder, is presently building several houses of a particular model. Davis had three partially built houses at the beginning of the second quarter of the year (April 1). Davis started four houses and completed five houses during the second quarter, and had two partially built houses at the end of the quarter (June 30). The contractor knows that she has spent $795,000 on construction materials, labor, and overhead for these houses during the second quarter and that the cost of the beginning work-in-process inventory for the three houses partially built on April 1 totals $42,000. The contractor wishes to know several other things, however, such as the cost of each house constructed in the second quarter, the cost of the ending work-in-process inventory, and the cost of the houses completed.

The contractor has several potential uses for the information about the cost of each house. First, the contractor had set prices based on market conditions and the estimate that each house would cost $145,000 to build. If she estimated incorrectly, the contractor would consider changing the prices on the houses or possibly would stop building this type of house if costs were so high that the contractor would make insufficient profits. Second, the contractor holds construction job supervisors responsible for managing and scheduling workers, for minimizing waste, and for other activities that affect construction costs. Product costs can provide feedback about their performance. Third, Davis Contractors prepares the external financial statements for its creditors that require ending inventory valuation and the cost of finished houses sold.

PROCEDURE FOR APPLYING COSTS TO UNITS PRODUCED

This section describes the five steps required to compute product costs, the cost of ending work-in-process inventory, and the cost of finished goods. Exhibit 15.8 presents the data required to do the analysis for the Davis Contractors example. Exhibit 15.8 shows that the contractor considered each of the three houses in the beginning work-in-process inventory to be 10 percent complete, on average, and the two houses in the ending work-in-process inventory each to be 30 percent complete,

EXHIBIT 15.8

DAVIS CONTRACTORS
Cost of Houses Produced
Data for Second Quarter, April 1 through June 30

	Units[a]	Product Costs	Percent of Processing Completed
Beginning Work-in-Process Inventory, April 1	3	$ 42,000	10%
Costs Incurred in Second Quarter	—	795,000	—
Completed and Transferred Out to Finished Goods Inventory	5	?	100
Ending Work-in-Process Inventory	2	?	30

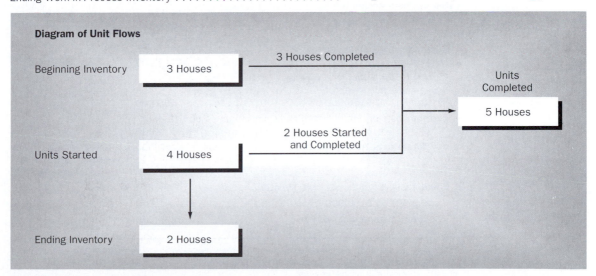

Diagram of Unit Flows

Beginning Inventory — 3 Houses
3 Houses Completed
Units Completed — 5 Houses
2 Houses Started and Completed
Units Started — 4 Houses
Ending Inventory — 2 Houses

[a]Some of these units are only partially completed.

EXHIBIT 15.9

DAVIS CONTRACTORS
Production Cost Report Using FIFO
Second Quarter, April 1 through June 30

	(Step 1) Physical Units	(Step 2) Compute Equivalent Units (E.U.)
Accounting for Units:		
Units to Account For:		
Beginning Work-in-Process (WIP) Inventory . .	3	
Units Started This Period	4	
Total Units to Account For	7	
Units Accounted For:		
Units Completed and Transferred Out:		
From Beginning Inventory	3	2.7[a] (90%)[b]
Started and Completed, Currently	2	2.0
Units in Ending WIP Inventory	2	0.6 (30%)[c]
Total Units Accounted For	7	5.3

	Total Costs	Unit Costs
Accounting for Costs:		
(Step 3) Costs to Be Accounted For:		
Costs in Beginning WIP Inventory	$ 42,000	
Current Period Costs	795,000	
Total Costs to Be Accounted For	$837,000	
(Step 4) Cost per Equivalent Unit of **Work Done This Period:**		
$795,000/5.3 E.U. . . . . =		$150,000 per E.U.
(Step 5) Costs Accounted For:		
Costs Assigned to Units Transferred Out:		
Costs from Beginning WIP Inventory	$ 42,000	
Current Costs Added to Complete Beginning WIP Inventory: 2.7 E.U. × $150,000 . . . . =	405,000	
Current Costs of Units Started and Completed: 2.0 E.U. × $150,000 . . . . =	300,000	
Total Costs Transferred Out	$747,000	$149,400 per Unit (= $747,000/5 Units Transferred Out)
Costs Assigned to Ending WIP Inventory:		
0.6 E.U. × $150,000 . . . . =	90,000	
Total Costs Accounted For	$837,000	

[a]Equivalent units required to complete beginning inventory. For example, 90 percent of 3 units must be added to the beginning inventory to complete it. Therefore, 2.7 (= 90% × 3) equivalent units are required to complete beginning inventory.

[b]Percent required to complete beginning inventory.

[c]Stage of completion of ending inventory.

on average. Assume the first-in, first-out (FIFO) cost flow assumption for inventory, for now. (Later, we discuss the effects of using the weighted-average method.) Exhibit 15.9 summarizes the five steps in the process and presents the analysis for Davis Contractors.

Step 1: Summarize the Flow of Physical Units This appears in the top of the production cost report in Exhibit 15.9.

Step 2: Compute Equivalent Units Since the firm has some partially completed units at the beginning and end of the period, accounting must convert the work into equivalent (finished) units produced. **Equivalent units (E.U.)** represent the translation of partially complete work into equivalent whole units. For example, two units, each 50 percent complete, represent one equivalent unit. Three categories of work done require equivalent unit computations to derive the equivalent work done in a period:

1. **Equivalent units to complete beginning work-in-process inventory.** For Davis Contractors, the three houses in beginning work-in-process (WIP) inventory were 10 percent complete when the period started. Since Davis completed them during this period, Davis did 90 percent of the work on these houses during the second quarter. Therefore, 2.7 equivalent units (= 3 houses × 90%) were required to complete the beginning inventory, as Exhibit 15.9 shows.
2. **Equivalent units for work started and completed during the period.** Exhibit 15.8 shows that Davis started and completed two houses during the period, representing two equivalent units produced, as shown in Exhibit 15.9.
3. **Units still in ending WIP inventory.** The ending WIP inventory represents the equivalent work done on units not completed and transferred out during the period. Two houses that Davis had 30 percent complete at the end of the period fit into this category, representing .6 equivalent units (= 2 houses × 30%).

The equivalent units produced for the second quarter are 5.3 units (= 2.7 + 2.0 + .6), as shown in Step 2 in Exhibit 15.9.

We base equivalent unit computations on the basic cost flow equation. If you know the equivalent work done in beginning and ending work-in-process inventories and the units transferred out, you can derive the equivalent units produced during the period as follows:

$$\begin{array}{c}\text{Equivalent Units} \\ \text{in the Beginning} \\ \text{Inventory}\end{array} + \begin{array}{c}\text{Equivalent Units} \\ \text{of Work Done} \\ \text{This Period}\end{array} = \begin{array}{c}\text{Equivalent Units} \\ \text{Transferred Out}\end{array} + \begin{array}{c}\text{Equivalent Units} \\ \text{in Ending} \\ \text{Inventory.}\end{array}$$

In our example, to find the work done this period, use the following formula:

$$\begin{array}{c}\text{Equivalent Units} \\ \text{of Work Done} \\ \text{This Period}\end{array} = \begin{array}{c}\text{Equivalent Units} \\ \text{Transferred Out}\end{array} + \begin{array}{c}\text{Equivalent Units} \\ \text{in Ending} \\ \text{Inventory}\end{array} - \begin{array}{c}\text{Equivalent Units} \\ \text{in Beginning} \\ \text{Inventory}\end{array}$$

$$= 5.0 + .6 - (3.0 \times 10\%)$$

$$= 5.3 \text{ Equivalent Units of Work Done.}$$

Step 3: Summarize Costs to Be Accounted For This step merely records the costs in beginning work-in-process inventory and the costs incurred during the period, as Step 3 of Exhibit 15.9 shows.

Step 4: Compute Unit Costs for the Current Period Exhibit 15.9 shows that the cost per equivalent unit produced this period is $150,000. Note that this cost represents work done during this period only; it does not include costs in beginning inventory. Davis would use this unit cost to evaluate performance in controlling costs, and it would provide information to management about the cost of building houses that Davis can use to assess prices and the profitability of continuing to build this type of house. Looking at Exhibit 15.9, what would be the total costs to be accounted for if the contractor considered the ending work-in-process inventory to be only 20 percent complete? (Answer: still $837,000.)

Step 5: Compute the Cost of Goods Completed and Transferred Out of Work-in-Process and the Cost of Ending Work-in-Process Inventory Exhibit 15.9 shows the cost of units transferred out, including the $42,000 from beginning inventory and the cost of the goods still in ending inventory, which accounting assigns a cost of $150,000 per equivalent unit.

Flow of Costs through Accounts Exhibit 15.10 presents the flow of costs through T-accounts. Looking at Exhibit 15.10, assuming the same beginning and ending inventory values, if current period costs were $805,000, what would be the value of Finished Goods Inventory? (Answer: $757,000.)

WEIGHTED-AVERAGE METHOD

The previous computations assumed FIFO, which means that accounting transferred out the cost of beginning inventory first and that the costs assigned to ending inven-

---

EXHIBIT 15.10

DAVIS CONTRACTORS
Cost Flow through T-Accounts (FIFO)
Second Quarter

	Work-in-Process Inventory			Finished Goods Inventory
Beginning Inventory	42,000	Cost Transferred Out:		
		Costs Already in Beginning Inventory ⟶	42,000	
		Cost to Complete Beginning Inventory ⟶	405,000	747,000[a]
Current Period Costs	795,000			
		Costs of Units Started and Completed in April ⟶	300,000	
Ending Inventory	90,000			

[a]Total costs transferred out of Work-in-Process Inventory

tory were the costs of goods produced during the current period.[3] If Davis used the weighted-average method instead of FIFO, accounting would assign the cost of goods transferred out and the cost of goods in ending inventory a weighted-average cost that considers both the current period cost and the beginning inventory cost. The weighted-average cost is $149,464 per unit, which equals the total costs Davis must account for, $837,000, divided by the total equivalent units, 5.6. The 5.6 equivalent units equal 5.3 equivalent units for the period plus .3 in beginning inventory. The 5.6 equivalent units also equal the 5.0 units transferred out plus .6 equivalent units in ending inventory. This result must be true because

$$BB + TI = TO + EB,$$

so

$$.3 + 5.3 = 5.0 + .6,$$

where TI is defined to be the equivalent units produced this period.

SOLUTIONS TO SELF-STUDY PROBLEMS

SUGGESTED SOLUTION TO PROBLEM 15.1 FOR SELF-STUDY

For each case, start with the formula:

$$BB + TI = TO + EB.$$

$$A: TI = TO + EB - BB$$

$$= \$61{,}000 + \$32{,}000 - \$40{,}000$$

$$= \$53{,}000.$$

$$B: BB = TO + EB - TI$$

$$= \$11{,}000 + \$16{,}000 - \$8{,}000$$

$$= \$19{,}000.$$

$$C: TO = BB + TI - EB$$

$$= \$35{,}000 + \$8{,}000 - \$27{,}000$$

$$= \$16{,}000.$$

---

[3]This statement assumes that the firm completed the units in beginning WIP inventory during the period. If some of the units in beginning inventory were still in WIP inventory at the end of the period, the firm would carry some beginning inventory costs to the ending inventory.

SUGGESTED SOLUTION TO PROBLEM 15.2 FOR SELF-STUDY

Compute the predetermined overhead rates as follows.

	Variable Overhead	Fixed Overhead
Labor hours	$\dfrac{\$108,000}{12,000} = \$9$ per hr.	$\dfrac{\$120,000}{12,000} = \$10$ per hr.
Labor dollars	$\dfrac{\$108,000}{(\$20 \times 12,000)} = \$.45$ per dollar	$\dfrac{\$120,000}{(\$20 \times 12,000)} = \$.50$ per dollar
Output	$\dfrac{\$108,000}{120,000} = \$.90$ per pizza	$\dfrac{\$120,000}{120,000} = \$1.00$ per pizza

SUGGESTED SOLUTION TO PROBLEM 15.3 FOR SELF-STUDY

- Lawsuit—job.
- Diet cola—process.
- Emergency room care—job.
- House painting—job.
- Paint—process.

SUGGESTED SOLUTION TO PROBLEM 15.4 FOR SELF-STUDY

a.

TOUCHE ANDERSEN & COMPANY
September

Accounts Receivable		Work in Process: Client A		Revenue	
(5a) 72,000		**(1)** 6,000 | 8,000 **(5b)**			72,000 **(5a)**
		(2) 2,000			

Wages and Accounts Payable		Work in Process: Client B		Cost of Services Billed	
	30,000 **(1)**	**(1)** 21,000 | 28,000 **(5b)**		**(5b)** 36,000	
		(2) 7,000			

		Overhead		Direct Labor— Unbillable	
	10,000 **(3)**	**(3)** 8,000 | 9,000 **(2)**		**(1)** 3,000	

				Marketing and Administrative Costs	
	5,000 **(4)**			**(4)** 5,000	

Entries: (1) Direct labor at $30 per hour. (2) Overhead as applied. (3) Actual overhead incurred. (4) Marketing and administrative costs. (5) Services billed.

b.

TOUCHE ANDERSEN & COMPANY
Income Statement for the Month Ended September 30

Revenue from Services	$72,000
Less Cost of Services Billed	36,000
Gross Margin	$36,000
Less:	
Direct Labor—Unbillable	3,000
Overhead (underapplied)	1,000[a]
Marketing and Administrative Costs	5,000
Operating Profit	$27,000

[a]Actual overhead $10,000 − $9,000 assigned to jobs.

SUGGESTED SOLUTION TO PROBLEM 15.5 FOR SELF-STUDY

a. Traditional Costing

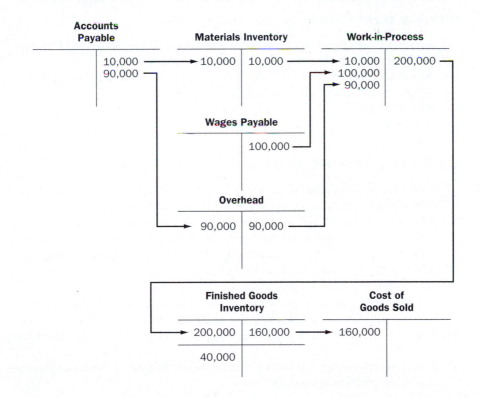

b. Backflush Costing

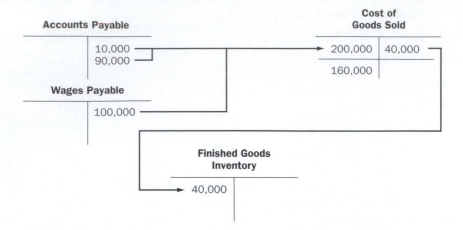

QUESTIONS, EXERCISES, PROBLEMS, AND CASES

REVIEW QUESTIONS

1. Review the meaning of the concepts or terms given in Key Terms and Concepts.
2. Compare and contrast job costing and process costing systems.
3. Why don't most service organizations have inventories (other than supplies)?
4. What is a production operation?
5. Why is operation costing called a hybrid costing method?
6. What is the basic cost flow equation?

CRITICAL ANALYSIS AND DISCUSSION QUESTIONS

7. Management of a company that manufactures small appliances is trying to decide whether to install a job or process costing system. The manufacturing vice-president has stated that job costing gives the best control. The controller, however, has stated that job costing would require too much record keeping. What do you think of the manufacturing vice-president's suggestion and why?
8. What operating conditions of companies make just-in-time methods feasible?
9. Discuss the impact of JIT methods at Hewlett-Packard.
10. Compare and contrast the problem of providing quality service in a service company to that of providing quality goods in a manufacturing company.
11. How does operation costing compare and contrast with job costing and process costing?
12. What types of savings can firms achieve with just-in-time methods compared to traditional production methods?
13. Explain the differences in accounting for the flow of costs using traditional accounting, where accounting charges costs first to inventory accounts, and using JIT.
14. Why must firms have reliable suppliers when using just-in-time methods?

15. Refer to the Managerial Application "Using the Basic Cost Flow Equation to Detect Fraud." How did the manager of the Gravins Division fraudulently increase profits? How was the fraud detected?

16. Name three companies not mentioned in the text that make products using processes.

17. Name three companies not mentioned in the text that produce jobs.

EXERCISES

Solutions to even-numbered exercises are at the end of this chapter after the cases.

18. **Cost flow model.** Horace Zontal is trying to compute unknown values in inventory accounts in three of his department stores. Knowing of your expertise in cost flows, he asks for your help and provides you with the following information about each store:

	Store		
	Downtown	Crossroads Mall	Northgate Mall
Beginning inventory	$ 30,000	?	?
Transfers in to inventory accounts	100,000	$200,000	$160,000
Transfers out of inventory accounts	110,000	180,000	150,000
Ending inventory	?	60,000	40,000

Tell Horace what the missing values are for each of his stores.

19. **Cost flow model.** A fire has destroyed the inventory of the Duroflame Company. Before paying for damages, the CMT Insurance Company wants to know the amount of ending inventory that is missing. You have been hired to dig through the ashes and find as much information as you can. You find the following information about four of Duroflame's big-selling inventory items:

	Product			
	Lighter Fluid	Waterproof Matches	Burn Ointment	Fireplace Screens
Beginning inventory	$20,000	$ 30,000	$30,000	?
Transfers into inventory accounts	90,000	170,000	60,000	$60,000
Transfers out of inventory accounts	40,000	190,000	70,000	60,000
Ending inventory	?	?	?	?

Compute the ending inventory, which is the amount destroyed by the fire, for any of the products that you can. You may not be able to compute ending inventory for all products. If you cannot compute the ending inventory, state what additional information you need.

20. **Cost flow model.** A flood has destroyed the inventory of the Colorado Flash Company. Before paying for damages, the Just-Say-No Insurance Company wants to know the amount of ending inventory that is missing. You have been hired to search through the water-sodden mess to find as much information as you can. You find the following information about four of Colorado Flash's big-selling inventory items:

	Item			
	Rubber Rafts	Rubber Duckies	Galoshes	Diving Equipment
Beginning inventory	$20,000	$10,000	?	$40,000
Transfers into inventory accounts	80,000	30,000	$40,000	60,000
Transfers out of inventory accounts	90,000	25,000	50,000	80,000
Ending inventory	?	?	?	?

Compute the ending inventory, which is the amount destroyed by the flood, for any of the products that you can. You may not be able to compute ending inventory for all products. If you cannot compute the ending inventory, state what additional information you need.

21. **Cost flow model.** The law firm of Kambert & Lowe has asked your help in computing damages in a lawsuit. The law firm's client claims an employee has stolen merchandise and is suspicious because this employee has just opened a discount electronics store. The law firm provides you with the following information from the accounting records:

	Product		
	Videocassette Recorders	Televisions	Compact Disc Players
Beginning inventory	$20,000	$20,000	$15,000
Transfers into inventory accounts	40,000	50,000	20,000
Transfers out of inventory accounts from sales	35,000	55,000	25,000
Ending inventory	?	?	?

You physically counted the ending inventory and found it to be as follows: videocassette recorders, $20,000; televisions, $5,000; and compact disc players, $10,000. Compute the ending inventory according to the accounting records and compare it to the physical count. What discrepancy between the physical count and the accounting records could be attributed to the theft, if any?

22. **Cost flow model.** Kaasa, Rah & Associates, an auditing firm, is reconstructing the records of a client called Chips 'R Us, which is concerned that some of its inventory is missing. The accounting records provide the following information about Chips' inventories:

	Product		
	Computer Chips	Potato Chips	Poker Chips
Beginning inventory	$100,000	$ 40,000	$ 10,000
Transfers into inventory accounts	400,000	300,000	100,000
Transfers out of inventory accounts from sales	450,000	280,000	105,000
Ending inventory	?	?	?

You physically counted the ending inventory and found it to be as follows: computer chips, $50,000; potato chips, $20,000; and poker chips, $5,000. Compute the ending inventory according to the accounting records and compare it to the physical count. What discrepancy do you find between the physical count and the accounting records, if any?

23. **Just-in-time methods.** Nunez Products uses a just-in-time system. To produce 2,000 units for an order, it purchased and used materials costing $50,000, and incurred other manufacturing costs of $30,000, of which $10,000 was labor. All costs were on account.

    After Nunez Products completed production of the 2,000 units and shipped 1,600 units, management needed the Finished Goods Inventory balance for the 400 units remaining in inventory for financial statement preparation. The firm incurred costs evenly across all products.

    Show the flow of costs using journal entries and T-accounts using backflush costing.

24. **Just-in-time methods.** Austin Tech uses just-in-time production methods. To produce 1,200 units for an order, Austin purchased and used materials costing $10,000 and incurred other manufacturing costs of $11,000, of which $4,000 was labor. All costs were on account.

    After Austin completed production on the 1,200 units and shipped 1,000 units, management needed the Finished Goods Inventory balance for the 200 units remaining.

    Prepare journal entries and T-accounts for these transactions using backflush costing.

25. **Job costs in a service organization.** Lafayette and Associates, a CPA firm, uses job costing. During April, the firm provided audit services for two clients and billed those clients for the services performed. Graham Productions was billed for 4,000 hours at $100 per hour and MCA Records was billed for 2,000 hours at $100 per hour. Direct labor costs were $60 per hour. Of the 6,400 hours worked in April, 400 hours were not billable. The firm assigns overhead to jobs at the rate of $20 per billable hour. During April, the firm incurred actual overhead of $140,000. The firm incurred marketing and administrative costs of $20,000. All transactions were on account.

    a. Show how Lafayette and Associates' accounting system would record these revenues and costs using journal entries.

    b. Prepare an income statement for April like the one in Exhibit 15.5.

26. **Job costs in a service organization.** Ads Unlimited, an advertising firm, uses job costing. During July, the firm provided advertising services for two clients and billed those clients for the services performed. MacLean River Soda was billed for $150,000 and Depardieu Productions was billed for $100,000. Direct labor costs were $80 per hour. Ads Unlimited worked 1,200 hours on the MacLean River Soda account and 900 hours on the Depardieu Productions account. The firm worked on additional 100 hours that it did not charge to either account. The firm assigns overhead to jobs at the rate of $30 per billable hour. During July, the firm incurred actual overhead of $70,000. The firm incurred marketing and administrative costs of $30,000. All transactions were on account.

    a. Show how Ads Unlimited's accounting system would record these revenues and costs using journal entries.

    b. Prepare an income statement for July like the one in Exhibit 15.5.

27. **Job costs in a service organization.** Kimbrell Architects uses job costing. During September, the firm provided architect services for three clients and billed those clients for the services performed. Seville Construction was billed for 900 hours, Hanford Homes was billed for 300 hours, Green Acres was billed for 200 hours, all at $100 per hour. Direct labor costs were $50 per hour. Of the 1,600 hours worked in September, 200 hours were not billable. The firm assigns overhead to jobs at the rate of $30 per billable hour. During September, the firm incurred actual overhead of $50,000. The firm incurred marketing and administrative costs of $20,000. All transactions were on account.

    a. Show how these revenues and costs would appear in T-accounts.

    b. Prepare an income statement for September like the one in Exhibit 15.5.

28. **Job costs in a service organization.** Creative Designs, a landscaping firm, uses job costing. During June, the firm provided landscaping services for two clients and billed those clients for the services performed. The city of Chicago was billed for $100,000 and Payfast Insurance was billed for $200,000. Direct labor costs were $50 per hour. Creative Designs worked 1,200 hours on the city of Chicago job, and 2,000 hours on the Payfast job. The firm could not charge 300 hours to either job. The firm assigns overhead to jobs at the rate of $20 per billable hour. During June, the firm incurred actual overhead of $70,000. The firm incurred marketing and administrative costs of $20,000. All transactions were on account.

    a. Show the flow of these revenues and costs through T-accounts.

    b. Prepare an income statement for June like the one in Exhibit 15.5.

29. **Computing equivalent units** (Appendix 15.1). The Assembly Department had 30,000 units 60 percent complete in Work-in-Process Inventory at the beginning of May. During May, the department started and completed 80,000 units. The department started another 20,000 units and completed 30 percent as of the end of May. Compute the equivalent units of work performed during May using FIFO. Assume the department incurred production costs evenly throughout processing.

30. **Computing product costs with incomplete products** (Appendix 15.1). Refer to the data in Exercise **29.** Assume that the cost assigned to beginning inventory on May 1 was $40,000 and that the department incurred $245,000 of production

costs during May. Prepare a production cost report like the one shown in Exhibit 15.9.

31. **Actual costs and normal costs.** Hudson Company uses a predetermined rate for applying overhead to production using normal costing. The rates for Year 1 follow: variable, 200 percent of direct labor dollars; fixed, 300 percent of direct labor dollars. Actual overhead costs incurred follow: variable, $20,000; fixed, $25,000. Actual direct materials costs were $5,000, and actual direct labor costs were $9,000. Hudson produced one job in Year 1.

    a. Calculate actual costs of the job.

    b. Calculate normal costs of the job using predetermined overhead rates.

32. **Applied overhead in a bank.** Holdup Interstate uses machine time as the basis for allocating overhead to its check processing activities. On January 1, Holdup Interstate estimated that production for the coming year would equal 800 million units. It also estimated that total overhead for the same year would equal $4,000,000 and that estimated machine time would equal 100,000 hours. The units produced and machine time for the four quarters follow:

Quarter	Actual Units of Production (in millions)	Actual Machine Time
1st	300 Checks	32,000 Hours
2nd	300 Checks	30,000 Hours
3rd	200 Checks	18,000 Hours
4th	100 Checks	12,000 Hours

    a. Compute the predetermined overhead rate for applying overhead on the basis of machine hours.

    b. Compute the amount of total overhead applied under normal costing for each quarter.

    c. Compute the overhead cost per unit (that is, per check processed) for each quarter using normal costing.

PROBLEMS

33. **Job costing for the movies.** Movies and television shows are jobs. Some are successful, some are not. Studios must decide what to do with the cost of unsuccessful shows ("flops"). Some studios have been criticized for assigning the cost of flops to successful shows, which in turn reduces profits available under profit-sharing agreements with actors, actresses, directors, and others associated with the successful show.

    Studios point out that flops have to be paid for out of the profits from successful shows. For example, Orion Pictures was criticized for carrying the cost of flops in inventory, instead of writing them off, thereby overstating assets and overstating profits.

    a. How does carrying "flops" in inventory overstate assets and profits?

    b. When do you think the cost of a movie that turns out to be a flop should be written off (that is, expensed)?

34. **Comparing job costs to management's expectations.** Illinois Construction Company uses a job costing system. It applies overhead to jobs at a rate of 55 percent of direct labor cost.

On August 1, the balance in the Work-in-Process Inventory account was $34,524. It had the following jobs in process on August 1:

Job No.	Materials	Direct Labor	Overhead	Total
478 (irrigation project)	$ 5,100	$ 9,620	$4,810	$19,530
479 (parking lot construction)	3,470	3,960	1,980	9,410
480 (street repair)	4,120	976	488	5,584
Total	$12,690	$14,556	$7,278	$34,524

Selected transactions for the month of August follow:
(1) Materials issued: Job 480, $682; Job 481, $4,200; Job 482, $2,600; indirect materials, $390; total, $7,872.
(2) It assigned labor costs as follows: Job 478, $331; Job 479, $2,651; Job 480, $7,800; Job 481, $5,891; Job 482, $1,720; indirect labor, $853; total, $19,246.
(3) It applies overhead for the month to jobs using an overhead rate of 55 percent of direct labor costs.
(4) It completed Jobs 478 and 479 in August.

Management of Illinois Construction Company is concerned that costs are higher than anticipated. Management had expected the cost of completed jobs to be as follows:

Job 478 $20,000, when complete.

Job 479 $13,000, when complete.

Job 480 $15,000, as of August 31.

Job 481 $10,000, as of August 31.

Job 482 $4,000, as of August 31.

Compare the actual job costs to management's expected costs, and report your results.

35. **Analyzing costs in a job company.** On June 1, Sierra Surveying Company had two jobs in process with the following costs:

	Direct Materials	Direct Labor
Toulumne	$1,000	$4,000
San Andreas	800	3,200

In addition, overhead is applied to these jobs at the rate of 100 percent of direct labor costs.

On June 1, Sierra had materials inventory (for example, plants and shrubs) totaling $2,000. During June, Sierra purchased $4,000 of materials and had none left in materials inventory at the end of the month. (However, Sierra had some materials in work-in-process inventory at the end of the month.)

During June, Sierra completed both the Toulumne and San Andreas jobs and recorded them as cost of goods sold. The Toulumne job required no more materials in June, but it did require $1,200 of direct labor to complete. The San Andreas job required $400 in indirect materials and $2,000 of direct labor to complete.

Sierra started a new job, Jackson, during June and put $1,600 of direct labor costs into this job. Unfortunately, Sierra lost the records of materials used on this job but knows all the materials available in June went into either San Andreas or Jackson. The Jackson job is still in work-in-process inventory at the end of the month.

Sierra needs to know the total cost of the Toulumne and San Andreas jobs, and the cost to date for the Jackson job, for billing purposes. (Otherwise, all the little Sierras at home will go hungry in July.) Please provide the cost of direct materials, direct labor, and overhead (at 100 percent of direct labor cost) for the three jobs.

36. **Compare just-in-time to a traditional accounting system.** Spoljarie Instruments produces heat measurement meters. The company received an order for 8,000 meters. The company purchased and used $250,000 of materials for this order. The company incurred labor costs of $125,000 and other nonlabor manufacturing costs of $400,000.

   The accounting period ended before the company completed the order. The firm had 10 percent of the total costs incurred still in Work-in-Process Inventory and 20 percent of the total costs incurred still in Finished Goods Inventory.
   a. Use T-accounts to show the flow of costs using backflush costing.
   b. Use T-accounts to show the flow of costs using a traditional costing system.

37. **Compare just-in-time to a traditional accounting system.** Sharp Manufacturing received an order for 10,000 units. The company purchased and used $200,000 of materials for this order. The company incurred labor costs of $90,000 and other nonlabor manufacturing costs of $150,000.

   The accounting period ended before the company completed the order. The firm had 5 percent of the total costs incurred still in Work-in-Process Inventory and 20 percent of the total costs incurred still in Finished Goods Inventory.
   a. Use T-accounts to show the flow of costs using backflush costing.
   b. Use T-accounts to show the flow of costs using a traditional costing system.

38. **Computing equivalent units and cost flows under process costing** (Appendix 15.1). Stephens Products Company has a process cost accounting system. Stephens incurred material, direct labor, and manufacturing overhead costs evenly during processing. On September 1, the firm had 10,000 units in process, 40 percent complete, with the following accumulated costs:

Material	$78,000
Direct Labor	40,000
Manufacturing Overhead	30,000

During September, Stephens started 55,000 units in process and incurred the following costs:

Material	$622,000
Direct Labor	490,000
Manufacturing Overhead	367,500

During September, Stephens completed 45,000 units. The units in ending inventory were, on average, 40 percent complete.

Prepare a production cost report such as the one in Exhibit 15.9 using FIFO.

39. **Equivalent units—solving for unknowns** (Appendix 15.1). For each of the following independent cases, calculate the information requested, using FIFO costing.

   a. Beginning inventory amounted to 2,000 units. The firm started and completed 4,500 units during this period. At the end of the period, the firm had 3,000 units in inventory that were 30 percent complete. Using FIFO costing, the equivalent production for the period was 5,600 units. What was the percentage of completion of the beginning inventory?

   b. The ending inventory included $8,700 for conversion costs. During the period, the firm required 4,200 equivalent units to complete the beginning inventory and started and completed 6,000 units. The ending inventory represented 2,000 equivalent units of work this period. What was the total conversion cost incurred during this period?

CASES

40. **Completing missing data.** After a dispute concerning wages, Ernest Arson tossed an incendiary device into the Flash Company's record vault. Within moments, only a few readable charred fragments remained from the company's factory ledger, as follows:

Direct Materials Inventory		Manufacturing Overhead	
Bal. 4/1 12,000		Actual Costs for April 14,800	

Work-in-Process Inventory		Accounts Payable	
Bal. 4/1 4,500			Bal. 4/30 8,000

Finished Goods Inventory		Cost of Goods Sold	
Bal. 4/30 16,000			

Sifting through the ashes and interviewing selected employees generated the following additional information:

(1) The controller remembers clearly that the firm based the predetermined overhead rate on an estimated 60,000 direct labor hours to be worked over the year and an estimated $180,000 in manufacturing overhead costs.

(2) The production superintendent's cost sheets showed only one job in process on April 30. The firm had added materials of $2,600 to the job and expended 300 direct labor hours at $6 per hour.

(3) The accounts payable are for direct materials purchases only, according to the accounts payable clerk. He clearly remembers that the balance in the account was $6,000 on April 1. An analysis of canceled checks (kept in the treasurer's office) shows that Flash made payments of $40,000 to suppliers during the month.

(4) A charred piece of the payroll ledger shows that the firm recorded 5,200 direct labor hours for the month. The employment department has verified that pay rates did not vary among employees (this infuriated Ernest, who thought that Flash underpaid him).

(5) Records maintained in the finished goods warehouse indicate that the finished goods inventory totaled $11,000 on April 1.

(6) From another charred piece in the vault you discern that the cost of goods manufactured (that is, finished) for April was $89,000.

Determine the following amounts:

a. Work-in-process inventory, April 30.

b. Direct materials purchased during April.

c. Overhead applied to work in process.

d. Cost of goods sold for April.

e. Over- or underapplied overhead for April.

f. Direct materials usage during April.

g. Direct materials inventory, April 30.

41. Evaluating cost systems used in financial services companies. John Frank, controller of Midwest Insurance Company, recently returned from a management education program where he talked to Peter Montgomery, his counterpart at Northern Insurance Company. Both companies had mortgage departments, but whereas Midwest gave loans only to businesses, Northern gave only home mortgage loans.

Peter Montgomery had described the use of standard costs at Northern as follows:

> We have collected data over several years that give us a pretty good idea how much each batch of loans costs to process. We receive loans in three main categories: (1) FHA and VA mortgages, (2) conventional home mortgages, and (3) development loans. Banks and other financial institutions make these loans initially and banks then package the loans and offer them to us as a package. The Mortgage Division establishes terms for ascertaining whether we accept the mortgage and for legal work on the loan. We assume that each loan in a category costs about the same. To calculate how much processing loans costs, we periodically have people in the Mortgage Division keep track of their time on each package of loans. Our overhead is about 130 percent of direct labor costs, so we assign overhead accordingly to each package of loans. We don't keep track of the actual costs of processing each package of loans. What we lose in knowing the actual cost of processing each package of loans, we make up by saving clerical costs that we would incur to keep track of the time spent on each package of loans.

A cost statement for a recent month appears in Exhibit 15.11.

Montgomery's comment about saving clerical costs struck a respondent chord with John Frank. Midwest's accounting costs had reached alarming levels,

---

EXHIBIT 15.11

Northern Insurance Company
Mortgage Division
Loan Processing Costs
Month of October

Category of Loans	Labor	Overhead	Number of Loan Packages Processed
Standard Costs			
FHA and VA	$ 4,200	$ 5,460	14
Conventional	31,160	40,508	82
Development	20,440	26,572	73
Total	$55,800	$72,540	
Actual Costs	$58,172	$74,626	
Variance	$ 2,372	$ 2,086	
	Unfavorable	Unfavorable	

according to the company president, and Frank was looking for ways to reduce costs. Midwest kept track of the following costs for each loan: labor; telephone costs; travel; and outside services, such as appraisals, legal fees, and the cost of consultants. The costs of processing these loans often amounted to several thousand dollars. A sample of these loans and their processing costs appears in Exhibit 15.12.

When Frank told the Mortgage Division manager about the methods Northern used, the manager responded: "That sounds fine for them because each package of loans in a category has about the same processing costs. The processing costs of each loan in our company vary considerably. I believe it would be invalid to establish standards for our loans."

EXHIBIT 15.12

Midwest Insurance Company
Mortgage Division
Loan Processing Costs
Month of July

Loan No.	Labor	Telephone	Travel	Outside Services		
				Appraisal	Legal	Other
A48-10136	$ 1,184	$ 113	$ 415	$ 1,500	—	—
A48-11237	3,63142	—2,300	— —			
B42-19361	814 78	— —	$1,500$	150		
C39-21341	4,191240	110 —	2,200—			
.	.	.	.	.	.	.
.	.	.	.	.	.	.
.	.	.	.	.	.	.
Total	$47,291	$4,843	$2,739	$11,800	$9,950	$1,470

Frank thought the Mortgage Division manager's comments were reasonable, but he wanted to find some way to save clerical costs by not recording the costs of processing each loan. At the same time, he knew the firm would potentially benefit from having a standard against which to compare actual costs.

a. What would you advise Mr. Frank to do? Compare the advantages and disadvantages of the system each company uses.

b. Diagram the flow of costs for each company using the data available in Exhibits 15.11 and 15.12. Treat each loan or category of loans as a separate product in your diagram.

SUGGESTED SOLUTIONS TO EVEN-NUMBERED EXERCISES

18. Cost flow model.

$$BB + TI = TO + EB.$$

Downtown: $\$30{,}000 + \$100{,}000 = \$110{,}000 + EB$

$$EB = \$30{,}000 + \$100{,}000 - \$110{,}000$$

$$EB = \$20{,}000.$$

Crossroads: $BB + \$200{,}000 = \$180{,}000 + \$60{,}000$

$$BB = \$180{,}000 + \$60{,}000 - \$200{,}000$$

$$BB = \$40{,}000.$$

Northgate: $BB + \$160{,}000 = \$150{,}000 + \$40{,}000$

$$BB = \$150{,}000 + \$40{,}000 - \$160{,}000$$

$$BB = \$30{,}000.$$

20. Cost flow model.

$$BB + TI = TO + EB.$$

Rubber rafts: $\$20{,}000 + \$80{,}000 = \$90{,}000 + EB$

$$EB = \$20{,}000 + \$80{,}000 - \$90{,}000$$

$$EB = \$10{,}000.$$

Rubber duckies: $\$10{,}000 + \$30{,}000 = \$25{,}000 + EB$

$$EB = \$10{,}000 + \$30{,}000 - \$25{,}000$$

$$EB = \$15{,}000.$$

Galoshes: Cannot compute because we do not have the beginning inventory amount.

Diving equipment: $\$40{,}000 + \$60{,}000 = \$80{,}000 + EB$

$$EB = \$40{,}000 + \$60{,}000 - \$80{,}000$$

$$EB = \$20{,}000.$$

22. **Cost flow model.** Use the cost flow equation, BB + TI = TO + EB, to find what the ending inventory should be per the records:

Computer chips: $100,000 + $400,000 = $450,000 + EB

$$EB = \$100,000 + \$400,000 - \$450,000$$

$$EB = \$50,000.$$

No discrepancy between the records and the physical count.

Potato chips: $40,000 + $300,000 = $28,000 + EB

$$EB = \$40,000 + \$300,000 - \$280,000$$

$$EB = \$60,000.$$

There appears to be a $40,000 (= $60,000 − $20,000 physical count) discrepancy between records and actual chips in inventory.

Poker chips: $10,000 + $100,000 = $105,000 + EB

$$EB = \$10,000 + \$100,000 - \$105,000$$

$$EB = \$5,000.$$

No discrepancy in poker chips.

24. **Just-in-time methods.**

Journal Entries:

(1) Cost of Goods Sold   21,000

        Accounts Payable—Materials   10,000

        Accounts Payable—Other Manufacturing Costs   7,000

        Wages Payable   4,000

   To record costs of production.

(2) Finished Goods Inventory ....   3,500[a]

        Costs of Goods Sold   3,500

   To record inventory.

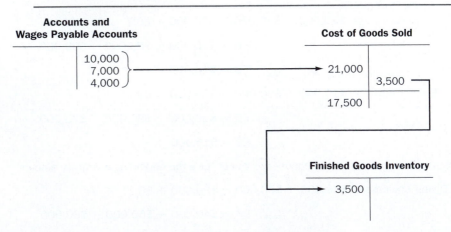

[a]$3,500 = 200 units at $17.50 per unit ($17.50 = $21,000/1,200 units).

26. Job costs in a service organization.

a. Journal entries

(1)	Work in Process: MacLean River Soda	96,000	
	Work in Process: Depardieu Productions	72,000	
	Direct Labor—Unbillable	8,000	
	Wages Payable		176,000
(2)	Work in Process: MacLean River Soda	36,000	
	Work in Process: Depardieu Productions	27,000	
	Overhead (applied)		63,000
(3)	Overhead	70,000	
	Wages and Accounts Payable		70,000
(4)	Marketing and Administrative Costs	30,000	
	Wages and Accounts Payable		30,000
(5a)	Accounts Receivable	250,000	
	Revenue		250,000
(5b)	Cost of Services Billed	231,000	
	Work in Process: MacLean River Soda		132,000
	Work in Process: Depardieu Productions		99,000

b. Income statement.

ADS UNLIMITED
Income Statement
For the Month Ending July 31

Revenue from Services	$250,000
Less Cost of Services Billed	231,000
Gross Margin	19,000
Less:	
Direct Labor—Unbillable	8,000
Overhead (underapplied)	7,000[a]
Marketing and Administrative	30,000
Operating Profit (Loss)	$(26,000)

[a]$7,000 = $70,000 actual overhead incurred − $63,000 applied to jobs and expensed as part of the Cost of Services Billed.

28. Job costs in a service organization.

a.

Wages and Accounts Payable			Work in Process: City of Chicago			Cost of Services Billed	
	175,000 (1)	(1)	60,000			(5b) 224,000	
	70,000 (3)			84,000 (5b)			
	20,000 (4)	(2)	24,000				

Overhead			Work in Process: Payfast Insurance			Marketing and Administrative Costs	
(3) 70,000	64,000 (2)	(1)	100,000			(4) 20,000	
				140,000 (5b)			
		(2)	40,000				

Accounts Receivable			Direct Labor— Unbillable			Revenue	
(5a) 300,000		(1)	15,000				300,000 (5a)

Entries:

(1) Labor costs at $50 per hour.

(2) Overhead at $20 per billable hour.

(3) Overhead actually incurred in June.

(4) Marketing and administrative costs.

(5) Services billed.

b. Income statement.

CREATIVE DESIGNS
Income Statement
For the Month Ending June 30

Revenue from Services	$300,000
Less Cost of Services Billed	224,000
Gross Margin	76,000
Less:	
Direct Labor—Unbillable	15,000
Overhead (underapplied)	6,000[a]
Marketing and Administrative	20,000
Operating Profit	$ 35,000

[a]$6,000 = $70,000 actual overhead incurred − $64,000 applied to jobs and expensed as part of the Cost of Services Billed.

30. Computing product costs with incomplete products (Appendix 15.1).

	Physical Units	% Completed During Period	Equivalent Units
Units to Account For:			
Beginning WIP	30,000	40%	12,000
Started and Completed	80,000	100	80,000
Ending WIP	20,000	30	6,000
Total	130,000		98,000

Costs to Be Accounted For:		
Beginning WIP	$ 40,000	
Current Period Costs	245,000	
Total Costs to Be Accounted For	$285,000	
Cost per E.U. Done This Period	$245,000 ÷ 98,000 E.U.	Cost per Unit $2.50 per E.U.
Costs Assigned to Units Transferred Out:		
Costs from Beginning WIP	$ 40,000	
Current Costs Added to Complete beginning WIP ($2.50 × 12,000 E.U.)	30,000	
Current Costs of Units Started & Completed ($2.50 × 80,000)	200,000	
Total Costs Transferred Out	$270,000	$2.45[a]
Costs Assigned to Ending WIP:		
($2.50 × 6,000 E.U.)	$ 15,000	
Total Costs Accounted For:	$285,000	

[a]$270,000 ÷ (30,000 units + 80,000 units).

32. Applied overhead in a bank.

a. Predetermined overhead rate $= \dfrac{\$4,000,000}{100,000 \text{ Hours}} = \$40$ per Machine

b. Total overhead applied.

Quarter	Normal Overhead
1st	32,000 × $40 = $1,280,000
2nd	30,000 × $40 = $1,200,000
3rd	18,000 × $40 = $ 720,000
4th	12,000 × $40 = $ 480,000

c. Overhead applied per check.

Quarter	Unit Cost
1st	$1,280,000 ÷ 300 million = $.00426
2nd	$1,200,000 ÷ 300 million = $.00400
3rd	$ 720,000 ÷ 200 million = $.00360
4th	$ 480,000 ÷ 100 million = $.00480

CHAPTER 16

COST ALLOCATION

LEARNING OBJECTIVES

1. Understand the nature of common (or indirect) costs.
2. Know why companies allocate common costs to departments and products.
3. Know how to allocate service department costs to production departments.
4. Understand methods of allocating marketing and administrative costs to departments.

This chapter discusses concepts and methods of assigning indirect costs, like overhead, to departments. We call such cost assignment *cost allocation.*

THE NATURE OF COMMON COSTS

Accountants distinguish between a direct cost and an indirect cost. (We also call indirect costs *common costs.*) A **direct cost** is one that firms can identify specifically with, or trace directly to, a particular product, department, or process. For example, direct materials and direct labor costs are direct with respect to products manufactured. A department manager's salary is a direct cost of the department, but indirect to the units the department produces.

A **common or indirect cost** results from the joint use of a facility or a service by several products, departments, or processes. For example, the cost of running an engine on a freight train for Union Pacific is common to the many cars on the train. The cost of grounds keeping at a university is common to its various schools and colleges. Many costs are common to different products manufactured. To develop product cost information, firms must allocate these common costs.

Firms allocate the costs of operating service departments (for example, computer services, maintenance department) to production departments for several purposes, discussed later in the chapter. We call this practice **service department cost allocation.**

546

Indirect cost allocations pervade accounting reports, both internal and external. To understand accounting reports and make appropriate interpretations, you must be familiar with the alternative allocation methods used and their effects on the resulting reports.

COST ALLOCATION

The following illustration demonstrates how companies allocate costs. Management could apply these methods to both manufacturing and nonmanufacturing settings.

A division of First Bank has four departments. The Commercial Department and Personal Department are production departments that handle banking services for businesses (commercial) and people (personal). Computer Services and Processing are **service departments.** That is, they exist to provide support to the production departments. First Bank keeps records of the direct material and direct labor costs incurred in both production departments. First Bank considers all other costs to be overhead. Exhibit 16.1 shows the relation among departments. Looking at

EXHIBIT 16.1

FIRST BANK
Organization Chart

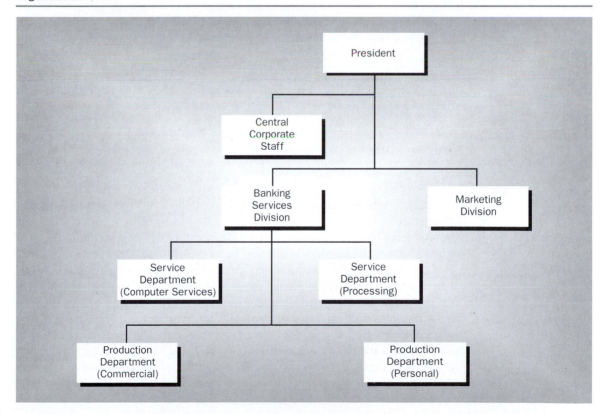

Exhibit 16.1, what department would be responsible for cost allocation and for preparing accounting reports for managerial use? (Answer: Central Corporate Staff.)

COST ALLOCATION TO PRODUCTION DEPARTMENTS

Exhibit 16.2 shows the steps in allocating costs.

First Bank first allocates overhead costs that it can attribute directly to one of the four departments. Costs in this category include salaries, labor costs, and supplies used.

Next First Bank allocates overhead costs that it cannot attribute directly to one of the departments. These costs include payments to an outside security agency, property taxes, rent and utilities, and miscellaneous costs. At this point First Bank must select a cost driver for each cost.

Using the chosen cost driver, First Bank allocates each of these costs to the four departments. Note the types of additional information that management must have to make these allocations, as shown below:

Cost	Cost Driver[a]	Allocation Appears in Suggested Solution to Problem 16.1 for Self-Study, Section ( )
(1) Security	Number of visits made to each department	Section (1)
(2) Property Taxes	Book value of equipment and inventory in each department	Section (2)
(3) Rent and Utilities	Floor space each department occupies	Section (3)
(4) Miscellaneous costs are distributed equally over the four production and service departments because the firm has no other logical basis for an allocation.		

[a]Managers and accountants selected these cost drivers as the bases to allocate security, property taxes, rent, and utilities.

The next step is to allocate the service department overhead costs to the production departments.

A simple and typical approach to cost allocation is the **step method.** The step method allocates costs in steps as follows: Begin with the service department that receives the smallest dollar amount of service from the other service departments. Allocate its cost to the other service and product departments. Next, distribute the total costs of the service department receiving the next smallest amount of service from other service departments and so on until all service department costs are allocated to the product departments. Once a given service department's cost has been allocated to other departments, do not allocate any costs back to that service department. Problem 16.1 for Self-Study on page 550 demonstrates the allocation process for First Bank.

EXHIBIT 16.2

Overhead Distribution and Allocation

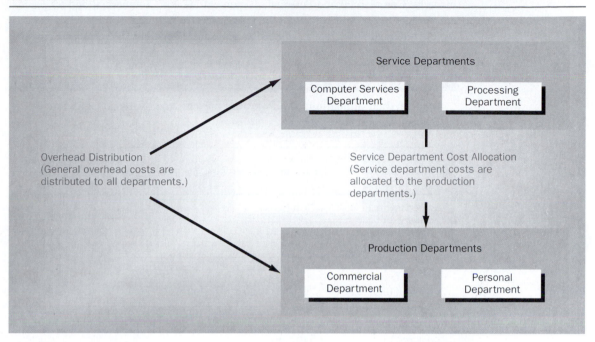

Assume the Computer Service Department provides service to the Processing Department, but receives little or no service from the Processing Department. Therefore, allocate Computer Services first, using the step method. Assume the cost driver for computer services costs is the number of computer hours required in each department. Computer hours used and the corresponding percent of usage by other departments appear below:

Department	Computer Hours	Percent[a]
Commercial	400 Hours	50%
Personal	200	25
Processing	200	25
Total	800 hours	100%

[a]50% = 400 hours/800 hours; etc.

Because the Commercial Department uses 50 percent of the computer hours, we allocate 50 percent of the computer services costs to it. In like fashion, we allocate 25 percent of the computer services costs to the Personal Department, and 25 percent of the computer services costs to the Processing Department.

Assume the cost driver for the Processing Department's costs is the quantity of transactions by the Commercial and Personal Departments. Of the total transactions made by Commercial and Personal, 40 percent are for Commercial and 60 percent are for Personal. So 40 percent of the Processing Department's costs are allocated to the Commercial Department, and 60 percent to the Personal Department.

PROBLEM 16.1 FOR SELF-STUDY

Step method allocation. The following presents the overhead costs for First Bank in the month of March:

	Total (1)	Commercial (2)	Personal (3)	Processing (4)	Computer Services (5)	Indirect Costs (6)
[a]Supervisor's Salary for Each Department ...	$11,930	$3,825	$4,300	$1,260	$2,545	
[a]Labor—Computer Services	6,000				6,000	
[a]Labor—Processing	1,000			1,000		
[a]Supplies Used ..	2,750	600	900	800	450	
Payment for Security	1,000					$1,000
Property Taxes ..	1,200					1,200
Rent and Utilities	1,440					1,440
Miscellaneous Costs	600					600
Total	$25,920	$4,425	$5,200	$3,060	$8,995	$4,240

[a]First Bank can assign each of these items directly to a department.

The overhead costs not assigned directly to a department (security, taxes, and rent and utilities) are assigned based on the following cost drivers:

Department	(1) Security Cost No. Visits	(2) Property Taxes Book Value of Assets	(3) Rent and Utilities Square Feet of Floor Space
Commercial	12	$100,000	15,000
Personal	12	70,000	15,000
Processing	16	26,000	6,000
Computer Services	0	4,000	4,000
Totals	40	$200,000	40,000

a. Calculate the percentage of cost drivers used by each department (e.g., Commercial security = 12/40 = 30%).

b. Assign the overhead to the four departments based on the percentage of cost drivers utilized.

c. Assign the service departments' costs using the step method based on computer hour usage and quantity of transactions as described in the text.

The solution to this self-study problem is at the end of the chapter on page 553.

SUMMARY OF ALLOCATION

Firms allocate costs to departments in three steps as shown in the Suggested Solution to Problem 16.1 for Self-Study: (1) allocation of costs directly to departments for costs that are directly traceable to departments (e.g., department managers' salaries at First Bank), (2) allocation of costs not directly traceable to departments using a reasonable method (e.g., security costs at First Bank), and (3) allocation of service department costs to the product departments using an arbitrary method (e.g., miscellaneous costs at First Bank).

MARKETING AND ADMINISTRATIVE EXPENSES

Management often applies techniques similar to those discussed above in allocating marketing and administrative costs. Macy's department store, for example, may wish to have its customer service and billing department costs allocated to men's clothing, furnishings, teenwear, and other departments for purposes of performance evaluation. A wholesaler of Honda motorcycles may wish to allocate the costs of advertising to different territories or types of customers (such as college students).

Exhibit 16.3 shows some of the bases of allocation that firms use for marketing and administrative costs. One striking aspect of the problem of such cost analysis

EXHIBIT 16.3

Allocation Bases

For Allocation Of	Basis
1. Insurance	Average Value of Finished Goods
2. Storage and Building Costs	Floor Space
3. Cost of Sending Monthly Statements, Credit Investigations, etc.	Number of Customers
4. Various Joint Costs Such as Advertising and Supervision of Selling Activities	Sales, Classified by Dealers, Territories, or Products
5. Credit Investigation, Postage, Stationery, and Other Such Expenses	Number of Orders Received
6. Handling Costs	Tonnage Handled
7. Salespersons' Expenses	Number of Salespersons' Calls
8. Order Writing and Filling	Number of Items on an Order
9. Stenographic Expense	Number of Letters Written
10. Automobile Operation, Delivery Expense, etc.	Number of Miles Operated

is that firms must accumulate extensive data in addition to the regular accounting information. Looking at Exhibit 16.3, what could be other bases for allocating salespersons' expenses to a geographic territory? (Answer: miles driven/traveled, dollar value of sales, or number of units sold.)

SUMMARY

The following items correspond to the learning objectives presented at the beginning of the chapter.

1. **Understand the nature of common (or indirect) costs.** A common, or indirect, cost results from the joint use of a facility or a service by several products, departments, or processes.
2. **Know why companies allocate common costs to departments and products.** Firms must allocate common costs to develop product cost information for purposes of pricing and bidding, contract cost reimbursement, motivation, asset valuation, and income determination.
3. **Know how to allocate service department costs to production departments.** First assign overhead costs that are directly attributable to a service or production department. Then allocate other overhead costs based on some cost driver.
4. **Understand methods of allocating and administrative costs to departments.** Management often applies techniques similar to those employed in allocating service department costs to allocate marketing and administrative costs for purposes of performance evaluation.

KEY TERMS AND CONCEPTS

Direct cost   Cost that can be directly attributable to a single cost object (such as a department or a unit of output).

Indirect or common cost   Cost resulting from use of raw materials, a facility, or a service that benefits several products or departments. An indirect cost cannot feasibly be attributed to a particular cost object.

Service department cost allocation   Allocation of service department costs to production departments.

Service department   A department that provides services to other departments, rather than direct work on a salable product.

Step method   The method for allocating service department costs that starts by allocating one service department's costs to a product department and to all other service departments. Then the firm allocates a second service department's costs, including costs allocated from the first, to product departments and to all other service departments except the first one. And so on.

SOLUTIONS TO SELF-STUDY PROBLEM

SUGGESTED SOLUTION TO PROBLEM 16.1 FOR SELF-STUDY

a.   Distribution of Various Overhead Costs for March

(1) Security Cost

Dept.	No. Visits	Percent[a]	Distribution of Security Cost to Department[b]
Commercial	12	30%	$ 300
Personal	12	30	300
Processing	16	40	400
Computer Services	0	—	—
Total	40	100%	$1,000

(2) Property Taxes

Dept.	Book Value of Equipment and Inventory	Percent	Distribution of Property Taxes to Department
Commercial	$100,000	50%	$ 600
Personal	70,000	35	420
Processing	26,000	13	156
Computer Services	4,000	2	24
Total	$200,000	100%	$1,200

(3) Rent and Utilities

Dept.	Square Feet of Floor Space	Percent	Distribution of Rent and Utilities to Department
Commercial	15,000	37.50%	$ 540
Personal	15,000	37.50	540
Processing	6,000	15.00	216
Computer Services	4,000	10.00	144
Total	40,000	100.00%	$1,440

[a]Percent equals number of visits to each department divided by the total visits in a typical night. For Commercial, 12 visits/40 total visits = 30%.

[b]Distribution to department equals percent times total cost. For example, for Commercial, $300 = 30% × $1,000.

b. Allocation of Overhead by Step Allocation
Overhead Allocation Schedule for Month Ending March 31

	Total	Commercial	Personal	Processing	Computer Services	Reference[a]
Supervisors' Salaries	$11,930	$3,825	$4,300	$1,260	$2,545	*
Labor—Computer Services	6,000	—	—	—	6,000	*
Labor—Processing	1,000	—	—	1,000	—	*
Supplies Used . .	2,750	600	900	800	450	*
Security	1,000	300	300	400	—	(1)
Property Taxes . .	1,200	600	420	156	24	(2)
Rent and Utility .	1,440	540	540	216	144	(3)
Miscellaneous[b] . .	600	150	150	150	150	
Total	$25,920	$6,015	$6,610	$3,982	$9,313	

[a]First Bank allocates each item marked with a star directly to a department. The number in parentheses refers to a section of part a above.

[b]Allocated evenly to departments as indicated above.

c. Allocation of Service Department Costs to Production Departments by Step Method

	Total	Commercial	Personal	Processing	Computer Services
Total before Allocation	$25,920	$ 6,015	$ 6,610	$ 3,982	$ 9,313
		50%	25%	25%	
Computer Services to the other departments[a]	—	4,657	2,328	2,328	(9,313)
	$25,920	$ 10,672	$ 8,938	$ 6,310	
		40%	60%		
Reallocation of Processing to Commercial and Personal[a]	—	2,524	3,786	(6,310)	
Total Production Department Overhead Costs	$25,920	$13,196	$12,724		

[a]Percentages for these allocations given in text.

QUESTIONS, EXERCISES, PROBLEMS, AND CASES

REVIEW QUESTIONS

1. Review the meaning of the concepts or terms given in Key Terms and Concepts.
2. Distinguish between a product department and a service department.
3. Distinguish between a direct cost and an indirect cost.
4. Give the steps in the cost allocation process.

CRITICAL ANALYSIS AND DISCUSSION QUESTIONS

5. For each of the types of common cost in the first column, select the most appropriate allocation base from the second column:

Common Cost	Allocation Base
Building Utilities	Value of Equipment and Inventories
Payroll Accounting	Number of Units Produced
Insurance	Number of Employees
Equipment Repair	Space Occupied
Quality Control Inspection	Number of Service Calls

6. When firms allocate service department costs to production departments, why do they first accumulate these costs at the service department level rather than assigning them directly to production departments?
7. Why do firms allocate service department costs to production departments?
8. Name some of the costs and benefits of cost allocation.
9. A critic of cost allocation noted, "You can avoid arbitrary cost allocations by not allocating any costs." Comment.
10. Discuss reasons for allocating costs to departments.

EXERCISES

Solutions to even-numbered exercises are at the end of the chapter after the cases.

11. **Allocating overhead to departments and jobs.** The accountants of Bowman Visuals made the following estimates for a year:

	Filming Department	Editing Department	Printing Department
Estimated Overhead	$ 66,000	$100,000	$120,000
Estimated Direct Labor Cost ...	$120,000	$100,000	$150,000
Estimated Direct Labor Time ...	11,000 Hours	12,500 Hours	15,000 Hours

a. Compute the overhead allocation rates for each department using direct labor hours as a basis.
b. Management wants to know how much the Casio commercial job cost. The following table shows the materials and labor costs; you will have to add the overhead costs using direct labor hours as the allocation base.

	Casio Commercial		
	Filming Department	Editing Department	Printing Department
Direct Material	$1,200	—	$160
Direct Labor Cost	$3,000	$4,000	$400
Direct Labor Time	250 Hours	400 Hours	38 Hours

12. **Allocating overhead.** The George Hamilton Sunscreen Company has two production departments and a maintenance department. In addition, the company

keeps other costs for the general plant in a separate account. The estimated cost data for Year 1 follow:

Cost	Product Dept. 1	Product Dept. 2	Maintenance	General Plant
Direct Labor	$50,000	$30,000	—	—
Indirect Labor	28,000	14,000	$22,500	$20,000
Indirect Materials ...	9,000	7,000	900	8,000
Miscellaneous	3,000	5,000	1,600	5,000
	$90,000	$56,000	$25,000	$33,000
Maintenance	7,000 Hours	13,000 Hours	—	—

The general plant services the three departments in the following proportions: 50 percent (Department 1); 30 percent (Department 2); 20 percent (Maintenance). Allocate maintenance costs based on maintenance hours.

Allocate maintenance department and general plant costs to the product departments. Use the step method, starting with general plant costs.

13. **Allocating overhead to jobs.** Johnson Inc., uses a job system of cost accounting. The data presented here relate to operations in its plant during January.

Johnson, Inc., has two product departments and one service department. The actual factory overhead costs during the month are $8,000. At the end of the month Mr. Johnson allocates overhead costs as follows: Department A, $4,200; Department B, $3,200, Department C, $600. He allocates the service department (Department C) overhead of $600 as follows: two-thirds to Department A, one-third to Department B.

Mr. Johnson applies factory overhead to jobs at the predetermined rates of 50 percent of direct labor costs in Department A and 75 percent in Department B. The firm delivers the jobs upon completion. The firm completed job nos. 789, 790, and 791 in January. Jobs 788 and 792 are still in process on January 31.

a. Complete the job production record in the following table by filling in the appropriate amounts. Be sure to show supporting calculations. (Job 788 has been done for you.)

b. For Departments A and B, compute the difference between the applied overhead using the predetermined rates and the actual overhead after allocating Department C overhead to Departments A and B.

Job Production Record

Job Order No.	Jobs in Process, Jan. 1	Direct Labor Dept. A	Direct Labor Dept. B	Direct Matl. Dept. A	Direct Matl. Dept. B	Applied Overhead Dept. A	Applied Overhead Dept. B	Total Costs	Jobs in Process, Jan. 31	Completed Jobs
788	$2,400	$ 600	$ 400	$ 500	$ 300	$300	$300	$4,800	$4,800	$—
789	1,700	1,200	600	900	600					
790		1,600	800	1,100	700					
791		2,000	1,200	1,200	900					
792		2,400	1,600	1,800	800					
Totals	$4,100	$7,800	$4,600	$5,500	$3,300	$	$	$	$	$

14. **Allocating service department costs using the step method.** Meridian Box Company has two service departments (maintenance and general factory administration) and two operating departments (cutting and assembly). Management has decided to allocate maintenance costs on the basis of the area in each department and general factory administration costs on the basis of labor hours the employees worked in each of their respective departments.

The following data appear in the company records for the current period:

	General Factory Administration	Maintenance	Cutting	Assembly
Area Occupied (square feet)	1,000	—	1,000	3,000
Labor Hours	—	100	100	400
Direct Labor Costs (operating departments only)			$1,500	$4,000
Service Department Direct Costs	$1,200	$2,400		

Use the step method to allocate service departments' costs to the operating departments, starting with maintenance.

15. **Using multiple cost drivers to allocate costs.** Assume Wong Manufacturing uses three allocation bases to allocate overhead costs from departments to jobs: number of different parts, number of machine hours, and number of job setup hours. The information needed to compute the allocation rates follows:

	Department A		Department B	
	Costs	Units of Activity	Costs	Units of Activity
1. Number of Different Parts	$ 1,000	40 Parts	$ 200	10 Parts
2. Number of Machine Hours Worked	$52,000	16,000 Hours	$15,000	1,500 Hours
3. Number of Hours to Set up Jobs	$ 6,000	300 Hours	$ 2,000	100 Hours

Job 300ZX required the following activities:

Department A: 10 parts, 1,000 machine hours, 20 setup hours.

Department B: 2 parts, 200 machine hours, 10 setup hours.

Allocate overhead costs to Job 300ZX using the two stages described in the chapter.

16. **Allocating service department costs directly to operating departments.** Joyner's Jolly Burgers has a commissary with two operating departments: P1, food inventory control, and P2, paper goods inventory control. It has two service departments: S1, computer services, and S2, administration, maintenance, and all other. Each department's direct costs are as follows:

P1	$90,000
P2	60,000
S1	30,000
S2	40,000

P1, P2, and S2 use S1's services as follows:

P1	10 Percent
P2	10 Percent
S2	80 Percent

P1 and P2 use S2's services as follows:

P1	62.5 Percent
P2	37.5 Percent

Compute the allocation of service center costs to operating departments. Allocate directly to operating departments. Do not allocate costs from one service department to another.

17. **Allocating service department costs using the step method.** Using the data for Exercise **16,** allocate service department costs using the step allocation method, in which the firm allocates service center costs to other service centers as well as to operating departments. Start by allocating S1 to S2, P1, and P2. Then allocate S1 to P1 and P2. For an example, see Suggested Solution to Problem 16.1 for Self-Study.

PROBLEMS

18. **Allocating overhead.** The Demski Company applies manufacturing overhead to the Melting and Molding departments. From the following data, prepare an overhead allocation schedule showing in detail the manufacturing overhead chargeable to each department. Some costs can be assigned directly (for example, indirect labor). Allocate machinery and equipment costs based on the cost of machinery and equipment, power based on horsepower rating, compensation insurance based on labor and indirect labor costs, and building-related costs based on floor space. Round all decimals to three places and all dollars to whole dollars.

DEMSKI COMPANY
Manufacturing Overhead Costs during the Month

Indirect Labor:	
Melting	$ 6,600
Molding	3,600
Supplies Used:	
Melting	1,500
Molding	900
Taxes (machinery and equipment, $72; building, $145)	217
Compensation Insurance	906
Power	300
Heat and Light	480
Depreciation: Building	390
Machinery and Equipment	360
Total	$15,253

Other Operating Data

	Floor Space (square feet)	Cost of Machinery and Equipment	Direct Labor per Month	Horsepower Rating
Department:				
Melting	4,000	$35,000	$ 2,000	120
Molding	6,000	25,000	10,000	180
Total	10,000	$60,000	$12,000	300

19. **Allocating unassigned costs to retail store departments.** The Schneider Specialty Shop has two departments, Clothing and Accessories. The operating expenses for the year ending December 31 follow.

a. Prepare a three-column statement of operating expenses with column headings: Clothing, Accessories, Total. Begin with direct departmental expenses and show a subtotal. Then continue with the allocated expenses, assigning each item to the various departments. Round all values to the nearest dollar and all percentages to one decimal place.

b. Prepare a condensed income statement with columns for Clothing, Accessories, and Total. Show the total operating expenses calculated in part **a** as a single deduction from gross margin.

SCHNEIDER SPECIALTY SHOP: Operating Expenses

	Clothing	Accessories	Unassigned	Total
Salaries:				
Clerks	$78,240	$69,360	—	$147,600
Others			$48,000	48,000
Supplies Used	3,800	3,200	1,400	8,400
Depreciation of Equipment	1,600	4,800	—	6,400
Advertising	3,726	8,586	3,888	16,200
Building Rent			19,000	19,000
Payroll Taxes			12,300	12,300
Worker's Compensation Insurance .			2,080	2,080
Fire Insurance			1,000	1,000
Delivery Expense			1,800	1,800
Miscellaneous Expenses	1,000	800	600	2,400

SCHNEIDER SPECIALTY SHOP

	Clothing	Accessories	Total
Sales	$600,000	$400,000	$1,000,000
Cost of Goods Sold	$440,000	$240,000	$680,000
Equipment	$10,080	$24,960	$35,040
Inventory (average)	$100,800	$139,200	$240,000
Floor Space (square feet)	2,400	3,600	6,000
Number of Employees	10	15	25

(Continued)

SCHNEIDER SPECIALTY SHOP

Expense	Bases of Allocation
Salaries—Other	Gross Margin
Supplies Used (unassigned)	Sales
Advertising (unassigned)	Sales
Building Rent	Floor Space
Payroll Taxes	Salaries (including both direct and other allocated salaries)
Worker's Compensation Insurance	Salaries (including both direct and other allocated salaries)
Fire Insurance	Cost of Equipment and Inventory
Delivery Expense	Sales
Miscellaneous Expenses (unassigned)	Number of Employees

20. **Allocating service department costs.** The Roselleti Spaghetti Company has two production departments, Tubing and Packing, and two service departments, Quality Control and Maintenance. In June, the Quality Control department provided 2,000 hours of service—1,047 hours to Tubing, 255 hours to Maintenance, and 698 hours to Packing. In the same month, Maintenance provided 2,750 hours to Tubing, 1,900 hours to Packing, and 350 hours to Quality Control. Quality Control incurred costs of $50,000, and Maintenance incurred costs of $105,000.

Use the step method to allocate service department costs sequentially based on hours of service provided. Start with Maintenance and then allocate Quality Control. Check your solution by making certain that the firm finally allocates $155,000 to the production departments.

21. **Allocating service department costs** (adapted from CPA exam). The Jurassic Company has three service departments (administration, maintenance, and computer support) and two production departments (creative and assembly). A summary of costs and other data for each department prior to allocation of service department costs for the year ended June 30, Year 1, follow:

	Administration	Maintenance	Computer Support	Creative	Assembly
Direct Material Costs	0	$65,000	$91,000	$3,130,000	$ 950,000
Direct Labor Costs	$90,000	$82,100	$87,000	$1,950,000	$2,050,000
Overhead Costs	$70,000	$56,100	$62,000	$1,650,000	$1,850,000
Direct Labor Hours	31,000	27,000	42,000	562,500	437,500
Number of Computers	12	8	20	280	200
Square Footage Occupied	1,750	2,000	4,800	88,000	72,000

Jurassic allocates the costs of the administration, maintenance, and computer services departments on the basis of direct labor hours, square footage occupied, and number of computers, respectively. Round all final calculations to the nearest dollar.

a. Assuming that Jurassic elects to distribute service department costs directly to production departments without interservice department cost allocation, what amount of maintenance department costs would Jurassic allocate to the creative department?

b. Assuming the same method of allocation as in part **a,** what amount of administration department costs would Jurassic allocate to the assembly department?

c. Assuming that Jurassic elects to distribute service department costs to other service departments (starting with the computer support department) as well as the production departments, what amounts of computer support department costs would Jurassic allocate to the maintenance department? (Note: Once the firm has allocated a service department's costs, no subsequent service department costs are allocated back to it.)

d. Assuming the same method of allocation as in part **c,** what amount of maintenance department costs would Jurassic allocate to the computer support department?

CASES

22. **Relating allocation methods to organizational characteristics for a retailer** (adapted from CMA exam). Columbia Company is a regional office supply chain with 26 independent stores. The firm holds each store responsible for its own credit and collections. The firm assigns the assistant manager in each store the responsibility for credit activities, including the collection of delinquent accounts, because the stores do not need a full-time employee assigned to credit activities. The company has experienced a sharp rise in uncollectibles the last two years. Corporate management has decided to establish a collections department in the home office that takes over the collection function companywide. The home office of Columbia Company will hire the necessary full-time personnel. The firm will base the size of this department on the historical credit activity of all the stores.

Top management discussed the new centralized collections department at a recent management meeting. Management has had difficulty deciding on a method to assign the costs of the new department to the stores because this type of home office service is unusual. Top management is reviewing alternative methods.

The controller favored using a predetermined rate for charging the costs to the stores. The firm would base the predetermined rate on budgeted costs. The vice-president for sales preferred an actual cost charging system.

In addition, management also discussed the basis for the collection charges to the stores. The controller identified the following four measures of services (allocation bases) that the firm could use:

(1) Total dollar sales.

(2) Average number of past-due accounts.

(3) Number of uncollectible accounts written off.

(4) One twenty-sixth of the cost to each of the stores.

The executive vice-president stated that he would like the accounting department to prepare a detailed analysis of the two charging methods and the four service measures (allocation bases).

a. Evaluate the two methods identified—predetermined rate versus actual cost—that the firm could use to charge the individual stores the costs of Columbia Company's new collections department in terms of

   (1) Practicality of application and ease of use.

   (2) Cost control.

   Also indicate whether a centralized or decentralized organization structure would be more conducive for each charging method.

b. For each of the four measures of services (allocation bases) the controller of Columbia Company identified:

   (1) Discuss whether using the service measure (allocation base) is appropriate in this situation.

   (2) Identify the behavioral problems, if any, that could arise as a consequence of adopting the service measure (allocation base).

23. **Allocation for economic decisions and motivation** (adapted from CMA exam). Bonn Company recently reorganized its computer and data processing system. Bonn has replaced the individual installations located within the accounting departments at its plants and subsidiaries with a single data-processing department at corporate headquarters responsible for the operations of a newly acquired large-scale computer system. The new department has been operating for 2 years and regularly producing reliable and timely data for the past 12 months.

   Because the department has focused its activities on converting applications to the new system and producing reports for the plant and subsidiary managements, it has devoted little attention to the costs of the department. Now that the department's activities are operating relatively smoothly, company management has requested that the departmental manager recommend a cost accumulation system to facilitate cost control and the development of suitable rates to charge users for service.

   For the past 2 years, the department has recorded costs in one account. The department has then allocated the costs to user departments on the basis of computer time used. The schedule below reports the costs and charging rate for Year 4.

   The department manager recommends that the five activity centers within the department accumulate the department costs. The five activity centers are systems analysis, programming, data preparation, computer operations (processing), and administration. She then suggests that the firm allocate the costs of the administration activity to the other four activity centers before developing a separate rate for charging users for each of the first four activities.

   After reviewing the details of the accounts, the manager made the following observations regarding the charges to the several subsidiary accounts within the department:

   (1) Salaries and benefits—records the salary and benefit costs of all employees in the department.

   (2) Supplies—records paper costs for printers and a small amount for other miscellaneous costs.

   (3) Equipment maintenance contracts—records charges for maintenance contracts that cover all equipment.

   (4) Insurance—records cost of insurance covering the equipment and the furniture.

Data Processing Department Costs for the Year Ended December 31, Year 4

(1) Salaries and Benefits	$ 622,600
(2) Supplies	40,000
(3) Equipment Maintenance Contract	15,000
(4) Insurance	25,000
(5) Heat and Air Conditioning	36,000
(6) Electricity	50,000
(7) Equipment and Furniture Depreciation	285,400
(8) Building Improvements Depreciation	10,000
(9) Building Occupancy and Security	39,300
(10) Corporate Administrative Charges	52,700
Total Costs	$1,176,000
Computer Hours for User Processing[a]	2,750
Hourly Rate ($1,176,000/2,750)	$ 428

[a]Use of available computer hours:

Testing and Debugging Programs	250
Setup of Jobs	500
Processing Jobs	2,750
Downtime for Maintenance	750
Idle Time	742
	4,992

---

(5) Heat and air conditioning—records a charge from the corporate heating and air conditioning department estimated to be the incremental costs to meet the special needs of the computer department.

(6) Electricity—records the charge for electricity based on a separate meter within the department.

(7) Equipment and furniture depreciation—records the depreciation charges for all equipment and furniture owned within the department.

(8) Building improvements—records the amortization charges for the building changes required to provide proper environmental control and electrical service for the computer equipment.

(9) Building occupancy and security—records the computer department's share of the depreciation, maintenance, heat, and security costs of the building; the firm allocates these costs to the department on the basis of square feet occupied.

(10) Corporate administrative charges—records the computer department's share of the corporate administrative costs. The firm allocates them to the department on the basis of number of employees in the department.

a. For each of the ten cost items, state whether or not the firm should distribute it to the five activity centers; and for each cost item that the firm should distribute, recommend the basis on which it should be distributed. Justify your conclusion in each case.

b. Assume that the costs of the computer operations (processing) activity will be charged to the user departments on the basis of computer hours. Using the analysis of computer utilization shown as a footnote to the department cost schedule presented in the problem, determine the total number of hours that should be employed to determine the charging rate for computer operations (processing). Justify your answer.

SUGGESTED SOLUTIONS TO EVEN-NUMBERED EXERCISES

12. Allocating overhead.

	Department			
	No. 1	No. 2	Maintenance	General Plant
Charged Directly to Department:				
Indirect Labor	$28,000	$14,000	$22,500	$20,000
Indirect Material	9,000	7,000	900	8,000
Miscellaneous	3,000	5,000	1,600	5,000
	$40,000	$26,000	$25,000	$33,000
Allocations:				
General Plant	16,500	9,900	6,600	(33,000)
Maintenance[a]	11,060	20,540	(31,600)	
Total Overhead[b]	$67,560	$56,440	0	0

[a]Total costs to be allocated: $25,000 + $6,600 = $31,600. Allocated on the basis of maintenance hours.

[b]$67,560 + $56,440 = $40,000 + $26,000 + $25,000 + $33,000.

14. Allocating service department costs using the step method.

	General Factory Administration	Maintenance	Cutting	Assembly
Service Department Costs	$1,200	$2,400	NA	NA
Maintenance Allocation . .	480($\frac{1}{5}$)	(2,400)	$480($\frac{1}{5}$)	$1,440($\frac{3}{5}$)
General Factory Administration Allocation	(1,680)		336($\frac{1}{5}$)	1,344($\frac{4}{5}$)
Total Costs Allocated			$816	$2,784

16. Allocating service department costs directly to operating departments.

	To	
From	P1	P2
S1	$15,000[a]	$15,000[a]
S2	25,000[b]	15,000[b]
	$40,000	$30,000

[a]$15,000 = $\dfrac{.10}{.10 + .10} \times$ $30,000. (The 80 percent of S1's costs used by S2 are ignored.)

[b]$25,000 = .625 \times$ $40,000.
$15,000 = .375 \times$ $40,000.

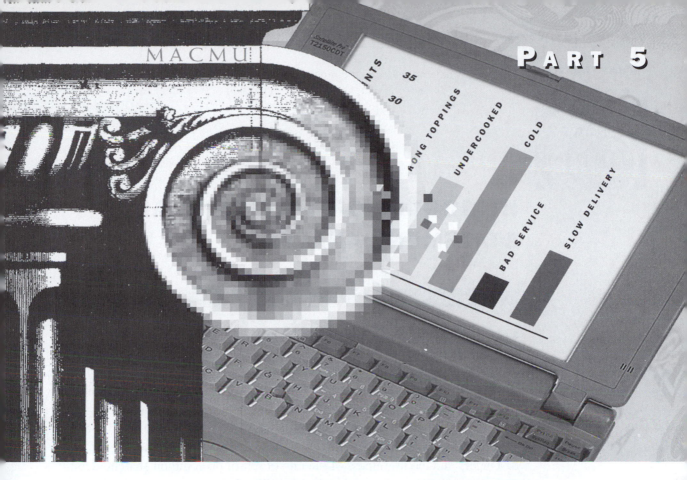

PART 5

OVERVIEW OF REPORTING

CHAPTER 17

INTRODUCTION TO FINANCIAL STATEMENT ANALYSIS

LEARNING OBJECTIVES

1. Understand the relation between the expected return and risk of investment alternatives and the role financial statement analysis can play in providing information about returns and risk.
2. Understand the usefulness of the rate of return on assets (ROA) as a measure of a firm's operating profitability independent of financing and the insights gained by disaggregating ROA into profit-margin and assets-turnover components.
3. Understand the usefulness of the rate of return on common shareholders' equity (ROCE) as a measure of profitability that incorporates a firm's particular mix of financing and the insights gained by disaggregating ROCE into profit-margin, assets-turnover, and leverage-ratio components.
4. Understand the strengths and weaknesses of earnings per common share as a measure of profitability.
5. Understand the distinction between short-term liquidity risk and long-term liquidity (solvency) risk and the financial statement ratios used to assess these two dimensions of risk.
6. Develop skills to interpret effectively the results of an analysis of profitability and risk.
7. (Appendix) Develop skills to prepare pro forma financial statements.
8. (Appendix) Understand the usefulness of pro forma financial statements in the valuation of a firm.

This chapter introduces tools and techniques for analyzing financial statements. Most financial statement analysis attempts to assess the profitability and risk of a firm. The analyst accomplishes this objective by examining relations between various financial statement items, expressed in the form of *financial statement ratios.* This chapter describes several commonly used financial statement ratios and illustrates their usefulness in assessing a firm's profitability and risk.

The results of such an analysis permit the analyst

1. to evaluate the past performance and current financial position of a firm (primarily a backward-looking exercise), and
2. to project its likely future performance and condition (primarily a forward-looking exercise).

Assessments by management of the performance of competitors, assessments by shareholders of the performance of management, and assessments by government antitrust regulators of a firm's performance use historical data. This chapter emphasizes such analyses. An examination of the financial statement effects of changes in strategies or policies, such as adding new products or substituting debt financing for equity financing, emphasizes the analysis of projected data. Management prepares a set of *pro forma financial statements* based on these new strategies or policies to study their impact. Analysts also use pro forma financial statements in valuing a firm, such as in evaluating an acquisition candidate. The appendix to this chapter discusses the preparation and use of pro forma financial statements.

OBJECTIVES OF FINANCIAL STATEMENT ANALYSIS

The first question the analyst asks in analyzing a set of financial statements is, "What do I look for?" The response to this question requires an understanding of investment decisions.

To illustrate, assume that you recently inherited $25,000 and must decide what to do with the bequest. You narrow the investment decision to purchasing either a certificate of deposit at a local bank or shares of common stock of Horrigan Corporation, currently selling for $50 per share. You will base your decision on the **return** you anticipate from each investment and the **risk** associated with that return.

The bank currently pays interest at the rate of 5 percent annually on certificates of deposit. Because the bank is unlikely to go out of business, you are virtually certain of earning 5 percent each year.

The return from investing in the shares of Horrigan Corporation's common stock has two components. First, the firm paid a cash dividend in its most recent year of $0.625 per share, and you anticipate that it will continue to pay this dividend in the future. Also, the market price of the stock will likely change between the date you purchase the shares and the date in the future when you sell them. The difference between the eventual selling price and the purchase price, often called a *capital gain* (or *loss,* if negative), is a second component of the return from buying the stock.

The common stock investment's return has more risk than does that of the certificate of deposit. The future profitability of the firm will likely affect future dividends and market price changes. Future income might be less than you currently anticipate if competitors introduce new products that erode Horrigan Corporation's share of its sales market. Future income might be greater than you currently anticipate if Horrigan Corporation makes important discoveries or introduces successful new products.

Economy-wide factors, such as inflation and changes in international tensions, will also affect the market price of Horrigan Corporation's shares. In addition, specific industry factors, such as raw materials shortages or government regulatory actions, may influence the market price of the shares. Because most individuals prefer less risk to more risk, you will probably demand a higher expected return if you purchase the Horrigan Corporation's shares than if you invest in a certificate of deposit.

Theoretical and empirical research has shown that the expected return from investing in a firm relates, in part, to the expected profitability of the firm.[1] The analyst studies a firm's past earnings to understand its operating performance and to help forecast its future profitability.

Investment decisions also require that the analyst assess the risk associated with the expected return.[2] A firm may find itself short of cash and unable to repay a short-term loan coming due. Or the amount of long-term debt in the capital structure may be so large that the firm has difficulty meeting the required interest and principal payments. The financial statements provide information for assessing how these and other elements of risk affect expected return.

Most financial statement analysis, therefore, explores some aspect of a firm's profitability or its risk, or both. Exhibit 17.1 summarizes the relation between financial statement analysis and investment decisions.

EXHIBIT 17.1

Relation between Financial Statement Analysis and Investment Decisions

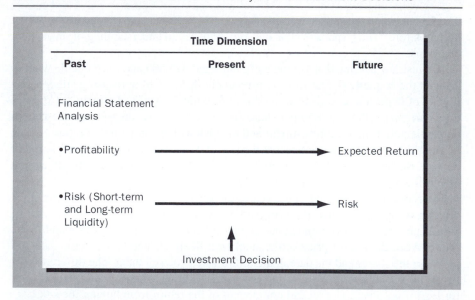

---

[1]Ray Ball and Phillip Brown, "An Empirical Evaluation of Accounting Income Numbers," *Journal of Accounting Research* (Autumn 1968), 159–178; Jane A. Ou and Stephen H. Penman, "Financial Statement Analysis and the Prediction of Stock Returns," *Journal of Accounting and Economics* (November 1989), 295–329.

[2]Modern finance distinguishes between systematic (market) risk and nonsystematic (firm-specific) risk. The discussion in this chapter does not distinguish between these two dimensions of risk.

USEFULNESS OF RATIOS

Readers may have difficulty answering their questions from the raw information in financial statements. For example, one cannot assess the profitability of a firm by noting the amount of net income. Comparing earnings with the assets or capital required to generate those earnings can help. The analyst expresses these (and other useful) relations between items in the financial statements in the form of ratios. Some ratios compare items within the income statement; some use only balance sheet data; others relate items from more than one of the three principal financial statements. Ratios aid financial statement analysis because they conveniently summarize data in a form easy to understand, interpret, and compare.

Ratios, by themselves out of context, provide little information. For example, does a rate of return on common shareholders' equity of 8.6 percent indicate satisfactory performance? Once calculated, the analyst must compare them with some standard. The following list provides several possible standards:

1. The planned ratio for the period.
2. The corresponding ratio during the preceding period for the same firm.
3. The corresponding ratio for a similar firm in the same industry.
4. The average ratio for other firms in the same industry.

Later sections of this chapter discuss difficulties encountered in using each of these bases for comparison.

The following sections describe several ratios useful for assessing profitability and various dimensions of risk. To demonstrate the calculation of various ratios, we use data for Horrigan Corporation for Years 2 through 4 appearing in Exhibit 17.2 (comparative income statements), Exhibit 17.3 (comparative balance sheets), and Exhibit 17.4 (comparative statements of cash flows). Our analysis for Horrigan

---

EXHIBIT 17.2

HORRIGAN CORPORATION
Comparative Income Statements
(all dollar amounts in millions)

	Years Ended December 31		
	Year 2	Year 3	Year 4
Sales Revenue	$210	$310	$475
Less Expenses:			
Cost of Goods Sold	$119	$179	$280
Selling	36	42	53
Administrative	15	17	22
Depreciation	12	14	18
Interest	5	10	16
Total	$187	$262	$389
Net Income before Taxes	$ 23	$ 48	$ 86
Income Tax Expense	7	14	26
Net Income	$ 16	$ 34	$ 60

EXHIBIT 17.3

HORRIGAN CORPORATION
Comparative Balance Sheets
(all dollar amounts in millions)

	December 31			
	Year 1	Year 2	Year 3	Year 4
Assets				
Cash	$ 10	$ 14	$ 8	$ 12
Accounts Receivable (net)	26	36	46	76
Inventories	14	30	46	83
Total Current Assets	$ 50	$ 80	$100	$171
Land	$ 20	$ 30	$ 60	$ 60
Building	150	150	150	190
Equipment	70	192	276	313
Less Accumulated Depreciation	(40)	(52)	(66)	(84)
Total Noncurrent Assets	$200	$320	$420	$479
Total Assets	$250	$400	$520	$650
Liabilities and Shareholders' Equity				
Accounts Payable	$ 25	$ 30	$ 35	$ 50
Salaries Payable	10	13	15	20
Income Taxes Payable	5	7	10	20
Total Current Liabilities	$ 40	$ 50	$ 60	$ 90
Bonds Payable	50	50	100	150
Total Liabilities	$ 90	$100	$160	$240
Common Stock ($10 par value)	$100	$150	$160	$160
Additional Paid-in Capital	20	100	120	120
Retained Earnings	40	50	80	130
Total Shareholders' Equity	$160	$300	$360	$410
Total Liabilities and Shareholders' Equity	$250	$400	$520	$650

Corporation studies changes in its various ratios over the three-year period. We call such an analysis a **time-series analysis,** in contrast with a **cross-section analysis,** which involves comparing a given firm's ratios with those of other firms for a specific period. Several exercises and problems at the end of the chapter involve cross-section analysis (Exercises 11, 12, 13, and Problem 28).

ANALYSIS OF PROFITABILITY

A firm engages in operations to generate net income. This section discusses three measures of **profitability:**

1. Rate of return on assets.
2. Rate of return on common shareholders' equity.
3. Earnings per common share.

EXHIBIT 17.4

HORRIGAN CORPORATION
Comparative Statements of Cash Flows
(all dollar amounts in millions)

	For the Year Ended December 31		
	Year 2	Year 3	Year 4
Operations			
Net Income	$ 16	$ 34	$ 60
Additions:			
Depreciation Expense	12	14	18
Increase in Accounts Payable	5	5	15
Increase in Salaries Payable	3	2	5
Increase in Income Taxes Payable	2	3	10
Subtractions:			
Increase in Accounts Receivable	(10)	(10)	(30)
Increase in Inventories	(16)	(16)	(37)
Cash Flow from Operations	$ 12	$ 32	$ 41
Investing			
Purchase of Land	$ (10)	$ (30)	—
Purchase of Building	—	—	$ (40)
Purchase of Equipment	(122)	(84)	(37)
Cash Flow from Investing	$(132)	$(114)	$ (77)
Financing			
Issuance of Bonds	—	$ 50	$ 50
Issuance of Common Stock	$ 130	30	—
Dividends	(6)	(4)	(10)
Cash Flow from Financing	$ 124	$ 76	$ 40
Net Change in Cash	$ 4	$ (6)	$ 4

RATE OF RETURN ON ASSETS

The **rate of return on assets (ROA)** measures a firm's performance in using assets to generate earnings independent of the financing of those assets. Previous chapters described three principal business activities: operating, investing, and financing. The rate of return on assets relates the results of *operating* performance to the *investments* of a firm without regard to how the firm *financed* the acquisition of those investments. Thus, ROA attempts to measure the success of a firm in creating and selling goods and services to customers, activities that fall primarily within the responsibility of production and marketing personnel. The rate of return on assets excludes consideration of the particular mix of financing used (debt versus shareholders' equity), an activity that falls within the responsibility of finance personnel. As with most rate of return computations the ratio divides some measure of income or performance by some measure of assets or capital required to generate that income.

The calculation of ROA is as follows:

$$\text{ROA} = \frac{\text{Net Income} + \text{Interest Expense Net of Income Tax Savings}}{\text{Average Total Assets}}$$

ROA uses an earnings figure in the numerator that recognizes income before any payments or distributions to the suppliers of capital. Because firms compute net income after subtracting interest expense on debt, the analyst must add back the interest expense to net income if the numerator is to exclude the costs of financing. Because firms can deduct interest expense in calculating taxable income, interest expense does not reduce *aftertax* net income by the full amount of interest expense. Thus, the analyst adds back interest expense reduced by the income taxes that interest deductions save to calculate the numerator of ROA.

For example, Horrigan Corporation reported interest expense for Year 4 (see Exhibit 17.2) of $16 million. The income tax rate is 30 percent of pretax income. Because Horrigan can deduct interest in computing taxable income, it saved income taxes of $4.8 million (= .30 × $16 million). The net *aftertax* cost of interest expense amounted $11.2 million (= $16.0 million − $4.8 million). To compute income before payments of interest to lenders, the analyst adds back to net income $11.2 million. The analyst need not add back dividends paid to shareholders because the firm does not deduct them as an expense in calculating net income; net income already represents an amount before payments to suppliers of shareholders' equity.

Because we are computing the earnings rate *for a year,* the measure of investment for the denominator should reflect the average amount of assets in use during the year. A crude but usually satisfactory figure for average total assets is one-half the sum of total assets at the beginning and at the end of the year.[3]

The calculation of rate of return on assets for Horrigan Corporation for Year 4 is as follows:[4]

$$\frac{\substack{\text{Net Income +} \\ \text{Interest Expense} \\ \text{Net of Income Tax} \\ \text{Savings}}}{\text{Average Total Assets}} = \frac{\$60 + (\$16 - \$4.8)}{.5(\$520 + \$650)} = 12.2 \text{ percent}$$

---

[3]Most financial economists would subtract average noninterest-bearing liabilities (for example, accounts payable, salaries payable) from average total assets in the denominator. Economists realize that when liabilities do not provide for explicit interest charges, the creditor adjusts the terms of the contract, such as setting a higher selling price or lower discount, for those who do not pay cash immediately. This ratio requires in the numerator the income amount before a firm accrues any charges to suppliers of funds. We cannot measure the interest charges implicit in the noninterest-bearing liabilities; items such as cost of goods sold and salary expense are somewhat larger because of these charges. Thus, implicit interest charges reduce the measure of operating income in the numerator. Subtracting average noninterest-bearing liabilities from average total assets likewise reduces the denominator for assets financed with such liabilities. The examples and problems in this book use average total assets in the denominator of the rate of return on assets, making no adjustment for noninterest-bearing liabilities.

[4]Throughout the remainder of this chapter, we omit reference to the fact that the amounts for Horrigan Corporation are in millions, so that, for example, $60 means $60 million and 16 shares means 16 million shares.

Thus, for each dollar of assets used, the management of Horrigan Corporation earned $.122 during Year 4 before payments to the suppliers of capital. The rate of return on assets was 8.9 percent in Year 3 and 6.0 percent in Year 2. Thus the rate of return increased steadily during this three-year period.

One might question the rationale for a measure of return that excludes the costs of financing. After all, the firm must finance the assets and must cover the cost of the financing if it is to be profitable.

The rate of return on assets has particular relevance to lenders, or creditors, of a firm. These creditors have a senior claim on earnings and assets relative to common shareholders. Creditors receive their return via contractual interest payments. The firm typically pays these amounts before it makes payments, often as dividends, to any other suppliers of capital. When extending credit or providing debt capital to a firm, creditors want to be sure that the firm can generate a rate of return on that capital (assets) exceeding its cost.

Common shareholders find the rate of return on assets useful in assessing financial leverage, which a later section of this chapter discusses.

DISAGGREGATING THE RATE OF RETURN ON ASSETS

To study changes in the rate of return on assets, the analyst can disaggregate ROA into the product of two other ratios. Improving either of these ratios will improve the overall rate of return. The disaggregation follows:

$$\text{Rate of Return on Assets} = \text{Profit Margin Ratio (before interest expense and related income tax effects)} \times \text{Total Assets Turnover Ratio}$$

or

$$\frac{\text{Net Income + Interest Expense Net of Income Tax Savings}}{\text{Average Total Assets}} = \frac{\text{Net Income + Interest Expense Net of Income Tax Savings}}{\text{Sales}} \times \frac{\text{Sales}}{\text{Average Total Assets}}$$

The **profit margin ratio** measures a firm's ability to control the level of expenses relative to sales. By holding down costs, a firm can increase the profits from a given amount of sales and thereby improve its profit margin ratio. The **total assets turnover ratio** measures a firm's ability to generate sales from a particular level of investment in assets. The smaller the amount of assets the firm needs to generate a given level of sales, the better (larger) the asset turnover. The total assets turnover measures a firm's ability to control the level of investment in assets for a particular level of sales.

Exhibit 17.5 disaggregates the rate of return on assets for Horrigan Corporation into profit margin and total assets turnover ratios for Year 2, Year 3, and Year 4. Much of the improvement in the rate of return on assets between Year 2 and Year 3 results from an increase in the profit margin ratio from 9.3 percent to 13.2 percent. The total

EXHIBIT 17.5

HORRIGAN CORPORATION
Disaggregation of Rate of Return on Assets for Year 2, Year 3, and Year 4

	Rate of Return on Assets		Profit Margin Ratio		Total Assets Turnover Ratio
	$\dfrac{\text{Net Income plus Interest Expense Net of Income Tax Savings}}{\text{Average Total Assets}}$	=	$\dfrac{\text{Net Income plus Interest Expense Net of Income Tax Savings}}{\text{Sales}}$	×	$\dfrac{\text{Sales}}{\text{Average Total Assets}}$
Year 2:	$\dfrac{\$16 + (\$5 - \$1.5)}{.5(\$250 + \$400)}$	=	$\dfrac{\$16 + (\$5 - \$1.5)}{\$210}$	×	$\dfrac{\$210}{.5(\$250 + \$400)}$
	6.0%	=	9.3%	×	.65
Year 3:	$\dfrac{\$34 + (\$10 - \$3)}{.5(\$400 + \$520)}$	=	$\dfrac{\$34 + (\$10 - \$3)}{\$310}$	×	$\dfrac{\$310}{.5(\$400 + \$520)}$
	8.9%	=	13.2%	×	.67
Year 4:	$\dfrac{\$60 + (\$16 - \$4.8)}{.5(\$520 + \$650)}$	=	$\dfrac{\$60 + (\$16 - \$4.8)}{\$475}$	×	$\dfrac{\$475}{.5(\$520 + \$650)}$
	12.2%	=	15.0%	×	.81

assets turnover ratio remained relatively stable between these two years. On the other hand, one can attribute most of the improvement in the rate of return on assets between Year 3 and Year 4 to the increased total assets turnover. The firm increased sales from each dollar invested in assets from $.67 of sales per dollar in Year 3 to $.81 of sales from each dollar invested in assets during Year 4. The increased total assets turnover, coupled with an improvement in the profit margin ratio, permitted Horrigan Corporation to increase its rate of return on assets during Year 4. To pinpoint the causes of the changes in Horrigan Corporation's profitability over this three-year period, we must analyze the changes in the profit margin ratio and total assets turnover ratio further. We will examine this analysis shortly.

Firms improve their rate of return on assets by increasing the profit margin ratio, the rate of assets turnover, or both. Some firms, however, have limited flexibility to alter one or the other of these components. For example, a firm selling commodity products in a highly competitive market may have little opportunity to increase its profit margin. Such a firm would likely take actions to improve its assets turnover (for example, tightening inventory controls to shorten the holding period for inventories) when attempting to increase its rate of return on assets. The activities of other firms might require substantial investments in property, plant, and equipment. The need for such investment might constrain the firm's ability to increase its rate of return on assets by increasing its assets turnover. Such a firm might have more flexibility to take actions that increase the profit margin (for example, creating brand loyalty for its products).

ANALYZING CHANGES IN THE PROFIT MARGIN RATIO

Changes in a firm's expenses relative to sales cause the profit margin ratio to change. To see the relation, one can express individual expenses and net income as a percentage of sales. Exhibit 17.6 presents such an analysis, called a common-size income statement, for Horrigan Corporation. This analysis alters the conventional income statement format by subtracting interest expense (net of its related income tax effects) as the last expense item. The percentages on the line Income before Interest and Related Income Tax Effect correspond to the profit margin ratios (before interest and related tax effects) in Exhibit 17.5.

The analysis in Exhibit 17.6 indicates that the improvement in Horrigan Corporation's profit margin ratio over the three years results primarily from decreased selling, administrative, and depreciation expenses as a percentage of sales. The analyst should explore further with management the reasons for these decreasing percentages.

- Does the decrease in selling expenses as a percentage of sales reflect a reduction in advertising expenditures that could hurt future sales?
- Does the decrease in depreciation expense as a percentage of sales reflect a failure to expand plant and equipment as sales increased?
- On the other hand, do these decreasing percentages result from economies of scale as the firm spreads fixed marketing, administrative, and depreciation expenses over a larger number of units?[5]

EXHIBIT 17.6

HORRIGAN CORPORATION
Common-Size Income Statement for Year 2, Year 3, and Year 4

| | Years Ended December 31 | | |
	Year 2	Year 3	Year 4
Sales Revenue	100.0%	100.0%	100.0%
Less Operating Expenses:			
Cost of Goods Sold	56.7%	57.7%	58.9%
Selling	17.1	13.6	11.2
Administrative	7.1	5.5	4.6
Depreciation	5.7	4.5	3.8
Total	86.6%	81.3%	78.5%
Income before Income Taxes and Interest	13.4%	18.7%	21.5%
Income Taxes at 30 Percent	4.1	5.5	6.5
Income before Interest and Related Income Tax Effect	9.3%	13.2%	15.0%
Interest Expense Net of Income Tax Effect	1.7	2.2	2.4
Net Income	7.6%	11.0%	12.6%

[5] *Operating leverage* is the term used to describe this phenomenon.

Neither the amount nor the trend in a particular ratio should, by itself, cause one to invest in a firm. Ratios indicate areas requiring additional analysis. For example, the analyst should explore further the increasing percentage of cost of goods sold to sales. The increase may reflect a pricing policy of reducing gross margin (selling price less cost of goods sold) to increase the volume of sales, successfully designed to generate increased profits even though the gross margin percentage declines. On the other hand, the replacement cost of inventory items may have increased without accompanying increases in selling prices. Or, the firm may have accumulated excess inventories that are physically deteriorating or are becoming obsolete.

ANALYZING CHANGES IN THE TOTAL ASSETS TURNOVER RATIO

The total assets turnover ratio aggregates the effects of the turnover ratios for the individual asset components. The analyst generally calculates three separate asset turnover ratios: accounts receivable turnover, inventory turnover, and plant asset turnover.

Accounts Receivable Turnover   The rate at which accounts receivable turn over indicates how quickly the firm collects cash. The **accounts receivable turnover ratio** equals net sales on account divided by average accounts receivable. Most firms, except some retailers (such as fast-food outlets) that deal directly with final consumers, sell their goods and services on account. For Horrigan Corporation, the accounts receivable turnover ratio for Year 4, assuming no sales for cash (that is, all sales on account), is as follows:

$$\frac{\text{Net Sales on Account}}{\text{Average Accounts Receivable}} = \frac{\$475}{.5(\$46 + \$76)} = 7.8 \text{ times per year}$$

The analyst often expresses the accounts receivable turnover in terms of the average number of days that elapse between the time that the firm makes the sale and later collects the cash, sometimes called "days accounts receivable are outstanding" or "days outstanding for receivables." To calculate this ratio, divide 365 days by the accounts receivable turnover ratio. The days outstanding for accounts receivable for Horrigan Corporation during Year 4 averages 46.8 days (= 365 days/7.8 times per year). Thus, on average, it takes slightly more than $1\frac{1}{2}$ months after the date of sale to collect its receivables. Whether this represents good performance or bad depends on the terms of sale. If the terms of sale are "net 30 days," the accounts receivable turnover indicates that collections do not accord with the stated terms. Such a result warrants a review of the credit and collection activity to ascertain the cause and derive corrective action. If the firm offers terms of "net 60 days," the ratio indicates that the firm handles accounts receivable well.

Inventory Turnover   The **inventory turnover ratio** indicates how fast firms sell their inventory items, measured in terms of rate of movement of goods into and out of the firm. Inventory turnover equals cost of goods sold divided by the average inventory during the period. The inventory turnover for Horrigan Corporation for Year 4 is as follows:

$$\frac{\text{Cost of Goods Sold}}{\text{Average Inventory}} = \frac{\$280}{.5(\$46 + \$83)} = 4.3 \text{ times per year}$$

Items remain in inventory about 85 days (= 365 days/4.3 times per year) before sale.

Managing inventory turnover involves two opposing considerations. Firms prefer to sell as many goods as possible with a minimum of capital tied up in inventories. An increase in the rate of inventory turnover between periods indicates reduced costs of financing the investment in inventory. On the other hand, management does not want to have so little inventory on hand that shortages result in lost sales. Increases in the rate of inventory turnover could signal a loss of customers, thereby offsetting any advantage gained by decreased investment in inventory. Firms must balance these opposing considerations in setting the optimum level of inventory and, thus, the accompanying rate of inventory turnover.

Some analysts calculate the inventory turnover ratio by dividing sales, rather than cost of goods sold, by the average inventory. As long as the ratio of selling price to cost of goods sold remains relatively constant, either measure will identify changes in the *trend* of the inventory holding period. Using sales in the numerator will lead, however, to incorrect measures of the inventory turnover ratio for calculating the average number of days that inventory is on hand until sale.

Plant Asset Turnover   The **plant asset turnover ratio** measures the relation between the investment in plant assets—property, plant, equipment—and sales. The plant asset turnover ratio for Horrigan Corporation for Year 4 is as follows:

$$\frac{\text{Sales}}{\text{Average Plant Assets}} = \frac{\$475}{.5(\$420 + \$479)} = 1.1 \text{ times per year}$$

Thus $1.00 invested in plant assets during Year 4 generated $1.10 in sales.

Some analysts find the reciprocal of this ratio helpful in comparing the operating characteristics of different firms. The reciprocal ratio measures dollars of plant assets required to generate one dollar of sales. For Horrigan Corporation, this reciprocal is $.90—Horrigan requires $.90 of plant assets to generate $1.00 of sales. Compare assets-per-dollar-of-sales, for example, of AT&T, with that for Safeway Stores in a recent year. AT&T has $2.70 of assets per dollar of sales, while Safeway Stores, a retailer with relatively modest plant assets, requires only $.16 (i.e., only 16 cents) of assets per dollar of sales. AT&T has large asset requirements to generate sales, while Safeway does not.

Interpret changes in the plant asset turnover ratio cautiously. Firms often invest in plant assets (for example, new production facilities) several periods before these assets generate sales from products manufactured in their plants. Thus, a low or decreasing rate of plant asset turnover may indicate an expanding firm preparing for future growth. On the other hand, a firm anticipating a decline in product sales could cut back its capital expenditures. Such an action could increase the plant asset turnover ratio.

Summary of Asset Turnovers We noted earlier that the total assets turnover for Horrigan Corporation remained stable between Year 2 and Year 3 but increased in Year 4. Exhibit 17.7 presents the four turnover ratios discussed for Horrigan Corporation over this three-year period. The accounts receivable turnover ratio increased steadily over the three years, indicating either more careful screening of credit applications or more effective collection efforts. The inventory turnover ratio decreased during the three years. Coupling this result with the increasing percentage of cost of goods sold to sales shown in Exhibit 17.6 indicates possibly excessive investments in deteriorating and obsolescent inventories.

Most of the increase in the total assets turnover between Year 3 and Year 4 results from an increase in the plant asset turnover. We note in the statement of cash flows for Horrigan Corporation in Exhibit 17.4 that total capital expenditures on land, buildings, and equipment decreased over the three-year period, possibly accounting for the increase in the plant asset turnover. The analyst should ask, "Why this decrease?"

SUMMARY OF THE ANALYSIS OF THE RATE OF RETURN ON ASSETS

The rate of return on assets helps you assess a firm's performance in using assets to generate earnings, independent of the financing of those assets. The rate of return on assets results from the interaction of its separate components: profit margin and total assets turnover.

- The profit margin ratio results from the relation of the various expenses to sales.
- Total assets turnover reflects the effects of turnover ratios for accounts receivable, inventory, and plant assets.

The analysis for Horrigan Corporation revealed the following:

1. The rate of return on assets increased over the three-year period from Year 2 to Year 4.
2. An increasing profit margin over all three years and an improved total assets turnover during Year 4 help to explain the improved rate of return on assets.
3. Decreases in the percentages of selling, administrative, and depreciation expenses to sales largely explain the improved profit margin. The analyst should question whether these decreases resulted from the firm's curtailing selling and administrative efforts that might adversely affect future sales and operations.

EXHIBIT 17.7

HORRIGAN CORPORATION
Asset Turnover Ratios for
Year 2, Year 3, and Year 4

	Year 2	Year 3	Year 4
Total Assets Turnover	.65	.67	.81
Accounts Receivable Turnover	6.80	7.60	7.80
Inventory Turnover	5.40	4.70	4.30
Plant Asset Turnover	.80	.80	1.10

4. The changes in the total assets turnover reflect the effects of increasing accounts receivable and plant asset turnover ratios and a decreasing inventory turnover. The increasing plant asset turnover, coupled with the decreased depreciation expense percentage, might relate to a reduced level of investment in new property, plant, and equipment that could hurt future productive capacity. The analyst should question whether the decreasing rate of inventory turnover, coupled with the increasing percentage of cost of goods sold to sales, indicates the buildup of obsolete inventory or some other inventory control problem.

PROBLEM 17.1 FOR SELF-STUDY

Analyzing the rate of return on assets.   Exhibit 17.8 presents profitability ratios for Abbott Corporation for 3 recent years.

a. Identify the likely reason for the decreasing rate of return on assets. Use common-size income statement percentages and individual asset turnover ratios in your interpretations.

b. What is the likely explanation for the decreasing cost of goods sold to sales percentage coupled with the increasing inventory turnover ratio?

The solution to this self-study problem is at the end of the chapter on page 604.

EXHIBIT 17.8

ABBOTT CORPORATION
Profitability Ratios
(Problem 17.1 for Self-Study)

		Common-Size Income Statements			**Individual Asset Turnovers**		
		Year 1	Year 2	Year 3		Year 1	Year 2	Year 3
Sales		100.0%	100.0%	100.0%	Accounts Receivable Turnover	4.3	4.3	4.2
Cost of Goods Sold		(79.7)	(79.6)	(79.4)	Inventory Turnover	3.2	3.4	3.6
Selling and Administrative		(10.3)	(10.2)	(10.4)	Plant Asset Turnover	.8	.7	.6
Income Taxes		(4.0)	(4.1)	(4.1)				
Profit Margin		6.0%	6.1%	6.1%				

RATE OF RETURN ON COMMON SHAREHOLDERS' EQUITY

The **rate of return on common shareholders' equity (ROCE)** measures a firm's performance in using and financing assets to generate earnings and is of primary interest to common shareholders. Unlike the rate of return on assets, the rate of return on shareholders' equity explicitly considers financing costs. Thus this measure of profitability incorporates the results of operating, investing, and financing decisions. The calculation of the rate of return on common shareholders' equity is as follows:

$$\text{ROCE} = \frac{\text{Net Income} - \text{Dividends on Preferred Stock}}{\text{Average Common Shareholders' Equity}}$$

The Numerator   To calculate the amount of earnings assignable to common shareholders' equity, the analyst subtracts all amounts required to compensate other providers of capital for the use of their funds. Expenses subtracted in computing net income already include amounts for interest expense, so the analysis requires no further adjustment for interest. Because expenses exclude all dividends, the analyst must subtract from net income any earnings allocable to preferred stock equity, usually the dividends on preferred stock declared during the period, to measure the returns solely to the common shareholders.

The Denominator   The capital provided by common shareholders during the period equals the average par value of common stock, capital contributed in excess of par value on common stock, and retained earnings for the period. (Alternatively, subtract average preferred shareholders' equity from average total shareholders' equity.)

The rate of return on common shareholders' equity of Horrigan Corporation for Year 4 is as follows:

$$\frac{\text{Net Income} - \text{Dividends on Preferred Stock}}{\text{Average Common Shareholders' Equity}} = \frac{\$60 - \$0}{.5(\$360 + \$410)} = 15.6 \text{ percent}$$

The rate of return on common shareholders' equity was 7.0 percent in Year 2 and 10.3 percent in Year 3. The rate of return on common shareholders' equity increased over the three years.

RELATION BETWEEN RETURN ON ASSETS AND RETURN ON COMMON SHAREHOLDERS' EQUITY

Exhibit 17.9 graphs the two measures of rate of return discussed thus far for Horrigan Corporation for Year 2, Year 3, and Year 4. In each year, the rate of return on common shareholders' equity exceeds the rate of return on assets. What accounts for this relation, and is it normal for profitable firms?

The rate of return on assets measures the profitability of a firm before any payments to the suppliers of capital. The calculation allocates to each of the various providers of capital some portion of this return on assets. The share allocated to creditors equals any contractual interest to which they have a claim (net of tax savings the firm realizes from deducting interest for tax purposes). The share allocated to preferred shareholders, if any, equals the stated dividend amounts on the preferred stock. Any remaining earnings belong to the common shareholders; that is, common

EXHIBIT 17.9
Rates of Return for Horrigan Corporation

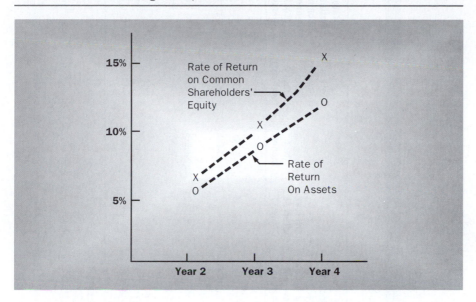

shareholders have a residual claim on all earnings after creditors and preferred share-holders receive amounts contractually owed them. Thus,

$$
\begin{array}{c}
\text{Rate of Return} \\
\text{on Assets}
\end{array}
\rightarrow
\begin{array}{c}
\text{Return to} \\
\text{Creditors} + \\
\text{(interest)}
\end{array}
+
\begin{array}{c}
\text{Return to} \\
\text{Preferred} \\
\text{Shareholders} \\
\text{(dividends)}
\end{array}
+
\begin{array}{c}
\text{Return to} \\
\text{Common} \\
\text{Shareholders} \\
\text{(residual).}
\end{array}
$$

We can now see that the rate of return on common shareholders' equity will exceed the rate of return on assets whenever the rate of return on assets exceeds the aftertax cost of debt (assuming, as here, that the firm has no preferred stock outstanding). For Year 4, the rate of return on assets was 12.2 percent (see Exhibit 17.5) and the aftertax cost of liabilities was 5.6 percent.[6] This return to assets exceeding the cost of aftertax debt belongs to the common shareholders.

The common shareholders earned a higher return but they undertook more risk in their investment. The risk results from the firm's incurring debt obligations with fixed payment amounts and dates. The next section discusses this phenomenon, called *financial leverage,* when common shareholders trade extra risk for a potentially higher return.

FINANCIAL LEVERAGE

The term **financial leverage** describes financing with debt and preferred stock to increase the potential return to the residual common shareholders' equity. As long as

---

[6]The 5.6 percent equals interest expense net of income tax savings divided by average total liabilities. For Year 4, the following facts are known from Exhibits 17.2, 17.3, and the discussion in the text: Interest expense (before income tax savings), $16; Income tax rate, 30%; Beginning of year liabilities, $160; End of year liabilities, $240. Therefore, 5.6 percent = [(1.0 − .3)$16]/[.5($160 + $240)] = $11.2/$200.

EXHIBIT 17.10

Effects of Financial Leverage on Rate of Return on Common Shareholders' Equity
(income tax rate is 30 percent of pretax income)

	Long-Term Equities		Income after Taxes but before Interest Charges[a]	Aftertax Interest Charges[b]	Net Income	Rate of Return on Total Assets[c] (percent)	Rate of Return on Common Shareholders' Equity (percent)
	Long-Term Borrowing at 10 Percent per Year	Shareholders' Equity					
Good Earnings Year							
Leveraged Company	$40,000	$ 60,000	$10,000	$2,800	$ 7,200	10.0%	12.0%
No-Debt Company	—	100,000	10,000	—	10,000	10.0	10.0
Neutral Earnings Year							
Leveraged Company	40,000	60,000	7,000	2,800	4,200	7.0	7.0
No-Debt Company	—	100,000	7,000	—	7,000	7.0	7.0
Bad Earnings Year							
Leveraged Company	40,000	60,000	4,000	2,800	1,200	4.0	2.0
No-Debt Company	—	100,000	4,000	—	4,000	4.0	4.0

[a]Not including any income tax savings caused by interest charges. Income before taxes and interest for *good* year is $14,286; for *neutral* year is $10,000; for *bad* year is $5,714.

[b]$40,000 (borrowed) × .10 (interest rate) × [1 − .30 (income tax rate)]. The numbers shown in the preceding column for aftertax income do not include the effects of interest charges on taxes.

[c]In each year, the rate of return on total assets is the same for both companies as the rate of return on common shareholders' equity for No-Debt Company: 10 percent, 7 percent, and 4 percent, respectively.

a firm earns a rate of return on assets that exceeds the rate it paid for the debt and preferred stock to acquire those assets, the rate of return to common shareholders will increase.

Illustration of Financial Leverage   Exhibit 17.10 explores this phenomenon. Leveraged Company and No-Debt Company both have $100,000 in assets. Leveraged Company borrows $40,000 at a 10 percent annual rate. No-Debt Company raises all its capital from common shareholders. Both companies pay income taxes at the rate of 30 percent.

Consider first, a good earnings year. Both companies earn $10,000 before interest charges (but after taxes, except for tax effects of interest charges).[7] This represents a rate of return on assets for both companies of 10 percent (= $10,000/ $100,000). Leveraged Company's net income is $7,200 [= $10,000 − (1.0 − .30 tax rate) × (.10 interest rate × $40,000 borrowed)], representing a rate of return on common shareholders' equity of 12.0 percent (= $7,200/$60,000). Net income of No-Debt Company is $10,000, representing a rate of return on shareholders' equity of 10 percent. Leverage increased the rate of return to shareholders of Leveraged Company, because the capital contributed by the long-term debtors earned 10 percent but required an aftertax interest payment of only 7 percent [= (1.0 − .30 tax rate) × (.10 interest rate)]. This additional 3 percent return on each dollar of assets financed by creditors increased the return to the common shareholders, as the following analysis shows.

Rate of Return to Common Shareholders

Excess Return on Assets Financed with Debt:

(.10 − .07) × ($40,000)	$ 1,200

Return on Assets Financed by Common Shareholders:

(.10) × ($60,000)	6,000
Total Return to Common Shareholders	$ 7,200
Common Shareholders' Equity	$60,000

Rate of Return on Common Shareholders' Equity:

$7,200/$60,000	12%

Although leverage increased the return to common stock equity during the good earnings year, a larger increase would occur if the firm financed a greater proportion of its assets with long-term borrowing, simultaneously increasing the firm's risk level. For example, assume that the firm financed its assets of $100,000 with $50,000 of long-term borrowing and $50,000 of shareholders' equity. Net income of Leveraged Company in this case would be $6,500 [= $10,000 − (1.0 − .30 tax rate) × (.10 × $50,000 borrowed)]. The rate of return on common stock equity would be 13 percent (= $6,500/$50,000). This compares with a rate of return on common stock equity of 12 percent when long-term debt was only 40 percent of the total capital provided. Increasing leverage from 40 percent to 50 percent, assuming the interest rate on the borrowings stayed constant, increased the rate of return from 12 percent to 13 percent.

---

[7]Income before taxes and before interest charges is $14,286; $10,000 = (1 − .30) × $14,286.

This 13 percent rate of return on common stock equity has the following components:

Rate of Return to Common Shareholders
Excess Return on Assets Financed with Debt:
   $(.10 - .07) \times (\$50,000)$ . . . . $ 1,500
Return on Assets Financed by Common Shareholders:
   $(.10) \times (\$50,000)$ 5,000
   Total Return to Common Shareholders . . . . $ 6,500
Common Shareholders' Equity $50,000
Rate of Return on Common Shareholders' Equity:
   $6,500/$50,000 . . . . 13%

Financial leverage increases the rate of return on common stock equity when the rate of return on assets exceeds the aftertax cost of debt. The greater the proportion of debt in the capital structure, however, the greater the risk the common shareholders bear. In addition, a firm cannot increase debt without increasing the cost of debt. As it adds more debt to the capital structure, the risk of default or insolvency becomes greater.[8] Lenders, including investors in a firm's bonds, require a higher and higher return (interest rate) to compensate for this additional risk. At some point, the aftertax cost of debt will exceed the rate of return earned on assets. At this point, leverage no longer increases the potential rate of return to common stock equity. For most large manufacturing firms, liabilities represent between 30 percent and 60 percent of total capital.

Exhibit 17.10 also demonstrates the effect of leverage in a neutral earnings year and in a bad earnings year. In the neutral earnings year, leverage neither increases nor decreases the rate of return to common shareholders, because the return on assets is 7 percent and the aftertax cost of long-term debt is also 7 percent. In the bad earnings year, the return on assets of 4 percent falls below the 7 percent aftertax cost of debt. The return on common stock equity then drops below the rate of return on assets to only 2 percent. Clearly, financial leverage—borrowing—can work in two ways. It can enhance owners' rate of return in good years, but owners run the risk that bad earnings years will be even worse than they would be without the borrowing.

DISAGGREGATING THE RATE OF RETURN ON COMMON SHAREHOLDERS' EQUITY

The rate of return on common shareholders' equity disaggregates into several components (in a manner similar to the disaggregation of the rate of return on assets) as follows:

---

[8]Firms want to avoid both insolvency and bankruptcy. The former refers to a condition where the firm has insufficient cash to pay its current debts, while the latter refers to a legal condition in which, usually, liabilities exceed assets.

EXHIBIT 17.11

HORRIGAN CORPORATION
Disaggregation of Rate of Return
on Common Shareholders' Equity

	Rate of Return on Common Shareholders' Equity[a] =	Profit Margin ×	Total Assets Turnover ×	Leverage Ratio
Year 2	7.0%	= 7.6% ×	.65 ×	1.4
Year 3	10.3%	= 11.0% ×	.67 ×	1.4
Year 4	15.6%	= 12.6% ×	.81 ×	1.5

[a]The amount for rate of return on common shareholders' equity may differ from the product of profit margin, total assets turnover, and leverage ratio, due to rounding.

$$
\begin{array}{c}
\text{Rate of Return} \\
\text{on Common} \\
\text{Shareholders'} \\
\text{Equity}
\end{array}
=
\begin{array}{c}
\text{Profit Margin Ratio} \\
\text{(after interest} \\
\text{expense and} \\
\text{preferred dividends)}
\end{array}
\times
\begin{array}{c}
\text{Total} \\
\text{Assets} \\
\text{Turnover} \\
\text{Ratio}
\end{array}
\times
\begin{array}{c}
\text{Leverage} \\
\text{Ratio.}
\end{array}
$$

The profit margin percentage indicates the portion of the sales dollar left over for the common shareholders after covering all operating costs and subtracting all claims of creditors and preferred shareholders. The total assets turnover indicates the sales generated from each dollar of assets. The **leverage ratio** indicates the relative proportion of capital provided by common shareholders contrasted with that provided by creditors and preferred shareholders. The larger the leverage ratio, the smaller the proportion of capital common shareholders provide and the larger the proportion creditors and preferred shareholders provide. Thus, the larger the leverage ratio, the greater the extent of financial leverage.

The disaggregation of the rate of return on common shareholders' equity ratio for Horrigan Corporation for Year 4 is as follows:

$$
\frac{\$60}{.5(\$360 + \$410)} = \frac{\$60}{\$475} \times \frac{\$475}{.5(\$520 + \$650)} \times \frac{.5(\$520 + \$650)}{.5(\$360 + \$410)}
$$

$$
15.6\% = 12.6 \text{ percent} \times .81 \times 1.5
$$

Exhibit 17.11 disaggregates the rate of return on common shareholders' equity for Horrigan Corporation for Year 2, Year 3, and Year 4. Most of the increase in the rate of return on common shareholders' equity results from an increasing profit margin over the three-year period and an increase in total assets turnover in Year 4. The leverage ratio remained reasonably stable over this period.

PROBLEM 17.2 FOR SELF-STUDY

Analyzing the rate of return on common shareholders' equity. Refer to the profitability analysis for Abbott Corporation in Problem 17.1 for Self-Study. Consider the following additional data.

	Year 1	Year 2	Year 3
Profit Margin (after subtracting financing costs) ..	5.1%	4.9%	4.6%
Total Assets Turnover	1.7	1.6	1.5
Leverage Ratio	1.6	1.8	2.1
Rate of Return on Common Shareholders' Equity[a] ..	14.0%	14.2%	14.2%

[a]Amounts may not equal the product of the three preceding ratios due to rounding.

a. What is the likely explanation for the increasing rate of return on common shareholders' equity?

b. Is financial leverage working to the advantage of the common shareholders in each year?

The solution to this self-study problem is at the end of the chapter on page 604.

EARNINGS PER SHARE OF COMMON STOCK

Earnings per share of common stock provides a third measure of profitability. Earnings per share equals net income attributable to common stock divided by the average number of common shares outstanding during the period. Earnings per share for Horrigan Corporation for Year 4 follows.

$$\frac{\text{Net Income} - \text{Preferred Stock Dividends Declared}}{\text{Weighted Average Number of Common Shares Outstanding during the Period.}^{9}} = \frac{\$60 - \$0}{16 \text{ shares}} = \$3.75 \text{ per share.}$$

Earnings per share were \$1.28 (= \$16/12.5) for Year 2 and \$2.19 (= \$34/15.5) for Year 3.

A firm with securities outstanding that holders can convert into or exchange for shares of common stock may report two earnings-per-share amounts: **basic earnings per share** (the amount that results from the calculations above) and **fully diluted earnings per share.** Convertible bonds and convertible preferred stock permit their holders to exchange these securities directly for shares of common stock. Many firms have employee stock option plans that allow employees to acquire shares of the company's common stock. When holders convert their securities or employees exercise their options, the firm will issue additional shares of common stock. Then, the amount shown as basic earnings per share will probably decrease. Accountants refer to such decreases as **dilution.** When a firm has securities outstanding that, if

---

[9]Exhibit 17.3 indicates that the par value of a common share is \$10 and that the common stock account has a balance of \$160 million throughout Year 4. The shares outstanding were therefore 16 million.

exchanged for shares of common stock, would decrease basic earnings per share by 3 percent or more, generally accepted accounting principles require a dual presentation: basic earnings per share and fully diluted earnings per share.[10]

Firms that do not have convertible or other potentially dilutive securities outstanding compute earnings per share in the conventional manner. Firms with outstanding securities that have the potential for materially diluting earnings per share as conventionally computed must present dual earnings-per-share amounts. Problem **29** at the end of this chapter explores more fully the calculation of earnings per share.

Interpreting Earnings per Share   Some accountants and financial analysts criticize earnings per share as a measure of profitability because it does not consider the amount of assets or capital required to generate that level of earnings. Two firms with the same earnings and earnings per share will not be equally profitable if one of the firms requires twice the amount of assets or capital to generate those earnings as does the other firm.

In comparing firms, earnings-per-share amounts have limited use. For example, assume that two firms have identical earnings, common shareholders' equity, and rates of return on common shareholders' equity. One firm may have a lower earnings per share simply because it has a larger number of shares outstanding (perhaps due to the use of a lower par value for its shares or to different earnings retention policies; see Exercise **20** at the end of this chapter).

Price-Earnings Ratio   Financial analysts often compare earnings-per-share amounts with the market price of the stock. They usually express this comparison as a price-earnings ratio (= market price per share/earnings per share). For example, the common stock of Horrigan Corporation sells for $50 per share at the end of Year 4. The price-earnings ratio, often called the P/E ratio, is 13.3 to 1 (= $50/ $3.75). The analyst often expresses the relation by saying that "the stock sells at 13.3 times earnings."

Tables of stock prices and financial periodicals often present price-earnings ratios. The analyst must interpret these published P/E ratios cautiously, however. In cases in which a firm has discontinued operations or has extraordinary gains and losses, the reader must ascertain whether the published ratio uses only income from continuing operations or final net income in the numerator. Also, the published P/E ratios for firms operating at a net loss for the most recent year are sometimes reported as positive numbers. This occurs because the publisher (for example, *Value Line*) converts the net loss for the year to a longer-run expected profit amount to calculate the P/E ratio. To serve their intended purpose, P/E ratios should use normal, ongoing earnings data in the denominator. The appendix to this chapter discusses more fully the use of earnings per share in the valuation of firms.

---

[10]Financial Accounting Standards Board, proposed *Statement of Financial Accounting Standards,* "Earnings per Share and Disclosure of Information about Capital Structure," 1996.

EXHIBIT 17.12
Profitability Ratios

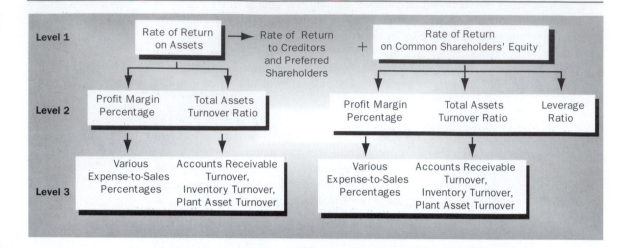

SUMMARY OF PROFITABILITY ANALYSIS

This chapter has introduced three broad measures for assessing a firm's profitability. Because the rate of return on assets and the rate of return on common shareholders' equity relate earnings to some measure of the capital required to generate those earnings, we have focused most of our attention on these two profitability measures.

Exhibit 17.12 summarizes the analysis discussed. Most generally (Level 1), the analysis concerns overall measures of profitability and the effectiveness of financial leverage. On the next level (Level 2), we disaggregate the overall measures of profitability into profit margin, asset turnover, and leverage components. Third, we further disaggregate the profit margin and asset turnover ratios to gain additional insights into reasons for changes in profitability. The depth of analysis required for an analyst to understand a particular case depends on the relative size of the observed differences or changes in profitability.

ANALYSIS OF RISK

Analysts deciding between investments must consider the comparative risks. Various factors affect the risk of business firms:

1. Economy-wide factors, such as increased inflation or interest rates, unemployment, or recessions.
2. Industry-wide factors, such as increased competition, lack of availability of raw materials, changes in technology, or increased government regulatory actions, such as antitrust or clean environment policies.
3. Firm-specific factors, such as labor strikes, loss of facilities due to fire or other casualty, or poor health of key managerial personnel.

Ultimately, analysts assess whether a firm will likely become bankrupt; creditors and investors may lose the capital they provided to a bankrupt firm.

Analysts assessing risk generally focus on the relative *liquidity* of a firm. Cash and near-cash assets provide a firm with the resources needed to adapt to the various types of risk; that is, liquid resources provide a firm with financial flexibility. Cash is also the connecting link that permits the operating, investing, and financing activities of a firm to run smoothly and effectively.

Assessing liquidity requires a time horizon. Consider the following three questions:

1. Does a firm have sufficient cash to repay a loan if it is due tomorrow?
2. Will the firm have sufficient cash to repay the same loan if it were due in six months?
3. Will the firm have sufficient cash to repay the same loan if it were due in five years?

In answering the first question, the analyst probably focuses on the amount of cash on hand and in the bank relative to the obligation coming due tomorrow. In answering the second question, the analyst compares the amount of cash expected from operations during the next six months, as well as from any new borrowings, with the obligations maturing during that period. In answering the third question, the focus shifts to the longer-run cash-generating ability of a firm relative to the amount of long-term debt maturing.

MEASURES OF SHORT-TERM LIQUIDITY RISK

This section discusses four measures for assessing **short-term liquidity risk:** (1) the current ratio, (2) the quick ratio, (3) the operating cash flow to current liabilities ratio, and (4) working capital turnover ratios.

Current Ratio   The **current ratio** equals current assets divided by current liabilities. Recall that current assets comprise cash and assets that a firm expects to turn into cash, sell, or consume within approximately one year of the balance sheet date. Current liabilities include obligations that will require cash (or the rendering of services) within approximately one year. Thus, the current ratio indicates a firm's ability to meet its short-term obligations. The current ratios of Horrigan Corporation on December 31, Year 1, Year 2, Year 3, and Year 4, is as follows:

	Current Ratio	=	Current Assets / Current Liabilities
December 31, Year 1	$\frac{\$\ 50}{\$\ 40}$	=	1.25 to 1.0
December 31, Year 2	$\frac{\$\ 80}{\$\ 50}$	=	1.60 to 1.0
December 31, Year 3	$\frac{\$100}{\$\ 60}$	=	1.67 to 1.0
December 31, Year 4	$\frac{\$171}{\$\ 90}$	=	1.90 to 1.0

Although the analyst generally prefers an excess of current assets over current liabilities, changes in the trend of the ratio can mislead. For example, when the current ratio exceeds 1 to 1, an increase of equal amount in both current assets and current liabilities (acquiring inventory on account) results in a decline in the ratio, whereas equal decreases (paying an accounts payable) result in an increased current ratio.[11]

In a recessionary period, a business may contract and use cash, a current asset, to pay its current liabilities. When the current ratio exceeds one, such action will increase it. In a boom period, firms sometimes conserve cash by delaying payment of current liabilities, causing the reverse effect. Thus, a high current ratio may accompany deteriorating business conditions, whereas a falling ratio may accompany profitable operations.

Furthermore, management can manipulate the current ratio. It can take deliberate steps to produce a financial statement that presents a better current ratio at the balance sheet date than the average, or normal, current ratio. For example, near the end of its fiscal year a firm might delay normal purchases on account. Or, it might collect receivables for loans to officers, classified as noncurrent assets, and use the proceeds to reduce current liabilities. When the current ratio exceeds one, the usual situation, such actions will increase the current ratio. Analysts refer to these manipulations as "window dressing."

Although analysts commonly use the current ratio in statement analysis, its trends do not necessarily indicate substantial changes and management can easily manipulate it.

Quick Ratio   A variation of the current ratio is the **quick ratio** (sometimes called the **acid test ratio**). The quick ratio includes in the numerator of the fraction only those current assets that a firm could convert quickly into cash. The numerator customarily includes cash, marketable securities, and receivables. Some businesses can convert their inventory of merchandise into cash more quickly than other businesses can convert their receivables. The facts in each case will indicate whether the analyst should include receivables or exclude inventories. The denominator includes all current liabilities.

Assuming that the quick ratios of Horrigan Corporation include accounts receivable but exclude inventory, the quick ratios on December 31, Year 1, Year 2, Year 3, and Year 4, are as follows:

	Quick Ratio	=	Cash, Marketable Securities, Accounts Receivable / Current Liabilities
December 31, Year 1	$\dfrac{\$36}{\$40}$	=	.90 to 1.0
December 31, Year 2	$\dfrac{\$50}{\$50}$	=	1.0 to 1.0
December 31, Year 3	$\dfrac{\$54}{\$60}$	=	.90 to 1.0
December 31, Year 4	$\dfrac{\$88}{\$90}$	=	.98 to 1.0

---

[11]The general rule is that adding equal amounts to both the numerator and the denominator of a fraction moves that fraction closer to the number 1, whereas subtracting equal amounts from both the numerator and the denominator of a fraction makes that fraction diverge from the number 1. To be even more general, adding a to (subtracting a from) the numerator while adding b to (subtracting b from) the denominator of the fraction makes the fraction converge to (diverge from) the fraction a/b.

Whereas the current ratio increased steadily over the period, the quick ratio remained relatively constant. The increase in the current ratio resulted primarily from a buildup of inventories.

Cash Flow from Operations to Current Liabilities Ratio   Some criticize the current ratio and the quick ratio because they use amounts at a specific point in time. If financial statement amounts at that particular time are unusually large or small, the resulting ratios will not reflect normal conditions.

The **cash flow from operations to current liabilities ratio** overcomes these deficiencies. The numerator of this ratio is cash flow from operations for the year. The denominator is average current liabilities for the year. The cash flow from operations to current liabilities ratios for Horrigan Corporation for Year 2, Year 3, and Year 4 are as follows:

	Cash Flow from Operations to Current Liabilities	=	Cash Flow from Operations Average Current Liabilities
Year 2	$\dfrac{\$12}{.5(\$40 + \$50)}$	=	26.7 percent
Year 3	$\dfrac{\$32}{.5(\$50 + \$60)}$	=	58.2 percent
Year 4	$\dfrac{\$41}{.5(\$60 + \$90)}$	=	54.7 percent

A healthy firm commonly has a ratio of 40 percent or more.[12] Thus the liquidity of Horrigan Corporation improved dramatically between Year 2 and Year 3.

Working Capital Turnover Ratios   During the *operating cycle* a firm:

1. Purchases inventory on account from suppliers,
2. Sells inventory on account to customers,
3. Collects amounts due from customers, and
4. Pays amounts due to suppliers.

This cycle occurs continually for most businesses. The number of days that a firm holds inventories (that is, 365 days/inventory turnover ratio) indicates the length of the period between the purchase and sale of inventory during each operating cycle. The number of days that a firm's receivables remain outstanding (that is, 365 days/accounts receivable turnover ratio) indicates the length of the period between the sale of inventory and the collection of cash from customers during each operating cycle.

Firms must finance their investments in inventories and accounts receivable. Suppliers typically provide a portion of the needed financing. The number of days that a firm's accounts payable remain outstanding (that is, 365 days/accounts payable turnover ratio) indicates the length of the period between the purchase of inventory

---

[12]Cornelius Casey and Norman Bartczak, "Using Operating Cash Flow Data to Predict Financial Distress: Some Extensions," *Journal of Accounting Research,* Spring 1985, pp. 384–401.

on account and the payment of cash to suppliers during each operating cycle. The **accounts payable turnover ratio** equals purchases on account divided by average accounts payable. Although firms do not disclose their purchases, the analyst can approximate the amount as follows:

Purchases = Cost of Goods Sold + Ending Inventory − Beginning Inventory.

The purchases of Horrigan Corporation appear below:

	Purchases	=	Cost of Goods Sold	+	Ending Inventory	−	Beginning Inventory
Year 2	$135	=	$119	+	$30	−	$14
Year 3	$195	=	$179	+	$46	−	$30
Year 4	$317	=	$280	+	$83	−	$46

The accounts payable turnover ratio for Year 4 is as follows:

$$\frac{\text{Purchases}}{\text{Average Accounts Payable}} = \frac{\$317}{.5(\$35 + \$50)} = 7.5$$

The accounts payable turnover was 4.3 for Year 2 and 5.5 for Year 3. The average number of days that payables were outstanding was 84.9 days for Year 2, 66.4 days for Year 3, and 48.7 days for Year 4. Thus, the days payable declined during the three years.

Interpreting the accounts payable turnover ratio involves opposing considerations. An increase in the accounts payable turnover ratio indicates that a firm pays its obligations to suppliers more quickly, requiring cash, even wasting it if the firm makes payments earlier than it needs to. On the other hand, a faster accounts payable turnover means a smaller relative amount of accounts payable that the firm must pay in the near future. Most firms want to extend their payables as long as they can, but they also want to maintain their reputations for honorable dealings. Ethical businesses, then, pay their bills on time, but negotiate hard for favorable payment terms.

A comparison of the days outstanding for inventories, accounts receivable, and accounts payable reveals the following:

Year	Days Inventory Held	Days Accounts Receivable Outstanding	Days Accounts Payable Outstanding
Year 2	67.6	53.7	84.9
Year 3	77.7	48.0	66.4
Year 4	84.9	46.8	48.7

The increased number of days that the firm held inventories suggests increased short-term liquidity risk. However, a reduction in the number of days that accounts receivable remain outstanding reduced short-term liquidity risk. Interpreting the decreased number of days that accounts payable remain outstanding involves the opposing considerations discussed earlier. Clearly, however, in Year 4 Horrigan Corporation must obtain more short-term financing for its investments in inventories than in Year 2. The operating cash flow to current liabilities ratio discussed in the preceding section suggests that operations have provided more than sufficient cash flow to finance this increased financing need.

SUMMARY OF SHORT-TERM LIQUIDITY ANALYSIS

The current and quick ratios measure liquidity at a particular date. These ratios for Horrigan Corporation indicate satisfactory conditions at the end of each year, although they indicate a buildup of inventories.

The cash flow from operations and working capital turnover ratios measure short-term liquidity for a period of time. The increase in the number of days the firm held inventory, coupled with a decrease in the number of days it delayed paying its accounts payable, suggests an increased need for short-term financing. However, Horrigan Corporation's increased profitability and accounts receivable turnover ratio resulted in an increasing cash flow from operations to current liabilities ratio, well above the 40 percent typically found for a financially healthy firm.

PROBLEM 17.3 FOR SELF-STUDY

Analyzing short-term liquidity risk. Refer to the profitability ratios for Abbott Corporation in Problems 17.1 and 17.2 for Self-Study. Consider the following additional data:

	Year 1	Year 2	Year 3
Current Ratio	1.4	1.3	1.2
Quick Ratio	1.0	.9	1.0
Cash Flow from Operations to			
Current Liabilities Ratio	38.2%	37.3%	36.4%
Days Accounts Receivable Outstanding	84.9	84.9	86.9
Days Inventories Held	114.1	107.4	101.4
Days Accounts Payable Outstanding	58.6	59.1	58.8

a. What is the likely explanation for the decreasing current ratio coupled with the stable quick ratio?

b. What is the likely explanation for the decline in the cash flow from operations to current liabilities ratio?

c. What is your assessment of the short-term liquidity risk of Abbott Corporation at the end of Year 3?

The solution to this self-study problem is at the end of the chapter on page 604.

MEASURES OF LONG-TERM LIQUIDITY RISK

Analysts use measures of **long-term liquidity risk** to evaluate a firm's ability to meet interest and principal payments on long-term debt and similar obligations as they come due. If a firm cannot make the payments on time, it becomes insolvent and may have to reorganize or liquidate.

A firm's ability to generate profits over several years provides the best protection against long-term liquidity risk. If a firm is profitable, it will either generate sufficient cash from operations or obtain needed capital from creditors and owners. The measures of profitability discussed previously therefore apply for this purpose as well. Analysts measure long-term liquidity risk with debt ratios, the cash flow from operations to total liabilities ratio, and the interest coverage ratio.

Debt Ratios   The debt ratio has several variations, but the **long-term debt ratio** commonly appears in financial analysis. It reports the portion of the firm's long-term capital that debt holders furnish. To calculate this ratio, divide total long-term debt by the sum of total long-term debt and total shareholders' equity.

Another form of the debt ratio is the **debt-equity ratio.** To calculate the debt-equity ratio, divide total liabilities (current and noncurrent) by total equities (= liabilities plus shareholders' equity = total assets). Some analysts compute the long-term debt ratio, as defined above, but call it "the debt-equity ratio." Be sure you know the definition the writer (or speaker) has in mind when you read (or hear) this term. No other financial statement ratio has so many variations in practice.

Exhibit 17.13 shows the two forms of the debt ratio for Horrigan Corporation on December 31, Year 1, Year 2, Year 3, and Year 4. In general, the higher these ratios, the higher the likelihood that the firm may be unable to meet fixed interest and principal payments in the future. Most firms must decide how much financial leverage, with its attendant risk, they can afford to take on. Funds obtained from issuing bonds or borrowing from a bank have a relatively low interest cost but require fixed, periodic payments that increase the likelihood of insolvency or even bankruptcy.

EXHIBIT 17.13

HORRIGAN CORPORATION
Debt Ratios

$\text{Long-Term Debt Ratio} = \dfrac{\text{Total Long-Term Debt}}{\text{Total Long-Term Debt} + \text{Shareholders' Equity}}$		$\text{Debt-Equity Ratio} = \dfrac{\text{Total Liabilities}}{\text{Total Liabilities} + \text{Shareholders' Equity}}$	
Dec. 31, Year 1 . . .	$\dfrac{\$50}{\$210} = 24$ percent	Dec. 31, Year 1 . . .	$\dfrac{\$90}{\$250} = 36$ percent
Dec. 31, Year 2 . . .	$\dfrac{\$50}{\$350} = 14$ percent	Dec. 31, Year 2 . . .	$\dfrac{\$100}{\$400} = 25$ percent
Dec. 31, Year 3 . . .	$\dfrac{\$100}{\$460} = 22$ percent	Dec. 31, Year 3 . . .	$\dfrac{\$160}{\$520} = 31$ percent
Dec. 31, Year 4 . . .	$\dfrac{\$150}{\$560} = 27$ percent	Dec. 31, Year 4 . . .	$\dfrac{\$240}{\$650} = 37$ percent

In assessing the debt ratios, analysts customarily vary the standard in relation to the stability of the firm's earnings and cash flows from operations. The more stable the earnings and cash flows, the higher the debt ratio they deem acceptable or safe. Public utilities frequently have high debt-equity ratios, frequently on the order of 60 percent to 70 percent. The stability of public utility earnings and cash flows makes these ratios acceptable to many investors. These investors might find such high leverage unacceptable for firms with less stable earnings and cash flows, such as a computer software developer or a biotechnology firm. Horrigan Corporation has debt ratios about average for an industrial firm.

Because several variations of the debt ratio appear in corporate annual reports, the analyst should take care when comparing debt ratios among firms.

Cash Flow from Operations to Total Liabilities Ratio   The debt ratios do not consider the availability of liquid assets to cover various levels of debt. The **cash flow from operations to total liabilities ratio** overcomes this deficiency. This cash flow ratio resembles the one for assessing short-term liquidity risk, but here the denominator includes *all* liabilities (both current and noncurrent). The cash flow from operations to total liabilities ratios for Horrigan Corporation are as follows:

	Cash Flow from Operations to Total Liabilities Ratio	=	Cash Flow from Operations Average Total Liabilities
Year 2	$\dfrac{\$12}{.5(\$90 + \$100)}$	=	12.6 percent
Year 3	$\dfrac{\$32}{.5(\$100 + \$160)}$	=	24.6 percent
Year 4	$\dfrac{\$41}{.5(\$160 + \$240)}$	=	20.5 percent

A financially healthy company normally has a cash flow from operations to total liabilities ratio of 20 percent or more. Thus the long-term liquidity risk decreased significantly between Year 2 and Year 3 but increased again in Year 4.

Interest Coverage Ratio   The number of times that earnings cover interest charges also measures long-term liquidity risk. The **interest coverage ratio** equals income before interest and income tax expenses divided by interest expense. For Horrigan Corporation, the interest coverage ratios for Year 2, Year 3, and Year 4 are as follows:

	Interest Coverage Ratio	=	Net Income before Interest and Income Taxes Interest Expense
Year 2	$\dfrac{\$16 + \$5 + \$7}{\$5}$	=	5.6 times
Year 3	$\dfrac{\$34 + \$10 + \$14}{\$10}$	=	5.8 times
Year 4	$\dfrac{\$60 + \$16 + \$26}{\$16}$	=	6.4 times

Thus, whereas the bonded indebtedness increased sharply during the three-year period, the growth in net income before interest and income taxes provided increasing coverage of the fixed interest charges.

This ratio attempts to indicate the relative protection that operating profitability provides bondholders, permitting them to assess the probability of a firm's failing to meet required interest payments. If bond indentures require periodic repayments of principal on long-term liabilities, the denominator of the ratio might include such repayments. The ratio would then be called the **fixed charges coverage ratio.**

One can criticize the interest or fixed charges coverage ratios as measures for assessing long-term liquidity risk because they use earnings rather than cash flows in the numerator. Firms pay interest and other fixed payment obligations with cash, not with earnings. When the value of the ratio is relatively low (for example, two to three times), the analyst should use some measure of cash flows, such as cash flow from operations, in the numerator.

SUMMARY OF LONG-TERM LIQUIDITY ANALYSIS

Long-term liquidity analysis focuses on the amount of debt (particularly long-term debt) in the capital structure and the adequacy of earnings and cash flows to service this debt (that is, to provide interest and principal payments as they mature). Although both short- and long-term debt of Horrigan Corporation increased over the three-year period, increases in sales, earnings, and cash flows from operations all appear to be increasing sufficiently to cover the current levels of debt.

PROBLEM 17.4 FOR SELF-STUDY

Analyzing long-term liquidity risk.   Refer to the profitability and short-term liquidity risk ratios for Abbott Corporation in Problems 17.1, 17.2, and 17.3 for Self-Study. Consider the following additional data:

	Year 1	Year 2	Year 3
Long-term Debt Ratio	27.2%	33.8%	43.3%
Debt-Equity Ratio	37.5%	44.4%	52.4%
Cash Flow from Operations to Total Liabilities Ratio	16.3%	13.4%	11.1%
Interest Coverage Ratio	6.7	5.1	4.1

a. What is the likely explanation for the decrease in the cash flow from operations to total liabilities ratio?

b. What is the likely explanation for the decrease in the interest coverage ratio?

c. What is your assessment of the long-term liquidity risk of Abbott Corporation at the end of Year 3?

The solution to this self-study problem is at the end of the chapter on page 605.

LIMITATIONS OF RATIO ANALYSIS

The analyst should be aware of limitations in the computations discussed in this chapter, such as the following:

1. Because ratios use financial statement data as inputs, the same factors that cause financial statements themselves to have shortcomings will affect the ratios computed from them. Such shortcomings, at least for some purposes, include the use of acquisition cost for assets rather than current replacement cost or net realizable value and the latitude permitted firms in selecting from among various generally accepted accounting principles.
2. Changes in many ratios correlate with each other. For example, the current ratio and the quick ratio often change in the same direction and proportionally. The analyst need not compute all the ratios to assess a particular dimension of profitability or risk.
3. When comparing the size of a ratio between periods for the same firm, one must recognize conditions that have changed between the periods being compared (for example, different product lines or geographic markets served, changes in economic conditions, changes in prices, changes in accounting principles, and corporate acquisitions).
4. When comparing ratios of a particular firm with those of similar firms, one must recognize differences between the firms (for example, use of different methods of accounting, differences in the methods of operations, type of financing, and so on).

Financial statement ratios alone cannot provide direct indicators of good or poor management. Such ratios indicate areas that the analyst should investigate further. For example, a decrease in the turnover of raw materials inventory, ordinarily considered an undesirable trend, may reflect the accumulation of scarce materials to keep the plant operating at full capacity during shortages. Such shortages may force competitors to restrict operations or to close down. The analyst must combine ratios derived from financial statements with an investigation of other facts before drawing conclusions.

AN INTERNATIONAL PERSPECTIVE

Analyzing the financial statements of a non-U.S. firm requires consideration of the following:

1. The format and terminology of financial statements in other countries often differs from those in the United States.
2. Economic, political, and cultural factors can differ from those in the United States in ways that affect the interpretation of financial statement ratios.
3. Firms may use accounting principles different from those U.S. firms use.

SUMMARY

For convenient reference, Exhibit 17.14 summarizes the calculation of the financial statement ratios discussed in this chapter.

This chapter began with the question, "Should you invest your inheritance in a certificate of deposit or in the shares of common stock of Horrigan Corporation?"

EXHIBIT 17.14

Summary of Financial Statement Ratios

Ratio	Numerator	Denominator
Profitability Ratios		
Rate of Return on Assets	Net Income + Interest Expense (net of tax effects)[a]	Average Total Assets during the Period[b]
Profit Margin Ratio (before interest effects) . . .	Net Income + Interest Expense (net of tax effects)[a]	Sales
Various Expense Ratios	Various Expenses	Sales
Total Assets Turnover Ratio	Sales	Average Total Assets during the Period
Accounts Receivable Turnover Ratio	Net Sales on Account	Average Accounts Receivable during the Period
Inventory Turnover Ratio	Cost of Goods Sold	Average Inventory during the Period
Plant Asset Turnover Ratio	Sales	Average Plant Assets during the Period
Rate of Return on Common Shareholders' Equity	Net Income − Preferred Stock Dividends	Average Common Shareholders' Equity during the Period
Profit Margin Ratio (after interest expense and preferred dividends)	Net Income − Preferred Stock Dividends	Sales
Leverage Ratio	Average Total Assets during the Period	Average Common Shareholders' Equity during the Period
Earnings per Share of Stock[c]	Net Income − Preferred Stock Dividends	Weighted-Average Number of Common Shares Outstanding during the Period

(continued)

---

[a]If the parent company does not own all of a consolidated subsidiary, the calculation also adds back to net income the minority interest share of earnings.

[b]See footnote 3 on page 572.

[c]This calculation is more complicated when there are convertible securities, options, or warrants outstanding.

Analysis of Horrigan Corporation's financial statements indicates that it has been a growing, profitable company with few indications of either short-term or long-term liquidity problems. You need at least three additional inputs before making the investment decision. First, you should consult sources of information other than the financial statements (for example, articles in the financial press, capital spending plans, and new product introduction plans by competitors) to understand a firm's fu-

EXHIBIT 17.14 *(continued)*

Ratio	Numerator	Denominator
Short-term Liquidity Ratios		
Current Ratio	Current Assets	Current Liabilities
Quick or Acid Test Ratio	Highly Liquid Assets (ordinarily cash, marketable securities, and receivables)[d]	Current Liabilities
Cash Flow from Operations to Current Liabilities Ratio	Cash Flow from Operations	Average Current Liabilities during the Period
Accounts Payable Turnover Ratio	Purchases[e]	Average Accounts Payable during the Period
Days Accounts Receivable Outstanding	365 days	Accounts Receivable Turnover Ratio
Days Inventories Held	365 days	Inventory Turnover Ratio
Days Accounts Payable Outstanding	365 days	Accounts Payable Turnover Ratio
Long-term Liquidity Ratios		
Long-term Debt Ratio	Total Long-term Debt	Total Long-term Debt Plus Shareholders' Equity
Debt-Equity Ratio	Total Liabilities	Total Equities (total liabilities plus shareholders' equity)
Cash Flow from Operations to Total Liabilities Ratio	Cash Flow from Operations	Average Total Liabilities during the Period
Times Interest Charges Earned	Net Income before Interest and Income Taxes	Interest Expense

[d]The calculation could conceivably exclude receivables for some firms and include inventories for others.

[e]Purchases = Cost of Goods Sold + Ending Inventories − Beginning Inventories.

ture profitability and risk. Second, you must decide your attitude toward, or willingness to assume, risk. Third, you must decide if you think the stock market price of the shares makes them an attractive current purchase.[13] Before making buy/sell recommendations to investors, analysts compare their assessments of the firm's profitability and risk to the firm's share price. Analysts might recommend the purchase of shares of a poorly run company whose shares they judge underpriced rather than recommend shares of a well-run company whose shares they judge overpriced in the market. At this stage in the investment decision the analysis requires intuition, judgment, and experience.

PROBLEM 17.5 FOR SELF-STUDY

Computing profitability and risk ratios. Exhibit 17.15 presents an income statement for Year 2, and Exhibit 17.16 presents a comparative balance sheet for Cox Corporation as of December 31, Year 1 and Year 2. Using information from these financial statements, compute the following ratios. The income tax rate is 30 percent. Cash flow from operations totals $3,300.

  a. Rate of return on assets.
  b. Profit margin ratio (before interest and related tax effects).

EXHIBIT 17.15

COX CORPORATION
Income and Retained Earnings Statement for Year 2
(Problem 17.5 for Self-Study)

Sales Revenue		$30,000
Less Expenses:		
Cost of Goods Sold	$18,000	
Selling	4,500	
Administrative	2,500	
Interest	700	
Income Taxes	1,300	
Total Expenses		27,000
Net Income		$ 3,000
Less Dividends:		
Preferred	$ 100	
Common	700	800
Increase in Retained Earnings for Year 2		$ 2,200
Retained Earnings, December 31, Year 1		4,500
Retained Earnings, December 31, Year 2		$ 6,700

[13]Finance texts discuss other important factors in the investment decision. Perhaps the most important question is how a particular investment fits in with the investor's entire portfolio. Modern research suggests that the suitability of a potential investment depends more on the attributes of the other components of an investment portfolio and the risk attitude of the investor than it does on the attributes of the potential investment itself.

EXHIBIT 17.16

COX CORPORATION
Comparative Balance Sheets
December 31, Year 1 and Year 2
(Problem 17.5 for Self-Study)

	December 31	
	Year 1	Year 2
Assets		
Current Assets		
Cash	$ 600	$ 750
Accounts Receivable	3,600	4,300
Merchandise Inventories	5,600	7,900
Prepayments	300	380
Total Current Assets	$10,100	$13,330
Property, Plant, and Equipment		
Land	$ 500	$ 600
Buildings and Equipment (net)	9,400	10,070
Total Property, Plant, and Equipment	$ 9,900	$10,670
Total Assets	$20,000	$24,000
Liabilities and Shareholders' Equity		
Current Liabilities		
Notes Payable	$ 2,000	$ 4,000
Accounts Payable	3,500	3,300
Other Current Liabilities	1,500	1,900
Total Current Liabilities	$ 7,000	$ 9,200
Noncurrent Liabilities		
Bonds Payable	4,000	2,800
Total Liabilities	$11,000	$12,000
Shareholders' Equity		
Preferred Stock	$ 1,000	$ 1,000
Common Stock	2,000	2,500
Additional Paid-in Capital	1,500	1,800
Retained Earnings	4,500	6,700
Total Shareholders' Equity	$ 9,000	$12,000
Total Liabilities and Shareholders' Equity	$20,000	$24,000

c. Cost of goods sold to sales percentage.
d. Selling expense to sales percentage.
e. Total assets turnover.
f. Accounts receivable turnover.
g. Inventory turnover.
h. Plant asset turnover.
i. Rate of return on common shareholders' equity.

    j. Profit margin ratio (after interest and preferred dividends).
    k. Leverage ratio.
    l. Current ratio (both dates).
   m. Quick ratio (both dates).
    n. Cash flow from operations to current liabilities ratio.
    o. Accounts payable turnover.
    p. Long-term debt ratio (both dates).
    q. Debt-equity ratio (both dates).
    r. Cash flow from operations to total liabilities ratio.
    s. Interest coverage ratio.

The solution to this self-study problem is at the end of the chapter on page 605.

KEY TERMS AND CONCEPTS

Return   The increase in wealth from an investment. Investments in common stock yield their return in the form of dividends and changes in market prices. Investments in debt securities yield their return in the form of interest and changes in market prices. Analysts generally express return as a percentage of the amount invested at the beginning of a period, where the period is generally one year.

Risk   A measure of the variability of the return on an investment. For a given expected amount of return, most people prefer less risk to more risk. Therefore, in rational markets, investments with more risk usually promise, or investors expect to yield, a higher rate or return than investments with lower risk.

Time-series analysis   Analysis of financial statements of a given firm for several periods of time.

Cross-section analysis   Analysis of financial statements of various firms for a single period of time.

Profitability   Analysis of a firm's ability to generate earnings from the use of capital.

Rate of return on assets (ROA)   A measure of operating profitability that excludes the effects of financing. ROA equals net income plus after-tax interest expense divided by average total assets.

Profit margin ratio   A measure of a firm's ability to generate earnings from sales. The profit margin ratio for ROA equals net income plus after-tax interest expense divided by sales. The profit margin ratio for the rate of return on common shareholders' equity (ROCE) equals net income divided by sales.

Total assets turnover ratio   A measure of the firm's ability to generate sales from a given level of assets. The total assets turnover ratio equals sales divided by average total assets.

Accounts receivable turnover ratio   A measure of the frequency during a period that a firm turns its accounts receivable into cash. Accounts receivable turnover equals net sales on account divided by average accounts receivable.

Inventory turnover ratio   A measure of the frequency during a period that a firm turns its inventory into sales. Inventory turnover equals cost of goods sold divided by average inventory.

Plant asset turnover ratio   A measure of the frequency during a period that a firm converts amounts invested in property, plant, and equipment into sales. Plant asset turnover equals sales divided by average property, plant, and equipment (net of accumulated depreciation).

Rate of return on common shareholders' equity (ROCE)   A measure of profitability that incorporates the effects of a firm's financing decisions. ROCE equals net income divided by average common shareholders' equity.

Financial leverage   The use of lower cost debt and preferred stock to increase the return to the residual common shareholders. Financial leverage works to the benefit of the common shareholders when the rate of return on assets exceeds the after-tax cost of debt and preferred stock.

Leverage ratio   The relative proportion of capital provided by common shareholders contrasted with that provided by creditors and preferred shareholders.

Basic earnings per share of common stock   A measure of profitability that relates net income allocable to the common shareholders to the weighted average number of share of common stock outstanding during a period.

Fully diluted earnings per share   A measure of profitability that reflects the dilutive effects of convertible securities and stock options and warrants.

Dilution   A potential reduction in earnings per share or book value per share by the potential conversion of securities or by the potential exercise of stock options or warrants.

Short-term liquidity risk   The risk that a firm will not have enough cash in the short-term to pay its debts.

Current ratio   A measure of short-term liquidity risk that relates current assets to current liabilities.

Quick ratio or asset test ratio   A measure of short-term liquidity risk that relates a firm's most liquid assets to current liabilities. Quick assets usually include cash, marketable securities classified as current assets and accounts receivable.

Cash flow from operations to current liabilities ratio   A measure of short-term liquidity risk that relates cash flow from operations to average current liabilities for a period.

Accounts payable turnover ratio   A measure of the frequency during a period that a firm pays its accounts payable. Accounts payable turnover equals purchases divided by average accounts payable.

Long-term liquidity risk   The risk that a firm will not have enough cash in the long-term to pay its debts.

Long-term debt ratio   A measure of long-term liquidity risk that relates long-term debt to the sum of long-term debt plus shareholders' equity.

Debt-equity ratio   A measure of long-term liquidity risk that relates long-term debt to shareholders' equity.

Cash flow from operations to total liabilities ratio   A measure of long-term liquidity risk that relates cash flow from operations to average total liabilities for a period.

Interest coverage ratio   A measure of long-term liquidity risk that relates net income before interest expense and income taxes to interest expense.

Fixed charges coverage ratio   A measure of long-term liquidity risk similar to the interest coverage ratio but includes other fixed payments, such as for leases.

Pro forma financial statements Financial statements as they would appear if some event, such as a merger or increased production and sales, had occurred or were to occur.

Capital gain The increase in the market value of an investment between two points in time.

Capital loss The decrease in the market value of an investment between two points in time.

SOLUTIONS TO SELF-STUDY PROBLEMS

SUGGESTED SOLUTION TO PROBLEM 17.1 FOR SELF-STUDY

Analyzing the rate of return on assets.

a. The declining rate of return on assets results from a decreasing total assets turnover. The profit margin ratio (before interest expense and related tax effects) was stable. The declining total assets turnover results primarily from a decreasing fixed assets turnover. Abbott Corporation has probably added productive capacity in recent years, anticipating higher sales in the future, which caused the plant asset turnover to decline.

b. Abbott Corporation has probably implemented more effective inventory control systems, resulting in an increasing inventory turnover ratio. The more rapid inventory turnover results in fewer writedowns of inventory items for product obsolescence and physical deterioration, thereby decreasing the cost of goods sold to sales percentage.

SUGGESTED SOLUTION TO PROBLEM 17.2 FOR SELF-STUDY

Analyzing the rate of return on common shareholders' equity.

a. The increasing rate of return on common shareholders' equity results from an increasing proportion of debt in the capital structure. Although the rate of return on assets declined, the increase in the leverage ratio more than offset the declining operating profitability.

b. The rate of return on common shareholders' equity exceeds the rate of return on assets, suggesting that the firm earned more on assets financed by creditors than the cost of creditors' capital. The excess return benefited the common shareholders.

SUGGESTED SOLUTION TO PROBLEM 17.3 FOR SELF-STUDY

Analyzing short-term liquidity risk.

a. Inventories are the principal asset that appears in the current ratio but not in the quick ratio. The declining current ratio indicates that inventories are not growing as rapidly as the overall level of operations. Note the decrease in the number of days inventory items are held, suggesting that the firm exerts more effective control over the level of inventories.

b. Abbott Corporation experienced a slight increase in the number of days receivables are outstanding, which tends to decrease cash flow from operations. The decrease in the number of days a firm holds inventories increases cash flow from operations and more than offsets the effect of accounts receivable on cash flow from operations. The stable accounts payable turnover also indicates that an acceleration or delay in paying accounts payable does not explain the decline in the cash flow from operations to current liabilities ratio. Most likely, declining profitability, which results in operations throwing off less cash with each revolution of the operating cycle, caused the decline. Note that the profit margin ratio excluding financing costs remained stable over the three years (see Problem 17.1 for Self-Study), whereas the profit margin ratio including financing costs declined (see Problem 17.2 for Self-Study). Thus, the declining profitability results from increased financing cost, probably related to the level of debt in the capital structure.

c. Abbott Corporation's cash flow from operations to current liabilities ratio is marginally less than the 40 percent considered desirable for a healthy firm. Its declining current ratio results from more effective inventory control systems, reducing short-term liquidity risk. A quick ratio around 1.0 indicates that the most liquid current assets are sufficient to pay current liabilities. These signals suggest a satisfactory level of short-term liquidity risk.

SUGGESTED SOLUTION TO PROBLEM 17.4 FOR SELF-STUDY

Analyzing long-term liquidity risk.

a. The response to question **b** in Problem 17.3 for Self-Study indicates that declining profitability helps explain the decrease in the cash flow from operations to total liabilities ratio. So does the increase in borrowing. This increased borrowing is both short-term and long-term, as the two debt ratios indicate.

b. The declining interest coverage ratio results primarily from increased interest expense on the increased debt loads. (Note from Problem 17.1 for Self-Study that the profit margin ratio excluding financing costs was stable during the last three years.)

c. The cash flow from operations to total liabilities ratio is below the 20 percent considered desirable for a healthy firm. Its interest coverage ratio remains four times earnings before interest and taxes. The growth in debt appears related to increases in plant assets (see the response to question **a** in Problem 17.1 for Self-Study). If Abbott Corporation experienced difficulty servicing its debt, it could perhaps sell some of these plant assets to obtain funds. Thus, the overall long-term liquidity risk level appears reasonable.

SUGGESTED SOLUTION TO PROBLEM 17.5 FOR SELF-STUDY

Computing profitability and risk ratios.

a. Rate of return on assets $= \dfrac{\$3,000 + (1 - .30)(\$700)}{.5(\$20,000 + \$24,000)} = 15.9$ percent.

b. Profit margin ratio $= \dfrac{\$3,000 + (1 - .30)(\$700)}{\$30,000} = 11.6$ percent.

c. Cost of goods sold to sales percentage $= \dfrac{\$18,000}{\$30,000} = 60.0$ percent.

d. Selling expense to sales percentage $= \dfrac{\$4{,}500}{\$30{,}000} = 15.0$ percent.

e. Total assets turnover $= \dfrac{\$30{,}000}{.5(\$20{,}000 + \$24{,}000)} = 1.4$ times per year.

f. Accounts receivable turnover $= \dfrac{\$30{,}000}{.5(\$3{,}600 + \$4{,}300)} = 7.6$ times per year.

g. Inventory turnover $= \dfrac{\$18{,}000}{.5(\$5{,}600 + \$7{,}900)} = 2.7$ times per year.

h. Plant asset turnover $= \dfrac{\$30{,}000}{.5(\$9{,}900 + \$10{,}670)} = 2.9$ times per year.

i. Rate of return on common shareholders' equity $= \dfrac{\$3{,}000 - \$100}{.5(\$8{,}000 + \$11{,}000)}$
$= 30.5$ percent.

j. Profit margin ratio (after interest) $= \dfrac{\$3{,}000 - \$100}{\$30{,}000} = 9.7$ percent.

k. Leverage ratio $= \dfrac{.5(\$20{,}000 + \$24{,}000)}{.5(\$8{,}000 + \$11{,}000)} = 2.3.$

l. Current ratio

December 31, Year 1: $\dfrac{\$10{,}100}{\$7{,}000} = 1.4{:}1.$

December 31, Year 2: $\dfrac{\$13{,}330}{\$9{,}200} = 1.4{:}1.$

m. Quick ratio

December 31, Year 1: $\dfrac{\$4{,}200}{\$7{,}000} = .6{:}1.$

December 31, Year 2: $\dfrac{\$5{,}050}{\$9{,}200} = .5{:}1.$

n. Cash flow from operations to current liabilities ratio $= \dfrac{\$3{,}300}{.5(\$7{,}000 + \$9{,}200)}$
$= 40.7$ percent.

o. Accounts payable turnover $= \dfrac{\$18{,}000 + \$7{,}900 - \$5{,}600}{.5(\$3{,}500 + \$3{,}300)} = 6.0$ times per year.

p. Long-term debt ratio

December 31, Year 1: $\dfrac{\$4{,}000}{\$13{,}000} = 30.8$ percent.

December 31, Year 2: $\dfrac{\$2{,}800}{\$14{,}800} = 18.9$ percent.

q. Debt-equity ratio

December 31, Year 1: $\dfrac{\$11,000}{\$20,000} = 55.0$ percent.

December 31, Year 2: $\dfrac{\$12,000}{\$24,000} = 50.0$ percent.

r. Cash flow from operations to total liabilities ratio $= \dfrac{\$3,300}{.5(\$11,000 + \$12,000)}$

$= 28.7$ percent.

s. Interest coverage ratio $= \dfrac{\$3,000 + \$1,300 + \$700}{\$700} = 7.1$ times.

APPENDIX 17.1: PRO FORMA FINANCIAL STATEMENTS AND VALUATION

Firms often project financial statement amounts for a year or more into the future. For example, a firm might project future sales, net income, assets, and cash flows to ascertain if operations will generate sufficient cash flows to finance capital expenditures or whether the firm will need to borrow more. A firm might change its product lines or pricing policies and might want to estimate the impact on rates of return. A firm might project future financial statement amounts for an acquisition target to ascertain the price it should pay.

Accountants use the term **pro forma financial statements** to refer to financial statements prepared under a particular set of assumptions. One set of assumptions might be that historical patterns (for example, growth rates or rates of return) will continue. Alternatively, the pro forma financial statements might reflect new assumptions about growth rates, debt levels, profitability, and so on.

This appendix describes and illustrates procedures for preparing pro forma financial statements, then demonstrates their usefulness in estimating the value of firms.

PREPARATION OF PRO FORMA FINANCIAL STATEMENTS

The preparation of pro forma financial statements requires the analyst to make assumptions about the future. The usefulness of the pro forma financial statements depends on the reasonableness of those assumptions. Various computer spreadsheet programs ease the calculations required in preparing these statements, but the warning "garbage-in, garbage-out" certainly applies—the results will have quality and validity no better than the input assumptions. Careful analysts will bring together in a single section of their work a list of all assumptions made and assumed values for parameters. Well-prepared pro forma allow the analyst to vary critical assumptions to see the effect on the results of interest.

The preparation of pro forma financial statements typically begins with the income statement, followed by the balance sheet and then the statement of cash flows. The level of operating activity usually dictates the required amount of assets, which in turn affects the required level of financing. Amounts for the statement of cash flows come directly from the income statement and comparative balance sheets.

To illustrate the preparation of pro forma financial statements, we use the data for Horrigan Corporation discussed previously in this chapter. We project amounts for Year 5.

PRO-FORMA INCOME STATEMENT

Sales The projection of income statement amounts begins with sales. The analyst studies the historical pattern of changes in sales and assesses whether this pattern will continue in the future. Among the questions raised are the following:

1. Does the firm plan to change product lines or pricing policies or make acquisitions of other companies that would alter the historical sales pattern?
2. Does the firm expect competitors to alter their strategies or new competitors to enter the market and thereby change the market shares?
3. Will conditions in the economy affect the firm's sales? For example, do the firm's sales fluctuate with economic cycles or do they remain steady or fluctuate with other variables, such as local population growth?

The assumption about sales drives most other items in the pro forma financial statements, which makes it perhaps the most important.

Exhibit 17.2 indicates that sales revenues for Horrigan Corporation increased from $210 million to $475 million between Year 2 and Year 4, a compound annual growth rate of 50.4 percent. This growth rate suggests a temporary high-growth phase, which will not continue indefinitely. Won't new competitors enter the market? Do any signs indicate market saturation of the firm's products, which will slow future growth? We assume here that this growth rate will continue for at least one more year. Thus, projected sales for Year 5 are $714 million (= $475 million × 1.504).

Operating Expenses Projecting operating expenses requires understanding the behavior of various operating costs. Do the expense items tend to vary with the level of sales, a behavior pattern characterized as a *variable cost?* Alternatively, does the expense item tend to remain relatively constant regardless of the level of sales, a behavior pattern characterized as a *fixed cost?*[14] Does the expense item have both variable and fixed cost characteristics, a pattern described as a *mixed cost* or a *step cost?* Does the firm have some discretion to change the amount of a fixed cost item in the short term in response to current conditions (for example, curtailing maintenance or advertising expenditures) or is there little discretion to change the level of fixed costs (for example, depreciation on equipment)? Understanding the behavior of each expense item aids in projecting its amount.

Exhibit 17.6 presents a common-size income statement for Horrigan Corporation for Year 2, Year 3, and Year 4. We use these common-size percentages in projecting operating expenses.

---

[14]In the long run, the firm can vary any cost: It can sell land and buildings, lay off salaried staff, omit research and development activity, and similarly change all costs. Still, in the short run, some costs do not vary much and the analyst will treat them as fixed. Thoughtful analysts will consider the time horizon pertinent for decisions and treat costs as variable or fixed depending on the length of that horizon. Managerial accounting and managerial economics texts discuss the importance of time horizon in assessing the variability of costs.

Cost of Goods Sold   The cost of goods sold percentage has increased slightly during the last three years. We learn from management that the increase results because of a pricing policy to keep prices low to maintain the high growth rate in sales. For sales revenue, we assume that the historical growth rate will continue. Thus, we project the cost of goods sold percentage to increase to 60 percent of sales. Projected cost of goods sold is $428 million (= .60 × $714 million).

Selling Expenses   The ratio of selling expense to sales decreased during the last three years. The decrease occurred because the firm compensated its sales staff based on a fixed salary each year but added few new salespeople. Thus, an increased sales level coupled with a relatively fixed compensation level caused the selling expense percentage to decrease. Horrigan Corporation indicates that it began switching to a commission-based compensation scheme in Year 4 and expects to fully implement this new system in Year 5. The firm expects selling expenses to average approximately 10 percent of sales in the future. Thus, projected selling expenses for Year 5 are $71 million (= .10 × $714 million).

Administrative Expense   The ratio of administrative expense to sales similarly decreased during the last three years. Discussions with management suggest that the decrease resulted from spreading the relatively fixed salaries of administrative personnel over a larger sales level. Management indicates that the administrative personnel are working at capacity so that additional increases in sales would require additional administrative personnel. We assume that the administrative expense percentage for Year 5 will decrease slightly to 4.5 percent of sales. Thus, projected administrative expenses for Year 5 are $32 million (= .045 × $714 million).

Depreciation Expense   The decrease in the ratio of depreciation expense to sales results from spreading the relatively fixed cost of operating capacity over ever-larger sales. Expenditures on depreciable assets have increased each year but at a decreasing rate (see the expenditures on buildings and equipment in Exhibit 17.4) and at a rate smaller than the increase in sales. The analyst must assess whether the firm has sufficient operating capacity to sustain a 50.4 percent growth rate in sales or whether it must acquire additional buildings and equipment. We note from the income statement in Exhibit 17.2 that depreciation expense increased approximately 22 percent annually during the last three years. Depreciable assets on the balance sheet increased at a similar rate during the last three years. Thus, we assume a growth rate in depreciation expense (and depreciable assets on the balance sheet) of 22 percent. Projected depreciation expense for Year 5 is $22 million (= $18 million × 1.22).

Interest Expense   Interest expense usually bears a relatively fixed relation to the level of borrowing. Interest expense for Horrigan Corporation averages approximately 10 percent of bonds payable. Projecting interest expense at this stage in the analysis is difficult. We must first project the asset side of the balance sheet and then the mix of financing needed to support that level of assets. We will assume at this stage that Horrigan Corporation will continue its historical pattern of adding $50 million to long-term debt early in Year 5. We can alter this assumption at a later point if the analysis shows that the firm does not need to borrow. Thus, projected interest expense for Year 5 is $20 million (= .10 × $200 million).

Income Tax Expense   Income tax expense remained a steady 30 percent of net income before income taxes during the last three years. We maintain this income tax rate in the projections for Year 5.

Exhibit 17.17 presents the pro forma income statement for Horrigan Corporation for Year 5.

PRO FORMA BALANCE SHEET

The analyst must make assumptions underlying the pro forma balance sheet consistent with those underlying the pro forma income statement. One approach assumes a total assets turnover similar to that of previous years. For example, the total assets turnover of Horrigan Corporation was .81 during Year 4. If the firm maintains this assets turnover during Year 5, then the calculation of its total assets at the end of Year 5 results from solving the following equation:

$$\frac{\text{Total}}{\text{Assets}} = \frac{\text{Sales}}{\text{Average Total Assets}} = \frac{\$714}{.5(\$650 + x)} = .81$$

Total assets at the end of Year 5 will be $1,113 million. The analyst can then use common-size balance sheet percentages to allocate this total to individual balance sheet accounts.

The above approach yields an unreasonable amount for total assets in this case relative to the historical growth rate in total assets. An alternative approach uses the his-

---

EXHIBIT 17.17

HORRIGAN CORPORATION
Pro Forma Income Statement for Year 5
(amounts in millions)

	Year 4 Actual	Assumption	Year 5 Pro Forma
Sales	$475	Growth Rate = 50.4%	$714
Less Expenses:			
Cost of Goods Sold	$280	60.0% of Sales	$428
Selling	53	10.0% of Sales	71
Administrative	22	4.5% of Sales	32
Depreciation	18	Growth Rate = 22.0%	22
Interest	16	10.0% of Bonds Payable[a]	20
Total Expenses	$389		$573
Net Income before Taxes	$ 86		$141
Income Tax Expense	26	30.0% of Net Income before Taxes	42
Net Income	$ 60		$ 99

[a]Including new bonds issued at the beginning of Year 5; see text.

torical growth rate in total assets of 37.5 percent during the last three years. This approach yields total assets of $894 million (= $650 million × 1.375). The analyst can then apply common-size balance sheet amounts to allocate this $894 million to individual balance sheet items.

A third approach combines both assets turnover and growth rate in analyzing separately each balance sheet item rather than applying an overall estimate to total assets. We illustrate this approach next. We will compute last the amount of cash at the end of Year 5 as the residual (or plug) necessary to equate total assets and total liabilities plus shareholders' equity.

Accounts Receivable   The accounts receivable turnover has trended upward during the last three years from 6.8 to 7.8. Most of the increase occurred between Year 2 and Year 3. We assume an accounts receivable turnover of 8.0 for Year 5. We solve the following equation to project accounts receivable at the end of Year 5.

$$\frac{\text{Accounts}}{\text{Receivable}}_{\text{Turnover Ratio}} = \frac{\text{Sales}}{\text{Average Accounts Receivable}} = \frac{\$714}{.5(\$76 + x)} = 8.0$$

Projected accounts receivable at the end of Year 5 are $103 million.

Inventory   We use the inventory turnover to project the ending inventory for Year 5. The inventory turnover ratio declined from 5.4 to 4.3 between Year 2 and Year 4. We assume an inventory turnover of 4.1 for Year 5.

$$\frac{\text{Inventory}}{\text{Turnover Ratio}} = \frac{\text{Cost of Goods Sold}}{\text{Average Inventories}} = \frac{\$428}{.5(\$83 + x)} = 4.1$$

Projected inventories at the end of Year 5 are $126 million.

Property, Plant, and Equipment   We could use the plant asset turnover to project property, plant, and equipment in a manner similar to accounts receivable and inventories above. Yet the plant asset turnover, like the total assets turnover, changed dramatically during the last three years and provides unreasonable projections for property, plant, and equipment. We instead use the historical growth rates for depreciation expense and depreciable assets of 22 percent. Projected property, plant, and equipment at the end of Year 5 is $584 million (= $479 million × 1.22).

Accounts Payable   The accounts payable turnover increased from 4.3 to 7.5 during the last three years. The analyst should attempt to learn whether the increase results from the firm's attempts to pay its suppliers more quickly, from pressure by suppliers to pay more quickly, or for some other reason. Such a clarification helps the analyst in projecting the likely accounts payable turnover during Year 5. Assume that the increase results from the firm's efforts to take advantage of cash discounts for prompt payment within 45 days of purchase. Paying within 45 days of purchase suggests an accounts payable turnover of 8.0. We solve the following equation to project accounts payable at the end of Year 5.

$$\text{Accounts Payable Turnover} = \frac{\text{Purchases}}{\text{Average Accounts Payable}} = \frac{\$428 + \$126 - \$83}{.5(\$50 + x)} = 8.0$$

Projected accounts payable at the end of Year 5 is $68 million.

Salaries Payable   The projected amount for salaries payable should consider both salary levels and the number of days since the last pay period as of the end of Year 5. Obtaining information on these items from published sources may sometimes be difficult. We project that salaries payable will grow at its historical annual growth rate of 26 percent during the last three years. Thus, projected salaries payable are $25 (= $20 × 1.26) million.

Income Taxes Payable   Income taxes payable have averaged 75 percent of income tax expense for the last two years. We assume a continuation of this pattern. Thus, projected income taxes payable are $32 (= .75 × $42) million.

Bonds Payable   The projection of interest expense assumed an increase of $50 million in bonds during Year 5.

Contributed Capital   We assume no change in common stock or additional paid-in capital during Year 5.

Retained Earnings   Retained earnings increases by the $99 million of net income and decreases by dividends declared and paid. Horrigan Corporation paid dividends totaling 17 percent of net income during Year 4. We assume a continuation of this dividend policy during Year 5, resulting in a dividend of $17 (= .17 × $99) million.[15] Thus, retained earnings at the end of Year 5 are $212 (= $130 + $99 − $17) million.

Exhibit 17.18 presents the pro forma balance sheet at the end of Year 5. A balance of $4 million in cash equates assets with liabilities and shareholders' equity. It appears that Horrigan Corporation needed the additional funds obtained from the $50 million long-term debt issued during Year 5 in order to maintain a positive balance in its cash account. The firm could, of course, have obtained the needed funds from other sources (for example, stretching accounts payable, short-term from banks, issuing additional common stock) or reduced its need for funds (for example, increasing its inventory turnover or curtailing expenditures on property, plant, and equipment and dividends). The preparation of pro forma financial statements permits the analyst to assess the effect of each of these alternatives.

---

[15]Corporate finance texts treat the interaction of dividend and borrowing policies.

EXHIBIT 17.18

HORRIGAN CORPORATION
Pro Forma Balance Sheet
December 31, Year 5
(amounts in millions)

	December 31, Year 4 Actual	Assumption	December 31, Year 5 Pro Forma
Assets			
Cash	$ 12	Residual	$ 4
Accounts Receivable	76	Turnover = 8.0	103
Inventories	83	Turnover = 4.1	126
Total Current Assets	$171		$233
Property, Plant, and Equipment (net)	479	Growth Rate = 22%	584
Total Assets	$650		$817
Liabilities and Shareholders' Equity			
Accounts Payable	$ 50	Turnover = 8.0	$ 68
Salaries Payable	20	Growth Rate = 26%	25
Income Taxes Payable	20	75% of Income Tax Expense . . .	32
Total Current Liabilities	$ 90		$125
Bonds Payable	150	Increase = $50	200
Total Liabilities	$240		$325
Common Stock	$160	No Change	$160
Additional Paid-in Capital	120	No Change	120
Retained Earnings	130	17% Dividend Payout Ratio	212
Total Shareholders' Equity	$410		$492
Total Liabilities and Shareholders' Equity	$650		$817

PRO FORMA STATEMENT OF CASH FLOWS

The analyst can prepare a pro forma statement of cash flows directly from the pro forma income statement and pro forma balance sheet. Exhibit 17.19 presents the pro forma statement of cash flows for Horrigan Corporation for Year 5. Note that the decrease in cash during Year 5 of $8 reconciles to the change in cash on the pro forma balance sheet. The only item not explicitly discussed previously is the cash outflow for acquisitions of property, plant, and equipment. The calculation of this amount is as follows:

Property, Plant, and Equipment (net) December 31, Year 4 (Exhibit 17.18)	$479
Plus Acquisitions during Year 5 (plug)	127
Less Depreciation Expense for Year 5 (Exhibit 17.17)	(22)
Property, Plant, and Equipment (net) December 31, Year 5 (Exhibit 17.18)	$584

EXHIBIT 17.19

HORRIGAN CORPORATION
Pro Forma Statement of Cash Flows for Year 5
(amounts in millions)

Operations

Net Income	$ 99
Depreciation	22
(Increase) Decrease in Accounts Receivable	(27)
(Increase) Decrease in Inventories	(43)
Increase (Decrease) in Accounts Payable	18
Increase (Decrease) in Salaries Payable	5
Increase (Decrease) in Income Taxes Payable	12
Cash Flow from Operations	$ 86

Investing

Acquisition of Property, Plant, and Equipment	$(127)
Cash Flow from Investing	$(127)

Financing

Issue of Long-term Debt	$ 50
Dividends	(17)
Cash Flow from Financing	$ 33
Change in Cash	$ (8)
Cash, December 31, Year 4	12
Cash, December 31, Year 5	$ 4

ANALYSIS OF PRO FORMA FINANCIAL STATEMENTS

The analyst can calculate various financial statement ratios from the pro forma financial statements. Exhibit 17.20 presents financial statement ratios for Horrigan Corporation based on its actual amounts for Year 2, Year 3, and Year 4 and its pro forma amounts for Year 5. The pro forma amounts indicate a continuing increase in profitability. The rate of return on assets increases because of both an increasing profit margin and increasing total assets turnover. The rate of return on common shareholders' equity increases because of improved operating profitability and increased financial leverage. The increased debt, however, does not appear to increase the short- or long-term liquidity risk of Horrigan Corporation. The projected increases in the cash flow and interest coverage ratios offset the slight increases in debt levels.

VALUATION

Managers, security analysts, and others analyze financial statements (both historical and pro forma) to form judgments about the market value of a firm. This section briefly describes the relation between financial statement items and market values. The analyst typically values a firm by several approaches to ascertain if a small range of values emerges. Entire textbooks and courses consider the valuation approaches introduced in the following sections.

EXHIBIT 17.20

HORRIGAN CORPORATION
Financial Statement Ratio Analysis

	Actual			Pro Forma
	Year 2	Year 3	Year 4	Year 5
Rate of Return on Assets	6.0%	8.9%	12.2%	15.4%
Profit Margin (before interest expense and related tax effects)	9.3%	13.2%	15.0%	15.8%
Total Assets Turnover	.65	.67	.81	.97
Cost of Goods Sold/Sales	56.7%	57.7%	58.9%	60.0%
Selling Expenses/Sales	17.1%	13.6%	11.2%	10.0%
Administrative Expenses/Sales	7.1%	5.5%	4.6%	4.5%
Depreciation Expenses/Sales	5.7%	4.5%	3.8%	3.1%
Interest Expense/Sales	2.4%	3.2%	3.4%	2.8%
Income Tax Expense/Sales	3.3%	4.5%	5.5%	5.9%
Accounts Receivable Turnover	6.8	7.6	7.8	8.0
Inventory Turnover	5.4	4.7	4.3	4.1
Plant Asset Turnover	.8	.8	1.1	1.3
Rate of Return on Common Shareholders' Equity	7.0%	10.3%	15.6%	22.0%
Profit Margin Ratio (after interest and preferred dividends)	7.6%	11.0%	12.6%	13.9%
Leverage Ratio	1.4	1.4	1.5	1.6
Current Ratio	1.60	1.67	1.90	1.86
Quick Ratio	1.00	.90	.98	.86
Cash Flow from Operations to Current Liabilities	26.7%	58.2%	54.7%	80.0%
Accounts Payable Turnover	4.3	5.5	7.5	8.0
Long-term Debt Ratio	14.3%	21.7%	26.8%	28.9%
Debt-Equity Ratio	25.0%	30.8%	36.9%	39.8%
Cash Flow from Operations to Total Liabilities	12.6%	24.6%	20.5%	30.4%
Interest Coverage Ratio	5.6	5.8	6.4	8.1

PRESENT VALUE OF FUTURE CASH FLOWS

An asset is a resource with the potential to generate future cash inflows (or to reduce future cash outflows). Likewise, the common stock of a firm has value to an investor because it can generate cash inflows to the investor in the form of dividends and cash proceeds on sale of the shares. If the sales price exceeds the investor's cost, the investor will have had a **capital gain.** When the cost exceeds the sales price, the investor has a **capital loss.** Dividends and capital gains or losses result from the future profitability and cash flows of a firm.

One valuation approach projects the net amount of cash flows a firm will generate from operating and investing activities over some number of years in the future. The analyst then discounts this net amount at an appropriate discount rate to find the present value of these future cash flows. (The appendix to this book discusses the procedure for discounting future cash flows to their equivalent present value.)

Refer to the pro forma statement of cash flows for Horrigan Corporation in Exhibit 17.19. Cash flow from operations totals $86 million and cash outflow for investing totals $127 million for Year 5. Thus, this firm does not project a positive net cash inflow from operating and investing activities during Year 5. Rapidly growing firms typically show such a pattern.

Assume for purposes of illustration that pro forma financial statements for Horrigan Corporation revealed the amounts in columns (1) through (4) in the table below. Column (5) shows the present value of the excess cash flow when discounted at 20 percent. The analyst expects excess cash flow after Year 9 to increase 28 percent each year. The $773.6 million represents the present value at the end of Year 4 of this excess cash flow after Year 9. Based on the 16 million shares of common stock outstanding (see Exhibit 17.3), the analyst estimates a market value of $50.91 per share (= $814.6 million/16 million shares).

Year (1)	Cash Flow from Operations (2)	Cash Flow from Investing (3)	Common Shareholders[a] (4)	Present Value of Excess Cash Flow (5)
5	$ 86	$(127)	$ (41)	$ (34.2)
6	129	(155)	(26)	(18.1)
7	194	(189)	5	2.9
8	290	(231)	59	28.5
9	435	(281)	154	61.9
After Year 9				773.6[b]
Total Present Value				$814.6

[a]Assumes that the firm will issue new debt to repay any debt coming due.

[b]Assumes a growth rate in excess cash flow of 28 percent per year and a discount rate of 20 percent.

MARKET MULTIPLES

A second valuation approach relies on market multiples of certain financial statement items for similar firms in the market. Identifying similar firms requires the analyst to consider such factors as the type of business, growth characteristics, and size.

Price Earnings Ratios   One common valuation approach relates market prices to multiples of earnings. The chain of logic runs as follows:

Market Price = Cash Flows from Dividends   × Appropriate
           and Residual Value   Discount Factors
                                ↓
        = Future Cash Flows of a Firm × Appropriate
                                Discount Factors
                                ↓
        = Future Earnings of a Firm   × Appropriate
                                Market Multiple
                                ↓
        = Current Earnings of a Firm × Appropriate
                                Market Multiple

The analyst uses current earnings as a surrogate for future earnings and cash flows (over sufficiently long periods net income equals cash inflows minus cash outflows from operating, investing, and nonequity financing activities). Future cash flows of the firm provide the source of cash flows to the investor. The market multiple serves the function of a discount rate in present value calculation.[16]

Assume that firms similar to Horrigan Corporation sell at 13 times Year 4 earnings from continuing operations. Based on the earnings of Horrigan Corporation for Year 4 of $60 million, a market multiple of 13 yields a total market value of $780 million, or $48.75 (= $780/16 shares) per share.

Market to Book Value Ratios Another valuation approach relates market values to the book values of common shareholders' equity of similar firms. Book values tend to exhibit less variability over time than earnings and provide perhaps less ambiguous indications of market values.

Assume that firms similar to Horrigan Corporation have average market value to book value ratios of 2.0 at the end of Year 4. The common shareholders' equity of Horrigan Corporation is $410 million at the end of Year 4, suggesting a total market value of $820 million or $51.25 (= $820 million/16 million) per share.

SUMMARY OF VALUATION APPROACHES

These three valuation approaches yielded market values for Horrigan Corporation of approximately $50 per share. We constructed the examples so that the values fell within a narrow range. Analysis of real data will likely show a wider range of market values, so the analyst must exercise judgment in choosing an approach to provide a reasonable estimate.

QUESTIONS, EXERCISES, PROBLEMS, AND CASES

QUESTIONS

1. Review the meaning of the terms and concepts listed in Key Terms and Concepts.
2. Describe several factors that might limit the comparability of a firm's financial statement ratios over several periods.
3. Describe several factors that might limit the comparability of one firm's financial statement ratios with those of another firm in the same industry.
4. "I can understand why the analyst adds back interest expense to net income in the numerator of the rate of return on assets, but I don't see why an adjustment is made for income taxes." Provide an explanation.

---

[16]Actually, the discount rate and the market multiple have a reciprocal relation. Refer to the discussion of perpetuities in this book's compound interest appendix. There you will see that the current value of an indefinite stream of constant payments, say $1 per period, has a current value of $1/r$ when the interest (or discount) rate is r per period. Thus, if the discount rate is 10 percent per period, the stream has current value of $10 (= $1/.10), but if the discount rate is 20 percent per period, then the stream has a current value of only $5 (= $1/.20). Market multipliers generally involve some variation of this relation between indefinite streams of payments and discount rates.

5. One company president stated, "The operations of our company are such that we must turn inventory over once every four weeks." Another company president in a similar industry stated, "The operations of our company are such that we can live comfortably with a turnover of four times each year." Explain what these two company presidents probably had in mind.

6. Some have argued that for any given firm at a particular time there is an optimal inventory turnover ratio. Explain.

7. Under what circumstances will the rate of return on common shareholders' equity exceed the rate of return on assets? Under what circumstances will it be less?

8. A company president recently stated, "The operations of our company are such that we can effectively use only a small amount of financial leverage." Explain.

9. Define financial leverage. As long as a firm's rate of return on assets exceeds its aftertax cost of borrowing, why doesn't the firm increase borrowing to as close to 100 percent of financing as possible?

10. Illustrate with amounts how a decrease in working capital can accompany an increase in the current ratio.

EXERCISES

Solutions to even-numbered exercises are at the end of the chapter after the cases.

11. **Calculating and disaggregating rate of return on assets.** Recent annual reports of The Coca-Cola Company and PepsiCo, Inc., reveal the following for Year 8 (in millions):

	Coca-Cola	Pepsi
Revenues	$16,172	$28,472
Interest Expense	199	645
Net Income	2,554	1,784
Average Total Assets	12,947	24,249

The Coca-Cola Company engages primarily in the soft-drink market, while PepsiCo's involvements include soft drinks, food snacks, and restaurants (Pizza Hut, KFC, Taco Bell). The income tax rate for Year 8 is 35 percent.

 a. Calculate the rate of return on assets for each company.

 b. Disaggregate the rate of return on assets in part **a** into profit margin and total assets turnover components.

 c. Comment on the relative profitability of the two companies for Year 8.

12. **Profitability analysis for two types of retailers.** Information taken from recent annual reports of two retailers appears below (amounts in millions). One of these companies is Wal-Mart, a discount store chain, and the other is The Limited, a specialty retailer of women's clothes. The income tax rate is 35 percent. Indicate which of these companies is Wal-Mart and which is The Limited. Explain.

	Company A	Company B
Sales	$7,321	$83,412
Interest Expense	65	706
Net Income	448	2,681
Average Total Assets	4,353	29,630

13. **Analyzing accounts receivable for two companies.** The annual reports of Campbell Soup Company and Heinz, two consumer foods companies, reveal the following for the current year (amounts in millions):

	Campbell Soup	Heinz
Sales	$6,690	$7,047
Accounts Receivable, January 1	646	979
Accounts Receivable, December 31	578	813

   a. Compute the accounts receivable turnover for each company.
   b. Compute the average number of days that accounts receivable are outstanding for each company.
   c. Which company is managing its accounts receivable more efficiently?

14. **Analyzing inventories over four years.** The following information relates to the activities of Bristol-Myers Squibb, a manufacturer of prescription drugs as well as nonprescription health products and toiletries (amounts in millions):

	Year 5	Year 6	Year 7	Year 8
Sales	$10,571	$11,156	$11,413	$11,984
Cost of Goods Sold	2,717	2,857	3,029	3,122
Average Inventory	1,409	1,471	1,408	1,360

   a. Compute the inventory turnover for each year.
   b. Compute the average number of days that inventories are held each year.
   c. Compute the cost of goods sold to sales percentage for each year.
   d. How well has Bristol-Myers Squibb managed its inventories over the four years?

15. **Analyzing plant asset turnover over four years.** The following information relates to Boise Cascade, a forest products company (amounts in millions):

	Year 2	Year 3	Year 4	Year 5
Sales	$3,950	$3,716	$3,958	$4,142
Average Plant Assets	3,550	3,503	3,232	2,951
Expenditures on Plant Assets	299	283	222	192

   a. Compute the plant asset turnover for each year.
   b. How well has Boise Cascade managed its investment in plant assets over the four years?

16. **Calculating and disaggregating rate of return on common shareholders' equity.** Information taken from the annual reports of Glaxo, a pharmaceutical company headquartered in the United Kingdom, for three recent years follows (amounts in millions):

	Year 4	Year 5	Year 6
Revenues	£4,096	£4,930	£5,656
Net Income	1,033	1,207	1,303
Average Total Assets	5,713	6,570	7,673
Average Common Shareholders' Equity	3,461	4,148	4,850

a. Compute the rate of return on common shareholders' equity for each year.
b. Disaggregate the rate of return on common shareholders' equity into profit margin, total assets turnover, and leverage ratio components.
c. How has the profitability of Glaxo changed over the three years?

17. **Profitability analyses for three companies.** The following data show five items from the financial statements of three companies for a recent year (amounts in millions):

	Company A	Company B	Company C
For Year			
Revenues	$ 6,373	$6,562	$12,223
Income before Interest and Related Taxes[a]	932	735	934
Net Income to Common Shareholders[b]	699	705	782
Average during Year			
Total Assets	13,493	4,352	9,136
Common Shareholders' Equity	5,192	1,760	3,887

[a]Net Income + [Interest Expense × (1 − Tax Rate)]
[b]Net Income − Preferred Stock Dividends

a. Compute the rate of return on assets for each company. Disaggregate the rate of return on assets into profit margin and total assets turnover components.
b. Compute the rate of return on common shareholders' equity for each company. Disaggregate the rate of return on common shareholders' equity into profit margin, total assets turnover, and leverage ratio components.
c. The three companies are May Department Stores, Kellogg's (breakfast cereals), and Consolidated Edison (electric utility). Which of the companies corresponds to A, B, and C? What clues did you use in reaching your conclusions?

18. **Relating profitability to financial leverage.**
a. Compute the rate of return on common shareholders' equity in each of the following independent cases.

Case	Average Total Assets	Average Interest-Bearing Debt	Average Common Share-holders' Equity	Rate of Return on Assets	Aftertax Cost of Interest-Bearing Debt
A	$200	$100	$100	6%	6%
B	200	100	100	8	6
C	200	120	80	8	6
D	200	100	100	4	6
E	200	50	100	6	6
F	200	50	100	5	6

b. In which cases is leverage working to the advantage of the common share-holders?

19. **Analyzing financial leverage.** The Borrowing Company has total assets of $100,000 during the year. The firm's borrowings total $20,000 at a 10 percent annual rate and it pays income taxes at a rate of 30 percent of pretax income. Shareholders' equity is $80,000.

   a. Calculate the amount of net income needed for the rate of return on share-holders' equity to equal the rate of return on assets.

   b. Compute the rate of return on common shareholders' equity for the net income determined in part **a**.

   c. Calculate the amount of income before interest and income taxes needed to achieve this net income.

   d. Repeat parts **a**, **b**, and **c**, assuming borrowing of $80,000 and common shareholders' equity of $20,000.

   e. Compare the results from the two different debt-equity relations, making generalizations where possible.

20. **Interpreting changes in earnings per share.** Company A and Company B both start Year 1 with $1 million of shareholders' equity and 100,000 shares of common stock outstanding. During Year 1, both companies earn net income of $100,000, a rate of return of 10 percent on common shareholders' equity at the beginning of Year 1. Company A declares and pays $100,000 of dividends to common shareholders at the end of Year 1, whereas Company B retains all its earnings and declares no dividends. During Year 2, both companies earn net income equal to 10 percent of shareholders' equity at the beginning of Year 2.

   a. Compute earnings per share for Company A and for Company B for Year 1 and for Year 2.

   b. Compute the rate of growth in earnings per share for Company A and Company B, comparing earnings per share in Year 2 with earnings per share in Year 1.

   c. Using the rate of growth in earnings per share as the criterion, which company's management appears to be doing a better job for its shareholders? Comment on this result.

21. **Calculating and interpreting short-term liquidity ratios.** Data taken from the financial statements of Sun Microsystems, a computer manufacturer, appear as follows (amounts in millions):

For the Year	Year 6	Year 7	Year 8
Revenues	$3,589	$4,309	$4,690
Cost of Goods Sold	1,963	2,518	2,753
Net Income	173	157	196
Cash Flow from Operations	508	336	355

On December 31	Year 5	Year 6	Year 7	Year 8
Cash and Marketable Securities	$ 834	$1,220	$1,139	$ 883
Accounts Receivable	515	504	627	853
Inventories	224	179	256	295
Prepayments	228	245	250	274
Total Current Assets	$1,801	$2,148	$2,272	$2,305
Accounts Payable	$ 212	$ 236	$ 271	$ 364
Bank Loans	80	133	129	117
Other Current Liabilities	421	470	547	667
Total Current Liabilities	$ 713	$ 839	$ 947	$1,148

a. Compute the current and quick ratios on December 31 of each year.
b. Compute the cash flow from operations to current liabilities ratio and the accounts receivable, inventory, and accounts payable turnover ratios for Year 6, Year 7, and Year 8.
c. How has the short-term liquidity risk of Sun Microsystems changed during the three-year period?

22. **Calculating and interpreting short-term liquidity ratios.** Data taken from the financial statements of International Paper Company, a forest products firm, appear as follows (amount in millions):

For the Year	Year 3	Year 4	Year 5
Revenues	$13,598	$13,685	$14,966
Cost of Goods Sold	10,987	11,089	12,028
Net Income	401	289	432
Cash Flow from Operations	1,078	929	1,275

On December 31	Year 2	Year 3	Year 4	Year 5
Cash and Marketable Securities	$ 238	$ 225	$ 242	$ 270
Accounts Receivable	1,841	1,861	1,856	2,241
Inventories	1,780	1,938	2,024	2,075
Prepayments	272	342	279	244
Total Current Assets	$4,131	$4,366	$4,401	$4,830
Accounts Payable	$1,110	$1,259	$1,089	$1,204
Bank Loans	1,699	2,356	2,089	2,083
Other Current Liabilities	918	916	831	747
Total Current Liabilities	$3,727	$4,531	$4,009	$4,034

a. Compute the current and quick ratios on December 31 of each year.
b. Compute the cash flow from operations to current liabilities ratio and the accounts receivable, inventory, and accounts payable turnover ratios for Year 3, Year 4, and Year 5.
c. How has the short-term liquidity risk of International Paper Company changed during the three-year period?

23. **Calculating and interpreting long-term liquidity ratios.** Data taken from the financial statement of Hasbro, a toy manufacturer, follow (amounts in millions). Hasbro acquired Tonka, also a toy company, in Year 2.

For the Year	Year 2	Year 3	Year 4
Net Income before Interest and Income Taxes ...	$248	$328	$370
Cash Flow from Operations	120	230	217
Interest Expense	43	36	30

On December 31	Year 1	Year 2	Year 3	Year 4
Long-term Debt	$ 57	$380	$ 206	$ 200
Total Liabilities	418	995	977	1,016
Total Shareholders' Equity	867	955	1,106	1,277

a. Compute the long-term debt ratio and the debt-equity ratio at the end of Year 2, Year 3, and Year 4.
b. Compute the cash flow from operations to total liabilities ratio and the interest coverage ratio for Year 2 through Year 4.
c. How has the long-term liquidity risk of Hasbro changed over this three-year period?

24. **Calculating and interpreting long-term liquidity ratios.** Data taken from the financial statements of Delta Airlines appear below (amounts in millions):

For the Year	Year 5	Year 6	Year 7
Net Income before Interest Expense and Income Taxes	$(635)	$(474)	$ (389)
Cash Flow from Operations	150	677	1,324
Interest Expense	151	177	271

On December 31	Year 4	Year 5	Year 6	Year 7
Long-term Debt	$2,059	$2,833	$3,716	$ 3,228
Total Liabilities	5,905	8,197	9,875	10,327
Total Shareholders' Equity	2,506	1,965	1,996	1,569

a. Compute the long-term debt ratio and the debt-equity ratio at the end of each year.
b. Compute the cash flow from operations to total liabilities ratio and the interest coverage ratio for Year 5 through Year 7.
c. How has the long-term liquidity risk of Delta Airlines changed over this period?

25. **Effect of various transactions on financial statement ratios.** Indicate the immediate effects (increase, decrease, no effect) of each of the following independent transactions on (1) the rate of return on common shareholders' equity, (2) the current ratio, and (3) the debt-equity ratio. State any necessary assumptions.

    a. A firm purchases merchandise inventory costing $205,000 on account.

    b. A firm sells for $150,000 on account merchandise inventory costing $120,000.

    c. A firm collects $100,000 from customers on accounts receivable.

    d. A firm pays $160,000 to suppliers on accounts payable.

    e. A firm sells for $10,000 a machine costing $40,000 and with accumulated depreciation of $30,000.

    f. A firm declares dividends of $80,000. It will pay the dividends during the next accounting period.

    g. A firm issues common stock for $75,000.

    h. A firm acquires a machine costing $60,000. It gives $10,000 cash and signs a note for $50,000 payable five years from now for the balance of the purchase price.

PROBLEMS

26. **Effect of various transactions on financial statement ratios.** Indicate the effects (increase, decrease, no effect) of the following independent transactions on (1) earnings per share, (2) working capital, and (3) the quick ratio, where accounts receivable are *included* but merchandise inventory is *excluded* from quick assets. State any necessary assumptions.

    a. A firm sells on account for $300,000 merchandise inventory costing $240,000.

    b. A firm declares dividends of $160,000. It will pay the dividends during the next accounting period.

    c. A firm purchases merchandise inventory costing $410,000 on account.

    d. A firm sells for $20,000 a machine costing $80,000 and with accumulated depreciation of $60,000.

    e. Because of defects, a firm returns to the supplier merchandise inventory purchased for $7,000 cash. The firm receives a cash reimbursement.

    f. A firm issues 10,000 shares of $10-par value common stock on the last day of the accounting period for $15 per share. It uses the proceeds to acquire the assets of another firm composed of the following: accounts receivable, $30,000; merchandise inventory, $60,000; plant and equipment, $100,000. The acquiring firm also agrees to assume current liabilities of $40,000 of the acquired company.

27. **Calculating and interpreting profitability and risk ratios.** Wal-Mart Stores, Inc., is the largest retailing company in the United States. It maintains a chain of discount stores in the southern and eastern sections of the United States. In recent years, it has expanded operations into warehouse clubs and food stores. Exhibit 17.21 presents comparative balance sheets, Exhibit 17.22 presents comparative income statements, and Exhibit 17.23 presents comparative statements of cash flows for Wal-Mart Stores for three recent years. Exhibit 17.24 presents a financial statement ratio analysis for Wal-Mart Stores for Year 3 and Year 4. The income tax rate is 35 percent.

    a. Compute the amounts of the ratios listed in Exhibit 17.24 for Year 5.

EXHIBIT 17.21

WAL-MART STORES, INC.
Comparative Balance Sheets
(amounts in millions)

	January 31			
	Year 2	Year 3	Year 4	Year 5
Assets				
Cash	$ 31	$ 12	$ 20	$ 45
Accounts Receivable	419	525	690	700
Inventories	7,384	9,268	11,014	14,064
Prepayments	741	393	391	529
Total Current Assets	$ 8,575	$10,198	$12,115	$15,338
Property, Plant, and Equipment (net) ...	6,434	9,792	13,175	15,874
Other Assets	434	575	1,151	1,607
Total Assets	$15,443	$20,565	$26,441	$32,819
Liabilities and Shareholders' Equity				
Accounts Payable	$ 3,454	$ 3,873	$ 4,104	$ 5,907
Notes Payable	494	1,648	1,646	1,882
Other Current Liabilities	1,056	1,233	1,656	2,184
Total Current Liabilities	$ 5,004	$ 6,754	$ 7,406	$ 9,973
Long-term Debt	3,278	4,845	7,960	9,709
Other Noncurrent Liabilities	172	207	322	411
Total Liabilities	$ 8,454	$11,806	$15,688	$20,093
Common Stock	$ 115	$ 230	$ 230	$ 230
Additional Paid-in Capital	625	527	536	539
Retained Earnings	6,249	8,002	9,987	11,957
Total Shareholders' Equity	$ 6,989	$ 8,759	$10,753	$12,726
Total Liabilities and Shareholders' Equity	$15,443	$20,565	$26,441	$32,819

EXHIBIT 17.22

WAL-MART STORES, INC.
Comparative Income Statements
(amounts in millions)

	Year 3	Year 4	Year 5
Sales Revenue	$55,985	$67,985	$83,412
Expenses:			
Cost of Goods Sold	$44,175	$53,444	$65,586
Marketing and Administrative	8,320	10,333	12,858
Interest	323	517	706
Income Taxes	1,172	1,358	1,581
Total Expenses	$53,990	$65,652	$80,731
Net Income	$ 1,995	$ 2,333	$ 2,681

EXHIBIT 17.23

WAL-MART STORES, INC.
Comparative Statements of Cash Flows
(amounts in millions)

	Year 3	Year 4	Year 5
Operations			
Net Income	$ 1,995	$ 2,333	$ 2,681
Depreciation	649	849	1,070
Other	13	(75)	21
(Increase) in Accounts Receivable	(106)	(165)	(84)
(Increase) in Inventories	(1,884)	(1,324)	(3,053)
(Increase) Decrease in Prepayments	(20)	(1)	(139)
Increase in Accounts Payable	420	230	1,914
Increase in Other Current Liabilities	211	349	496
Cash Flow from Operations	$ 1,278	$ 2,196	$ 2,906
Investing			
Acquisition of Property, Plant, and Equipment	$(3,366)	$(3,644)	$(3,734)
Other	(140)	(842)	(58)
Cash Flow from Investing	$(3,506)	$(4,486)	$(3,792)
Financing			
Increase (Decrease) in Short-term Borrowing	$ 1,135	$ (14)	$ 220
Increase in Long-term Borrowing	1,367	3,108	1,250
Increase in Common Stock	16	10	—
Decrease in Long-term Borrowing	(68)	(456)	(107)
Acquisition of Common Stock	—	—	—
Dividends	(241)	(299)	(391)
Other	—	(51)	(61)
Cash Flow from Financing	$ 2,209	$ 2,298	$ 911
Change in Cash	$ (19)	$ 8	$ 25
Cash, Beginning of Year	31	12	20
Cash, End of Year	$ 12	$ 20	$ 45

b. What are the likely reasons for the changes in Wal-Mart's rate of return on assets during the three-year period? Analyze the financial ratios to the maximum depth possible.

c. What are the likely reasons for the changes in Wal-Mart's rate of return on common shareholders' equity during the three-year period?

d. How has the short-term liquidity risk of Wal-Mart changed during the three-year period?

e. How has the long-term liquidity risk of Wal-Mart changed during the three-year period?

28. **Calculating and interpreting profitability and risk ratios.** Nike and Reebok maintain dominant market shares in the athletic footwear market. Nike places somewhat greater emphasis on the performance characteristics of footwear while Reebok places somewhat greater emphasis on the fashion characteristics of its footwear. Exhibit 17.25 presents comparative balance sheets for Nike and

EXHIBIT 17.24

WAL-MART STORES, INC.
Financial Ratio Analysis

	Year 3	Year 4	Year 5
Rate of Return on Assets	12.3%	11.4%	
Profit Margin for Rate of Return on Assets	3.9%	3.9%	
Total Assets Turnover	3.1	2.9	
Cost of Goods Sold/Sales	78.9%	78.6%	
Marketing and Administrative Expenses/Sales	14.9%	15.2%	
Interest Expense/Sales	.6%	.8%	
Income Tax Expense/Sales	2.1%	2.0%	
Accounts Receivable Turnover Ratio	118.6	111.9	
Inventory Turnover Ratio	5.3	5.3	
Plant Assets Turnover Ratio	6.9	5.9	
Rate of Return on Common Shareholders' Equity	25.3%	23.9%	
Profit Margin for Rate of Return on Common Shareholders' Equity	3.6%	3.4%	
Leverage Ratio	2.3	2.4	
Current Ratio	1.5	1.6	
Quick Ratio	.1	.1	
Cash Flow from Operations to Current Liabilities Ratio	21.7%	31.0%	
Accounts Payable Turnover Ratio	12.1	13.8	
Long-term Debt Ratio	35.6%	42.5%	
Debt-Equity Ratio	57.4%	59.3%	
Cash Flow from Operations to Total Liabilities Ratio	12.6%	16.0%	
Interest Coverage Ratio	10.8	8.1	

Reebok at the end of Year 10 and Year 11. Exhibit 17.26 presents an income statement for each firm for Year 11. Cash flows from operations for Year 11 were $255 million for Nike and $173 million for Reebok. The income tax rate is 35 percent. On the basis of this information and appropriate financial statement ratios, which company is

a. more profitable?

b. less risky in terms of short-term liquidity?

c. less risky in terms of long-term solvency?

CASES

29. **Case introducing earnings-per-share calculations for a complex capital structure.** The Layton Ball Corporation has a relatively complicated capital structure. In addition to common shares, it has issued stock options, warrants, and convertible bonds. Exhibit 17.27 summarizes some pertinent information about these items. Net income for the year is $9,500, and the income tax rate used in computing income tax expense is 40 percent of pretax income.

a. First, ignore all items of capital except for the common shares. Calculate earnings per common share.

EXHIBIT 17.25

NIKE AND REEBOK
Comparative Balance Sheets
(amounts in millions)

	Nike		Reebok	
	Year 10	Year 11	Year 10	Year 11
Assets				
Cash	$ 519	$ 216	$ 79	$ 84
Accounts Receivable	703	1,053	457	532
Inventories	470	630	514	625
Prepayments	78	147	77	96
Total Current Assets	$1,770	$2,046	$1,127	$1,337
Property, Plant, and Equipment (net)	406	555	131	165
Other Assets	198	542	134	147
Total Assets	$2,374	$3,143	$1,392	$1,649
Liabilities and Shareholders' Equity				
Accounts Payable	$ 211	$ 298	$ 282	$ 171
Bank Loans	131	429	27	69
Other Current Liabilities	220	381	87	266
Total Current Liabilities	$ 562	$1,108	$ 396	$ 506
Long-term Debt	12	10	134	132
Other Noncurrent Liabilities	59	60	15	21
Total Liabilities	$ 633	$1,178	$ 545	$ 659
Common Stock	$ 3	$ 4	$ 1	$ 1
Additional Paid-in Capital	108	122	267	168
Retained Earnings	1,630	1,839	1,182	1,424
Treasury Stock	—	—	(603)	(603)
Total Shareholders' Equity	$1,741	$1,965	$ 847	$ 990
Total Liabilities and Shareholders' Equity	$2,374	$3,143	$1,392	$1,649

EXHIBIT 17.26

NIKE AND REEBOK
Comparative Income Statements
(amounts in millions)

	For Year 11	
	Nike	Reebok
Sales Revenue	$4,761	$3,280
Expenses:		
Cost of Goods Sold	$2,865	$1,966
Selling and Administrative	1,222	889
Interest	24	17
Income Taxes	250	154
Total Expenses	$4,361	$3,026
Net Income	$ 400	$ 254

b. In past years, employees have been issued options to purchase shares of stock. Exhibit 17.27 indicates that the price of the common stock throughout the year was $25 but that the stock options could be exercised at any time for $15 each. The option allows the holder to surrender it along with $15 cash and receive one share in return. Thus the number of shares would increase, which would decrease the earnings-per-share figure. The company would, however, have more cash. Assume that the holders of options tender them, along with $15 each, to purchase shares. Assume that the company uses the cash to purchase shares for its own treasury at a price of $25 each. Compute a new earnings-per-share figure. (The firm does *not* count shares in its own treasury in the denominator of the earnings-per-share calculation.)

c. Exhibit 17.27 indicates that there were also warrants outstanding in the hands of the public. The warrant allows the holder to turn in that warrant, along with $30 cash, to purchase one share of stock. If holders exercised the warrants, the number of outstanding shares would increase, which would reduce earnings per share. However, the company would have more cash, which it could use to purchase shares for the treasury, reducing the number of shares outstanding. Assume that all holders of warrants exercise them. Assume that the company uses the cash to purchase outstanding shares for the treasury. Compute a new earnings-per-share figure. (Ignore the information about options and the calculations in part **b** at this point.) Note that a rational warrant holder would *not* exercise his or her warrants for $30 when a share could be purchased for $25.

d. There were also convertible bonds outstanding. The convertible bond entitles the holder to trade in that bond for 10 shares. If holders convert the bonds, the number of shares would increase, which would tend to reduce

---

EXHIBIT 17.27

LAYTON BALL CORPORATION
Information on Capital Structure for Earnings-per-Share Calculations

Assume the following data about the capital structure and earnings
 for the Layton Ball Corporation for the year:

Number of Common Shares Outstanding throughout the Year	2,500 shares
Market Price per Common Share throughout the Year	$25
Options Outstanding during the Year:	
Number of Shares Issuable on Exercise of Options	1,000 shares
Exercise Price per Share	$15
Warrants Outstanding during the Year:	
Number of Shares Issuable on Exercise of Warrants	2,000 shares
Exercise Price per Share	$30
Convertible Bonds Outstanding:	
Number (issued 15 years ago)	100 bonds
Proceeds per Bond at Time of Issue (= par value)	$1,000
Shares of Common Issuable on Conversion (per bond)	10 shares
Coupon Rate (per year)	$4\frac{1}{8}$ percent

earnings per share. On the other hand, the company would not have to pay interest and thus would have no interest expense on the bond, because it would no longer be outstanding. This would tend to increase income and earnings per share. Assume that all holders of convertible bonds convert their bonds into shares. Compute a new net income figure (do not forget income tax effects on income of the interest saved) and a new earnings-per-share figure. (Ignore the information about options and warrants and the calculations in parts **b** and **c** at this point.)

e. Now consider all the previous calculations. Which sets of assumptions from parts **b, c,** and **d** lead to the lowest possible earnings per share when they are all made simultaneously? Compute a new earnings per share under the most restrictive set of assumptions about reductions in earnings per share.

EXHIBIT 17.28

Data for Ratio Detective Exercise

	Company Numbers						
	(1)	**(2)**	**(3)**	**(4)**	**(5)**	**(6)**	**(7)**
Balance Sheet at End of Year							
Current Receivables	1.20%	29.11%	15.80%	13.70%	22.65%	14.11%	8.38%
Inventories	9.18	0.00	6.87	23.19	16.40	14.02	8.54
Net Plant and Equipment[a]	5.12	9.63	10.77	16.01	29.68	17.62	24.97
All Other Assets	3.64	7.02	37.91	25.63	13.49	38.18	46.45
Total Assets	19.14%	45.76%	71.35%	78.53%	82.22%	83.93%	88.34%
[a]Cost of Plant and Equipment (gross)	17.71%	14.80%	21.50%	29.47%	42.79%	27.07%	38.41%
Current Liabilities	7.87%	9.82%	21.87%	14.09%	14.34%	22.39%	35.58%
Long-term Liabilities	2.06	7.96	12.30	16.07	41.56	39.38	14.51
Owners' Equity	9.21	27.98	37.18	48.37	26.32	22.16	38.25
Total Equities	19.14%	45.76%	71.35%	78.53%	82.22%	83.93%	88.34%
Income Statement for Year							
Revenues	100.00%	100.00%	100.00%	100.00%	100.00%	100.00%	100.00%
Cost of Goods Sold (excluding depreciation) or Operating Expenses[b]	77.17	53.77	53.93	33.99	69.14	45.37	40.17
Depreciation	1.23	1.39	7.55	1.95	3.01	2.65	2.26
Interest Expense	2.44	0.52	2.88	.91	2.98	2.92	1.66
Advertising Expense	.89	0.00	0.00	1.38	2.53	4.29	8.54
Research and Development Expense	0.00	1.00	10.95	0.00	0.00	0.70	0.00
Income Taxes	1.08	0.53	2.88	5.09	2.65	5.39	6.61
All Other Items (net)	15.29	18.87	15.98	47.05	14.84	31.72	26.78
Total Expenses	98.10%	76.08%	94.17%	90.37%	95.15%	93.04%	86.02%
Net Income	1.90%	23.92%	5.83%	9.63%	4.85%	6.96%	13.98%

f. Accountants publish several earnings-per-share figures for companies with complicated capital structures and complicated events during the year. *The Wall Street Journal,* however, publishes only one figure in its daily columns (where it reports the price-earnings ratio—the price of a share of stock divided by its earnings per share). Which of the figures computed previously for earnings per share do you think *The Wall Street Journal* should report as *the* earnings-per-share figure? Why?

30. **Detective analysis—identify company.** In this problem, you become a financial analyst/detective. Exhibit 17.28 expresses condensed financial statements for 13 companies on a percentage basis. In all cases, total sales revenues appear as 100.00%. All other numbers were divided by sales revenue for the year. The

EXHIBIT 17.28 (CONTINUED)

	Company Numbers					
	(8)	(9)	(10)	(11)	(12)	(13)
Balance Sheet at End of Year						
Current Receivables	9.22%	14.58%	6.89%	113.30%	48.15%	295.65%
Inventories	7.81	13.92	7.72	0.00	0.00	0.00
Net Plant and Equipment[a]	55.55	66.06	152.60	13.07	8.97	10.95
All Other Assets	18.71	50.38	18.99	62.50	241.21	647.73
Total Assets	91.29%	144.94%	186.20%	188.87%	298.33%	954.33%
[a]Cost of Plant and Equipment (gross)	146.54%	92.26%	207.74%	17.81%	15.12%	12.21%
Current Liabilities	15.96%	39.68%	16.73%	129.32%	228.94%	515.13%
Long-term Liabilities	37.18	18.53	79.94	22.30	11.19	320.34
Owners' Equity	38.15	86.73	89.53	37.25	58.20	118.86
Total Equities	91.29%	144.94%	186.20%	188.87%	298.33%	954.33%
Income Statement for Year						
Revenues	100.00%	100.00%	100.00%	100.00%	100.00%	100.00%
Cost of Goods Sold (excluding depreciation) or Operating Expenses[b]	83.78%	28.89%	75.03%	87.69%	87.78%	26.86%
Depreciation	6.20	5.23	5.97	2.02	0.08	0.00
Interest Expense	1.23	.70	4.45	1.38	0.00	55.48
Advertising Expense	0.00	.37	0.00	0.00	0.00	0.00
Research and Development Expense	.55	13.39	0.00	0.00	0.00	0.00
Income Taxes	.23	9.86	5.04	5.23	2.83	7.82
All Other Items (net)	3.33	18.60	(.45)	(2.17)	0.00	(2.01)
Total Expenses	95.32%	77.04%	90.04%	94.15%	90.69%	88.15%
Net Income	4.68%	22.96%	9.96%	5.85%	9.31%	11.85%

[b]Represents operating expenses for the following companies: Advertising agency, insurance company, finance company, and the public accounting partnership.

13 companies (all corporations except for the accounting firm) shown here represent the following industries:

(1) Advertising agency.
(2) Computer manufacturer.
(3) Department store chain (that carries its own receivables).
(4) Distiller of hard liquor.
(5) Electric utility.
(6) Finance company (lends money to consumers).
(7) Grocery store chain.
(8) Insurance company.
(9) Pharmaceutical company.
(10) Public accounting (CPA) partnership.
(11) Soft drink company.
(12) Steel manufacturer.
(13) Tobacco products company.

Use whatever clues you can to match the companies in Exhibit 17.28 with the industries listed above. You may find it useful to refer to average industry ratios compiled by Dun & Bradstreet, Prentice-Hall, Robert Morris Associates, and the Federal Trade Commission. Most libraries carry copies of these documents.

31. **Interpreting profitability and risk ratios.** Texas Instruments (TI) manufactures and sells semiconductors and other electronics products. Its manufacturing facilities are capital intensive (property, plant, and equipment compose approximately 43 percent of total assets). Recent rapid increases in demand for semiconductors forced TI to outsource the manufacture of some of its products. Exhibit 17.29 presents financial statement ratios for TI for three recent years.

    a. What are the likely reasons for the increasing profit margin for rate of return on assets?
    b. What are the likely reasons for the increasing inventory and plant asset turnovers?
    c. What are the likely reasons for the decreases in the leverage ratio?
    d. What are the likely reasons for the increasing cash flow from operations to average current and average total liabilities ratios?
    e. What are the likely reasons for the increasing current ratio?

32. **Interpreting profitability and risk ratios.** The Limited operates specialty retail stores in shopping malls throughout the United States. Exhibit 17.30 (p. 634) presents financial ratios for The Limited for Year 3, Year 4, and Year 5. Selected additional data appear below:

Data for Case 32

	Sales Mix			Operating Income Mix		
	Year 3	Year 4	Year 5	Year 3	Year 4	Year 5
Women's Apparel	72%	66%	59%	72%	49%	41%
Lingerie	19	22	25	25	38	40
Men's Apparel	6	8	10	5	9	10
Personal Care	3	4	6	(2)	4	9
	100%	100%	100%	100%	100%	100%

EXHIBIT 17.29

TEXAS INSTRUMENTS
Financial Statement Ratios

	Year 2	Year 3	Year 4
Profit Margin for Rate of Return on Assets	3.8%	5.9%	7.0%
Assets Turnover	1.5	1.5	1.6
Rate of Return on Assets	5.5%	9.1%	11.1%
Cost of Goods Sold ÷ Sales	76.9%	73.6%	72.4%
Selling and Administrative Expenses ÷ Sales	17.5%	17.8%	17.1%
Income Tax Expense (excluding tax effects of interest expense) ÷ Sales	1.9%	2.8%	3.6%
Accounts Receivable Turnover	7.9	7.8	7.8
Inventory Turnover	7.4	8.1	8.8
Plant Asset Turnover	3.3	3.9	4.3
Profit Margin for Rate of Return on Common Shareholders' Equity	3.3%	5.6%	6.7%
Leverage Ratio	3.1	2.8	2.4
Current Ratio	1.6	1.7	1.8
Quick Ratio	1.1	1.1	1.2
Cash Flow from Operations ÷ Average Current Liabilities	49.6%	51.0%	73.0%
Days Accounts Payable	29	29	30
Long-term Debt Ratio	31.8%	23.1%	21.0%
Debt-Equity Ratio	62.4%	61.4%	56.5%
Cash Flow from Operations ÷ Average Total Liabilities	25.5%	27.0%	40.2%
Interest Coverage Ratio	8.2	15.8	24.2
Sales (Year 1 = 100)	110	126	152
Assets (Year 1 = 100)	104	120	140

Data for Case 32 (continued)

Operating Income ÷ Sales			
	Year 3	Year 4	Year 5
Women's Apparel	10.7%	6.6%	6.9%
Lingerie	13.5%	15.5%	16.1%
Men's Apparel	7.2%	9.3%	10.4%
Personal Care	(6.5)%	8.7%	15.0%

	Year 3	Year 4	Year 5
Sales per Square Foot . . .	$ 304	$ 297	$ 286
Sales per Employee	$68,960	$74,309	$69,326

a. What are the likely reasons for the increase in the cost of goods sold to sales percentage from 71.3 percent in Year 3 to 73.0 percent in Year 4?

EXHIBIT 17.30

THE LIMITED
Financial Ratios

	Year 3	Year 4	Year 5
Profit Margin for Rate of Return on Assets	7.1%	6.0%	6.7%
Assets Turnover	1.9	1.8	1.7
Rate of Return on Assets	13.6%	10.8%	11.3%
Cost of Goods Sold ÷ Sales....................	71.3%	73.0%	71.1%
Selling and Administrative Expenses ÷ Sales	17.3%	17.3%	18.0%
Income Tax Expense (excluding tax savings from interest expense) ÷ Sales	4.5%	3.8%	4.4%
Interest Expense (net of tax savings) ÷ Sales	.6%	.6%	.6%
Accounts Receivable Turnover	8.8	7.7	6.2
Inventory Turnover	6.5	6.9	6.5
Plant Asset Turnover	4.0	4.2	4.4
Profit Margin for Rate of Return on Common Shareholders' Equity	6.6%	5.4%	6.1%
Leverage Ratio	1.8	1.7	1.7
Rate of Return on Common Shareholders' Equity	22.0%	16.6%	17.2%
Current Ratio	2.48	3.14	3.20
Quick Ratio	1.22	1.95	1.93
Days Accounts Payable	18	20	18
Cash Flow from Operations ÷ Average Current Liabilities	121.6%	62.8%	48.0%
Long-term Debt Ratio	19.3%	21.0%	19.0%
Debt-Equity Ratio	41.0%	40.9%	39.6%
Cash Flow from Operations ÷ Average Total Liabilities	48.3%	27.4%	20.6%
Interest Coverage Ratio	13.0	11.1	12.3
Sales (1992 = 100)	112.9	117.8	119.0
Net Income (1992 = 100)	112.9	97.0	111.2
Assets (1992 = 100)	112.5	120.9	133.7
Capital Expenditures (1992 = 100)	82.2	57.6	61.3

b. What are the likely reasons for the increase in the selling and administrative expenses to sales percentage from 17.3 percent in Year 4 to 18.0 percent in Year 5?

c. What are the likely reasons for the increases in the plant asset turnover during the three years?

d. Did financial leverage work to the benefit of the common shareholders in each year? Explain.

e. What is the likely reasons for the *increase* in the current ratio from 3.14 in Year 4 to 3.20 in Year 5, but a *decrease* in the quick ratio from 1.95 in Year 4 to 1.93 in Year 5?

f. What are the likely reasons for the decreases in the cash flow operations to liabilities ratios between Year 4 and Year 5?

EXHIBIT 17.31

W. T. GRANT COMPANY
Comparative Balance Sheets

	January 31				
	1971	**1972**	**1973**	**1974**	**1975**
Assets					
Cash and Marketable Securities	$ 34,009	$ 49,851	$ 30,943	$ 45,951	$ 79,642
Accounts Receivable	419,731	477,324	542,751	598,799	431,201
Inventories	260,492	298,676	399,533	450,637	407,357
Other Current Assets	5,246	5,378	6,649	7,299	6,581
Total Current Assets	$719,478	$831,229	$ 979,876	$1,102,686	$ 924,781
Investments	23,936	32,367	35,581	45,451	49,764
Property, Plant, and Equipment (net)	61,832	77,173	91,420	100,984	101,932
Other Assets	2,382	3,901	3,821	3,862	5,790
Total Assets	$807,628	$944,670	$1,110,698	$1,252,983	$1,082,267
Equities					
Short-term Debt	$246,420	$237,741	$ 390,034	$ 453,097	$ 600,695
Accounts Payable	118,091	124,990	112,896	103,910	147,211
Current Deferred Taxes	94,489	112,846	130,137	133,057	2,000
Total Current Liabilities	$459,000	$475,577	$ 633,067	$ 690,064	$ 749,906
Long-term Debt	32,301	128,432	126,672	220,336	216,341
Noncurrent Deferred Taxes	8,518	9,664	11,926	14,649	—
Other Long-term Liabilities	5,773	5,252	4,694	4,195	2,183
Total Liabilities	$505,592	$618,925	$ 776,359	$ 929,244	$ 968,430
Preferred Stock	$ 9,600	$ 9,053	$ 8,600	$ 7,465	$ 7,465
Common Stock	18,180	18,529	18,588	18,599	18,599
Additional Paid-in Capital	78,116	85,195	86,146	85,910	83,914
Retained Earnings	230,435	244,508	261,154	248,461	37,674
Total	$336,331	$357,285	$ 374,488	$ 360,435	$ 147,652
Less Cost of Treasury Stock	(34,295)	(31,540)	(40,149)	(36,696)	(33,815)
Total Shareholders' Equity	$302,036	$325,745	$ 334,339	$ 323,739	$ 113,837
Total Equities	$807,628	$944,670	$1,110,698	$1,252,983	$1,082,267

33. **Case analysis of bankruptcy.** On October 2, 1975, W. T. Grant Company filed for bankruptcy protection under Chapter XI of the Bankruptcy Act. At that time, assets totaled $1.02 billion, and liabilities totaled $1.03 billion. The company operated at a profit for most years before 1974, but reported an operating loss of $177 million for its fiscal year January 31, 1974, to January 31, 1975.

The accompanying Exhibits 17.31 through 17.34 on pages 635–638 contain the following kinds of information:

1. Balance sheets, income statements, and statements of cash flows for W. T. Grant Company for the 1971 through 1975 fiscal periods.

EXHIBIT 17.32

W. T. GRANT COMPANY
Statement of Income and Retained Earnings

	Years Ended January 31				
	1971	**1972**	**1973**	**1974**	**1975**
Sales	$1,254,131	$1,374,811	$1,644,747	$1,849,802	$1,761,952
Concessions	4,986	3,439	3,753	3,971	4,238
Equity in Earnings	2,777	2,383	5,116	4,651	3,086
Other Income	2,874	3,102	1,188	3,063	3,376
Total Revenues	$1,264,768	$1,383,735	$1,654,804	$1,861,487	$1,772,652
Cost of Goods Sold	$ 843,192	$ 931,237	$1,125,261	$1,282,945	$1,303,267
Selling, General, and Administration	329,768	373,816	444,377	518,280	540,953
Interest	18,874	16,452	21,127	51,047	199,238
Taxes: Current	21,140	13,487	9,588	(6,021)	(19,439)
Deferred	11,660	13,013	16,162	6,807	(98,027)
Other Expenses	557	518	502	—	24,000
Total Expenses	$1,225,191	$1,348,523	$1,617,017	$1,853,058	$1,949,992
Net Income	$ 39,577	$ 35,212	$ 37,787	$ 8,429	$ (177,340)
Dividends	(20,821)	(21,139)	(21,141)	(21,122)	(4,457)
Other	—	—	—	—	(28,990)
Change in Retained Earnings	$ 18,756	$ 14,073	$ 16,646	$ (12,693)	$ (210,787)
Retained Earnings— Beg. of Period	211,679	230,435	244,508	261,154	248,461
Retained Earnings— End of Period	$ 230,435	$ 244,508	$ 261,154	$ 248,461	$ 37,674

2. Additional financial information about W. T. Grant Company, the retail industry, and the economy for the same period.

Prepare an analysis that explains the major causes of Grant's collapse. Assume an income tax rate of 48 percent.

34. **Preparing pro forma financial statements (requires Appendix 17.1).** Problem 27 presents financial statements for Wal-Mart Stores, Inc., for Year 3, Year 4, and Year 5, as well as financial statement ratios.

a. Prepare a set of pro forma financial statements for Wal-Mart Stores, Inc., for Year 6 through Year 9 using the following assumptions:

Income Statement

1. Sales will grow 22 percent.
2. Cost of goods sold will equal 78.6 percent of sales.
3. Selling and administrative expenses will equal 15.5 percent of sales.
4. Interest expense will equal 7 percent of average interest-bearing debt.
5. Income tax expense will equal 37 percent of income before income taxes.

EXHIBIT 17.33

W. T. GRANT COMPANY
Statement of Cash Flows

	Years Ended January 31				
	1971	**1972**	**1973**	**1974**	**1975**
Operations					
Net Income	$39,577	$ 35,212	$ 37,787	$ 8,429	($177,340)
Additions:					
Depreciation and Other	9,619	10,577	12,004	13,579	14,587
Decrease in Accounts Receivable	—	—	—	—	121,351
Decrease in Inventories	—	—	—	—	43,280
Increase in Accounts Payable	13,947	6,900	—	—	42,028
Increase in Deferred Taxes	14,046	18,357	17,291	2,920	—
Subtractions:					
Equity in Earnings and Other	(2,470)	(1,758)	(1,699)	(1,344)	(16,993)
Increase in Accounts Receivable	(51,464)	(57,593)	(65,427)	(56,047)	—
Increase in Inventories	(38,365)	(38,184)	(100,857)	(51,104)	—
Increase in Prepayments	(209)	(428)	(1,271)	(651)	(11,032)
Decrease in Accounts Payable	—	—	(12,093)	(8,987)	—
Decrease in Deferred Taxes	—	—	—	—	(101,078)
Cash Flow from Operations	($15,319)	($ 26,917)	($114,265)	($ 93,205)	($ 85,197)
Investing					
Noncurrent Assets:					
Property, Plant, and Equipment	($16,141)	($ 25,918)	($ 26,250)	($ 23,143)	($ 15,535)
Investments in Securities	(436)	(5,951)	(2,040)	(5,700)	(5,182)
Cash Flow from Investing	($16,577)	($ 31,869)	($ 28,290)	($ 28,843)	($ 20,717)
Financing					
New Financing:					
Short-Term Bank Borrowing	$64,288	—	$152,293	$ 63,063	$ 147,898
Issue of Long-Term Debt	—	$100,000	—	100,000	—
Sale of Common Stock:					
To Employees	5,218	7,715	3,492	2,584	886
On Open Market	—	2,229	174	260	—
Reduction in Financing:					
Repayment of Short-Term Borrowing (net)	—	(8,680)	—	—	—
Retirement of Long-Term Debt	(1,538)	(5,143)	(1,760)	(6,336)	(3,995)
Reacquisition of Preferred Stock	(948)	(308)	(252)	(618)	—
Reacquisition of Common Stock	(13,224)	—	(11,466)	(133)	—
Dividends	(20,821)	(21,138)	(21,141)	(21,122)	(4,457)
Cash Flow from Financing	$32,975	$ 74,675	$121,340	$137,698	$140,332
Other	(47)	(47)	2,307	(642)	(727)
Net Change in Cash	$ 1,032	$ 15,842	($ 18,908)	$ 15,008	$ 33,691

EXHIBIT 17.34

Additional Information

	Fiscal Years Ending January 31				
	1971	**1972**	**1973**	**1974**	**1975**
W. T. Grant Company					
Range of Stock Price, Dollar per Share[a]	$41\frac{7}{8}$–$70\frac{5}{8}$	$34\frac{3}{4}$–$48\frac{3}{4}$	$9\frac{7}{8}$–$44\frac{3}{8}$	$9\frac{5}{8}$–41	$1\frac{1}{2}$–12
Earnings per Share in Dollars	$2.64	$2.25	$2.49	$0.76	$(12.74)
Dividends per Share in Dollars	$1.50	$1.50	$1.50	$1.50	$ 0.30
Number of Stores	1,116	1,168	1,208	1,189	1,152
Total Store Area, Thousands of Square Feet	38,157	44,718	50,619	53,719	54,770

	Calendar Year Ending December 31				
	1970	**1971**	**1972**	**1973**	**1974**
Retail Industry[b]					
Total Chain Store Industry Sales in Millions of Dollars	$6,969	$6,972	$7,498	$8,212	$8,714

	Calendar Year Ending December 31				
	1970	**1971**	**1972**	**1973**	**1974**
Aggregate Economy[c]					
Gross National Product in Billions of Dollars	$1,075.3	$1,107.5	$1,171.1	$1,233.4	$1,210
Bank Short-term Lending Rate	8.48%	6.32%	5.82%	8.30%	11.28%

[a]Source: *Standard and Poor's Stock Reports.*

[b]Source: *Standard Industry Surveys.*

[c]Source: *Survey of Current Business.*

Balance Sheet

6. Cash will equal the amount necessary to equate total assets with total liabilities plus shareholders' equity.

7. Accounts receivable will increase at the growth rate in sales.

8. Inventory will turn over 5.2 times per year.

9. Prepayments will increase at the growth rate in sales.

10. Plant assets (net) will grow at 18.9 percent per year.

11. Other assets will increase at the growth rate in sales.

12. Accounts payable will turn over 13.0 times per year.

13. Notes payable will increase to $2,000 million in Year 6 and thereafter increase $100 million each year.

14. Other current liabilities will grow at the growth rate in sales.

15. Long-term debt will grow at the growth rate in property, plant, and equipment.

16. Other noncurrent liabilities will increase at the growth rate in sales.

17. Common stock and additional paid-in capital will not change.
18. Dividends will increase at a 25 percent growth rate.
Statement of Cash Flows
19. Depreciation expense will increase at the growth rate in property, plant, and equipment.
20. The change in Other Noncurrent Assets is an investing activity.
21. The change in Other Noncurrent Liabilities is an operating activity.
   b. Describe actions that Wal-Mart Stores, Inc., might take to deal with the shortage of cash projected in part **a**.

SUGGESTED SOLUTIONS TO EVEN-NUMBERED EXERCISES

12. **Profitability analysis for two types of retailers.** Company A is the specialty retailer (The Limited) because of its higher profit margin and lower total assets turnover, relative to Company B (Wal-Mart).

	Rate of Return on Assets	=	Profit Margin Ratio	×	Total Assets Turnover Ratio
Company A:	$\dfrac{\$448 + (1 - .35)(\$65)}{\$4,353}$	=	$\dfrac{\$448 + (1 - .35)(\$65)}{\$7,321}$	×	$\dfrac{\$7,321}{\$4,353}$
	11.3 percent	=	6.7 percent	×	1.68
Company B:	$\dfrac{\$2,681 + (1 - .35)(\$706)}{\$29,630}$	=	$\dfrac{\$2,681 + (1 - .35)(\$706)}{\$83,412}$	×	$\dfrac{\$83,412}{\$29,630}$
	10.6 percent	=	3.8 percent	×	2.82

14. **Analyzing inventories over four years.**

a.

Year	Numerator	Denominator	Inventory Turnover
5	$2,717	$1,409	1.93
6	2,857	1,471	1.94
7	3,029	1,408	2.15
8	3,122	1,360	2.30

b.

Year	Numerator	Denominator	Days Inventory Held
5	365	1.93	189
6	365	1.94	188
7	365	2.15	170
8	365	2.30	159

c.

Year	Numerator	Denominator	Cost of Goods Sold Percentage
5	$2,717	$10,571	25.7%
6	2,857	11,156	25.6%
7	3,029	11,413	26.5%
8	3,122	11,984	26.1%

d. The increasing inventory turnover coupled with the increased cost of goods sold percentage suggests a shift in product mix toward faster-moving, lower-margin products. A shift in sales mix toward nonprescription health products and toiletries is consistent with faster inventory turnover and lower gross margin.

16. **Calculating and disaggregating rate of return on common shareholders' equity.**

a.

Year	Numerator	Denominator	Rate of Return on Common Shareholders' Equity
4	£1,033	£3,461	29.8%
5	1,207	4,148	29.1%
6	1,303	4,850	26.9%

b. **Profit Margin**

Year	Numerator	Denominator	Profit Margin
4	£1,033	£4,096	25.2%
5	1,207	4,930	24.5%
6	1,303	5,656	23.0%

Total Asset Turnover

Year	Numerator	Denominator	Total Asset Turnover
4	£4,096	£5,713	.72
5	4,930	6,570	.75
6	5,656	7,673	.74

Leverage Ratio

Year	Numerator	Denominator	Leverage Ratio
4	£5,713	£3,461	1.65
5	6,570	4,148	1.58
6	7,673	4,850	1.58

c. The rate of return on common shareholders' equity declined during the three years. The decline between Year 4 and Year 5 results from a decrease in capital structure leverage. The decline in the profit margin between Year 4 and Year 5 is offset by an increase in the total assets turnover, so that Glaxo's operating profitability improved between these two years. The decline in the rate of return on common shareholders' equity between Year 5 and Year 6 is due to decreased operating profitability, given that the leverage ratio remained constant. Both the profit margin and total assets turnover declined. Sales increased 20.4 percent [= (£4,930/£4,096) − 1] between Year 4 and Year 5 and 14.7 percent [= (£5,656/£4,930) − 1] between Year 5 and Year 6. The decrease in the rate of sales growth might have squeezed the profit margin and resulted in some diseconomies of scale with Glaxo's manufacturing, selling, or administrative facilities.

18. Relating profitability to financial leverage.

a.

Case	Net Income Plus Aftertax Interest Expense[a]	Aftertax Interest Expense[b]	Net Income[c]	Rate of Return on Common Shareholders' Equity
A	$12	$6.0	$ 6	$ 6/$100 = 6%
B	$16	$6.0	$10	$10/$100 = 10%
C	$16	$7.2	$ 8.8	$8.8/$ 80 = 11%
D	$ 8	$6.0	$ 2	$ 2/$100 = 2%
E	$12	$3.0	$ 9	$ 9/$100 = 9%
F	$10	$3.0	$ 7	$ 7/$100 = 7%

[a]Numerator of the rate of return on assets. In Case A, $12 = .06 × $200.
[b]Aftertax cost of borrowing times interest-bearing debt. In Case A, $6.0 = .06 × $100.
[c]Net income plus aftertax interest expense minus aftertax interest expense. In Case A, $6 = $12 − $6.

b. Leverage works successfully in Cases B, C, E, and F with respect to total debt. With respect to interest-bearing debt, leverage works successfully in Cases B and C.

20. Interpreting changes in earnings per share.
a. Company A Earnings per Share:

Year 1 .... $\dfrac{\$100,000}{100,000 \text{ Shares}} = \$1$ per Share.

Year 2 .... $\dfrac{\$100,000}{100,000 \text{ Shares}} = \$1$ per Share.

Company B Earnings per Share:

Year 1 .... $\dfrac{\$100,000}{100,000 \text{ Shares}} = \$1$ per Share.

Year 2 .... $\dfrac{.10 \times (\$1,000,000 + \$100,000)}{100,000 \text{ Shares}} = \$1.10$ per Share.

b. Company A: No growth.

Company B: 10 percent annual growth.

c. Company B: This result is misleading. Comparisons of growth in earnings per share are valid only if firms employ equal amounts of assets in the business. Both the rate of return on assets and on shareholders' equity are better measures of growth performance. Earnings per share results do not, in general (as in this problem), take earnings retention into account.

22. **Calculating and interpreting short-term liquidity ratios.**

   a. **Current Ratio**

Year End	Numerator	Denominator	Current Ratio
2	$4,131	$3,727	1.11
3	4,366	4,531	.96
4	4,401	4,009	1.10
5	4,830	4,034	1.20

   Quick Ratio

Year End	Numerator	Denominator	Quick Ratio
2	$2,079	$3,727	.56
3	2,086	4,531	.46
4	2,098	4,009	.52
5	2,511	4,034	.62

   b. **Cash Flow from Operations to Current Liabilities Ratio**

Year	Numerator	Denominator	Cash Flow from Operations to Current Liabilities Ratio
3	$1,078	$4,129.0[a]	26.1%
4	929	4,270.0[b]	21.8%
5	1,275	4,021.5[c]	31.7%

[a].5($3,727 + $4,531) = $4,129.0.
[b].5($4,531 + $4,009) = $4,270.0.
[c].5($4,009 + $4,034) = $4,021.5.

Accounts Receivable Turnover Ratio

Year	Numerator	Denominator	Accounts Receivable Turnover Ratio
3	$13,598	$1,851.0[a]	7.35
4	13,685	1,858.5[b]	7.36
5	14,966	2,048.5[c]	7.31

[a].5($1,841 + $1,861) = $1,851.0.
[b].5($1,861 + $1,856) = $1,858.5.
[c].5($1,856 + $2,241) = $2,048.5.

Inventory Turnover Ratio

Year	Numerator	Denominator	Inventory Turnover Ratio
3	$10,987	$1,859.0[a]	5.91%
4	11,089	1,981.0[b]	5.60%
5	12,028	2,049.5[c]	5.87%

[a].5($1,780 + $1,938) = $1,859.0.
[b].5($1,938 + $2,024) = $1,981.0.
[c].5($2,024 + $2,075) = $2,049.5.

Accounts Payable Turnover Ratio

Year	Numerator	Denominator	Accounts Payable Turnover Ratio
3	$11,145[a]	$1,184.5[d]	9.41
4	11,175[b]	1,174.0[e]	9.52
5	12,079[c]	1,146.5[f]	10.54

[a]$10,987 + $1,938 − $1,780 = $11,145.   [d].5($1,110 + $1,259) = $1,184.5.
[b]$11,089 + $2,024 − $1,938 = $11,175.   [e].5($1,259 + $1,089) = $1,174.0.
[c]$12,028 + $2,075 − $2,024 = $12,079.   [f].5($1,089 + $1,204) = $1,146.5.

c. The short-term liquidity risk of International Paper declined slightly over the three-year period. The current and quick ratios showed steady improvement. The accounts receivable and inventory turnover ratios changed relatively little, so one must look at current liabilities to understand the reasons for the improvements in the current and quick ratios. The accounts payable turnover ratio increased, indicating that International Paper paid its suppliers more quickly. Also, International Paper reduced its short-term borrowing. The cash flow from operations to average current liabilities ratio decreased between Year 3 and Year 4 but increased between Year 4 and Year 5. The decline between Year 3 and Year 4 is due primarily to reduced profitability in Year 4. Sales were relatively flat between these two years and the profit margin declined. Improved profitability in Year 5 resulted in increased cash flow from operations. The levels of these short-term liquidity ratios suggest that International Paper still has considerable short-term liquidity risk. Its quick ratio is considerably less than 1.0 and its cash flow from operations to average current liabilities ratio is less than the 40 percent commonly found for a financially healthy firm.

24. Calculating and interpreting long-term liquidity ratios.

a. Long-Term Debt Ratio

Year End	Numerator	Denominator	Long-Term Debt Ratio
4	$2,059	$2,059 + $2,506	45.1%
5	2,833	2,833 + 1,965	59.0%
6	3,716	3,716 + 1,996	65.1%
7	3,228	3,228 + 1,569	67.3%

Debt-Equity Ratio

Year End	Numerator	Denominator	Debt-Equity Ratio
4	$ 5,905	$ 5,905 + $2,506	70.2%
5	8,197	8,197 + 1,965	80.7%
6	9,875	9,875 + 1,996	83.2%
7	10,327	10,327 + 1,569	86.8%

b. Cash Flow from Operations to Total Liabilities Ratio

Year	Numerator	Denominator	Cash Flow from Operations to Total Liabilities Ratio
5	$ 150	.5($5,905 + $8,197)	2.1%
6	677	.5($8,197 + $9,875)	7.5%
7	1,324	.5($9,875 + $10,327)	13.1%

Interest Coverage Ratio

Year	Numerator	Denominator	Times Interest Charges Earned
5	$(635)	$151	Neg.
6	(474)	177	Neg.
7	(389)	271	Neg.

c. The debt ratios increased during the three-year period, suggesting increased long-term solvency risk. The cash flow from operations to average total liabilities increased during the three years, but its level is less than that usually encountered for a healthy firm. Delta's interest coverage ratio is negative. Thus, Delta evidences significant long-term solvency risk.

COMPOUND INTEREST EXAMPLES AND APPLICATIONS

LEARNING OBJECTIVES

1. Understand why accountants and financial managers need to master compound interest methods.
2. Distinguish between future and present value and between single payments and annuities.
3. Practice converting written problem descriptions into a form suitable for analytic solution.
4. Practice finding internal rate of return on a series of equally spaced cash flows.

Managerial accountants and managers deal with interest calculations because expenditures for an asset most often precede the receipts for services that asset produces. Money received sooner has more value than money received later. The difference in timing can affect whether or not acquiring an asset is profitable. Amounts of money received at different times are different commodities. Managers use interest calculations to make valid comparisons among amounts of money their firm will pay or recieve at different times.

Managers evaluate a series of money payments over time, such as from an investment project, by finding the present value of the series of payments. The *present value* of a series of payments is a single amount of money at the present time that is the economic equivalent of the entire series.

This appendix illustrates the use of compound interest techniques with a comprehensive series of examples, which use the tables appearing after this appendix. Calculators can do the same computations.

FUTURE VALUE

If you invest $1 today at 10 percent compounded annually, it will grow to $1.10000 at the end of 1 year, $1.21000 at the end of 2 years, $1.33100 at the end of 3 years, and so on, according to the following formula

$$F_n = P(1 + r)^n,$$

where

$$F_n = \text{accumulation or future value}$$
$$P = \text{one-time investment today}$$
$$r = \text{interest rate per period}$$
$$n = \text{number of periods from today.}$$

The amount F_n is the future value of the present payment, P, compounded at r percent per period for n periods. Table 1, at the end of this appendix, shows the future values of $P = \$1$ for various periods and for various interest rates.

Example 1   How much will $1,000 deposited today at 8 percent compounded annually be worth 10 years from now?

One dollar deposited today at 8 percent will grow to $2.15892; therefore $1,000 will grow to $1,000(1.08)^{10} = \$1,000 \times 2.15892 = \$2,158.92$.

PRESENT VALUE

This section deals with the problems of calculating how much principal, P, you must invest today to have a specified amount, F_n, at the end of n periods. You know the future amount, F_n, the interest rate, r, and the number of periods, n; you want to find P. To have $1 one year from today when deposits earn 8 percent, you must invest P of $.92593 today. That is, $F_1 = P(1.08)^1$ or $\$1 = \$.92593 \times 1.08$. Because $F_n = P(1 + r)^n$, dividing both sides of the equation by $(1 + r)^n$ yields

$$\frac{F_n}{(1 + r)^n} = P, \quad \text{or} \quad P = \frac{F_n}{(1 + r)^n} = F_n(1 + r)^{-n}.$$

Table 2 at the end of this appendix shows discount factors or, equivalently, present values of $1 for various interest (or discount) rates for various periods.

Example 2   What is the present value of $1 due 10 years from now if the interest rate (or, equivalently, the discount rate) r is 12 percent per year?

From Table 2, 12-percent column, 10-period row, the present value of $1 to be received 10 periods hence at 12 percent is $.32197.

EXHIBIT A.1			

Verification of Net Present Value of $10,717 Single Cash Flow of $13,500 at the End of Year 3 Discounted at 8 Percent per Year

Year	Beginning Amount	+ Interest at 8 Percent	= Ending Amount
1	$10,717	$ 857	$11,574
2	11,574	926	12,500
3	12,500	1,000	13,500

Example 3   You project that an investment will generate cash of $13,500 three years from today. What is the net present value today of this cash receipt if the discount rate is 8 percent per year?

One dollar received 3 years hence discounted at 8 percent has a present value of $.79383. See Table 2, 3-period row, 8-percent column. Thus the project has a present value of $13,500 × .79383 = $10,717. Exhibit A.1 shows how $10,717 grows to $13,500 in 3 years.

CHANGING THE COMPOUNDING PERIOD: NOMINAL AND EFFECTIVE RATES

"Twelve percent, compounded annually" is the price for a loan; this price means interest increases, or converts to, principal once a year at the rate of 12 percent. Often, however, the price for a loan states that compounding will take place more than once a year. A savings bank may advertise that it pays interest of 6 percent, compounded quarterly. This kind of payment means that at the end of each quarter the bank credits savings accounts with interest calculated at the rate 1.5 percent (= 6 percent/4). The investor can withdraw the interest payment or leave it on deposit to earn more interest.

If you invest $10,000 today at 12 percent compounded annually, it will grow to a future value 1 year later of $11,200. If the rate of interest is 12 percent compounded semiannually, the bank adds 6-percent interest to the principal every 6 months. At the end of the first 6 months, $10,000 will have grown to $10,600; that amount will grow to $10,600 × 1.06 = $11,236 by the end of the year. Notice that 12 percent compounded semiannually results in the same amount as 12.36 percent compounded annually.

Suppose that the bank quotes interest as 12 percent, compounded quarterly. It will add an additional 3 percent of the principal every 3 months. By the end of the year, $10,000 will grow to $10,000 × $(1.03)^4$ = $10,000 × 1.12551 = $11,255. Twelve percent compounded quarterly is equivalent to 12.55 percent compounded annually. At 12 percent compounded monthly, $1 will grow to $1 × $(1.01)^{12}$ = $1.12683, and $10,000 will grow to $11,268. Thus, 12 percent compounded monthly is equivalent to 12.68 percent compounded annually.

For a given *nominal* rate, such as the 12 percent in the preceding examples, the more often interest compounds, the higher the *effective* rate of interest paid. If a nominal rate, r, compounds m times per year, the effective rate is equal to $(1 + r/m)^m - 1$.

In practice, to solve problems that require computation of interest quoted at a nominal rate r percent per period compounded m times per period for n periods, use the tables for rate r/m and $m \times n$ periods. For example, 12 percent compounded quarterly for 5 years is equivalent to the rate found in the interest tables for $r = 12/4 = 3$ percent for $m \times n = 4 \times 5 = 20$ periods.

Example 4   What is the future value 5 years hence of $600 invested at 8 percent compounded quarterly?

Eight percent compounded four times per year for 5 years is equivalent to 2 percent per period compounded for 20 periods. Table 1 shows the value of $F_{20} = (1.02)^{20}$ to be 1.48595. Six hundred dollars, then, would grow to $600 × 1.48595 = $891.57.

Example 5 How much money must you invest today at 12 percent compounded semiannually to have $1,000 four years from today?

Twelve percent compounded two times a year for 4 years is equivalent to 6 percent per period compounded for 8 periods. The *present value,* Table 2, of $1 received 8 periods hence at 6 percent per period is $.62741; that is, $.62741 invested today for 8 periods at an interest rate of 6 percent per period will grow to $1. To have $1,000 in 8 periods (4 years), you must invest $627.41 (= $1,000 × $.62741) today.

Example 6 A local department store offers its customers credit and advertises its interest rate at 18 percent per year, compounded monthly at the rate of $1\frac{1}{2}$ percent per month. What is the effective annual interest rate?

One and one-half percent per month for 12 months is equivalent to $(1.015)^{12} - 1 = 19.562$ percent per year. See Table 1, 12-period row, $1\frac{1}{2}$-percent column, where the factor is 1.19562.

Example 7 If prices increased at the rate of 6 percent during each of two consecutive 6-month periods, how much did prices increase during the entire year?

If a price index is 100.00 at the start of the year, it will be $100.00 \times (1.06)^2 = 112.36$ at the end of the year. The price change for the entire year is $(112.36/100.00) - 1 = 12.36$ percent.

ANNUITIES

An *annuity* is a series of equal payments, one per equally spaced period of time. Examples of annuities include monthly rental payments, semiannual corporate bond coupon (or interest) payments, and annual payments to a lessor under a lease contract. Armed with an understanding of the tables for future and present values, you can solve any annuity problem. Annuities arise so often, however, and their solution is so tedious without special tables or calculator functions that annuity problems merit special study and the use of special tables or functions.

TERMINOLOGY FOR ANNUITIES

Annuity terminology can confuse you because not all writers use the same terms.

An annuity with payments occurring at the end of each period is an *ordinary annuity* or an *annuity in arrears.* Semiannual corporate bonds usually promise coupon payments paid in arrears or, equivalently, the first payment does not occur until after the bond has been outstanding for 6 months.

An annuity with payments occurring at the beginning of each period is an *annuity due* or an *annuity in advance.* Rent paid at the beginning of each month is an annuity due.

In a *deferred annuity,* the first payment occurs some time later than the end of the first period.

Annuities payments can go on forever. Such annuities are *perpetuities.* Bonds that promise payments forever are *consols.* The British and the Canadian governments have issued consols from time to time. A perpetuity can be in arrears or in advance. The two differ only in the timing of the first payment.

Annuities may confuse you. Studying them is easier with a time line such as the one shown below.

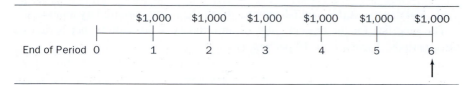

A time line marks the end of each period, numbers the period, shows the payments the investor receives or pays, and shows the time in which the accountant wants to value the annuity. The time line above represents an ordinary annuity (in arrears) for six periods of $1,000 to be valued at the end of period 6. The end of period 0 is "now." The first payment occurs one period from now. The arrow points to the valuation date.

ORDINARY ANNUITIES (ANNUITIES IN ARREARS)

The future values of ordinary annuities appear in Table 3 at the end of this appendix.

Consider an ordinary annuity for three periods at 12 percent. The time line for the future value of such an annuity is

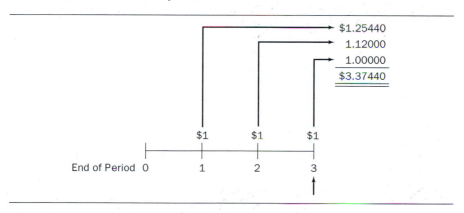

The $1 received at the end of the first period earns interest for two periods, so it is worth $1.25440 at the end of period 3. (see Table 1). The $1 received at the end of the second period grows to $1.12000 by the end of period 3, and the $1 received at the end of period 3 is, of course, worth $1.00000 at the end of period 3. The entire annuity is worth $3.37440 at the end of period 3. This amount appears in Table 3 for the future value of an ordinary annuity for three periods at 12 percent. Factors for the future value of an annuity for a particular number of periods sum the factors for the future value of $1 for each of the periods. The future value of an ordinary annuity is

$$\begin{matrix} \text{Future Value of} \\ \text{Ordinary Annuity} \end{matrix} = \begin{matrix} \text{Periodic} \\ \text{Payment} \end{matrix} \times \begin{matrix} \text{Factor for} \\ \text{the Future} \\ \text{Value of an} \\ \text{Ordinary Annuity.} \end{matrix}$$

Thus,

$$\$3.37440 \quad = \quad \$1 \quad \times \quad 3.37440.$$

Table 4 at the end of this appendix shows the present value of ordinary annuities.

The time line for the present value of an ordinary annuity of $1 per period for three periods, discounted at 12 percent, is

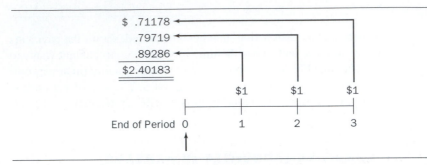

The $1 the investor receives at the end of period 1 has a present value of $.89286, the $1 investor receives at the end of period 2 has a present value of $.79719, and the $1 the investor receives at the end of the third period has a present value of $.71178. Each of these numbers comes from Table 2. The present value of the annuity is the sum of these individual present values, $2.40183, shown in Table 4.

The present value of an ordinary annuity for n periods is the sum of the present value of $1 received one period from now plus the present value of $1 received two periods from now, and so on until we add on the present value of $1 received n periods from now. The present value of an ordinary annuity is

$$\begin{array}{c} \text{Present Value} \\ \text{of an} \\ \text{Ordinary Annuity} \end{array} = \begin{array}{c} \text{Periodic} \\ \text{Payment} \end{array} \times \begin{array}{c} \text{Factor for} \\ \text{the Present} \\ \text{Value of an} \\ \text{Ordinary Annuity.} \end{array}$$

Thus,

$$\$2.40183 \quad = \quad \$1 \quad \times \quad 2.40183.$$

Example 8 Accountants project an investment to generate $1,000 at the end of each of the next 20 years. If the interest rate is 8 percent compounded annually, what will the future value of these flows be at the end of 20 years?

The time line for this problem is

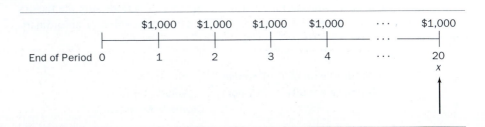

The symbol x denotes the amount you must calculate. Table 3 indicates that the factor for the future value of an annuity at 8 percent for 20 periods is 45.76196. Thus,

$$\begin{array}{l} \text{Future Value} \\ \text{of an} \\ \text{Ordinary Annuity} \end{array} = \begin{array}{l} \text{Periodic} \\ \text{Payment} \end{array} \times \begin{array}{l} \text{Factor for} \\ \text{the Future} \\ \text{Value of an} \\ \text{Ordinary Annuity} \end{array}$$

$$x = \$1{,}000 \times 45.76196$$
$$x = \$45{,}762.$$

The cash flows have future value \$45,762.

Example 9   Parents want to accumulate a fund to send their child to college. The parents will invest a fixed amount at the end of each calendar quarter for the next 10 years. The funds will accumulate in a savings certificate that promises to pay 8-percent interest compounded quarterly. What amount must the parents invest to accumulate a fund of \$50,000?

The time line for this problem is

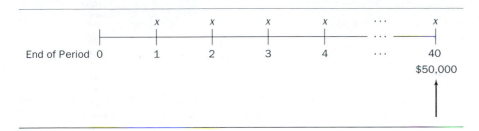

This problem is similar to Example 8 both involve periodic investments of cash that accumulate interest over time until a specific time in the future. In Example 8, you know the periodic investment and compute the future value. In Example 9, you know the future value and compute the period investment. Table 3 indicates that the future value of an annuity at 2 percent (= 8 percent per year/4 quarters per year) per period for 40 (= 4 quarters per year $\times$ 10 years) periods is 60.40198. Thus,

$$\begin{array}{l} \text{Future Value} \\ \text{of an} \\ \text{Ordinary Annuity} \end{array} = \begin{array}{l} \text{Periodic} \\ \text{Payment} \end{array} \times \begin{array}{l} \text{Factor for} \\ \text{the Future} \\ \text{Value of an} \\ \text{Ordinary Annuity} \end{array}$$

$$\$50{,}000 = x \times 60.40198$$
$$x = \frac{\$50{,}000}{60.40198}$$
$$x = \$828.$$

Because you want to find the periodic payment, you divide the future value amount of \$50,000 by the future value factor.

Example 10   A firm borrows \$30,000 from an insurance company. The interest rate on the loan is 8 percent compounded semiannually. The firm agrees to repay the loan in equal semiannual installments over the next 5 years and make the first payment 6 months from now. What is the amount of the required semiannual payment?

The time line is

You know the present value and must compute the periodic payment. Table 4 indicates that the present value of an annuity at 4 percent (= 8 percent per year/2 semiannual periods per year) for 10 periods (= 2 periods per year × 5 years) is 8.11090. Thus,

$$
\begin{array}{ccc}
\text{Present Value} & & \text{Factor for} \\
\text{of an} & = & \text{Periodic} \quad \times \quad \text{the Present} \\
\text{Ordinary Annuity} & & \text{Payment} \qquad \text{Value of an} \\
& & \text{Ordinary Annuity} \\
\$30{,}000 & = & x \quad \times \quad 8.11090 \\
x & = & \dfrac{\$30{,}000}{8.11090} \\
x & = & \$3{,}699.
\end{array}
$$

Because you are finding the periodic payment, you divide the present value amount of $30,000 by the present value factor. Exhibit A.2 shows how periodic payments of

---

EXHIBIT A.2

Amortization Schedule for $30,000 Mortgage, Repaid in Semiannual Installments of $3,700, Interest Rate of 8 Percent, Compounded Semiannually

6-Month Period (1)	Mortgage Principal Start of Period (2)	Interest Expense for Period (3)	Payment (4)	Portion of Payment Reducing Principal (5)	Mortgage Principal End of Period (6)
0					$30,000
1	$30,000	$1,200	$3,700	$2,500	27,500
2	27,500	1,100	3,700	2,600	24,900
3	24,900	996	3,700	2,704	22,196
4	22,196	888	3,700	2,812	19,384
5	19,384	775	3,700	2,925	16,459
6	16,459	658	3,700	3,042	13,417
7	13,417	537	3,700	3,163	10,254
8	10,254	410	3,700	3,290	6,964
9	6,964	279	3,700	3,421	3,543
10	3,543	142	3,685	3,543	0

Column **(2)** = column **(6)** from previous period.

Column **(3)** = .04 × column **(2)**.

Column **(4)** is given, except row 10, where it is the amount such that column **(4)** = column **(2)** + column **(3)**.

Column **(5)** = column **(4)** − column **(3)**.

Column **(6)** = column **(2)** − column **(5)**.

Present Value of Cost Savings Guides Pricing Decision

In the 1970s, Robert Mendenhall discovered a process that enables highway and road builders to reuse asphalt pavement in constructing rebuilt or new roads. He patented the process. Mendenhall's discovery promised large cost savings in road building. Mendenhall licensed his patent to CMI Corp. CMI began to produce and sell recycling plants capable of producing high-quality road surface materials from recycled asphalt.

In the 1980s, competitors, such as Barber-Greene (BG), approached CMI about obtaining licenses to use the patent. Management at CMI wanted some method for thinking about the license fees it might reasonably expect to collect from others' use of the patent. Management believed that the cost savings from incorporating the new process into asphalt plants justified prices at least 25 percent larger than prices for equipment using the old processes.

Data pertinent to the analysis:

- Prices for asphalt plants using the old processes averaged $735,000.
- The new recycling plants had a capacity to produce 150,000 to 300,000 tons of new road surfaces per year.
- Contractors expect the recyling plants to last for 15 to 18 years but depreciate them

over 10 years on a straight-line basis for tax reporting.
- Because of air pollution problems, a contractor cannot use 100-percent recycled asphalt in producing new paving materials. Instead, the contractor must use a mixture of recycled and new, virgin asphalt. Depending on the application, the ratio of recycled to virgin asphalt ranges from 70/30 to 50/50.
- To produce a ton of paving materials from virgin asphalt costs the contractors from $14 to $17 per ton in materials and plant operating costs, not counting the cost of the plant itself.
- Various industry studies indicate a cost savings from using recycled asphalt of $.50 to $11.40 per ton of new paving materials produced from recycled asphalt.
- The risk of the contracting process for road builders suggests a discount rate for plant acquisitions of 15 to 20 percent per year before taxes.

CMI's financial analysts constructed the analysis of two examples appearing in Exhibit A.3 to help management think about its opportunity. These examples helped management understand that cost savings justify price increases for asphalt plants of even larger than 25 percent and license fees in excess of $100,000 per plant.

$3,700 amortize the loan. We call such a schedule an *amortization schedule*. If the periodic payments were $3,699, not $3,700, the "error" in the final payment would be even smaller.

Example 11 A company signs a lease acquiring the right to use property for 3 years. The company promises to make lease payments of $19,709 annually at the end of this and the next 2 years. The discount, or interest, rate is 15 percent per year. What is the present value of the lease payments, which is the equivalent cash purchase price for this property?

EXHIBIT A.3

Derivation of Price Increase for Recycling Asphalt Drum Plant Justified by Cost Savings

First Illustration: Worst-case assumptions

Second Illustration: Best-case assumptions

Price (List) of New Asphalt Plant	$735,000	
Capacity of New Plant to Produce Output In tons per year		
First Illustration	150,000	
Second Illustration	300,000	
Life of New Asphalt Plant in Years		
First Illustration	10	
Second Illustration	15	
Savings per Ton of Output Produced[a]		
First Illustration	$1.50	
Second Illustration	$2.50	
Dollar Savings per Year		
First Illustration	$225,000	= 150,000 tons × $1.50 per ton
Second Illustration	$750,000	= 300,000 tons × $2.50 per ton
Annual Discount Rate for Owner of Plant		
First Illustration	20.0%	
Second Illustration	15.0%	
Present Value of Dollar Savings Over Life of Plant		
First Illustration	$943,306	= present value of $225,000 per year for 10 years discounted at 20 percent per year. = $225,000 × 4.19247
Second Illustration	$4,385,528	= present value of $750,000 per year for 15 years discounted at 15 percent per year. = $750,000 × 5.84737
Percentage Increase in Selling Price of New Asphalt Plant Justified by Cost Savings		
First Illustration	128%	= $943,306/$735,000
Second Illustration	597%	= $4,385,528/$735,000

[a]If each ton of output requires as much as 70 percent, or as little as 50 percent, of new material, then the savings per ton of output ranges from $1.50 (= .30 × $5.00) to $2.50 (= .50 × $5.00) per ton of output.

The time line is

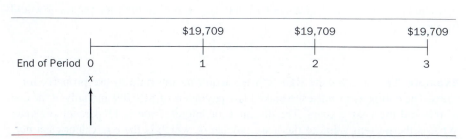

The factor from Table 4 for the present value of an annuity at 15 percent for 3 periods is 2.28323. Thus,

$$
\begin{array}{c}
\text{Present Value} \\
\text{of an} \\
\text{Ordinary Annuity}
\end{array}
=
\begin{array}{c}
\text{Periodic} \\
\text{Payment}
\end{array}
\times
\begin{array}{c}
\text{Factor for} \\
\text{the Present} \\
\text{Value of an} \\
\text{Ordinary Annuity}
\end{array}
$$

$$X = \$19{,}709 \times 2.28323$$

$$X = \$45{,}000$$

Example 12 Mr. Mason is 62 years old. He wishes to invest equal amounts on his sixty-third, sixty-fourth, and sixty-fifth birthdays so that starting on his sixty-sixth birthday he can withdraw $50,000 on each birthday for 10 years. His investments will earn 8 percent per year. How much should he invest on the sixty-third through sixty-fifth birthdays?

The time line for this problem is

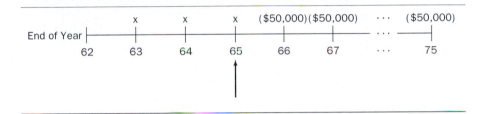

At 65, Mr. Mason needs to have accumulated a fund equal to the present value of an annuity of $50,000 per period for 10 periods, discounted at 8 percent per period. The factor from Table 4 for 8 percent and 10 periods is 6.71008. Thus,

$$
\begin{array}{c}
\text{Present Value} \\
\text{of an} \\
\text{Ordinary Annuity}
\end{array}
=
\begin{array}{c}
\text{Periodic} \\
\text{Payment}
\end{array}
\times
\begin{array}{c}
\text{Factor for} \\
\text{the Present} \\
\text{Value of an} \\
\text{Ordinary Annuity}
\end{array}
$$

$$X = \$50{,}000 \times 6.71008$$
$$X = \$335{,}504.$$

The time line now appears as follows:

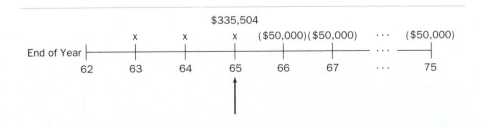

The question now becomes: How much must Mr. Mason invest on his sixty-third, sixty-fourth, and sixty-fifth birthdays to accumulate a fund of $335,504 on his sixty-fifth birthday? The factor for the future value of an annuity for three periods at 8 percent is 3.24640. Thus,

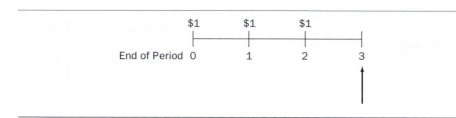

$$
\begin{array}{ccc}
\text{Future Value} & & \text{Factor for} \\
\text{of an} & = \text{Periodic} \times & \text{the Future} \\
\text{Ordinary Annuity} & \text{Payment} & \text{Value of an} \\
& & \text{Ordinary Annuity} \\
\$335,504 & = x \times & 3.24640 \\
x & = \dfrac{\$335,504}{3.24640} & \\
x & = \$103,346. &
\end{array}
$$

ANNUITIES IN ADVANCE (ANNUITIES DUE)

The time line for the future value of a three-period annuity in advance is

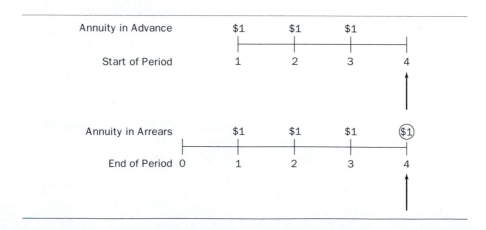

Notice that we calculated the future value for the *end* of the period in which the last payment occurs. When you have tables of ordinary annuities, tables for annuities due are unnecessary.

To see this, compare the time line for the future value of an annuity in advance for three periods with the time axis relabeled to show the start of the period and the time line for the future value of an ordinary annuity (in arrears) for four periods.

A $1 annuity in advance for *n* periods has a future value equal to the future value of a $1 annuity in arrears for *n* + 1 periods *minus* $1. The $1 circled in the time line for the annuity in arrears is the $1 that you must subtract to calculate the future value of an annuity in advance. No annuity payment occurs at the end of period 3. The note at the foot of Table 3 states: "To convert from this table to values of an annuity in advance, find the annuity in arrears above for one more period and subtract 1.00000."

EXAMPLE PROBLEM INVOLVING FUTURE VALUE OF ANNUITY DUE

Example 13   A student plans to invest $1,000 a year at the beginning of each of the next 10 years in certificates of deposit paying interest at 12 percent per year, making the first payment today. What will be the amount of the certificates at the end of the tenth year?
   The time line is

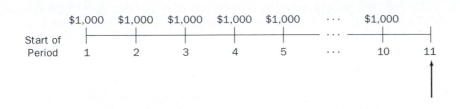

The factor for the future value of an annuity for 11 (= 10 + 1) periods is 20.65458. Because a $1,000 investment does not occur at the end of the tenth year, you subtract 1.000000 from 20.65458 to obtain the factor for the annuity in advance of 19.65458. The future value of the annuity in advance is

$$\begin{matrix} \text{Future Value} \\ \text{of an} \\ \text{Annuity in Advance} \end{matrix} = \begin{matrix} \text{Periodic} \\ \text{Payment} \end{matrix} \times \begin{matrix} \text{Factor for the} \\ \text{Future Value of} \\ \text{an Annuity in} \\ \text{Advance} \end{matrix}$$

$$x = \$1,000 \times 19.65458$$
$$x = \$19,655.$$

PRESENT VALUE OF ANNUITY DUE

The time line for the present value of an annuity in advance for three periods is

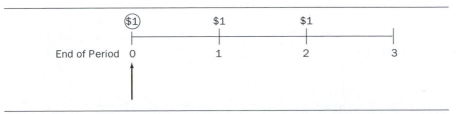

Notice that except for the first, circled payment, it looks just like the present value of an ordinary annuity for two periods. A $1 annuity in advance for *n* periods has a present value equal to the present value of a $1 annuity in arrears for *n* − 1 periods *plus* $1. The note at the foot of Table 4 states: "To convert from this table to values of an annuity in advance, find the annuity in arrears above for one fewer period and add 1.00000."

Example 14   What is the present value of rents of $350 paid monthly, in advance, for 1 year when the discount rate is 1 percent per month?

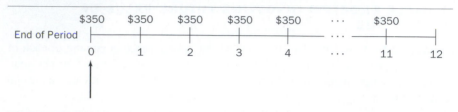

The present value of $1 per period *in arrears* for 11 periods at 1 percent per period is $10.36763; the present value of $1 per period in advance for 12 periods is $10.36763 + $1.00 = $11.36763, and the present value of this year's rent is $350 × 11.36763 = $3,979.

DEFERRED ANNUITIES

When the first payment of an annuity occurs some time after the end of the first period, the annuity is *deferred.* The time line for an ordinary annuity of $1 per period for four periods deferred for two periods is

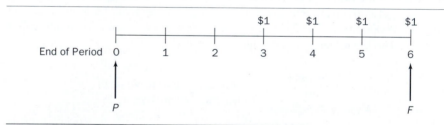

The arrow marked *P* shows the time of the present value calculation; the arrow marked *F* shows the future value calculation. The deferral does not affect the future value, which equals the future value of an ordinary annuity for four periods.

Notice that the time line for the present value looks like one for an ordinary annuity for six periods *minus* an ordinary annuity for two periods:

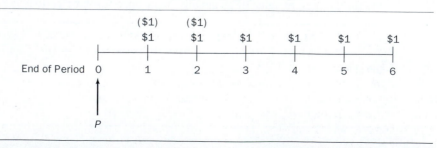

Calculate the present value of an annuity of *n* payments deferred for *d* periods by subtracting the present value of an annuity for *d* periods from the present value of an annuity for *n* + *d* periods.

Example 15   Refer to the data in Example 12. Recall that Mr. Mason wants to withdraw $50,000 per year on his sixty-sixth through his seventy-fifth birthdays. He wishes to invest a sufficient amount on his sixty-third, sixty-fourth, and sixty-fifth birthdays to provide a fund for the later withdrawals.
    The time line is

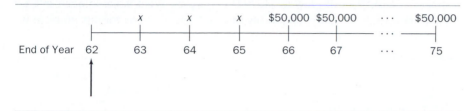

As of his sixty-second birthday, the $50,000 series of payments on Mr. Mason's sixty-sixth through seventy-fifth birthdays is a deferred annuity. The interest rate is 8 percent per year.
    You can find the present value using the factor for the present value of an annuity for 13 periods (10 payments deferred for three periods) of 7.90378 and subtracting the factor for the present value of an annuity for three periods of 2.57710. The net amount is 5.32668 (= 7.90378 − 2.57710). Multiplying by the $50,000 payment amount, you find the present value of the deferred annuity on Mr. Mason's sixty-second birthday of $266,334 (= $50,000 × 5.32668).

PERPETUITIES

A periodic payment to be received forever is a *perpetuity*. Future values of perpetuities are undefined. One dollar to be received at the end of every period discounted at rate *r* percent has a present value of $1/*r*. Observe what happens in the expression for the present value of an ordinary annuity of $*A* per payment as *n*, the number of payments, approaches infinity:

$$P_A = \frac{A[1 - (1 + r)^{-n}]}{r} \ .$$

As *n* approaches infinity, $(1 + r)^{-n}$ approaches zero, so that P_A approaches $A(1/r)$. If the first payment of the perpetuity occurs now, the present value is $A[1 + (1/r)]$.

Example 16   The Canadian government offers to pay $30 every 6 months forever in the form of a perpetual bond. What is that bond worth if the discount rate is 10 percent compounded semiannually?
    Ten percent compounded semiannually is equivalent to 5 percent per 6-month period. If the first payment occurs six months from now, the present value is $30/.05 = $600. If the first payment occurs today, the present value is $30 + $600 = $630.

IMPLICIT INTEREST RATES: FINDING INTERNAL RATES OF RETURN

The preceding examples computed a future value or a present value given the interest rate and stated cash payment. Or, they computed the required payments given their known future value or their known present value. In some calculations, we know the present or future value and the periodic payments; we must find the implicit interest rate. Assume, for example, a case in which we know that a cash investment of $10,500 will grow to $13,500 in 3 years. What is the implicit interest rate, or market rate of return, on this investment? The time line for this problem is

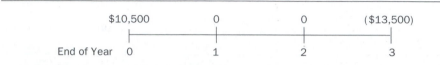

$10,500   0   0   ($13,500)

End of Year   0   1   2   3

The implicit interest rate is r, such that

(A.1)
$$\$10{,}500 = \frac{\$13{,}500}{(1 + r)^3} \,.$$

(A.2)
$$0 = \$10{,}500 + \frac{\$13{,}500}{(1 + r)^3} \,.$$

In other words, the present value of $13,500 discounted three periods at r percent per period is $10,500. The present value of all current and future cash flows nets to zero when future flows are discounted at r percent per period. In general, the only way to find such an r is a trial-and-error procedure.[1] The procedure is finding the internal rate of return of a series of cash flows. The *internal rate of return* of a series of cash flows is the discount rate that equates the net present value of that series of cash flows to zero. Follow these steps to find the internal rate of return:

1. Make an educated guess, called the "trial rate," at the internal rate of return. If you have no idea what to guess, try zero.
2. Calculate the present value of all the cash flows (including the one at the end of year 0).
3. If the present value of the cash flows is zero, stop. The current trial rate is the internal rate of return.
4. If the amount found in step 2 is less than zero, try a larger interest rate as the trial rate and go back to step 2.
5. If the amount found in step 2 is greater than zero, try a smaller interest rate as the new trial rate and go back to step 2.

---

[1] In cases where r appears in only one term, as here, you can find r analytically. Here, $r = (\$13{,}500/\$10{,}500)^{1/3} - 1 = .087380$.

The following iterations illustrate the process for the example in Equation A.1.

Iteration Number	Trial Rate = r	Net Present Values: Right-Hand Side of A.2
1	0.00%	($3,000)
2	10.00	357
3	5.00	(1,162)
4	7.50	(367)
5	8.75	3

With a trial rate of 8.75 percent, the right-hand side is close enough to zero so that you can use 8.75 percent as the implicit interest rate. Continued iterations would find trial rates even closer to the true rate, which is about 8.7380 percent.

You may find calculating the internal rate of return for a series of cash flows tedious, and you should not attempt it unless you have at least a calculator. An exponential feature, the feature that allows the computation of $(1 + r)$ raised to various powers, helps.[2] Computer spreadsheets, such as Lotus 1-2-3® and Excel®, have a built-in function to find the internal rate of return.

Example 17   The Alexis Company acquires a machine with a cash price of $10,500. It pays for the machine by giving a note for $12,000 promising to make payments equal to 7 percent of the face value, $840 (= .07 × $12,000), at the end of each of the next 3 years and a single payment of $12,000 in 3 years. What is the implicit interest rate in the loan?

The time line for this problem is

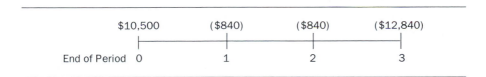

The implicit interest rate is r, such that[3]

(A.3) $$\$10,500 = \frac{\$840}{(1 + r)} + \frac{\$840}{(1 + r)^2} + \frac{\$840}{(1 + r)^3}.$$

---

[2]You may use other methods to guess the trial rate that will approximate the true rate in fewer iterations than the method described here. If you want to find internal rates of return efficiently with successive trial rates, refer to a mathematical reference book to learn about the "Newton search" method, sometimes called the "method of false position."

[3]Compare this formulation to that in Equation A.2. Note that the left-hand side is zero in one case but not in the other. The left-hand side can be either nonzero or zero, depending on what seems convenient for the particular context.

The iteration process finds an internal rate of return of 12.2 percent to the nearest tenth of 1 percent:

Iteration Number	Trial Rate	Right-Hand Side of A.3
1	7.0%	$12,000
2	15.0	9,808
3	11.0	10,827
4	13.0	10,300
5	12.0	10,559
6	12.5	10,428
7	12.3	10,480
8	12.2	10,506
9	12.1	10,533

Example 18   In some contexts, such as mortgages or leases, one knows the amount of a series of future periodic payments, which are identical in all periods, and the present value of those future payments. For example, a firm may borrow $100,000 and agree to repay the loan, in 20 payments of $11,746 each, at the end of each of the next 20 years. To calculate interest expense each period, you must find the interest rate implicit in the loan.

You have the following information:

$$\begin{matrix} \text{Present Value} \\ \text{of an} \\ \text{Ordinary Annuity} \end{matrix} = \begin{matrix} \text{Periodic} \\ \text{Payment} \end{matrix} \times \begin{matrix} \text{Factor for} \\ \text{the Present} \\ \text{Value of an} \\ \text{Ordinary Annuity} \end{matrix}$$

$$\$100,000 = \$11,746 \times x$$

$$x = \frac{\$100,000}{\$11,746}$$

$$x = 8.51354.$$

The factor to discount 20 payments of $11,746 to a present value of $100,000 is 8.51354. To find the interest rate implicit in the discounting, scan the 20-payment row of Table 4 to find the factor 8.51354. The interest rate at the head of the column is the implicit interest rate, approximately 10 percent in the example.

Example 19   An investment costing $11,400 today provides the following after-tax cash inflows at the ends of each of the next five periods: $5,000, $4,000, $3,000, $2,000, $1,000. What is the internal rate of return on these flows? That is, find r such that

$$\textbf{(A.2)} \quad 0 = (\$11,400) + \frac{\$5,000}{(1+r)} + \frac{\$4,000}{(1+r)^2} + \frac{\$3,000}{(1+r)^3} + \frac{\$2,000}{(1+r)^4} + \frac{\$1,000}{(1+r)^5}.$$

Trial rates r produced the following sequences of estimates of the internal rate of return:

Iteration Number	Trial Rate	Right-Hand Side of A.4
1	0.00%	$3,600
2	10.00	692
3	15.00	(414)
4	12.50	115
5	13.50	(102)
6	13.00	6
7	13.10	(16)
8	13.01	4
9	13.01	2
10	13.03	(1)

The estimating proceeds several steps farther than necessary. To the nearest whole percentage point, the internal rate of return is 13 percent.

To the nearest one-hundredth of a percent, the internal rate of return is 13.03 percent. Further trials finds an even more precise answer, $r = 13.027$ percent. Physical scientists learn early in their training not to use more significant digits in calculations than the accuracy of the measuring devices merits. Accountants, too, should not carry calculations beyond the point of accuracy. Given the likely uncertainty in the estimates of cash flows, an estimate of the internal rate of return accurate to the nearest whole percentage point will serve its intended purpose.

COMPOUND INTEREST AND ANNUITY TABLES

TABLE 1

Future Value of $1

$F_n = P(1 + r)^n$

r = interest rate; n = number of periods until valuation; $P = \$1$

Periods = n	½%	1%	1½%	2%	3%	4%	5%	6%	7%	8%	10%	12%	15%	20%	25%
1	1.00500	1.01000	1.01500	1.02000	1.03000	1.04000	1.05000	1.06000	1.07000	1.08000	1.10000	1.12000	1.15000	1.20000	1.25000
2	1.01003	1.02010	1.03023	1.04040	1.06090	1.08160	1.10250	1.12360	1.14490	1.16640	1.21000	1.25440	1.32250	1.44000	1.56250
3	1.01508	1.03030	1.04568	1.06121	1.09273	1.12486	1.15763	1.19102	1.22504	1.25971	1.33100	1.40493	1.52088	1.72800	1.95313
4	1.02015	1.04060	1.06136	1.08243	1.12551	1.16986	1.21551	1.26248	1.31080	1.36049	1.46410	1.57352	1.74901	2.07360	2.44141
5	1.02525	1.05101	1.07728	1.10408	1.15927	1.21665	1.27628	1.33823	1.40255	1.46933	1.61051	1.76234	2.01136	2.48832	3.05176
6	1.03038	1.06152	1.09344	1.12616	1.19405	1.26532	1.34010	1.41852	1.50073	1.58687	1.77156	1.97382	2.31306	2.98598	3.81470
7	1.03553	1.07214	1.10984	1.14869	1.22987	1.31593	1.40710	1.50363	1.60578	1.71382	1.94872	2.21068	2.66002	3.58318	4.76837
8	1.04071	1.08286	1.12649	1.17166	1.26677	1.36857	1.47746	1.59385	1.71819	1.85093	2.14359	2.47596	3.05902	4.29982	5.96046
9	1.04591	1.09369	1.14339	1.19509	1.30477	1.42331	1.55133	1.68948	1.83846	1.99900	2.35795	2.77308	3.51788	5.15978	7.45058
10	1.05114	1.10462	1.16054	1.21899	1.34392	1.48024	1.62889	1.79085	1.96715	2.15892	2.59374	3.10585	4.04556	6.19174	9.31323
11	1.05640	1.11567	1.17795	1.24337	1.38423	1.53945	1.71034	1.89830	2.10485	2.33164	2.85312	3.47855	4.65239	7.43008	11.64153
12	1.06168	1.12683	1.19562	1.26824	1.42576	1.60103	1.79586	2.01220	2.25219	2.51817	3.13843	3.89598	5.35025	8.91610	14.55192
13	1.06699	1.13809	1.21355	1.29361	1.46853	1.66507	1.88565	2.13293	2.40985	2.71962	3.45227	4.36349	6.15279	10.69932	18.18989
14	1.07232	1.14947	1.23176	1.31948	1.51259	1.73168	1.97993	2.26090	2.57853	2.93719	3.79750	4.88711	7.07571	12.83918	22.73737
15	1.07768	1.16097	1.25023	1.34587	1.55797	1.80094	2.07893	2.39656	2.75903	3.17217	4.17725	5.47357	8.13706	15.40702	28.42171
16	1.08307	1.17258	1.26899	1.37279	1.60471	1.87298	2.18287	2.54035	2.95216	3.42594	4.59497	6.13039	9.35762	18.48843	35.52714
17	1.08849	1.18430	1.28802	1.40024	1.65285	1.94790	2.29202	2.69277	3.15882	3.70002	5.05447	6.86604	10.76126	22.18611	44.40892
18	1.09393	1.19615	1.30734	1.42825	1.70243	2.02582	2.40662	2.85434	3.37993	3.99602	5.55992	7.68997	12.37545	26.62333	55.51115
19	1.09940	1.20811	1.32695	1.45681	1.75351	2.10685	2.52695	3.02560	3.61653	4.31570	6.11591	8.61276	14.23177	31.94800	69.38894
20	1.10490	1.22019	1.34686	1.48595	1.80611	2.19112	2.65330	3.20714	3.86968	4.66096	6.72750	9.64629	16.36654	38.33760	86.73617
22	1.11597	1.24472	1.38756	1.54598	1.91610	2.36992	2.92526	3.60354	4.43040	5.43654	8.14027	12.10031	21.64475	55.20614	135.5253
24	1.12716	1.26973	1.42950	1.60844	2.03279	2.56330	3.22510	4.04893	5.07237	6.34118	9.84973	15.17863	28.62518	79.49685	211.7582
26	1.13846	1.29526	1.47271	1.67342	2.15659	2.77247	3.55567	4.54938	5.80735	7.39635	11.91818	19.04007	37.85680	114.4755	330.8722
28	1.14987	1.32129	1.51722	1.74102	2.28793	2.99870	3.92013	5.11169	6.64884	8.62711	14.42099	23.88387	50.06561	164.8447	516.9879
30	1.16140	1.34785	1.56308	1.81136	2.42726	3.24340	4.32194	5.74349	7.61226	10.06266	17.44940	29.95992	66.21177	237.3763	807.7936
32	1.17304	1.37494	1.61032	1.88454	2.57508	3.50806	4.76494	6.45339	8.71527	11.73708	21.11378	37.58173	87.56507	341.8219	1262.177
34	1.18480	1.40258	1.65900	1.96068	2.73191	3.79432	5.25335	7.25103	9.97811	13.69013	25.54767	47.14252	115.80480	492.2235	1972.152
36	1.19668	1.43077	1.70914	2.03989	2.89828	4.10393	5.79182	8.14725	11.42394	15.96817	30.91268	59.13557	153.15185	708.8019	3081.488
38	1.20868	1.45953	1.76080	2.12230	3.07478	4.43881	6.38548	9.15425	13.07927	18.62528	37.40434	74.17966	202.54332	1020.675	4814.825
40	1.22079	1.48886	1.81402	2.20804	3.26204	4.80102	7.03999	10.28572	14.97446	21.72452	45.25926	93.05097	267.86355	1469.772	7523.164
45	1.25162	1.56481	1.95421	2.43785	3.78160	5.84118	8.98501	13.76461	21.00245	31.92045	72.89048	163.9876	538.76927	3657.262	22958.87
50	1.28323	1.64463	2.10524	2.69159	4.38391	7.10668	11.46740	18.42015	29.45703	46.90161	117.3909	289.0022	1083.65744	9100.438	70064.92
100	1.64667	2.70481	4.43205	7.24465	19.21863	50.50495	131.5013	339.3021	867.7163	2199.761	13780.61	83522.27	117×10^4	828×10^5	491×10^7

TABLE 2

Present Value of $1

$P = F_n(1 + r)^{-n}$

r = discount rate; n = number of periods until payment; $F_n = \$1$

Periods = n	½%	1%	1½%	2%	3%	4%	5%	6%	7%	8%	10%	12%	15%	20%	25%
1	.99502	.99010	.98522	.98039	.97087	.96154	.95238	.94340	.93458	.92593	.90909	.89286	.86957	.83333	.80000
2	.99007	.98030	.97066	.96117	.94260	.92456	.90703	.89000	.87344	.85734	.82645	.79719	.75614	.69444	.64000
3	.98515	.97059	.95632	.94232	.91514	.88900	.86384	.83962	.81630	.79383	.75131	.71178	.65752	.57870	.51200
4	.98025	.96098	.94218	.92385	.88849	.85480	.82270	.79209	.76290	.73503	.68301	.63552	.57175	.48225	.40960
5	.97537	.95147	.92826	.90573	.86261	.82193	.78353	.74726	.71299	.68058	.62092	.56743	.49718	.40188	.32768
6	.97052	.94205	.91454	.88797	.83748	.79031	.74622	.70496	.66634	.63017	.56447	.50663	.43233	.33490	.26214
7	.96569	.93272	.90103	.87056	.81309	.75992	.71068	.66506	.62275	.58349	.51316	.45235	.37594	.27908	.20972
8	.96089	.92348	.88771	.85349	.78941	.73069	.67684	.62741	.58201	.54027	.46651	.40388	.32690	.23257	.15777
9	.95610	.91434	.87459	.83676	.76642	.70259	.64461	.59190	.54393	.50025	.42410	.36061	.28426	.19381	.13422
10	.95135	.90529	.86167	.82035	.74409	.67556	.61391	.55839	.50835	.46319	.38554	.32197	.24718	.16151	.10737
11	.94661	.89632	.84893	.80426	.72242	.64958	.58468	.52679	.47509	.42888	.35049	.28748	.21494	.13459	.08590
12	.94191	.88745	.83639	.78849	.70138	.62460	.55684	.49697	.44401	.39711	.31863	.25668	.18691	.11216	.06872
13	.93722	.87866	.82403	.77303	.68095	.60057	.53032	.46884	.41496	.36770	.28966	.22917	.16253	.09346	.05498
14	.93256	.86996	.81185	.75788	.66112	.57748	.50507	.44230	.38782	.34046	.26333	.20462	.14133	.07789	.04398
15	.92792	.86135	.79985	.74301	.64186	.55526	.48102	.41727	.36245	.31524	.23939	.18270	.12289	.06491	.03518
16	.92330	.85282	.78803	.72845	.62317	.53391	.45811	.39365	.33873	.29189	.21763	.16312	.10686	.05409	.02815
17	.91871	.84438	.77639	.71416	.60502	.51337	.43630	.37136	.31657	.27027	.19784	.14564	.09293	.04507	.02252
18	.91414	.83602	.76491	.70016	.58739	.49363	.41552	.35034	.29586	.25025	.17986	.13004	.08081	.03756	.01801
19	.90959	.82774	.75361	.68643	.57029	.47464	.39573	.33051	.27651	.23171	.16351	.11611	.07027	.03130	.01441
20	.90506	.81954	.74247	.67297	.55368	.45639	.37689	.31180	.25842	.21455	.14864	.10367	.06110	.02608	.01153
22	.89608	.80340	.72069	.64684	.52189	.42196	.34185	.27751	.22571	.18394	.12285	.08264	.04620	.01811	.00738
24	.88719	.78757	.69954	.62172	.49193	.39012	.31007	.24698	.19715	.15770	.10153	.06588	.03493	.01258	.00472
26	.87838	.77205	.67902	.59758	.46369	.36069	.28124	.21981	.17220	.13520	.08391	.05252	.02642	.00874	.00302
28	.86966	.75684	.65910	.57437	.43708	.33348	.25509	.19563	.15040	.11591	.06934	.04187	.01997	.00607	.00193
30	.86103	.74192	.63976	.55207	.41199	.30832	.23138	.17411	.13137	.09938	.05731	.03338	.01510	.00421	.00124
32	.85248	.72730	.62099	.53063	.38834	.28506	.20987	.15496	.11474	.08520	.04736	.02661	.01142	.00293	.00079
34	.84402	.71297	.60277	.51003	.36604	.26355	.19035	.13791	.10022	.07305	.03914	.02121	.00864	.00203	.00051
36	.83564	.69892	.58509	.49022	.34503	.24367	.17266	.12274	.08754	.06262	.03235	.01691	.00653	.00141	.00032
38	.82735	.68515	.56792	.47119	.32523	.22529	.15661	.10924	.07646	.05369	.02673	.01348	.00494	.00098	.00021
40	.81914	.67165	.55126	.45289	.30656	.20829	.14205	.09722	.06678	.04603	.02209	.01075	.00373	.00068	.00013
45	.79896	.63905	.51171	.41020	.26444	.17120	.11130	.07265	.04761	.03133	.01372	.00610	.00186	.00027	.00004
50	.77929	.60804	.47500	.37153	.22811	.14071	.08720	.05429	.03395	.02132	.00852	.00346	.00092	.00011	.00001
100	.60729	.36971	.22563	.13803	.05203	.01980	.00760	.00295	.00115	.00045	.00007	.00001	.00000	.00000	.00000

TABLE 3

Future Value of Annuity of $1 in Arrears

$$F_A = \frac{(1 + r)^n - 1}{r}$$

r = interest rate; n = number of payments

[handwritten note: "f at beginning of year ... both at ... either y + deduct $1"]

No. of Payments

= n	½%	1%	1½%	2%	3%	4%	5%	6%	7%	8%	10%	12%	15%	20%	25%
1	1.00000	1.00000	1.00000	1.00000	1.00000	1.00000	1.00000	1.00000	1.00000	1.00000	1.00000	1.00000	1.00000	1.00000	1.00000
2	2.00500	2.01000	2.01500	2.02000	2.03000	2.04000	2.05000	2.06000	2.07000	2.08000	2.10000	2.12000	2.15000	2.20000	2.25000
3	3.01503	3.03010	3.04523	3.06040	3.09090	3.12160	3.15250	3.18360	3.21490	3.24640	3.31000	3.37440	3.47250	3.64000	3.81250
4	4.03010	4.06040	4.09090	4.12161	4.18363	4.24646	4.31013	4.37462	4.43994	4.50611	4.64100	4.77933	4.99338	5.36800	5.76563
5	5.05025	5.10101	5.15227	5.20404	5.30914	5.41632	5.52563	5.63709	5.75074	5.86660	6.10510	6.35285	6.74238	7.44160	8.20703
6	6.07550	6.15202	6.22955	6.30812	6.46841	6.63298	6.80191	6.97532	7.15329	7.33593	7.71561	8.11519	8.75374	9.92992	11.25879
7	7.10588	7.21354	7.32299	7.43428	7.66246	7.89829	8.14201	8.39384	8.65402	8.92280	9.48717	10.08901	11.06680	12.91590	15.07349
8	8.14141	8.28567	8.43284	8.58297	8.89234	9.21423	9.54911	9.89747	10.25980	10.63663	11.43589	12.29969	13.72682	16.49908	19.84186
9	9.18212	9.36853	9.55933	9.75463	10.15911	10.58280	11.02656	11.49132	11.97799	12.48756	13.57948	14.77566	16.78584	20.79890	25.80232
10	10.22803	10.46221	10.70272	10.94972	11.46388	12.00611	12.57789	13.18079	13.81645	14.48656	15.93742	17.54874	20.30372	25.95868	33.25290
11	11.27917	11.56683	11.86326	12.16872	12.80780	13.48635	14.20679	14.97164	15.78360	16.64549	18.53117	20.65458	24.34928	32.15042	42.56613
12	12.33556	12.68250	13.04121	13.41209	14.19203	15.02581	15.91713	16.86994	17.88845	18.97713	21.38428	24.13313	29.00167	39.58050	54.20766
13	13.39724	13.80933	14.23683	14.68033	15.61779	16.62684	17.71298	18.88214	20.14064	21.49530	24.52271	28.02911	34.35192	48.49660	68.75958
14	14.46423	14.94742	15.45038	15.97394	17.08632	18.29191	19.59863	21.01507	22.55049	24.21492	27.97498	32.39260	40.50471	59.19592	86.94947
15	15.53655	16.09690	16.68214	17.29342	18.59891	20.02359	21.57856	23.27597	25.12902	27.15211	31.77248	37.27971	47.58041	72.03511	109.6868
16	16.61423	17.25786	17.93237	18.63929	20.15688	21.82453	23.65749	25.67253	27.88805	30.32428	35.94973	42.75328	55.71747	87.44213	138.1085
17	17.69730	18.43044	19.20136	20.01207	21.76159	23.69751	25.84037	28.21288	30.84022	33.75023	40.54470	48.88367	65.07509	105.9306	173.6357
18	18.78579	19.61475	20.48938	21.41231	23.41444	25.64541	28.13238	30.90565	33.99903	37.45024	45.59917	55.74971	75.83636	128.1167	218.0446
19	19.87972	20.81090	21.79672	22.84056	25.11687	27.67123	30.53900	33.75999	37.37896	41.44626	51.15909	63.43968	88.21181	154.7400	273.5558
20	20.97912	22.01900	23.12367	24.29737	26.87037	29.77808	33.06595	36.78559	40.99549	45.76196	57.27500	72.05244	102.44358	186.6880	342.9447
22	23.19443	24.47159	25.83758	27.29898	30.53678	34.24797	38.50521	43.39229	49.00574	55.45676	71.40275	92.50258	137.63164	271.0307	538.1011
24	25.43196	26.97346	28.63352	30.42186	34.42647	39.08260	44.50200	50.81558	58.17667	66.76476	88.49733	118.15524	184.16784	392.4842	843.0329
26	27.69191	29.52563	31.51397	33.67091	38.55304	44.31174	51.11345	59.15638	68.67647	79.95442	109.18177	150.33393	245.71197	567.3773	1319.489
28	29.97452	32.12910	34.48148	37.05121	42.93092	49.96758	58.40258	68.52811	80.69769	95.33883	134.20994	190.69889	327.10408	819.2233	2063.952
30	32.28002	34.78489	37.53868	40.56808	47.57542	56.08494	66.43885	79.05819	94.46079	113.28321	164.49402	241.33268	434.74515	1181.881	3227.174
32	34.60862	37.49407	40.68829	44.22703	52.50276	62.70147	75.29883	90.88978	110.21815	134.21354	201.13777	304.84772	577.10046	1704.109	5044.710
34	36.96058	40.25770	43.93309	48.03380	57.73018	69.85791	85.06696	104.18375	128.25876	158.62667	245.47670	384.52098	765.36535	2456.118	7884.609
36	39.33610	43.07688	47.27597	51.99437	63.27594	77.59831	95.83632	119.12087	148.91346	187.10215	299.12681	484.46312	1014.34568	3539.009	12321.95
38	41.73545	45.95272	50.71989	56.11494	69.15985	85.97034	107.70955	135.90421	172.56102	220.31595	364.04343	609.83053	1343.62216	5098.373	19255.30
40	44.15885	48.88637	54.26789	60.40198	75.40126	95.02552	120.79977	154.76197	199.63511	259.05652	442.59256	767.09142	1779.09031	7343.858	30088.66
45	50.32416	56.48107	63.61420	71.89271	92.71986	121.0294	159.7002	212.7435	285.7493	386.5056	718.9048	1358.230	3585.12846	18281.31	91831.50
50	56.64516	64.46318	73.68283	84.57940	112.7969	152.6671	209.3480	290.3359	406.5289	573.7702	1163.909	2400.018	7217.71628	45497.19	280255.7
100	129.33370	170.4814	228.8030	312.2323	607.2877	1237.624	2610.025	5638.368	12381.66	27484.52	137796.1	696010.5	783×10^4	414×10^6	196×10^8

Note: To convert from this table to values of an annuity in advance, determine the annuity in arrears above for one more period and subtract 1.00000.

TABLE 4

Present Value of Annuity of $1 in Arrears

$$P_A = \frac{1 - (1+r)^{-n}}{r} \times \$1.00$$

r = discount rate; n = number of payments

n Periods = Payments — Payments in Arrears

P_A (Value in Table 4) → $\sum$ (Individual Values from Table 2); P_F (Value in Table 4)

No. of Payments = n	½%	1%	1½%	2%	3%	4%	5%	6%	7%	8%	10%	12%	15%	20%	25%
1	.99502	.99010	.98522	.98039	.97087	.96154	.95238	.94340	.93458	.92593	.90909	.89286	.86957	.83333	.80000
2	1.98510	1.97040	1.95588	1.94156	1.91347	1.88609	1.85941	1.83339	1.80802	1.78326	1.73554	1.69005	1.62571	1.52778	1.44000
3	2.97025	2.94099	2.91220	2.88388	2.82861	2.77509	2.72325	2.67301	2.62432	2.57710	2.48685	2.40183	2.28323	2.10648	1.95200
4	3.95050	3.90197	3.85438	3.80773	3.71710	3.62990	3.54595	3.46511	3.38721	3.31213	3.16987	3.03735	2.85498	2.58873	2.36160
5	4.92587	4.85343	4.78264	4.71346	4.57971	4.45182	4.32948	4.21236	4.10020	3.99271	3.79079	3.60478	3.35216	2.99061	2.68928
6	5.89638	5.79548	5.69719	5.60143	5.41719	5.24214	5.07569	4.91732	4.76654	4.62288	4.35526	4.11141	3.78448	3.32551	2.95142
7	6.86207	6.72819	6.59821	6.47199	6.23028	6.00205	5.78637	5.58238	5.38929	5.20637	4.86842	4.56376	4.16042	3.60459	3.16114
8	7.82296	7.65168	7.48593	7.32548	7.01969	6.73274	6.46321	6.20979	5.97130	5.74664	5.33493	4.96764	4.48732	3.83716	3.32891
9	8.77906	8.56602	8.36052	8.16224	7.78611	7.43533	7.10782	6.80169	6.51523	6.24689	5.75902	5.32825	4.77158	4.03097	3.46313
10	9.73041	9.47130	9.22218	8.98259	8.53020	8.11090	7.72173	7.36009	7.02358	6.71008	6.14457	5.65022	5.01877	4.19247	3.57050
11	10.67703	10.36763	10.07112	9.78685	9.25262	8.76048	8.30641	7.88687	7.49867	7.13896	6.49506	5.93770	5.23371	4.32706	3.65640
12	11.61893	11.25508	10.90751	10.57534	9.95400	9.38507	8.86325	8.38384	7.94269	7.53608	6.81369	6.19437	5.42062	4.43922	3.72512
13	12.55615	12.13374	11.73153	11.34837	10.63496	9.98565	9.39357	8.85268	8.35765	7.90378	7.10336	6.42355	5.58315	4.53268	3.78010
14	13.48871	13.00370	12.54338	12.10625	11.29607	10.56312	9.89864	9.29498	8.74547	8.24424	7.36669	6.62817	5.72448	4.61057	3.82408
15	14.41662	13.86505	13.34323	12.84926	11.93794	11.11839	10.37966	9.71225	9.10791	8.55948	7.60608	6.81086	5.84737	4.67547	3.85926
16	15.33993	14.71787	14.13126	13.57771	12.56110	11.65230	10.83777	10.10590	9.44665	8.85137	7.82371	6.97399	5.95423	4.72956	3.88741
17	16.25863	15.56225	14.90765	14.29187	13.16612	12.16567	11.27407	10.47726	9.76322	9.12164	8.02155	7.11963	6.04716	4.77463	3.90993
18	17.17277	16.39827	15.67256	14.99203	13.75351	12.65930	11.68959	10.82760	10.05909	9.37189	8.20141	7.24967	6.12797	4.81219	3.92794
19	18.08236	17.22601	16.42617	15.67846	14.32380	13.13394	12.08532	11.15812	10.33560	9.60360	8.36492	7.36578	6.19823	4.84350	3.94235
20	18.98742	18.04555	17.16864	16.35143	14.87747	13.59033	12.46221	11.46992	10.59401	9.81815	8.51356	7.46944	6.25933	4.86958	3.95388
22	20.78406	19.66038	18.62082	17.65805	15.93692	14.45112	13.16300	12.04158	11.06124	10.20074	8.77154	7.64465	6.35866	4.90943	3.97049
24	22.56287	21.24339	20.03041	18.91393	16.93554	15.24696	13.79864	12.55036	11.46933	10.52876	8.98474	7.78432	6.43377	4.93710	3.98111
26	24.32402	22.79520	21.39863	20.12104	17.87684	15.98277	14.37519	13.00317	11.82578	10.80998	9.16095	7.89566	6.49056	4.95632	3.98791
28	26.06769	24.31644	22.72672	21.28127	18.76411	16.66306	14.89813	13.40616	12.13711	11.05108	9.30657	7.98442	6.53351	4.96967	3.99226
30	27.79405	25.80771	24.01584	22.39646	19.60044	17.29203	15.37245	13.76483	12.40904	11.25778	9.42691	8.05518	6.56598	4.97894	3.99505
32	29.50328	27.26959	25.26714	23.46833	20.38877	17.87355	15.80268	14.08404	12.64656	11.43500	9.52638	8.11159	6.59053	4.98537	3.99683
34	31.19555	28.70267	26.48173	24.49859	21.13184	18.41120	16.19290	14.36814	12.85401	11.58693	9.60857	8.15656	6.60910	4.98984	3.99797
36	32.87102	30.10751	27.66068	25.48884	21.83225	18.90828	16.54685	14.62099	13.03521	11.71719	9.67651	8.19241	6.62314	4.99295	3.99870
38	34.52985	31.48466	28.80505	26.44064	22.49246	19.36786	16.86789	14.84602	13.19347	11.82887	9.73265	8.22099	6.63375	4.99510	3.99917
40	36.17223	32.83469	29.91585	27.35548	23.11477	19.79277	17.15909	15.04630	13.33171	11.92461	9.77905	8.24378	6.64178	4.99660	3.99947
45	40.20720	36.09451	32.55234	29.49016	24.51871	20.72004	17.77407	15.45583	13.60552	12.10840	9.86281	8.28252	6.65429	4.99863	3.99983
50	44.14279	39.19612	34.99969	31.42361	25.72976	21.48218	18.25593	15.76186	13.80075	12.23348	9.91481	8.30450	6.66051	4.99945	3.99994
100	78.54264	63.02888	51.62470	43.09835	31.59891	24.50500	19.84791	16.61755	14.26925	12.49432	9.99927	8.33323	6.66666	5.00000	4.00000

Note: To convert from this table to values of an annuity in advance, determine the annuity in arrears above for one fewer period and add 1.00000.

GLOSSARY

The definitions of many words and phrases in the Glossary use other Glossary terms. In a given definition (definiens), we *italicize* terms that themselves (or variants thereof) appear elsewhere under their own listings (as definienda). The cross-references generally take one of two forms:

1. **absorption costing.** See *full absorption costing.*
2. **ABC.** *Activity-based costing.*

Form 1 refers you to another term for discussion of this **bold-faced** term (definiendum). Form 2 tells you that this **bold-faced** term (definiendum) is synonymous with the *italicized* term, which you can consult for discussion if necessary.

A

AAA. *American Accounting Association.*

ABC. *Activity-based costing.*

abnormal spoilage. Actual spoilage exceeding that expected when operations are normally efficient. Usual practice treats this cost as an *expense* of the period rather than as a *product cost.* Contrast with *normal spoilage.*

absorbed overhead. *Overhead costs* allocated to individual products at some *overhead rate;* also called *applied overhead.*

absorption costing. See *full absorption costing.*

Abstracts of the EITF. See *Emerging Issues Task Force.*

accelerated depreciation. In calculating *depreciation* charges, any method in which the charges become progressively smaller each period. Examples are *double declining-balance depreciation* and *sum-of-the-years'-digits depreciation* methods.

account. A device for representing the amount (*balance*) for any line (or a part of a line) in the *balance sheet* or *income statement.* Because income statement accounts explain the changes in the balance sheet account Retained Earnings, the definition does not require the last three words of the preceding sentence. An account is any device for accumulating additions and subtractions relating to a single *asset, liability,* or *owners' equity* item, including *revenues* and *expenses.*

account analysis method. A method of separating *fixed costs* from *variable costs* based on the analyst's judgment of whether the cost is fixed or variable. Based on

their names alone, the analyst might classify *direct labor (material) costs* as variable and *depreciation* on a factory building as fixed. In our experience, this method results in too many fixed costs and not enough variable costs—that is, analysts have insufficient information to judge management's ability to reduce costs that appear to be fixed.

accountability center. *Responsibility center.*

accountancy. The British word for *accounting.* In the United States, it means the theory and practice of accounting.

accountant's opinion. *Auditor's report.*

accountant's report. *Auditor's report.*

accounting. A system conveying information about a specific *entity.* The information is in financial terms and will appear in accounting statements only if the accountant can measure it with reasonable precision. The *AICPA* defines accounting as a service activity whose "function is to provide quantitative information, primarily financial in nature, about economic entities that is intended to be useful in making economic decisions."

accounting conventions. Methods or procedures used in accounting. Writers tend to use this term when the method or procedure has not yet received official authoritative sanction by a pronouncement of a group such as the *APB, EITF, FASB,* or *SEC.* Contrast with *accounting principles.*

accounting cycle. The sequence of accounting procedures starting with *journal entries* for ast due; normally, a *current liability.*

accounting entity. See *entity.*

accounting equation. *Assets = Equities; Assets = Liabilities + Owners' Equity.*

accounting event. Any occurrence that is recorded in the accounting records.

accounting methods. *Accounting principles;* procedures for carrying out accounting principles.

accounting period. The time period between consecutive *balance sheets;* the time period for which the firm prepares *financial statements* that measure *flows,* such as the *income statement* and the *statement of cash flows.*

accounting policies. *Accounting principles* adopted by a specific *entity.*

accounting principles. The methods or procedures used in accounting for events reported in the *financial statements.* We tend to use this term when the method or procedure has received official authoritative sanction from a pronouncement of a group such as the *APB, EITF, FASB,* or *SEC.* Contrast with *accounting conventions* and *conceptual framework.*

Accounting Principles Board. See *APB.*

accounting procedures. See *accounting principles.* However, this term usually refers to the methods for implementing accounting principles.

accounting rate of return. Income for a period divided by average investment during the period; based on income, rather than discounted cash flows, and hence a poor decision-making aid or tool. See *ratio.*

accounting standards. *Accounting principles.*

accounting system. The procedures for collecting and summarizing financial data in a firm.

accounts payable. A *liability* representing an amount owed to a *creditor,* usually arising from the purchase of *merchandise* or materials and supplies, not necessarily due or past due; normally, a *current liability.*

accounts receivable. Claims against a *debtor* usually arising from sales or services rendered, not necessarily due or past due; normally, a *current asset.*

accounts receivable turnover. Net sales on account divided by average accounts receivable. See *ratio.*

accretion. When a *book value* grows over time, such as a *bond* originally issued at a *discount,* the correct technical term is "accretion," not "amortization." This term also refers to an increase in economic worth through physical change caused by natural growth, usually said of a natural resource such as timber. Contrast with *appreciation.* See *amortization.*

accrual. Recognition of an *expense* (or *revenue*) and the related *liability* (or *asset*) resulting from an *accounting event,* frequently from the passage of time but not signaled by an explicit cash transaction; for example, the recognition of interest expense or revenue (or wages, salaries, or rent) at the end of a period even though the firm makes no explicit cash transaction at that time. Cash flow follows accounting recognition; contrast with *deferral.*

accrual basis of accounting. The method of recognizing *revenues* as a firm sells *goods* (or delivers them) and as it renders *services,* independent of the time when it receives cash. This system recognizes *expenses* in the period when it recognizes the related revenue, independent of the time when it pays out cash. *SFAC No. 1* says "Accrual accounting attempts to record the financial effects on an enterprise of transactions and other events and circumstances that have cash consequences for the enterprise in the periods in which those transactions, events, and circumstances occur rather than only in the periods in which cash is received or paid by the enter-

prise." Contrast with the *cash basis of accounting.* See *accrual* and *deferral.* We could more correctly call this "accrual/deferral" accounting.

accrue. See *accrued,* and contrast with *incur.*

accrued. Said of a *revenue (expense)* that the firm has earned (recognized) even though the related *receivable (payable)* has a future due date. We prefer not to use this adjective as part of an account title. Thus, we prefer to use Interest Receivable (Payable) as the account title rather than Accrued Interest Receivable (Payable). See *matching convention; accrual.* Contrast with *incur.*

accumulated depreciation. A preferred title for the asset *contra account* that shows the sum of *depreciation* charges on an asset since the time the firm acquired it. Other account titles are *allowance* for *depreciation* (acceptable term) and *reserve* for *depreciation* (unacceptable term).

accurate presentation. The qualitative accounting objective suggesting that information reported in financial statements should correspond as precisely as possible with the economic effects underlying transactions and events. See *fair presentation* and *full disclosure.*

acid test ratio. *Quick ratio.*

acquisition cost. Of an *asset,* the net *invoice* price plus all *expenditures* to place and ready the asset for its intended use. The other expenditures might include legal fees, transportation charges, and installation costs.

activity accounting. *Responsibility accounting.*

activity-based costing (ABC). Method of assigning *indirect costs,* including nonmanufacturing *overhead costs,* to products and services. ABC assumes that almost all overhead costs associate with activities within the firm and vary with respect to the *drivers* of those activities. Some practitioners suggest that ABC attempts to find the drivers for all indirect costs; these people note that in the long run, all costs are *variable,* so *fixed* indirect costs do not occur. This method first assigns costs to activities and then to products based on the products' usages of the activities.

activity-based management (ABM). Analysis and management of activities required to make a product or produce a service. Focuses attention to enhance activities that add value to the customer and reduce activities that do not. Its goal is to satisfy customer needs while making smaller demands on costly resources. Sometimes called "activity management."

activity basis. *Costs* are *variable* or *fixed* (*incremental* or *unavoidable*) with respect to some activity, such as production of units (or the undertaking of some new project). Usage calls this activity the "activity basis."

activity center. Unit of the organization that performs a set of tasks.

activity variance. *Sales volume variance.*

actual cost (basis). *Acquisition* or *historical cost.* Also contrast with *standard cost.*

actual costing (system). Method of allocating costs to products using actual *direct materials*, actual *direct labor*, and actual *factory overhead.* Contrast with *normal costing* and *standard costing.*

actuarial. An adjective describing computations or analyses that involve both *compound interest* and probabilities, such as the computation of the *present value* of a life-contingent *annuity.* Some writers use the word even for computations involving only one of the two.

additional paid-in capital. An alternative acceptable title for the capital contributed in excess of par (or stated) value account.

additional processing cost. *Costs* incurred in processing *joint products* after the *split-off point.*

adjunct account. An *account* that accumulates additions to another account. For example, Premium on Bonds Payable is adjunct to the liability Bonds Payable; the effective liability is the sum of the two account balances at a given date. Contrast with *contra account.*

adjusted acquisition (historical) cost. Sometimes said of the *book value* of a *plant asset*, that is, *acquisition cost* less *accumulated depreciation.* Also, cost adjusted to a *constant dollar* amount to reflect *general price level changes.*

adjusted trial balance. *Trial balance* taken after *adjusting entries* but before *closing entries.* Contrast with *pre-* and *post-closing trial balances.* See *unadjusted trial balance* and *post-closing trial balance.*

adjusting entry. An entry made at the end of an *accounting period* to record a *transaction* or other *accounting event* that the firm has not yet recorded or has improperly recorded during the accounting period; an entry to update the accounts.

administrative costs (expenses). *Costs (expenses)* incurred for the firm as a whole, in contrast with specific functions, such as manufacturing or selling; includes such items as salaries of top executives, general office rent, legal fees, and auditing fees.

advances from (by) customers. A preferred title for the *liability* account representing *receipts* of *cash* in advance of delivering the *goods* or rendering the *service.* After the firm delivers the goods or services, it will recognize *revenue.* This is sometimes called "deferred revenue" or "deferred income."

advances to suppliers. A preferred term for the *asset* account representing *disbursements* of cash in advance of receiving *assets* or *services.*

affiliated company. A company controlling or controlled by another company.

agency theory. A branch of economics relating the behavior of *principals* (such as owner nonmanagers or bosses) and that of their *agents* (such as nonowner managers or subordinates). The principal assigns responsibility and authority to the agent, but the agent's own risks and preferences differ from those of the principal. The principal cannot observe all activities of the agent. Both the principal and the agent must consider the differing risks and preferences in designing incentive contracts.

agent. One authorized to transact business, including executing contracts, for another.

aging accounts receivable. The process of classifying *accounts receivable* by the time elapsed since the claim came into existence for the purpose of estimating the amount of uncollectible accounts receivable as of a given date. See *allowance for uncollectibles.*

aging schedule. A listing of *accounts receivable*, classified by age, used in *aging accounts receivable.*

AICPA (American Institute of Certified Public Accountants). The national organization that represents *CPAs.* It oversees the writing and grading of the Uniform CPA Examination. Each state sets its own requirements for becoming a CPA in that state. See *certified public accountant.*

all-capital earnings rate. *Rate of return on assets.*

all-current method. *Foreign currency translation* in which all *financial statement* items are translated at the *current exchange rate.*

all-inclusive (income) concept. A concept that does not distinguish between *operating* and *nonoperating revenues* and *expenses.* Thus, the only entries to retained earnings are for *net income* and *dividends.* Under this concept the *income statement* reports all *income, gains*, and *losses*; thus, net income includes events usually reported as prior-period adjustments and as corrections of errors. *GAAP* do not include this concept in its pure form, but *APB Opinions Nos. 9 and 30* move far in this direction. They do permit retained earnings entries for prior-period adjustments and correction of errors.

allocate. To divide or spread a *cost* from one *account* into several accounts, to several products or activities, or to several periods.

allocation base. The systematic method that assigns *joint costs* to *cost objectives.* For example, a firm might assign the cost of a truck to periods based on miles driven during the period; the allocation base is miles. Or, the firm might assign the cost of a factory supervisor to a product based on *direct labor* hours; the allocation base is direct labor hours.

allowance. A balance sheet *contra account* generally used for *receivables* and depreciable assets.

allowance for uncollectibles (accounts receivable). A *contra account* that shows the estimated amount of *accounts receivable* the firm expects not to collect. When the firm uses such an allowance, the actual write-off of specific accounts receivable (*debit* allowance, *credit* specific customer's account) does not affect *revenue* or *expense* at the time of the write-off. The firm reduces revenue when it debits *bad debt expense* (or, preferred by your authors, a revenue contra account) and credits the allowance; the firm can base the amount of the credit to the allowance on a percentage of sales on account for a period of time or compute it from *aging accounts receivable*. This contra account enables the firm to show an estimate of the amount of receivables that it expects to collect without identifying specific uncollectible accounts. See *allowance method*.

allowance method. A method of attempting to match all *expenses* of a transaction with their associated *revenues;* usually involves a debit to expense and a credit to an *estimated liability*, such as for estimated warranty expenditures, or a debit to a revenue (*contra*) account and a credit to an asset (*contra*) account, such as in some firms' accounting for uncollectible accounts. See *allowance for uncollectibles* for further explanation. When the firm uses the allowance method for *sales discounts*, the firm records sales at gross invoice prices (not reduced by the amounts of discounts made available). The firm debits an estimate of the amount of discounts to be taken to a revenue contra account and *credits* an allowance account, shown contra to *accounts receivable*.

American Accounting Association (AAA). An organization primarily for academic accountants, but open to all interested in accounting. It publishes the *Accounting Review* and several other journals.

American Institute of Certified Public Accountants. See *AICPA*.

amortization. Strictly speaking, the process of liquidating or extinguishing ("bringing to death") a *debt* with a series of payments to the *creditor* (or to a *sinking fund*). From that usage has evolved a related use involving the accounting for the payments themselves: "amortization schedule" for a mortgage, which is a table showing the allocation between *interest* and *principal*. The term has come to mean writing off ("liquidating") the cost of an asset. In this context it means the general process of *allocating* the *acquisition cost* of an asset either to the periods of benefit as an *expense* or to *inventory* accounts as a *product cost*. This is called *depreciation* for *plant assets, depletion* for *wasting assets* (natural resources), and "amortization" for *intangibles*. *SFAC No. 6* refers to amortization as "the accounting process of reducing an amount by periodic payments or write-downs." The expressions "unamortized debt discount or premium" and "to amortize debt discount or premium" relate to *accruals*, not to *deferrals*. The expressions "amortization of long-term assets" and "to amortize long-term assets" refer to deferrals, not accruals. Contrast with *accretion*.

analysis of variances. See *variance investigation*.

annual report. A report prepared once a year for shareholders and other interested parties. Includes a *balance sheet*, an *income statement*, a *statement of cash flows*, a reconciliation of changes in *owners' equity* accounts, a *summary of significant accounting principles*, other explanatory *notes*, the *auditor's report*, and comments from management about the year's events. See *financial statements*.

annuitant. One who receives an *annuity*.

annuity. A series of payments of equal amount, usually made at equally spaced time intervals.

annuity certain. An *annuity* payable for a definite number of periods. Contrast with *contingent annuity*.

annuity due. An *annuity* whose first payment occurs at the start of period 1 (or at the end of period 0). Contrast with *annuity in arrears*.

annuity in advance. An *annuity due*.

annuity in arrears. An *ordinary annuity* whose first payment occurs at the end of the first period.

APB. Accounting Principles Board of the *AICPA*. It set *accounting principles* from 1959 through 1973, issuing 31 *APB Opinions* and 4 *APB Statements*. The *FASB* superseded it.

APB Opinion. The name for pronouncements of the *APB* that compose much of *generally accepted accounting principles*; the APB issued 31 *APB Opinions* from 1962 through 1973.

applied cost. A *cost* that a firm has *allocated* to a department, product, or activity; not necessarily based on actual costs incurred.

applied overhead. *Overhead costs* charged to departments, products, or activities. Also called *absorbed overhead*.

appreciation. An increase in economic value caused by rising market prices for an *asset*. Contrast with *accretion*.

approximate net realizable value method. A method of assigning joint costs to *joint products* based on revenues minus *additional processing costs* of the end products.

arbitrary. Having no causation basis. Accounting theorists and practitioners often, properly, say, "Some cost allocations are arbitrary." In that sense, the accountant does not mean that the allocations are capricious or haphazard but does mean that theory suggests no unique solution to the allocation problem at hand. Accountants require that arbitrary allocations be systematic, rational, and consistently followed over time.

arm's length. A transaction negotiated by unrelated parties, both acting in their own self-interests; the basis for a *fair market value* estimation or computation.

articulate. The relation between any operating statement (for example, *income statement* or *statement of cash flows*) and comparative balance sheets, where the operating statement explains (or reconciles) the change in some major balance sheet category (for example, *retained earnings* or *working capital*).

asset. The *FASB* defines assets as "probable future economic benefits obtained or controlled by a particular entity as a result of past transactions. . . . An asset has three essential characteristics: (a) it embodies a probable future benefit that involves a capacity, singly or in combination with other assets, to contribute directly or indirectly to future net cash inflows, (b) a particular entity can obtain the benefit and control others' access to it, and (c) the transaction or other event giving rise to the entity's right to or control of the benefit has already occurred." A footnote points out that "probable" means that which we can reasonably expect or believe but that is not certain or proved. You may understand condition (c) better if you think of it as requiring that a future benefit cannot be an asset if it arises from an *executory contract*, a mere exchange of promises. Receiving a purchase order from a customer provides a future benefit, but it is an executory contract, so the order cannot be an asset. An asset may be *tangible* or *intangible*, short-term (current) or long-term (noncurrent).

asset turnover. Net sales divided by average assets. See *ratio*.

at par. A *bond* or *preferred shares* issued (or selling) at *face amount*.

attest. Rendering of an *opinion* by an auditor that the *financial statements* are fair. Common usage calls this procedure the "attest function" of the CPA. See *fair presentation*.

attestor. Typically independent *CPAs*, who *audit financial statements* prepared by management for the benefit of users. The *FASB* describes accounting's constituency as comprising preparers, attestors, and users.

attribute measured. The particular *cost* reported in the balance sheet. When making physical measurements, such as of a person, one needs to decide the units with which to measure, such as inches or centimeters or pounds or grams. One chooses the attribute height or weight independently of the measuring unit, English or metric. Conventional accounting uses *historical cost* as the attribute measured and *nominal dollars* as the measuring unit. Some theorists argue that accounting would better serve readers if it used *current cost* as the attribute measured. Others argue that accounting would better serve readers if it used *constant dollars* as the measuring unit. Some, including us, think accounting should change both the measuring unit and the attribute measured. One can measure the attribute historical cost in nominal dollars or in constant dollars. One can also measure the attribute current cost in nominal dollars or constant dollars. Choosing between the two attributes and the two measuring units implies four different accounting systems. Each of these four has its uses.

attribute(s) sampling. The use of sampling technique in which the observer assesses each item selected on the basis of whether it has a particular qualitative characteristic in order to ascertain the rate of occurrence of this characteristic in the population. See also *estimation sampling*. Compare *variables sampling*. Example of attributes sampling: Take a sample population of people, note the fraction male (say, 40 percent), and then infer that the entire population contains 40 percent males. Example of variables sampling: Take a sample population of people, observe the weight of each sample point, compute the mean of those sampled people's weights (say, 160 pounds), and then infer that the mean weight of the entire population equals 160 pounds.

audit. Systematic inspection of accounting records involving analyses, tests, and *confirmations*. See *internal audit*.

audit committee. A committee of the board of directors of a *corporation*, usually comprising outside directors, who nominate the independent auditors and discuss the auditors' work with them. If the auditors believe the shareholders should know about certain matters, the auditors, in principle, first bring these matters to the attention of the audit committee; in practice, the auditors may notify management before they notify the audit committee.

audit program. The procedures followed by the *auditor* in carrying out the *audit*.

audit trail. A reference accompanying an entry, or *post,* to an underlying source record or document. Efficiently checking the accuracy of accounting entries requires an audit trail. See *cross-reference*.

auditing standards. Standards promulgated by the *AICPA*, including general standards, standards of field work, and standards of reporting. According to the

AICPA, these standards "deal with the measures of the quality of the performance and the objectives to be attained" rather than with specific *auditing* procedures.

auditor. Without modifying adjective, usually refers to an external auditor—one who checks the accuracy, fairness, and general acceptability of accounting records and statements and then *attests* to them. See *internal auditor.*

auditor's opinion. *Auditor's report.*

auditor's report. The auditor's statement of the work done and an opinion of the *financial statements.* The auditor usually gives unqualified ("clean") opinions but may qualify them, or the auditor may disclaim an opinion in the report. Often called the "accountant's report."

available for sale, securities. *Marketable securities* a firm holds that are classified as neither trading securities nor held-to-maturity (debt) securities. This classification is important in *SFAS No. 115,* which requires the owner to carry marketable equity securities on the balance sheet at market value, not at cost. Under *SFAS No. 115,* the income statement reports *holding gains and losses* on trading securities but not on securities available for sale. The required accounting *credits* (*debits*) holding gains (losses) on securities available for sale directly to an *owners' equity* account. On sale, the firm reports realized gain or loss as the difference between the selling price and the original cost, for trading securities, and as the difference between the selling price and the book value at the beginning of the period of sale, for securities available for sale and for debt securities held to maturity. By their nature, however, the firm will only rarely sell debt securities "held to maturity."

average. The arithmetic mean of a set of numbers; obtained by summing the items and dividing by the number of items.

average collection period of receivables. See *ratio.*

average-cost flow assumption. An inventory *flow assumption* in which the cost of units equals the *weighted average* cost of the *beginning inventory* and purchases. See *inventory equation.*

average tax rate. The rate found by dividing *income tax* expense by *net income* before taxes. Contrast with *marginal tax rate.*

avoidable cost. A *cost* that ceases if a firm discontinues an activity. An *incremental* or *variable cost.* See *programmed cost.*

B

backflush costing. A method of *allocating indirect costs* and *overhead;* used by companies that hope to have zero or small *work-in-process inventory* at the end of the period. The method *debits* all *product costs* to *cost* of goods sold (or *finished goods inventory*) during the period. To the extent that work in process actually exists at the end of the period, the method then debits work-in-process and *credits* cost of goods sold (or finished goods inventory). This method is "backflush" in the sense that costing systems ordinarily, but not in this case, allocate first to work in process and then forward to cost of goods sold or to finished goods. Here, the process allocates first to cost of goods sold (or finished goods) and then, later if necessary, to work-in-process.

backlog. Orders for which a firm has insufficient *inventory* on hand for current delivery and will fill in a later period.

bad debt. An *uncollectible account;* see *bad debt expense.*

bad debt expense. The name for an *account debited* in both the *allowance method* for *uncollectible accounts* and the direct write-off method. Under the allowance method, some prefer to treat the account as a revenue contra, not as an expense, and give it an account title such as Uncollectibles Accounts Adjustment.

bailout period. In a *capital budgeting* context, the total time that elapses before accumulated cash inflows from a project, including the potential *salvage value* of assets at various times, equal or exceed the accumulated cash outflows. Contrast with *payback period,* which assumes completion of the project and uses terminal salvage value. Bailout, in contrast with payback, takes into account, at least to some degree, the *present value* of the cash flows after the termination date that the analyst is considering. The potential salvage value at any time includes some estimate of the flows that can occur after that time.

balance. As a noun, the opening balance in an *account* plus the amounts of increases less the amounts of decreases. (In the absence of a modifying adjective, the term means closing balance, in contrast to opening balance. The closing balance for a period becomes the opening balance for the next period.) As a verb, "balance" means to find the value of the arithmetic expression described above.

balance sheet. Statement of financial position that shows Total *Assets* = Total *Liabilities* + *Owners' Equity.* The balance sheet usually classifies Total Assets as (1) *current assets,* (2) *investments,* (3) *property, plant, and equipment,* or (4) *intangible assets.* The balance sheet accounts composing Total Liabilities usually appear under the headings Current Liabilities and Long-term Liabilities.

balance sheet account. An account that can appear on a balance sheet. A *permanent account*; contrast with *temporary account.*

balanced scorecard. A set of performance targets, not all set in dollar amounts, for setting an organization's goals for its individual employees or groups or divisions. A community relations employee might, for example, set targets in terms of number of employee hours devoted to local charitable purposes.

balloon. Most *mortgage* and *installment loans* require relatively equal periodic payments. Sometimes, the loan requires relatively equal periodic payments with a large final payment. Usage calls the large final payment a "balloon" payment and the loan a "balloon" loan. Although a coupon bond meets this definition, usage seldom, if ever, applies this term to bond loans.

bankrupt. Occurs when a company's *liabilities* exceed its *assets* and the firm or one of its creditors has filed a legal petition that the bankruptcy court has accepted under the bankruptcy law. A bankrupt firm is usually, but need not be, insolvent.

basic earnings per share (BEPS). The *FASB* proposes, following guidance from the *IASC*, to replace primary earnings per share computations and disclosures with basic earnings-per-share computations and disclosures. Basic earnings per share will equal *net income* attributable to common shareholders divided by the *weighted-average* number of common shares outstanding during the period. See *primary earnings per share (PEPS)* for contrast. Because BEPS does not deal with common-stock equivalents, it will almost always give a larger earnings-per-share figure than PEPS.

basis. *Acquisition cost*, or some substitute therefor, of an *asset* or *liability* used in computing gain or loss on disposition or retirement; *attribute measured*. This term appears in both financial and *tax* reporting, but the basis of a given item need not be the same for both purposes.

basket purchase. Purchase of a group of *assets* (and *liabilities*) for a single price; the acquiring firm must assign *costs* to each item so that it can record the individual items with their separate amounts in the *accounts*.

bear. One who believes that security prices will fall. A "bear market" refers to a time when stock prices are generally declining. Contrast with *bull*.

beginning inventory. Valuation of *inventory* on hand at the beginning of the *accounting period;* equals *ending inventory* from the preceding period.

behavioral congruence. *Goal congruence.*

benchmarking. Process of measuring a firm's performance, products, and services against standards based on best levels of performance achievable or, sometimes, achieved by other firms.

BEPS. *Basic earnings per share.*

bid. An offer to purchase, or the amount of the offer.

Big Six. The six largest U.S. *public accounting* partnerships; in alphabetical order: Arthur Andersen & Co.; Coopers & Lybrand; Deloitte & Touche; Ernst & Young; KPMG Peat Marwick; and Price Waterhouse.

bill. An *invoice* of charges and *terms of sale* for *goods* and *services;* also, a piece of currency.

bill of materials. A specification of the quantities of *direct materials* a firm expects to use to produce a given job or quantity of output.

board. *Board of directors.*

board of directors. The governing body of a corporation; elected by the shareholders.

bond. A certificate to show evidence of debt. The *par value* is the *principal* or *face amount* of the bond payable at maturity. The coupon rate is the amount of the yearly payments divided by the principal amount. Coupon bonds have attached to them coupons that the holder can redeem at stated dates. Increasingly, firms issue not coupon bonds but instead registered bonds, where the firm or its agent keeps track of the owner. Normally, bonds call for semiannual payments.

bond ratings. Ratings of corporate and municipal *bond* issues by Moody's Investors Service and by Standard & Poor's Corporation, based on the issuer's existing *debt* level, its previous record of payment, the coupon rate on the bonds, and the safety of the *assets* or *revenues* that are committed to paying off *principal* and *interest*. Moody's top rating is Aaa; Standard & Poor's is AAA.

bond redemption. Retirement of *bonds.*

bond refunding. To incur *debt*, usually through the issue of new *bonds*, intending to use the proceeds to retire an *outstanding* bond issue.

bonus. Premium over normal *wage* or *salary*, paid usually for meritorious performance.

book. As a verb, to record a transaction; as a noun, usually plural, the *journals* and *ledgers*; as an adjective, see *book value.*

book cost. *Book value.*

book inventory. An *inventory* amount that results not from physical count but from the amount of beginning inventory plus *invoice* amounts of net purchases less invoice amounts of requisitions or withdrawals; implies a *perpetual inventory* method.

book of original entry. *Journal.*

book value. The amount shown in the books or in the *accounts* for an *asset, liability*, or *owners' equity* item. The term is generally used to refer to the *net* amount of an asset or group of assets shown in the account that records the asset and reductions, such as for *amortization*, in its cost. Of a firm, it refers to the excess of total assets over total liabilities; *net assets.*

book value per share of common stock. Common *shareholders' equity* divided by the number of shares of common stock outstanding. See *ratio*.

bookkeeping. The process of analyzing and recording transactions in the accounting records.

borrower. See *loan*.

breakeven analysis. See *breakeven chart*.

breakeven chart. Two kinds of breakeven charts appear here. The charts use the information for a month shown below. Revenue is $30 per unit.

Cost Classification	Variable Cost, Per Unit	Fixed Cost, Per Month
Manufacturing costs:		
Direct material	$ 4	—
Direct labor	9	—
Overhead.	4	$3,060
Total manufacturing costs. .	$17	$3,060
Selling, general, and administrative costs.	5	1,740
Total costs	$22	$4,800

The cost-volume-profit graph presents the relation between changes in volume to the amount of *profit*, or *income*. Such a graph shows total *revenue* and total *costs* for each volume level, and the user reads profit or loss at any volume directly from the chart. The profit-volume graph does not show revenues and costs but more readily indicates profit (or loss) at various output levels. Keep in mind two caveats about these graphs:

1. Although the curve depicting *variable cost* and total cost appears as a straight line for its entire length, at low or high levels of output, variable cost will probably differ from $22 per unit. The variable cost figure usually results from studies of operations at some broad central area of production, called the *relevant range*. The chart will not usually provide accurate results for low (or high) levels of activity. For this reason, the total cost and the profit-loss curves sometimes appear as dotted lines at lower (or higher) volume levels.

2. This chart, simplistically, assumes a single-product firm. For a multiproduct firm, the horizontal axis would have to be stated in dollars rather than in physical units of output. Breakeven charts for multiproduct firms necessarily assume that the firm sells constant proportions of the several products so that changes in this mixture, as well as in costs or selling prices, invalidate such a chart.

(a) Cost-Volume-Profit Graph

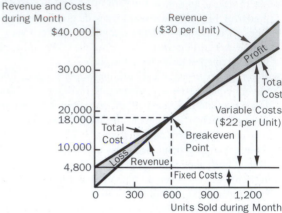

(b) Profit-Volume Graph

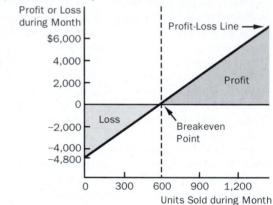

breakeven point. The volume of sales required so that total *revenues* equal total *costs;* may be expressed in units (*fixed costs/contribution per unit*) or in sales dollars [selling price per unit × (fixed costs/contribution per unit)].

budget. A financial plan that a firm uses to estimate the results of future operations; frequently used to help control future operations. In governmental operations, budgets often become the law. See *standard costs* for further elaboration and contrast.

budgeted cost. See *standard costs* for definition and contrast.

budgeted statements. *Pro forma statements* prepared before the event or period occurs.

bull. One who believes that security prices will rise. A "bull market" refers to a time when stock prices are generally rising. Contrast with *bear*.

burden. See *overhead costs*.

burn rate. A new business usually begins life with cash-absorbing operating losses but with a limited amount of cash. The "burn rate" measures how long the new business can survive before operating losses must stop or the firm must receive a new infusion of cash. Writers usually express the burn rate in months.

business entity. *Entity*.

by-product. A *joint product* whose sales value is so small relative to the sales value of the other joint product(s) that it does not receive normal accounting treatment. The costs assigned to by-products reduce the costs of the main product(s). Accounting allocates by-products a share of joint costs such that the expected gain or loss at their sale is zero. Thus, by-products appear in the *accounts* at *net realizable value*.

bylaws. The rules adopted by the shareholders of a corporation; specify the general methods for carrying out the functions of the corporation.

c

capacity. Stated in units of product, the amount that a firm can produce per unit of time; stated in units of input, such as *direct labor* hours, the amount of input that a firm can use in production per unit of time. A firm uses this measure of output or input in allocating *fixed costs* if the amounts producible are normal, rather than maximum, amounts.

capacity cost. A *fixed cost* incurred to provide a firm with the capacity to produce or to sell. Consists of *standby costs* and *enabling costs*. Contrast with *programmed costs*.

capacity variance. *Production volume variance*.

capital. *Owners' equity* in a business; often used, equally correctly, to mean the total assets of a business; sometimes used to mean *capital assets*.

capital asset. Properly used, a designation for income tax purposes that describes property held by a taxpayer, except *cash*, inventoriable *assets*, goods held primarily for sale, most depreciable property, real estate, *receivables*, certain *intangibles*, and a few other items. Sometimes writers use this term imprecisely to describe *plant* and equipment, which are clearly not capital assets under the income-tax definition. Writers often use the term to refer to an *investment* in *securities*.

capital budget. Plan of proposed outlays for acquiring long-term *assets* and the means of *financing* the acquisition.

capital budgeting. The process of choosing *investment* projects for an enterprise by considering the *present value* of cash flows and deciding how to raise the funds the investment requires.

capital expenditure (outlay). An *expenditure* to acquire long-term *assets*.

capital gain. The excess of proceeds over *cost*, or other *basis*, from the sale of a *capital asset* as defined by the Internal Revenue Code. If the taxpayer has held the capital asset for a sufficiently long time before sale, then the gain is taxed at a rate lower than that used for other gains and ordinary income.

capital lease. A *lease* treated by the lessee as both the borrowing of funds and the acquisition of an *asset* to be *amortized*. The lessee (tenant) recognizes both the *liability* and the asset on its *balance sheet*. Expenses consist of *interest* on the *debt* and *amortization* of the asset. The lessor (landlord) treats the lease as the sale of the asset in return for a series of future cash receipts. Contrast with *operating lease*.

capital loss. A negative capital gain; see *capital gain*.

capital rationing. In a *capital budgeting* context, the imposition of constraints on the amounts of total capital expenditures in each period.

capital stock. The ownership shares of a corporation. Consists of all classes of *common* and *preferred shares*.

capital structure. The composition of a corporation's equities; the relative proportions of short-term debt, long-term debt, and *owners' equity*.

capitalization of a corporation. A term used by investment analysts to indicate *shareholders' equity* plus bonds outstanding.

capitalization of earnings. The process of estimating the *fair value* of a firm by computing the *net present value* of the predicted *net income* (not *cash flows*) of the firm for the future.

capitalization rate. An *interest rate* used to convert a series of payments or receipts or earnings into a single *present value*.

capitalize. To record an *expenditure* that may benefit a future period as an *asset* rather than to treat the expenditure as an *expense* of the period of its occurrence. Whether expenditures for advertising or for research and development should be capitalized is controversial, but *SFAS No. 2* forbids capitalizing *R&D* costs. We believe GAAP should allow firms to capitalize expenditures when they lead to future benefits and thus meet the criterion to be an asset.

carrying cost. Costs (such as property taxes and insurance) of holding, or storing, *inventory* from the time of purchase until the time of sale or use.

carrying value (amount). *Book value*.

CASB (Cost Accounting Standards Board). A board authorized by the U.S. Congress to "promulgate cost-accounting standards designed to achieve uniformity and consistency in the cost-accounting principles followed by defense contractors and subcontractors under federal contracts." The *principles* the CASB promulgated since 1970 have considerable weight in practice wherever the *FASB* has not established a standard. Congress allowed the CASB to go out of existence in 1980 but reinstated it in 1990.

cash. Currency and coins, negotiable checks, and balances in bank accounts. For the *statement of cash flows*, "cash" also includes *marketable securities* held as *current assets*.

cash basis of accounting. In contrast to the *accrual basis of accounting*, a system of accounting in which a firm recognizes *revenues* when it receives *cash* and recognizes *expenses* as it makes *disbursements*. The firm makes no attempt to match *revenues* and *expenses* in measuring *income*.

cash budget. A schedule of expected cash *receipts* and *disbursements*.

cash cycle. The period of time that elapses during which a firm converts *cash* into *inventories*, inventories into *accounts receivable*, and *receivables* back into cash. Sometimes called *earnings cycle*.

cash discount. A reduction in sales or purchase price allowed for prompt payment.

cash dividend. See *dividend*.

cash equivalent value. A term used to describe the amount for which an *asset* could be sold. Sometimes called market value or *fair market price (value)*.

cash flow. Cash *receipts* minus *disbursements* from a given *asset*, or group of assets, for a given period. Financial analysts sometimes use this term to mean *net income + depreciation + depletion + amortization*. See also *operating cash flow* and *free cash flow*.

cash flow from operations. Receipts from customers and from investments less expenditures for inventory, labor, and services, used in the usual activities of the firm, less interest expenditures. See *statement of cash flows* and *operations*. Same as *cash provided by operations*.

cash flow statement. *Statement of cash flows*.

cash provided by operations. An important subtotal in the *statement of cash flows*. This amount equals the total of revenues producing *cash* less *expenses* requiring cash. Often, the amount appears as *net income* plus expenses not requiring cash (such as *depreciation* charges) minus revenues not producing cash (such as revenues recognized under the equity method of accounting for a long-term investment). The statement of cash flows maintains the same distinctions between *continuing operations*, discontinued operations, and *income* or *loss* from *extraordinary items* as does the *income statement*.

cash yield. See *yield*.

cashier's check. A bank's own check drawn on itself and signed by the cashier or other authorized official. It is a direct obligation of the bank.

central corporate expenses. General *overhead expenses* incurred in running the corporate headquarters and related supporting activities of a corporation. Accounting treats these expenses as *period expenses*. Contrast with *manufacturing overhead*. Line of business reporting must decide how to treat these expenses—whether to allocate them to the individual segments and, if so, how to allocate them.

central processing unit (CPU). The component of a computer system carrying out the arithmetic, logic, and data transfer.

certificate. The document that is the physical embodiment of a *bond* or a *share of stock;* a term sometimes used for the *auditor's report*.

certified internal auditor. See *CIA*.

certified management accountant. *CMA*.

certified public accountant (CPA). An accountant who has satisfied the statutory and administrative requirements of his or her jurisdiction to be registered or licensed as a public accountant. In addition to passing the Uniform CPA Examination administered by the *AICPA*, the CPA must meet certain educational, experience, and moral requirements that differ from jurisdiction to jurisdiction. The jurisdictions are the 50 states, the District of Columbia, Guam, Puerto Rico, and the Virgin Islands.

CGA (Certified General Accountant). Canada: an accountant who has satisfied the experience, education, and examination requirements of the Certified General Accountants' Association.

charge. As a noun, a *debit* to an account; as a verb, to debit.

charge off. To treat as a *loss* or *expense* an amount originally recorded as an *asset;* use of this term implies that the charge is not in accord with original expectations.

chart of accounts. A list of names and numbers, systematically organized, of *accounts*.

charter. Document issued by a state government authorizing the creation of a corporation.

chartered accountant (CA). The title used in Australia, Canada, and the United Kingdom for an accountant who has satisfied the requirements of the institute of his or her jurisdiction to be qualified to serve as a *pub-*

lic accountant. In Canada, each provincial institute or order has the right to administer the examination and set the standards of performance and ethics for Chartered Accountants in its province. For a number of years, however, the provincial organizations have pooled their rights to qualify new members through the Inter-provincial Education Committee, and the result is that there are nationally set and graded examinations given in English and French. Deviation from the pass/fail grade awarded by the Board of Examiners (a subcommittee of the Inter-provincial Education Committee) is rare.

CIA (Certified Internal Auditor). One who has satisfied certain requirements of the *Institute of Internal Auditors,* including experience, ethics, education, and passing examinations.

CICA. Canadian Institute of Chartered Accountants.

clean opinion. See *auditor's report.*

close. As a verb, to transfer the *balance* of a *temporary* or *contra* or *adjunct account* to the main account to which it relates; for example, to transfer *revenue* and *expense* accounts directly, or through the *income summary* account, to an *owners' equity* account or to transfer purchase discounts to purchases.

closed account. An *account* with equal *debits* and *credits,* usually as a result of a *closing entry.*

closing entries. The entries that accomplish the transfer of balances in *temporary accounts* to the related *balance sheet accounts.*

closing inventory. *Ending inventory.*

CMA (Certified Management Accountant) certificate. Awarded by the *Institute of Certified Management Accountants* of the *Institute of Management Accountants* to those who pass a set of examinations and meet certain experience and continuing-education requirements.

collateral. *Assets* pledged by a *borrower* who will surrender those assets if he or she fails to repay a *loan.*

collectible. Capable of being converted into *cash*—now if due, later otherwise.

collusion. Cooperative effort by employees to commit fraud or another unethical act.

commercial paper. Short-term notes issued by corporate borrowers.

commission. Remuneration, usually expressed as a percentage, to employees based on an activity rate, such as sales.

committed costs. *Capacity costs.*

common cost. *Cost* resulting from the use of *raw materials,* a facility (for example, plant or machines), or a service (for example, fire insurance) that benefits several products or departments. A firm must allocate this cost to those products or departments. Common costs result when two or more departments produce multiple products together even though the departments could produce them separately; *joint costs* occur when two or more departments must produce multiple products together. Many writers use "common costs" and "joint costs" synonymously. See *joint cost, indirect costs,* and *overhead costs.* See *sterilized allocation.*

common shares. *Shares* representing the class of owners who have residual claims on the *assets* and *earnings* of a *corporation* after the firm meets all *debt* and *preferred shareholders'* claims.

common-size statement. A *percentage statement* usually based on total *assets* or *net sales* or *revenues.*

companywide control. See *control system.*

comparative (financial) statements. *Financial statements* showing information for the same company for different times, usually two successive years for balance sheets and three for *income* and *cash flow statements.* Nearly all published financial statements are in this form. Contrast with *historical summary.*

compliance audit. Objectively obtaining and evaluating evidence regarding assertions, actions, and events to ascertain the degree of correspondence between them and established performance criteria.

compliance procedure. An *audit* procedure used to gain evidence as to whether the prescribed internal controls are operating effectively.

composite cost of capital. See *cost of capital.*

compound interest. *Interest* calculated on *principal* plus previously undistributed interest.

compounding period. The time period, usually a year or a portion of a year, for which a firm calculates *interest.* At the end of the period, the borrower may pay interest to the lender or may add the interest (that is, convert it) to the principal for the next interest-earning period.

comprehensive budget. *Master budget.*

comptroller. Same meaning and pronunciation as *controller.*

conceptual framework. A coherent system of interrelated objectives and fundamentals, promulgated by the *FASB* expected to lead to consistent standards for *financial accounting* and reporting.

confidence level. The measure of probability that the actual characteristics of the population lie within the stated precision of the estimate derived from a sampling process. A sample estimate may be expressed in the following terms: "Based on the sample, we are 95 percent sure [confidence level] that the true population value is within the range of X to Y [precision]." See *precision.*

conservatism. A *reporting objective* that calls for anticipation of all *losses* and *expenses* but defers recognition of *gains* or *profits* until they are *realized* in *arm's-length* transactions. In the absence of certainty, report events to minimize cumulative income. Conservatism does not mean reporting low income in every *accounting period*. Over long-enough time spans, income is cash-in less cash-out. If a (conservative) reporting method shows low income in early periods, it must show higher income in some later period.

consistency. Treatment of like *transactions* in the same way in consecutive periods so that financial statements will be more comparable than otherwise; the reporting policy implying that a reporting *entity*, once it adopts specified procedures, should follow them from period to period.

consolidated financial statements. Statements issued by legally separate companies that show financial position and income as they would appear if the companies were one economic *entity*.

contingency. A potential *liability*. If a specified event occurs, such as a firm's losing a lawsuit, it would recognize a liability. The notes disclose the contingency, but so long as it remains contingent, it does not appear in the *balance sheet*. *SFAS No. 5* requires treatment as a contingency until the outcome is "probable" and the amount of payment can be reasonably estimated, perhaps within a range. When the outcome becomes probable (the future event is "likely" to occur) and the firm can reasonably estimate the amount (using the lower end of a range if it can estimate only a range), then the firm recognizes a liability in the accounts, rather than just disclosing it. A *material* contingency may lead to a qualified, "*subject to*," auditor's opinion. Firms do not record *gain* contingencies in the accounts but merely disclose them in notes.

contingent annuity. An *annuity* whose number of payments depends on the outcome of an event whose timing is uncertain at the time the annuity begins; for example, an annuity payable until death of the *annuitant*. Contrast with *annuity certain*.

contingent liability. *Contingency*. Avoid this term because it refers to something not (yet) a *liability* on the *balance sheet*.

continuous budget. A *budget* that adds a future period as the current period ends. This budget, then, always reports on the same number of periods.

continuous compounding. *Compound interest* in which the *compounding period* is every instant of time. See *e* for the computation of the equivalent annual or periodic rate.

continuous improvement. Modern TQM practitioners believe that the process of seeking quality is never complete. An attitude reflecting that assumption, seeking always to improve activities.

continuous inventory method. The *perpetual inventory* method.

contra account. An *account*, such as *accumulated depreciation*, that accumulates subtractions from another account, such as *machinery*. Contrast with *adjunct account*.

contributed capital. Name for the *owners' equity* account that represents amounts paid in, usually in *cash*, by owners; the sum of the balances in *capital stock* accounts plus capital contributed in excess of par (or stated) value accounts.

contribution approach. Method of preparing *income statements* that reports *contribution margin*, by separating *variable costs* from *fixed costs*, in order to emphasize the importance of cost behavior patterns for purposes of planning and control.

contribution margin. *Revenue* from *sales* less all variable *expenses*. Contrast with *gross margin*.

contribution margin ratio. *Contribution margin* divided by *net sales*; usually measured from the price and cost of a single unit; sometimes measured in total for companies with multiple products.

contribution per unit. Selling price less *variable costs* per unit.

control (controlling) account. A summary *account* with totals equal to those of entries and balances that appear in individual accounts in a *subsidiary ledger*. Accounts Receivable is a control account backed up with an account for each customer. Do not change the balance in a control account unless you make a corresponding change in one of the subsidiary accounts.

control system. A device used by top management to ensure that lower-level management carries out its plans or to safeguard assets. Control designed for a single function within the firm is "operational control"; control designed for autonomous segments that generally have responsibility for both revenues and costs is "divisional control"; control designed for activities of the firm as a whole is "companywide control." Systems designed for safeguarding *assets* are "internal control" systems.

controllable cost. A *cost* influenced by the way a firm carries out operations. For example, marketing executives control advertising costs. These costs can be *fixed* or *variable*. See *programmed costs*.

controller. A title for the chief accountant of an organization; often spelled *comptroller*.

conversion cost. *Direct labor* costs plus factory *overhead* costs incurred in producing a product; that is, the cost to convert *raw materials* to finished products. *Manufacturing cost.*

conversion period. *Compounding period;* also, period during which the holder of a *convertible bond* or convertible *preferred stock* can convert it into *common shares.*

convertible bond. A *bond* whose owner may convert it into a specified number of shares of *capital stock* during the *conversion period.*

coproduct. A product sharing production facilities with another product. For example, if an apparel manufacturer produces shirts and jeans on the same line, these are coproducts. Distinguish coproducts from *joint products* and *by-products* that, by their very nature, a firm must produce together, such as the various grades of wood a lumber factory produces.

copyright. Exclusive right granted by the government to an individual author, composer, playwright, and the like for the life of the individual plus 50 years. If a firm receives the copyright, then the right extends 75 years after the original publication. The *economic life* of a copyright can be less than the legal life, such as, for example, the copyright of this book.

corporation. A legal entity authorized by a state to operate under the rules of the entity's *charter.*

cost. The sacrifice, measured by the *price* paid or required to be paid, to acquire *goods* or *services.* See *acquisition cost* and *replacement cost.* Terminology often uses "cost" when referring to the valuation of a good or service acquired. When writers use the word in this sense, a cost is an *asset.* When the benefits of the acquisition (the goods or services acquired) expire, the cost becomes an *expense* or *loss.* Some writers, however, use "cost" and "expense" as synonyms. Contrast with *expense.* The word "cost" appears in more than 50 terms, each with sometimes subtle distinctions in meaning, used in accounting. See *cost terminology* for elaboration.

cost accounting. Classifying, summarizing, recording, reporting, and allocating current or predicted *costs;* a subset of *managerial accounting.*

Cost Accounting Standards Board. See *CASB.*

cost accumulation. Bringing together, usually in a single *account*, all *costs* of a specified activity. Contrast with *cost allocation.*

cost allocation. Assigning *costs* to individual products or time periods. Contrast with *cost accumulation.*

cost-based transfer price. A *transfer price* based on *historical costs.*

cost behavior. The functional relation between changes in activity and changes in *cost;* for example: *fixed* versus *variable costs*; linear versus *curvilinear cost.*

cost/benefit criterion. Some measure of *costs* compared with some measure of benefits for a proposed undertaking. If the costs exceed the benefits, then the analyst judges the undertaking not worthwhile. This criterion will not yield good decisions unless the analyst estimates all costs and benefits flowing from the undertaking.

cost center. A unit of activity for which a firm accumulates *expenditures* and *expenses.*

cost driver. A factor that causes an activity's costs. See *driver* and *activity basis.*

cost-effective. Among alternatives, the one whose benefit, or payoff, per unit of cost is highest; sometimes said of an action whose expected benefits exceed expected costs whether or not other alternatives exist with larger benefit–cost ratios.

cost estimation. The process of measuring the functional relation between changes in activity levels and changes in cost.

cost flow assumption. See *flow assumption.*

cost-flow equation. Beginning Balance + Transfers In = Transfers Out + Ending Balance; BB + TI = TO + EB.

cost flows. Costs passing through various classifications within an entity.

cost object(ive). Any activity for which management desires a separate measurement of *costs.* Examples include departments, products, and territories.

cost of capital. *Opportunity cost* of funds invested in a business; the rate of return rational owners require an asset to earn before they will devote that asset to a particular purpose; sometimes measured as the average rate per year a company must pay for its *equities.* In efficient capital markets, this cost is the *discount rate* that equates the expected *present value* of all future cash flows to common shareholders with the market value of common stock at a given time. Analysts often measure the cost of capital by taking a *weighted average* of the firm's *debt* and various equity securities. We sometimes call the measurement so derived the "composite cost of capital," and some analysts confuse this measurement of the cost of capital with the cost of capital itself. For example, if the equities of a firm include substantial amounts for the deferred income tax liability, the composite cost of capital will underestimate the true cost of capital, the required rate of return on a firm's assets, because the deferred income tax liability has no explicit cost.

cost of goods manufactured. The sum of all costs allocated to products completed during a period, including materials, labor, and *overhead.*

cost of goods purchased. Net purchase price of goods acquired plus costs of storage and delivery to the place where the owner can productively use the items.

cost of goods sold. Inventoriable *costs* that firms *expense* because they sold the units; equals *beginning inventory* plus *cost of goods purchased* or *manufactured* minus *ending inventory*.

cost of sales. Generally refers to *cost of goods sold*, occasionally to *selling expenses*.

cost pool. *Indirect cost pool*; groupings or aggregations of costs, usually for subsequent analysis.

cost principle. The *principle* that requires reporting *assets* at *historical* or *acquisition cost*, less accumulated *amortization*. This principle relies on the assumption that cost equals *fair market value* at the date of

acquisition and that subsequent changes are not likely to be significant.

cost sheet. Statement that shows all the elements composing the total cost of an item.

cost structure. For a given set of total costs, the percentages of fixed and variable costs, typically two percentages adding to 100 percent.

cost terminology. The word "cost" appears in many accounting terms. The accompanying exhibit classifies some of these terms according to the distinctions between the terms in accounting usage. Joel Dean was, to our knowledge, the first to attempt such distinctions; we have used some of his ideas here. We discuss some of the terms in more detail under their own listings.

Cost Terminology Chart: Distinctions among Terms Containing the Word "Cost"

Terms (Synonyms in Parentheses)			Distinctions and Comments
1. The following pairs of terms distinguish the basis measured in accounting.			
Historical Cost (Acquisition Cost)	v.	Current Cost	A distinction used in financial accounting. Current cost can be used more specifically to mean replacement cost, net realizable value, or present value of cash flows. "Current cost" is often used narrowly to mean replacement cost.
Historical Cost (Actual Cost)	v.	Standard Cost	The distinction between historical and standard costs arises in product costing for inventory valuation. Some systems record actual costs while others record the standard costs.
2. The following pairs of terms denote various distinctions among historical costs. For each pair of terms, the sum of the two kinds of costs equals total historical cost used in financial reporting.			
Variable Cost	v.	Fixed Cost (Constant Cost)	Distinction used in breakeven analysis and in designing cost accounting systems, particularly for product costing. See (4), below, for a further subdivision of fixed costs and (5), below, for an economic distinction closely paralleling this one.
Traceable Cost	v.	Common Cost (Joint Cost)	Distinction arises in allocating manufacturing costs to product. Common costs are allocated to product, but the allocations are more-or-less arbitrary. The distinction also arises in segment reporting and in separating manufacturing from nonmanufacturing costs.
Direct Cost	v.	Indirect Cost	Distinction arises in designing cost accounting systems and in product costing. Direct costs can be traced directly to a cost object (e.g., a product, a responsibility center), whereas indirect costs cannot.
Out-of-Pocket Cost (Outlay Cost; Cash Cost)	v.	Book Cost	Virtually all costs recorded in financial statements require a cash outlay at one time or another. The distinction here separates expenditures to occur in the future from those already made and is used in making decisions. Book costs, such as for depreciation, reduce income without requiring a future outlay of cash. The cash has already been spent. See future v. past costs in (5), below.

Terms (Synonyms in Parentheses)			Distinctions and Comments
Incremental Cost (Marginal Cost; Differential Cost)	v.	Unavoidable Cost (Inescapable Cost; Sunk Cost)	Distinction used in making decisions. Incremental costs will be incurred (or saved) if a decision is made to go ahead (or to stop) some activity, but not otherwise. Unavoidable costs will be reported in financial statements whether the decision is made to go ahead or not, because cash has already been spent or committed. Not all unavoidable costs are book costs, as, for example, a salary promised but not yet earned, that will be paid even if a no-go decision is made.
			The economist restricts the term "marginal cost" to the cost of producing one more unit. Thus the next unit has a marginal cost; the next week's output has an incremental cost. If a firm produces and sells a new product, the related new costs would properly be called incremental, not marginal. If a factory is closed, the costs saved are incremental, not marginal.
Escapable Cost	v.	Inescapable Cost (Unavoidable Cost)	Same distinction as incremental v. sunk costs, but this pair is used only when the decision maker is considering stopping something—ceasing to produce a product, closing a factory, or the like. See next pair.
Avoidable Cost	v.	Unavoidable Cost	A distinction sometimes used in discussing the merits of variable and absorption costing. Avoidable costs are treated as product cost and unavoidable costs are treated as period expenses under variable costing.
Controllable Cost	v.	Uncontrollable Cost	The distinction here is used in assigning responsibility and in setting bonus or incentive plans. All costs can be affected by someone in the entity; those who design incentive schemes attempt to hold a person responsible for a cost only if that person can influence the amount of the cost.

3. In each of the following pairs, used in historical cost accounting, the word "cost" appears in one of the terms where "expense" is meant.

Expired Cost	v.	Unexpired Cost	The distinction between *expense* and *asset*.
Product Cost	v.	Period Cost	The terms distinguish product cost from period expense. When a given asset is used, is its cost converted into work in process and then into finished goods on the balance sheet until the goods are sold, or is it an expense shown on this period's income statement? Product costs appear on the income statement as part of cost of goods sold in the period when the goods are sold. Period expenses appear on the income statement with an appropriate caption for the item in the period when the cost is incurred or recognized.

4. The following subdivisions of fixed (historical) costs are used in analyzing operations. The relation between the components of fixed costs is:

$$\text{Fixed Costs} = \text{Capacity Costs} + \text{Programmed Costs}$$

Semifixed Costs + "Pure" Fixed Costs + Fixed Portions of Semivariable Costs = Standby Costs + Enabling Costs

Terms (Synonyms in Parentheses)			Distinctions and Comments
Capacity Cost (Committed Cost)	v.	Programmed Cost (Managed Cost; Discretionary Cost)	Capacity costs give a firm the capability to produce or to sell. Programmed costs, such as for advertising or research and development, may not be essential, but once a decision to incur them is made, they become fixed costs.
Standby Cost	v.	Enabling Cost	Standby costs will be incurred whether capacity, once acquired, is used or not, such as property taxes and depreciation on a factory. Enabling costs, such as for security force, can be avoided if the capacity is unused.
Semifixed Cost	v.	Semivariable Cost	A cost fixed over a wide range but that can change at various levels is a semifixed cost or "step cost." An example is the cost of rail lines from the factory to the main rail line where fixed cost depends on whether there are one or two parallel lines, but are independent of the number of trains run per day. Semivariable costs combine a strictly fixed component cost plus a variable component. Telephone charges usually have a fixed monthly component plus a charge related to usage.

5. The following pairs of terms distinguish among economic used or decision-making uses or regulatory uses of cost terms.

Fully Absorbed Cost	v.	Variable Cost (Direct Cost)	Fully absorbed costs refer to costs where fixed costs have been allocated to units or departments as required by generally accepted accounting principles. Variable costs, in contrast, may be more relevant for making decisions, such as in setting prices.
Fully Absorbed Cost	v.	Full Cost	In full costing, all costs, manufacturing costs as well as central corporate expenses (including financing expenses) are allocated to product or divisions. In full absorption costing, only manufacturing costs are allocated to product. Only in full costing will revenues, expenses, and income summed over all products or divisions, equal corporate revenues, expenses, and income.
Opportunity Cost	v.	Outlay Cost (Out-of-Pocket Cost)	Opportunity cost refers to the economic benefit foregone by using a resource for one purpose instead of for another. The outlay cost of the resource will be recorded in financial records. The distinction arises because a resource is already in the possession of the entity with a recorded historical cost. Its economic value to the firm, opportunity cost, generally differs from the historical cost; it can be either larger or smaller.
Future Cost	v.	Past Cost	Effective decision making analyzes only present and future outlay costs, or out-of-pocket costs. Opportunity costs are relevant for profit maximizing; past costs are used in financial reporting.
Short-Run Cost	v.	Long-Run Cost	Short-run costs vary as output is varied for a given configuration of plant and equipment. Long-run costs can be incurred to change that configuration. This pair of terms is the economic analog of the accounting pair, see (2), above, variable and fixed costs. The analogy is not perfect because some short-run costs are fixed, such as property taxes on the factory, from the point of view of breakeven analysis.

Terms (Synonyms in Parentheses)			Distinctions and Comments
Imputed Cost	v.	Book Cost	In a regulatory setting some costs, for example the cost of owners' equity capital, are calculated and used for various purposes; these are imputed costs. Imputed costs are not recorded in the historical costs accounting records for financial reporting. Book costs are recorded.
Average Cost	v.	Marginal Cost	The economic distinction equivalent to fully absorbed cost of product and direct cost of product. Average cost is total cost divided by number of units. Marginal cost is the cost to produce the next unit (or the last unit).
Differential Cost (Incremental Cost)	v.	Variable Cost	Whether a cost changes or remains fixed depends on the activity basis being considered. Typically, but not invariably, costs are said to be variable or fixed with respect to an activity basis such as changes in production levels. Typically, but not invariably, costs are said to be differential or not with respect to an activity basis such as the undertaking of some new venture. For example, consider the decision to undertake the production of food processors, rather than food blenders, which the manufacturer has been making. To produce processors requires the acquisition of a new machine tool. The cost of the new machine tool is incremental with respect to a decision to produce food processors instead of food blenders, but once acquired, becomes a fixed cost of producing food processors. If costs of direct labor hours are going to be incurred for the production of food processors or food blenders, whichever is produced (in a scenario when not both are to be produced), such costs are variable with respect to production measured in units, but not incremental with respect to the decision to produce processors rather than blenders. This distinction is often blurred in practice, so a careful understanding of the activity basis being considered is necessary for understanding of the concepts being used in a particular application.

cost-volume-profit analysis. A study of the sensitivity of *profits* to changes in units sold (or produced) or costs or prices.

cost-volume-profit graph (chart). A graph that shows the relation between *fixed costs, contribution per unit, breakeven point,* and *sales.* See *breakeven chart.*

costing. The process of calculating the cost of activities, products, or services; the British word for *cost accounting.*

CPA. See *certified public accountant.* The *AICPA* suggests that no periods appear in the abbreviation.

Cr. Abbreviation for *credit,* always with initial capital letter.

credit. As a noun, an entry on the right-hand side of an *account;* as a verb, to make an entry on the right-hand side of an account; records increases in *liabilities, own-* ers' equity, revenues, and *gains;* records decreases in *assets* and *expenses.* See *debit and credit conventions.* This term also refers to the ability or right to buy or borrow in return for a promise to pay later.

creditor. One who lends.

Critical Path Method (CPM). A method of *network analysis* in which the analyst estimates normal duration time for each activity within a project. The critical path identifies the shortest completion period based on the most time-consuming sequence of activities from the beginning to the end of the network. Compare *PERT.*

cross-reference (index). A number placed beside each *account* in a *journal entry* indicating the *ledger* account to which the recordkeeper posted the entry and placing in the ledger the page number of the journal where the record keeper first recorded the journal entry; used to link the *debit* and *credit* parts of an entry in the ledger accounts back to the original entry in the journal.

cross-section analysis. Analysis of *financial statements* of various firms for a single period of time; contrast with time-series analysis, in which analysts examine statements of a given firm for several periods of time.

current assets. *Cash* and other *assets* that a firm expects to turn into cash, sell, or exchange within the normal operating cycle of the firm or one year, whichever is longer. One year is the usual period for classifying asset balances on the *balance sheet*. Current assets include *cash, marketable securities, receivables, inventory,* and current prepayments.

current cost. *Cost* stated in terms of current values (of *productive capacity*) rather than in terms of *acquisition cost*. See *net realizable value, current selling price*.

current cost accounting. The *FASB's* term for *financial statements* in which the *attribute measured* is *current cost*.

current liability. A *debt* or other obligation that a firm must discharge within a short time, usually the *earnings cycle* or one year, normally by expending *current assets*.

current ratio. Sum of *current assets* divided by sum of *current liabilities*. See *ratio*.

current replacement cost. Of an *asset*, the amount currently required to acquire an identical asset (in the same condition and with the same service potential) or an asset capable of rendering the same service at a current *fair market price*. If these two amounts differ, use the lower. Contrast with *reproduction cost*.

current selling price. The amount for which an *asset* could be sold as of a given time in an *arm's-length* transaction rather than in a forced sale.

currently attainable standard cost. *Normal standard cost*.

curvilinear (variable) cost. A continuous, but not necessarily linear (straight-line), functional relation between activity levels and *costs*.

cutoff rate. *Hurdle rate*.

D

data bank. An organized file of information, such as a customer name and address file, used in and kept up to date by a processing system.

database. A comprehensive collection of interrelated information stored together in computerized form to serve several applications.

database management system. Generalized software programs used to handle physical storage and manipulation of databases.

DCF. *Discounted cash flow*.

debit. As a noun, an entry on the left-hand side of an *account;* as a verb, to make an entry on the left-hand side of an account; records increases in *assets* and *expenses;* records decreases in *liabilities, owners' equity,* and *revenues*. See *debit and credit conventions*.

debit and credit conventions. The conventional use of the *T-account* form and the rules for debit and credit in *balance sheet accounts* (see below). The equality of the two sides of the *accounting equation* results from recording equal amounts of *debits* and *credits* for each transaction.

Any Asset Account

Opening Balance Increase + Dr. Ending Balance	Decrease − Cr.

Any Liability Account

Decrease − Dr.	Opening Balance Increase + Cr. Ending Balance

Any Owners' Equity Account

Opening Balance Decrease − Dr.	Increase + Cr. Ending Balance

Revenue and expense accounts belong to the owners' equity group. The relation and the rules for debit and credit in these accounts take the following form:

Owners' Equity

Decrease − Dr.	Increase + Cr.

Expenses		**Revenues**	
Dr.	Cr.	Dr.	Cr.
+	−	−	+
*			*

*Normal balance before closing

debt. An amount owed. The general name for *notes, bonds, mortgages*, and the like that provide evidence of amounts owed and have definite payment dates.

debt capital. *Noncurrent liabilities.* See *debt financing,* and contrast with *equity financing.*

debt-equity ratio. Total *liabilities* divided by total *equities.* See *ratio.* Some analysts put only total *shareholders' equity* in the denominator. Some analysts restrict the numerator to *long-term debt.*

debt financing. Raising *funds* by issuing *bonds, mortgages*, or *notes.* Contrast with *equity financing. Leverage.*

debt ratio. *Debt-equity ratio.*

debt service payment. The payment required by a lending agreement, such as periodic coupon payment on a bond or installment payment on a loan or a lease payment. It is sometimes called "interest payment," but this term will mislead the unwary. Only rarely will the amount of a debt service payment equal the interest expense for the period preceding the payment. A debt service payment will always include some amount for interest, but the payment will usually differ from the interest expense.

debt service requirement. The amount of cash required for payments of *interest*, current maturities of *principal* on outstanding *debt*, and payments to sinking funds (corporations) or to the debt service fund (governmental).

debtor. One who borrows.

decentralized decision making. Management practice in which a firm gives a manager of a business unit responsibility for that unit's *revenues* and *costs*, freeing the manager to make decisions about prices, sources of supply, and the like, as though the unit was a separate business that the manager owns. See *responsibility accounting* and *transfer price.*

defalcation. Embezzlement.

default. Failure to pay *interest* or *principal* on a *debt* when due.

deferral. The accounting process concerned with past *cash receipts* and payments; in contrast to *accrual;* recognizing a liability resulting from a current cash receipt (as for magazines to be delivered) or recognizing an asset from a current cash payment (as for prepaid insurance or a long-term depreciable asset).

deferred annuity. An *annuity* whose first payment occurs sometime after the end of the first period.

deferred charge. *Expenditure* not recognized as an *expense* of the period when made but carried forward as an *asset* to be *written off* in future periods, such as for advance rent payments or insurance premiums. See *deferral.*

deficit. A *debit balance* in the Retained Earnings account; presented on the *balance sheet* in a *contra account* to *shareholders' equity;* sometimes used to mean negative *net income* for a period.

deflation. A period of declining general price changes.

demand deposit. *Funds* in a checking account at a bank.

denominator volume. Capacity measured in the number of units the firm expects to produce this period; when divided into *budgeted fixed costs*, results in fixed costs applied per unit of product.

department(al) allocation. Obtained by first accumulating *costs* in *cost pools* for each department and then, using separate rates or sets of rates for each department, allocating from each cost pool to products produced in that department.

dependent variable. See *regression analysis.*

depletion. Exhaustion or *amortization* of a *wasting asset* or *natural resource.*

depreciable cost. That part of the *cost* of an *asset,* usually *acquisition cost* less *salvage value*, that the firm will charge off over the life of the asset through the process of *depreciation.*

depreciable life. For an *asset*, the time period or units of activity (such as miles driven for a truck) over which the firm allocates the *depreciable cost*. For tax returns, depreciable life may be shorter than estimated *service life.*

depreciation. *Amortization* of *plant assets*; the process of allocating the cost of an asset to the periods of benefit— the *depreciable life;* classified as a *production cost* or a *period expense*, depending on the asset and whether the firm uses *full absorption* or *variable costing.*

Descartes' rule of signs. In a *capital budgeting* context, a rule that says a series of cash flows will have a nonnegative number of *internal rates of return*. The number equals the number of variations in the sign of the cash flow series or is less than that number by an even integer. Consider the following series of cash flows, the first occurring now and the others at subsequent yearly intervals: $-100, -100, +50, +175, -50, +100$. The internal rates of return are the numbers for r that satisfy the following equation:

$$-100 - \frac{100}{(1+r)} + \frac{50}{(1+r)^2} + \frac{175}{(1+r)^3} - \frac{50}{(1+r)^4} + \frac{100}{(1+r)^5}$$
$$= 0.$$

The series of cash flows has three variations in sign: a change from minus to plus, a change from plus to minus, and a change from minus to plus. The rule says that this series must have either one or three internal rates of return; in fact, it has only one, about 12 percent. But also see *reinvestment rate.*

detective controls. *Internal controls* designed to detect, or maximize the chance of detection of, errors and other irregularities.

determination. See *determine*.

determine. A term often used (in our opinion, overused) by accountants and those who describe the accounting process. A leading dictionary associates the following meanings with the verb "determine": settle, decide, conclude, ascertain, cause, affect, control, impel, terminate, and decide upon. In addition, accounting writers can mean any one of the following: measure, allocate, report, calculate, compute, observe, choose, and legislate. In accounting, there are two distinct sets of meanings—those encompassed by the synonym "cause or legislate" and those encompassed by the synonym "measure." The first set of uses conveys the active notion of causing something to happen, and the second set of uses conveys the more passive notion of observing something that someone else has caused to happen. An accountant who speaks of cost or income "determination" generally means measurement or observation, not causation; management and economic conditions cause costs and income to be what they are. One who speaks of accounting principles "determination" can mean choosing or applying (as in "determining depreciation charges" from an allowable set) or causing to be acceptable (as in the *FASB*'s "determining" the accounting for *leases*). In the long run, income is cash in less cash out, so management and economic conditions "determine" (cause) income to be what it is. In the short run, reported income is a function of accounting principles chosen and applied, so the accountant "determines" (measures) income. A question such as "Who determines income?" has, therefore, no unambiguous answer. The meaning of "an accountant determining acceptable accounting principles" is also vague. Does the clause mean merely choosing one principle from the set of generally acceptable principles, or does it mean using professional judgment to decide that some of the generally accepted principles are not correct under the current circumstances? We try never to use "determine" unless we mean "cause." Otherwise we use "measure," "report," "calculate," "compute," or whatever specific verb seems appropriate. We suggest that careful writers will always "determine" to use the most specific verb to convey meaning. "Determine" seldom best describes a process in which those who make decisions often differ from those who apply technique. The term *predetermined (factory) overhead rate* contains an appropriate use of the word.

diagnostic signal. See *warning signal* for definition and contrast.

differentiable cost. The cost increments associated with infinitesimal changes in volume. If a total cost curve is smooth (in mathematical terms, differentiable), then we say that the curve graphing the derivative of the total cost curve shows differentiable costs.

differential. An adjective used to describe the change (increase or decrease) in a *cost, expense, investment, cash flow, revenue, profit,* and the like as the firm produces or sells one or more additional (or fewer) units or undertakes (or ceases) an activity. This term has virtually the same meaning as *incremental*, but if the item declines, "decremental" better describes the change. Contrast with *marginal*, which means the change in cost or other item for a small (one unit or even less) change in number of units produced or sold.

differential analysis. Analysis of *differential costs, revenues, profits, investment, cash flow,* and the like.

differential cost. See *differential*.

direct access. Access to computer storage where information can be located directly, regardless of its position in the storage file. Compare *sequential access*.

direct cost. Cost of *direct material* and *direct labor* incurred in producing a product. See *prime cost*. In some accounting literature, writers use this term to mean the same thing as *variable cost*.

direct costing. Another, less-preferred, term for *variable costing*.

direct labor (material) cost. Cost of labor (material) applied and assigned directly to a product; contrast with *indirect labor (material)*.

direct labor variance. Difference between actual and standard direct labor allowed.

direct method. See *statement of cash flows*.

direct posting. A method of bookkeeping in which the firm makes entries directly in *ledger accounts*, without using a *journal*.

disbursement. Payment by *cash* or by check. See *expenditure*.

disclaimer of opinion. An *auditor's report* stating that the auditor cannot give an opinion on the *financial statements*. Usually results from *material* restrictions on the scope of the audit or from material uncertainties, which the firm has been unable to resolve by the time of the audit, about the accounts.

disclosure. The showing of facts in *financial statements, notes* thereto, or the *auditor's report*.

discount. In the context of *compound interest, bonds* and *notes*, the difference between *face amount* (or *future value*) and *present value* of a payment; in the context of *sales* and purchases, a reduction in price granted for prompt payment. See also *quantity discount*.

discount factor. The reciprocal of one plus the *discount rate*. If the discount rate is 10 percent per period, the discount factor for three periods is $1/(1.10)^3 = (1.10)^{-3} = 0.75131$.

discount rate. *Interest rate* used to convert future payments to *present values*.

discounted bailout period. In a *capital budgeting* context, the total time that must elapse before discounted value of net accumulated cash flows from a project, including potential *salvage value* at various times of assets, equals or exceeds the *present value* of net accumulated cash outflows. Contrast with *discounted payback period*.

discounted cash flow (DCF). Using either the *net present value* or the *internal rate of return* in an analysis to measure the value of future expected cash *expenditures* and *receipts* at a common date. In discounted cash flow analysis, choosing the alternative with the largest internal rate of return may yield wrong answers given *mutually exclusive projects* with differing amounts of initial investment for two of the projects. Consider, to take an unrealistic example, a project involving an initial investment of $1 with an *IRR* of 60 percent and another project involving an initial investment of $1 million with an IRR of 40 percent. Under most conditions, most firms will prefer the second project to the first, but choosing the project with the larger IRR will lead to undertaking the first, not the second. Usage calls this shortcoming of choosing between alternatives based on the magnitude of the internal rate of return, rather than the magnitude of the *net present value* of the cash flows, the "scale effect."

discounted payback period. The shortest amount of time that must elapse before the discounted present value of cash inflows from a project, excluding potential *salvage value,* equals the discounted *present value* of the cash outflows.

discovery sampling. Acceptance sampling in which the analyst accepts an entire population if and only if the sample contains no disparities.

discretionary cost center. See *engineered cost center* for definition and contrast.

discretionary costs. *Programmed cost.*

Discussion Memorandum. A neutral discussion of all the issues concerning an accounting problem of current concern to the *FASB*. The publication of such a document usually signals that the FASB will consider issuing an *SFAS* or *SFAC* on this particular problem. The discussion memorandum brings together material about the particular problem to facilitate interaction and comment by those interested in the matter. A public hearing follows before the FASB will issue an *Exposure Draft*.

distributed processing. Processing in a computer information network in which an individual location processes data relevant to it while the operating system transmits information required elsewhere, either to the central computer or to another local computer for further processing.

distribution expense. *Expense* of selling, advertising, and delivery activities.

dividend. A distribution of assets generated from *earnings* to owners of a corporation. The firm may distribute cash (cash dividend), stock (stock dividend), property, or other securities (dividend in kind). Dividends, except stock dividends, become a legal liability of the corporation when the corporation's board declares them. Hence, the owner of stock ordinarily recognizes *revenue* when the board of the corporation declares the dividend, except for stock dividends.

dividend yield. *Dividends* declared for the year divided by market price of the stock as of the time for which the analyst computes the yield.

division. A more or less self-contained business unit that is part of a larger family of business units under common control.

divisional control. See *control system.*

dollar sign rules. In accounting statements or schedules, the placement of a dollar sign beside the first figure in each column and beside any figure below a horizontal line drawn under the preceding figure.

double entry. In recording transactions, a system that maintains the equality of the *accounting equation* or the *balance sheet*. Each entry results in recording equal amounts of *debits* and *credits.*

Dr. The abbreviation for *debit*, always with initial capital letter.

driver, cost driver. A cause of costs incurred. Examples include order processing, issuing an engineering change order, changing the production schedule, and stopping production to change machine settings. The notion arises primarily in product costing, particularly *activity-based costing.*

dual transfer prices. The *transfer price charged* to the buying *division* differs from that *credited* to the selling division. Such prices make sense when the selling division has excess capacity and, as usual, the *fair market value* exceeds the *incremental cost* to produce the goods or services being transferred.

duality. The axiom of *double entry* record keeping that every *transaction* must result in equal *debit* and *credit* amounts.

dumping. A foreign firm's selling a good or service in the United States at a price below market price at home or, in some contexts, below some measure of cost (which concept not clearly defined). Illegal in the United States if the practice harms (or threatens to harm) an industry in the United States.

E

e. The base of natural logarithms; 2.71828 . . . . If *interest* compounds continuously during a period at stated rate of r per period, then the effective *interest rate* is equivalent to interest compounded once per period at rate I where $I = e^r - 1$. Tables of e^r are widely available. If 12 percent annual interest compounds continuously, the effective annual rate is $e^{.12} - 1 = 12.75$ percent. Interest compounded continuously at rate r for d days is $e^{rd/365} - 1$. For example, interest compounded for 92 days at 12 percent is $e^{.12 \times 92/365} - 1 = 3.07$ percent.

earnings. A term with no precise meaning, used to mean *income* or sometimes *profit*. When the *FASB* requires firms to report *comprehensive income,* it will encourage firms to use the term "earnings" for the total formerly reported as *net income*.

earnings cycle. The period of time that elapses for a given firm, or the series of transactions, during which the firm converts *cash* into *goods* and *services*, then sells goods and services to customers, and finally collects cash from customers. *Cash cycle.*

economic depreciation. Decline in *current cost* (or *fair value*) of an *asset* during a period.

economic entity. See *entity.*

economic life. The time span over which the firm expects to receive the benefits of an *asset*. The economic life of a *patent, copyright*, or *franchise* may be less than the legal life. *Service life.*

economic order quantity (EOQ). In mathematical *inventory* analysis, the optimal amount of stock to order when demand reduces inventory to a level called the "reorder point." If A represents the *incremental cost* of placing a single order, D represents the total demand for a period of time in units, and H represents the incremental holding cost during the period per unit of inventory, then the economic order quantity is $Q = 2AD/H$. Usage sometimes calls Q the "optimal lot size."

EDP. *Electronic data processing.*

effective (interest) rate. Of a liability such as a *bond,* the *internal rate of return* or *yield to maturity* at the time of issue. If the borrower issues the bond for a price below *par*, the effective rate is higher than the coupon rate; if it issues the bond for a price greater than par, then the effective rate is lower than the coupon rate. In the context of *compound interest*, when the *compounding period* on a *loan* differs from one year, such as a nominal interest rate of 12 percent compounded monthly. The effective interest is the single rate that one could use at the end of the year to multiply the *principal* at the beginning of the year and give the same amount as results from compounding interest each period during the year. For example, if 12 percent per year compounds monthly, the effective annual interest rate is 12.683 percent. That is, if you compound $100 each month at 1 percent per month, the $100 will grow to $112.68 at the end of the year. In general, if the nominal rate of r percent per year compounds m times per year, then the effective rate is $(1 - r/m)^m - 1$.

efficiency variance. A term used for the *quantity variance* for materials or labor or variable overhead in a *standard costing system.*

electronic data processing. Performing computations and other data organizing steps in a computer, in contrast to doing these steps by hand or, several decades earlier, with mechanical calculators.

Emerging Issues Task Force (EITF). A group convened by the *FASB* to deal more rapidly with accounting issues than the FASB's due-process procedures can allow. The task force comprises about 20 members from public accounting, industry, and several trade associations. It meets every six weeks. Several FASB board members usually attend and participate. The chief accountant of the *SEC* has indicated that the SEC will require that published financial statements follow guidelines set by a consensus of the EITF. The EITF requires that nearly all its members agree on a position before that position receives the label of "consensus." Such positions appear in *Abstracts of the EITF*, published by the FASB. Since 1984, the EITF has become one of the promulgators of *GAAP*.

enabling costs. A type of *capacity cost* that a firm will stop incurring if it shuts down operations completely but will incur in full if it carries out operations at any level. Examples include costs of a security force or of a quality control inspector for an assembly line. Contrast with *standby costs*.

ending inventory. The *cost* of *inventory* on hand at the end of the *accounting period*, often called "closing inventory." Ending inventory from the end of one period becomes the *beginning inventory* for the next period.

engineered cost center. Responsibility center with sufficiently well established relations between inputs and outputs that the analyst can predict the outputs given data on inputs or, conversely, given the outputs can estimate the amounts of inputs that the process should have used. Consider the relation between pounds of flour (input) and loaves of bread (output). In contrast to discretionary cost center where such relations are so imprecise that analysts have no reliable way to relate inputs to outputs. Consider the relation between advertising the corporate logo or trademark (input) and future revenues (output).

engineering method (of cost estimation). To estimate unit cost of product from study of the materials, labor, and overhead components of the production process.

enterprise. Any business organization, usually defining the accounting *entity*.

entity. A person, *partnership, corporation*, or other organization. The *accounting entity* that issues accounting statements may not be the same as the entity defined by law. For example, a sole proprietorship is an accounting entity, but the individual's combined business and personal assets are the legal entity in most jurisdictions. Several affiliated corporations may be separate legal entities but issue *consolidated financial statements* for the group of companies operating as a single economic entity.

EOQ. *Economic order quantity*.

EPVI. *Excess present value index*.

equities. *Liabilities* plus *owners' equity*. See *equity*.

equity. A claim to *assets*; a source of assets. *SFAC No. 3* defines equity as "the residual interest in the assets of an entity that remains after deducting its liabilities." Thus, many knowledgeable people use "equity" to exclude liabilities and count only owners' equities. We prefer to use the term to mean all liabilities plus all owners' equity because there is no other single word that serves this useful purpose. We fight a losing battle.

equity financing. Raising *funds* by issuing *capital stock*. Contrast with *debt financing*.

equity ratio. *Shareholders' equity* divided by total *assets*. See *ratio*.

equivalent production. *Equivalent units*.

equivalent units (of work). The number of units of completed output that would require the same costs as a firm would actually incur for production of completed and partially completed units during a period. For example, if at the beginning of a period the firm starts 100 units and by the end of the period has incurred costs for each of these equal to 75 percent of total costs to complete the unit, then the equivalent units of work for the period is 75. Used primarily in *process costing* calculations to measure in uniform terms the output of a continuous process.

escapable cost. *Avoidable cost*.

estimated liability. The preferred terminology for estimated costs the firm will incur for such uncertain things as repairs under *warranty*. An estimated liability appears on the *balance sheet*. Contrast with *contingency*.

estimation sampling. The use of sampling technique in which the sampler infers a qualitative (e.g., fraction female) or quantitative (e.g., mean weight) characteristic of the population from the occurrence of that characteristic in the sample drawn. See *attribute(s) sampling*; *variables sampling*.

except for. Qualification in *auditor's report*, usually caused by a change, approved by the auditor, from one acceptable accounting principle or procedure to another.

excess present value. In a *capital budgeting* context, *present value* (of anticipated net cash inflows minus cash outflows including initial cash outflow) for a project. The analyst uses the *cost of capital* as the *discount rate*.

excess present value index. *Present value* of future *cash* inflows divided by initial cash outlay.

exchange. The generic term for a transaction (or, more technically, a reciprocal transfer) between one *entity* and another; in another context, the name for a market, such as the New York Stock Exchange.

executory contract. A mere exchange of promises; an agreement providing for payment by a payor to a payee on the performance of an act or service by the payee, such as a labor contract. Accounting does not recognize benefits arising from executory contracts as *assets,* nor does it recognize obligations arising from such contracts as *liabilities*.

exit value. The proceeds that would be received if assets were disposed of in an *arm's-length transaction. Current selling price. Net realizable value*.

expected value. The mean or arithmetic *average* of a statistical distribution or series of numbers.

expected value of (perfect) information. Expected net benefits from an undertaking with (perfect) information minus expected net benefits of the undertaking without (perfect) information.

expenditure. Payment of *cash* for *goods* or *services* received. Payment may occur at the time the purchaser receives the goods or services or at a later time. Virtually synonymous with *disbursement* except that disbursement is a broader term and includes all payments for goods or services. Contrast with *expense*.

expense. As a noun, a decrease in *owners' equity* accompanying the decrease in *net assets* caused by selling *goods* or rendering *services* or by the passage of time; a "gone" (net) asset; an expired cost. Measure expense as the *cost* of the (net) assets used. Do not confuse with *expenditure* or *disbursement*, which may occur before, when, or after the firm recognizes the related expense. Use the word "cost" to refer to an item that still has service potential and is an asset. Use the word "expense" after the firm has used the asset's service potential. As a verb, "expense" means to designate an expenditure— past, current, or future—as a current expense.

Exposure Draft (ED). A preliminary statement of the *FASB* showing the contents of a pronouncement being considered for enactment by the board.

extraordinary item. A *material expense* or *revenue* item characterized both by its unusual nature and by its infrequency of occurrence; appears along with its income tax effects separately from ordinary income and income from discontinued operations on the *income statement*. Accountants would probably classify a *loss* from an earthquake as an extraordinary item. Accountants treat gain (or loss) on the retirement of *bonds* as an extraordinary item under the terms of *SFAS No. 4*.

F

face amount (value). The nominal amount due at *maturity* from a *bond* or *note* not including the contractual periodic payment that may also come due on the same date. Good usage calls the corresponding amount of a stock certificate the *par* or *stated value*, whichever applies.

factory. Used synonymously with manufacturing as an adjective.

factory burden. *Manufacturing overhead.*

factory cost. *Manufacturing cost.*

factory expense. *Manufacturing overhead. Expense* is a poor term in this context because the item is a *product cost*.

factory overhead. Usually an item of *manufacturing cost* other than *direct labor* or *direct materials*.

fair market price (value). See *fair value*.

fair presentation (fairness). One of the qualitative standards of financial reporting. When the *auditor's report* says that the *financial statements* "present fairly . . . ," the auditor means that the accounting alternatives used by the entity all comply with *GAAP*. In recent years, however, courts have ruled that conformity with *generally accepted accounting principles* may be insufficient grounds for an opinion that the statements are fair. *SAS No. 5* requires that the auditor judge the accounting principles used to be "appropriate in the circumstances" before attesting to fair presentation.

fair value, fair market price (value). *Price* (value) negotiated at *arm's length* between a willing buyer and a willing seller, each acting rationally in his or her own self-interest. The accountant may estimate this amount in the absence of a monetary transaction. This is sometimes measured as the present value of expected cash flows.

FASAC. *Financial Accounting Standards Advisory Council.*

FASB (Financial Accounting Standards Board). An independent board responsible, since 1973, for establishing *generally accepted accounting principles*. Its official pronouncements are *Statements of Financial Accounting Concepts (SFAC)*, *Statements of Financial Accounting Standards (SFAS)*, and *FASB Interpretations*. See also *Discussion Memorandum*.

FASB Interpretation. An official statement of the *FASB* interpreting the meaning of *Accounting Research Bulletins*, *APB Opinions*, and *Statements of Financial Accounting Standards*.

favorable variance. An excess of actual *revenues* over expected revenues; an excess of *standard cost* over actual cost.

federal income tax. *Income tax* levied by the U.S. government on individuals and corporations.

feedback. The process of informing employees about how their actual performance compares with the expected or desired level of performance in the hope that the information will reinforce desired behavior and reduce unproductive behavior.

FICA (Federal Insurance Contributions Act). The law that sets Social Security taxes and benefits.

fiduciary. Someone responsible for the custody or administration of property belonging to another; as an executor (of an estate), agent, receiver (in *bankruptcy*), or trustee (of a trust).

FIFO (first-in, first-out). The *inventory flow assumption* that firms use to compute *ending inventory* cost from most recent purchases and *cost of goods sold* from oldest purchases including beginning inventory. FIFO describes cost flow from the viewpoint of the income statement. From the balance sheet perspective, *LISH* (last-in, still-here) describes this same cost flow. Contrast with *LIFO*.

finance. As a verb, to supply with *funds* through the *issue* of *stocks, bonds, notes,* or *mortgages* or through the retention of earnings.

financial accounting. The accounting for *assets, equities, revenues*, and *expenses* of a business. Primarily concerned with the historical reporting of the financial position and operations of an *entity* to external users on a regular, periodic basis. Contrast with *managerial accounting*.

Financial Accounting Foundation. The independent foundation (committee) that raises funds to support the *FASB* and *GASB*.

Financial Accounting Standards Advisory Council (FASAC). A committee of academics, preparers, attestors, and users giving advice to the *FASB* on matters of strategy and emerging issues. The council spends much of each meeting learning about current developments in standard setting from the FASB staff.

Financial Accounting Standards Board. *FASB*.

Financial Executives Institute (FEI). An organization of financial executives, such as chief accountants, *controllers*, and treasurers, of large businesses. In recent years, the FEI has been a critic of the *FASB* because it views many of the FASB requirements as burdensome while not *cost-effective*.

financial expense. An *expense* incurred in raising or managing *funds*.

financial statements. The *balance sheet, income statement, statement of retained earnings, statement of cash flows*, statement of changes in *owners' equity accounts*, and *notes* thereto.

financial structure. *Capital structure*.

financial vice-president. Person in charge of the entire accounting and finance function; typically one of the three most influential people in the company.

financing activities. Obtaining resources from (a) owners and providing them with a return on and a return of their *investment* and (b) *creditors* and repaying amounts borrowed (or otherwise settling the obligation). See *statement of cash flows*.

financing lease. *Capital lease*.

finished goods (inventory account). Manufactured product ready for sale; a *current asset* (inventory) account.

firm. Informally, any business entity. (Strictly speaking, a firm is a *partnership*.)

first-in, first-out. See *FIFO*.

fiscal year. A period of 12 consecutive months chosen by a business as the *accounting period* for *annual reports*, not necessarily a *natural business year* or a calendar year.

fixed assets. *Plant assets*.

fixed assets turnover. *Sales* divided by average total *fixed assets*.

fixed budget. A plan that provides for specified amounts of *expenditures* and *receipts* that do not vary with activity levels; sometimes called a "static budget." Contrast with *flexible budget*.

fixed charges earned (coverage) ratio. *Income* before *interest expense* and *income tax* expense divided by interest expense.

fixed cost (expense). An *expenditure* or *expense* that does not vary with volume of activity, at least in the short run. See *capacity costs*, which include *enabling costs* and *standby costs*, and *programmed costs* for various subdivisions of fixed costs. See *cost terminology*.

fixed interval sampling. A method of choosing a sample in which the analyst selects the first item from the population randomly, with the remaining sample items drawn at equally spaced intervals.

fixed liability. *Long-term liability*.

fixed manufacturing overhead applied. The portion of fixed *manufacturing overhead* cost allocated to units produced during a period.

fixed overhead variance. Difference between actual fixed manufacturing costs and fixed manufacturing costs applied to production in a *standard costing system*.

flexible budget. *Budget* that projects *receipts* and *expenditures* as a function of activity levels. Contrast with *fixed budget*.

flexible budget allowance. With respect to *manufacturing overhead*, the total cost that a firm should have incurred at the level of activity actually experienced during the period.

flow. The change in the amount of an item over time. Contrast with *stock*.

flow assumption. An assumption used when the firm makes a withdrawal from *inventory*. The firm must compute the cost of the withdrawal by a flow assumption if the firm does not use the *specific identification* method. The usual flow assumptions are *FIFO, LIFO*, and *weighted average*.

flow of costs. *Costs* passing through various classifications within an *entity* engaging, at least in part, in manufacturing activities. See the accompanying diagram for a summary of *product* and *period cost* flows.

footing. Adding a column of figures.

footnotes. More detailed information than that provided in the *income statement, balance sheet, statement of retained earnings*, and *statement of cash flows*. These are an integral part of the statements, and the *auditor's report* covers them. They are sometimes called "notes."

forward price. The price of a commodity for delivery at a specified future date. In contrast to the "spot price," the price of that commodity on the day of the price quotation.

franchise. A privilege granted or sold, such as to use a name or to sell products or services.

Flow of Costs (and Sales Revenue)

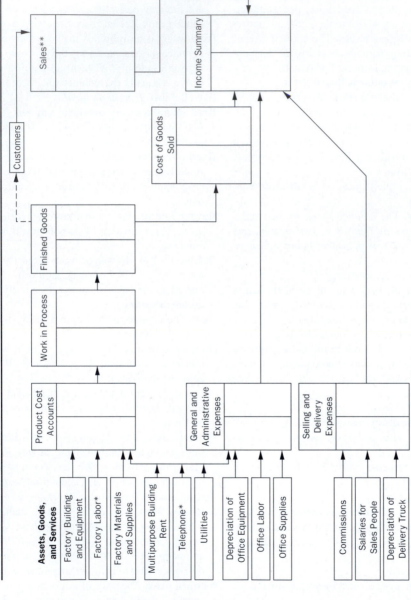

*The credit in the entry to record these items is usually to a payable, for all others, the credit is usually to an asset, or to an asset contra account.
**When the firm records sales to customers, it credits the Sales account. The debit is usually to Cash or Accounts Receivable.

fraudulent financial reporting. Intentional or reckless conduct that results in materially misleading *financial statements*.

free cash flow. Financial statement analysts' term meaning *cash flow from operations + interest expense + income tax expense*.

full absorption costing. The *costing* method that assigns all types of manufacturing costs (*direct material, direct labor,* fixed and variable overhead) to units produced; required by *GAAP;* also called "absorption costing." Contrast with *variable costing.*

full costing, full costs. The total cost of producing and selling a unit; often used in *long-term* profitability and pricing decisions. Full cost per unit equals *full absorption cost* per unit plus *marketing, administrative, interest*, and other *central corporate expenses*, per unit. The sum of full costs for all units equals total costs of the firm.

full disclosure. The reporting policy requiring that all significant or *material* information appear in the financial statements.

fully diluted earnings per share. Smallest earnings per share figure on common stock that one can obtain by computing an earnings per share for all possible combinations of assumed exercise or conversion of potentially dilutive securities. This figure must appear on the *income statement* if it is less than 97 percent of earnings available to common shareholders divided by the average number of *common shares* outstanding during the period.

function. In mathematics, a rule for associating a number, called the dependent variable, with another number (or numbers), called independent variable(s).

funding. Replacing *short-term* liabilities with *long-term* debt.

funds. Generally *working capital*; *current assets* less *current liabilities;* sometimes used to refer to *cash* or to cash and *marketable securities.*

funds provided by operations. See *cash provided by operations.*

FUTA (Federal Unemployment Tax Act). Provides for taxes to be collected at the federal level, to help subsidize the individual states' administration of their unemployment compensation programs.

future value. Value at a specified future date of a sum increased at a specified *interest rate.*

G

GAAP. *Generally accepted accounting principles.* A plural noun.

GAAS. *Generally accepted auditing standards.* A plural noun. Do not confuse with *GAS.*

gain. Increase in *owners' equity* caused by a *transaction* that is not part of a firm's typical, day-to-day operations and not part of owners' *investment* or withdrawals. Accounting distinguishes the meaning of the term "gain" (or *loss*) from that of related terms. First, gains (and losses) generally refer to nonoperating, incidental, peripheral, or nonroutine transactions: gain on sale of land in contrast to *gross margin* on *sale of inventory.* Second, gains and losses are *net* concepts, not gross concepts: gain or loss results from subtracting some measure of *cost* from the measure of inflow. *Revenues* and *expenses*, on the other hand, are gross concepts; their difference is a net concept. Gain is nonroutine and net, *profit* or *margin* is routine and net; revenue from continuing operations is routine and gross; revenue from discontinued operations is nonroutine and gross. Loss is net but can be either routine ("loss on sale of inventory") or not ("loss on disposal of segment of business").

GAS. *Goods available for sale.* Do not confuse with *GAAS.*

GASB (Governmental Accounting Standards Board). An independent body responsible, since 1984, for establishing accounting standards for state and local government units. It is part of the *Financial Accounting Foundation*, parallel to the *FASB*, and currently consists of five members.

general expenses. *Operating expenses* other than those specifically identified as cost of goods sold, selling, and administration.

generally accepted accounting principles (GAAP). As defined by the *FASB*, the conventions, rules, and procedures necessary to define accepted accounting practice at a particular time; includes both broad guidelines and relatively detailed practices and procedures. In the United States the FASB defines GAAP to include accounting pronouncements of the *SEC* and other government agencies as well as a variety of authoritative sources, such as this book.

generally accepted auditing standards (GAAS). The standards, as opposed to particular procedures, that are promulgated by the *AICPA* (in *Statements on Auditing Standards*) and that concern "the auditor's professional quantities" and "the judgment exercised by him in the performance of his examination and in his report." Currently, there are ten such standards: three general ones (concerned with proficiency, independence, and degree of care to be exercised), three standards of field work, and four standards of reporting. The first standard of reporting requires that the *auditor's report* state whether the firm prepared the *financial statements* in accordance with *generally accepted accounting principles*. Thus the typical auditor's report says that the auditor conducted the examination in accordance with generally accepted auditing standards and that the firm prepared the statements in accordance with generally accepted accounting principles. See *auditor's report*.

goal congruence. The idea that all members of an organization have incentives to perform for a common interest, such as shareholder wealth maximization for a *corporation*.

going-concern assumption. For accounting purposes, accountants' assumption that a business will remain in operation long enough to carry out all its current plans. This assumption partially justifies the *acquisition cost* basis, rather than a liquidation or *exit value* basis, of accounting.

going public. Said of a business when its *shares* become widely traded rather than being closely held by relatively few shareholders; issuing shares to the general investing public.

goods. Items of merchandise, supplies, raw materials, or finished goods. Sometimes the meaning of "goods" is extended to include all *tangible* items, as in the phrase "goods and services."

goods available for sale. The sum of *beginning inventory* plus all acquisitions of merchandise or finished goods during an *accounting period*.

goods-in-process. *Work-in-process.*

goodwill. The excess of cost of an acquired firm (or operating unit) over the current *fair market value* of the separately identifiable *net assets* of the acquired unit. Before the acquiring firm can recognize goodwill, it must assign a fair market value to all identifiable assets, even when not recorded on the books of the acquired unit. Informally, the term indicates the value of good customer relations, high employee morale, a well respected business name, and so on, all of which the firm or analyst expects to result in greater-than-normal earning power.

Governmental Accounting Standards Board. *GASB.*

gross. Not adjusted or reduced by deductions or subtractions. Contrast with *net,* and see *gain* for a description of how the difference between net and gross affects usage of the terms *revenue, gain, expense,* and *loss*.

gross margin. *Net sales* minus *cost of goods sold*.

gross margin percent. $100 \times (1 - cost\ of\ goods\ sold/net\ sales) = 100 \times (gross\ margin/net\ sales)$.

gross profit. *Gross margin.*

gross profit ratio. *Gross margin* divided by *net sales*.

gross sales. All *sales* at *invoice* prices, not reduced by *discounts*, allowances, *returns*, or other adjustments.

guarantee. A promise to answer for payment of debt or performance of some obligation if the person liable for the debt or obligation fails to perform. A guarantee is a *contingency* of the *entity* making the promise. Often, writers use the words "guarantee" and "warranty" to mean the same thing. In precise usage, however, "guarantee" means a promise to fulfill the promise of some person to perform a contractual obligation such as to pay a sum of cash, whereas "warranty" refers to promises about pieces of machinery or other products. See *warranty*.

H

hardware. The physical equipment or devices forming a computer and peripheral equipment.

hash total. Used to establish accuracy of data processing; a control that takes the sum of data items not normally added together (e.g., the sum of a list of part numbers) and subsequently compares that sum with a computer-generated total of the same values. If the two sums are identical, then the analyst takes some comfort that the two lists are identical.

Hasselback. An annual directory of accounting faculty at colleges and universities; gives information about the faculty's training and fields of specialization. James R. Hasselback, of Florida State University, has compiled the directory since the 1970s; Prentice-Hall distributes it.

historical cost. *Acquisition cost; original cost;* a *sunk cost.*

historical summary. A part of the *annual report* to shareholders that shows items, such as *net income, revenues, expenses, asset* and *equity* totals, earnings per share, and the like, for five or ten periods including the current one. Usually not as much detail appears in the historical summary as in *comparative statements,* which typically report as much detail for the two preceding years as for the current year. Annual reports may contain both comparative statements and a historical summary.

holding gain or loss. Difference between end-of-period price and beginning-of-period price of an asset held during the period. The *financial statements* ordinarily do not separately report realized holding gains and losses. Income does not usually report unrealized gains at all, except on trading securities. See *lower of cost or* *market.* See *inventory profit* for further refinement, including *gains* on *assets* sold during the period.

horizontal analysis. *Time-series analysis.*

horizontal integration. The extension of activity by an organization in the same general line of business or expansion into supplementary, complementary, or compatible products. Compare *vertical integration.*

human resource accounting. A term used to describe a variety of proposals that seek to report the importance of human resources—knowledgeable, trained, and loyal employees—in a company's earning process and total assets.

hurdle rate. Required rate of return in a *discounted cash flow* analysis.

I

I. *Identity matrix.*

IASC. *International Accounting Standards Committee.*

ICMA (Institute of Certified Management Accountants). See *CMA* and *Institute of Management Accountants.*

ideal standard costs. *Standard costs* set equal to those that a firm would incur under the best possible conditions.

identity matrix. A square *matrix* with ones on the main diagonal and zeros elsewhere; a matrix **I** such that for any other matrix **A, IA = AI = A.** The matrix equivalent to the number one.

IIA. *Institute of Internal Auditors.*

IMA. *Institute of Management Accountants.*

impairment. Reduction in *market value* of an *asset.* When the firm has information indicating that its long-lived *assets,* such as *plant,* identifiable *intangibles,* and *goodwill,* have declined in market value or will provide a smaller future benefit that originally anticipated, it tests to see if the decline in value is so drastic that the expected future cash flows from the asset have declined below *book value.* If then-current book value exceeds the sum of expected cash flows, an asset impairment has occurred. At the time the firm judges that an impairment has occurred, the firm writes down the book value of the asset to its then-current *fair value,* which is the market value of the asset or, if the firm cannot assess the market value, the expected *net present value* of the future cash flows.

implicit interest. *Interest* not paid or received. See *interest, imputed.* All transactions involving the deferred payment or receipt of *cash* involve interest, whether explicitly stated or not. The implicit interest on a single-payment *note* equals the difference between the amount collected at maturity and the amount lent at the start of the loan. One can compute the implicit *interest rate* per year for loans with a single cash inflow and a single cash outflow from the following equation:

$$\left[\frac{\text{Cash Received at Maturity}}{\text{Cash Lent}} \right]^{(1/t)} - 1$$

where *t* is the term of the loan in years; *t* need not be an integer.

imputed cost. A cost that does not appear in accounting records, such as the *interest* that a firm could earn on cash spent to acquire inventories rather than, say, government bonds. Or, consider a firm that owns the buildings it occupies. This firm has an imputed cost for rent in an amount equal to what it would have to pay to use similar buildings owned by another or to the amount it could collect from someone else who rents the same premises from the firm. *Opportunity cost.*

imputed interest. See *interest, imputed.*

in the black (red). Operating at a *profit* (*loss*).

incentive compatible compensation. Said of a compensation plan that induces managers to act for the interests of owners while acting also in their own interests. For example, consider a time of rising prices and increasing inventories when using a *LIFO* cost flow assumption implies paying lower *income taxes* than using *FIFO.* A bonus scheme for managers based on accounting *net income* is not incentive-compatible because owners likely benefit more under LIFO, whereas managers benefit more if they report using FIFO. See *LIFO conformity rule; goal congruence.*

income. Excess of *revenues* and gains over *expenses* and *losses* for a period; *net income.*

income accounts. *Revenue* and *expense accounts.*

income before taxes. On the *income statement,* the difference between all *revenues* and *expenses* except *income tax* expense. Contrast with *net income.*

income determination. See *determine.*

income smoothing. A method of timing business *transactions* or choosing *accounting principles* so that the firm reports smaller variations in *income* from year to year than it otherwise would. Although some managements set income smoothing as an objective, no standard setter does.

income statement. The statement of *revenues, expenses, gains,* and *losses* for the period, ending with *net income* for the period. Accountants usually show the earnings-per-share amount on the income statement; the *reconciliation* of beginning and ending balances of *retained earnings* may also appear in a combined statement of income and retained earnings.

income tax. An annual tax levied by the federal and other governments on the income of an entity.

incremental. An adjective used to describe the increase in *cost, expense, investment, cash flow, revenue, profit,* and the like if the firm produces or sells one or more units or if it undertakes an activity. See *differential.*

incremental cost. See *incremental.*

incur. Said of an obligation of a firm, whether or not that obligation is *accrued.* For example, a firm incurs interest expense on a loan as time passes but accrues that interest only on payment dates or when it makes an *adjusting entry.*

independence. The mental attitude required of the *CPA* in performing the *attest* function. It implies that the CPA is impartial and that the members of the auditing CPA firm own no stock in the corporation being audited.

independent accountant. The *CPA* who performs the *attest* function for a firm.

independent variable. See *regression analysis.*

indirect cost pool. Any grouping of individual costs that a firm does not identify with a *cost objective.*

indirect costs. Costs of production not easily associated with the production of specific goods and services; *overhead costs.* Accountants may *allocate* them on some *arbitrary* basis to specific products or departments.

indirect labor (material) cost. An *indirect cost* for labor (material), such as for supervisors (supplies).

indirect method. See *statement of cash flows.*

inescapable cost. A *cost* that the firm or manager cannot avoid (see *avoidable*) because of an action. For example, if management shuts down two operating rooms in a hospital but still must employ security guards in unreduced numbers, the security costs are "inescapable" with respect to the decision to close the operating rooms.

inflation. A time of generally rising prices.

information system. A system, sometimes formal and sometimes informal, for collecting, processing, and communicating data that are useful for the managerial functions of decision making, planning, and control and for financial reporting under the *attest* requirement.

installment. Partial payment of a debt or partial collection of a receivable, usually according to a contract.

Institute of Certified Management Accountants (ICMA). See *CMA* and *Institute of Management Accountants.*

Institute of Internal Auditors (IIA). The national association of accountants who are engaged in internal auditing and are employed by business firms; administers a comprehensive professional examination. Those who pass the exam qualify to be designated *CIA (Certified Internal Auditor).*

Institute of Management Accountants (IMA). Formerly, the National Association of Accountants, NAA; a society open to those engaged in management accounting; parent organization of the *ICMA,* which oversees the *CMA* program.

insurance. A contract for reimbursement of specific losses; purchased with insurance premiums. "Self-insurance" is not insurance but is merely the noninsured's willingness to assume the risk of incurring losses while saving the premium.

intangible asset. A nonphysical, *noncurrent* right that gives a firm an exclusive or preferred position in the marketplace. Examples are *copyright, patent, trademark, goodwill,* organization costs, *capitalized* advertising cost, computer programs, licenses for any of the preceding, government licenses (e.g., broadcasting or the right to sell liquor), *leases, franchises,* mailing lists, exploration permits, import and export permits, construction permits, and marketing quotas. Commonly, accountants define "intangible" with a "for example" list, as we have just done, because accounting has been unable to devise a definition of "intangible" that will include items such as those listed above but exclude stock and bond certificates. Accountants classify these items as tangibles, even though they give their holders a preferred position in receiving dividends and interest payments.

intercompany transaction. *Transaction* between parent company and *subsidiary* or between subsidiaries in a consolidated entity; the accountant must eliminate the effects of such a transaction when preparing *consolidated financial statements.*

intercorporate investment. When a given *corporation* owns *shares* or *debt* issued by another.

interdepartment monitoring. An *internal control* device. An advantage of allocating *service department costs* to *production departments* stems from the incentives it gives those charged with the costs to control the costs incurred in the service department. That process of having one group monitor the performance of another is interdepartment monitoring.

interest. The charge or cost for using *cash,* usually borrowed funds. Interest on one's own cash used is an *opportunity cost, imputed interest.* The amount of interest for a loan is the total amount paid by a borrower to a lender less the amount paid by the lender to the borrower. Accounting seeks to allocate that interest over the time of the loan so that the interest rate (= interest charge/amount borrowed) stays constant each period. See *interest rate* for discussion of quoted amount. See *effective interest rate* and *nominal interest rate*.

interest, imputed. The difference between the face amount and the present value of a promise. If a borrower merely promises to pay a single amount, sometime later than the present, then the face amount the borrower will repay at *maturity* will exceed the present value (computed at a *fair market* interest rate, called the "imputed interest rate") of the promise. See also *imputed cost*.

interest factor. One plus the *interest* rate.

interest rate. A basis used for computing the cost of borrowing funds usually expressed as a ratio per period of time between the number of currency units (e.g., dollars) charged per number of currency units borrowed for that same period of time. When the writers and speakers do not state a period, they almost always mean a period of one year.

internal audit, internal auditor. An *audit* conducted by the firm's own employees, called "internal auditors," to ascertain whether the firm's *internal control* procedures work as planned. Contrast with an external audit conducted by a *CPA*.

internal controls. Policies and procedures designed to provide management with reasonable assurances that employees behave in a way that enables the firm to meet its organizational goals. See *control system*.

internal rate of return (IRR). The discount rate that equates the net *present value* of a stream of cash outflows and inflows to zero.

internal reporting. Reporting for management's use in planning and control. Contrast with external reporting for *financial statement* users.

Internal Revenue Service (IRS). Agency of the U.S. Treasury Department responsible for administering the Internal Revenue Code and collecting income and certain other taxes.

International Accounting Standards Committee (IASC). An organization that promotes the international harmonization of accounting standards.

interpolation. The estimation of an unknown number intermediate between two (or more) known numbers.

inventoriable costs. *Costs* incurred that the firm adds to the cost of manufactured products; *product costs* (*assets*) as opposed to *period expenses*.

inventory. As a noun, the *balance* in an asset *account* such as raw materials, supplies, work in process, and finished goods; as a verb, to calculate the *cost* of goods on hand at a given time or to count items on hand physically.

inventory equation. *Beginning inventory* + net additions − withdrawals = *ending inventory.* Ordinarily, additions are net purchases, and withdrawals are *cost of goods sold*. Notice that ending inventory, appearing on the balance sheet, and cost of goods sold, appearing on the income statement, must add to a fixed sum. The larger is one; the smaller must be the other. In valuing inventories, the firm usually knows beginning inventory and net purchases. Some inventory methods (for example, some applications of the retail inventory method) measure costs of goods sold and use the equation to find the cost of ending inventory. Most methods measure cost of ending inventory and use the equation to find the cost of goods sold (withdrawals).

inventory profit. A term with several possible meanings. Consider the data in the accompanying illustration. The firm uses a *FIFO cost flow assumption* and derives its *historical cost* data. The assumed *current cost* data resemble those that the *FASB* suggested in *SFAS No. 89*. The term "income from continuing operations" refers to revenues less expenses based on current, rather than historical, costs. To that subtotal, add realized holding gains to arrive at realized (conventional) income. To that, add unrealized holding gains to arrive at economic income. The term "inventory profit" often refers (for example in some *SEC* releases) to the realized holding gain, $110 in the illustration. The amount of inventory profit will usually be material when the firm uses FIFO and when prices rise. Other analysts, including us, prefer to use the term "inventory profit" to refer to the total *holding gain*, $300 (= $110 + $190, both realized and unrealized), but writers use this meaning less often. In periods of rising prices and increasing inventories, the realized holding gains under a FIFO cost flow assumption will exceed those under LIFO. In the illustration, for example, assume under LIFO that the historical cost of goods sold is $4,800, that historical LIFO cost of beginning inventory is $600, and that historical LIFO cost of ending inventory is $800. Then income from continuing operations, based on current costs, remains $350 (= $5,200 − $4,850), realized holding gains are $50 (= $4,850 − $4,800), realized income is $400 (= $350 + $50), the unrealized holding gain for the year is $250 [= ($1,550 − $800) − ($1,100 − $600)], and economic income is $650 (= $350 + $50 + $250).

The cost flow assumption has only one real effect on this series of calculations: the split of the total holding gain into realized and unrealized portions. Thus, economic income does not depend on the cost flow assumption. Holding gains total $300 in the illustration. The choice of cost flow assumption determines the portion reported as realized.

Inventory Profit Illustration

	(Historical) Acquisition Cost Assuming FIFO	Current Cost
ASSUMED DATA		
Inventory, 1/1.	$ 900	$1,100
Inventory, 12/31.	1,160	1,550
Cost of Goods Sold for the Year .	4,740	4,850
Sales for the Year	$5,200	$5,200
INCOME STATEMENT FOR THE YEAR		
Sales	$5,200	$5,200
Cost of Goods Sold	4,740	4,850
(1) Income from Continuing Operations		$ 350
Realized Holding Gains		110[a]
(2) Realized Income = Conventional Net Income (under FIFO)	$ 460	$ 460
Unrealized Holding Gain		190[b]
(3) Economic Income		$ 650

[a]Realized holding gain during a period is current cost of goods sold less historical cost of goods sold; for the year the realized holding gain under FIFO is $110 = $4,850 − $4,740. Some refer to this as "inventory profit."

[b]The total unrealized holding gain at any time is current cost of inventory on hand at that time less historical cost of that inventory. The unrealized holding gain during a period is unrealized holding gain at the end of the period less the unrealized holding gain prior to this year is $200 = $1,100 − $900. Unrealized holding gain during the year = ($1,550 − $1,160) − ($1,100 − $900) = $390 − $200 = $190.

inventory turnover. Number of times the firm sells the average *inventory* during a period; *cost of goods sold* for a period divided by average inventory for the period. See *ratio*.

investing activities. Lending funds and collecting *principal* (but not *interest*, which is an *operating activity*) on those loans; acquiring and selling *securities* or produc-

tive *assets* expected to produce *revenue* over several *periods*.

investment. An *expenditure* to acquire property or other *assets* in order to produce *revenue*; the asset so acquired; hence a current expenditure made in anticipation of future income; said of other companies' *securities* held for the long term and appearing in a separate section of the *balance sheet;* in this context, contrast with *marketable securities*.

investment center. A *responsibility center,* with control over *revenues, costs,* and *assets*.

investment decision. The decision whether to undertake an action involving production of goods or services.

investment turnover ratio. A term that means the same thing as *total assets turnover ratio*. We sometimes use it for a *division,* something less than the entire firm.

investments. A *balance sheet* heading for *tangible assets* held for periods longer than the operating cycle and not used in *revenue* production (assets not meeting the definitions of *current assets* or *property, plant, and equipment*).

invoice. A document showing the details of a sale or purchase *transaction*.

I.O.U. An informal document acknowledging a debt, setting out the amount of the debt and signed by the debtor.

IRR. *Internal rate of return*.

IRS. *Internal Revenue Service*.

isoprofit line. On a graph showing feasible production possibilities of two products that require the use of the same, limited resources, a line showing all feasible production possibility combinations with the same *profit* or, perhaps, *contribution margin*.

issue. A corporation exchange of its stock (or *bonds*) for *cash* or other *assets*. Terminology says the corporation "issues," not "sells," that stock (or bonds). Also used in the context of withdrawing supplies or materials from inventory for use in operations and of drawing a check.

J

JIT. See *just-in-time inventory*.

job cost sheet. A schedule showing actual or budgeted inputs for a special order.

job (-order) costing. Accumulation of *costs* for a particular identifiable batch of product, known as a job, as it moves through production.

joint cost. Cost of simultaneously producing or otherwise acquiring two or more products, called *joint products,* that a firm must, by the nature of the process, produce or acquire together, such as the cost of beef and hides of cattle. Generally, accounting allocates the joint costs of production to the individual products in proportion to their respective sales value (or, sometimes and usually not preferred, their respective physical quantities) at the *split-off* point. Other examples include *central corporate expenses* and *overhead* of a department when it manufactures several products.

joint cost allocation. See *joint cost*.

joint product. One of two or more outputs with significant value produced by a process that a firm must produce or acquire simultaneously. See *by-product* and *joint cost*.

journal. The place where the firm records *transactions* as they occur; the book of original entry.

journal entry. A dated recording in a *journal,* showing the accounts affected, of equal *debits* and *credits,* with an explanation of the *transaction,* if necessary.

judgment(al) sampling. A method of choosing a sample in which the analyst subjectively selects items for examination, in contrast to selecting them by statistical methods. Compare *random sampling*.

just-in-time inventory (production) (JIT). In managing *inventory* for manufacturing, system in which a firm purchases or manufactures each component just before the firm uses it. Contrast with systems in which firms acquire or manufacture many parts in advance of needs. JIT systems have much smaller carrying costs for inventory, ideally none, but run higher risks of incurring *stockout* costs.

K

k. Two to the tenth power (2^{10} or 1,024), when referring to computer storage capacity. The one-letter abbreviation derives from the first letter of the prefix "kilo-" (which means 1,000 in decimal notation).

Kaizen costing. A management concept that seeks continuous improvements, likely occurring in small, incremental amounts, by refinements of all components of a production process.

L

labor variances. The *price* (or *rate*) and *quantity* (or *usage*) *variances* for *direct labor* inputs in a *standard costing system*.

lapping (accounts receivable). The theft, by an employee, of cash sent in by a customer to discharge the latter's *payable*. The employee conceals the theft from the first customer by using cash received from a second customer. The employee conceals the theft from the second customer by using cash received from a third customer, and so on. The process continues until the thief returns the funds or can make the theft permanent by creating a fictitious *expense* or receivable write-off or until someone discovers the fraud.

lead time. The time that elapses between placing an order and receiving the *goods* or *services* ordered.

learning curve. A mathematical expression of the phenomenon that incremental unit costs to produce decrease as managers and labor gain experience from practice.

lease. A contract calling for the lessee (user) to pay the lessor (owner) for the use of an asset. A cancelable lease allows the lessee to cancel at any time. A noncancelable lease requires payments from the lessee for the life of the lease and usually shares many of the economic characteristics of *debt financing*.

least and latest rule. Paying the least amount of taxes as late as possible within the law to minimize the *present value* of tax payments for a given set of operations. Sensible taxpayers will follow this rule. When a taxpayer knows that tax rates will increase later, the taxpayer may reduce the present value of the tax burden by paying smaller taxes sooner. Each set of circumstances requires its own computations.

ledger. A book of accounts; book of final entry. Contrast with *journal*.

leverage. Some measure of output increases faster than the measure of input. "Operating leverage" refers to the tendency of *net income* to rise at a faster rate than sales in the presence of *fixed costs*. A doubling of sales, for example, usually implies a more than doubling of net income. "Financial leverage" (or "capital leverage") refers to an increase in rate of return larger than the increase in explicit financing costs—the increased rate of return on *owners' equity* (see *ratio*) when an *investment* earns a return larger than the after-tax *interest rate* paid for *debt financing*. Because the interest charges on debt usually do not change, any *incremental* income benefits owners and none benefits debtors. When writers use the term "leverage" without a qualifying adjective, the term usually refers to financial leverage, the use of *long-term* debt in securing *funds* for the *entity*.

liability. An obligation to pay a definite (or reasonably definite) amount at a definite (or reasonably definite) time in return for a past or current benefit (that is, the obligation arises from a transaction that is not an *executory contract*); a probable future sacrifice of economic benefits arising from present obligations of a particular *entity* to transfer *assets* or to provide services to other entities in the future as a result of past *transactions* or events. The *FASB* says that "probable" refers to that which we can reasonably expect or believe but that is neither certain nor proved. A liability has three essential characteristics: (1) the obligation to transfer assets or services has a specified or knowable date, (2) the entity has little or no discretion to avoid the transfer, and (3) the event causing the obligation has already happened, that is, it is not executory.

LIFO (last-in, first-out). An *inventory* flow assumption in which the *cost of goods sold* equals the cost of the most recently acquired units and a firm computes the *ending inventory cost* from the costs of the oldest units. In periods of rising prices and increasing inventories, LIFO leads to higher reported expenses and therefore lower reported income and lower balance sheet inventories than does FIFO. Contrast with *FIFO*. See *inventory profit*.

LIFO conformity rule. The *IRS* rule requiring that companies that use a *LIFO cost flow assumption* for *income taxes* also use LIFO in computing *income* reported in *financial statements* and forbidding the disclosure of pro forma results from using any other cost flow assumption.

LIFO inventory layer. A portion of LIFO inventory cost reported on *balance sheet*. The *ending inventory* in physical quantity will usually exceed the *beginning inventory*; the *LIFO cost flow assumption* assigns to this increase in physical quantities a cost computed from the prices of the earliest purchases during the year. The LIFO inventory then consists of layers, sometimes called "slices," which typically consist of relatively small amounts of physical quantities from each of the past years when purchases in physical units exceeded sales in units. Each layer carries the prices from near the beginning of the period when the firm acquired it. The earliest layers will typically (in periods of rising prices) have prices much less than current prices. If inventory quantities should decline in a subsequent period—a "dip into old LIFO layers"—the latest layers enter cost of goods sold first.

line of credit. An agreement with a bank or set of banks for short-term borrowings on demand.

linear programming. A mathematical tool for finding profit-maximizing (or cost-minimizing) combinations of products to produce when a firm has several products that it can produce but faces linear constraints on the resources available in the production processes or on maximum and minimum production requirements.

liquid. Said of a business with a substantial amount (the amount is unspecified) of *working capital,* especially *quick assets*.

liquid assets. *Cash,* current *marketable securities,* and, sometimes, current *receivables*.

liquidity. Refers to the availability of *cash,* or near-cash resources, for meeting a firm's obligations.

loan. An arrangement in which the owner of property, called the lender, allows someone else, called the borrower, the use of the property for a period of time, which the agreement setting up the loan usually specifies. The borrower promises to return the property to the lender and, often, to make a payment for the use of the property. This term is generally used when the property is *cash* and the payment for its use is *interest*.

LOCOM. *Lower of cost or market.*

long-lived (term) asset. An asset whose benefits the firm expects to receive over several years; a *noncurrent* asset, usually includes *investments, plant assets,* and *intangibles*.

long-term liability (debt). *Noncurrent liability.*

long-term, long-run. A term denoting a time or time periods in the future. How far in the future depends on context. For some securities traders, "long-term" can mean anything beyond the next hour or two. For most managers, it means anything beyond the next year or two. For government policymakers, it can mean anything beyond the next decade or two. For geologists, it can mean millions of years.

long-term solvency risk. The risk that a firm will not have sufficient *cash* to pay its *debts* sometime in the *long run*.

loophole. Imprecise term meaning a technicality allowing a taxpayer (or *financial statements*) to circumvent the intent, without violating the letter, of the law (or *GAAP*).

loss. Excess of *cost* over net proceeds for a single transaction; negative *income* for a period; a cost expiration that produced no *revenue*. See *gain* for a discussion of related and contrasting terms and how to distinguish loss from *expense*.

lower of cost or market (LOCOM). A basis for valuation of *inventory*. This basis sets inventory value at the lower of *acquisition cost* or *current replacement cost* (market), subject to several constraints, not illustrated here.

M

MACRS. Modified Accelerated Cost Recovery System.

maintenance. *Expenditures* undertaken to preserve an *asset's* service potential for its originally intended life. These expenditures are *period expenses* or *product costs*. See *repair*.

make-or-buy decision. A managerial decision about whether the firm should produce a product internally or purchase it from others. Proper make-or-buy decisions in the short run result only when a firm considers *incremental costs* in the analysis.

management. Executive authority that operates a business.

management accounting. See *managerial accounting.*

management audit. An audit conducted to ascertain whether a firm or one of its operating units properly carries out its objectives, policies, and procedures; generally applies only to activities for which accountants can specify qualitative standards. See *audit* and *internal audit.*

management by exception. A principle of management in which managers focus attention on performance only if it differs significantly from that expected.

management by objective (MBO). A management approach designed to focus on the definition and attainment of overall and individual objectives with the participation of all levels of management.

management information system (MIS). A system designed to provide all levels of management with timely and reliable information required for planning, control, and evaluation of performance.

managerial (management) accounting. Reporting designed to enhance the ability of management to do its job of decision making, planning, and control. Contrast with *financial accounting.*

manufacturing cost. Cost of producing goods, usually in a factory.

manufacturing expense. An imprecise, and generally incorrect, alternative title for *manufacturing overhead.* The term is generally incorrect because these costs are usually *product costs,* not expenses.

manufacturing overhead. General manufacturing *costs* that are not directly associated with identifiable units of product and that the firm incurs in providing a capacity to carry on productive activities. Accounting treats fixed manufacturing overhead cost as a *product cost* under *full absorption costing* but as an *expense* of the period under *variable costing.*

margin. *Revenue* less specified expenses. See *contribution margin* and *gross margin.*

margin of safety. Excess of actual, or budgeted, sales over *breakeven* sales. Usually expressed in dollars; may be expressed in units of product.

marginal cost. The *incremental cost* or *differential cost* of the last unit added to production of the first unit subtracted from production. See *cost terminology* and *differential* for contrast.

marginal costing. *Variable costing.*

marginal revenue. The increment in *revenue* from the sale of one additional unit of product.

marginal tax rate. The amount, expressed as a percentage, by which income taxes increase when taxable income increases by one dollar. Contrast with *average tax rate.*

market-based transfer price. A *transfer price* based on external market data rather than internal company data.

market price. See *fair value.*

market rate. The rate of *interest* a company must pay to borrow *funds* currently. See *effective rate.*

market value. *Fair market value.*

marketable securities. Other companies' *stocks* and *bonds* held that can be readily sold on stock exchanges or over-the-counter markets and that the company plans to sell as cash is needed; classified as *current assets* and as part of "cash" in preparing the *statement of cash flows.* If the firm holds these same securities for *long-term* purposes, it will classify them as *noncurrent assets. SFAS No. 115* requires that all marketable equity and all debt securities (except those debt securities the holder has the ability and intent to hold to maturity) appear at market value on the balance sheet. The firm reports changes in market value in income for trading securities but debits holding losses (or credits holding gains) directly to owners' equity accounts for securities available for sale.

marketing costs. Costs incurred to sell; includes locating customers, persuading them to buy, delivering the goods or services, and collecting the sales proceeds.

master budget. A *budget* projecting all *financial statements* and their components.

matching convention. The concept of recognizing cost expirations *(expenses)* in the same accounting period during which the firm recognizes related *revenues;* combining or simultaneously recognizing the revenues and expenses that jointly result from the same *transactions* or other events.

material. As an adjective, it means relatively important, capable of influencing a decision (see *materiality*); as a noun, *raw material.*

materiality. The concept that accounting should disclose separately only those events that are relatively important (no operable definition yet exists) for the business or for understanding its statements. The *FASB* says that accounting information is material if "the judgment of a reasonable person relying on the information would have been changed or influenced by the omission or misstatement."

materials variances. *Price* and *quantity variances* for *direct materials* in *standard costing systems;* difference between actual cost and standard cost.

matrix. A rectangular array of numbers or mathematical symbols.

matrix inverse. For a given square *matrix* **A,** the *matrix,* A^{-1} such that $AA^{-1} = A^{-1}A = I$, the *identity matrix.* Not all square matrices have inverses. Those that do not are "singular"; those that do are nonsingular.

maturity. The date at which an obligation, such as the *principal* of a *bond* or a *note*, becomes due.

MBO. *Management by objective.*

merchandise. *Finished goods* bought by a retailer or wholesaler for resale; contrast with finished goods of a manufacturing business.

merchandise costs. Costs incurred to sell a product, such as commissions and advertising.

merchandise turnover. *Inventory turnover* for merchandise. See *ratio.*

merchandising business. As opposed to a manufacturing or service business, one that purchases (rather than manufactures) *finished goods* for resale.

merger. The joining of two or more businesses into a single *economic entity.*

MIS. *Management information system.*

mix variance. One of the manufacturing *variances.* Many *standard cost* systems specify combinations of inputs, for example, labor of a certain skill and materials of a certain quality grade. Sometimes combinations of inputs used differ from those contemplated by the standard. The mix variance attempts to report the cost difference caused by those changes in the combination of inputs.

mixed cost. A *semifixed* or a *semivariable* cost.

money. A word seldom used with precision in accounting, at least in part because economists have not yet agreed on its definition. Economists use the term to refer to both a medium of exchange and a store of value. See *cash.*

mortgage. A claim given by the borrower (mortgagor) to the lender (mortgagee) against the borrower's property in return for a loan.

moving average. An *average* computed on observations over time. As a new observation becomes available, analysts drop the oldest one so that they always compute the average for the same number of observations and use only the most recent ones.

moving average method. *Weighted-average inventory method.*

multiple-step. Said of an *income statement* that shows various subtotals of *expenses* and *losses* subtracted from *revenues* to show intermediate items such as *operating income,* income of the enterprise (operating income plus *interest* income), income to investors (income of the enterprise less *income taxes*), net income to shareholders (income to investors less interest charges), and income retained (net income to shareholders less dividends).

mutually exclusive (investment) projects. Competing investment projects where accepting one project eliminates the possibility of undertaking the remaining projects.

N

National Association of Accountants (NAA). Former name for the *Institute of Management Accountants (IMA).*

natural business year. A 12-month period chosen as the reporting period so that the end of the period coincides with a low point in activity or inventories. See *ratio* for a discussion of analyses of financial statements of companies using a natural business year.

natural resources. Timberland, oil and gas wells, ore deposits, and other products of nature that have economic value. Terminology uses the term *depletion* to refer to the process of *amortizing* the cost of natural resources. Natural resources are "nonrenewable" (for example, oil, coal, gas, ore deposits) or "renewable" (timberland, sod fields); terminology often calls the former *wasting assets.*

negotiated transfer price. A *transfer price* set jointly by the buying and the selling divisions.

net. Reduced by all relevant deductions.

net assets. Total *assets* minus total *liabilities;* equals the amount of *owners' equity.*

net current assets. *Working capital* = *current assets* − *current liabilities.*

net income. The excess of all *revenues* and *gains* for a period over all *expenses* and *losses* of the period. The *FASB* is proposing to discontinue use of this term and substitute *earnings.*

net loss. The excess of all *expenses* and *losses* for a period over all *revenues* and *gains* of the period; negative *net income.*

net present value. Discounted or *present value* of all cash inflows and outflows of a project or of an *investment* at a given *discount rate.*

net realizable (sales) value. A method for *allocating joint costs* in proportion to *realizable values* of the joint products. For example, joint products A and B together cost $100; A sells for $60, whereas B sells for $90. Then a firm would allocate to A ($60/$150) × $100 = .40 × $100 = $40 of cost while it would allocate to B ($90/$150) × $100 = $60 of cost.

net sales. Sales (at gross invoice amount) less *returns*, allowances, freight paid for customers, and *discounts* taken.

net worth. A misleading term with the same meaning as *owners' equity*. Avoid using this term; accounting valuations at historical cost do not show economic worth.

network analysis. A method of planning and scheduling a project, usually displayed in a diagram, that enables management to identify the interrelated sequences that it must accomplish to complete the project.

next-in, first-out. See *NIFO*.

NIFO (next-in, first-out). A *cost flow assumption,* one not allowed by *GAAP*. In making decisions, many managers consider *replacement costs* (rather than *historical costs*) and refer to them as NIFO costs.

no par. Said of *stock* without a *par value*.

nominal accounts. *Temporary accounts,* such as *revenue* and *expense* accounts; contrast with *balance sheet accounts*. The firm *closes* all nominal accounts at the end of each *accounting period*.

nominal amount (value). An amount stated in dollars, in contrast to an amount stated in constant dollars. Contrast with real amount (value).

nominal dollars. The measuring unit giving no consideration to differences in the general purchasing power of the dollar over time. The face amount of currency or coin, a *bond,* an *invoice,* or a *receivable* is a nominal dollar amount. When the analyst adjusts that amount for changes in general purchasing power, it becomes a constant dollar amount.

nominal interest rate. A rate specified on a *debt* instrument; usually differs from the market or *effective rate;* also, a rate of *interest* quoted for a year. If the interest compounds more often than annually, then the *effective interest rate* exceeds the nominal rate.

noncontrollable cost. A cost that a particular manager cannot control.

noncurrent. Of a *liability,* due in more than one year (or more than one *operating cycle*). Of an *asset,* the firm will enjoy the future benefit in more than one year (or more than one operating cycle).

nonmanufacturing costs. All *costs* incurred other than those necessary to produce goods. Typically, only manufacturing firms use this designation.

nonoperating. In the *income statement* context, said of *revenues* and *expenses* arising from *transactions* incidental to the company's main line(s) of business; in the *statement of cash flows* context, said of all financing and investing sources or uses of cash in contrast with cash provided by operations. See *operations*.

nonrecurring. Said of an event that is not expected to happen often for a given firm. *APB Opinion No. 30* requires firms to disclose separately the effects of such events as part of ordinary items unless the event is also unusual. See *extraordinary* item.

nonvalue-added activity. An activity that causes costs without increasing a product's or service's value to the customer.

normal costing. Method of charging costs to products using actual *direct materials,* actual *direct labor,* and predetermined *factory overhead* rates.

normal costing system. *Costing* based on *actual material* and labor *costs* but using *predetermined overhead* rates per unit of some *activity basis* (such as *direct labor* hours or machine hours) to apply overhead to production. Management decides the rate to charge to production for overhead at the start of the period. At the end of the period the accounting multiplies this rate by the actual number of units of the base activity (such as actual direct labor hours worked or actual machine hours used during the period) to apply overhead to production.

normal spoilage. Costs incurred because of ordinary amounts of spoilage. Accounting prorates such costs to units produced as *product costs*. Contrast with *abnormal spoilage*.

normal standard cost, normal standards. The *cost* a firm expects to incur under reasonably efficient operating conditions with adequate provision for an average amount of rework, spoilage, and the like.

normal volume. The level of production over a time span, usually one year, that will satisfy purchasers' demands and provide for reasonable *inventory* levels.

note. An unconditional written promise by the maker (borrower) to pay a certain amount on demand or at a certain future time. See *footnotes* for another context.

number of days sales in inventory (or receivables). Days of average inventory on hand (or average collection period for receivables). See *ratio*.

O

objective function. In *linear programming,* the name of the profit (or cost) criterion the analyst wants to maximize (or minimize).

objectivity. The reporting policy implying that the firm will not give formal recognition to an event in financial statements until the firm can measure the magnitude of the events with reasonable accuracy and check that amount with independent verification.

obsolescence. A decline in *market value* of an *asset* caused by improved alternatives becoming available that will be more *cost-effective*. The decline in market value does not relate to physical changes in the asset itself. For example, computers become obsolete long before they wear out. See *partial obsolescence*.

open account. Any *account* with a nonzero *debit* or *credit balance*.

operating. An adjective used to refer to *revenue* and *expense* items relating to the company's main line(s) of business. See *operations*.

operating accounts. *Revenue, expense,* and *production cost accounts.* Contrast with *balance sheet accounts*.

operating activities. For purposes of the *statement of cash flows,* all *transactions* and events that are neither *financing activities* nor *investing activities*. See *operations*.

operating budget. A formal *budget* for the *operating cycle* or for a year.

operating cash flow. *Cash flow from operations*. Financial statement analysts sometimes use this term to mean *cash flow from operations − capital expenditures − dividends.* This usage leads to such ambiguity that the reader should always confirm the definition the writer uses before drawing inferences from the reported data.

operating cycle. *Earnings cycle*.

operating expenses. *Expenses* incurred in the course of *ordinary* activities of an *entity;* frequently, a classification including only *selling, general,* and *administrative expenses,* thereby excluding *cost of goods sold, interest,* and *income tax* expenses.

operating lease. A *lease* accounted for by the lessee without showing an *asset* for the lease rights (leasehold) or a *liability* for the lease payment obligations. The lessee reports only rental payments during the period, as *expenses* of the period. The asset remains on the lessor's *books,* where rental collections appear as *revenues*.

operating leverage. Usually said of a firm with a large proportion of *fixed costs* in its total costs. Consider a book publisher or a railroad: Such a firm has large costs to produce the first unit of service; then, the *incremental costs* of producing another book or transporting another freight car are much less than the average cost, so the *gross margin* on sale of the subsequent units is relatively large. Contrast, for example, a grocery store, where the *contribution margin* equals less than 5 percent of the selling price. For firms with equal profitability, however defined, we say that the one with the larger percentage increase in income from a given percentage increase in dollar sales has the larger operating leverage. See *leverage* for contrast of this term with "financial leverage."

operating ratio. See *ratio*.

operational control. See *control system*.

operations. A word not precisely defined in *accounting.* Generally, analysts distinguish operating activities (producing and selling *goods* or *services*) from *financing activities* (raising funds) and *investing activities.* Acquiring goods on account and then paying for them one month later, though generally classified as an operating activity, has the characteristics of a financing activity. Or consider the transaction of selling *plant assets* for a price in excess of *book value.* On the *income statement,* the gain appears as part of income from operations ("continuing operations" or "discontinued" operations, depending on the circumstances), but the *statement of cash flows* reports all the funds received below the Cash from Operations section, as a nonoperating source of cash, "disposition of noncurrent assets."

opinion. The *auditor's report* containing an attestation or lack thereof.

opinion paragraph. Section of *auditor's report,* generally following the scope paragraph, giving the auditor's conclusion that the *financial statements* are (rarely, are not) in accordance with *GAAP* and present fairly the financial position, changes in financial position, and the results of *operations*.

opportunity cost. The *present value* of the *income* (or *costs*) that a firm could earn (or save) from using an *asset* in its best alternative use to the one under consideration.

opportunity cost of capital. *Cost of capital*.

option. The legal right to buy something during a specified period at a specified price, called the exercise price. Do not confuse employee stock options with put and call options traded in various public markets.

ordinary annuity. An *annuity in arrears*.

original cost. *Acquisition cost;* in public utility accounting, the acquisition cost of the *entity* first devoting the *asset* to public use.

outlay. The amount of an *expenditure*.

outlier. Said of an observation (or data point) that appears to differ significantly in some regard from other observations (or data points) of supposedly the same phenomenon; in a *regression analysis,* often used to describe an observation that falls far from the fitted regression equation (in two dimensions, line).

out-of-pocket. Said of an *expenditure* usually paid for with cash. An *incremental* cost.

out-of-stock cost. The estimated decrease in future *profit* as a result of losing customers because a firm has insufficient quantities of *inventory* currently on hand to meet customers' demands.

output. Physical quantity or monetary measurement of *goods* and *services* produced.

outside director. A member of a corporate *board of directors* who is not a company officer and does not participate in the corporation's day-to-day management.

outstanding. Unpaid or uncollected; when said of *stock,* refers to the shares issued less treasury stock; when said of checks, refers to a check issued that did not clear the drawer's bank prior to the bank statement date.

overapplied (overabsorbed) overhead. Costs applied, or *charged,* to product exceeding actual *overhead costs* during the period; a credit balance in an overhead account after overhead is assigned to product.

overhead costs. Any *cost* not directly associated with the production or sale of identifiable *goods* and *services;* sometimes called "burden" or *indirect costs* and, in Britain, "oncosts"; frequently limited to manufacturing overhead. See *central corporate expenses* and *manufacturing overhead.*

overhead rate. Standard, or other predetermined rate, at which a firm applies *overhead costs* to products or to services.

owners' equity. *Assets* minus *liabilities;* paid-in capital plus *retained earnings* of a corporation.

P

P&L. Profit-and-loss statement; *income statement.*

paper profit. A *gain* not yet realized through a *transaction;* an *unrealized holding gain.*

par value. *Face amount* of a *security.*

Pareto chart. In many business settings, a relatively small percentage of the potential population causes a relatively large percentage of the activity at interest. For example, some businesses find that the top 20 percent of the customers buy 80 percent of the goods sold. Or, the top 10 percent of products account for 60 percent of the revenues or 70 percent of the profits. The statistical distribution known as the Pareto distribution has this property of skewness, so a graph of a phenomenon with such skewness has come to be known as a Pareto chart, even if the underlying data do not actually well fit the Pareto distribution. Practitioners of TQM find that in many businesses a small number of processes account for a large fraction of the quality problems so they advocate charting potential problems and actual occurrences of problems to identify the relatively small number of sources of trouble. They call such a chart a "Pareto chart."

partial obsolescence. One cause of decline in *market value* of an *asset.* As technology improves, the economic value of existing assets declines. In many cases, however, it will not pay a firm to replace the existing asset with a new one, even though it would acquire the new type rather than the old if it did make a new acquisition currently. In these cases, the accountant should theoretically recognize a loss from partial obsolescence from the firm's owning an old, out-of-date asset, but *GAAP* do not permit recognition of partial obsolescence until the sum of future cash flows from the asset total less than *book value;* see *impairment.* The firm will carry the old asset at *cost* less *accumulated depreciation* until the firm retires it from service so long as the undiscounted future *cash flows* from the asset exceed its book value. Thus management that uses an asset subject to partial obsolescence reports results inferior to those reported by similar management that uses a new asset. See *obsolescence.*

partnership. Contractual arrangement between individuals to share resources and operations in a jointly run business.

patent. A right granted for up to 20 years by the federal government to exclude others from manufacturing, using, or selling a claimed design, product, or plant (e.g., a new breed of rose) or from using a claimed process or method of manufacture; an *asset* if the firm acquires it by purchase. If the firm develops it internally, current *GAAP* require the firm to *expense* the development costs when incurred.

pay-as-you-go. Said of an *income tax* scheme in which the taxpayer makes periodic payments of income taxes during the period when it earns the income to be taxed; in contrast to a scheme in which the taxpayer owes no payments until the end of, or after, the period when it earned the income being taxed (Called PAYE—pay-as-you-earn—in Britain). The phrase is sometimes used to describe an unfunded pension plan, or retirement benefit plan, in which the firm makes payments to pension plan beneficiaries from general corporate funds, not from cash previously contributed to a fund. Under this method, the firm debits expense as it makes payments, not as it incurs the obligations.

payable. Unpaid but not necessarily due or past due.

payback period. Amount of time that must elapse before the cash inflows from a project equal the cash outflows.

payback reciprocal. One divided by the *payback period.* This number approximates the *internal rate of return* on a project when the project life exceeds twice the payback period and the cash inflows are identical in every period after the initial period.

P/E ratio. *Price-earnings ratio.*

percentage statement. A statement containing, in addition to (or instead of) dollar amounts, ratios of dollar amounts to some base. In a percentage *income state-*

ment, the base is usually either *net sales* or total *revenues,* and in a percentage *balance sheet,* the base is usually total *assets.*

period. *Accounting period.*

period cost. An inferior term for *period expense.*

period expense (charge). *Expenditure,* usually based on the passage of time, charged to operations of the accounting period rather than *capitalized* as an asset. Contrast with *product cost.*

periodic inventory. In recording *inventory,* a method that uses data on beginning inventory, additions to inventories, and ending inventory to find the cost of withdrawals from inventory. Contrast with *perpetual inventory.*

periodic procedures. The process of making *adjusting entries* and *closing entries* and preparing the *financial statements,* usually by use of *trial balances* and *work sheets.*

permanent account. An account that appears on the *balance sheet.* Contrast with *temporary account.*

perpetual annuity. *Perpetuity.*

perpetual inventory. Records on quantities and amounts of *inventory* that the firm changes and makes current with each physical addition to or withdrawal from the stock of goods; an inventory so recorded. The records will show the physical quantities and, frequently, the dollar valuations that should be on hand at any time. Because the firm explicitly computes *cost of goods sold,* it can use the *inventory equation* to compute an amount for what *ending inventory* should be. It can then compare the computed amount of ending inventory to the actual amount of ending inventory as a *control* device to measure the amount of *shrinkages.* Contrast with *periodic inventory.*

perpetuity. An *annuity* whose payments continue forever. The *present value* of a perpetuity in arrears is *p/r* where *p* is the periodic payment and *r* is the *interest rate* per period. If a perpetuity promises $100 each year, in arrears, forever and the interest rate is 8 percent per year, then the perpetuity has a value of $1,250 = $100/.08.

PERT (*Program Evaluation and Review Technique*). A method of *network analysis* in which the analyst makes three time estimates for each activity—the optimistic time, the most likely time, and the pessimistic time— and gives an expected completion date for the project within a probability range.

physical units method. A method of allocating a *joint cost* to the *joint products* based on a physical measure of the joint products; for example, allocating the cost of a cow to sirloin steak and to hamburger, based on the weight of the meat. This method usually provides non-

sensical (see *sterilized allocation*) results unless the physical units of the joint products tend to have the same value.

physical verification. *Verification,* by an *auditor,* performed by actually inspecting items in *inventory, plant assets,* and the like, in contrast to merely checking the written records. The auditor may use statistical sampling procedures.

planning and control process. General name for the techniques of management comprising the setting of organizational goals and *strategic plans, capital budgeting, operations* budgeting, comparison of plans with actual results, performance evaluation and corrective action, and revisions of goals, plans, and budgets.

plant. *Plant assets.*

plant asset turnover. Number of dollars of *sales* generated per dollar of *plant assets;* equal to sales divided by average plant assets.

plant assets. *Assets* used in the revenue-production process. Plant assets include buildings, machinery, equipment, land, and natural resources. The phrase "property, plant, and equipment" (though often appearing on balance sheets) is therefore a redundancy. In this context, "plant" used alone means buildings.

plantwide allocation method. A method for *allocating overhead costs* to product. First, use one *cost pool* for the entire plant. Then, allocate all costs from that pool to product using a single overhead *allocation* rate, or one set of rates, to all the products of the plant, independent of the number of departments in the plant.

plug. Process for finding an unknown amount. For any *account,* beginning balance + additions − deductions = ending balance; if you know any three of the four items, you can find the fourth with simple arithmetic, called "plugging." In making a *journal entry,* often you know all *debits* and all but one of the *credits* (or vice versa). Because *double-entry* bookkeeping requires equal debits and credits, you can compute the unknown quantity by subtracting the sum of the known credits from the sum of all the debits (or vice versa), also called "plugging." Accountants often call the unknown the "plug."

population. The entire set of numbers or items from which the analyst samples or performs some other analysis.

post. To record entries in an *account* to a *ledger,* usually as transfers from a *journal.*

post-closing trial balance. *Trial balance* taken after the accountant has *closed* all *temporary accounts.*

PPB. *Program budgeting.* The second "P" stands for "plan."

practical capacity. Maximum level at which the plant or department can operate efficiently.

precision. The degree of accuracy for an estimate derived from a sampling process, usually expressed as a range of values around the estimate. The analyst might express a sample estimate in the following terms: "Based on the sample, we are 95 percent sure [confidence level] that the true population value is within the range of X to Y [precision]." See *confidence level.*

pre-closing trial balance. *Trial balance* taken at the end of the period before *closing entries;* in this sense, an *adjusted trial balance;* sometimes taken before *adjusting entries* and then synonymous with *unadjusted trial balance.*

predatory prices. Setting prices below some measure of cost in an effort to drive out competitors with hope of recouping losses later by charging monopoly prices. Illegal in the United States if the prices set are below long-run variable costs. We do not know of any empirical evidence that firms are successful at recoupment.

predetermined (factory) overhead rate. Rate used in applying overhead to products or departments developed at the start of a period. Compute the rate as estimated overhead cost divided by the estimated number of units of the overhead allocation base (or *denominator volume*) activity. See *normal costing.*

preferred shares. *Capital stock* with a claim to *income* or *assets* after *bondholders* but before *common shares. Dividends* on preferred shares are *income distributions,* not *expenses.*

prepaid expense. An *expenditure* that leads to a *deferred charge* or prepayment. Strictly speaking, this is a contradiction in terms because an *expense* is a gone asset, and this title refers to past expenditures, such as for rent or insurance premiums, that still have future benefits and thus are *assets.* We try to avoid this term and use "prepayment" instead.

present value. Value today (or at some specific date) of an amount or amounts to be paid or received later (or at other, different dates), discounted at some *interest* or *discount rate;* an amount that, if invested today at the specified rate, will grow to the amount to be paid or received in the future.

price. The quantity of one *good* or *service,* usually *cash,* asked in return for a unit of another good or service. See *fair value.*

price-earnings (P/E) ratio. At a given time, the market value of a company's *common share,* per share, divided by the *earnings per* common *share* for the past year. The analyst usually bases the denominator on income from continuing operations or, if the analyst thinks the

current figure for that amount does not represent a usual situation—such as when the number is negative or, if positive, close to zero—on some estimate of the number. See *ratio.*

price index. A series of numbers, one for each period, that purports to represent some *average* of prices for a series of periods, relative to a base period.

price level. The number from a *price index* series for a given period or date.

price variance. In accounting for *standard costs,* an amount equal to (actual cost per unit − standard cost per unit) times actual quantity.

primary earnings per share (PEPS). Net *income* to common shareholders plus *interest* (net of tax effects) or *dividends* paid on common-stock equivalents divided by (weighted average of common shares outstanding plus the net increase in the number of common shares that would become *outstanding* if the holders of all common stock equivalents were to exchange them for common shares with cash proceeds, if any, used to retire common shares). The *FASB* proposes to change the computation and to use the new title *basic earnings per share.*

prime cost. Sum of *direct materials* plus *direct labor* costs assigned to product.

prime rate. The loan rate charged by commercial banks to their creditworthy customers. Some customers pay even less than the prime rate and others, more. The *Federal Reserve Bulletin* is the authoritative source of information about historical prime rates.

principal. An amount in which *interest* accrues, either as *expense* (for the borrower) or as *revenue* (for the lender); the *face amount* of a *loan;* also, the absent owner (principal) who hires the manager (agent) in a "principal-agent" relationship.

principle. See *generally accepted accounting principles.*

pro forma statements. Hypothetical statements; financial statements as they would appear if some event, such as a *merger* or increased production and sales, had occurred or were to occur; sometimes spelled as one word, "proforma."

proceeds. The *funds* received from the disposition of assets or from the issue of securities.

process costing. A method of *cost accounting* based on average costs (total cost divided by the *equivalent units* of work done in a period); typically used for assembly lines or for products that the firm produces in a series of steps that are more continuous than discrete.

product. *Goods* or *services* produced.

product cost. Any *manufacturing cost* that the firm can—or, in some contexts, should—debit to an *inventory* account. See *flow of costs,* for example. Contrast with *period expenses.*

product life cycle. Time span between initial concept (typically starting with *research and development*) of a *good* or *service* and time when firm ceases to support customers who have purchased the good or service.

production cost. *Manufacturing cost.*

production cost account. A *temporary account* for accumulating *manufacturing costs* during a period.

production department. A department producing salable *goods* or *services;* contrast with *service department.*

production volume variance. Standard fixed overhead rate per unit of normal *capacity* (or base activity) times (units of base activity budgeted or planned for a period minus actual units of base activity worked or assigned to product during the period); often called a "volume variance."

productive capacity. One *attribute measured* for *assets.* The *current cost* of *long-term* assets means the cost of reproducing the productive capacity (for example, the ability to manufacture one million units a year), not the cost of reproducing the actual physical assets currently used (see *reproduction cost*). *Replacement cost* of productive capacity will be the same as reproduction cost of assets only in the unusual case when no technological improvement in production processes has occurred and the relative prices of goods and services used in production have remained approximately the same as when the firm acquired the currently used ones.

profit. Excess of *revenues* over *expenses* for a *transaction;* sometimes used synonymously with *net income* for the period.

profit center. A *responsibility center* for which a firm accumulates both *revenues* and *expenses.* Contrast with *cost center.*

profit margin. *Sales* minus all *expenses.*

profit margin percentage. *Profit margin* divided by *net sales.*

profit maximization. The doctrine that the firm should account for a given set of operations so as to make reported *net income* as large as possible; contrast with *conservatism.* This concept in accounting differs from the profit-maximizing concept in economics, which states that the firm should manage operations to maximize the present value of the firm's wealth, generally by equating *marginal costs* and *marginal revenues.*

profit variance analysis. Analysis of the causes of the difference between budgeted profit in the *master budget* and the profits earned.

profit-volume analysis (equation). Analysis of effects, on *profits,* caused by changes in volume or *contribution margin* per unit or *fixed costs.* See *breakeven chart.*

profit-volume graph. See *breakeven chart.*

profit-volume ratio. *Net income* divided by net sales in dollars.

profitability accounting. *Responsibility accounting.*

program budgeting (PPB). Specification and analysis of inputs, outputs, costs, and alternatives that link plans to *budgets.*

programmed cost. A *fixed cost* not essential for carrying out operations. For example, a firm can control costs for research and development and advertising designed to generate new business, but once it commits to incur them, they become fixed costs. These costs are sometimes called managed costs or *discretionary costs.* Contrast with *capacity costs.*

projected financial statement. *Pro forma* financial statement.

property, plant, and equipment. See *plant assets.*

prorate. To *allocate* in proportion to some base; for example, to allocate *service department* costs in proportion to hours of service used by the benefited department or to allocate *manufacturing variances* to product sold and to product added to *ending inventory.*

prorating variances. See *prorate.*

provision. Part of an *account* title. Often the firm must recognize an *expense* even though it cannot be sure of the exact amount. The entry for the estimated expense, such as for *income taxes* or expected costs under *warranty,* is as follows:

Expense (Estimated)	X	
Liability (Estimated)		X

American terminology often uses "provision" in the expense account title of the above entry. Thus, Provision for Income Taxes means the estimate of income tax expense. (British terminology uses "provision" in the title for the estimated liability of the above entry, so that Provision for Income Taxes is a balance sheet account.)

public accountant. Generally, this term is synonymous with *certified public accountant.* Some jurisdictions, however, license individuals who are not CPAs as public accountants.

public accounting. That portion of accounting primarily involving the *attest* function, culminating in the *auditor's report.*

purchase investigation. An investigation of the financial affairs of a company for the purpose of disclosing matters that may influence the terms or conclusion of a potential acquisition.

purchase order. Document issued by a buyer authorizing a seller to deliver goods, with the buyer to make payment later.

Q

qualified report (opinion). *Auditor's report* containing a statement that the auditor was unable to complete a satisfactory examination of all things considered relevant or that the auditor has doubts about the financial impact of some *material* item reported in the financial statements. See *except for* and *subject to*.

quality. In modern usage, a product or service has quality to the extent it conforms to specifications or provides customers the characteristics promised them.

quantitative performance measure. A measure of output based on an objectively observable quantity, such as units produced or *direct costs* incurred, rather than on an unobservable quantity or a quantity observable only nonobjectively, like quality of service provided.

quantity discount. A reduction in purchase price as quantity purchased increases. The Robinson-Patman Act constrains the amount of the discount. Do not confuse with *purchase discount*.

quantity variance. *Efficiency variance.* In *standard cost* systems, the standard price per unit times (actual quantity used minus standard quantity that should be used).

quick assets. *Assets* readily convertible into *cash;* includes cash, current marketable securities, and current receivables.

quick ratio. Sum of (cash, current marketable securities, and current receivables) divided by *current liabilities;* often called the "acid test ratio." The analyst may exclude some nonliquid receivables from the numerator. See *ratio*.

R

R^2. The proportion of the statistical variance of a *dependent variable* explained by the equation fit to *independent variable(s)* in a *regression analysis*.

Railroad Accounting Principles Board (RAPB). A board brought into existence by the Staggers Rail Act of 1980 to advise the Interstate Commerce Commission on accounting matters affecting railroads. The RAPB was the only cost-accounting body authorized by the government during the decade of the 1980s (because Congress ceased funding the CASB during the 1980s). The RAPB incorporated the pronouncements of the CASB and became the government's authority on cost accounting principles.

R & D. See *research and development*.

random number sampling. For choosing a sample, a method in which the analyst selects items from the *population* by using a random number table or generator.

random sampling. For choosing a sample, a method in which all items in the population have an equal chance of being selected. Compare *judgment(al) sampling*.

RAPB. *Railroad Accounting Principles Board*.

rate of return on assets. *Return on assets*.

rate of return on common stock equity. See *ratio*.

rate of return on shareholders' (owners') equity. See *ratio*.

rate of return (on total capital). See *ratio* and *return on assets*.

rate variance. *Price variance,* usually for *direct labor costs*.

ratio. The number resulting when one number divides another. Analysts generally use ratios to assess aspects of profitability, solvency, and liquidity. The commonly used financial ratios fall into three categories: (1) those that summarize some aspect of *operations* for a period, usually a year, (2) those that summarize some aspect of financial position at a given moment—the moment for which a balance sheet reports, and (3) those that relate some aspect of operations to some aspect of financial position. Exhibit 17.14 lists the most common financial ratios and shows separately both the numerator and the denominator for each ratio.

raw material. Goods purchased for use in manufacturing a product.

real accounts. *Balance sheet accounts,* as opposed to *nominal accounts*. See *permanent accounts*.

real interest rate. Interest rate reflecting the productivity of capital, not including a premium for inflation anticipated over the life of the *loan*.

realizable value. *Fair value* or, sometimes, *net realizable (sales) value*.

realize. To convert into *funds;* when applied to a *gain* or *loss,* implies that an *arm's-length transaction* has taken place. Contrast with *recognize;* the firm may recognize a loss (as for example on *marketable equity securities*) in the financial statements even though it has not yet realized the loss via a transaction.

realized holding gain. See *inventory profit* for definition and an example.

receipt. Acquisition of *cash*.

receivable. Any *collectible,* whether or not it is currently due.

receivable turnover. See *ratio*.

recognize. To enter a transaction in the accounts; not synonymous with *realize*.

reconciliation. A calculation that shows how one balance or figure derives from another, such as a reconciliation of retained earnings or a bank reconciliation schedule. See *articulate*.

refinancing. An adjustment in the *capital structure* of a *corporation*, involving changes in the nature and amounts of the various classes of *debt* and, in some cases, *capital* as well as other components of *shareholders' equity*. *Asset* carrying values in the accounts remain unchanged.

regression analysis. A method of *cost estimation* based on statistical techniques for fitting a line (or its equivalent in higher mathematical dimensions) to an observed series of data points, usually by minimizing the sum of squared deviations of the observed data from the fitted line. Common usage calls the cost that the analysis explains the "dependent variable"; it calls the variable(s) we use to estimate cost behavior "independent variable(s)." If we use more than one independent variable, the term for the analysis is "multiple regression analysis." See R^2, *standard error, t-value*.

reinvestment rate. In a *capital budgeting* context, the rate at which the firm invests cash inflows from a project occurring before the project's completion. Once the analyst assumes such a rate, no project can ever have multiple *internal rates of return*. See *Descartes' rule of signs*.

relative performance evaluation. Setting performance targets and, sometimes, compensation in relation to the performance of others, perhaps in different firms or divisions, that face a similar environment.

relevant cost. Cost used by analyst in making a decision. *Incremental cost. Opportunity cost.*

relevant range. Activity levels over which costs are linear or for which *flexible budget* estimates and *breakeven charts* will remain valid.

rent. A charge for use of land, buildings, or other assets.

repair. An *expenditure* to restore an *asset's* service potential after damage or after prolonged use. In the second sense, after prolonged use, the difference between repair and maintenance is one of degree and not of kind. A repair is treated as an *expense* of the period when incurred. Because the firm treats repairs and maintenance similarly in this regard, the distinction is not important. A repair helps to maintain capacity at the levels planned when the firm acquired the asset.

replacement cost. For an asset, the current fair market price to purchase another, similar asset (with the same future benefit or service potential). *Current cost.* See *reproduction cost* and *productive capacity*. See also *inventory profit*.

reporting objectives (policies). The general purposes for which the firm prepares *financial statements*. The *FASB* has discussed these in *SFAC No. 1*.

representative item sampling. Sampling in which the analyst believes the sample selected is typical of the entire population from which it comes. Compare *specific item sampling*.

reproduction cost. The *cost* necessary to acquire an *asset* similar in all physical respects to another asset for which the analyst requires a current value. See *replacement cost* and *productive capacity* for contrast.

required rate of return (RRR). *Cost of capital.*

research and development. A form of economic activity with special accounting rules. Firms engage in research in hopes of discovering new knowledge that will create a new product, process, or service or improving a present product, process, or service. Development translates research findings or other knowledge into a new or improved product, process, or service. *SFAS No.2* requires that firms expense costs of such activities as incurred on the grounds that the future benefits are too uncertain to warrant *capitalization* as an asset. This treatment seems questionable to us because we wonder why firms would continue to undertake R&D if there was no expectation of future benefit; if future benefits exist, then R&D *costs* should be assets that appear, like other assets, at *historical cost*.

residual income. In an external reporting context, a term that refers to *net income* to *common shares* (= net income less preferred stock dividends). In *managerial accounting*, this term refers to the excess of income for a *division* or segment of a company over the product of the *cost of capital* for the company multiplied by the average amount of capital invested in the division during the period over which the division earned the income.

residual value. At any time, the estimated or actual *net realizable value* (that is, proceeds less removal costs) of an *asset*, usually a depreciable *plant asset*. In the context of depreciation accounting, this term is equivalent to *salvage value* and is preferred to scrap value because the firm need not scrap the asset. It is sometimes used to mean net *book value*. In the context of a noncancelable lease, it is the estimated value of the leased asset at the end of the lease period. See *lease*.

resources supplied. Expenditures made for an activity.

resources used. Cost driver rate times cost driver volume.

responsibility accounting. Accounting for a business by considering various units as separate entities, or *profit centers*, giving management of each unit responsibility for the unit's *revenues* and *expenses*. See *transfer price*.

responsibility center. An organization part or segment that top management holds accountable for a specified set of activities. Also called "accountability center." See *cost center, investment center, profit center, revenue center.*

retained earnings. Net *income* over the life of a corporation less all *dividends* (including capitalization through stock dividends); *owners' equity* less *contributed capital.*

retained earnings statement. A *reconciliation* of the beginning and the ending balances in the retained earnings account; required by *generally accepted accounting principles* whenever the firm presents comparative balance sheets and an *income statement.* This reconciliation can appear in a separate statement, in a combined statement of income and retained earnings, or in the balance sheet.

return. A schedule of information required by governmental bodies, such as the tax return required by the *Internal Revenue Service;* also the physical return of merchandise. See also *return on investment.*

return on investment (ROI), return on capital. *Income* (before distributions to suppliers of capital) for a period; as a rate, this amount divided by average total assets. The analyst should add back *interest,* net of tax effects, to *net income* for the numerator. See *ratio.*

return on assets (ROA). *Net income* plus after-tax *interest charges* plus minority interest in income divided by average total *assets;* perhaps the single most useful ratio for assessing management's overall operating performance. Most financial economists would subtract average noninterest-bearing *liabilities* from the denominator. Economists realize that when liabilities do not provide for explicit interest charges, the creditor adjusts the terms of contract, such as setting a higher selling price or lower discount, to those who do not pay cash immediately. (To take an extreme example, consider how much higher salary a worker who receives a salary once per year, rather than once per month, would demand.) This ratio requires in the numerator the income amount before the firm accrues any charges to suppliers of funds. We cannot measure the interest charges implicit in the noninterest-bearing liabilities because they cause items such as cost of goods sold and salary expense to be somewhat larger, since the interest is implicit. Subtracting their amounts from the denominator adjusts for their implicit cost. Such subtraction assumes that assets financed with noninterest-bearing liabilities have the same rate of return as all the other assets.

revenue. The increase in *owners' equity* accompanying the increase in *net assets* caused by selling goods or rendering services; for short, a service rendered. *Sales* of products, merchandise, and services, and earnings from *interest, dividends, rents,* and the like. Measure

revenue as the expected *net present value* of the net assets the firm will receive. Do not confuse with *receipt* of *funds,* which may occur before, when, or after revenue is recognized. Contrast with *gain* and *income.* See also *holding gain.* Some writers use the term "gross income" synonymously with *revenue;* avoid such usage.

revenue center. Within a firm, a *responsibility center* that has control only over revenues generated. Contrast with *cost center.* See *profit center.*

risk. A measure of the variability of the *return on investment.* For a given expected amount of return, most people prefer less risk to more risk. Therefore, in rational markets, investments with more risk usually promise, or investors expect to receive, a higher rate of return than investments with lower risk. Most people use "risk" and "uncertainty" as synonyms. In technical language, however, these terms have different meanings. We use "risk" when we know the probabilities attached to the various outcomes, such as the probabilities of heads or tails in the flip of a fair coin. "Uncertainty" refers to an event for which we can only estimate the probabilities of the outcomes, such as winning or losing a lawsuit.

risk-adjusted discount rate. Rate used in discounting cash flows for projects more or less risky than the firm's average. In a *capital budgeting* context, a decision analyst compares projects by comparing their net *present values* for a given *interest* rate, usually the cost of capital. If the analyst considers a given project's outcome to be much more or much less risky than the normal undertakings of the company, then the analyst will use a larger interest rate (if the project is riskier) or smaller interest rate (if less risky) in discounting, and the rate used is "risk-adjusted."

risk free rate. An interest rate reflecting only the pure interest rate plus an amount to compensate for inflation anticipated over the life of a loan, excluding a premium for the risk of default by the borrower. Financial economists usually measure the risk free rate in the United States from United States government securities, such as Treasury bills and notes.

risk premium. Extra compensation paid to employees or extra *interest* paid to lenders, over amounts usually considered normal, in return for their undertaking to engage in activities riskier than normal.

ROA. *Return on assets.*

ROI. *Return on investment;* usually used to refer to a single project and expressed as a ratio: *income* divided by average *cost* of *assets* devoted to the project.

royalty. Compensation for the use of property, usually a patent, copyrighted material, or natural resources. The amount is often expressed as a percentage of receipts from using the property or as an amount per unit produced.

RRR. Required rate of return. See *cost of capital.*

rule of 69. Rule stating that an amount of cash invested at r percent per period will double in $69/r + .35$ periods. This approximation is accurate to one-tenth of a period for interest rates between 1/4 and 100 percent per period. For example, at 10 percent per period, the rule says that a given sum will double in $69/10 + .35 = 7.25$ periods. At 10 percent per period, a given sum actually doubles in 7.27+ periods.

rule of 72. Rule stating that an amount of cash invested at r percent per period will double in $72/r$ periods. A reasonable approximation for interest rates between 4 and 10 percent but not nearly as accurate as the *rule of 69* for interest rates outside that range. For example, at 10 percent per period, the rule says that a given sum will double in $72/10 = 7.2$ periods.

S

safety stock. Extra items of *inventory* kept on hand to protect against running out.

salary. Compensation earned by managers, administrators, and professionals, not based on an hourly rate. Contrast with *wage.*

sale. A *revenue* transaction in which the firm delivers *goods* or *services* to a customer in return for cash or a contractual obligation to pay.

sale and leaseback. A financing transaction in which the firm sells improved property but takes it back for use on a long-term *lease.* Such transactions often have advantageous income tax effects but usually have no effect on *financial statement income.*

sales activity variance. *Sales volume variance.*

sales discount. A sales *invoice* price reduction usually offered for prompt payment.

sales return. The physical return of merchandise. The seller often accumulates amounts of such returns in a temporary revenue contra account.

sales-type (capital) lease. A form of *lease.* See *capital lease.* When a manufacturer (or other firm) that ordinarily sells goods enters a capital lease as lessor, the lease is a "sales-type lease." When a financial firm, such as a bank or insurance company or leasing company, acquires the asset from the manufacturer and then enters a capital lease as lessor, the lease is a "direct-financing-type lease." The manufacturer recognizes its ordinary profit (sales price less *cost of goods sold,* where sales price is the *present value* of the contractual lease payments plus any down payment) on executing

the sales-type capital lease, but the financial firm does not recognize profit on executing a capital lease of the direct-financing type.

sales volume variance. Budgeted *contribution margin* per unit times (planned sales volume minus actual sales volume).

salvage value. Actual or estimated selling price, net of removal or disposal costs, of a used *plant asset* that the firm expects to sell or otherwise retire.

scale effect. See *discounted cash flow.*

scatter diagram. A graphic representation of the relation between two or more variables within a population.

schedule. A supporting set of calculations, with explanations, that show how to derive figures in a *financial statement* or tax return.

SEC (Securities and Exchange Commission). An agency authorized by the U.S. Congress to regulate, among other things, the financial reporting practices of most public corporations. The SEC has indicated that it will usually allow the *FASB* to set accounting principles, but it often requires more disclosure than the FASB requires. The SEC states its accounting requirements in its *Accounting Series Releases (ASR), Financial Reporting Releases,* Accounting and Auditing Enforcement Releases, *Staff Accounting Bulletins* (these are, strictly speaking, interpretations by the accounting staff, not rules of the commissioners themselves), and *Regulations S–X.*

security. Document that indicates ownership, such as a *share* of *stock,* or indebtedness, such as a *bond,* or potential ownership, such as an *option* or warrant.

self-check(ing) digit. A digit forming part of an account or code number, normally the last digit of the number, which is mathematically derived from the other numbers of the code and is used to detect errors in transcribing the code number. For example, assume the last digit of the account number is the remainder after summing the preceding digits and dividing that sum by nine. Suppose the computer encounters the account numbers 7027261-7 and 9445229-7. The program can tell that something has gone wrong with the encoding of the second account number because the sum of the first seven digits is 35, whose remainder on division by 9 is 8, not 7. The first account number does not show such an error because the sum of the first seven digits is 25, whose remainder on division by 9 is, indeed, 7. The first account number may be in error, but the second surely is.

selling and administrative expenses. *Expenses* not specifically identifiable with, or assigned to, production.

semifixed costs. *Costs* that increase with activity as a step function.

semivariable costs. *Costs* that increase strictly linearly with activity but that are positive at zero activity level. Royalty fees of 2 percent of sales are variable; royalty fees of $1,000 per year plus 2 percent of sales are semivariable.

sensitivity analysis. A study of how the outcome of a decision-making process changes as one or more of the assumptions change.

sequential access. Access to computer storage where the analyst can locate information only by a sequential search of the storage file. Compare *direct access*.

service bureau. A commercial data-processing center providing service to various customers.

service department. A department, such as the personnel or computer department, that provides services to other departments rather than direct work on a salable product. Contrast with *production department*. A firm must allocate costs of service departments whose services benefit manufacturing operations to *product costs* under *full absorption costing*.

service life. Period of expected usefulness of an asset; may differ from *depreciable life* for income tax purposes.

service potential. The future benefits that cause an item to be classified as an *asset*. Without service potential, an item has no future benefits, and accounting will not classify the item as an asset. The *FASB* suggests that the primary characteristic of service potential is the ability to generate future net cash inflows.

services. Useful work done by a person, a machine, or an organization. See *goods*.

setup. The time or costs required to prepare production equipment for doing a job.

SFAC. *Statement of Financial Accounting Concepts* of the *FASB*.

SFAS. *Statement of Financial Accounting Standards*. See *FASB*.

shadow price. An opportunity cost. A *linear programming* analysis provides as one of its outputs the potential value of having available more of the scarce resources that constrain the production process, for example, the value of having more time available on a machine tool critical to the production of two products. Common terminology refers to this value as the "shadow price" or the "dual value" of the scarce resource.

share. A unit of stock representing ownership in a corporation.

shareholders' equity. Proprietorship or *owners' equity* of a corporation. Because "stock" means inventory in Australia, Britain, and Canada, their writers use the term "shareholders' equity" rather than the term "stockholders' equity."

short-run, short-term. The opposite of *long-run* or *long-term*.

short-term. Current; ordinarily, due within one year.

short-term liquidity risk. The risk that an *entity* will not have enough *cash* in the *short run* to pay its *debts*.

shrinkage. An excess of *inventory* shown on the *books* over actual physical quantities on hand; can result from theft or shoplifting as well as from evaporation or general wear and tear. Some accountants, in an attempt to downplay their own errors, use the term to mean record keeping mistakes that they later must correct, with some embarrassment, and that result in material changes in reported income. One should not use the term "shrinkage" for the correction of mistakes because adequate terminology exists for describing mistakes.

shutdown cost. Those fixed costs that the firm continues to incur after it has ceased production. The costs of closing down a particular production facility.

simple interest. *Interest* calculated on *principal* where interest earned during periods before maturity of the loan does not increase the principal amount earning interest for the subsequent periods and the lender cannot withdraw the funds before maturity. Interest = principal $\times$ interest rate $\times$ time, where the rate is a rate per period (typically a year) and time is expressed in units of that period. For example, if the *rate* is annual and the time is two months, then in the formula, use 2/12 for time. Simple interest is seldom used in economic calculations except for periods of less than one year and then only for computational convenience. Contrast with *compound interest*.

skeleton account. *T-account*.

slide. The name of the error made by a bookkeeper in recording the digits of a number correctly with the decimal point misplaced; for example, recording $123.40 as $1,234.00 or as $12.34. If the only errors in a *trial balance* result from one or more slides, then the difference between the sum of the *debits* and the sum of the *credits* will be divisible by nine. Not all such differences divisible by nine result from slides. See *transposition error*.

SMAC (Society of Management Accountants of Canada). The national association of accountants whose provincial associations engage in industrial and governmental accounting. The association undertakes research and administers an educational program and comprehensive examinations; those who pass qualify to be designated CMA (Certified Management

Accountants), formerly called RIA (Registered Industrial Accountant).

software. The programming aids, such as compilers, sort and report programs, and generators, that extend the capabilities of and simplify the use of the computer, as well as certain operating systems and other control programs. Compare *hardware.*

solvent. Able to meet debts when due.

source of funds. Any *transaction* that increases *cash* and *marketable securities* held as *current assets.*

sources and uses statement. *Statement of cash flows.*

specific identification method. Method for valuing *ending inventory* and *cost of goods sold* by identifying actual units sold and remaining in inventory and summing the actual costs of those individual units; usually used for items with large unit values, such as precious jewelry, automobiles, and fur coats.

specific item sampling. Sampling in which the analyst selects particular items because of their nature, value, or method of recording. Compare *representative item sampling.*

spending variance. In *standard cost systems*, the *rate* or *price variance* for *overhead costs.*

split. *Stock split.* Sometimes called "split-up."

split-off point. In accumulating and allocating costs for *joint products*, the point at which all costs are no longer *joint costs* but at which an analyst can identify costs associated with individual products or perhaps with a smaller number of *joint products.*

spoilage. See *abnormal spoilage* and *normal spoilage.*

spreadsheet. For many years, a term that referred specifically to a work sheet organized like a *matrix* that provides a two-way classification of accounting data. The rows and columns both have labels, which are *account* titles. An entry in a row represents a *debit,* whereas an entry in a column represents a *credit.* Thus, the number "100" in the "cash" row and the "accounts receivable" column records an entry debiting cash and crediting accounts receivable for $100. A given row total indicates all debit entries to the account represented by that row, and a given column total indicates the sum of all credit entries to the account represented by the column.

Since personal computer software has become widespread, this term refers to any file created by programs such as Lotus 1-2-3® and Microsoft Excel®. Such files have rows and columns, but they need not represent debits and credits. Moreover, they can have more than two dimensions.

standard cost. Anticipated *cost* of producing a unit of output; a predetermined cost to be assigned to products produced. Standard cost implies a norm—what costs should be. Budgeted cost implies a forecast—

something likely, but not necessarily, a "should," as implied by a norm. Firms use standard costs as the benchmark for gauging good and bad performance. Although a firm may similarly use a budget, it need not. A budget may be a planning document, subject to changes whenever plans change, whereas standard costs usually change annually or when technology significantly changes or costs of labor and materials significantly change.

standard costing. *Costing* based on *standard costs.*

standard costing system. *Product costing* using *standard costs* rather than actual costs. The firm may use either *full absorption* or *variable costing* principles.

standard error (of regression coefficients). A measure of the uncertainty about the magnitude of the estimated parameters of an equation fit with a *regression analysis.*

standard manufacturing overhead. *Overhead costs* expected to be incurred per unit of time and per unit produced.

standard price (rate). Unit price established for materials or labor used in *standard cost systems.*

standard quantity allowed. The direct material or direct labor (inputs) quantity that production should have used if it produced the units of output in accordance with preset standards.

standby costs. A type of *capacity cost*, such as property taxes, incurred even if a firm shuts down operations completely. Contrast with *enabling costs.*

stated capital. Amount of capital contributed by shareholders; sometimes used to mean legal capital.

statement of cash flows. A schedule of *cash receipts* and payments, classified by *investing, financing,* and *operating activities;* required by the *FASB* for all for-profit companies. Companies may report operating activities with either the direct method (which shows only receipts and payments of cash) or the indirect method (which starts with *net income* and shows adjustments for *revenues* not currently producing cash and for *expenses* not currently using cash). "Cash" includes cash equivalents such as Treasury bills, commercial paper, and *marketable securities* held as *current assets.* This is sometimes called the "funds statement."

Statement of Financial Accounting Concepts (SFAC). One of a series of *FASB* publications in its *conceptual framework* for *financial accounting* and reporting. Such statements set forth objectives and fundamentals to be the basis for specific financial accounting and reporting standards.

Statement of Financial Accounting Standards (SFAS). See *FASB.*

statement of financial position. *Balance sheet.*

statement of retained earnings (income). A statement that reconciles the beginning-of-period and the end-of-period balances in the *retained earnings* account. It shows the effects of *earnings, dividend* declarations, and prior-period adjustments.

statement of significant accounting policies (principles). A summary of the significant *accounting principles* used in compiling an *annual report;* required by *APB Opinion No. 22.* This summary may be a separate exhibit or the first *note* to the financial statements.

static budget. *Fixed budget.* Budget developed for a set level of the driving variable, such as production or sales, which the analyst does not change if the actual level deviates from the level set at the outset of the analysis.

status quo. Events or cost incurrences that will happen or that a firm expects to happen in the absence of taking some contemplated action.

step allocation method. *Step-down method.*

step cost. *Semifixed cost.*

step-down method. In *allocating service department* costs, a method that starts by allocating one service department's costs to *production departments* and to all other service departments. Then the firm allocates a second service department's costs, including costs allocated from the first, to production departments and to all other service departments except the first one. In this fashion, a firm may allocate all service departments' costs, including previous allocations, to production departments and to those service departments whose costs it has not yet allocated.

step(ped) cost. *Semifixed cost.*

sterilized allocation. Desirable characteristics of cost allocation methods. Optimal decisions result from considering *incremental costs* only. Optimal decisions never require *allocations* of *joint* or *common costs.* A "sterilized allocation" causes the optimal decision choice not to differ from the one that occurs when the accountant does not allocate joint or common costs "sterilized" with respect to that decision. Arthur L. Thomas first used the term in this context. Because *absorption costing* requires that product costs absorb all manufacturing costs and because some allocations can lead to bad decisions, Thomas (and we) advocate that the analyst choose a sterilized allocation scheme that will not alter the otherwise optimal decision. No single allocation scheme is always sterilized with respect to all decisions. Thus, Thomas (and we) advocate that decisions be made on the basis of incremental costs before any allocations.

stewardship. Principle by which management is accountable for an *entity's* resources, for their efficient use, and for protecting them from adverse impact. Some theo-

rists believe that accounting has as a primary goal aiding users of *financial statements* in their assessment of management's performance in stewardship.

stock. A measure of the amount of something on hand at a specific time. In this sense, contrast with *flow.* See *inventory, capital stock.*

stock split(-up). Increase in the number of common shares outstanding resulting from the issuance of additional shares to existing shareholders without additional capital contributions by them. Does not increase the total *value* (or stated value) of *common shares* outstanding because the *board* reduces the par (or stated) value per share in inverse proportion. A three-for-one stock split reduces par (or stated) value per share to one-third of its former amount. A stock split usually implies a distribution that increases the number of shares outstanding by 20 percent or more.

stockholders' equity. See *shareholders' equity.*

stockout. Occurs when a firm needs a unit of *inventory* to use in production or to sell to a customer but has none available.

stockout costs. *Contribution margin* or other measure of *profits* not earned because a seller has run out of *inventory* and cannot fill a customer's order. A firm may incur an extra cost because of delay in filling an order.

stores. *Raw materials,* parts, and supplies.

strategic plan. A statement of the method for achieving an organization's goals.

stratified sampling. In choosing a sample, a method in which the investigator divides the entire *population* first into relatively homogeneous subgroups (strata) and then selects random samples from these subgroups.

subject to. In an *auditor's report,* qualifications usually caused by a *material* uncertainty in the valuation of an item, such as future promised payments from a foreign government or outcome of pending litigation.

subsidiary. A company in which another company owns more than 50 percent of the voting shares.

summary of significant accounting principles. *Statement of significant accounting policies (principles).*

sunk cost. Past *costs* that current and future decisions cannot affect and, hence, that are irrelevant for decision making aside from *income tax* effects. Contrast with *incremental costs* and *imputed costs.* For example, the *acquisition cost* of machinery is irrelevant to a decision of whether to scrap the machinery. The current *exit value* of the machine is the *opportunity cost* of continuing to own it, and the cost of, say, the electricity to run the machine is an incremental cost of its operation. Sunk costs become relevant for decision making when the analysis requires taking *income taxes (gain* or *loss* on disposal of asset) into account, since the cash payment for income taxes depends on the tax basis of the asset. Avoid the term in careful writing because it is ambiguous. Consider, for example, a machine costing $100,000 with current *salvage value* of $20,000. Some (including us) would say that $100,000 is "sunk"; others would say that only $80,000 is "sunk."

supplementary statements (schedules). Statements (schedules) in addition to the four basic *financial statements* (*balance sheet, income statement, statement of cash flows,* and the *statement of retained earnings*).

T

T-account. Account form shaped like the letter T with the title above the horizontal line. *Debits* appear on the left of the vertical line, *credits* on the right.

t-statistic. For an estimated *regression* coefficient, the estimated coefficient divided by the *standard error* of the estimate.

t-value. In *regression analysis*, the ratio of an estimated regression coefficient divided by its *standard error*.

take-home pay. The amount of a paycheck; earned *wages* or *salary* reduced by deductions for *income taxes,* Social Security taxes, contributions to fringe-benefit plans, union dues, and so on. Take-home pay might be as little as half of earned compensation.

take-or-pay contract. As defined by *SFAS No. 47,* a purchaser-seller agreement that provides for the purchaser to pay specified amounts periodically in return for products or services. The purchaser must make specified minimum payments even if it does not take delivery of the contracted products or services.

tangible. Having physical form. Accounting has never satisfactorily defined the distinction between tangible and intangible assets. Typically, accountants define intangibles by giving an exhaustive list, and everything not on the list is defined as tangible. See *intangible asset* for such a list.

target cost. *Standard cost*. Sometimes, target price less expected profit margin.

target price. Selling price based on customers' value in use, constrained by competitors' prices of similar items, of a good or service.

tax. A nonpenal, but compulsory, charge levied by a government on income, consumption, wealth, or other basis, for the benefit of all those governed. The term does not include fines or specific charges for benefits accruing only to those paying the charges, such as licenses, permits, special assessments, admission fees, and tolls.

tax shield. The amount of an *expense,* such as *depreciation,* that reduces taxable income but does not require

working capital. Sometimes this term includes expenses that reduce taxable income and use working capital. A depreciation deduction (or *R&D* expense in the expanded sense) of $10,000 provides a tax shield of $3,700 when the marginal tax rate is 37 percent.

technology. The sum of a firm's technical *trade secrets* and know-how, as distinct from its *patents*.

temporary account. *Account* that does not appear on the *balance sheet; revenue* and *expense* accounts, their *adjuncts* and *contras, production cost accounts, dividend distribution accounts*, and purchases-related accounts (which close to the various inventories); sometimes called a *nominal account.*

term structure. A phrase with different meanings in *accounting* and financial economics. In accounting, it refers to the pattern of times that must elapse before *assets* turn into, or produce, *cash* and the pattern of times that must elapse before *liabilities* require cash. In financial economics, the phrase refers to the pattern of interest rates as a function of the time that elapses for loans to come due. For example, if six-month loans cost 6 percent per year and 10-year loans cost 9 percent per year, this is called a "normal" term structure because the longer-term loan carries a higher rate. If the six-month loan costs 9 percent per year and the 10-year loan costs 6 percent per year, the term structure is said to be "inverted."

terms of sale. The conditions governing payment for a sale. For example, the terms *2/10, n(et)/30* mean that if the purchaser makes payment within 10 days of the invoice date, it can take a *discount* of 2 percent from *invoice* price; the purchaser must pay the invoice amount, in any event, within 30 days, or it becomes overdue.

theory of constraints (TOC). Concept of improving operations by identifying and reducing botttlenecks in process flows.

thin capitalization. A state of having a high *debt-equity ratio*. Under income tax legislation, the term has a special meaning.

throughput contribution. Sales dollars minus the sum of all short-run variable costs.

tickler file. A collection of *vouchers* or other memoranda arranged chronologically to remind the person in charge of certain duties to make payments (or to do other tasks) as scheduled.

time-adjusted rate of return. *Internal rate of return.*

time cost. *Period cost.*

time deposit. Cash in bank earning interest. Contrast with *demand deposit.*

time-series analysis. See *cross-section analysis* for definition and contrast.

times-interest (charges) earned. Ratio of pretax *income* plus *interest* charges to interest charges. See *ratio*.

total assets turnover. *Sales* divided by average total *assets*.

total quality management (TQM). Concept of organizing a company to excel in all its activities in order to increase the quality of products and services.

traceable cost. A *cost* that a firm can identify with or assign to a specific product. Contrast with a *joint cost*.

trade-in. Acquiring a new *asset* in exchange for a used one and perhaps additional cash.

trade secret. Technical or business information such as formulas, recipes, computer programs, and marketing data not generally known by competitors and maintained by the firm as a secret; theoretically capable of having an indefinite, finite life. A famous example is the secret process for Coca-Cola® (a registered *trademark* of the company). The firm will capitalize this intangible asset only if purchased and then will amortize it over a period not to exceed 40 years. If the firm develops the intangible internally, the firm will *expense* the costs as incurred and show no asset.

trademark. A distinctive word or symbol that is affixed to a product, its package, or its dispenser and that uniquely identifies the firm's products and services. See *trademark right*.

trademark right. The right to exclude competitors in sales or advertising from using words or symbols that are so similar to the firm's *trademarks* as possibly to confuse consumers. Trademark rights last as long as the firm continues to use the trademarks in question. In the United States, trademark rights arise from use and not from government registration. They therefore have a legal life independent of the life of a registration. Registrations last 20 years, and the holder may renew them as long as the holder uses the trademark.

trading on the equity. Said of a firm engaging in *debt financing;* frequently said of a firm doing so to a degree considered abnormal for a firm of its kind. *Leverage*.

transaction. A transfer (of more than promises—see *executory contract*) between the accounting *entity* and another party or parties.

transfer price. A substitute for a *market*, or *arm's length, price* used in *profit*, or *responsibility center, accounting* when one segment of the business "sells" to another segment. Incentives of profit center managers will not coincide with the best interests of the entire business unless a firm sets transfer prices properly.

transfer-pricing problem. The problem of setting *transfer prices* so that both buyer and seller have *goal congruence* with respect to the parent organization's goals.

transposition error. An error in record keeping resulting from reversing the order of digits in a number, such as recording "32" for "23." If the only errors in a *trial balance* result from one or more transposition errors, then the difference between the sum of the *debits* and the sum of the *credits* will be divisible by nine. Not all such differences result from transposition errors.

treasurer. The financial officer responsible for managing cash and raising funds.

trial balance. A two-column listing of *account balances*. The left-hand column shows all accounts with *debit* balances and their total. The right-hand column shows all accounts with *credit* balances and their total. The two totals should be equal. Accountants compute trial balances as a partial check of the arithmetic accuracy of the entries previously made.

turnover. The number of times that *assets,* such as *inventory* or *accounts receivable,* are replaced on average during the period. Accounts receivable turnover, for example, is total sales on account for a period divided by average accounts receivable balance for the period. See *ratio*.

turnover of plant and equipment. See *ratio*.

U

unadjusted trial balance. *Trial balance* taken before the accountant makes *adjusting* and *closing entries* at the end of the period.

unavoidable cost. A *cost* that is not an *avoidable cost*.

uncertainty. See *risk* for definition and contrast.

uncollectible account. An *account receivable* that the *debtor* will not pay. If the firm uses the preferable *allowance method,* the entry on judging a specific account to be uncollectible *debits* the allowance for uncollectible accounts and *credits* the specific account receivable. See *bad debt expense*.

uncontrollable cost. The opposite of *controllable cost*.

underapplied (underabsorbed) overhead. An excess of actual *overhead costs* for a period over costs applied, or charged, to products produced during the period; a *debit balance* remaining in an overhead account after the accounting assigns overhead to product.

unexpired cost. An *asset*.

unfavorable variance. In *standard cost* accounting, an excess of expected revenue over actual revenue or an excess of actual cost over standard cost.

unqualified opinion. See *auditor's report*.

unrealized holding gain. See *inventory profit* for definition and an example.

unrealized gain (loss) on marketable securities. An *income statement account* title for the amount of *gain (loss)* during the current period on the portfolio of *mar-*

ketable securities held as trading securities. *SFAS No. 115* requires the firm to recognize in the income statement gains and losses caused by changes in market values, even though the firm has not yet *realized* them.

unrecovered cost. *Book value* of an *asset*.

unused capacity. The difference between resources supplied and resources used.

usage variance. *Efficiency variance.*

V

value. Monetary worth. This term is usually so vague that you should not use it without a modifying adjective unless most people would agree on the amount. Do not confuse with cost. See *fair market price (value), exit value.*

value added. *Cost* of a product or *work-in-process,* minus the cost of the material purchased for the product or work-in-process.

value-added activity. Any activity that increases the usefulness to a customer of a product or service.

value chain. The set of business functions that increase the usefulness to the customer of a product or service; typically including research and development, design of products and services, production, marketing, distribution, and customer service.

value engineering. An evaluation of the activities in the *value chain* to reduce costs.

value variance. *Price variance.*

variable budget. *Flexible budget.*

variable costing. In allocating costs, a method that assigns only variable manufacturing costs to products and treats fixed manufacturing costs as *period expenses.* Contrast with *full absorption costing.*

variable costs. *Costs* that change as activity levels change. Strictly speaking, variable costs are zero when the activity level is zero. See *semivariable costs.* In accounting, this term most often means the sum of *direct costs* and variable *overhead.*

variable overhead variance. Difference between actual and standard variable overhead costs.

variables sampling. The use of a sampling technique in which the sampler infers a particular quantitative characteristic of an entire population from a sample (e.g., mean amount of accounts receivable). See also *estimation sampling.* See *attribute(s) sampling* for contrast and further examples.

variance. Difference between actual and *standard costs* or between *budgeted* and actual *expenditures* or, sometimes, *expenses.* The word has completely different meanings in accounting and in statistics, where it means a measure of dispersion of a distribution.

variance analysis. *Variance investigation.* This term's meaning differs in statistics.

variance investigation. A step in managerial control processes. *Standard costing systems* produce *variance* numbers of various sorts. These numbers seldom exactly equal to zero. Management must decide when a variance differs sufficiently from zero to study its cause. This term refers both to deciding when to study the cause and to the study itself.

variation analysis. Analysis of the causes of changes in financial statement items of interest such as *net income* or *gross margin.*

verifiable. A qualitative objective of financial reporting specifying that accountants can trace items in *financial statements* back to underlying documents—supporting *invoices,* canceled checks, and other physical pieces of evidence.

verification. The auditor's act of reviewing or checking items in *financial statements* by tracing back to underlying documents—supporting *invoices,* canceled checks, and other business documents—or sending out confirmations to be returned.

vertical analysis. Analysis of the *financial statements* of a single firm or across several firms for a particular time, as opposed to *horizontal* or *time-series analysis,* in which the analyst compares items over time for a single firm or across firms.

vertical integration. The extension of activity by an organization into business directly related to the production or distribution of the organization's end products. Although a firm may sell products to others at various stages, a vertically integrated firm devotes the substantial portion of the output at each stage to the production of the next stage or to end products. Compare *horizontal integration.*

visual curve fitting method. One crude form of cost *estimation.* Sometimes, when a firm needs only rough approximations of the amounts of *fixed* and *variable costs,* management need not perform a formal *regression analysis* but can plot the data and draw in a line that seems to fit the data. Then it can use the parameters of that line for the rough approximations.

volume variance. *Production volume variance;* less often, used to mean *sales volume variance.*

voucher. A document that signals recognition of a *liability* and authorizes the *disbursement* of *cash;* sometimes used to refer to the written evidence documenting an *accounting entry,* as in the term "journal voucher".

W

wage. Compensation of employees based on time worked or output of product for manual labor. But see *take-home pay.*

warning signal. Tools used to identify quality control problems can either merely signal a problem (warning) or both signal a problem and suggest its cause (diagnostic).

warranty. A promise by a seller to correct deficiencies in products sold. When the seller gives warranties, proper accounting practice recognizes an estimate of warranty *expense* and an *estimated liability* at the time of sale. See *guarantee* for contrast in proper usage.

waste. Material that is a residue from manufacturing operations and that has no sale value. Frequently, this has negative value because a firm must incur additional costs for disposal.

wasting asset. A *natural resource* having a limited *useful life* and, hence, subject to *amortization,* called *depletion.* Examples are timberland, oil and gas wells, and ore deposits.

weighted average. An average computed by counting each occurrence of each value, not merely a single occurrence of each value. For example, if a firm purchases one unit for $1 and two units for $2 each, then the simple average of the purchase prices is $1.50, but the weighted average price per unit is $5/3 = $1.67. Contrast with *moving average*.

weighted-average inventory method. Valuing either withdrawals or *ending inventory* at the *weighted-average* purchase price of all units on hand at the time of withdrawal or of computing ending inventory. The firm uses the *inventory equation* to calculate the other quantity. If a firm uses the *perpetual inventory* method, accountants often call it the *moving average method.*

window dressing. The attempt to make financial statements show *operating* results, or financial position, more favorable than they would otherwise show.

work-in-process (inventory account). Partially completed product; appears on the *balance sheet* as *inventory*.

working capital. *Current assets* minus *current liabilities;* sometimes called "net working capital" or *net current assets.*

work(ing) papers. The schedules and analyses prepared by the *auditor* in carrying out investigations before issuing an *opinion* on *financial statements*.

worth. *Value.* See *net worth.*

write down. To *write off,* except that the firm does not charge all the assets' cost to expense or *loss;* generally used for nonrecurring items.

write off. To *charge* an *asset* to *expense* or *loss;* that is, to *debit* expense (or loss) and *credit* asset.

Y

yield. *Internal rate of return* of a stream of cash flows. Cash yield is cash flow divided by book value. See also *dividend yield*.

yield to maturity. At a given time, the *internal rate of return* of a series of cash flows; usually said of a *bond;* sometimes called the "effective rate."

yield variance. Measures the input-output relation while holding the standard mix of inputs constant: (standard price multiplied by actual amount of input used in the standard mix) − (standard price multiplied by standard quantity allowed for the actual output). It is the part of the *efficiency variance* not called the *mix variance*.

Z

zero-base(d) budgeting (ZBB). One philosophy for setting budgets. In preparing an ordinary *budget* for the next period, a manager starts with the budget for the current period and makes adjustments as seem necessary because of changed conditions for the next period. Since most managers like to increase the scope of the activities managed and since most prices increase most of the time, amounts in budgets prepared in the ordinary, incremental way seem to increase period after period. The authority approving the budget assumes that managers will carry out operations in the same way as in the past and that next period's expenditures will have to be at least as large as those of the current period. Thus, this authority tends to study only the increments to the current period's budget. In ZBB, the authority questions the process for carrying out a program and the entire budget for the next period. The authority studies every dollar in the budget, not just the dollars incremental to the previous period's amounts. The advocates of ZBB claim that in this way, (1) management will more likely delete programs or divisions of marginal benefit to the business or governmental unit, rather than continuing with costs at least as large as the present ones, and (2) management may discover and implement alternative, more cost-effective ways of carrying out programs. ZBB implies questioning the existence of programs and the fundamental nature of the way that firms carry them out, not merely the amounts used to fund them. Experts appear to divide evenly as to whether the middle word should be "base" or "based."

INDEX

Note: Companies and entities in **bold** represent real companies and entities.